Underdeveloped Areas

A BOOK OF READINGS
AND RESEARCH

LYLE W. SHANNON

UNIVERSITY OF WISCONSIN

HARPER & BROTHERS PUBLISHERS
NEW YORK

Library of Congress catalog card number: 57–9866

CONTENTS

PREFACE

SOCIOLOGISTS have failed to take maximum advantage of research opportunities in underdeveloped areas, in part because of their reluctance to move into an area that has unfortunately, but traditionally, been the private preserve of other disciplines. Too, there has been reluctance on the part of some sociologists to recognize the work of those who have strayed too far from the fold, i.e., who have sallied forth on research that approaches what is believed to be the area of competence of other disciplines. The sociologist, however, may possess research techniques and an awareness of the crucial variables that give him a particular competence in this area of study. It is even likely that problems once considered central to another discipline, are basically sociological.

But, on the other hand, in recent years we have had increasing numbers of social scientists actively taking part in interdisciplinary research. One might correctly assume that if their experience in interdisciplinary research has been pleasant they are more receptive to the offerings of other disciplines from that time on, but if it has been unpleasant they are convinced that their own substantive field can make the greatest contribution to an understanding of the problems in that area. Nevertheless a number of interdisciplinary research teams are in the field in underdeveloped areas; their ongoing and incompletely reported activities will no doubt prove of value both from a strictly scientific viewpoint and for their applicability to administrative problems of governmental agencies. Many of the people whose articles appear in this volume are pioneers in interdisciplinary research. While primarily qualified in one discipline, they have seen the importance of taking a variety of sets of variables into consideration in explaining human behavior.

It is possible that part of the difficulties experienced by sociologists pioneering in this field has been due to the fact that they have spoken of their research in terms of "area research," i.e., have given the impression that they were conducting research in a geographical or cultural area with the idea of knowing about that area in itself, rather than having an interest in basic social processes that have made the area what it is. For this reason, the sociologist interested in underdeveloped areas may be incorrectly thought of or defined as a person whose basic interests differ from those of other sociologists. He has not made it clear that he is interested in how various social processes operate under some conditions to curtail development and under others to facilitate it. The articles in this volume, it may be said, deal with conditions and social and economic processes that have resulted in some areas developing their resources more fully than others. How those that are underdeveloped may be stimulated to fuller development and a higher level of living is the essential problem.

It should be noted that some professional and scientific journals have been more aware of the crucial importance of what is going on in underdeveloped areas than have others. Some journals have made it a policy to report on research taking place in underdeveloped areas and others have felt that this type of research is only peripheral to their primary interest.

Another indication of the increasing focus of attention on problems of underdeveloped areas is the establishment of institutes for the study of problems of underdeveloped areas at some of the leading universities in the United States. One outstanding example of such an institute is the Research Center on Economic Development and Cultural Change at the University of Chicago. One of the first objectives of this center has been to synthesize the unorganized body of knowledge dealing with problems of underdeveloped areas in order to arrive at general principles. The center has recognized the need for interdisciplinary research and is composed of economists, sociologists, anthropologists, and geographers. Another such center, The Center for International Studies, is located at Massachusetts Institute of Technology.

The Social Science Research Council, the Ford Foundation, the Rockefeller Foundation, and the Near East Foundation have subsidized extensive research, experimentation, or development projects in underdeveloped areas. It should be added that sociologists are far down the list among those who have taken advantage of research positions and fellowships made available by those organizations. The academic situation is mentioned at this point; the activities of large private corporations, individual governments, and the United Nations are discussed in detail in various chapters to follow.

Internationally known figures have said that competition between the two powerful opposing camps will increasingly shift from the military phase to the economic, and that success will hinge on their ability to develop underdeveloped areas. It might be remarked, with tongue in cheek, that so much attention has been focused on underdeveloped areas and their problems that the social scientists, if they could deliver, would gain increased prestige and status at the expense of the military.

This book of readings and research should be of assistance to those who are interested in some of the better articles that have appeared in professional journals on the subject of underdeveloped areas during the past ten years. In selecting items for this volume, about 200 different professional or scholarly journals were perused for a period covering the past 10 years. These journals contained about 2000 articles whose content made them pertinent to the subject. Many were not research oriented, but of the total, around 200 seemed more helpful than the others. These were in turn sifted and the final selections are found in this volume. Many excellent articles were excluded for reasons of space.

An attempt has been made to contribute some data and analysis aside from that which appears in the readings. Most of the articles appearing in this volume have been adapted from the original. All articles appear with the permission of both the publisher and the author. Permission to use these articles is appreciated. It is the hope of the editor that the meaning of none has been distorted by editing, by the position in which they appear, by their title or by comments made by way of introduction. Many of these articles have been authored by social scientists or others with government positions. Needless to say, their professional publications represent their own opinions and not necessarily those of the government agency with which they are associated.

This volume may be useful in an interdisciplinary course on problems of underdeveloped areas or in courses on underdeveloped areas presented by various disciplines within the social sciences. It is hoped that it will stimulate further interdisciplinary inquiry into the problems of underdeveloped areas.

LYLE W. SHANNON

October, 1957
Department of Sociology and Anthropology
University of Wisconsin

Underdeveloped Areas

I

DEFINITION AND DISTRIBUTION
OF UNDERDEVELOPED AREAS

INTRODUCTION

UNDERDEVELOPED areas became a focal point of world interest early in 1949 when President Truman gave almost singular attention to their problems in his inaugural address. Since that time public attention has been drawn to the activities of a multitude of public and private agencies engaged in a wide variety of developmental programs in underdeveloped areas. It has been suggested that the development of underdeveloped countries will be an area of intense competition between the United States and the U.S.S.R. for many years in the future. Underdeveloped areas containing either vast natural resources needed by major world powers, millions of potential workers or soldiers, or having strategic locations from a military viewpoint, will be of particular interest from a standpoint of their importance in world affairs.

Unfortunately the term, "underdeveloped areas," has been carelessly used and ill-defined. "Underdeveloped" has been used almost interchangeably with "undeveloped," although listings of each type would have both similarities and differences. An "undeveloped" area may be "underdeveloped" and then again it may offer little in the way of developmental possibilities, its "undeveloped" condition being due to a lack of natural or human resources. An "underdeveloped" area may be relatively developed but capable of further development.

Although one might expect the concept of "underdeveloped areas" to refer to the existing level of development in relation to the human and natural resources available, this has not always been the practice. "Underdeveloped" seems to refer to a low level of economic development, quite apart from the potentialities of an area. An area that might more properly be classified as "developed but still impoverished," is characterized as "underdeveloped." An area that is "undeveloped" may be referred to as "underdeveloped" when the facts of the case are that it is not capable of or amenable to development; it is undeveloped and

1

impoverished and not much can be done about it. An area may be "developed," i.e., industrialization and mechanization of agriculture may have resulted in a high level of living among the people, but remain "underdeveloped" in the sense that its vast resources, natural and human, are still comparatively untapped.

The following table should clarify the 4 possibilities suggested by the preceding paragraph. At one time all areas were undeveloped and underdeveloped. The Sudan might be suggested as an example of this type of area, while India represents an area that is no longer undeveloped but remains underdeveloped. Great Britain is still a third type, neither underdeveloped nor undeveloped. It might be shown that all areas are somewhere in transition between the first type and the third type unless they are in the fourth category, undeveloped but not underdeveloped. Greenland might be used as an example of the latter.

TABLE 1.   Types of Undeveloped and Underdeveloped Areas

		Underdeveloped	
		Yes	No
	Yes	Sudan ←	Greenland
Undeveloped		↓	
	No	India →	Great Britain

It is conceivable that scientific advance will in due time reveal Greenland to be the possessor of extensive mineral resources now unknown, thus changing Greenland's classification according to the scheme presented in Table 1. The arrows in Table 1 indicate the successive classifications of a country as it changes from an undeveloped resourceless type to the highly developed category. If the examples presented in Table 1 do not fit the reader's evaluation of these countries, it is suggested that other examples be selected that are considered more suitable as illustrations of points on the development continuum.

The question arises, how may we precisely define "underdeveloped" in such a manner that the various countries or political entities of the world may be reliably classified as being either developed or underdeveloped? Is it possible to set up a definition that may be used by a panel of judges or by independent researchers, who, following this definition, will arrive at identical or almost identical lists of countries. Several definitions of underdeveloped areas follow and may be used as a starting point.

DEFINING UNDERDEVELOPED AREAS

Norman S. Buchanan and Howard S. Ellis state that, "An economically underdeveloped country is one which on the average affords its inhabitants an end product of consumption and material well-being appreciably inferior to that provided by the economies of the developed countries. Poor is a relative term." They continue, "To designate a country as underdeveloped also implies that its present economic performance—as evidenced by the average of consumption and material well-being—could be improved by means which are known and understood."[1]

In a similar fashion, Eugene Staley defines an underdeveloped country as, "A country characterized by mass poverty which is chronic and not the result of some temporary misfortune, and by obsolete methods of production and social organization, which means that the poverty is not entirely due to poor natural resources and hence could presumably be lessened by methods already proved in other countries."[2]

A third definition of underdeveloped areas is presented by Jacob Viner, ". . . an underdeveloped country . . . is a country which has good potential prospects for using more capital or more labor or more available natural resources, or all of these to support its present population on a higher level of living, or, if its *per capita* income level is already fairly high, to support a larger population on a not lower level of living."[3]

If we accept any one of these definitions or a similar definition, is it then possible to divide the world into a dichotomy of developed and underdeveloped areas or into a number of categories according to varying degrees of development? This cannot readily be accomplished for a number of reasons. Much of the pertinent data have not been collected for the political areas that would be used if we were to attempt to make the division on such a basis. It is also possible that development within political boundaries is more variable than development between political entities. On the other hand, even fewer data are available if we attempt to establish natural areas of development. Land forms, rainfall, temperature, resources, and other physical characteristics of the world have nonpolitical patterns of occurrence; although data are available on their distribution, the necessary developmental and level of living data are unavailable on the same basis.

These definitions of underdeveloped areas, as we have noted, imply that we need more than a simple level of development index; they call for a level of development index related to possibilities of development. Strictly speaking, we should construct an index of underdevelopment using such items as the ratio of developed waterpower to potential waterpower or other similar kinds of information. Data of this type, however, are available for relatively few of the various political areas.

CLASSIFYING AREAS AS DEVELOPED OR UNDERDEVELOPED

Exhaustive examination and appraisal of the available data lead one to conclude that we must turn to data indicative of the level of living in political

[1] Norman S. Buchanan and Howard S. Ellis, *Approaches to Economic Development*, New York, The Twentieth Century Fund, 1955, pp. 3–4.

[2] Eugene Staley, *The Future of Underdeveloped Countries*, New York, Harper & Brothers, 1954, p. 13.

[3] Jacob Viner, *International Trade and Economic Development*, Glencoe, The Free Press, 1952, p. 125.

entities or areas in order to classify them as developed or underdeveloped. These data do not enable us to distinguish between underdeveloped and undeveloped areas so that references to underdeveloped areas always include the possibility of the area being undeveloped but not underdeveloped. While this is not entirely satisfactory, it is all that can be done with the available data.

Buchanan and Ellis point out that 2 kinds of statistical data are available for the purpose of measuring development. There are statistical indices representing the quality and texture of life as end product; an example of this type of index would be infant mortality rates. Secondly, there are indices that describe economic performances and explain or at least correlate with poor end-product data, such as infant mortality rates. An example of this type of index would be low agricultural productivity per person or per acre. Other indices may be of a mixed type. An absence of all-weather roads might be an example of the mixed type since they are an end product as well as essential to efficient marketing.

A vast amount of social and economic data has been collected by the United Nations in the past 10 years, representing a step forward in international social bookkeeping. Assuming that we are willing to overlook the heterogeneity of many political areas and that we are likewise willing to settle for less data than appears to be called for by typical definitions of underdeveloped areas, it is possible to make use of these data in the construction of a scale measuring the level of development of political entities.[4] These data could be combined, using appropriate techniques, so that each of the 195 political entities in the world could be placed on a continuum, resulting in a range of countries from those that are highly developed to those with a relatively low level or complete lack of development.

Several researchers have, on previous occasions, divided the various political entities of the world into the dichotomy, developed or underdeveloped and undeveloped, or into classification systems with 3 or more categories, using developmental data similar to that which we have just mentioned. These classifications have usually been made, taking into consideration only a very few variables that were considered crucial by the researcher. It may well be, however, that more elaborate efforts with a larger number of variables will result in a very similar classification.

Staley, for example, has grouped countries into three categories, mainly on a basis of *per capita* income as of 1950 or thereabouts, although degree of urbanization and proportion of working people engaged in nonagricultural occupations were taken into account. He places 1.6 billion or two-thirds of the world's population in underdeveloped countries. Other sources have presented very similar estimates of the population of underdeveloped areas. They are found principally

---

[4] The United Nations has listed major political entities of the world for statistical purposes and has consistently collected data on a basis of these established political areas. See *Nomenclature of Geographical Areas for Statistical Purposes, Statistical Papers, Series M., No. 1*, Lake Success, Statistical Office of the United Nations, January 1949.

in Latin America, Africa, the Middle East, south and southeast Asia, and Oceania.

It should be helpful at this point to present a preliminary classification of the 195 political entities in the world as developed or underdeveloped. We shall follow the usual systems of classification, following broad continental lines or geographical regions for the most part, with certain important exceptions. This classification is presented in Table 2 and summarized in Tables 3 and 4. Table 2 not only presents a system of classification according to developmental status but, in addition, indicates the political status of each entity.

North American political entities are classified as developed; almost 100 percent of the residents of North America are to be found in the most developed areas, Canada and the United States. The existence of a few people in other parts of the continent is relatively unimportant in determining the classification of this continent.

Central America, including the Caribbean and adjacent island areas, is usually classified as underdeveloped, although parts of this scattered and diverse area are highly developed as contrasted to the average level of development in the area. The heterogeneity of this area will be of some interest to us when we reach the chapter on measuring development.

South America has been classified on most occasions as underdeveloped but an examination of various indices of economic activity indicates that Argentina, Chile, and Uruguay, the most southern self-governing areas, can scarcely be considered underdeveloped in comparison with other political entities. The remainder of South America is classified as underdeveloped.

Europe is classified as developed although several of the areas included here might be considered underdeveloped or undeveloped. Spitzbergen is an example of the latter, and at most, is inhabited only a part of each year by a temporary mining population. Nevertheless, the population of Europe is found in countries which are for the most part well developed.

Africa, with the exception of the Union of South Africa, is classified as underdeveloped.

The Middle East is usually considered underdeveloped but the level of development is varied with some of the oil-producing countries scoring very high on indices of economic activity. For the present, however, we shall follow the usual practice of classifying the entire region as underdeveloped.

Although central, eastern, and southern Asia are separated from southeast Asia in our regional system of classification, we may note that all of Asia, with the exception of the Soviet Union and Japan, is classified as underdeveloped.

Oceania is classified as underdeveloped with the exception of Australia, New Zealand, and Hawaii.

The picture of underdeveloped areas that is presented varies considerably, depending on whether we are referring to the number of underdeveloped political entities, the size of these areas in square miles of area, or their size in popula-

TABLE 2. Political Entities of the World Arranged According to Region, Political Status, and Development: 1950; Listing Population, Land Area, and Percent of World's Population and Land Area in Various Subcategories

A. North America
Developed
Self-governing

	Population	Area
United States	151,689,000	7,827,680
Canada	13,712,000	9,960,170

% of World Population and Land Area
6.87%   13.27%

Non-self-governing

	Population	Area
Alaska	136,000	1,518,717
St. Pierre & Miquelon	5,000	240
Greenland	23,000	2,175,600

% of World Population and Land Area
−.01%   2.75%

B. Central America
Underdeveloped or Undeveloped
Self-governing

	Population	Area
Panama	797,000	74,010
Cuba	5,362,000	114,525
Costa Rica	800,000	51,011
Nicaragua	1,053,000	148,000
Dominican Rep.	2,116,000	49,543
Mexico	25,706,000	1,969,367
Salvador	1,859,000	34,162
Guatemala	2,803,000	108,889
Honduras	1,505,000	115,205
Haiti	3,112,000	27,750

% of World Population and Land Area
1.87%   2.00%

Non-self-governing

	Population	Area
Puerto Rico	2,216,000	8,896
Virgin Is.	27,000	344
Jamaica	1,403,000	11,424
Neth. W. Indies	163,000	947
Bermuda	37,000	54
Leeward Is.	113,000	1,094
Barbados	210,000	431
Bahama Is.	79,000	11,404
Trinidad & Tobago	632,000	5,128
Windward Is.	276,000	2,126
Brit. Honduras	66,000	22,965
Canal Zone	52,000	1,432
Martinique	273,000	1,102
Guadaloupe	289,000	1,780

% of World Population and Land Area
.24%   .05%

C. South America
Developed
Self-governing

	Population	Area
Chile	5,809,000	741,767
Argentina	17,197,000	2,808,492
Uruguay	2,353,000	186,926

% of World Population and Land Area
1.05%   2.79%

Non-self-governing
(None)

Underdeveloped or Undeveloped
Self-governing

	Population	Area
Paraguay	1,406,000	406,752
Bolivia	3,019,000	1,098,581
Ecuador	3,203,000	275,000
Venezuela	4,927,000	912,050
Peru	8,405,000	1,249,049
Brazil	52,124,000	8,516,037
Colombia	11,260,000	1,138,355

% of World Population and Land Area
3.50%   10.14%

Non-self-governing

	Population	Area
British Guiana	420,000	214,962
Falkland Is.	2,000	11,960
Surinam	219,000	142,822
French Guiana	26,000	91,000

% of World Population and Land Area
.02%   .34%

D. Europe
Developed

Self-governing

	Population	Area
Luxembourg	297,000	2,582
Belgium	8,639,000	30,507
Switzerland	4,694,000	41,295
Denmark	4,270,000	42,936
Finland	4,012,000	337,009
Austria	6,906,000	83,851
France	41,944,000	550,986
Norway	3,264,000	324,222
Sweden	7,017,000	440,122
Iceland	143,000	103,000
Netherlands	10,114,000	32,388
Portugal	8,490,000	91,721
Czechoslovakia	12,340,000	127,827
Ireland	2,969,000	70,282
Poland	24,977,000	311,730
United Kingdom	50,616,000	244,002
Spain	27,868,000	503,061
Germany	69,000,000	353,352
Yugoslavia	16,148,000	256,880
Hungary	9,313,000	93,011
Italy	46,280,000	301,055
Monaco	21,000	1
Liechtenstein	14,000	157
Romania	16,094,000	237,502
Bulgaria	7,235,000	110,842
San Marino	13,000	61
Andorra	5,000	453
Greece	7,960,000	132,562
Albania	1,200,000	28,748

% of World Population and Land Area
16.28%   3.62%

Non-self-governing

	Population	Area
Gibralter	25,000	6
Malta & Gozo	313,000	316
Channel Is.	103,000	195
Spitzbergen	0	64,477
Isle of Man	54,000	572

% of World Population and Land Area
.02%   .04%

E. Africa
Developed

Self-governing

	Population	Area
Union of S. Africa	12,320,000	1,224,206

% of World Population and Land Area
.51%   .91%

Non-self-governing
(None)

Underdeveloped or Undeveloped

Self-governing

	Population	Area
Egypt	20,439,000	1,000,000
Ethiopia	15,000,000	1,060,000
Sudan	8,350,000	2,505,700
Libya	1,124,000	1,759,500
Liberia	1,648,000	111,370

Non-self-governing

	Population	Area
St. Helena	5,000	210
Seychelles	36,000	405
Madagascar	4,469,000	592,200
Mauritius	465,000	1,865
Sierra Leone	1,880,000	72,323
Sp. Poss. in N. Af.	141,000	213
Zanzibar & Pemba	269,000	2,642

Algeria	8,753,000	2,191,464
Belgian Congo	11,258,000	2,343,930
Kenya	5,555,000	582,624
Tunisia	2,470,000	1,558,830
Reunion	258,000	2,511
Swaziland	197,000	17,364
Nyasaland	2,330,000	125,465
Gold Coast	3,870,000	204,089
Uganda	5,125,000	243,401
Fr. Cameroons	3,085,000	439,000
Mozambique	5,717,000	771,125
Morocco	8,410,000	390,800
Nigeria	24,000,000	876,922
Somaliland Prot.	500,000	176,113
Br. Cameroons	1,000,000	88,266
Br. Togoland	397,000	33,775
Ruandi Urundi	3,914,000	54,172
Gambia	273,000	10,537
Togoland (Fr.)	998,000	55,000
Tanganyika	7,707,000	939,326
Basutoland	574,000	30,343
Somaliland (It.)	1,246,000	513,533
Fr. Somaliland	55,000	21,700
Fr. Equa. Afri.	4,406,000	2,510,000
Sao Tome & Prin.	60,000	964
Sp. Guinea	175,000	28,051
Morrocan Prot.	1,192,000	45,656
Cape Verde Is.	138,000	4,033
No. Rhodesia	1,866,000	751,908
Port. Guinea	511,000	36,125
Bechuanaland	289,000	712,200
Fr. West Afri.	17,208,000	4,752,700
So. Rhodesia	2,090,000	389,347
S. W. Africa	379,000	822,876
Angola	4,093,000	1,246,700
Tangier	111,000	349
Spanish W. Africa	80,000	269,150

% of World Population and Land Area
1.93%   4.81%

% of World Population and Land Area
5.75%   17.84%

F. Middle East
Underdeveloped or Undeveloped
Self-governing

	Population	Area
Israel	1,258,000	21,000
Syria	3,215,000	181,337
Lebanon	1,257,000	10,400
Iraq	5,100,000	435,415
Jordan	1,269,000	96,513
Iran	18,772,000	1,630,000
Kuwait	170,000	20,719
Yemen	4,500,000	195,000
Saudi Arabia	6,000,000	135,135

Non-self-governing

	Population	Area
Cyprus	484,000	9,251
Aden Colony	100,000	207
Aden Protectorate	650,000	315,968

Afghanistan	12,000,000	650,000
Muscat & Oman	550,000	212,400
Trucial Oman	80,000	15,000
Qatar	20,000	2,200
Bahrein	110,000	598
Turkey	20,935,000	767,119

% of World Population and Land Area
    3.12%   3.27%

% of World Population and Land Area
    .05%   .24%

G. Southeast Asia
Underdeveloped and Undeveloped
Self-governing

	Population	Area
Philippines	19,868,000	299,404
Indonesia	75,500,000	1,411,564
Thailand	18,313,000	511,937
Burma	18,489,000	677,544

% of World Population and Land Area
    5.49%   1.48%

Non-self-governing

	Population	Area
Singapore	1,018,000	755
Malaya	5,227,000	131,049
New Guinea	1,018,000	412,781
Portuguese Timor	434,000	18,990
Indochina	30,000,000	705,400
British Borneo	956,000	203,786

% of World Population and Land Area
    1.60%   1.10%

H. Central, Eastern, and Southern Asia
Developed
Self-governing

	Population	Area
Japan	82,900,000	368,303
U.S.S.R.	193,000,000	22,270,600

% of World Population and Land Area
    11.46%   16.89%

Non-self-governing
(None)

Underdeveloped and Undeveloped
Self-governing

	Population	Area
Ceylon	7,544,000	65,607
India	358,000,000	3,288,241
Korea	29,500,000	220,769
Pakistan	75,040,000	947,663
Formosa	7,476,000	35,961
China	463,500,000	9,736,288
Bhutan	300,000	50,000
Nepal	7,000,000	140,000
Mongolia	885,000	1,621,000

% of World Population and Land Area
    39.43%   12.00%

Non-self-governing

	Population	Area
French India	337,000	501
Portuguese India	637,000	3,983
Ryukyu Is.	929,000	3,344
Maldive Is.	85,000	298
Bonin Is.	148	104
Macau	188,000	16
Hong Kong	2,260,000	1,013

% of World Population and Land Area
    .18%   −.01%

I. Oceania
Developed
Self-governing

	Population	Area
New Zealand	1,920,000	267,985
Australia	8,186,000	7,703,867

% of World Population and Land Area
    .41%   5.94%

Non-self-governing

	Population	Area
Hawaii	497,000	16,635

% of World Population and Land Area
    .02%   .01%

TABLE 2. Political Entities of the World Arranged According to Region, Political Status, and Development: 1950; Listing Population, Land Area, and Percent of World's Population and Land Area in Various Subcategories

Underdeveloped and Undeveloped Self-governing (None)	Non-self-governing		
		Population	Area
	Amer. Samoa	497,000	16,635
	Guam	59,000	534
	Fiji	289,000	18,233
	Cook Is.	15,000	259
	Niue	4,000	259
	Norfolk Is.	1,000	35
	Western Samoa	79,000	2,927
	Tonga	46,000	697
	Gilbert & Ellice Is.	38,000	956
	Pacific Is. (U.S.)	55,000	1,713
	Nauru	3,000	21
	New Hebrides	49,000	14,762
	New Caledonia	63,000	18,635
	Papua	369,000	234,490
	Tokelau	1,000	10
	Br. Solomon Is.	100,000	29,784
	New Guinea	1,071,000	241,000
	Pitcairn	130	5
	Fr. Oceania	60,000	3,998
	% of World Population and Land Area	.11%	.43%

% of World Population Developed and Self-governing 36.58%
% of World Land Area 43.52%

% of World Population Developed and Non-self-governing .04%
% of World's Land Area 2.80%

% of World Population Underdeveloped or Undeveloped and Self-governing 55.34%
% of World's Land Area 33.70%

% of World Population Underdeveloped or Undeveloped and Non-self-governing 7.95%
% of World's Land Area 20.00%

tion. The number of political entities and the percent of the world's population that is classified as developed or underdeveloped are presented in a region-by-region summary in Table 3.

Examination of Table 3 clearly reveals that it matters very little whether we classify Central American political entities as developed or underdeveloped when the proportion of the world's population that they constitute is taken into consideration. For all practical purposes, and this will become clearer as we proceed, the real problem of underdeveloped areas is to be found in Africa, the Middle East between Africa and Asia, and in Asia. In this area alone we find about 60 percent of the world's population.

It must be emphasized that the classification of underdeveloped areas presented at this point is frequently found in other volumes on underdeveloped areas, that its advantage lies in the fact that broad geographical lines are followed for the most part, and that, in spite of a certain degree of heterogeneity within each geographical region or continent, attention is focused on the most crucial areas of underdevelopment.

TABLE 3. World Population According to Development
Number of Political Entities and Percent of World's Population in Each of Nine Regions:
1950

Region	Developed		Underdeveloped	
	Number of Political Entities	Percent of World's Population	Number of Political Entities	Percent of World's Population
North America	5	6.87	0	.00
Central America	0	0.00	24	2.11
South America	3	1.05	11	3.52
Europe	34	16.30	0	.00
Africa	1	.51	49	7.69
Middle East	0	0.00	18	3.17
Southeast Asia	0	0.00	10	7.09
Central, Eastern, and Southern Asia	2	11.46	16	39.61
Oceania	3	.43	19	.11
Total	48	36.62	147	63.29

Table 4 is set up in the same manner as Table 3 with the exception that the number of political entities in each category is contrasted with the percent of the world's land area in that category.

TABLE 4. World Land Area According to Development
Number of Political Entities and Percent of World's Land Area in Each of Nine Regions:
1950

Region	Number of Political Entities		Percent of World's Land Area	
	Developed	Under-developed	Developed	Under-developed
North America	5	0	16.02	.00
Central America	0	24	.00	2.05
South America	3	11	2.79	10.48
Europe	34	0	3.66	.00
Africa	1	49	.91	22.65
Middle East	0	18	.00	3.51
Southeast Asia	0	10	.00	2.58
Central, Eastern and Southern Asia	2	16	16.89	12.00
Oceania	3	19	5.95	.43
Total	48	147	46.22	53.70

The data in Table 4 reveal that the vast areas of underdevelopment are found in Africa, Asia, and South America. The dissimilarity of the picture when land area is taken into consideration rather than population is due in part to the influence of India and China as densely populated underdeveloped areas and the quite different influence of Brazil as a large but sparsely populated under-developed area. The considerable difference in population size, land area, and density of the various political entities is a factor with which we must reckon in various other computations but this may be discussed in fuller detail at the proper time.

The readings presented in this chapter are designed as an introduction to the subject of underdeveloped areas and the problems involved in planning for their development.

The first article by Douglas F. Dowd, "Two-Thirds of the World," briefly describes the impact of Western penetration on the underdeveloped world, the economic and political institutions of these areas, and their relation to the low level of living. In order to present a picture of national income and its variability from country to country, a short selection is presented from the United Nations publication, *National Income and Its Distribution in Under-Developed Countries*. The concentration of low income areas in Africa, Latin America, and Asia is clearly shown by Table 1 and Table 2.

TWO-THIRDS OF THE WORLD*

DOUGLAS F. DOWD

THE spectacular upsurge of interest in underdeveloped areas, although belated, is a welcome recognition of the importance which should be attached to an impoverished and disturbed two-thirds of the world. It has now become popular to advocate steps to aid in the economic and social development of these areas, with the expressed aim of alleviating widespread poverty and unrest, and of utilizing more fully the resources of these areas. Although one would not wish to quarrel with the aim thus expressed, there remains good reason to differ with the basic assumption underlying most proposals for developing these areas—the assumption that such development can at once be beneficial to all

* Reprinted by permission from the Fall 1953 issue of *The Antioch Review*, Yellow Springs, Ohio. Copyright 1953 by the Antioch Review, Inc.

concerned and take place within an institutional framework basically the same as that which now exists. What is required to bring about the economic development of the underdeveloped areas is nothing less than a comprehensive social transformation, and a substantial modification of their place in the world economy. Isolated attacks on specific scarcities (though such scarcities must be removed, of course), where they do not represent a naïve approach to the problem, may well lend themselves to a perpetuation of colonial relationships.

This contention will be supported by an examination of the modern history of these areas, and of their prevailing economic, political, and social characteristics. In the following desperately synoptic treatment, I shall highlight the character and importance of institutional relationships in the underdeveloped world, suggest the nature of the foundation which must be laid for beneficial economic development, and point toward some implications for the industrialized world.

The underdeveloped areas comprise most of the land surface of the world, and contain most of its people. They differ widely with respect to resources, climate, and terrain, and in cultural heritage. However, if our concern is with the problem of economic development, we may discern similar clusters of relevant institutions through the entire underdeveloped world. On specific points, important differences between any two areas (or within one area) may be found. But, so far as the general nature of the problem is concerned, similarities far outweigh differences.

I

Conditions in the underdeveloped areas, and proposals for their future development, cannot sensibly be appraised without some understanding of the impact of Western (i.e., European and American) penetration upon them.

This process began with the mercantilist adventurers and trading companies around the beginning of the sixteenth century. It recurred in a new wave with the imperialist ventures of the nineteenth century. The expansion did not always stem from the same motivations, it affected different areas in different fashions and at different times, and its effect changed through the years. Nonetheless, we can make several generalizations about its results.

Of prime importance economically was the fact that previously isolated communities were drawn into the world economy. This entailed the gradual breakdown of the former village economy—subsistence agriculture and handicrafts—and the introduction of a money economy. The peasant was pushed into commercialized agriculture, the role which his handicrafts had

played seriously deteriorated, and he was crushed by debt. A rural proletariat—wage laborers and tenants—was created, and the economies of these areas became dependent, i.e., subordinate to the needs of the Western powers.

It may not have been the intention of the Western nations to bring about such sweeping changes. But it was inevitable that the intrusion of the plantation economy, of intensive mineral exploitation, and of Western manufactures and capital would bring forth a whole new set of social relationships.

The new society generally meant a net decline in the peasant's already unfortunate position. His level of material comfort had always been low according to Western standards. He had often lived in an oppressive social environment. But it had been a world which, if not of his own making, was at least of his own people. Now he had become a pawn in the world economy, pushed and hauled by movements of world prices, and by a correspondingly worsened economic position in his own locale. What had been good in his old world diminished, while at the same time he became subject to buffets from distant lands.

The political and social consequences of the process of Western expansion were not less important than those of an economic nature. The increasing scope and complexity of the relationships between the metropolitan and dependent areas ultimately developed into a political as well as economic domination. Though he had perhaps been ruled autocratically or even cruelly since time began, the native was now subject to foreign rulers, who scorned not only his welfare but frequently his culture and the color of his skin.

Ironically, even otherwise laudable steps taken by the intruding powers had unfortunate consequences. Their economic needs for orderly and continuous trading

and production often led them in time to
introduce minimal health and sanitary
measures. These in turn reduced mortality
rates without altering birth rates, and in
many areas a dangerous population problem developed.

The vigor of Western technology, and
its accompanying military power, led to
the disintegration of what had often been
a high level of culture and social unity.
Security was replaced by insecurity; dignity
by degradation; a low level of wants by
poverty; autonomy by dependence. This is
not to romanticize the largely hidden past;
rather, it is to speak in relative terms, and
to emphasize that whatever colonialism has
meant to the West, it has meant social
disintegration to the now dependent societies and has furnished the ingredients
for a powerful, unstable ferment throughout the world.

The modern result of Western political
domination and economic exploitation in
the underdeveloped world has been political unrest, a drive toward nationalism,
and the "urge to industrialize." This is not
a new phenomenon; it has now become
significant because it can no longer be denied. In the postwar world the drive has
become stronger, and the power of the
West to resist weaker.

This has been the impact of Western
penetration on the underdeveloped world.
The symmetrical conclusion does not follow that the removal of Western domination—as necessary as that may be—would
by itself reverse these trends or significantly ameliorate prevailing conditions.
The continuing deplorable conditions in
those underdeveloped countries which
have achieved "political independence"
alone (e.g., in Latin America) serves as
testimony to this point. Existing distributions of power and wealth among indigenous groups, and the associated social
framework, remain as significant obstacles
to economic and social development.

II

A review of the salient characteristics of
the underdeveloped areas takes on the
quality of a melancholy catalogue of obstacles to economic and social development. It is, nevertheless, the realistic basis
for understanding their problems.

Their economies are geared predominantly to primary production. Their people, except for a privileged few, live in
grinding poverty—the outcome of a cir-
cular chain of relationships, intimately interrelated and feeding upon each other.

A key link in this chain is the typically
small-sized holding (tropical Africa is an
important exception) worked by the peasant—a holding so small that the peasant
is less a farmer than a gardener. In the
villages of South China, for example, peasant families are classified as "poor," "middle," and "rich," who possess three-fourths
of an acre, just over an acre, and just under two and one-half acres, respectively.
Fragmentary holdings and large families,
with primitive and wasteful farming techniques, furnish a grim example of the
meaning of the law of diminishing returns.

The peasant's low level of output typically runs behind his consumption needs,
adding the heavy link of permanent indebtedness to the chain around his neck.
Whether he be a small independent culti-
vator, tenant, sharecropper, or landless laborer, his perpetual need for money—for
taxes, rent, interest, consumer goods, ceremonial and religious expenses, fodder—
drives the peasant ever deeper into the
hands of the moneylender. The greater his
need for money, the more likely that interest rates will rise, that his market produce will sell for less, that his rents and
forced services will increase. Furthermore,
because he incurs debt for current needs
rather than for investment, the peasant is
not provided with a lever to escape his
indebtedness. In the best of circumstances,

he is precariously independent; more commonly he falls into peonage.

These circumstances, combined with insecurity of tenure, do not encourage or allow the peasant to adopt improvements which constitute economic development in agriculture. He cannot afford to experiment nor does he have the incentive. It is of little value to him to increase his productivity if it is the moneylender, the landlord, or the tax collector, among others, who will reap the benefit.

The peasant is, on the whole, a subsistence producer; still, he markets an increasingly large portion of his crops over time. He has been drawn ineluctably into the market economy, not by a desire for profit, but by his permanent need for money. He receives little for his pains. If a tenant, he loses close to half his crop to the landowner. If in debt, as he always is, the moneylender (often the landowner, again) may seize an arbitrarily-valued portion of his crop at harvest time. The peasant takes what is left to market. He goes at the earliest possible moment—harvest time—for he needs money, and he lacks storage facilities. Lack of adequate transportation allows him to go only to the nearest market. He there sells as one of a large group of similarly-stricken peasants, and he sells to a small group of collusively organized buyers (if not to one buyer alone). His selling price is with rare exceptions the lowest price of the year.

The price he receives is established on the world market, thereafter to be scaled down to him through innumerable middlemen's transactions (as high as fifty, in India). The peasant receives the residue —out of which he must pay taxes. The final turn of the screw comes when, assuming the peasant has grown a food crop, he is forced to buy back a quantity of that food for his own consumption later in the year—at a substantially higher price.

The weak position of the peasant in his immediate surroundings is shared by his country in the world economy. It is a one-sided, nondiversified economy, specializing in primary production (food and raw materials). Its structure of production is generally divided between a large subsistence element, and a smaller, frequently foreign-controlled set of productive facilities specializing in primary production for export. These two sectors intermingle to the extent that a "surplus" of food (e.g., rice in Burma) enters into the export trade. On the fringes of both sectors is commonly found an excessively large group of petty traders ("small business"), whose activities are more a measure of disguised unemployment than of productive effort. Complementing export production is the appropriate amount of relatively large-scale activity in commerce and finance.

The performance of such an economy does little to enhance the material welfare of its people, precludes any significant steps toward economic development, and renders the society weak economically, politically, and militarily. This is so for a variety of connected reasons. 1) Because it is selling its primary goods largely to the industrialized sector of the world, the underdeveloped country is subject to the periodic cyclical fluctuations originating there. 2) As a primary producer, it is selling goods the demand for which is typically inelastic—geared to the demand for food or raw materials to supply manufacturing. Although inelasticity can benefit the primary producing countries in inflationary periods, they are harder hit than the industrialized nations in depressed periods. Since they are importers of manufactured goods, there is for them a periodic cyclical deterioration in the terms of trade, for the prices of manufactured goods do not fall in the same proportion as those of the extractive industries. And their recovery must depend upon actions taken elsewhere. 3) The native worker in these industries—whether a laborer on a plantation or a worker in the mines—is severely jeopardized by the sensitivity of his industry to international business fluctuations. Because of the generally abundant supply of labor, he cannot expect his wages to rise above subsistence levels in periods of high prices, but a fall in world prices leads to disastrous wage cuts, and in addition threatens him with loss of work. He shares little in prosperity, but he carries the full burden of depression. 4) In addition to cyclical deterioration, the long-term trend in the price relations between primary commodities and manufactured goods has, since the last quarter of the nineteenth century, turned against the primary producers. A recent United Nations study reports that on the average, a given quantity of primary exports in 1939 would pay for only sixty per cent of the quantity of manufactured goods which it could buy in the late nineteenth century. Such a falling trend *can* be accompanied by rising standards of living for the affected country. This will be true where prices fall because of increased productivity and where markets expand more than proportionately—such was the case in England in the nineteenth century. But, where demand is relatively inelastic, and the economy one-sided, a fall in the terms of trade amounts to a deterioration of national purchasing power.

In the postwar context of inflation it has frequently been argued that the very reliance of the underdeveloped countries on the export of primary commodities is to their advantage. Apart from the fact that this inflationary pressure on primary goods has been disappearing for the last year (recessions in cotton, rubber, copper and other prices are continuing), it generally is not true that worldwide pressure on primary goods, leading to inflated prices, has a beneficial impact on the prospects for economic development. Several factors combine to mitigate the possible benefits of the situation. 1) Much—perhaps most—of the benefits from inflated prices goes either to foreign owners or a tiny minority of the indigenous population—neither group seriously interested either in economic development or the welfare of the affected peoples. 2) The upward trend in the terms of trade since 1939 has been in the context of war and large-scale military production, and the goods needed for development (principally capital equipment) have been difficult or impossible to purchase. 3) The "good times" of inflated prices reduce the desire to industrialize, by allowing easy gains to be made in speculative trade and the like, and by ameliorating some of the more severe problems of these countries.

One-sidedness has its further consequences in the clear dangers of putting all of one's economic eggs in one basket. A change in technology abroad (e.g., synthetic rubber), a change in the investment plans of the one or two major (often foreign) export firms, new trade barriers, a crop failure—any or all of these are omnipresent threats to the economic welfare of the nondiversified economy. Such an economy lacks the ability to adapt; it cannot roll with the punch. What would be a relatively minor shock to a diversified economy can mean disaster to the underdeveloped country.

There are, finally, "noneconomic" consequences of one-sidedness. A nonindustrialized nation is a weak nation—weak in its ability to defend itself militarily and in its ability to resist unfavorable trade agreements or other commercial policies originating in the metropolitan areas. Because it is economically inferior, it is politically and militarily inferior. Where it is not in the status of a colony, it is likely to be a pawn in some more powerful nation's game.

Additional institutional features of strategic importance acting as obstacles to economic development are to be found in the structural characteristics of the underdeveloped country. Wherever we look into the structure of ownership and control —of land, industry, commerce, or finance —we find concentration.

Land ownership, the basis of wealth and power, is with relatively few exceptions heavily concentrated. In Egypt, for example, in 1947, less than half of one per cent of landowners (11,000 out of 2,662,- 000) owned close to thirty-seven per cent of the land; less than six per cent owned over sixty-six per cent. In contrast, three-quarters of the landowners possessed one acre or less, and their aggregate holdings amounted to slightly over thirteen per cent of the total. In Chile, in 1937, less than one-third of one per cent of all land-owners held over half of the land; over forty-three per cent of landowners held only one-half of one per cent of the land. In India, two-thirds of all the cultivated land is owned by fewer than a million large landowners; over a hundred million small cultivators hold less than one-quarter of the land. Where exceptions to this pattern are found, the pressure of population on the land generally plays the same oppressive role as that of concentrated land ownership elsewhere. And in some areas these two scourges are combined (e.g., in India).

In many instances the large landholdings are foreign-owned, and devoted to the production of exports (sugar, rubber, cotton). The foreigner has generally interested himself in the ownership of land where it is utilized for export crops or for the exploitation of mineral resources. More commonly, the large landowner is himself a native of the underdeveloped country (in Southeast Asia he will often be not a Westerner, but a Chinese or Indian). Although his activities may extend into the plantation-type economy, he is more likely to resemble the feudal baron of medieval Europe. The resemblance is not complete, however. The recognition of mutual rights and responsibilities which often characterized manorial relationships in Western Europe is generally absent, on the one hand, and the economic activities of the landlord are more extensive in the modern underdeveloped country, on the other. Frequently he is at once landowner, moneylender, and merchant. The activities are complementary in nature, each reinforcing the power and strategic position of its possessor in the other fields.

In the "business" world in the underdeveloped country, we are confronted with an interlinked, noncompetitive pattern of business enterprise; a veritable spider web of economic controls. J. S. Furnivall, an authority on colonial areas, points out that in such areas

big business reaches out towards a comprehensive monopoly. In Burma we have noted that the more important business houses do not concentrate on trade only but are importers, exporters, millers, estate and ship owners at the same time, and may have considerable interests outside Burma. Similarly, a few firms, closely interlinked, have dominated the economic life of Netherlands India. The United Africa Company is a signal illustration of the same tendency in Africa.[1]

Typically the number of firms (outside petty trade and production) is small and organized on a large scale. Each firm readily merges into a community of interests with its like members in other fields of endeavor. In such an environment, as has been remarked concerning India, "private enterprise is far from free enterprise." This structure of ownership and control, dominated as it is by a native ruling clique and a handful of foreigners, stands as an imposing obstacle to eco-

[1] *Colonial Policy and Practice*, p. 479.

nomic development. Where, with relative absence of risk, high returns can be made with ease from real estate, moneylending, speculative trade, and the like, it is hardly to be expected that the greater risks and slower returns of industrial investment will be undertaken.

Out of such concentration of ownership comes a highly unequal *distribution* of income, while the *level* of national income is held down by the economic situation of the peasant producer and the position of his country in the world economy. Although precise national income statistics for the underdeveloped areas are notoriously meagre, the general quality of their income situation is clear. These are, in the fullest sense of the term, poor countries. They are poor in the sense that per capita real income is relatively much lower than that of the industrialized nations. They are poor in the sense that income is not sufficient in absolute terms to sustain health, working efficiency, or a "normal" span of years.

The net national income of the United States in 1949 was around $216 billion, for a population of roughly 150 million —over $1400 per capita. After making all conceivable adjustments for purposes of realistic comparison, one is struck, if not shocked, by the vast difference in per capita income between ourselves and the underdeveloped countries. In Asia in that same year, India, with a population more than twice as large as our own, had a recorded national income of less than one-tenth of ours—$57 per capita. Indonesia, with 72 million people, had a national income of slightly over $2 billion—$30 per capita. The Philippine Islands had a national income of $850 million for a population of close to 20 million—$44 per capita.[2] This national poverty was increased by the drain to foreign investors.

[2] United Nations, *Economic Survey of Asia and the Far East, 1950*, p. 112.

Moreover, in parts of Southeast Asia (at least) the trend in per capita income has been down since the war, and the gap between the very wealthy and the very poor (there is no appreciable middle class) has widened in the inflation of the postwar years. If we add to this general picture the reminder that a greatly disproportionate share of the national income goes to a tiny privileged group, the per capita income of the underlying population falls below its already grossly low figure.

The low level of national income precludes the possibility of any substantial margin of savings, and thus of investment (except through foreign gifts or loans— the latter currently at near prohibitive rates). Subsistence needs in such an atmosphere act as a sponge. We might expect the distribution of income, deplorable though it may be on egalitarian grounds, to allow large savings in the privileged group, and a proportionate amount of real investment. Savings *do* take place, but find their way into land, hoards, speculation, and other nonproductive ventures. And a good deal of these high incomes waste away into conspicuous consumption.

Over and above the attractions to available capital in the underdeveloped country held out by nonindustrial investment, positive deterrents for the potential industrial investor exist because of the absence of 1) wide markets for the goods which would flow from industrial production, 2) the principal sources of "external economies"—flowing from developed transportation, communications, power, marketing, and financial systems, and 3) the bases for an efficient labor force— health services, adequate training and educational systems, and reasonable living facilities. These deficiencies exist because the areas *are* underdeveloped, and, taken together with the numerous other points mentioned above and below, they combine to *keep* an area underdeveloped. So far as markets and external economies are concerned, the private investor is either unable or disinclined to take the steps which might remedy the situation. So far as the condition of the labor force is concerned, this is in part a product of the low level of development, in part a product of the poverty of the people, and in part a consequence of the social irresponsibility characterizing government in these areas.

Poverty, poor health, inadequate shelter, low productivity, illiteracy, and a short life expectancy (in India, average life expectancy is 27 years) all go together. Poverty and overcrowding, combined, are a potent force making for malnutrition and disease, and increased susceptibility to further disease, sapping vitality and ultimately life. Low productivity and short life expectancies together yield further unfortunate consequences: because close to half the new born children will die before they reach, say, fifteen, "a substantial share of the low national income is used for children who never attain the productive years of adulthood. Correspondingly, the average working life of those who do attain the productive ages is curtailed by high death rates."[3]

The native of the underdeveloped country is often thought of as ignorant, lazy, and as a ne'er-do-well. He is illiterate, but not stupid; his ignorance stems from his poverty and his need to concentrate his time and energy on staying alive. He is not lazy; he is ill. He is not a ne'er-do-well; he has been demoralized by an oppressive social environment. Unless and until social conditions are markedly improved, the labor force in the underdeveloped countries will remain sadly ill-equipped for the tasks of economic development in skills, morale, and energy.

[3] U.S. Department of State, *Point Four*, p. 105.

Associated as a partial cause and result of the whole string of conditions outlined above is another major source of concern: the problem of population. In parts of Asia, the Caribbean, and the Middle East, the threat of overpopulation has become a reality. Less well-recognized is the nature of this problem as it affects large sections of the entire underdeveloped world—most of Asia and the Far East, the Middle East, Central Africa, the Caribbean Islands, Central America, and northern and western South America. These are classified by the demographer as "unstable societies"—lands whose populations are poised between decimation should there be a reduction of available subsistence, on the one hand, or tremendous growth brought about by lowering the mortality rate (achieved relatively easily through epidemic control, slightly improved agricultural techniques, and so on) without a concomitant lowering of the birth rate (quite difficult to achieve).

Clearly, this constitutes a thorny obstacle to economic development. Overpopulation leads to an undue, though understandable, emphasis on subsistence, rather than investment. In nations where the margin of surplus is slender the basis for capital formation is thus lacking. Particularly today, the political pressures playing upon the governments of these areas lead to a strong emphasis on subsistence (as well as upon economic development). The existence of this problem in itself sets the requirement for rapid and comprehensive development, if development is to yield a net gain. Piecemeal improvements (a new dam, refinery, or mill, exchange controls, technical assistance, and the like) in such a setting are not likely to lead to a growth in national income which will outstrip the growth of population.

Finally, what of the governments of these countries? The nature of government and of the political atmosphere in the underdeveloped world is conducive to the development of unrest, but not of the economy. Frequently, it means corruption and petty graft, despotism and misrule. Since the war, certain countries (e.g., India and Burma) have won political independence; in others, already established national governments have begun to take notice, more often on paper than in practice, of the needs of their people. Still dominating the picture, however, are governments composed of a ruling oligarchy of native landowners, financiers, and merchants, often kept or controlled by outside interests.

The taxing power is used regressively and heavily, as might be expected where those who would be hit hardest by a progressive tax structure are those who legislate. Governments are unstable, often requiring the alert support of the military for maintenance. Instability and fiscal confusion are enhanced by the wide fluctuations in revenue attendant upon fluctuations in prices and volume of exports. Schooled in irresponsibility by their past or present colonial masters, these governments are at best sluggish in their response to social problems.

What was set in motion over three centuries ago by the expanding Western powers now gives every appearance of being out of control. Varying from restlessness in tropical Africa to revolt in Asia, the current political atmosphere in the underdeveloped world is one of tension, uncertainty, and eager striving. In some cases the peasantry pushes against its native rulers; in colonial areas agrarian unrest combines with nationalism to reach feverish heights. Whatever the sources of these movements, the goal is a higher level of social welfare, and the path to economic and political strength is that of industrialization.

It is now appropriate to ask what is

entailed—for the countries themselves, and for the industrialized world—if this path is to be traveled successfully.

III

Economic development, quite narrowly construed, is a process comprising capital formation, increased productivity, and a more nearly optimum utilization of resources, and its yield is (over and above important political and social changes) a higher level of material welfare. Such a process, sounding like simplicity itself to contemporary Western ears, does not begin easily. An adequate resource base is required, but, more importantly, the appropriate social framework must first exist, or be created.

In the past, economic development has begun in either of two general types of social environment: 1) within a regime of economic liberalism—entailing a more or less competitive economy and a permissive government (and one generous with subsidies and the like when needed); or, 2) where there has been a considerable amount of centralized government direction and control. England and the United States are examples of the former, and Japan and the Soviet Union of the latter type.

The comparative importance of resource availability and social institutions becomes clear when we compare two areas such as North and Latin America. North America is more abundantly endowed with resources than Latin America (so far as we know), but the difference in that respect is a small fraction of the vast difference in real income between the two areas. Indeed, we may look to our own backyard—the American South—for a confirmation of this point.

The crucial role of institutional arrangements for economic development may be discovered in the histories of already industrialized areas. There it may be seen that although reasonably good to excellent resource bases existed, the industrialization process did not get under way until a significant wrench away from the old order of things had been accomplished. Flexibility of institutional arrangements was enhanced, as were resources, by the possibilities of geographic (and commercial) expansion during the process. The general lack of these same opportunities for the countries now trying to develop would seem to strengthen an argument for the need deliberately to structure the institutions of these countries to the needs of economic development, if such development is to take place. As the generosity of nature, time, and place declines, intelligence and design must intrude. The leading characteristics of the underdeveloped countries indicate that the degree to which institutional restructuring is necessary, if they are to develop, is formidable.

The situation of the peasant (and thus, to a large degree, the economy) can be relieved only by a sweeping program of agricultural improvements and agrarian reorganization. Land reform, though a necessary ingredient of any successful program in these areas, is not the panacea which it is popularly conceived to be. Mexican (in the '30's) and Japanese (in the postwar years) land reforms indicate that land reform unaccompanied by a whole set of other changes is likely to be an illusory and purely temporary device, which, though it will reduce fever will not cure the disease. Marketing, credit, storage, transportation facilities, agricultural extension services, irrigation, medical care —all these, *plus* land reform, *and more* are required before the peasant can lift himself from his precarious and unproductive condition, and thereby contribute to economic development. These require-

ments in turn set up the need for diversification and industrialization of the economy—a need intensified where a population problem exists, if there are to be productive outlets for surplus people.

These changes do not have to be, nor could they be, put into effect simultaneously or in their final form. But decisive steps in that direction must be taken, and the people must believe that they will continue. Government is the only agency capable of initiating and directing such a program. This in turn requires that the governments of these areas turn their eyes from the past to the future, and become more responsive to the needs of the people as a whole than to their own interests. Those governments which persist in clinging to the past will certainly not bring the conditions for economic development to their nations, and may, where popular movements are strong, be swept away.

Successful development programs will require honest and efficient government administration, carefully worked out plans, resource surveys, decisions as to the relative importance of the public and private sectors of the economy, improved national income investigations, and a host of other technical, legal, and economic changes. These matters are individually of sufficient importance that their handling may make or break a country's program. The point is that the achievement of each segment of the program to a large extent depends upon the corresponding achievement of the others. Separately conceived and executed improvements will do little to better the over-all situation, and may even worsen it. Sweeping institutional changes are required; in many countries the magnitude of such change is tantamount to social revolution.

LEVELS AND SOURCES OF INCOME
IN VARIOUS COUNTRIES*

INTERNATIONAL comparisons of income are subject to serious reservations owing to the crudeness of the available estimates in domestic currency for many countries, to differences in concepts and institutional arrangements, and to the difficulties of converting the estimates into a common currency. The data presented in this study are, nevertheless, reasonably adequate for broad comparisons of the orders of magnitude of the per capita national income levels of the various countries covered and for indicating the disparities between the under-developed and industrialized countries, while the differences in the sources of income, according to major industry groupings, throw light on the factors accounting for the disparities.

Although the term "national income" is used in this chapter, the concept employed is that of national income produced within the country, or net geographical product at factor cost, rather than the more usual concept of national income of residents or net national income at factor cost. The former concept includes income which is paid to foreign investors holding assets in the country concerned but excludes income which is received from foreign assets owned by the residents of that country. In most cases the difference between these items is small.

* Reprinted from *National Income and Its Distribution in Under-Developed Countries*, Statistical Papers, Series E, No. 3, Department of Economic Affairs, United Nations, New York, 1951, pp. 2–3.

Table 1 presents information regarding the level of per capita incomes in fifty-seven countries measured in terms of United States dollars. This table classifies the countries by range of income per head and continental area, and also indicates what percentage of the combined population of all the countries is accounted for by the countries in each income range. Of the countries shown, twelve of them, with a total population amounting to 34 per cent of the population of all fifty-seven countries (covering 63 per cent of the world's population (cf. table 2)) are classified as having per capita incomes below $100 in 1949, and thirty-three countries, with 59 per cent of the population, have per capita incomes below $300. Only eight countries, with 16 per cent of the population, have per capita incomes in excess of $600.

Of the countries shown in table 1, the greatest concentration of very low-income countries is to be found in Asia, while the countries of Western Europe (with some exceptions) and Oceania, and parts of North America are to be found in the uppermost ranges. In general, the Eastern European countries and most of South America are in the intermediate ranges in respect of the level of per capita income. Since only a small part of Africa (about 20 per cent by population) is covered in the table, the bunching of the African countries in the lowest range, which one would expect and which is confirmed by table 2, is not brought out. Indeed, the countries not shown for the various continental divisions have, generally, considerably lower per capita incomes than those covered by table 1, so that the inequality among countries is actually greater than suggested by this table.

Table 2 shows the figures for total population and total national (and per capita) income by continental areas, the latter being arrived at by including rough estimates for the national incomes of the

TABLE 1. Countries Classified by Size of *Per Capita* Income in 1949 and Continental Division

Income Per Capita in US Dollars	Population		Africa	America, North	America, South	Asia	Europe and USSR	Oceania
	Number (million)	Per Cent						
Under $100	509	34	Kenya N. Rhodesia	Dominican Republic	Ecuador Paraguay	Burma Ceylon India Iran Pakistan Philippines Thailand		
$100–200	284	19	Egypt S. Rhodesia	Mexico	Brazil Chile Colombia Peru Surinam	Japan Syria Turkey	Bulgaria Greece Spain Yugoslavia	
$200–300	82	6	Union of S. Africa	Cuba Puerto Rico			Austria Hungary Italy	
$300–450	305	20			Argentina Uruguay	Israel	Czechoslovakia Finland Germany (Western) Ireland Poland USSR	
$450–600	69	5			Venezuela		Belgium France Iceland Luxembourg Netherlands Norway	
$600–900	89	6		Canada			Denmark Sweden Switzerland United Kingdom	Australia New Zealand
$900 and over	149	10		U.S.A.				
Total	1,487	100						

General Note: The countries are listed alphabetically in each group. The concept of income used to calculate the per capita data is national income produced within the territorial boundaries of the country or net geographical product at factor cost.

TABLE 2. Population, Income, and *Per Capita* Income of Continental Divisions, 1949

Continent	Population		Continental Income		Percentages of Continental Totals Covered by Countries in Table 1		Per Capita Income in Terms of US Dollars		
	Number (thousand)	Percentage of World Total	Amount ($ US billion)	Percentage of World Total	Population	Income	All Countries	Countries in Table 1	Other Areas
Africa	197,881	8.3	14.0	2.6	20.9	42.8	75	140	60
America, North	213,316	9.0	237.0	43.6	92.3	99.6	1,100	1,200	70
America, South	107,519	4.5	18.0	3.5	95.3	98.1	170	175	90
Asia	1,253,514	53.0	58.0	10.5	48.0	65.4	50	70	30
Europe	392,789	16.6	148.5	27.3	87.2	92.3	380	400	240
USSR[a]	193,000[b]	8.1	59.5	11.0	100.0	100.0	310	310	—
Oceania	12,434	0.5	7.0	1.5	77.8	98.6	560	710	50
WORLD TOTAL	2,370,453	100.0	542.0	100.0	62.7	92.0	230	350	50

[a] Includes the Byelorussian and the Ukrainian Soviet Socialist Republic.
[b] Population figures refer to 1946.

countries not contained in table 1. In addition, the percentage of the total continental population and national income covered by the countries included in this table is indicated. From table 2 it appears that the areas distinguished may be ranked in terms of declining income or output per head of population as follows: North America ($1,100), Oceania ($560), Europe ($380), the USSR ($310), South America ($170), Africa ($75), and Asia ($50).

This marked inequality of incomes may also be brought out by relating a continent's share in the world population to its share in world national income. Thus, Asia, with over half the world's population, produces only one-tenth of the world's national income. North America, on the other hand, with less than 10 per cent of the world's population, accounts for nearly 45 per cent of the world's national income. Asia, Africa and South America together, with over 65 per cent of the world's population, generate somewhat in excess of 15 per cent of the world's national income, while the remaining areas, with only 25 per cent of the world's population, produce about 40 per cent of the world's income.

It should be borne in mind that the figures presented are more appropriate for comparing levels of production than levels of welfare. In any attempt to make inter-country comparisons of living standards many additional factors would have to be taken into account. For example, it would be necessary to adjust the figures for the distributive and other services that are important in industrialized countries but relatively uncommon in underdeveloped areas, and which therefore serve to inflate the incomes of the former without necessarily raising welfare correspondingly. Without such adjustments, the figures tend to magnify the differences in the levels of welfare between countries in different stages of development. The disparity between rich and poor countries is further exaggerated as the result of the under-estimation in certain cases of the important sectors of activity carried on outside the monetary sphere in subsistence economies.

Dr. Douglas F. Dowd is an Assistant Professor of Economics at Cornell University. He developed an interest in the problems of underdeveloped areas during World War II when he spent 2½ years in New Guinea and the Philippines. Professor Dowd is also the author of *Modern Economic Problems in Historical Perspective*.

II

THE POLITICAL STATUS
OF UNDERDEVELOPED AREAS

In this chapter we shall attempt to classify political entities according to their status as self-governing or non-self-governing and according to the variable, developed or underdeveloped.

The Statistical Office of the United Nations has classified the 195 political entities of the world as self-governing or non-self-governing.[1] A self-governing political entity is one in which there are internal executive authorities and/or legislative bodies representing the inhabitants of the territory and who are free to regulate the economic conditions and social rights of their own people. A non-self-governing political entity is one in which the rights of the inhabitants, their economic status, and social privileges are regulated by another political entity in charge of the administration of the territory.[2]

Our familiarity with the political status of most African political entities immediately suggests that underdeveloped areas will be non-self-governing or so-called "colonies" or "protectorates." While this conclusion would be justified for Africa and parts of Asia, underdeveloped areas may, in reality, be found with a variety of political systems ranging from those with little or no self-government at any level to those that have had a history of self-government for hundreds of years. The non-self-governing as well as the self-governing political entities exist under a wide variety of governments, some with elected representatives and executives and others with the decision-making power concentrated in the hands of a few persons who have acquired their status in a traditional but nonelective fashion.

Rather than list each political entity according to its development and political status the following tables present an overall view of world population and political entities by regions.[3] The classification as developed or underdeveloped

[1] *Nomenclature of Geographical Areas for Statistical Purposes*, Statistical Papers, Series M., No. 1, Lake Success: United Nations, 1949.

[2] Modified from suggested definitions in *Problems of Transmission and Organization: Report of the Secretary-General of the United Nations*, A/74, 21 October 1946, pp. 4–5.

[3] Some modification of the United Nations' classification of political entities was necessitated by changes in the political status of various entities since the United Nations' list was published.

is identical to that previously mentioned and presented in detail in Chapter I.

A glance at Table 5 is sufficient to show that Africa and Oceania are largely composed of underdeveloped non-self-governing political entities. The Middle East is self-governing and underdeveloped; Central America and Asia are underde-

TABLE 5.   World Population According to Political Status and Development
Number of Political Entities and Percent of World Population According to Distribution in Nine Regions: 1950

| | Developed | | | | Underdeveloped | | | |
| | Self-Governing | | Non-self-Governing | | Self-Governing | | Non-self-Governing | |
	No. of Political Entities	% of World Pop.	No. of Political Entities	% of World Pop.	No. of Political Entities	% of World Pop.	No. of Political Entities	% of World Pop.
North America	2	6.87	3	−.01	0	.00	0	.00
Central America	0	.00	0	.00	10	1.87	14	.24
South America	3	1.05	0	.00	7	3.50	4	.02
Europe	29	16.28	5	.02	0	.00	0	.00
Africa	1	.51	0	.00	5	1.93	44	5.75
Middle East	0	.00	0	.00	15	3.12	3	.05
Southeast Asia	0	.00	0	.00	4	5.49	6	1.60
Central, Eastern, and Southern Asia	2	11.46	0	.00	9	39.43	7	.18
Oceania	2	.41	1	.02	0	.00	19	.11
Total	39	36.58	9	.04	50	55.34	97	7.95

veloped, about half of the political entities being self-governing and the other half non-self-governing. It should be noted that, although a large number of our political entities are non-self-governing, they constitute only 8 percent of the world's population. Africa and southeast Asia are the location of almost all the non-self-governing underdeveloped peoples. Even as this is written the indigenous inhabitants of these areas are struggling for self-government.

If we combine regions into one table the following result is obtained.

TABLE 6.   World Population and Political Entities According to Political Status and Development: 1950

| | Underdeveloped | | Developed | | Total | |
	Number	% of World Population	Number	% of World Population	Number	% of World Population
Self-Governing	50	55.34	39	36.58	89	91.92
Non-self-Governing	97	7.95	9	.04	106	7.99
Total	147	63.29	48	36.62	195	99.91

The relationship between political status and underdevelopment is now more clearly seen. This is the kind of relationship that might be called "one-way." If a political entity is non-self-governing it is almost always underdeveloped; if it is self-governing it may be developed or underdeveloped. If an area is developed it is probably self-governing and if it is underdeveloped it may be either self-governing or non-self-governing.

The question is frequently raised, what degree of development must a political entity have in order to be self-governing? This question appears to assume that development is the basis of capacity for self-government. Actually, this is an *a priori* viewpoint; it is a viewpoint based on a hypothesis rather than previous research. While it is possible to describe the joint occurrence of the two variables, development and self-government, one cannot assume that development is therefore a prerequisite to self-government. Neither can one assume that self-government is a prerequisite or condition necessary before development. That underdeveloped and undeveloped areas are non-self-governing may be an indication of retardation brought about by colonial policy, or of the relative difficulty in developing these areas as contrasted to others with more readily available resources. The arrangement of political entities in either of the tables just presented cannot be said to have been determined exclusively by economic or other forms of development or by political status. In some instances political status may be a determinant of level of development and in other cases it may be shown that level of development has been a determinant of political status. In still other cases, and these probably constitute the majority, both political status and development are "causes" and "consequences."

Since there has been such an active interest in the hypothesis that development of various kinds is related to political status, we shall present in detail in a later chapter the results of various pieces of research attempting to test this hypothesis. We may state now, however, that the research thus far conducted has failed to find the close relationship hypothesized between political status and various factors considered crucial in determining whether or not an area is capable of self-government. It is doubtful if anyone should have expected to find a single factor or group of factors differentiating self-governing from non-self-governing political entities. However, the possibility of various combinations of developmental factors differentiating between political entities or countries according to their political status must also be considered. It is possible that some complex configuration of traits differentiate self-governing from non-self-governing areas and that this configuration of traits is a function of the level of development of a political entity.

Nevertheless, the student should be sensitized to the role of government in underdeveloped areas. The characteristics of numerous underdeveloped, self-governing areas have received considerable attention in the media of mass communication in recent years and several have been publicized by prominent Americans in accounts of their travels in these lands.[4] While the existence of a despotic government in a self-governing area may be a handicap to development of human

---

[4] An excellent example of this type of report is William O. Douglas's volume, *Strange Lands and Friendly People*, Harper & Brothers, 1954.

and natural resources, these difficulties are multiplied if a non-self-governing entity is under the control of a despotic controlling power.

The first article in this chapter, "The Changing Structure of a Micronesian Society," by John Useem, illustrates the instability and lack of continuity that may be found in a program of economic and social development in underdeveloped areas. One can scarcely expect development to proceed in an orderly fashion under the conditions herein described.

"Nationalism in Tropical Africa," by James S. Coleman presents a systematic description of nationalistic movements in Africa and lists the factors that have contributed to their growth.

THE CHANGING STRUCTURE OF A MICRONESIAN SOCIETY*

JOHN USEEM

ONE of the most significant social phenomena of the past century has been the impact of the larger society on local cultures. The urbanization of rural life, the secularization of sacred structures, the acculturation of minority groups, the modernizing of primitive peoples are but different manifestations of the same social process. This process is modifying not only surface relationships but also the entire organization of community life; native ways of living, traditional patterns of social inter-action, and preexisting systems of values are reoriented. While we now know the characteristic features of this transition, and can even forecast its successive stages, we are exceedingly limited in our skill in directing it as a social program.

The writer, as a Naval Military Gov-

* Adapted and reprinted by permission from *American Anthropologist*, Vol. 47, No. 4, October–December, 1945, pp. 567–588.

ernment officer, spent six months in the Palau group of Caroline Islands in charge of the population of Angaur. In order to develop effective techniques for the administration of Angaur, a systematic study was made of its past and more recent social order. During the course of a hundred years, Spanish, Germans, and Japanese in sequence endeavored to reshape the social contours of Palau. Now the United States is continuing that historic process.

THE IMPACT OF SPANISH, GERMAN, AND JAPANESE CONTROL ON THE NATIVE SOCIAL ORDER

In characteristic fashion each colonial power, during its period of control, sought to reform native ways to conform to its preconceptions of the proper modes of behavior. Though they differed in the means employed in bringing about the change and in the aspects of the local culture they concentrated on, their ends were essentially alike.

While it is customary to think of the Japanese as an Oriental influence, their objectives, in reality, differed little from those of their predecessors. For example, the Japanese stressed the capitalistic mores surrounding labor and individual advancement, the concept of progress and change as values *per se*, and sought to disseminate numerous mechanical devices which are usually thought of as uniquely Western. Hence, the supplanting of one colonial power by another did not entail a major break in the controlling group's attitude towards Palau's way of living.

The Spanish formally exercised control over Palau for fourteen years, from 1885 to 1899, the Germans for fifteen years between 1899 and 1914, and the Japanese in the thirty-year span 1914–1944. The brevity of the Spanish and German eras, in contrast to the Japanese, limited their influence on native life.

Spanish administration was almost entirely in the hands of the Capuchin order of monks. The principal efforts of this governing body were directed at evangelization, "uplifting" of native morals, and the preservation of order. While the first missionaries were received with indifference, continuous efforts eventually resulted in the conversion of the bulk of the population to Catholicism. To achieve these ends, tabus, totemism, sorcery, the worship of ancestral spirits, and interisland warfare were discouraged by all possible methods. Native styles of dancing were declared to be sinful. The fourteen years of Spanish control were of primary significance in their impact on the religious life of Angaur. The loss of supernatural sanctions of the social hierarchy indirectly weakened the social order and thereby made possible other changes in the subsequent period.

The Germans, in keeping with their national mind-set, sought to systematize native life. While the Germans did not intervene in the details of the social life of Angaur, they established a series of regulations concerning native institutions. These were not deliberately designed to modify the total culture but rather to alter those items in conflict with German conceptions of the good life. Missionary activities were encouraged, the native religious practices were outlawed, mission schools were made compulsory, women companions for the club prohibited. Palau style dances were permitted but not encouraged. Chiefs were retained in control but subjected to detailed supervision from above and their authority curtailed. Heavy emphasis was placed on health measures. The first hospitals were established, toilets were introduced and their use made compulsory, the homes of dysentery cases were destroyed to prevent contagion, and a program to combat yaws was begun. The one-room long-houses were viewed with disfavor and so newlyweds were required to build small palm-thatch huts. A network of roads linking all the communities of the island was constructed. The greatest effort of all was directed toward the development of a capitalistic economy. Scientists quickly located phosphate deposits, and the German South Seas Phosphate Company immediately entered into production. Everything possible was done to replace the cooperative-subsistence economy by an individualistic commercial economy. Native money which had more social than fiduciary significance was exchanged for German money. Extension of credit was stopped so that people would work regularly to acquire purchasing power. Club-controlled labor and trade, and the family-clan inheritance of property were declared inoperative. Every man between twenty and sixty was required to plant eight coconut trees a year, and to accept wage work. Men were not allowed to loaf in the club during the work day. Collective land holdings were liquidated, on the theory that each person would then have to work to gain a livelihood, and none would be free of labor. Within a short time much of the island lands were owned by the phosphate company. The German era was of lasting effect in that it inaugurated many of the social and economic policies subsequently pursued by the Japanese. But the inner life of the community was hardly troubled by the German superimposed values. The shift from German to Japanese control took place with no local conflict between the two powers. During the transition the former officials aided the incoming ones in setting up their administration.

Japanese administration of Angaur passed through three phases: the Navy period of control (1914–1918), a mixed Navy and civil service organization (1918–1922), and finally the South Seas Bureau (1922–1944). The Navy retained the pre-existing legislation but relaxed its enforcement. Navy personnel were friendly to the natives and in general allowed the people to run their own society. The same outlook prevailed in the mixed period. The Navy held the key positions while the Japanese civil servants carried out the routine governmental programs. No major effort was made to alter local institutions but a great number of minor regulations were introduced by the bureaucracy. The South Seas Bureau adopted all of the socio-economic programs typical of an enlightened colonial imperialism—namely, the controlled exploitation of local resources, the improvement of the population's well-being, and the maintenance of a responsible government.

A wide variety of measures was undertaken to facilitate the modernization of native life. To inculcate further the incentives necessary to workers in a capital-istic system, stress was placed on the prestige which surrounds persons of wealth and the moral values of industry and continuous labor. Similarly, time-consuming ceremonies and dances which disrupted the daily work schedule were frowned upon. To encourage a desire for wage work and higher levels of living, quantities of manufactured articles ranging from canned fish to electric light bulbs were imported for sale to natives. In order to offset native indifference to modern health procedures, a hospital was opened, medical care was given free, and an extensive sanitary program was undertaken. Public schools were designed to give the usual elementary courses in language (Japanese), mathematics, natural sciences, geography, agriculture and craftsmanship, and also to acquaint the younger generation with a new code of ethics and mode of behavior. School teachers constantly emphasized the need for "modernization." While a series of lectures was given on native history, the lesson pointed out was the importance of progress.

The most drastic alteration was in the system of governing. Native officials had fled to their homes during the shift from German to Japanese control; while soon recalled to duty, they were never restored to their original positions. For a brief time the Japanese tried the German scheme of indirect rule, using native chiefs and council as their intermediary, but then abandoned it. Direct intervention in the internal affairs of Angaur society became the standard operating procedure. In the German period native chiefs retained most of their traditional prerogatives including the issuance of all orders to the members of their group. Councils also wielded much influence, for they continued to exercise their right to pass on the chiefs' edicts. But with Japanese direct rule, the chiefs and the councils were stripped of much of their authority. Laws were promulgated by the Bureau and the chiefs merely carried out the enactments. Hence the weakened chieftainship became the only recognized native office. When the people objected to an ordinance they no longer appealed to their chiefs or council but assembled as a body and went directly to the Japanese official. Such an appeal, however, was not an easy enterprise, for it entailed traveling to Korror, the headquarters of the South Sea Bureau, and often the official responsible was in Truk or Tokio.

The focal point of local enterprise, the phosphate works, were enlarged and their ownership transferred to the quasi-governmental South Seas Colonial Company. The company in cooperation with the South Seas Bureau provided social security benefits for aged and injured workers, honored the terms of its labor contracts, paid its workers a fairly high wage and, according to its former employees, treated them with fairness and humanity. Natives were not encouraged to set up their own small enterprises and while many local industries declined, such as seamanship and seafaring trades, a few natives did open stores and artisans made handicrafts for the souvenir market. Commercial relations displaced bartering, and Japanese money became the only legal tender. No ceiling was placed on the wealth accumulated by the Angaurese and some succeeded in saving considerable sums of money. Taxes were low, the South Seas Bureau meeting most of the costs of its own personnel and public utilities. Skilled Japanese carpenters were brought to the island to build Japanese-style wooden homes which the population viewed as a distinct gain in health conditions.

Through informal but constant pressure, other innovations took place. The wearing of clothing became universal and tatooing no longer was done by the younger generations. The use of the Japanese language, the practice of bowing, the cover-ing up of the mouth while laughing, pre-occupation with cleanliness in the home and in appearance, the gearing of the day's routine to the clock, the use of rice as the staple food, refraining from outward show of romantic love in courtship were but a few indications of the range of innovations. Young men in line for leadership were selected from each village to visit Japan. Upon return these persons were encouraged to win adherents to the new manners and morals. One of the most far-reaching influences was the daily social interaction between the Japanese residents and the Angaurese. This was especially true among the children who played together and shared a common daily routine. The emulation of the group with high prestige was inevitable, and so unconsciously and in many subtle ways the Angaurese took on Japanese mores and folkways.

The South Seas Bureau policy of gradualism and of piecemeal alterations, however, evoked unforseen results. The withdrawal of one traditional practice dislocated a series of others, some of which were deemed desirable.

Uncapitalistic behavior was never stamped out, and social voids remained where no adequate substitutes were forthcoming. The ceremonial feasts which accompanied the passage rites were contravening the recently introduced capitalistic modes of behavior. For instance, after death an expensive feast lasting several days was held in the home of the deceased. In former times the clan assumed the burden of promoting such feasts, but the conversion of some of the population to individual savings rather than group-sharing precipitated sharp conflicts. The Japanese housing program evoked a new type of parasitism. Families would call upon their clan to meet the cost of the new home in accordance with traditional practices. But while in the old days once a home was built the families remained in it permanently, now, enterprising families would soon sell their new household, keep the profit, and then call on the clan to meet the cost of building another. While waiting the construction of the second place, the ambitious family would move into the dwelling of any member of its clan. These practices were declared illegal. A series of similar rules was worked out for other difficulties but at no time was a complete adjustment reached. The reciprocal rights and duties of the two sexes were obscured by the reforms which had been made in the clan-family system. The role of women which originally had been clearly defined was now ambiguous. Marital ties also were confused. A native would be deemed married to two women under Angaur custom; the Japanese regarded the additional mate as a "friend"; and the missionaries denied that the second marital relationship legally existed.

The last year of Japanese dominance was marked by a renaissance of the indigenous social order. The Japanese were too preoccupied to combat this revival and so relinquished control over the daily lives of the natives. Conflicting orders between officials of the South Seas Bureau and the army officers created a situation in which the natives could choose their own course of action from a series of alternatives. Informed that they would be hideously treated should the Americans come, the Angaurese decided they would be better off if their own ingroup was made strong to meet the difficult period ahead.

THE ESTABLISHMENT OF AMERICAN NAVAL MILITARY GOVERNMENT

The assumption of American control of Angaur was accompanied by the total destruction which surrounds war. Unlike the previous transitions, there was no continuity in the economic or community life of the island. Native homes and villages were uninhabitable, the principal source of livelihood—the phosphate mine—ceased operations, and even the topography of the island was greatly modified by hyperactive engineers.

The Angaurese slipped through the Japanese lines into the American lines. They arrived in rags, many were ill, and everyone was filled with anxiety. They looked with concern upon a large hole being dug for a latrine, fearing it might be their grave. They were exceedingly meek and extremely anxious to please the Americans. When asked to perform a job, it was soon necessary to tell them to slow down for they worked as fast and as hard as humanly possible. Thus, when unloading sand from a truck they would try to make the floor immaculate, brushing off all the loose particles with their hands.

The liberation of a primitive society proved to be a far more complex affair than anticipated. Liberation from Japanese control created a political vacuum. There being no fixed, long-range foreign policy for guidance of military government, it was necessary to confine all programs to the immediate, short-range objectives. Liberation connotes freedom, which was not practicable in an area of military operations. To offset the enemy's indoctrination regarding America, the civil-affairs staff relied on personal social relations rather than formal lectures. Enlisted men from small midwestern towns proved to be especially effective in communicating a sense of sympathetic understanding. While occasionally, in their brash informal American way, they ran counter to local mores, their genuine naïveté, utter lack of arrogance, and regard for natives as equals quickly elicited an exceedingly friendly response. The preconceived American notion of "primitiveness" also was quickly found to be a meaningless construct. A half century of acculturation and capitalistic industrial development had brought to the people of Angaur most of the attributes of modern civilization. It was quite a shock for military personnel to be asked if they knew about moving pictures, ice cream, and table tennis. The civil-affairs planners had been misled by the anthropological literature perused prior to invasion; it presented an antiquated picture of native life at the level of the German era, and was permeated with propagandistic stereotypes of Japanese actions. As a result, supplies were taken for an aboriginal people, whereas in reality what was needed were items of the same type as would be brought to a South Dakota rural community. The issuance of emergency relief precipitated some unforeseen cultural complications. An attempt to ascertain who needed shoes evoked a community-wide controversy. Shoes were not merely an article of wear but also a mark of status. Those who previously were without shoes insisted that everyone urgently needed them, and persons who once possessed them maintained with great feeling that only the elite were entitled to shoes. American democratic concepts of social equality clashed with native concepts of social stratification. The issue was finally resolved by the compromise provision of shoes to all workers, thereby setting up a new social category. These were thereafter worn regardless of personal comfort and correctness of fit. Communication, as it had amongst previous incoming governments, turned out to be a vexing problem. Nothing is more frustrating than the urgent need to convey or comprehend some idea and be confronted by the blockage of language differences. Having a single interpreter who spoke Japanese and no Palau, the more ingenious soon resorted to a special brand of elementary English accompanies by gestures; such phrases as O.K., *very good, got, all-a-same* were rapidly assimilated by the natives who were

more adept (and perhaps more motivated as well as experienced) at acquiring a new speech. But the more subtle social relationships involving abstract concepts were either untangled by the interpreter or passed over by default. To overcome this barrier, classes in English were soon established for the Angaurese and a study of native institutions undertaken.

The writer had established as the goal of all civil-affairs actions the restoration of the indigenous ways of living, but it was soon found that reconstruction of a culture brings forth at least as many societal problems as the process of destruction. It was not possible or even entirely desirable to eliminate all of the cultural modifications which had occurred in the past fifty years.

Changing subordinate-superordinate relationships brought forth serious psychological problems. Angaur people have so long played the role of the subordinate that they have developed fixed habit patterns for this social status. For example, they never would object outwardly to any proposal, regardless of its intrinsic demerits, and even when patently absurd orders were issued they invariably would carry them out. Despite much prompting they would not express their wishes unless specifically asked to do so, and then the response was that they would do whatever the governors wished them to do. The latter would state they would like to do what the people desired. After some hesitation a definite preference would be given but with many apologies. Whenever native leaders were asked to recommend policies, elicited answers were in terms of a projected role of a superordinate, rather than in terms of the subordinate's interests. The suggested course was highly demanding on themselves. Thus in a case of a person violating the sanitary orders, the chief's proposal of discipline was far harsher than warranted by the act, by native penalties or American norms. In the theoretical framework of Mead, their experience with prior authorities had built up a "generalized other" of superordinates whose social acts would be satisfactory for the elite and inconvenient for themselves. Hence, when called upon to assume the role of policy-making, heretofore denied them, they made decisions which would call forth in themselves previously established emotional responses of subordinates. Intellectually they could assume coordinate status in the new "democratic" era but habitual anticipatory behavior led them to act as superordinates to themselves. Following the practice of emulating the dominant group in outward behavior, in part a by-product of the high prestige of the American and in part to please him, miscellaneous American traits were indiscriminately copied; young men modeled themselves after the G.I., and girls tried to imitate the women shown in moving pictures and magazines. The jitterbug dances were tried out with great interest, and samples of other types of American dances were constantly requested. This outlook persisted even when social interaction had continued for some time and they had gained completely a sense of security.

Attempts to restore Palau life brought disagreements over the exact nature of old institutions. Individuals live a social pattern rather than intellectually comprehend it in all its ramifications. Hence, knowledge of former ways was uncertain and the correct procedures became the topic of debate. The restoration of different cultural complexes led to internal contradictions requiring further modifications.

The appraisal of former customs in order to decide whether or not they should be reinstated is an exceedingly difficult task. It brings into the foreground the whole question of values. Past practices must be judged in the perspective of future goals, hedonistic folkways balanced with practicalities, etc. It also entails consideration of the intrinsic merits of the modifications made during the Spanish, German and Japanese regimes. The enterprise would be impossible if Angaur lacked a basic cultural orientation that is shared by the entire group. It would be inconceivable to procure a consensus in a heterogeneous, disorganized, large population with conflicting interests and rival factions.

With the alleviation of the emergency and the commencement of the restoration of a semi-autonomous society the focus of attention began to turn toward the restoration of a sound economy. The prewar earnings of Japanese currency were exchanged at the current low rates, thus resulting in a considerable loss of wealth. Only a small proportion of the money held by the people was released to them after the exchange, the rest being held in trust until the end of the war. Savings accounts were not honored despite the fact that the bank funds were found intact and receipts were available. Clan and village funds were frozen. Wages were low and such household goods as were placed on sale scaled at a high price. To take an extreme case, a formerly wealthy native owned $2,450.00 in postal savings and $750.00 in cash. After the exchange he had $10.00.

Because of the experience of the last half century, the Angaurese are convinced they can never fully reestablish a static ancestral type of order or return to a subsistence economy. The acculturation process continues within the American framework as it has under the Spanish, German, and Japanese predecessors.

NATIVE REACTIONS TO THE ACCULTURATION PROCESS

A society which believes it is being persecuted or exploited, and without the power of overt retaliation, develops techniques for counteracting the dominant power. The opposition may take the form of a well-organized underground, a nativistic movement, or may assume a more subtle form of passive resistance. Likewise a group convinced that its rulers are hostile to its indigenous culture and determined to eradicate it will develop strong ingroup cohesiveness and intensify its efforts to preserve its cultural integrity. Strong pressure will be exerted against the deviate who seeks to gain personal advantage through either escaping into the dominant group or acting as a "quisling." But it does not follow that a society subjected to social reorganization and cultural indoctrination responds in these ways if it deems the motives of the elite to be honorable and their premises historically sound. Such is the case of Angaur. With the single exception of its early rebellion against conversion to Christianity, the people have never consciously fought the outsider. The absence of opposition was not due to a sense of total defeat and resignation to the inevitable, as is true of the Sioux Indians. Rather, it emanates from a realistic acknowledgement that to survive as a culture Palau society must accommodate itself to the modern colonial-capitalistic world. Native hostility to the Germans centered primarily on the ruthless, unyielding methods they used to gain their ends. There was no resentment of the Germans' objectives and no feeling that they were unjust in their dealings with the Angaurese. So, too, discontentment with the Japanese stemmed not from the changes they imposed but rather from the limits placed on native advancement in the newer social institutions. Their eagerness today to learn American ways is but another indication of this desire to adjust to new circumstances.

It is apparent that Angaur has not experienced cultural collapse. The weakening of the native social system did not produce a void in the island's social or-

ganization. The Angaurese never have so identified themselves with the outgroup as to lose their sense of ingroup unity. Without any formal agreement, factions refrain from allying themselves with the government officials in order to overcome their opposition. Though there is no conscious plot to maintain a private sphere, some group-arrived-at decisions are not communicated to non-members, and some social actions are not performed in the presence of outsiders. Within the confines of native society, emotions are freer and the old mores (intermingled with new ones) guide behavior, whereas in dealing with persons of the outgroup, emotions are circumscribed and the prevailing conduct norms are carefully observed. The control group each time sought to introduce an alternative pattern to replace the one curtailed. Though the substitutions were not always successful, they did provide meaningful goals. Thus the replacement of the local faith by Christianity, the introduction of a new style of dancing in place of the older forms, the establishment of a responsible colonial government in lieu of the pre-existing native political organization, the offering of tangible rewards as compensation for the loss of leisure time, the provision of manufactured goods as a substitute for handicrafts, etc., meant a shift but not lack of a pattern of social action. The Angaurese, as previously noted, were not hostile to change *per se* but were never confronted by a sequence of contradictory programs. New modes of behavior were welcomed as additions to the island's culture rather than viewed as threats to it. The consistency of attitudes among the various successive control groups, and their willingness to continue what had been started by their predecessor precluded any confusion on the ultimate ends being sought. The reformations, while affecting nearly every aspect of group life, modified but did not destroy the traditional ways of living. The absence of any coercion, the tolerance of native views, the avoidance of ruthless suppression of ancestral institutions eased the process of adjustment and prevented the building up of a deep sense of inner tension and overt rebellion. The changes that came were usually accompanied by a rise in scale of living rather than a decline of the population to poverty and insecurity. They engendered a sense of progress and hope of an even better future rather than one of frustration and total defeat. While the controlling powers made mistakes in their efforts to manipulate the social structure, their genuine desire to improve the welfare of the population created no serious hostility to the agents of change, and found tangible expression in considerable material aid to the natives in their times of need. Within the native society itself the persistence of its indigenous value system, the adaptability of the people, and their maintenance of integrated personalities despite numerous upsets in their lives, made possible reorganization without demoralization.

This case and others like it cast doubts on the popular sociological generalization that the secularization of primitive-rural life can only result in social demoralization. But it also gives further support to the conclusion that the successful alteration of a going social system is an exceedingly difficult task. Primary social groups can be readily altered by the actions of an outside group, but the reconstruction of a balanced social order that is capable of operating on its own within the framework of the larger society remains an unknown social technique.

NATIONALISM IN TROPICAL AFRICA*

JAMES S. COLEMAN

POSTWAR uprisings and nationalist assertions in Tropical Africa—that part of the continent south of the Sahara and north of the Union—have directed increased attention towards the nature and implications of the awakening of the African to political consciousness. Among scholars this neglected area has long been the preserve of the scientific linguist or of the social anthropologist; only recently have American sociologists, economists, and political scientists developed an active interest in its problems. As a consequence,

* Adapted and reprinted by permission from *The American Political Science Review*, Vol. XLVIII, No. 2, June, 1954, pp. 404–424.

apart from certain efforts by anthropologists to popularize their findings we have been obliged to rely primarily upon the somewhat contradictory accounts of colonial governments seeking to explain imperial connections, or of African nationalists determined to achieve self-government and the good life of which national self-determination has become the symbol. Thus, we have been placed in the uncomfortable position of having to formulate opinions and policy and to render judgments without sufficient knowledge, or, what could be worse, on the basis of evaluations provided by participants in the nationalist struggle. There is, therefore, a very real need for independent and objective research regarding the character and probable course of African nationalist development.

I. WHAT IS AFRICAN NATIONALISM?

On the level of abstraction at which the political scientist is accustomed to roam, a nation is not a loose catch-all term denoting a larger grouping of tribes (e.g., Zulus, Basutos, Mende, Buganda, or Hausa); rather it is a post-tribal, post-feudal terminal *community* which has emerged from the shattering forces of disintegration that characterize modernity. This does not mean that the Hausa peoples of Northern Nigeria cannot become a nation, nor does it mean that the "national" consciousness of the ordinary Hausaman must reach the level of intensity of the average Frenchman before there is a nation. It does suggest, however, that there must be a much greater awareness of a closeness of contact with "national" compatriots as well as with the "national" government.[1] This closeness of contact on the horizontal and vertical levels has been a distinctly Western phenomenon, for the obvious reason that it is the result of modern technology.

Not only is a political scientist quite precise in his use of the concept "nation," but in poaching on the insights of the Africanists he also finds it difficult to place under the cover of "nationalism" all forms of past and present discontent and organizational development in Africa. Thus, it is believed useful at the outset to distinguish the following:

A. TRADITIONALIST MOVEMENTS

1. Spontaneous movements of resistance to the initial European occupation or post-

[1] Royal Institute of International Affairs, *Nationalism* (London, 1939), pp. 1–7; Karl W. Deutsch, *Nationalism and Social Communication* (New York, 1953), pp. 1–14.

pacification revolts against the imposition of new institutions, or new forms of coercion, referred to herein as "primary resistance."

2. Nativistic, mahdistic, or messianic mass movements—usually of a magico-religious character—which are psychological or emotional outlets for tensions produced by the confusions, frustrations, or socio-economic inequalities of alien rule, referred to herein as "nativism."[2]

B. SYNCRETISTIC MOVEMENTS

1. Separatist religious groups, which have seceded and declared their independence from white European churches either because of the desire for religious independence or because the white clerics were intolerant regarding certain African customs; hereafter referred to as "religious separatism."

2. Kinship associations, organized and led by the Western-educated and urbanized "sons abroad" for the purposes of preserving a sense of identity with the kinfolk in the bush and "brothers" in the impersonal urban center, as well as of providing vehicles for pumping modernity—including the ideas and sentiment of nationalism—into the rural areas.

3. Tribal associations, organized and led by Western-educated elements—usually in collaboration with some traditionalists—who desire to resurrect, or to create for

[2] Nativism is here used in its broad and universal sense, as defined by the late Professor Ralph Linton: "Any conscious, organized attempt on the part of a society's members to revive or perpetuate selected aspects of its culture." See his "Nativistic Movements," *American Anthropologist*, Vol. 45, pp. 230–240, at p. 230 (April–June, 1943). The concept thus includes traditionalist movements in either the European or non-European world. This point is stressed because of the understandable sensitivity of many educated Africans to the root word "native," which as a result of the colonial experience tends to carry with it the connotation of inferiority.

the first time, a tribal sentiment ("tribalism"), for the purpose of establishing large-scale political units, the boundaries of which will be determined by tribal affiliation (i.e., those who accept the *assumption* of common blood and kinship) and the forms of government by a syncretism of tribal and Western institutions.

C. MODERNIST MOVEMENTS

1. Economic-interest groups (labor unions, cooperative societies, professional and middle-class associations) organized and led by Western-educated elements for the purpose of advancing the material welfare and improving the socio-economic status of the members of those groups.

2. Nationalist movements, organized and led by the Westernized elite which is activated by the Western ideas of democracy, progress, the welfare state, and national self-determination, and which aspires *either:* (a) to create modern independent African nation-states possessing an internal state apparatus and external sovereignty and all of the trappings of a recognized member state of international society (e.g., Sudan, Gold Coast, Nigeria, and possibly Sierra Leone); *or* (b) to achieve absolute social and political equality and local autonomy within a broader Eur-African grouping (e.g., French and Portuguese Africa) or within what is manifestly a plural society (e.g., except for Uganda, the territories of British East and Central Africa).[3]

3. Pan-African or trans-territorial movements, organized and led by the Westernized elite, frequently in association with or under the stimulus of American Negroes or West Indians abroad, for the purposes of creating a global *racial* consciousness and unity, or of agitating for the advancement and welfare of members of the *African* race wherever they may be, or of devising plans for future nationalist activity in specific regions.

Once these very arbitrary analytical distinctions are drawn it should be stressed that none of the categories can be treated in isolation. Each of the movements is in one way or another a response to the challenge of alien rule, or of the intrusion of the disintegrating forces—and consequently the insecurity—of modernity. The recent so-called nationalism in Central Africa has been a mixture of "primary resistance" by the chiefs and traditionalists of Northern Rhodesia and Nyasaland and the nationalist agitation of the Westernized elite. Until the project of Federation became an active issue, African movements in this area were confined principally to religious separatist groups, tribal associations, or, in the case of Northern Rhodesia, labor unions. On the West Coast, where nationalism is far more advanced, traditionalist and syncretistic movements have not been and are not absent. In some instances, kinship associations and separatist religious groups have been the antecedents of nationalist organi-

[3] The difference between the goal orientations of the two categories of movements is partly the result of the objectives of differing colonial policies (i.e., the British policy of self-government and differentiation versus the French, Portuguese, and in a qualified sense the Belgian policies of assimilation and identity) and in part the result of the presence or absence of a settled white population. Confronted with the overwhelming obstacles to the full realization of *African self-government*, African leaders in the second category tend towards the extreme either of accommodation (Union of South Africa) or of violence (Kenya). In the territories of the Central African Federation the leaders of the African Congress have tended not to define their ultimate objectives, preferring to act empirically. The strength and persistence of the autonomic drive is reflected, however, in their reported attraction to the original Gore-Brown partition plan adopted by the European Confederate party. See David Cole, "How Strong is the African National Congress," *New Commonwealth*, Vol. 27, pp. 5–10, at p. 9 (Jan. 4, 1954).

zations; in others they have provided the principal organizational bases of the latter (e.g., the National Council of Nigeria and the Cameroons was first inaugurated as a federation mainly of kinship associations, and the African National Congress of the Rhodesias and Nyasaland was the product of fusion of several African welfare societies). In certain cases unrest or protest of a nativistic flavor has been instigated by nationalists for their modernist ends; in others nationalists have claimed such uncoordinated uprisings, as well as purely economic protest movements, to be manifestations of "nationalism," when in reality the participants were unaware of such implications.

One of the interesting differences between prewar and postwar nationalism on the West Coast of Africa is that in the former period nationalism tended to be—as Lord Lugard insisted—the esoteric pasttime of the tiny educated minorities of Lagos, Accra, Freetown, and Dakar; whereas in the latter period these minorities—greatly expanded and dispersed in new urban centers throughout the interior—have made positive efforts to popularize and energize the nationalist crusade in two ways.[4] The first has been to preach education, welfare, progress, and the ideal of self-government among the masses, largely through the nationalist press, independent African schools, and kinship and tribal associations. The aim here has been, in the words of one of their leading prophets, Dr. Nnamdi Azikiwe of Nigeria, to bring about "mental emancipation" from a servile colonial mentality.[5] The second method has been to tap all existing nativistic and religious tensions and economic grievances among the traditionbound masses, as well as the grievances

[4] Sir F. D. Lugard, *The Dual Mandate in British Tropical Africa* (London, 1923), pp. 83 ff.

[5] *Renascent Africa* (Lagos, 1937).

and aspirations of the urbanized clerks and artisans, and channel the energies thus unleashed into support of the nationalist drive. The technique here has been (1) to make nationalism, and in particular its objective of self-government, an integrating symbol in which even the most disparate goals could find identification, and (2) to politicize—one would like to say nationalize—all existing thought and associations. Until recently, many observers —including colonial administrators— tended to live in the prewar climate of opinion and therefore underestimated the power which had thus been harnessed to the nationalist machine.

In the case of the Mau Mau movement in Kenya we are confronted with a complex mixture of nationalism, with a strong traditional bias on the part of the Westernized leaders, and nativism, manipulated by the leaders, on the part of the masses. Both have been generated to an especially high level of intensity as a consequence of the acute and largely unassuaged sense of frustration on the part of the Westernized elite, growing out of the very bleak outlook arising from the almost total absence, until recently, of meaningful career and prestige opportunities within either the old or the new systems, and of the masses, resulting from the land shortage and the overcrowding on the reservations. The presence of a sizable Asian "third force," which virtually monopolizes the middle-class sector, and which has been and is politically conscious, provides a new variable of no little significance in the total situation. The fact that the pattern of organization and the strategy and tactics of the Mau Mau revolt indicate a higher level of sophistication than sheer nativism would imply suggests that our analytical categories need further refinement or qualification.

A particularly striking feature of African nationalism has been the literary and cultural revival which has attended it. A renewed appreciation of and interest in "African" culture has been manifested, in most instances by the most sophisticated and acculturated Africans. In some cases this cultural renaissance has had a purely tribal emphasis; in others it has taken a "neo-African" form, such as the African dress of Dr. Nnamdi Azikiwe, nationalist leader in Nigeria. It has usually been accompanied by a quest for an African history which would in general reflect glory and dignity upon the African race and in particular instill self-confidence in the Western-educated African sensitive to the prejudiced charge that he has no history or culture. In short, there has emerged a new pride in being African. In French areas, the accent until recently has been upon French culture and literature, but there are increasing signs of a shift to African themes amongst the French African literati. The important point is that African nationalism has this cultural content, which renders more difficult any effort to separate rigidly the cultural nationalism of the urban politician from the nativism of the bush peasant.

Yet the differences are important to the student of African nationalism. Primary resistance and nativism tend to be negative and spontaneous revolts or assertions of the unacculturated masses against the disruptive and disorganizing stranger-invader. They are a reflection of a persistent desire of the masses to preserve or recreate the old by protesting against the new. Syncretism is different in that it contains an element of rationality—an urge to recapture those aspects of the old which are compatible with the new, which it recognizes as inevitable and in some respects desirable. Whereas all forms of protest are politically consequential—at least to colonial administrators—only nationalism is primarily political in that it is irrevocably committed to a positive and radical altera-

tion of the power structure. In brief, nationalism is the terminal form of colonial protest.

Another reason for distinguishing between the various categories of assertion, which are basically differences in goal orientation, is not only to provide some basis for judging the nature of the popular support of a nationalist movement during its buildup, but also to have some means of predicting the stability and viability of the political order established by the nationalists once they achieve self-government. The governments of Pakistan, Burma, India, and Indonesia have each been plagued by internal tensions arising from what are fundamentally South Asian variants of traditionalism and tribalism. If a colonial nationalist movement comes to power atop a wave of mass protest which is primarily or even in part nativistic in character, this would have a direct bearing upon the capacity of the Westernized leaders of that movement, not only to maintain political unity and stability but also to carry out what is at the core of most of their programs—rapid modernization by a centralized bureaucratic machine. Any thorough study of the anatomy of a nationalist movement, therefore, must seek to determine the linkages and compatibilities between the goal orientations of the several forces from which that movement derives its élan and strength.

II. FACTORS CONTRIBUTING TO THE RISE OF NATIONALISM

It is far easier to define and describe nationalism than it is to generalize about the factors which have contributed to its manifestation. Put most briefly, it is the end product of the profound and complex transformation which has occurred in Africa since the European intrusion. It is a commonplace that the imposition of Western technology, socio-political institutions, and ideology upon African societies has been violently disruptive of the old familistic order in that they have created new values and symbols, new techniques for the acquisition of wealth, status, and prestige, and new groups for which the old system had no place. The crucial point here is not that nationalism as a matter of fact happened to appear at a certain point in time after the "Western impact," but rather that the transformation the latter brought about has been an indispensable precondition for the rise of nationalism. Nationalism, as distinguished from primary resistance or nativism, requires considerable gestation. A few of the constituent elements have been:

A. ECONOMIC

1. *Change from a subsistence to a money economy.* This change, consciously encouraged by colonial governments and European enterprise in order to increase the export of primary products, introduced the cash nexus and economic individualism, altered the patterns of land tenure and capital accumulation, and, in general, widened the area of both individual prosperity and insecurity.

2. *Growth of a wage-labor force.* This development has resulted in the proletarianization of substantial numbers of Africans, which has weakened communal or lineage responsibility and rendered those concerned vulnerable to economic exploitation and grievances.

3. *Rise of a new middle class.* Laissez-faire economics and African enterprise, coupled with opportunities for university and professional education, have been factors contributing to the growth of a middle class. This class is most advanced in Senegal, the Gold Coast, and Southern Nigeria, where it has developed despite successive displacement or frustration by the intrusion of Levantines and the monopolistic practices of European firms.

B. SOCIOLOGICAL

1. *Urbanization.* The concentration of relatively large numbers of Africans in urban centers to meet the labor demands of European enterprise has loosened kinship ties, accelerated social communication between "detribalized" ethnic groups, and, in general, contributed to "national" integration.

2. *Social mobility.* The European-imposed *pax* coupled with the development of communications and transport has provided the framework for travel, the growth of an internal exchange economy, and socio-political reintegration.

3. *Western education.* This has provided certain of the inhabitants of a given territory with a common lingua franca; with the knowledge and tools to acquire status and prestige and to fulfill aspirations within the new social structure; and with some of the ideas and values by which alien rule and colonialism could be attacked. It has been through Western education that the African has encountered the scientific method and the idea of progress with their activistic implications, namely, an awareness of alternatives and the conviction that man can creatively master and shape his own destiny.

C. RELIGIOUS AND PSYCHOLOGICAL

1. *Christian evangelization.* The conscious Europeanization pursued by Christian missionary socieites has been a frontal assault upon traditional religious systems and moral sanctions. Moreover, the Christian doctrine of equality and human brotherhood challenged the ethical assumptions of imperialism.

2. *Neglect or frustration of Western-educated elements.* Susceptibility to psychological grievance is most acute among the more acculturated Africans. Social and economic discrimination and the stigma of inferiority and backwardness have precipitated a passionate quest for equality and

modernity, and latterly self-government. Rankling memories of crude, arrogant, or insulting treatment by a European have frequently been the major wellspring of racial bitterness and uncompromising nationalism.

D. POLITICAL

1. *Eclipse of traditional authorities.* Notwithstanding the British policy of indirect rule, the European superstructure and forces of modernity have tended to weaken the traditional powers of indigenous authorities and thereby to render less meaningful pre-colonial socio-political units as objects of loyalty and attachment. There has been what Professor Daryll Forde calls a "status reversal"; that is, as a result of the acquisition by youth of Western education and a command over Western techniques in all fields, there has been ". . . an increasing transfer of command over wealth and authority to younger and socially more independent men at the expense of traditional heads. . . ."[6]

2. *Forging of new "national" symbols.* The "territorialization" of Africa by the European powers has been a step in the creation of new nations, not only through the erection of boundaries within which the intensity of social communication and economic interchange has become greater than across territorial borders, but also as a consequence of the imposition of a common administrative superstructure, a common legal system, and in some instances common political institutions which have become symbols of territorial individuality.

These are a few of the principal factors in the European presence which have contributed to the rise of nationalism. As any casual observer of African developments is aware, however, there have been and are

[6] Daryll Forde, "The Conditions of Social Development in West Africa," *Civilisations,* Vol. 3, pp. 471–485 (No. 4, 1953).

marked areal differences in the overt manifestation of nationalism. Such striking contrasts as the militant Convention People's party of the Gold Coast, the conservative Northern People's Congress of Nigeria, the pro-French orientation of the African editors of *Présence Africaine,* the cautious African editors of *La Voix du Congolais,* and the terroristic Mau Mau of Kenya are cases in point.

There are a number of explanations for these areal variations. One relates to the degree of acculturation in an area. This is a reflection of the duration and intensity of contact with European influences. The contrast between the advanced nationalism of the British West Coast and of Senegal and the nascent nationalism of British and French Central Afria is partly explicable on this basis.

A second explanation lies in the absence or presence of alien settlers. On this score the settler-free British West Coast is unique when contrasted to the rest of Africa. The possibility of a total fulfillment of nationalist objectives (i.e., *African* self-government) has been a powerful psychological factor which partly explains the confident and buoyant expectancy of West Coast nationalists. On the other hand, as previously noted, the tendencies toward accommodation or terrorism in the white-settler areas is a reflection of the absence of such moderating expectancy.

Certain African groups exposed to the same forces of acculturation and the same provocation have demonstrated radically different reactions. The Kikuyu versus the Masai peoples of Kenya, the Ibo versus the Hausa peoples of Nigeria, and the Creole and Mende of Sierra Leone are cases in point. It is suggested that the dynamism, militancy, and nationalist élan of the Ibo peoples of Nigeria are rooted partly in certain indigenous Ibo culture traits (general absence of chiefs, smallness in scale and the democratic character of indigenous political organization, emphasis upon achieved status, and individualism). Much of the same might be said for the Kikuyu peoples of Kenya.

Differing colonial policies constitute another cause of these areal differences. Nationalism is predominantly a phenomenon of British Africa, and to a lesser extent of French Africa. Apart from the influence of the foregoing historical, sociological, and cultural variables, this fact, in the case of British Africa, is explained by certain unique features of British colonial policy.

It was inevitable that Britain, one of the most liberal colonial powers in Africa, should have reaped the strongest nationalist reaction. A few of the principal features of British policy which have stimulated nationalism deserve mention:

1. *Self-government as the goal of policy.* Unlike the French and Portuguese who embrace their African territories as indivisible units of the motherland, or the Belgians who until recently have been disinclined to specify the ultimate goals of policy, the British have remained indiscriminately loyal to the Durham formula.[7]

[7] Regarding Belgian policy, see Pierre Wigny, "Methods of Government in the Belgian Congo," *African Affairs*, Vol. 50, pp. 310–317 (Oct., 1951). Wigny remarks (p. 311) that ". . . Belgians are reluctant to define their colonial policy. They are proud of their first realisations, and sure of the rightness of their intentions." Since this was written, there have been some very dramatic changes in Belgian policy, especially regarding the educated elite, the potential nationalists. The great debate in Belgian colonial circles on "le statut des Congolais civilisés" was terminated by four decrees of May 17, 1952 according to which educated Congolese are assimilated to Europeans in civil law. Regarding Portuguese policy, see Marcelo Caetano, *Colonizing Traditions, Principles and Methods of the Portuguese* (Lisbon, 1951). The keynote of the policy is the "spiritual assimilation" of the Africans to a "Portuguese nation dwelling in European, African, Asiatic and Indonesian Provinces." The African *civilisado* is thus a citizen of Portugal.

In West Africa, this has enthroned the African nationalists; in Central and East Africa, the white settlers.

2. *Emphasis upon territorial individuality.* More than any other colonial power, the British have provided the institutional and conceptual framework for the emergence of nations. Decentralization of power, budgetary autonomy, the institution of territorial legislative councils and other "national" symbols—all have facilitated the conceptualization of a "nation."

3. *Policy on missionaries and education.* The comparative freedom granted missionaries and the laissez-faire attitude toward education, and particularly post-primary education, has distinguished and continued to distinguish British policy sharply from non-British Africa.

4. *Neglect, frustration, and antagonism of educated elite.* Not only have more British Africans been exposed to higher education, but the British government until recently remained relatively indifferent to the claims and aspirations of this class, which forms the core of the nationalist movements.

5. *Freedom of nationalist activity.* The *comparative* freedom of activity (speech, association, press, and travel abroad) which British Africans have enjoyed—within clearly defined limits and varying according to the presence of white settlers—has been of decisive importance.

All of this suggests that African nationalism is not merely a peasant revolt. In fact, as already noted, nationalism where it is most advanced has been sparked and led by the so-called detribalized, Western-educated, middle-class intellectuals and professional Africans; by those who in terms of improved status and material standards of living have benefitted most from colonialism; in short, by those who have come closest to the Western World but have been denied entry on full terms of equality. From this comparatively affluent—but psychologically aggrieved—group have come the organizers of tribal associations, labor unions, co-operative groups, farmers' organizations, and—more recently—nationalist movements. They are the Africans whom British policy has done most to create and least to satiate.[8]

This brief and selective treatment of a few of the factors which have contributed to the African nationalist awakening suggests certain avenues which might be profitably explored and more fully developed by subsequent research. Specifically, what is the relationship between the nature and intensity of nationalism and the degree of urbanization, the degree of commercialization of agriculture, and the size and geographical distribution of the wage-labor force and salariat? In short, what is the causal connection between "detribalization" and nationalism? Certain aspects of such an inquiry could be subjected to statistical analysis, but the results could only be suggestive, and in some instances might be positively deceptive. In the case of urbanization, for example, the highly urbanized and acculturated Yoruba peoples of Nigeria for nearly a decade lagged far behind the Ibo peoples in nationalist vigor and élan. Ibadan, the largest urban center in tropical Africa, has been until recently one of the most politically inert towns of Nigeria. Again, in terms of the proletarianization of labor and urbaniza-

[8] The thesis here is that there are at least four ingredients in the psychology of colonial nationalism, and that British policy in Africa has come closest towards inculcating or providing them: (a) an awareness of the existence or possibility of alternatives to the status quo, a state of mind produced by Western education and particularly by study and travel abroad; (b) and intense desire to change the status quo; (c) a system within which the major alternative to the status quo—self-government—has the status of legitimacy; and (d) an area of relative freedom in which that legitimate alternative may be pursued.

tion resulting from European industrialism and commercial activity, the Belgian Congo is one of the most advanced territories, but one in which nationalism is least in evidence.[9] Freetown, Sierra Leone, one of the oldest non-traditional urban centers, became a haven of respectability and conservatism, being eclipsed by the less-developed Protectorate in the push towards nationalist objectives. Urbanization has been an important ingredient in the nationalist awakening, but it has been a certain type of urban development—mainly the impersonal and heterogeneous "new towns"—which has occurred in conjunction with other equally decisive factors.

In the case of the relationship between the degree of commercialization of land and labor and the degree of nationalism, the figures set forth for the Gold Coast in Table 1 suggest either a causal connection or a parallel development. Yet in turning to similar figures for other territories—especially the Belgian Congo and Nigeria—it is clear that the relationship between commercialization and nationalism, important though it may be, must be considered and interpreted in the light of other variables.

Again, the fact that the nationalist movements have been organized and led by intellectuals and the so-called middle class suggests a relationship between nationalism and the number of Africans with higher education, the size of per capita income, the degree of the individualization of land tenure, the size of middle-class and professional groups (i.e., independent traders, produce middlemen, farmers employing labor, druggists, lorry owners, lawyers, doctors, etc.), and the degree of vertical

[9] The Belgian policy of stabilization of labor in the urban centers of the Congo, in which 83% of the men have their families with them, is one of the several factors which may help to explain this.

TABLE 1.   Commercialization and Nationalism in Certain African Territories

Territory	Percentage of Cultivated Land Used by Africans for Commercial Production (1947–1950) [a]	African Wage Earners as Percentage of Total African Population (1950) [b]	Degree of Overt Nationalism
Gold Coast	75%	9.0%	Advanced
Belgian Congo	42	7.6	None
Nigeria	41	1.2	Advanced
Uganda	33	3.9	Nascent
Kenya	7	7.6	Nascent

[a] E. A. Keukjian, "Commercializing Influence of the Development of Exports on Indigenous Agricultural Economics in Tropical Africa," unpub. diss. (Harvard Univ., June, 1953); United Nations, Economic and Social Council (15th session). *World Economic Situation. Aspects of Economic Development in Africa.* New York, Document E/2377, March 20, 1953.
[b] United Nations, Department of Economic Affairs. *Review of Economic Conditions in Africa (Supplement to World Economic Report, 1949–50).* New York, Document E/1910/Add. 1 Rev. 1-ST/ECA/9/Add. 1, April, 1951, p. 76.

mobility within the emergent socio-economic structure. In any event, the insights of an economist are indispensable for a complete anatomy of African nationalism.

The Christian missionaries have been blamed frequently for their ruthless assault upon native religious systems and the thoroughgoing Europeanization, conscious or implicit, in their evangelization. This has suggested the formula: missionaries = detribalization = nationalism.   Yet   the postwar figures shown in Table 2 do not bear out this assumption.[10] Missionaries

activities and nationalist assertion cannot be established by mere quantitative analysis. The figures in Table 2 hint at a possible causal relationship between proponderant Protestant evangelization and advanced nationalism (viz., Gold Coast and Nigeria) and preponderant Catholic evangelization and the absence of nationalism (viz., Portuguese Angola and the Belgian Congo). Yet this connection must be examined in the light of other relevant factors, such as the degree of control and direction extended to missionary societies by colonial governments; the freedom al-

TABLE 2.   Christianity and Nationalism in Certain African Territories

Territory	Percentage of Christians to Total Population	Percentage of Protestants to All Christians	Percentage of Catholics to All Christians	Degree of Overt Nationalism
Belgian Congo	37%	29%	71%	None
Nayasaland	26	49	51	Nascent
Gold Coast	15	58	42	Advanced
Angola	15	22	78	None
Kenya	10	51	49	Nascent
Nigeria	5	67	33	Advanced

have been important catalytic agents in the transformation of African societies, but the causal connection between their

[10] *World Christian Handbook* (London, 1949).

lowed such societies to establish schools—particularly secondary schools—and to determine the curriculum; the tolerance accorded anti-white or anti-colonial sects (e.g., the Jehovah's Witnesses are permitted in most of British Africa but proscribed in non-British Africa); the latitude allowed African sects of a syncretistic, revivalistic, or puritanical character; the extent to which evangelical bodies have *Africanized* their church organization, the priesthood, and the propagation of the gospel; and, finally, the strength of Islam.

The corrosive influence of Western education has been a significant ingredient in the rise of nationalism. Yet the Belgian Congo claims a higher percentage of literacy than any other colonial territory in Africa.[11] In order to establish a relationship we must move beyond the superficial analysis of literacy statistics and ask the following questions:

1. *The nature of the curriculum.* Has it been and is it literary and based upon the model of a European grammar school, or is it practical and designed to train the student to be a good farmer, artisan, or clerk in European employ, and incidentally to limit his sophistication and contact with unsettling ideas? Is instruction conducted in the vernacular or in a European language?

2. *Opportunities for post-primary education.* Are secondary schools (particularly those operated by missionary societies or by enterprising and nationalist-minded Africans such as Eyo Ita in Nigeria or Jomo Kenyatta in Kenya) allowed to mushroom into existence, or are they carefully planned and rigidly controlled by the colonial government as to both number and curriculum? What are the opportunities for study in universities abroad? What is the latitude granted students to determine their own careers? Here we touch upon a crucial factor—in 1945, Freetown, Sierra Leone, and Lagos, Nigeria, each had more Western-type secondary schools than all of the non-British territories in Africa combined. In 1952 over 4,000 Africans from British territories were studying in universities and technical schools abroad and nearly 1,000 in territorial universities in Africa, whereas only a handful had such opportunity or inclination in Belgian and Portuguese Africa. This is in part a reflection of the existence of a larger African middle-class in British Africa, but it is also the result of the unique British attitude regarding the relationship between higher education and emergent African leadership. French policy and practice, despite differing assumptions, most closely approximate those of the British.[12]

3. *Openings of careers for the talented.* The stability of any political or social order is determined by this factor. Is there any planned relationship between the output of the schools and opportunities for satisfying employment or careers? In French and Belgian Africa, colonial governments have maintained a stringent control over the supply-demand situation as between *post-primary* schools and the requirements of government and the developing economy. In British Africa there are hundreds of thousands of unemployed or underemployed "Standard VI" boys clus-

[11] United Nations, *Non-Self-Governing Territories.* Vol. III: *Special Study on Education.* New York, Document ST/TRI/SER.A./5/Add. 2, January, 1951.

[12] By decree of April 16, 1950, the *Institut des Hautes Études* was established at Dakar; and on January 1, 1952, there were 1,640 scholarship holders in continental France, of whom 572 were pursuing higher education. *Civilisations,* Vol. 3, pp. 575–83 (No. 4, 1953). On British educational policy in tropical Africa see *African Education* (Oxford: The Nuffield Foundation and the Colonial Office, 1953). The Belgians within the past few years have dramatically reoriented their policy regarding higher education for the Congolese. Since 1952 Congo students have been admitted to the Albert I College at Leopoldville; the first Negro University of the Congo is scheduled for opening in 1954; and recently the Belgian press has drawn attention to the admission to Louvain University of a Negro student from the Congo. *Civilisations,* Vol. 3, pp. 599–602 (No. 4, 1953).

tered in the coastal towns and urban centers of the interior.

The most potent instrument used in the propagation of nationalist ideas and racial consciousness has been the *African-owned* nationalist pι ess. In Nigeria alone nearly 100 newspapers or periodicals have been published by Africans since the British intrusion, of which 12 dailies and 14 weeklies—all African owned—are currently in circulation. The crucial role performed in the nationalist awakening by African journalistic enterprise on the British West Coast is well known.[13] Until the publication of *Afrique Noire* (organ of the *Rassemblement Démocratique Africaine* of French West Africa) there was nothing in non-British Africa which even closely approximated this development. And even this journal is no match for the pungent criticism and racial consciousness one finds in the pages of Dr. Nnamdi Azikiwe's *West African Pilot* in Nigeria.[14] Needless to say, the nationalist press is one of our major sources of data regarding nationalist motivation, objectives, and organization. It is not the number of newspapers published which is significant, but rather the volume of circulation and areal distribution, the news and editorial content and the nature of the appeal, the types of readers, the existence of competitive papers

[13] Compare with the number of *African-owned-and-edited* dailies and weeklies (combined total) in the following territories: *British Africa*: Gold Coast (17), Uganda (8), Sierra Leone (7), Gambia (3); *French West Africa* (10); and none, insofar as is known, in Belgian, Portuguese, or Spanish Africa; or in Kenya, the territories of the Central African Federation, or in the Union of South Africa.

[14] On the other hand, there appears to be no newspaper in British West Africa comparable with the European-owned-and-edited journal of French West Africa entitled *Les Echos de l'A.O.F.*, which "week after week passionately attacks the administration. . . ." See Thomas Hodgkin, "The Metropolitan Axis," *West Africa*, January 9, 1954, at p. 6.

sponsored by colonial governments, the financial stability of the paper, and other factors which would reflect its impact and influence upon the ideas, aspirations, and activities of those literate groups predisposed towards nationalism.

These are but a few of the more important factors in the rise of nationalism which require evaluation and weighting before the student of comparative colonial nationalism can go beyond the mere description of the history and anatomy of a particular nationalist movement. There is great danger in doing a disservice to scholarly research in Africa if one generalizes on the basis of observations made and data assembled in one territory. As has been suggested, there are certain general predisposing and precipitating causes of modern nationalism which are applicable to the whole continent; yet once these are mentioned, it is necessary to examine each area of nationalist activity for that special combination of factors which explains the origin, strength, and orientation of its nationalist movement.

III. FACTORS CONDITIONING NATIONALIST DEVELOPMENT

Normally, a colonial nationalist movement directs its efforts towards the attainment of two main objectives: (1) the achievement of self-government, and (2) the creation of a cultural or political sense of nationality and unity within the boundaries of the area of the nation to be. Nationalists are obliged to adopt the second objective because imperial powers either did not or could not establish political boundaries which embraced only one self-conscious cultural unit; and certainly those powers made no conscious effort to build nations.

The major factor conditioning the development of a particular nationalist movement, therefore, is the degree of internal politico-cultural unity, tolerance, or compatibility amongst the peoples of the area moving into its national era. Disunities can exist in a given territory for a variety of reasons:

1. Traditional pre-colonial hostilities and cultural incompatibilities such as exist between the Kikuyu and Masai peoples of Kenya, or the Ibo and the Tiv peoples of Nigeria. In some instances these have been exacerbated as a result of imperial policies; in others as a consequence of the mere fact of lumping them together and endeavoring to impose territorial uniformity.

2. Tensions between groups resulting from unevenness in development, acculturation, and the acquisition of modernity. These can be the product of original cultural differences (i.e., the variations between groups in their receptivity and adaptability to modernity—e.g., the Ibo and Hausa); historical circumstances (i.e., differences in the duration and intensity of the European impact—e.g., the Creoles of Freetown vs. the Mende peoples of the Protectorate of Sierra Leone); or of constitutional reforms pointing towards African self-government. One could argue that Ibo-Yoruba hostility in Nigeria is the product of all three factors. Just as the advance towards independence precipitated a cleavage between Muslims and Hindus in India, so has the development of nationalism and the move towards self-government in Africa brought to light a multitude of disunities. Fear of domination by the more advanced and acculturated groups—European or African —is one obvious explanation.

3. Tensions between the Westernized elite—the nationalists—and the traditionalists and the masses. This nationalist disability has tended to be exaggerated in the past, usually by imperial spokesmen endeavoring to repudiate the nationalists or to isolate them from the traditionalists.

The intensity of the cleavage varies widely according to circumstances. In several areas such as the Protectorate of Sierra Leone, the Northern Territories of the Gold Coast, Western and Northern Nigeria, amongst the Kikuyu in Kenya, and in Northern Rhodesia and Nyasaland the educated nationalists and some leading traditionalists have cooperated in varying degrees.

4. Differences within the ranks of the Westernized elite. These disagreements —and one is struck by their persistence, strength, and virulence—may arise from several causes, including normal competition for power and prestige or honest differences over aims, timing, or methods to be employed in the nationalist drive.

These nationalist disabilities are the product of a complex mixture of hard historical and cultural facts, of changes introduced and differentials created by the Western intrusion, as well as of the provocations of the nationalist drive itself. The success of any nationalist movement will in a large measure depend upon the extent to which these internal tensions are softened or dissipated. The latter will depend, in turn, upon the degree of repressive opposition, or unwitting or intentional cooperation, of colonial governments; upon the development of pan-territorial political associations, the membership of which is rooted in all ethnic groups and in which there is free vertical mobility into the "upper crust" which that membership constitutes; upon the emergence of pan-territorial economic-interest groups (e.g., middle-class associations or labor organizations); and upon many other sociological processes (outgroup marriages, commonsality, etc.) which Professor Karl W. Deutsch has suggested are essential building blocks of any new national community.[15]

[15] "The Growth of Nations," *World Politics,* Vol. 5, pp. 168–196 (Jan., 1953).

It would be naive and unhistorical to argue that a large measure of politico-cultural integration is required—as distinguished from being desirable—in order for a nationalist movement to succeed in wresting self-government from an imperial power. Most successful colonial nationalist movements have been organized and led by small minorities which have been able either to gain the support of the masses or to capitalize upon their inertia and apathy. It would be unrealistic, however, to contemplate the success of a movement which did not have at least a minimum of unity or tolerance within the "upper crust."

Some of these forces contributing towards integration are measurable and provide rough indices upon which the research scholar can base predictions of the development of a particular nationalist movement. In an interesting new theory regarding the growth of nations, Professor Deutsch has suggested certain criteria which might be profitably employed in seeking to determine the prospects of success of a nationalist movement in its nation-building endeavors.[16] His central thesis is that cases of successful political integration in history show a number of patterns which seem to recur. As he puts it, a nation "is the result of the transformation of people, or of several ethnic elements, in the process of social mobilization." The prospects of success are indicated by the completeness of that transformation and the intensity of social mobilization around the symbols of the new national community. A nation is not only a subjective affirmation of will of zealous nationalists; it is also the product of the operation of powerful objective forces, several of which have been mentioned.

[16] Ibid. See also Deutsch's Nationalism and Social Communication (cited in note 5), pp. 81 ff.

Thus far it has been assumed that the leaders of nationalist movements in Africa will seek to build new national communities out of the diverse human materials located within the artificial boundaries of the existing colonial territories.

In general, it would seem that where nationalism manifests itself in considerable strength it is evidence that disintegration of the old and social mobilization around the symbols of the new order have occurred on a scale sufficient to weaken or destroy attachments and loyalties of the nationalists to pre-colonial socio-political units, either because they have been crushed and are beyond memory or because they are unattractive or manifestly unsuitable as "nations" in a modern world of nation-states. The European presence has done much towards the creation of new nations, the "national" sentiment of the nationalists being a reflection of this.

A few of the many factors which might be observed and evaluated in order to determine the probable success, as well as the territorial implications, of an African nationalist movement or nation-building endeavor are as follows:[17] (1) the degree of internal social mobility, economic interchange and interdependence, intermarriage and commonsality, and the intensity and level of social communication among the ethnic groups comprising a given territory; (2) the location of population clusters and "core areas," as well as of "sub-national" regions of more intense economic interchange or of cultural focus; (3) the powers and functions of "sub-national" political institutions (i.e., regional, tribal, etc.), and the degree of meaningful participation in them by the

[17] For several of the concepts used here the author is indebted to the works of Professor Karl W. Deutsch, previously cited. See especially his Nationalism and Social Communication, pp. 15–45.

Western-educated elements; (4) the rate at which "national" institutions and activities are capable of attracting and absorbing new social strata from all ethnic groups into the "national" life (e.g., the ethnic composition of the central administrative and technical services); (5) the centrality and nationalness of educational institutions, particularly the professional schools and universities; (6) the degree of pan-territorial circulation of nationalist newspapers and literature and the extent to which these play up "national" events and personalities; (7) the differentials in the material development, per capita income and wealth, the acquisition of modern skills and knowledge, and the concentration and capacity for accumulation of capital amongst the different subnational areas and ethnic groups; (8) the ethnic makeup of the Western-educated categories and particularly of the active membership of nationalist or proto-nationalist groups; (9) the development and extent of usage of a trans-tribal pan-territorial language, be it English, French, Portuguese, Swahili, or Hausa; (10) the compatibility of the "detribalized" basic personality types produced by the indigenous cultures; (11) the extent to which the territory concerned embraces total cultural groups, or, put another way, the degree to which artificial colonial boundaries have bifurcated ethnic groups whose division may be the source of later irredentism; and (12) the rapport between the Western-educated nationalist elements and the traditionalists, including the existence of nativistic tensions or economic grievances which the nationalists could manipulate or exploit in their mobilization of mass support.

Results obtained from inquiries along these lines would go far to explain the present orientation of a nationalist movement, as well as possible future trends. And yet an emphatic note of caution should be sounded: objective forces of integration and disintegration are powerful determinants in the nation-building process, but so also are subjective factors.[18] By all laws of geography and economics Northern Ireland should belong to Eire, and East Pakistan to the Republic of India; but they do not. By the same laws, the Gambia should belong to Senegal, French Guinea to Sierra Leone and Liberia, Mozambique to the Central African Federation, and so forth; and yet present trends suggest that such will not be the case. The principal forces currently operating to shape Africa's emergent nations are either tribalism or a nationalism following artificial imperial boundaries; and, with few exceptions, neither of these is directed towards the creation of political units which the geographer or economist would classify as ideal. In this respect, of course, Africa is not unique.

The foregoing raises the crucial question of whether it is possible for the peoples of Africa—in their own interest—to avoid the balkanization implicit in the full application of the national principle to their continent. So long as the rest of the world is organized according to that principle, and so long as the national idea universally embodies aspirations which cannot be satisfied by other forms of human organization, the answer would seem to be in the negative. The quest for racial equality and acceptance is as important an ingredient in the African revolt as is the desire to determine one's own destiny. Rightly or wrongly, self-government within the confines of the sovereign nation-state has become the supreme symbol of the equality of peoples. The only possible

[18] Given suitable conditions, including a politically favorable milieu and the proper techniques, there would seem to be no reason why subjective factors such as loyalties, attitudes, and attachments to national or "sub-national" symbols, could not to some extent be measured.

alternative would be broader Eur-African political groupings or self-governing plural societies in which emergent African leaders could play what they would feel to be an equal role. In the light of the persistence of national self-determination as a symbol, and particularly in view of the growing strength and contagion of African nationalism, the future of such multi-racial experiments will depend in a large measure upon the rapidity with which European governments and leaders provide for such a role.

Dr. John Useem is a Professor of Sociology and Anthropology at Michigan State University. He is coauthor of *The Western-Educated Man in India*, 1955, and has contributed to *Planning Micronesia's Future; Cultural Patterns and Technical Charge;* and *Human Problems and Technological Change.* His field of research is cross-cultural relations, a topic on which he has published numerous articles in professional journals.

Dr. James S. Coleman is an Assistant Professor of Political Science at the University of California at Los Angeles. In addition to the article included in this volume, he has published other articles in professional journals and was a contributor to *Africa, A Continent in Transition.*

III

THE DEMOGRAPHIC CHARACTERISTICS OF UNDERDEVELOPED AREAS

IT HAS been said that none of the basic demographic data necessary for scientific social planning are available for most of the underdeveloped areas of the world and the available data must be treated with extreme skepticism. This has unfortunately continued to be the case in spite of the efforts of the United Nations to collect and evaluate data from each of the world's political entities. Although the available data are admittedly inadequate, an effort may be made to describe the demographic characteristics of underdeveloped areas as contrasted to the characteristics of developed areas.

POPULATION TYPES

Demographers have hypothesized that populations tend to evolve through various stages, and have classified the populations of various political entities according to their evolutionary stage or population type.

Warren S. Thompson has stated that there are 3 types: (1) that type in which both birth and death rates are low and under control and the population is stationary or almost so because of the low rate of natural increase; in this type the birth rate may continue to decline so that natural increase ceases or population declines; (2) that type in which both high birth and death rates are declining, but death rates are declining more rapidly at first than birth rates so that the rate of natural increase is increasing; and (3) that type in which neither high birth rates nor high death rates have come under reasonable control, where famine or epidemics may take a large toll of lives at any time, and where rate of growth fluctuates although the potential rate of growth is high.[1] Thompson has suggested examples for each of these population types. Underdeveloped

---

[1] See Thompson, Warren S., "Population," *The American Journal of Sociology*, Vol. 34, No. 6, May 1929, pp. 959–975; Thompson, *Plenty of People*, New York, Ronald Press Co., 1948, Chap. 6; and Thompson, *Population and Peace in the Pacific*, Chicago, University of Chicago Press, 1946, Chap. 2.

areas, we would hypothesize, would belong in the third type listed, were data available on them. The most advanced among developed areas would have the demographic characteristics of type 1. Those political entities that are now industrializing would be classified as type 2 in the Thompson system.

In very much the same fashion, C. P. Blacker has hypothesized 5 population types: (1) *declining*, with a low death rate but even lower birth rate and an excess of deaths over births, i.e., a declining population; (2) *low stationary*, with low birth rates balanced by low death rates; (3) *late expanding*, with declining birth but more rapidly declining death rates; (4) *early expanding*, characterized by high birth and death, but declining death rates; and (5) *high stationary*, marked by high birth and death rates.[2] We would expect the underdeveloped areas to be found in Blacker's fourth and fifth population types. The developed areas would fall in population types 1 and 2; type 3 would contain a group of political entities now in the process of industrialization.

If we take all the various combinations of birth, death, and natural increase rates into consideration, each continuum of birth, death, and natural increase rates having been divided into a dichotomy, 8 different population types are possible. The most parsimonious way of representing these types is in a table as follows.

TABLE 7.   Population Types Possible with Three Dichotomized Demographic Variables

Population Type	Birth Rate	Natural Increase	Death Rate
I	low	low	low
II	high	low	low
III	low	low	high
IV	low	high	low
V	high	high	low
VI	low	high	high
VII	high	low	high
VIII	high	high	high

Each population type consists of a different combination of the 3 dichotomized variables, the variables having been placed on a continuum and dichotomized in such a way as to maximize their ability to differentiate between developed and underdeveloped or undeveloped areas. More will be said about each variable very shortly. Population type I is comparable to Thompson's type (1) and Blacker's *low stationary* type or *declining* type. Population type II, as well as possibly type IV, although type IV is not likely to be found, represent different stages in the transition from Thompson's population type (2) to type (1) and are also

[2] See Blacker, C. P., "Stages in Population Growth," *The Eugenics Review*, Vol. 39, No. 3, October 1947, pp. 88–102. For a general discussion of the problem see "History of Population Theories," Chapter 3, *The Determinants and Consequences of Population Trends*, Population Studies No. 17, Population Division, Department of Social Affairs, United Nations, New York, 1953.

similar to Blacker's *late expanding* type. Population type V is comparable to Thompson's type (2) and Blacker's *early expanding* type. Population type VI obviously does not exist. Population types VII and VIII are similar to Thompson's type (3) and Blacker's *high stationary* type. J. S. Davis has suggested that neither Thompson nor Blacker has made provision for another type in which births, although relatively low and stable, remain above deaths and result in a considerable rate of increase.[3] This type is provided for by our population type IV and is essentially another variation of the *late expanding* type of Blacker.

While this approach, that is, taking births, deaths, and rates of natural increase for a given year, measures a static aspect of population type, the results are essentially the same as those obtained by using trend data in place of demographic data for the latest available year. If we are willing to assume that population types have some common content, that within population type there is a unidimensional variable, and that there is consistent variation in the characteristics of population types as one goes from the "most desirable" as indicated by low birth rate, low death rate, and low natural increase to the "least desirable" type, only 4 of the 8 population types shown in Table 7 should have any members. If we were to accept this as a model of the universe of population types, we would expect all political entities, within certain limits of error, to fall in Types I, II, V, and VIII. We would expect Type I to consist of developed political entities, Type II to consist of those in the process of development and not always to be classified as developed, Type V to consist of political entities in an intermediate position and probably not be classified as developed, and Type VIII to consist of underdeveloped areas. This classification assumes a unidimensional model with each type having the same or a more favorable rating on each characteristic than the population type below it. This model assumes that differences between population types are a matter of degree and that each political entity evolves over a period of years from Type VIII to Type I. We may, of course, find that this is not a very good model and discard it for a model that permits differences in kind as well as degree. Were we to do that, 7 of the 8 population types that we have shown in Table 7 would be definite possibilities.

Before comparing either model with the data, we will make an item by item examination of the demographic variables and show their relationship to the dichotomy that we have set up, developed or underdeveloped. As previously described, in each case the variables have been dichotomized so as to maximize their ability to separate developed from underdeveloped areas.

CRUDE BIRTH RATE

If more extensive data were available it might be that a different picture would be presented of the relationship between birth rates and development. As in

---

[3] See Davis, J. S., "Population and Resources," *Journal of the American Statistical Association*, Vol. 45, No. 251, September 1950, pp. 346–349.

the case of other variables, large variations are found within both developed and underdeveloped areas, births ranging from less than 15 per 1000 population per year to more than 50 per 1000 population per year. Birth rates for areas with data available are presented in Table 8.

TABLE 8. Distribution of Political Entities According to
Crude Birth Rate per 1000 Population and Development[4]

Birth Rate	Developed	Under-developed	Total
−26	28	9	37
26+	9	54	63
Total	37	63	100

The phi coefficient of correlation is .964, indicating a relatively high relationship of crude birth rates to development. Since we have expressed some concern over the representativeness of the birth rate for any single year as the birth rate of the country for recent years or as indicative of the birth rate type in determining population type, the data from the *Demographic Yearbook* were plotted for each political entity for all years available. This enables us to determine the trend of the birth rate in each political entity. Each political entity was classified as having a low, medium, or high birth rate that was either stable, fluctuating, rising, or declining. Sufficient data were available to classify only 77 political entities in this fashion. Using this trend data, the political entities actually fell into a dichotomy with low birth rates on one hand and medium or high birth rates on the other. The phi coefficient of correlation between birth rates and development was 1.087.[5]

CRUDE DEATH RATE

The relationship of deaths to development, exclusive of stillbirths, per 1000 population, is shown in Table 9. Deaths range from less than 6 to more than 26 per 1000 population per year. If the age composition of the population of each political entity were known, comparison would be more meaningful. The phi coefficient of correlation of the data in Table 9 is .469.

As in the case of birth rates, there was some hesitancy in accepting the most recently reported death rate as necessarily representative of the type of death rate that is characteristic of the country. In most cases the death rates, if available, extended back to 1920–24 or thereabouts and enabled one to obtain some

[4] The demographic data in Tables 8 through 11 are from the *Demographic Yearbook—1951 and 1952*, United Nations, New York, 1952 and 1953, Tables 10, 16, and 19.

[5] The phi coefficient of correlation is used merely as an index of relationships existing within the 2 by 2 tables presented in the introductory section of each chapter. It is possible for the phi coefficient, unlike the Pearsonian coefficient of correlation, to exceed 1.000, particularly when a correction has been made for the dichotonization of 2 continuous variables.

idea of the trend. Populations were classified as having a low, medium, or high death rate that was stable, fluctuating, declining, or rising. Having combined categories for computational purposes, the phi coefficient of correlation was .297. These findings should not be surprising because our demographic model suggests that some of the underdeveloped areas will have falling death rates although still retaining high birth rates.

TABLE 9.   Distribution of Political Entities According to Crude Death Rates per 1000 Population and Development

Death Rates	Developed	Under-developed	Total
−13.5	34	41	75
13.5+	3	22	25
Total	37	63	100

INFANT MORTALITY RATE

The number of deaths per 1000 live births, exclusive of still births, is usually considered to be quite a sensitive index of social conditions in an area. Such information is not available for a large proportion of our political entities but the data are presented for a sufficient number of them to be suggestive. Political entities with the most favorable infant mortality rate have fewer than 40 deaths per 1000 live births per year, while others exceed 200 or one-fifth of all live births per year. The data are shown in Table 10. The phi coefficient of correlation is .478 between infant mortality rates and development.

TABLE 10.   Distribution of Political Entities According to Infant Mortality Rates per 1000 Population and Development

Infant Mortality Rates	Developed	Under-developed	Total
70+	13	39	52
−70	23	19	42
Total	36	58	94

CRUDE RATE OF NATURAL INCREASE

The relationship of natural increase to development is shown in Table 11. Natural increase varies from 2 per 1000 population per year to more than 40 persons per 1000 population per year. The phi coefficient of correlation was 1.009. When the trend data were substituted for the most recent year available data, the phi coefficient of correlation became 1.048.

TABLE 11. Distribution of Political Entities According to
Crude Rate of Natural Increase and Development

Rate of Natural Increase	Developed	Under-developed	Total
21+	0	42	42
−21	37	21	58
Total	37	63	100

COMPARING THE DATA WITH THE MODEL

With the basic data in mind, let us now refer back to the demographic model presented in Table 7. How are the various political entities actually distributed according to the 8 possible combinations of birth rates, death rates, and rates of natural increase? If the data are manipulated according to a general technique known variously as the Guttman technique, scale analysis, or the Cornell technique,[6] our 100 political entities are distributed among the eight possible population types as shown in column (2) of Table 12.

TABLE 12. A Demographic Model and the Distribution of 100 Political Entities in
Relation to the Model

(1) Population Type	(2) No. Political Entities in Each Type	(3) Expected Developed	(4) Actual Developed	(5) Expected Under-developed	(6) Actual Under-developed
I *	35	35	27	0	8
II *	13	6	7	7	6
III	3	3	1	0	2
IV	0	0	0	0	0
V *	27	0	2	27	25
VI	0	0	0	0	0
VII	8	0	2	8	6
VIII*	14	0	0	14	14
Total	100	44	39	56	61

If the unidimensional demographic model were a perfect model of population types, we would expect all cases to fall in those population types marked with an asterisk in column (1). This is not the result, however, and 11 of the 100 political entities are found in other types, as seen in column (2). The distribution of political entities in column (2) is due to a variety of factors. Developed areas are represented out of proportion to their numbers, while underdeveloped areas are underrepresented in the political entities for which we have data. Some geographic and cultural areas are represented to a greater extent than others.

[6] A description of these techniques with numerous examples may be found in Samuel A. Stouffer *et al.*, *Measurement and Prediction, Studies in Social Psychology in World War II*, Vol. 4, Princeton, Princeton University Press, 1950.

This means that demographic data are available to a greater extent for political entities that are likely to be population type I on a basis of their other social characteristics than for other population types. The reverse could be said concerning types V and VIII. Since a large proportion of our total number of political entities are underdeveloped we should have a large number of types V and VIII if the model is a correct representation of the universe of political entities and the entities for which data are available are representative of the universe.

On a basis of the marginal totals shown in column (2), how many developed or underdeveloped political entities would we expect to find in each population type, if the general hypothesis of development is accepted as a determinant of population type? The figures shown in columns (3) and (5) might reasonably be expected if development is a determinant of population type. The actual results are seen in columns (4) and (6) and although the figures show some deviation from the expected pattern, the deviation may not only be explained in terms of shortcomings of the model but in shortcomings of the data. Nonetheless, the data do suggest that our model has some use as a representation of a universe comprising neither a random sample nor a complete enumeration.

A complete listing of each of the 100 political entities for which demographic data are available may be found in Appendix I. This appendix, in addition to classifying political entities according to population types, classifies them according to major geographic areas, developmental status, and political status as self-governing or non-self-governing. The data in Appendix I are arranged in such a way as to show which political entities may be found in each of the various combinations of the categories just mentioned, and the percent of the world's population that may be found in each of these categories and combinations of categories. The reader may wish to refer to Appendix I from time to time while studying the data presented in Table 12. The reader may wish to hypothesize the characteristics of the 95 political entities shown in neither Appendix I nor Table 12 and attempt to construct the distribution that would be found in Appendix I or Table 12 if the data were available.

It should also be noted that, in line with our expectations, no cases were found of type VI, and in addition no cases were found of type IV, a category that could have members but would be unlikely to have them. Manipulation of the cutting points reveals that essentially the same outcome is achieved regardless of the exact location of cutting points on the continuum of birth rates, death rates, and natural increase rates.

In the articles that follow one may find a more detailed description of the relationship of demographic characteristics to development. The first article, "Population Growth and Economic Development," by Hope Tisdale Eldridge, describes the changing demographic characteristics of political entities and their present and possible future meaning in light of the dire predictions of Malthusians and neo-Malthusians. The reader should note that there are points of disagreement in the Eldridge article and the Kingsley Davis article that follows,

"Population and Change in Backward Areas." One should ask if these differences are based on research or differences in estimates concerning the future rate of progress in various areas of science. These articles are followed by a selection from *The Determinants and Consequences of Population Trends.* The latter should be of particular interest to persons concerned with the development of underdeveloped areas, since it suggests the direction that demographic evolution may take in underdeveloped countries today in contrast to the course of demographic evolution in Europe. This article in itself would make us inclined to reject the unidimensional model of population types that has been briefly mentioned in this chapter and in its place create a model with differences in kind rather than differences in degree alone. An article by Wilbert Moore, "Migration and Native Laborers in South Africa," describes the demographic effects of large-scale migration of native laborers from the village subsistence economy to the industrial plant or mine.

This chapter concludes with "Institutional Patterns Favoring High Fertility in Underdeveloped Areas," by Kingsley Davis. Davis points out that nearly all underdeveloped areas not only have high fertility rates but have in common even more basic characteristics. This uniformity enables us to predict a number of things about an area if we are given certain basic information. The high fertility rates of quite diverse cultures in underdeveloped areas are explained in terms of family structure and group values.

POPULATION GROWTH AND ECONOMIC DEVELOPMENT*

HOPE TISDALE ELDRIDGE

ONE of the most striking evidences of mankind's success in the struggle to ameliorate the conditions of life is the conquest of mortality. The implications of this achievement go far beyond the simple fact of an increase in the average length of life, for mortality could not have been reduced without a host of

* Reprinted by permission from *Land Economics*, Vol. XXVIII, No. 1, February 1952, pp. 1–9.

changes in the physical, economic, cultural and intellectual spheres. Not that all the preconditions and concomitants of declining mortality have been directly experienced by each individual in the society. Nevertheless, the gains in health and longevity through improved nutrition, personal hygiene, public sanitation, and availability of medical services and facilities have resulted from pervasive social changes associated with improved agricultural methods, the spread of education, and technological progress.

With the increased availability of demographic statistics, evidence is accumulating that the fall in death rates is not confined to the western industrialized nations (though these countries undoubtedly now enjoy the lowest mortality levels) but that there have also been significant declines in other parts of the world in recent decades. Statistics recently compiled by the United Nations indicate that crude death rates have been reduced by one-third to one-half since 1930 in a considerable number of the so-called "under-developed" countries. This marked downward shift in mortality levels shows clearly in the data for 27 such countries for which statistics are available for the year 1930 (in one case the data relate to 1932) and for 1950 (in a few cases the data relate to 1949).[1] These areas have the following distributions with respect to the crude death rate:

Crude death rate	1930	1950
(per 1,000)	(number of countries)	
Under 10.0	—	4
10.0–14.9	4	17
15.0–19.9	9	4
20.0–24.9	13	2
25.0 or over	3	—

These data may not be taken as representative of all underdeveloped areas, for they include chiefly the more advanced among such areas. Very large and important regions such as China, Indochina, Indonesia, most of Africa and parts of Latin America, where death rates may range up to 40 per 1,000, are excluded entirely be-

[1] These countries are: Barbados, British Guiana, British Honduras, Cape Verde Islands, Ceylon, Chile, Colombia, Costa Rica, Cyprus, Egypt, El Salvador, Fiji Islands, Guatemala, Honduras, India, Jamaica, Japan, Mauritius, Mexico, Panama, Puerto Rico, Singapore, Surinam, Thailand, Trinidad, Venezuela, Western Samoa. Source: United Nations *Demographic Yearbook, 1951,* Table 14.

cause of the absence of statistical information. However, they represent a rather broad geographic range and at least suggest that similar changes may be occurring in parts of the world where vital data are not systematically collected.

The median death rate among the 27 countries was 20.4 per 1,000 in 1930 and 12.2 in 1950, indicating a reduction of 40 percent in about two decades. These figures are subject to considerable error, stemming mainly from the underregistration of deaths. Absolute levels are no doubt understated both at the beginning and at the end of the 20-year period, perhaps by as much as 50 percent in some cases. But, in view of the probable improvement in registration during this period, it is quite possible that the magnitude of the actual decline is understated by the statistics.

Data on natality indicate that, while mortality has been falling sharply, birth rates continue at relatively high levels. The same 27 countries as listed above have the following distribution with respect to crude birth rates in 1930 and in 1950:

Crude birth rate	1930	1950
(per 1,000)	(number of countries)	
Under 30.0	1	3
30.0–34.9	11	5
35.0–39.9	8	7
40.0–44.9	1	5
45.0 or more	6	7

While these data suggest that there was something of a rise in fertility between 1930 and 1950, it seems probable that they are merely reflecting an improvement in the registration of births. Indeed, it is quite possible that, in some areas at least, the improvement in registration may be masking an actual decline in fertility.

Data for recent postwar years are more widely available as well as more accurate than data for 1930. These statistics show that crude birth rates in the neighborhood of 30 to 45 per 1,000 are prevalent in Latin America. Information for the Asian countries is limited and that for Africa is only fragmentary, but available data indicate that rates of over 35 per 1,000 are not uncommon. Such rates, no doubt underestimated, may be compared with rates of 15 to 25 per 1,000 in the more heavily industrialized countries of Western Europe and northern North America (including Australia and New Zealand).

The combination of high fertility and diminishing mortality results in accelerating rates of natural increase. Of the 125 countries for which statistics for a recent postwar year (in most cases, 1950) are available, 43 report rates of natural increase of two percent or more (see table below). More than half of these are Latin American countries. In this region, 25 of the 39 countries supplying vital data report rates of natural increase higher than two percent and five a rate of more than three percent. Seven of the 17 Asian countries show rates of two percent or more and five of the ten countries in Oceania report rates at this level. In contrast, 21 of the 39 European countries are increasing at a rate of less than one percent per year.

Although the reliability of the basic data for most of the countries (except those of Europe, the northern part of North America, Australia and New Zealand) is subject to considerable question, the indicated rates must be regarded as minimum estimates of the rates at which the populations are increasing, unless we are willing to assume that births are more fully registered than deaths. There is evidence that in some cases the coverage of births is relatively better than that of deaths. However, death registration is generally held to be more complete than birth registration. If so, an appropriate

DISTRIBUTION OF 125 COUNTRIES WITH RESPECT TO ANNUAL RATES OF NATURAL INCREASE *
(Data refer to most recent year for which statistics are available)

Continent	All Countries	Number of countries with specified rates of increase		
		Under 1.0%	1.0–1.9%	2.0% or more
Total.........	125	33	49	43
Africa........	20	9	7	4
America.......	44	1	18	25
U.S. and Canada[1].....	5	..	5	..
Latin America.....	39	1	13	25
Asia..........	17	1	9	7
Europe........	34	21	11	2
Oceania.......	10	1	4	5

[1] Including all of North America north of Mexico.
* Source: "Population and Vital Statistics Reports," *Statistical Papers*, Series A. Vol. III, No. 3–4, October 1951, United Nations, New York.

correction for under-registration would yield still higher rates of increase for those countries where recorded rates are already relatively high.[2]

It should be remembered that the frequency distribution shown in the table represents units that vary greatly as to population size. Consequently, no conclusion as to the proportion of the world's population that is growing at the various rates may be drawn from it.

The statistics summarized in the table cover about nine-tenths of the population of Europe and Oceania, about four-fifths of the population of the Americas (all of

[2] For example, Kingsley Davis estimates crude birth and death rates for India 1931–1941 at 45 and 31 per 1,000, respectively. The official data for this period yield average rates of 34 and 23 per 1,000. The implied rates of natural increases are 11 per 1,000 on the basis of the official data and 14 per 1,000 on the basis of Davis' estimates. See Kingsley Davis, *The Population of India and Pakistan* (Princeton University Press, 1951). Chapters 5, 9, and 11.

northern North America and two-thirds of Latin America) about one-fourth of Africa (mostly North African Moslems and Europeans) and less than one-fifth of the Asian population. Together they comprise approximately 40 percent of the world's population. The vast populations of China, the USSR, Southeastern Asia and most of Africa, do not figure in these data. China alone, with a population somewhere between 400 million and a half-a-billion, holds perhaps one-sixth of the world's inhabitants. Speculative estimates for this country place both the birth and the death rates at high levels. A recent report on demographic conditions in the Far East, prepared by experts in the fields of population and public health states:

"There is every reason to believe that the birth rate is over 40 per 1,000 population. For anyone familiar with the behavior of birth rates throughout the world and with China's social organization, it would be surprising to find a lower rate and equally surprising if that rate were to undergo any very substantial decline in the next two decades except as a temporary result of sweeping catastrophe.

"The trend of the death rate is much less predictable. Even in the good years with no major epidemics or famines, the death rate is probably above 30 per 1,000. Some studies suggest that year in and year out it might even average 40. There is little doubt that a period of peace and strong government, even one that merely improves the functioning of the economy along existing lines, would bring considerably more favorable conditions than have existed in the past two decades and would reduce death rates for at least some time."[3]

[3] Marshall C. Balfour, Roger F. Evans, Frank W. Notestein and Irene B. Taeuber, *Public Health and Demography in the Far East* (Rockefeller Foundation, 1950), pp. 74-75.

The present situation of China cannot be assessed, but conditions may have changed considerably since the observations on which these paragraphs are based were made.

Conditions similar to those described above may prevail in some of the other areas for which statistics are not available, high fertility being largely cancelled by high mortality with the result that rates of natural increase resemble those of the industrial countries where low fertility and low mortality yield low rates of natural increase. This probably does not apply to the USSR, however, a country which industrialized rapidly after 1920 and which may now have achieved relatively low death rates and possibly has experienced an appreciable decline in fertility.

In spite of the limitations of the data and the extent of our ignorance, the evidences of progress in the reduction of mortality are real and impressive. As is often the case with important discoveries or profound social changes that represent great achievement in a given direction, this piece of progress has precipitated conditions that may in the course of time stifle further achievements in the direction of economic development and higher levels of living.

The story of the demographic evolution of the Western World since the middle of the seventeenth century is well-known and needs only be sketched here. The decline in mortality which began at about the same time as the Industrial Revolution was accompanied by a rapid and sustained growth that resulted in a seven-fold increase in the population of Europe and "Europe overseas" within the space of about 300 years. The fall in birth rates, which began later than the fall in mortality, considerably reduced the rate of natural increase and, on the eve of the second World War, several countries were actually recording a small natural decrease. During and after the war, fertility levels in these areas rose significantly. Current rates of natural increase are still higher than during the inter-war period, but they now show some signs of a moderate decrease.

Upon this story, combined with a recognition of the widening gap between fertility and mortality in economically under-developed or densely populated countries, rests a growing concern over the prospect of diminishing natural resources before a rising tide of starving and shivering humanity. We hear of precious top soil washing down the mountain sides and into the sea, forests melting before fire and axe, coal veins approaching exhaustion, petroleum deposits running low, while mankind spawns and multiplies, heedless of the future and oblivious to the approach of disaster.

There is no doubt that this concern is justified in large measure, but the proclivity for seeing only one aspect of a problem, and preferably the dreary one, should not be allowed to make us forget to examine alternative possibilities with some care. Above all, the paralysis of despair should be avoided. The record of man's progress is one of increasing ingenuity in controlling his environment and planning his future. While resourcefulness is not a complete substitute for resources, the latter cannot be exploited without the former. Furthermore, it is clear that what constitutes a resource is subject to the most startling changes. It is quite impossible to foretell very far into the future just which among the presently unused objects and forces lying about on our planet or perhaps drifting through outer space may be transformed overnight into valuable resources.

This is not to say that we must not attack our present problems in terms of what is known and attainable here and now and in the foreseeable future. But we need not break our hearts too irreparably over the grim fate of mankind 1,000 or even 100 years from now, for their problems are certain not to be the same as our problems, and their fate may well be happier than our own.

Consider the problem of food, for example. Opinions differ as to how far we can go in expanding world food production.

We are reminded, on the one hand, that practically all fertile and accessible land is already under cultivation, that much of the land that is now under cultivation should not even be planted to crops, that much of what was once fertile land has deteriorated or been forced out of cultivation by poor farming methods. According to this school, the end is in sight for agricultural expansion. The threat of further substantial increases in population can only mean creeping starvation, as numbers plunge ahead of production, agricultural resources contract, and available average supplies drop below the danger point.

This is not an unreasonable view, if we assume the worst in all directions. Resources *have* been wasted in the past; good land *has* been misused; most of the world's most fertile land *is* already under cultivation; population *is* likely to increase; no doubt there *are* limits to what the world can be made to produce. In some regions of the world the density of the population with respect to agricultural land and the recurrent periods of distress resulting from crop failures, droughts, floods, etc. give the effect of over-population. There are areas in India, for example, where the density of the agricultural population exceeds 600 persons per square mile of cultivated land. There are regions in Japan where every available piece of soil is under cultivation, including the small strips of land along the railways and even between the cross-ties. In

China before the revolution the evidences of exhausted land and pressure of the population upon agricultural resources were wide-spread. In such crowded areas the parcelling of farm land, whereby farms have been cut into smaller and smaller fragments as they passed from one generation to another, has probably reinforced the loss in productive capacity caused by agricultural malpractice of other types. With respect to these areas it is difficult to imagine how the population tolerance of the land could be significantly increased.

According to another point of view, such conditions as those described above obviously call for radical social and economic reorganization. They do not necessarily attest to the absolute inability of the land to produce sufficient food for an even larger population than is now forced to draw sustenance from it. For now that we are aware of past mistakes, it is not necessary that we continue to make them in the future. If we do continue to make them, no doubt we shall have to pay the price. The choice is ours. Furthermore, the long run and the short run may not be looked at within the same frame of reference. The calamity-howlers have their eyes on the long run and their minds on the present state of the world. At any time in history, a look at the distant future in the perspective of contemporary ways and means must have been alarming. It does not do to assume that the dynamics of population growth are eternal while those of resources development are approaching stalemate and retrogression, for this has not been so in the past.

The outlook for the short run, in terms of what is possible, appears to be much less depressing than the one that is so popular among recent best-sellers. Perhaps the reason for this is that scientists and technicians are inclined to deal with problems into which they can really sink

their teeth, rather than to indulge in imaginary extrapolation of certain trends, selected for their scare-value and press-appeal.

Richard Bradfield, agronomist at Cornell University has said, "In the majority of cases the most optimistic views of the world's potentialities for sustained and increased food production are expressed by the agricultural scientists and the most pessimistic views by the nonagriculturists!"[4] Bradfield indicates that the earth's crust contains, for all practical purposes, an inexhaustible supply of all known plant nutrients except nitrogen, of which there is an inexhaustible supply in the atmosphere, and that the earth is not going to run out of the raw materials for soil building in the foreseeable future. He concludes that the great advances of agricultural science in the past have brought the world to a stage where the problem of food can be attacked with confidence and that, to this end, programs of research should be intensified all over the world. If, in the future, the world is not better fed, it will not be the shortage of physical resources that is the cause, but poverty and ignorance.

Salter of the U.S. Department of Agriculture estimates that the goals set by the Food and Agriculture Organization of the United Nations for agricultural production in 1960 which represent an adequate diet for all people (including allowance for population increase) can be met through the utilization of resources known to exist. Increases obtainable through more intensive use of present cropland and through the development of additional land not now cultivated

[4] Richard Bradfield, "Soil Resources and the World's Potential Food Supply," *Studies in Population*, Proceedings of the Annual Meeting of the Population Association of America at Princeton, New Jersey, May, 1949. (Princeton University Press, Princeton, New Jersey, 1949).

would more than meet these goals for 5 out of the 7 basic classes of food, and could be made to meet the others also if shifts in the utilization of certain raw products were made. "To meet world food needs, then, much less than all these sources of production are required, if efforts are made to produce primarily those classes of foods in deficit."[5]

Kellogg, also of the U.S. Department of Agriculture, similarly estimates that the improvement of agricultural methods and the bringing into cultivation of additional land (estimated by both Salter and Kellogg at about 1.3 billion acres as compared with about 3 billion acres already under cultivation) would meet food requirements for some time to come.[6] Kellogg emphasizes the need for further research and points out that practices that are good in one place can be ruinous in another. The goal of conservation should not be conservation itself but a sustained productivity whereby, for example, erosive lands are under a protective cover that is also a productive cover.

There is often a considerable gap between what is possible and what is achieved. The possibilities are all rather firmly based on known resources and established techniques of production. It is some years now since they were plainly stated. But only a few months ago, the Food and Agriculture Organization of the United Nations, which was founded precisely for the purpose of implementing the kind of program declared possible by Bradfield, Salter, Kellogg and others, was forced to announce that perhaps three-fifths of the world's population is under-

nourished and that food supplies per capita are estimated to be four per cent below prewar levels.

FAO is not to be blamed for this state of affairs. Its heroic efforts could not transcend its puny budget and limited powers. The United Nations technical assistance program and the United States Point Four program also represent but a small beginning. In a divided world, throwing much of its strength and substance into non-productive enterprises, it is not surprising that food production has not kept pace with population growth.

The practical problems involved in a successful and effective program are enormous and complex, both in terms of the world as a whole and in terms of conditions, resources and people as they exist in the various regions of the world.[7] Meanwhile, the possibilities are still there. The world is still rich and waiting.

In the face of the slow grinding of the mills of man's corporate intelligence, a certain desperation sets in. Man's very numbers take on a sinister significance and we arrive at an interesting paradox in which we see his extinction implicit in his prolixity, the same mechanism whereby he gained life and welfare becoming the mechanism whereby he loses them. Hence the advocacy of controlled population growth. Few doubt that the small-family system will develop spontaneously in the East with industrialization, urbanization and the "emancipation" of women, just as it developed in the West. But now that the open spaces are gone, there is fear that the rapid expansion of population, which is already under way in

[5] Robert M. Salter, "World Soil and Fertilizer Resources in Relation to Food Needs," Freedom from Want (E. E. DeTurk, ed.) Chronica Botanica, Vol. 11, No. 4, 1948.

[6] See Charles E. Kellogg, "Food Production Potentialities and Problems," Journal of Farm Economics, Proceedings Number, February 1949.

[7] For a more specific treatment of these, see Findings of Studies on the Relationships between Population Trends and Economic and Social Factors, especially Chapter IX, "World Population and Resources," United Nations Document E/CN.9/77. United Nations, New York, March 22, 1951.

a considerable number of countries, as we have seen, will thrust ahead of economic development bringing down the social structure in a morass of poverty and frustration.

For obvious reasons, the under-privileged peoples of the world are largely unaware of any need to reduce their birth rates, of any threat of a "population explosion," of the possibility that they can control the number of children they have; they are in general quite without the means of practicing birth control as it is practiced in industrial society, even if they wanted to do so.

On the whole it is difficult to judge which approach represents the more formidable problem in social engineering, the economic or the contraceptive. Not that either approach precludes the other. Indeed, most of the proponents of population control regard their program as a holding operation while economic development gets under way. Their position is that it will be easier to raise levels of living if the increase in numbers is held in check.

Many feel that the outlook is hopeless in the absence of a simple contraceptive that can be taken orally, or by injection, or in some manner that would be appropriate and convenient in peasant populations living under relatively primitive conditions. Recent research in this field holds out the promise that such a cheap and simple contraceptive may be available in a matter of years. So, even as the possibility of greatly increased food supplies appears to be just around the corner, the possibility of controlling the rate of population growth seems also to be almost within our grasp. The impact of such a product on the patterns of human behavior and incidentally on the problem of population cannot be estimated in advance.

While we watch the development of these varied prospects and possibilities, there is one aspect of the problem of population and resources that should be considered carefully. The very word "balance" implies that population is on one side of the scales and food or natural resources on the other side. This antithesis is to a considerable degree unreal. Population and resources will not line up on opposite sides of a balance sheet, for population is itself both a resource and a consumer of resources. Even if a distinction is made between resources as raw materials and resources as human labor and ingenuity, the logical dilemma is not entirely avoided. We are so long past the stage when subsistence could be gained by foraging and browsing that almost no raw materials are utilized in their free and native state, i.e., without cultivation, processing, preservation, transportation or some form of manipulation that goes far beyond the simple acts of picking and gathering.

On the surface, it seems a matter of elementary arithmetic that, if consumer goods are in short supply, a quick curtailment of population growth or even a reduction in numbers would enhance the goods available for each member of the population. Actually, the immediate effects of population control are not so easy to evaluate. It does not necessarily follow that a reduction in numbers will automatically produce a signally higher level of living for the existing population. For this reason the advocates of population control are often accused of evading the basic issue, of substituting family limitation for a positive program of economic development. This accusation is perhaps partly justified. Nevertheless, it cannot be denied that a considerable amount of strength and energy go into the bearing and rearing of large families and that a significant proportion of available supplies is consumed by the non-producing part of the population. Much of that strength would be freed for more directly productive kinds of work if the number of births were reduced. If, however, some provision is not made so that this strength and energy are used effectively, very little gain will have been made.

From the economic point of view there is not much to choose between unused energies and constant child-bearing. Under these circumstances, the economic cost of high fertility, with its attendant high infant mortality, is probably not excessive. In areas where high fertility is not cancelled by high mortality, the gains that are reflected in the lower mortality will in any case be negated if human capacities are not fully utilized. From the ethical point of view there is a certain irresponsibility, whether individual or collective, about bringing large numbers of children into the world without adequate provision for feeding and clothing them and bringing them safely to maturity.

By and large, it does not make sense to worry over the depletion of material resources when the human agent is not employed to its utmost, both in the exploita-

tion and in the judicious conservation of these resources. It *does* make sense to divert energy from child-bearing to economic development wherever poverty and malnutrition are prevalent, wherever the difference from year to year between death and survival is largely a matter of luck with the crops and the weather.

One thing is certain. Birth control is not a panacea. It is only a means to an end and in some ways a negative means. Surely, the chief object is to build a modern, literate, well-nourished, technologically competent society in all the presently under-developed areas of the world.

Those who take a dim view like to compound population increases at various percentages per annum and terrify us with the results. But it is useless to calculate numbers of persons without qualifying the other variables in the equation of the future. The prospect of a doubling of the world's population by the end of the twentieth century holds no terrors unless we can be certain that the physical appurtenances of life cannot be more than doubled in the same period.

POPULATION AND CHANGE IN
BACKWARD AREAS*

KINGSLEY DAVIS

* Reprinted by permission from the *Columbia Journal of International Affairs*, Vol. IV, No. 2, Spring 1950, pp. 43–49.

THE preoccupation with "two worlds" in the sense of communism versus democracy has obscured another dichotomy that

is probably more profound—that between the archaic agricultural nations and the modern industrial nations. This division, which cuts across the other, results from the fact that the industrial revolution has spread from its point of origin in Europe to only a few other areas of the globe. In the meantime, the industrial nations have enjoyed such an advantage that they have been able to dominate the still agricultural nations politically and economically, and this dominance has resulted in conditions that make it difficult for the latter to emerge from their non-industrial state.

THE ARCHAIC AGRICULTURAL COUNTRIES

A country can be regarded as still agricultural if 50 per cent or more of its occupied males are engaged in farming and allied pursuits. This excludes countries such as Argentina and New Zealand whose agriculture is mechanized and thus supports a substantial labor force in secondary and tertiary industry. Applying the 50-per-cent criterion and using computations and estimates made by the Bureau of Applied Social Research, we find that the archaic agricultural countries and colonies embrace three-fourths of the world's area and people. They embrace a far larger proportion of the tropics than of the temperate zone. By continents the percentage of the population in this type of country is as follows:

TABLE 1

	Per Cent
World	76
Africa	100
Asia (exc. USSR)	93
Central & Caribbean America	87
South America	77
Europe (exc. USSR)	30
Anglo-America	None

One of the striking facts about the archaic agricultural countries is that they have a much higher agricultural density than the industrial countries. They have, for example, an average of approximately 106 males engaged in agriculture per square mile of agricultural land, whereas in the industrial countries the figure is only about 34. Table 2 shows that the more agricultural a country is (in our sense of the term) the more densely settled is its agricultural population.

TABLE 2. Agricultural Density According to Degree of Agriculturalism

Per Cent of Occupied Males in Agriculture	Agricultural Males per Square Mile of Agricultural Land
0–29.9	21.00
30–49.9	54.64
50–69.9	68.07
70+	130.88

Japan is the major exception to the general rule. Although an industrial country, it has almost 400 agriculturally engaged males per square mile of agricultural land. Its case is interesting, because it shows that labor-intensive agriculture can be combined with modern industrialization. Japan, of course, started its industrialization with a much higher rural density than any other industrial country ever started with.

The gap between industrial and agricultural countries can be illustrated in numerous ways. In 1939 the average per capita income for 29 countries that were agricultural according to our definition was $68 per annum, whereas in 21 industrial countries it was $305 per annum, or four-and-a-half times as great.[1] In 1947 the average proportion illiterate aged 10 and over was 68 per cent in the agricultural countries but only 3.3 per cent in industrial countries. In the same year the agricultural countries had 9.9 per cent of their population living in cities of 50,000 or more, whereas the industrial countries

[1] Computed from Howard S. Piquet, "Point Four and World Production," *Annals of the American Academy of Political and Social Science*, Vol. 268 (March, 1950), pp. 150–151. The averages are not weighted by population.

had 31.3 per cent living in such places.[2] It can be seen that a very wide chasm separates the two countries not only in terms of rural density of population but also in terms of the earmarks of civilization.

THE IMPACT OF THE WEST

Although the agricultural countries have remained non-industrial they have nevertheless been greatly affected by industrialization in other areas. They have evolved a new mixed type of society based on contact with and subordination to the industrial peoples. Their agriculture has tended to become commercialized. Their people have been drawn into a money economy. Their handicrafts have been destroyed or reduced in importance by cheap foreign manufactures. Their leaders have become identified with foreign masters. The profits of their work have been siphoned off, with a little left over to finance local industrial progress. Their death rate has been reduced, but their birth rate has remained static because the people have remained agricultural and uninstructed. As a consequence their population has grown less rapidly than in industrializing countries but nevertheless rapidly enough to add greatly to already heavy densities. They have therefore reached, in many cases at least, a melancholy state in which great numbers in relation to developed resources live at extremely low levels. The demographic situation makes it very difficult for them to industrialize and thus escape from their poverty, especially since rapid population growth has been the normal accompaniment of industrial development. These heavily peopled industrial areas therefore

face the prospect of very great increases in numbers if they industrialize, although the population is already so great that industrialization is difficult.

It has naturally occurred to many people that if somehow the threat of great future increases of population could be obviated, the process of industrial development and modernization could be facilitated, and that certainly the ultimate standard of living would be greater than it would otherwise be. But the prospects of removing the demographic threat do not appear promising.

MIGRATION, BIRTH CONTROL AND INDUSTRIALIZATION

It has sometimes been suggested, for example, that migration might hold a solution. Indeed, since many of the industrial peoples have reached a stage when their numbers are no longer growing, it has sometimes been maintained that they should open their doors to Asiatics and others from densely settled agricultural countries, thus relieving population pressure in the rest of the world and aiding the process of modernization. It has also been suggested that the world's "empty spaces" controlled by European peoples, such as the western part of the United States, much of Australia, Central and South America, and parts of Africa, be opened up to Chinese, Indian, and Indonesian settlement.[3] The truth is, however, that the industrial countries with a declining rate of population growth either already have dense populations (as in Europe) or have very restrictive immigration policies with respect to Asiatics. Short of conquest, most of the so-called empty spaces are not open to colonization by the only kind of people who can settle in

[2] Based on computations and estimates of literacy and urbanization for the world's countries and colonies made by the Division of Population Research, Bureau of Applied Social Research.

[3] See Radhakamal Mukerjee, *Races, Lands, and Food* (New York: Dryden Press, 1946) and *Migrant Asia* (Rome: Tipografia Failli, 1936).

them under conditions of low capitalization.[4] Furthermore, since the proportion of the world's population now living in overcrowded agricultural regions is quite high, the amount of emigration required to really aid them in solving their demographic problems would be astronomical in comparison to any previous mass migration in human history, and unless somehow the basic structure and economy of the rural societies were changed, they would simply build up again to their old population densities. In turn, the same patterns of dense settlement in agriculture at low levels of living might be repeated in the remaining open spaces of the globe, with a net loss rather than gain to human civilization. Migration therefore does not offer a promising solution.

The next question is whether other forms of population control might be exercised in the crowded regions of archaic agriculturalism. Here, too, the prospects are far from promising. In the past history of modern nations a decline in fertility has accompanied or followed industrialization. It therefore seems questionable to assume that such a decline can be made to precede and thus help along the process of economic development. Actually, we do not know enough about peasant attitudes toward family size. Not enough scientific research using modern methods of attitude and opinion measurement has been utilized in western countries, and certainly not enough in the crowded agricultural regions of the world. It would therefore

[4] See W. D. Forsyth, *The Myth of Open Spaces* (Melbourne: Melbourne University Press, 1942); Isaiah Bowman (ed.), *Limits of Land Settlement* (New York: Council on Foreign Relations, 1937); Wilbert E. Moore, "Economic Limits of International Resettlement," *American Sociological Review*, Vol. 10 (April, 1945), pp. 274–281; Kingsley Davis, "Future Migration into Latin America" in *Postwar Problems of Migration* (New York: Milbank Memorial Fund, 1947), pp. 30–48.

be rash to state categorically that a decline in peasant birth rates would be impossible to bring about. The invention of long-term and more convenient birth control techniques than those now in use, the employment of modern means of public education and propaganda, and the experiment of an all-out government campaign to bring down fertility might conceivably yield results in countries such as India, China, Java, and Egypt. But the truth is that no government is likely to throw its weight entirely behind such a movement, because the reproductive mores are too embedded in non-rational sentiment for the public to give its strong support.

We are left, then, with the only apparent solution—namely, a program of rapid industrialization. The hope is that industrial growth can be made so quickly that it will get ahead of population growth and eventually solve the population problem not only by providing a higher standard of living for the population and the inevitable growth of numbers during the process of economic development, but also by bringing those new social conditions that will cause people voluntarily to limit their offspring. In short, it is hoped to repeat the experience of the now industrialized countries, but more rapidly.

THE PRIORITY OF HUMAN NECESSITIES

Actually nearly all of the governments in underdeveloped areas are pinning their faith on industrialization. The obstacles, however, are many—not the least of which is population density, which is one of the problems that the program is designed to solve. Most of the crowded rural countries have long been the victims of a colonialism or semi-colonialism which has built up their population without giving them a sense of national statesmanship and self-discipline or a balanced economy. Their people have become a sort of agricultural proletariat serving the industrial world. They are faced with superior competition even on the agricultural side from countries that have a high ratio of resources to population. In fact, the areas that have recently become industrial or mechanized seem to be those that are sparsely settled, such as Australia, New Zealand, Argentina, Brazil, Russia, Canada, and the United States. It is not easy to believe that the heavily peopled rural areas of today, especially when they embrace huge population aggregates like India, Pakistan, Egypt, and Java, can rapidly and smoothly make the transition to an industrial regime.

In general, heavy density and potentially fast population growth tend to focus economic effort on consumption rather than heavy industry. The swollen masses are so deprived of the immediate necessities of existence that everything is expended on the imperative task of simply maintaining life. As their bare necessities are met the masses tend to multiply so fast that the supply of food must be constantly expanded. This makes it hard to accumulate the surplus and invest the time necessary to develop heavy industries, even though in the end the heavy industries would yield a greater amount of consumption goods. Most of the crowded people are so near the subsistence point that they cannot save. They tend to borrow for consumption purposes and thus to get into the vicious circle of impoverished indebtedness. Even when they can save they feel so insecure that they prefer a high liquidity of their assets to a modest interest through investment. In this way the amount of investment capital produced by the population tends to be small, and for this reason too, the amount of capital that can be borrowed from foreign sources is not great, especially since the new nation-

alism in many of the countries in question makes for suspicion and limitation of the use of foreign capital under conditions acceptable to the lenders. Finally, it is particularly difficult for a democratic government to ignore the tragic wants of the majority of its citizens in order to build a heavy industry for the future. It feels constrained to use its economic means to feed, clothe, and shelter the people when they are in dire poverty and when there will be many more of them tomorrow than there are today.

An agricultural country has mainly its agriculture as the means for financing an industrial program. But peasant agriculture does not furnish the technical personnel and the experience required for industrialization. An industrial revolution does not depend solely on capital; it also depends on a tradition of science, or impersonal law, of competent government administration, and of competitive enterprise. These traditions cannot be acquired overnight. At the same time an overcrowded peasant population makes for inefficiency in agriculture itself. It carries a tremendous burden of unemployment and underemployment, of fragmentation of holdings, of dispiriting and wasteful subinfeudation, of unproductive indebtedness, and of low capitalization and soil erosion. Most of the land is devoted to food crops for subsistence rather than to commercial crops for the accumulation of an investment surplus. The country thus has little that it can export to pay for the importation of machinery and other necessities of heavy industry. The situation reaches its ultimate futility when the food requirements of the swollen population become so great that an agricultural country becomes an importer of agricultural produce—that is, when the total value of agricultural imports exceeds the total value of agricultural exports. Actually, this paradoxical condition is impossible to reach except when shipments of food are received through the charity of other nations, but several countries of the world are headed in that direction.

It should be mentioned, also, that a country with rapid population growth attributable to an extremely high fertility and a high but somewhat lower death rate is one that has an unusual burden of young-age dependency. The proportion of dependents to people in the productive ages is unusually large. Also, much of the energy of the people is wasted in useless reproduction. Women give birth to and nurse millions of babies each year who are destined to die before they reach a productive age. In addition, the inevitably high mortality in such a population—high but not high enough to cancel the higher birth rate—is always associated with excessive morbidity. Disease, undernourishment, malnutrition, and injury lead to lethargy and absenteeism, and hence to inefficiency.[5]

There seems little doubt that mechanization and modernization will eventually come to all major areas of the world. There is no reason to think that this newest stage in human cultural evolution will remain only partially diffused, that the countries of the earth will permanently remain divided into two distinct worlds, the one of illiterate agriculturalism and the other of literate urban-industrialism. The statistics on literacy, urbanization, and manufacturing indeed show that modernization is going forward nearly everywhere, though in some cases at a slow

[5] A fuller analysis of the economic ills of crowded areas and agriculturalism is contained in the writer's volume, *The Population of India and Pakistan* (Princeton: Princeton University Press). See also D. Ghosh, *Pressure of Population and Economic Efficiency in India* (New Delhi: Indian Council on World Affairs, 1946) and Harvey S. Perloff, *Puerto Rico's Economic Future* (Chicago: University of Chicago Press, 1950).

pace. The main question is how, and under what conditions, the diffusion of industrial civilization will be completed.

WAS MALTHUS RIGHT?

In view of the formidable obstacles to industrialization in underdeveloped and crowded regions, it seems utopian to look for a smooth transition to modernism. The sheer size of prospective population gains alone discourages this view. Much more likely seems the possibility that strife and turmoil, which at once reduce the existing demographic glut and sweep away old institutions and vested interests, will be the mechanism by which the present vicious circle will be broken. One indication that this may be the actual course of events is the present struggle going on between two massive politico-economic systems. The underdeveloped areas may become the battleground of still another major conflict, one fought with new material and psychological weapons and more deadly than any past conflict. Out of such a major struggle might come a new stability and eventually a new population balance based on low birth rates and low death rates, more efficient than the old and consequently giving human beings a higher standard of living.

Such a prospective means to a solution of rural overpopulation is, of course, distasteful. One hopes, therefore, that other means may be found. One likes to think that a combined program of rapid industrialization (with help from the older industrial countries), of strategic emigration, and of all-out birth control campaigns might furnish the basis for a less disastrous transition to modern civilization in the great underdeveloped and heavily peopled areas of the world. There is, indeed, a good deal of effort designed in one way or another to implement such a program. But from a strictly scientific, or dispassionate, point of view the chances do not appear good. The democratic nations must therefore be prepared to face a struggle of major proportions, and to fight their battle wherever and however it may become necessary. Unfortunately, the world demographic situation, partly the consequence of Western dominance and the partial diffusion of industrial culture, is one of the reasons why this unwelcome but possible eventuality must be faced.

IMPLICATIONS OF POPULATION TRENDS IN UNDER-DEVELOPED COUNTRIES*

THE preceding sections demonstrate that much remains to be learned concerning the relationships between demographic trends and economic and social development in the under-developed countries, and that much controversy exists among writers concerning these relationships. Discussion of controversial questions could be made more fruitful were better statistics assembled, especially for those under-developed countries which at the present possess very few statistics. However, quite a large measure of agreement on certain points and conclusions may be achieved among researchers making a rational use of already available information. These conclusions constitute the point of departure for further study of economic and social development problems in the under-developed countries.

Demographic considerations have a practical bearing on two major aspects of developmental programmes. First, they are involved in the formulation of pro-

* From "Implications of Population Trends in Under-Developed Countries," Chapter XV, *The Determinants and Consequences of Population Trends*, Population Studies No. 17, Population Division, Department of Social Affairs, United Nations, New York, 1953, pp. 284–287.

gramme objectives. The purpose of economic and social development is to build a society and an economy which can more fully meet the needs of the people. The specific needs depend not only on the size of the population but also on its composition and geographical distribution. It is not sufficient to consider the population at the time the programme is initiated; probable future population changes should also be taken into account in so far as that is possible, in order that appropriate provision may be made for them. In particular, it is important to take account of the population changes which may result from economic development and social reforms. Second, demographic considerations are involved in developing and applying the nations's productive resources to meet the specific needs. A major resource is the labour supply; its volume and characteristics are determined mainly by the size, composition and distribution of the population. The development and utilization of other resources, including land and capital, are also affected by demographic factors.

Among the least controversial points which emerge from the foregoing is the probability of a fairly rapid increase in the population of under-developed countries, provided the tempo of economic development is sufficient to provide food and other necessities for the growing numbers. This increase will result from the decline in the death rate which, in most cases is not likely to be compensated for by a comparable reduction in the birth rate. It is therefore important that plans for social and economic development should take population growth into account.

The evidence supports a presumption —though by no means a certainty—that economic development in the areas now under-developed may eventually result in declining fertility, much as it did in Europe and Europe overseas, and as it has recently done to some extent in a few other areas. However, if such fertility declines do occur, it is nearly certain that they will lag behind the declines in mortality, at least in the initial stages. In fact, this lag already exists, and has existed for some time, throughout most of the under-developed regions of the world. The available facts indicate that economic development in most of Asia, Africa and much of Latin America has not yet been accompanied by any substantial changes in fertility, though the decline of mortality is nearly universal. In the planning of measures for social welfare and economic development, it would be useful to know how long the discrepancy between fertility and mortality rates can be expected to continue, and under what conditions, how soon, and at what rate fertility rates can be expected to fall.

Emigration may drain off a part of the excess of births over deaths in some of the under-developed countries, as it did in Europe especially during the latter half of the nineteenth century and the first decade of the twentieth. But the possibilities of international migration are at present less favourable than they were in the days of the great European exodus. The "new world" then offered huge areas with good economic opportunities where migrants could locate almost without restriction. No such areas exist today. Many of the vacant or sparsely settled regions which remain are either unsuitable for habitation under present conditions or require large capital investments to make settlement practicable. Almost everywhere legal barriers have been erected, severely restricting numbers and prescribing the types of immigrants allowed. Potential emigrants from Asian countries in particular find it difficult to gain admission to other regions of the world. Moreover, the very size of the population in some of the most important under-developed countries is such that emigration probably could not occur on a sufficiently large scale to have any major influence on the rate of population growth.

On the other hand, economic and social development in some areas where the local population cannot furnish the volume or the type of labour supply required may create the need for a substantial amount of immigration. Many obstacles, however, hinder large-scale immigration to such areas, notably the high capitalization required and the difficulty of attracting the types of immigrants most desired for developmental purposes. It appears probable that the trend of population, especially in those under-developed countries which are now heavily populated, will henceforth be governed primarily by the changing relationships between birth and death rates, and only to a relatively minor extent by migration.

Thus the increase of production which must be achieved if there is to be definite economic and social progress must provide not only for those vital needs of the existing population which are not adequately met at present, but also for the needs of the additional population resulting from the present and future declines in mortality rates and also perhaps from the social and economic development measures themselves.

The growth of population in the under-developed countries will not necessarily follow an identical course with that of the population in the European countries during their period of development. Initially, the growth in population is likely to be more rapid because of the rapid introduction of public health safeguards and superior medical techniques. On the other hand, it is possible that the governments of the under-developed countries will promote birth control programmes to lessen the discrepancy between the existing birth and death rates. The reduction of birth rates involves, however, far more difficult problems than the reduction of death rates.

These possibilities require careful attention when plans are drawn for economic and social development programmes, especially in those countries where the population is now very dense in relation to usable land and other resources. On the one hand, it is essential that development be planned, if possible, on a sufficient scale to meet the needs of the growing population, in so far as they may be foreseen. It is important, in this connexion, to take into account not only the expected changes in the total number of consumers, but also the changes in their wants which will accompany a rise in *per capita* real income. Special attention should be paid to the means of providing for adequate satisfaction of basic needs for food, housing, clothing, education, medical care, etc. In the calculation of these needs, not only expected changes in the size of the population, but also shifts in its composition with respect to sex, age, and number of families are important. Methods of quantifying more exactly the relationships of population size and structure to needs for certain types of

goods and services need to be improved. It is not impossible that should certain countries encounter difficulty in achieving a sufficiently rapid economic development, their governments may consider devoting greater efforts to implementing a policy of limiting population growth.

While population growth increases the needs of a nation, it also adds to one of the chief economic resources, the labour supply. The size of the labour supply, however, does not vary in direct proportion to the size of the population. It is influenced, *inter alia*, by the structure of the population in terms of age groups, and by social and economic conditions determining the proportions of men and women at different ages who engage in economic activities. In the design of a programme for economic and social development it is evidently desirable to take account of demographic and other factors which influence the size and growth of this productive asset.

Where a large proportion of the population consists of children, the economically active population tends to be small in proportion to the total population. Such is the situation of most under-developed countries at the present time. The high proportion of children is thus to be regarded as a symptom of an economically inefficient process of reproduction. A disproportionately large share of income is spent on rearing large numbers of children, many of whom do not survive to take their places in the labour force. The vital problem of education is also rendered much more difficult by this age structure. Only large reductions in the birth rates of the under-developed countries, such as have occurred in Europe, North America, and parts of Oceania, would greatly increase the ratio of adults.

The advantage that can be derived from an increasing labour supply depends on the productivity with which it can be employed. Among the determinants of productivity is the quantity of physical resources with which the labour force works, including land and other natural resources as well as man-made capital equipment. Where the population is large in proportion to the available physical resources, it may be difficult to employ an increasing labour supply without allowing output per unit of labour to fall. On the other hand, where physical resources lie idle for lack of the manpower needed to exploit them, a rapidly increasing labour supply may be necessary if a higher standard of living is to be achieved. The rate of increase in the population and the labour supply may itself directly affect the rate at which these resources are built up or destroyed. Thus, a careful consideration of the relationships between population growth and the development and utilization of physical resources is important in the planning of economic and social development.

The review of the literature reveals wide agreement on the thesis that an increase of population in agricultural areas possessing an abundance of good unused land may be favourable to a rising level of living. In many of the under-developed countries, for example, in Africa and Latin America, agricultural productivity and levels of living are low in spite of the presence of large areas of unoccupied land. This situation results largely from ignorance of more efficient methods of cultivation and lack of the capital equipment necessary to utilize the idle resources. In many of these areas major resources in the form of minerals, forests, and water-power also lie idle or are only partially or inefficiently exploited for lack of adequate capital or a sufficiently large and capable labour force. Under these conditions population growth could, if accompanied by adequate capitalization and technological improvements, often play an important, positive role in economic development.

There is a wider range of disagreement in the findings with regard to the relationship of population growth to economic development and social advancement in such countries as India, China, and Egypt, where natural resources are much scarcer in relation to the size of the population. Few writers would disagree that the food problem will be aggravated by a rapid growth of population. On the other hand, it is also generally agreed that suitable measures to increase the area of land under cultivation, improve agricultural methods, provide better equipment, and correct cultural and political conditions which impede economic and social advancement, would permit a higher return to the agricultural labour force. It is recognized that the amount of improvement possible through these measures would differ from country to country. Disagreement is found chiefly in the degree of importance attached to population size and to other factors affecting agricultural productivity in these countries. According to one view, no appreciable progress in raising productivity and living standards is possible if the present population on the land increases substantially. Another view is that considerable population increases even in the most densely populated agricultural areas could be accommodated, with a rising standard of living, if proper care were taken in extending cultivation, improving methods and equipment, etc. But apparently most proponents of the latter argument would agree, in any case, that the problem would be considerably simplified if the rate of growth of the agricultural population were kept to a minimum in the future. In other words, in the types of areas mentioned, either a reduction in the birth rate or industrialization which would permit a rapid flow of workers from agriculture into other branches of economic activity, or both, would be advantageous from an economic point of view.

Industrialization is generally accepted as particularly necessary in heavily populated countries where agriculture cannot absorb additional manpower. Many, but not all, writers believe that rapid population growth and the heavy burden of dependent children constitute obstacles to industrialization, since they make savings difficult and increase the needs for investments that do not raise productivity. In any event, all are agreed on the need for more abundant and rapid capital formation at home or the contribution of capital from outside. Some writers believe that with sufficient capital, industrialization could proceed more rapidly than population growth even in the event of the heavy mortality reductions and the maintenance of the high levels of fertility which now characterize under-developed countries. Others fear that unless fertility rates are greatly reduced within the near future, most of the benefits from industrialization, like those deriving from agricultural improvements, will be cancelled by population growth.

In their efforts to industrialize, the peoples of the under-developed countries face many other obstacles besides the handicaps of an excessively large population and a heavy load of childhood dependency. Many lack adequate supplies of strategic minerals and energy resources and suffer from a lack of industrial skills, of aptitude for technical and commercial occupations, and of general education. Their efficiency is further impaired by poor health and inadequate equipment. Moreover, such countries are newcomers competing with the established economic power of nations which began their industrialization earlier. The existence of these difficulties lends support to the view that the under-developed countries cannot afford to neglect any means of improving their situation, but must press forward energetically with a broad programme of social and economic development linked with practical population policies.

Finally, the social and political institutions suitable in an epoch of stationary population and technique are not adapted to the new problems created by the growth of the population. Although there is almost unanimous agreement on the need for institutional reforms, there is no such agreement on their nature and scope, either within the framework of "planned" or of "free" societies. Many writers have warned of the social evils which may result from the breakdown of ancient institutions and the formation of an urban proletariat, and steps have been proposed for avoiding such dangers. Development must not be concerned solely with material production but also with culture. Education is still markedly insufficient, even in countries which are already undergoing economic and social development.

THE MIGRATION OF NATIVE LABORERS
IN SOUTH AFRICA*

WILBERT E. MOORE

In the development of European colonial administration and economic exploitation of the African continent, the problem of making productive use of native labor has been continuously paramount. Indeed, the labor resources of the continent figured in the world economy long before the completion of political subjugation and regular colonial administration. The slave trade provided one kind of answer to the problem of using native labor, representing in a sense the removal for processing elsewhere of a replaceable natural resource. With the development of tropical agriculture, mining, and permanent white colonization, the problem became one of using tribal natives for local economic production. Although slavery, called by one name or another, has been practiced at one time or another in all parts of the continent, there has gradually been established an indirect, less openly coercive expedient for the integration of culturally and economically backward peoples into modern economic life. This coercion by indirection, which is more in keeping with European canons of law and ethics and conceptions of productive relationships, has been accomplished mainly by the use of the power of taxation as a prerogative of constituted governmental authority. Tribal natives have been brought within a wage and money economy by levying head taxes or hut taxes, payable only in cash, and thus obtainable only by wage employment or by selling agricultural produce. The taxation policy has been supplemented in South and East Africa by the seizure of good agricultural land by Europeans and the confinement of tribal natives to ever narrowing territories or preserves.

Aside from a whole range of questions concerning the difficult adaptations of native institutions to European culture and civilization as represented in piecemeal contacts,[1] the full utilization of native labor resources has been blocked by inconsistencies in the policies of Europeans. Throughout British South Africa (as well as in most of East Africa, namely, where there is a strong white settlement) a racial caste system prevails. This inevitably affects the division of labor, and its particular form in South Africa affects also the actual territorial disposition and mobility of labor. Not only are some jobs regarded as exclusively African occupations and others as exclusively European, but also some territories are regarded as appropriate permanent residences of natives and others as exclusively under the ownership and control, if not the exclusive occupancy, of Europeans.

* Adapted and reprinted by permission from *The Milbank Memorial Fund Quarterly*, Vol. XXIV, October 1946, pp. 401–419.

[1] See, for example, Hunter, Monica: *Reaction to Conquest: Effects of Contact with Europeans on the Pondo of South Africa.* London, Humphrey Milford, Oxford University Press, 1936.

TABLE 1.   Economic activity of native males and females, 1936[1]

Economic Group	Males		Females	
	Number	Per Cent	Number	Per Cent
Agriculture	1,437,087	62.4	1,659,349	86.5
Mining	393,020	17.1	—	—
Manufacturing	210,407	9.1	3,358	0.2
Transport and communication	90,193	3.9	146	—[a]
Commerce and finance	6,447	0.3	242	—[a]
Professions, sport, entertainment	17,605	0.8	4,335	0.2
Personal services	112,901	4.9	243,369	12.7
Other	35,411	1.5	8,520	0.4
Totals	2,303,071	100.0	1,919,319	100.0

[a] Less than one-tenth of one per cent.
[1] Union of South Africa, Sixth Census, 1936, Vol. IX, pp. 71, 74.

This dual separation between Europeans and natives—of strata in the social scale and of areas within the country—has its inconsistencies. The territorial segregation assumes completely separate communities; this is in exact opposition to the demand for cheap and exploitable native labor in the white community. To some extent this inconsistency is resolved by the use of more or less temporary laborers who retain tribal affiliations and are considered as residents of the native reserves. This in turn creates a number of serious difficulties, not only for the white employer but also for the economy and social structure of the native villages. On the other hand, the caste system of occupational distinction would bar full qualitative use of native labor, even if the labor force were less transitory and mobile.

It is only against this background of dual separation that the particular features of migratory native labor in South Africa can be understood.

MIGRATORY LABOR AND NATIVE EMPLOYMENT

In British South Africa there are four main types of demand for native labor in the white community: agriculture, mining, manufacturing, and domestic service. Table 1 indicates the relative importance of these modes of economic activity among natives in the Union of South Africa, but unfortunately does not distinguish within the category of "agriculture" between tribal natives and those employed by European farmers or "squatting" on land legally owned by white cultivators. In any event, European agricultural production does not depend heavily upon migratory farm labor but rather enjoys a more or less permanent native labor force in various degrees of personal dependency upon the white land owner.[2] Similarly, migratory labor is rarely recruited in the native territories specifically for domestic service, which rather depends upon fairly permanent resident natives, whether in urban or rural areas. Manufacturing depends to a considerable extent upon unskilled native labor recruited on a temporary basis, but, because of the typically small size of establishments and their territorial dispersion, is less exclusively dependent on nonresident labor than is mining with its predominant concentration in the Witwatersrand area of Transvaal Province. The gold mines

[2] See Tinley, J. M.: THE NATIVE LABOR PROBLEM OF SOUTH AFRICA. Chapel Hill, University of North Carolina Press, 1942, pages 85–98.

of the Rand provide the most important single source of employment for migratory workers within the Union, with much smaller numbers employed in diamond mines and manufacturing establishments. Copper and tin mines have an analogous significance in the economic structure of the Rhodesias. Thus the most outstanding economic feature of native labor migration is the recruitment of laborers in the native reserves under contract or indenture for work in the fairly limited mining areas.

This clear territorial concentration of economic activity employing large numbers of native workers would seem to facilitate the statistical analysis of labor mobility. And in fact the movement of labor to the mining areas is sufficiently marked to make its main features clear. However, numerous difficulties impede precise statement of the situation.

As previously noted, European employers for the most part do not recruit a *permanent* labor force for work in the mines, nor can they rely upon a resident urban proletariat attracted and held by employment opportunities. However much individual employers might find a dependable, resident labor force advantageous, they are barred from fostering such a development by the principle of territorial segregation and the attempt to maintain natives in tribal conditions. This policy is naturally reinforced by the limited, although increasing, interest of tribal natives in modern economic life and their preference for traditional modes of agricultural life functionally related to the whole institutional framework. Concretely, this means that the native labor force as enumerated, for example, by any given census may be quite different from that which would have been enumerated a few months earlier or later. The infrequent censuses of the Union do not attempt to classify natives according to permanent residence; they

are enumerated *de facto* and not *de jure.* Thus, although natives in 1936 were tabulated according to place of birth, there is no way of determining how many of the migrants at the time of the census were temporarily at employment centers and how many were more or less permanent additions to the labor force (the so-called "detribalized natives"). The direction of the flow can be determined, but not its exact size for a given period or its duration with respect to individual components.

Workers for the principal centers employing native laborers are recruited both from the predominantly native areas within the Union and from neighboring territories. The data concerning native immigration[3] from the three High Commission Territories—Basutoland, Swaziland, and Bechuanaland—from Mozambique, or from British colonies to the north are no more satisfactory than those relating to migration within the Union. Statistics of immigration for the Union exclude natives. The number of natives leaving the High Commission Territories during any year may be approximately determined from passes issued in those territories; how many return in the course of the year is completely unknown. For Basutoland the 1936 and earlier censuses enumerated "absentees," but the difficulty of length of residence remains. Even less evidence exists with respect to other areas of labor recruitment, except that the annual number of workers under indenture from Mozambique is fixed in round numbers by treaty. These scattered bits of evidence, supplemented by statistics on place of birth and by statistics of employment, provide only

[3] "Native" as used in this discussion refers uniformly to Negroid natives of the African continent, primarily Bantu in the areas here under consideration. This explains the use of such otherwise contradictory terms as "native immigrants."

rough measures of the ebb and flow of migratory movements.

In general, therefore, the possible statistical description of native labor migration in British South Africa is considerably less than could be desired. Data on place of birth, for example, do not have the same significance as similar data where migration involves a definite change of legal residence, and where census data present *de jure* as well as *de facto* enumerations. On the other hand, the significance of temporary migration with more or less frequent turnover of labor supply should not be misinterpreted. As long as the total labor force remains reasonably constant, or is at most subject only to long-term variations, the enumerated native population may for some purposes be regarded as permanently resident in the places where enumerated. This would be true even if no laborer gained legal residence at his place of work and remained only for one year under indenture and never returned. If each departing worker is replaced by another during the same year, or any shorter or longer period under consideration, the total for the period obviously remains constant.

The foregoing should not obscure other demographic, as well as economic and social, consequences of such labor mobility. The "permanent" labor force by statistical artifact would still not be self-reproducing by natural increase. Moreover, extended periods of absence on the part of the laborers from their truly permanent places of residence may affect the demographic balance in those areas. Unfortunately the available data do not allow adequate appraisal of these effects. They permit, indeed, only the determination of the direction of labor mobility, its approximate extent in terms of statistics on place of birth and employment in labor centers, and the more obvious changes in population composition resulting from the movement.

INTERNAL MIGRATION

The census enumeration of natives by place of birth allows the tracing of migratory movements only among the four provinces of the Union and not by smaller administrative districts. Indirect evidence, however, in the form of age and sex distributions allows a more definite identification of the two principal sources within the Union of native laborers recruited for work in the Transvaal, namely, the Transkeian district of Cape Province and the Zululand district of Natal. The data on place of birth in the 1936 census allow calculation of the net balance of movement among the provinces as represented by the enumerated native population in 1936. Aside from a quite minor movement from Natal to Orange Free State, these data show the Cape Province to be something of a "universal donor," and the Transvaal to be a "universal receiver." As might be expected from knowledge of the South African economy, the most significant movement is that from all of the other provinces to the Transvaal. The predominant importance of that movement is made even clearer if the calculation is limited to native males enumerated in urban areas. On this basis other inter-provincial movements are substantially reduced or even reversed, whereas the volume of native male migration from all provinces to the urban areas of the Transvaal represents virtually half of the total migration to the province.

Three points will bear reiteration for their relevance to the interpretation of these balances in migratory movements: (1) There is no satisfactory way of separating permanent migration of detribalized natives to places of employment in predominantly white areas from the temporary migration of tribal natives to labor

Natives, Union of South Africa, 1936

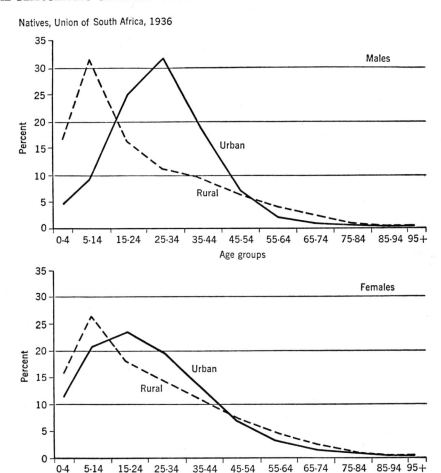

FIGURE 1. Age distribution of native males and females in rural and urban areas of the Union of South Africa, 1936. From Union of South Africa: Sixth Census, 1936, Vol. IX, page xi.

centers. (2) The reliability of the size of these balances is relative to the numerical stability of native employment.[4] (3) The

[4] Independent evidence on native employment in the chief labor centers indicates some seasonal variation, with a low point around the end of December and a high point in June or July. These variations are by no means uniform from one year to the next, however, and are partly affected by longer-term trends in employment. In general, May, the month of the 1936 census, seems fairly representative, at least for

particular composition of the enumerated native population is unstable in the degree that there is a continual ebb and flow of migrants.

The effects of these migratory movements, however temporary the stay of particular migrants, is reflected in the age and sex composition of the native populations

that year. *See:* Union of South Africa, *Monthly Bulletin of Union Statistics,* issues for 1936 and other years.

in the areas of supply and in the areas of labor demand. The percentage age distribution of rural and urban native males (Figure 1) indicates that one aspect of the migratory movement is a concentration of native males of working ages in urban areas. The selective aspect of the migration with respect to sex is emphasized by comparison of rural and urban age distributions of native females (Figure 1) which shows no such marked contrast as found with native males. Another aspect of the movement is a shift out of agriculture into other economic activities, particularly mining. The results of this movement may be seen in the contrasting age distributions of native males in agriculture and in mining (Figure 2).

As previously indicated, the data on place of birth of the native population of the Union of South Africa as enumerated in 1936 allow only the determination of net balances of movement among the four provinces. However, a closer identification of the areas of origin and of destination may be gained from the age-sex composition of the native population by smaller areas. Figures 3 and 4 show the per cent of total native population represented by each quinquennial age-sex group in Zululand in Natal and the Witwatersrand urban concentration in Transvaal. The Zululand area of the Union of South Africa has an almost entirely native population, and constitutes one of the principal areas of origin within the Union of the heavy concentration of males of working ages evident in the Witwatersrand gold mining area. It should be observed that this is a rough and indirect measure of the size and direction of migratory flow, as the native laborers found in the Witwatersrand are also drawn in lesser numbers from other parts of the Union and in substantial numbers from outside the country, as will be noted below.

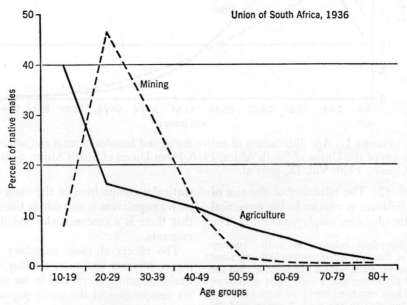

FIGURE 2. Age distribution of native males engaged in agriculture and mining, Union of South Africa, 1936. From Union of South Africa: Sixth Census, 1936, Vol. IX, page xvi.

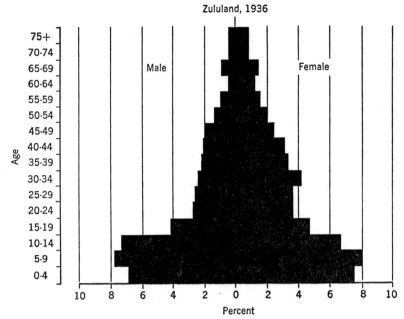

FIGURE 3. Age and sex distribution of natives in Zululand, Natal Province, Union of South Africa, 1936. From Union of South Africa: Sixth Census, 1936, *Ages and Marital Conditions of the Bantu Population*, Table 3, pages 6–27.

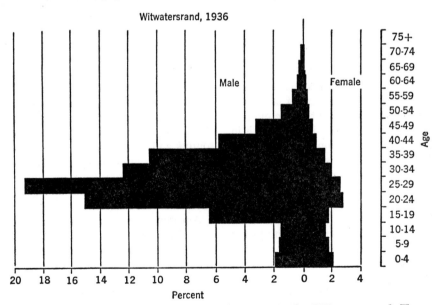

FIGURE 4. Age and sex distribution of natives in the Witwatersrand, Transvaal Province, Union of South Africa, 1936. From Union of South Africa: Sixth Census, 1936, Vol. IX, Table 5, page 27.

MIGRATION FROM OUTSIDE THE UNION

The pull of the labor markets of the Union of South Africa extends beyond the political boundaries of the state. It is essential to an understanding of substantial flow of native migratory workers from surrounding areas to bear in mind certain peculiar features of South African economy. The social structure includes a somewhat unstable combination of three elements of particular importance in this connection. Those elements are (1) white supremacy, enforced in law and custom and applied in a caste division of labor; (2) territorial segregation of natives; and (3) economic activity, especially mining, that rests in large measure on cheap gang labor by natives. *This is an economic regime based upon cheap labor used with deliberate waste:* there is the waste arising from the failure to develop and use potential skills of native workers, owing to the institution of white supremacy, and the waste of rapid turnover and expenses of continual recruiting, owing to the refusal to develop a stable resident labor supply in the employment centers.

It is understandable that this combination of structural elements may produce recurring or chronic shortages of labor supply, somewhat independent of the number of native nationals of working ages. This in fact has been the situation in the Union of South Africa and it has given rise to the recruiting of native workers in other parts of British South and East Africa, and in the Portuguese colony of Mozambique.

At the time of the 1936 census there were in the Union about one-third of a million natives born outside the country. This represented 5 per cent of the total native population.

Although no official statistics record the annual number of native immigrants into the Union of South Africa, data are available on native employees, by territory of origin, in the principal labor centers. These labor centers comprise, besides the Witwatersrand gold mines, a number of scattered mining and manufacturing areas, and probably account for nearly all natives employed in the two major types of economic activity that depend upon migratory workers.

From the employment statistics it is possible to arrive at a fairly adequate picture of the annual average number of immigrant laborers during the period 1925–1939. These averages are shown in Figure 5.

These data leave quite unanswered the question of the total number of immigrant laborers entering the Union during any year, as they represent only average numbers of employees. In other words, they reveal nothing concerning the amount of turnover required to keep the given average numbers of workers in employment.

A comparison of the number of passes issued to natives in Bechuanaland, Basutoland, and Swaziland to proceed to the Union for employment, with the average number from those areas actually employed in established labor centers suggests annual turnover ratios substantially less than 100 per cent for Basutoland and Bechuanaland natives, and considerably over 100 per cent for Swaziland. Because these data come from completely different sources and because there is no assurance that natives uniformly equip themselves with passes to cross generally unguarded borders, these ratios cannot be regarded as any more than suggestive.

A reasonably safe and comfortably round guess from this evidence, then, is that the average number of workers employed in the labor centers is an approximate representation of the number of migratory workers entering and leaving the Union each year. How many of these migrants in any year are newly weaned from tribal conditions and how many are former wage earn-

Native Employment in Native Centers

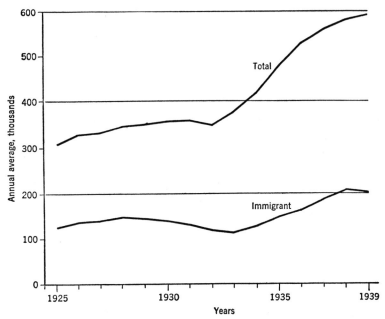

FIGURE 5. Total and immigrant native laborers in established labor centers, Union of South Africa, annual averages, 1925–1939. From monthly averages as given in Union of South Africa, Monthly Bulletin of Union Statistics, Nos. 27–180 (1925–1936) and Vols. XVI–XIX (1937–1940).

ers returning, there is no evidence at all to determine. Because of the unskilled nature of the work performed this is a question of small importance to the individual employer, and of no apparent concern to any other white South African.

CONCLUSION

The labor system of South Africa presents a nice case of what might be called the relation of migration to social opportunity. If it is the economic development of mining and manufacturing that provides the pull attracting workers from tribal reserves within the Union and immigrants from beyond the national boundaries, it is the network of barriers to social mobility that accounts for an almost equal push back to tribal areas and a constant ebb and flow of unskilled native workers.

If this system provides a sort of statistical equilibrium it does not follow that it produces anything like a stable social equilibrium. Native labor migration serves as a bridge between rigid and otherwise incompatible types of social restraint—the caste system and territorial segregation. It makes possible the limited use of native labor while keeping it out of the way. Yet it is probably impossible to bring backward peoples within a money economy without giving them material aspirations that go with that economy. As those aspirations replace the indirect coercion of taxation and territorial restriction, the natives may be expected to protest against their limited opportunities. The restraints thus appear to be subject to pressure that may lead to their collapse.

INSTITUTIONAL PATTERNS FAVORING HIGH
FERTILITY IN UNDERDEVELOPED AREAS*

KINGSLEY DAVIS

PRACTICALLY all of the world's underde-veloped areas, embracing something like three-fourths of the world's population, still have high birth rates, that is, more than 30 births per 1000 inhabitants an-nually and more than 4 births per woman during her reproductive life. In fact, the rates in many underdeveloped areas today are about as high as they have ever been.

In explaining why the rates are so high, we have to ask two questions: First, why were birth rates high in the past? Second, why are they that way now?

The answer to the first question is found, interestingly enough, in the death rate. Until twenty to eighty years ago, de-pending on the area in question, death rates were extremely high by modern standards. The underdeveloped societies therefore had to have a high fertility to match their high mortality, else they would not survive. Probably many societies in the past failed to survive, their members being killed off faster than they could reproduce. The societies we know about today are necessarily the ones that did survive. They did so because they evolved an institu-tional structure having an incentive sys-tem strong enough to induce their people to reproduce abundantly.

In recent times, however, the necessity imposed by a high mortality has tended to disappear. The death rate in most under-developed areas has been declining for a considerable period, and in many it has dropped rapidly in recent years, often faster than it ever did in the now indus-trialized countries. As a result, many of these areas have today a death rate almost as low as that of industrial nations. In Cey-lon, for example, the crude death rate fell by 43 per cent in four years (it was 22.0 per 1000 in 1945, and 12.6 in 1949—and had reached 11.6 in 1951). In Puerto Rico it declined by 46 per cent during the ten years from 1940 to 1950, the rate now resembling that in continental United States; and during the same decade in For-mosa it declined by 42 per cent. Compara-ble reductions have been experienced in parts of the British Caribbean and in parts of Latin America and Africa.

The phenomenally rapid drops in mor-tality in recent years have generally come on the heels of longer but less spectacular declines in the past. Consequently, our sec-ond question is peculiarly relevant—why, in the absence of the necessity that once existed, has the institutional structure of economically retarded areas continued to support a high rate of reproduction?

In beginning an answer to this second question, one must recall that the under-developed regions are still in the peasant-agricultural stage of development.[1] This is

* Reprinted by permission from *Eugenics Quarterly*, Vol. 2, No. 1, March, 1955, pp. 33–39.

[1] To be clear as to what is meant by "under-developed," we draw the line in terms of the oc-cupational structure. A country with more than 50 per cent of its gainfully employed males oc-

the stage of economic progress that most of them have been in for many centuries, the stage to which their institutional structure is accordingly well adapted. The rise of industrial nations elsewhere in the world has had an impact on the less advanced areas; it has brought commerce and political change, and it has brought, as we have seen, a marked decline in mortality. But it has not fundamentally altered the agrarian character of the society and to this extent has not forced a change in the institutional structure. Supported by time-honored agrarian conditions, the social organization has retained many of its elaborate mechanisms for inducing a high rate of reproduction. It has done so even though a high birth rate, once functional, has now become strictly disfunctional.

To push the inquiry further, we must try to understand the particular institutional patterns which, in agrarian societies, give rise to this high but disfunctional fertility. Important and clear-cut as the problem is, it has been the subject of surprisingly little research, with the result that misleading theories still persist. Furthermore, since the backward areas embrace cultures of great diversity, students of social structure have been overly impressed and distracted by cultural differences among these areas, overlooking the basic uniformities underlying the surface variations. In other words, if nearly all underdeveloped areas have in common a high fertility, the mech-

anisms by which they reach this result doubtless also have some things in common. It thus seems wise to look for the deeper uniformities.

In analyzing the institutional factors responsible for fertility, one finds the main key in the family, for human society accomplishes the function of bearing, nourishing, and socializing children primarily through the universal instrumentality of the nuclear family.[2] It is through the relations of the nuclear family to the rest of society, then, that we can expect to find the social factors controlling the level of fertility.

EFFECT OF THE COMPOSITE FAMILY AND JOINT HOUSE-HOLD

In primitive and agrarian societies, as is well known, the nuclear family is less independent of the wider kinship structure than it is in industrial societies. Its formation through marriage, its economic position, and the conduct of its members are all governed by elder relatives to a greater degree. In sociological terms, the nuclear family of procreation tends in agrarian societies to be controlled by other kinship groups, notably by the two families of orientation.

One common arrangement in terms of which such control is facilitated is the joint household, which arises when the newly married couple are required to live with the parents of one or the other partner. Such an arrangement is quite prevalent in underdeveloped areas,[3] but even where it is

---

cupied in agriculture, fishing, and forestry, we designate as underdeveloped. On this basis, three-fourths of the world's people and three-fourths of its area are in countries in this category. See the writer's paper, "Population and the Further Spread of Industrial Society," *Proceedings of the American Philosophical Society*, Vol. 95 (Feb. 13, 1951), pp. 8–19. For the most part the underdeveloped societies are not primitive. Only a small portion of the world's inhabitants live in societies without any literacy and without other accoutrements of modern civilization.

[2] The term "nuclear family" is used by Geo. P. Murdock, *Social Structure* (New York: Macmillan, 1949), Ch. 1, to describe the unit consisting of mother, father, and children. This unit has also been variously characterized as the "primary" or "immediate" family, as in the works of Lloyd Warner.

[3] For the 159 societies for which he secured adequate information on residence and inheritance rules, Murdock found 149 to require resi-

absent the nuclear family tends to dwell close to and be under the surveillance of the in-laws. Furthermore, it is not simply a matter of dwelling arrangements and social control but also a matter of economic solidarity. The joint household and the composite family often function as an economic unit.

Given this subordination and incorporation of the nuclear family by wider kinship groups, several consequences tend to follow which are conducive to abundant reproduction.

1. *The economic cost of rearing children does not impinge directly on the parents* to the same extent that it does where the nuclear family is a more independent unit. With a common household and a joint economy, with three or more generations present, one's own child draws out of the general exchequer, not out of his parents' income alone.

2. *The inconvenience and effort of child care do not fall so heavily on the parents alone.* With grandparents, aunts, uncles, and older cousins in the household, the care of the young children may be so distributed among the entire menage that no particular strain is put upon the parents. In fact, as has often been pointed out, the joint household is an excellent arrangement whereby young mothers, in the prime of life and thus capable of maximum productivity, are freed during working hours for work in the fields or in handicraft, while older women and older children, less productive economically, look after the infants and younger children. Thus the mother's maternal function does not have to compete with her economic function as in an industrial society.

3. *The age at marriage can be quite young,* because, under joint household conditions, there is no necessary implication that the husband must be "able to support a wife and family" before he gets married. In this respect there seems to have been a difference between West European society, even prior to industrialism, and that of most other parts of the pre-industrial world. The historian, Russell, has pointed out that in the Middle Ages there was a tradition linking the nuclear family with a piece of land adequate to maintain the family.

"In each village there were usually certain number of holdings of similar character which required the efforts of a mature male, physically and mentally; about thirty acres of land together with a quota of animals upon the manor. . . . Obviously only the full holdings could be expected to care for a family satisfactorily in the eyes of the lay population. Thus naturally marriage would be restricted to those who had holdings. . . . The principle of no holding, no marriage, operated as a fairly effective check upon population increase. The conditions of mortality tended to make the average age of marriage for the young men vary between twenty-two and twenty-five years. It also meant that the weak in mind or body were not permitted to marry. . . ."[4]

Thus West European society tended to set the nuclear family apart a long time ago—a fact which is borne out by Western legal history, kinship terminology, and courtship custom. As Western peoples became more commercial and more urban, the rule that land is necessary to form a marriage became extended to mean that a job is necessary. In this way, as commercial and industrial positions came to require ap-

---

dence with extended relatives. *Op. cit.*, p. 38. The majority of these societies, 98 in all, required patrilocal residence. It is hard, however, to reconcile his table on p. 38 with that on p. 32, where the proportion of "independent" families is higher.

[4] Josiah C. Russell, "Demographic Values in the Middle Ages," in Geo. F. Mair (ed.), *Studies In Population* (Princeton: Princeton Univ. Press, 1949), p. 104.

prenticeship and training, and as land became scarce, the way was paved for the postponement of marriage to fairly advanced ages.[5] The more one looks into the matter, the more it appears that the structure of the family in Western industrial societies is not wholly a product of urban-industrialism but is in part a product of cultural peculiarities extending back at least into Medieval times. In fact, it can be argued that the West European family structure was one factor in the origin of the industrial revolution in Northwestern Europe.

Family organization in non-European agrarian societies, however, is different from that of pre-industrial Europe. Especially in Asia, it often embodies the principles of joint residence and joint economic responsibility. Furthermore, the parents in many of these societies are morally obligated to find mates for their children and to marry them at an early age. In the patrilocal joint household the bride simply joins her husband's family and the groom continues to live there. The bride can contribute to the joint economy even though young, and the groom is not required to be financially independent. In India, in 1891, nearly a fifth of the girls below 15 years of age, and 89 per cent of those aged 15–19, had been married. The marriage age in India is rising, but as late as 1951 nearly 10 per cent of Indian girls under 15 and three-fourths of those 15–19 had been married.[6] In such countries as In-

dia, Korea, Formosa, and Turkey, practically no women 20–24 are single. It is obvious that, other things equal, the younger the age at marriage, the higher the ultimate fertility, especially since a woman's reproductive capacity is apparently greatest in her late teens and early twenties.

4. With an emphasis on kin solidarity *the compulsion to marry is often quite strong*. Especially with patrilocal residence arrangements, the daughter may be viewed as a potential liability to her family of orientation, to be satisfactorily married at all costs. From the standpoint of the groom's family, a marriage represents not only an alliance with another strong family line but also an essential means of expanding one's own agnatic line. The necessity of getting one's children married may indeed be viewed as a religious and moral obligation. As a consequence, fewer persons go through life without marrying than in the case of the industrial nations. In fact, in India in 1891, a higher proportion of women aged 20–24 had been married (97.3 per cent) than were ever married by any age in Western countries. In Denmark in 1787, for example, only 91 per cent of the women aged 45–49 had ever been married; and in France in 1881 only 87 per cent of the women of this age had ever been wed.

5. *The young wife is motivated to have offspring as early as possible and in considerable number*. Given the joint family and the prevailing rule of patrilocal residence, the bride is a stranger among her husband's relatives. Because of her newness and because of her youth, she is often assigned a low position in the restricted hierarchy of women. She has little she can

---

[5] Such postponement, especially noticeable in the latter half of the nineteenth and early twentieth century, was carried to an extreme in Ireland and the Scandinavian countries. See David V. Glass (ed.), *Introduction to Malthus* (London: Watts, 1953), pp. 25–54; Conrad M. Arensberg and Solon T. Kimball, *Family and Community in Ireland* (Cambridge: Harvard University Press, 1940); John Hajnal, "The Marriage Boom," *Population Index*, Vol. 19 (April 1953), pp. 80–101.

[6] See K. Davis, "Fertility Control and the Demographic Transition in India" in Milbank

Memorial Fund, *The Interrelations of Demographic, Economic, and Social Problems in Selected Underdeveloped Areas* (New York: Milbank Fund, 1954), pp. 85–86.

call her own until a child is born. The birth of a son proves her contribution to her husband's line and thus begins her rise to a higher position within the domestic circle. Offspring also give her something to lavish her affection on, something on the basis of which she can stand up for herself. In cultures where the father's bond with the child is a strong one, the birth of offspring gives the wife extra standing in his eyes; and in cultures where divorce is easily possible for the male, as in most Muslim countries, the wife views offspring as a means of holding her husband. Under such circumstances it is not strange that a young married woman has little incentive to avoid childbirth.

6. *The man is strongly motivated to demand offspring.* The structure of the joint family ordinarily rewards not only the mother's but also the father's reproduction. Often the children are viewed as belonging to him and his family, and the sons as perpetuating his family line. More tangibly, numerous children help to strengthen the patrilineally organized composite family by the sheer weight of numbers. Insofar as this family remains a viable economic and social unit, it gains economic and political strength by having an abundance of youthful members. Young adults can thus provide security for their old age even when few other means are available, and they are encouraged to do so by their elders.

The male's motivation is seen further in what may be called "sociological cures" for sterility. A barren wife not only suffers stigma, but she may be divorced to make room for a new and presumably more fertile wife. A woman who bears only daughters may suffer the same fate. In addition, in some agrarian cultures at least, the wife's barrenness may be a just cause for the acquisition of a concubine or a second wife or for the adoption of children of her husband's relatives.

THE SEGREGATION OF MALE AND FEMALE ROLES

So far we have traced some of the effects of subordinating the nuclear family to wider kinship groups. An additional influence on fertility is the tendency of stable agrarian societies to segregate sharply the roles of men and women. This tendency is often connected with the dependent status of the nuclear family in the joint household, because when several related men and several women dwell together, strong avoidance rules are required to reduce the possibility of prohibited sexual contact and sexual rivalry. But the segregation of male and female roles is found in agrarian societies with or without joint household arrangements, and thus may be viewed as a somewhat independent factor in high fertility.

The institutional restriction of the feminine sphere may reach an extreme degree —as in the practice of purdah in Muslim and to some extent in Hindu culture, and in the seclusion of females in agrarian Latin cultures. The effect of such limitation is to confine women largely to the household and to identify them with reproduction, so that their lives revolve around home and children. Female education is regarded as unnecessary if not actually immoral. Women, therefore, have little knowledge, sophistication, or independence. They cannot conceive of a glamor role or a career role which would compete with the childbearing role. They cannot complain that children prevent their getting outside the home, because outside activities are excluded anyway.

With the segregation of roles, the gulf between the man's and the woman's world becomes so wide that communication between husband and wife is reduced to a minimum—particularly with reference to sexual topics, for the woman is supposed to have no knowledge or initiative in such matters. Curiously, husband and wife in many cases may never discuss the one thing that presumably represents their special bond, sex and reproduction. Toward this aspect of life the woman has mainly a non-rational approach—religious, superstitious, and incurious. The husband views reproduction as his prerogative, something taken for granted and involving simple compliance on the wife's part.[7]

A further consequence of feminine seclusion is that, when economic development first begins, women do not proportionately enter the industrial and commercial labor market. As a result the cities in many underdeveloped areas (notably in Asia) are heavily masculine.[8] The occupations that Westerners now regard as chiefly feminine—nursing, teaching, stenography, domestic service, retail selling—are generally staffed by men. Entry into such occupations would take women out of the home and give them a sense of conflict between pregnancy and economic gain. Also it would take them to towns and cities, where rearing children is more difficult. The exclusion of women from the labor market therefore continues for them the conditions favorable to high fertility even after considerable economic development has occurred.

AGRARIAN SOCIETY AND THE FAMILY

The features of family organization barely sketched above are well adapted to a peasant mode of existence. In traditional

[7] J. M. Stycos and Reuben Hill have particularly emphasized the lack of communication between husband and wife as a factor in high fertility. "Prospects of Birth Control in Puerto Rico," *Annals of the American Academy of Political and Social Science*, Vol. 285 (Jan. 1953), pp. 140–142. Also, "Cultural Checks on Birth Control Use in Puerto Rico" in Milbank, *op. cit.*, p. 61.

[8] See Eunice Cooper, "Urbanization in Malaya," *Population Studies*, Vol. 5 (Nov. 1951), pp. 125–126; K. Davis, *Population of India and Pakistan* (Princeton: Princeton University Press,

agriculture the main instrument of production, apart from land, is human labor. To learn any skill involved does not require formal education but merely observation and practice. Children can thus start producing at an early age. Women can work in the fields and in the household handicrafts without much hindrance from constant childbearing. Furthermore, the type of agriculture in which most of the product is consumed at home rather than sold, in which hand labor substitutes for capital, and in which the level of living is consequently extremely low—this is the type in which the means of transportation and communication are scant, and in which consequently the rural village is extremely isolated. The state, in such circumstances, tends to be a distant mechanism scarcely less rapacious and unpredictable than the marauding thieves from which it supposedly protects the village. The village must therefore protect itself as best it can. Its means of social control must be strong, and thus family controls and the authority of the elders can be easily enforced. Without much geographical or social mobility, kinship can serve as a principal basis of social position. The division of labor can be simple, resting heavily on the ascription of status on the basis of kinship, caste, age, and sex. With mortality high from disease, occasional famine, disaster, and war, the constant struggle is to maintain the population. Children strengthen and continue both the family and the village, and the institutional mechanisms favoring their appearance are strongly rooted.

The whole economic and family context represents an intricate and tightly integrated complex which can survive an amazing number of vicissitudes and last for an amazing length of time. Favorable conditions are responded to by an irrepressible

1951), pp. 139–141. The cities of 500,000 or more in India in 1931 had 173 males for every 100 females.

expansion of numbers; unfavorable conditions are met by a remarkable power of survival and recuperation. As a consequence the stable agrarian mode of life has achieved a wide distribution over the world and still includes over half of humanity. It has in recent times encountered a force strong enough to liquidate it—the impact of urban-industrial civilization. But the corrosive power of this impact is not always manifest. Sometimes it affects the stable agrarian society, not as an unfavorable condition, but as a favorable one. If the underdeveloped area continues to remain agricultural, its participation in the world economy being that of a supplier of raw materials; if security is guaranteed by a colonial government or by world peace; and if mortality is reduced by the impact of modern medical science and public health—if these things happen, as they often have, the effect is to maintain those parts of the social structure most favorable to a high birth rate. The agrarian society therefore expands; it may even send millions of people overseas while its home population is growing rapidly. Eventually, however, the expansion runs into problems of congestion. Conditions either must become worse and the expansion cease, or industrialism must destroy the agrarian institutional complex and thus substitute a new economic and social order which no longer responds to economic growth by an automatic, reflex increase of population.

RELIGIOUS AND ETHICAL VALUES

Little has been said thus far about the role of religious values in maintaining a high birth rate. The omission is deliberate, for it seems more reliable to reason in terms of social organization than in terms of avowed values. Above all, care must be exercised in accepting sacred literature or priestly doctrine as evidence of a society's actual values. Motivation is always moti-

vation within a situation. Without an awareness of the circumstances in which people are placed, we can say little or nothing about their values. The latter at best tend to be vague and protean, furnishing the observer with a skimpy basis for predicting behavior.

However, it is worth noting that the religious paraphernalia of agrarian societies is generally in consonance with the institutions producing a high fertility. The desire for sons in patrilineal societies—whether the religion be Muslim, Hindu, or Buddhist—is reinforced by supernatural beliefs and ritualistic practices. The authority of the elders is strengthened by the tendency to regard them as somewhat sacred, as being near the other world. The segregated role of the woman is ritualistically defined, so that its violation becomes a religious as well as a moral offense; and the wife's subordination to the husband may be expressed by worship of him and his lineal ancestors. All told, despite the diversity found in different cultures, the value system seemingly serves to bolster the institutional arrangements already described.

BALANCING FACTORS

Our intention has not been to imply that every feature of agrarian social structure favors fertility. On the contrary, any social order has functions other than reproduction which its members must perform, and some of these are both partly antithetical to reproduction and equally as important for societal survival. It follows that no society is so organized as to get from its women anything near the maximum childbearing of which they are biologically capable. Some of the mechanisms that dampen fertility are the prejudice against widow remarriage (Hindu), the taboo on intercourse after childbirth (many cultures), easy divorce (Muslim), monogamy, an insistence on legitimacy, restraints on medical knowledge and practice with reference to pregnancy and parturition, and the prejudice against procreation after grandchildren have already appeared.

However, our purpose here has been merely to consider some of the widespread institutional patterns favoring reproduction, particularly in the massive agrarian societies that are archaic rather than strictly primitive. These societies respond to urban-industrial penetration usually by maintaining much of their social and familial organization. Truly primitive peoples, on the other hand, experience more of a shock on direct contact with advanced peoples. In this case both a rise in mortality and a decline in fertility often occur, making survival extremely difficult. Primitive societies which survive such a shock sometimes have their institutional organization so altered that, when mortality is reduced, the disfunctionally high fertility may not persist long. It seems likely, for example, that the societies formed from slave populations in the West Indies will achieve a modern demographic balance sooner than those formed by Asian peasants (e.g. in Formosa). At first it might be thought that family disorganization, as observed currently in the British West Indies, would be conducive to high fertility in virtue of the lack of institutional restraint on sexual relations. But no society can avoid placing responsibility on somebody to take care of the child—if not the father, then either the woman who bears the child or whose daughter does so. The institutional system, being disorganized, puts no particular restraint upon the woman's protecting herself by reducing childbearing.

All told, the big agrarian societies appear to be the ones where the institutional supports to functionless reproduction are likely to be strongest, to persist longest, and to cause the greatest demographic imbalances. It is of great sociological interest to study the process of change by which this functionless fertility is gradually eliminated through alterations in the reproductive institutions.

Dr. Hope Tisdale Eldridge is currently engaged in demographic research under the auspices of the International Union for the Scientific Study of Population. She is the author of *Population Policies: A Survey of Recent Developments,* 1954, and of articles in various sociological and statistical journals since 1942. She was formerly a population analyst with the U.S. Bureau of the Census, a population statistician with the United Nations Food and Agriculture Organization, and Editor of the *Demographic Yearbook* of the United Nations.

Dr. Kingsley Davis is a Professor of Sociology at the University of California at Berkeley. He was formerly a Professor of Sociology on the Graduate Faculty of Columbia University and Director of the University's Bureau of Applied Social Research. His main interests lie in the social and economic aspects of population trends. He is the author of *Human Society,* 1949, and *The Population of India and Pakistan,* 1951, in addition to numerous articles appearing in professional journals in the field of sociology and population.

Dr. Wilbert E. Moore is a Professor of Sociology in the Department of Economics and Sociology at Princeton University. He is author of *Industrialization and Labor,* 1951 and *Economic Demography of Eastern and South-eastern Europe,* 1945, as well as numerous articles in professional journals.

IV

COMMUNICATION, MASS MEDIA, AND EDUCATION IN UNDERDEVELOPED AREAS

SEVERAL crucial factors in the general pattern of deficiencies in underdeveloped areas are the absence of adequate transportation and communication systems, the quality and quantity of the mass media of communication, and of course, the poorly attended and inadequately financed educational institutions.

Numerous articles have appeared on these subjects, but however fascinating they may have been, they dealt with specific cases of educational or transportation or communication systems rather than with the presentation of the relation of various indices of these variables to the classification of a country as either developed or underdeveloped. While studies of a case nature are of value in sensitizing persons to the problem, the overall view is also of considerable value. The available statistical material enables us to make generalized statements about the relation of numerous variables to the criterion, developed and underdeveloped or undeveloped. This approach is different than some others because it attempts to show the likelihood that certain conditions will be found in underdeveloped areas, and that these conditions are found with such regularity that they may be predicted as present in a certain proportion of the cases that one will encounter. This observed regularity or uniformity in the characteristics of underdeveloped areas then becomes the basis for a general program of development, but a flexible program that may be manipulated in order to deal most effectively with varied economies and cultures.

We shall immediately turn to an examination of the relation of general development to some of these variables for which we have obtained data from the United Nations' *Demographic and Statistical Yearbooks*, as well as the *Communications Yearbook*.

NEWSPAPER CIRCULATION

The circulation of daily newspapers appears to be closely related to the status of an area as developed or underdeveloped. The circulation of daily newspapers varies from none to over 600 newspapers per 1000 population. By cutting the continuum of newspaper circulation for political entities at that point which most efficiently separates the developed from underdeveloped areas, the distribution shown in Table 13 is obtained. The phi coefficient of correlation is 1.007,

TABLE 13. Distribution of Political Entities According to Newspaper Circulation and Status as Developed or Underdeveloped[1]

Newspaper Circulation per 1000 Population	Developed	Under-developed	Total
−85	7	60	67
85+	30	11	41
Total	37	71	108

indicating a comparatively high degree of relationship between newspaper circulation and development.

One must, as in the case of other similar tables, remember that these findings are very suggestive but not necessarily conclusive as far as the total picture is concerned, since a complete enumeration of our 195 political entities is not possible.

RADIOS

The number of radios per 1000 population, as in the case of newspapers, is highly correlated with development. From the data at hand we see that radios vary from less than 1 radio per 1000 population to almost 700 radios per 1000 population. The United States has the largest *per capita* ownership of radios in the world; in recent years half of the radios sold in the United States have been for autos rather than the home, particularly since television has become available to such a large part of the United States. The distribution of radios per 1000 population has been divided as shown in Table 14, and the phi coefficient of correlation is 1.022.

TABLE 14. Distribution of Political Entities According to Radios per 1000 Population and Status as Developed or Underdeveloped[2]

Radios per 1000 Population	Developed	Under-developed	Total
−45	9	80	89
45+	32	11	43
Total	41	91	132

[1] Data from *Statistical Yearbook, 1952*, New York, United Nations, 1953, Table 174.
[2] Data from *Statistical Yearbook, 1952*, New York, United Nations, 1953, Table 177.

TELEPHONES

The number of telephones per 100 population varies from none to more than 20. The cutting point between developed and underdeveloped areas is 2, and the phi coefficient of correlation between development and telephones per 100 population is .855. The meaning of this particular index as another index of communication facilities depends somewhat upon other variables such as density of population, urbanism, and distance between persons who have need or desire for communication with each other. The data are shown in Table 15.

TABLE 15.   Distribution of Political Entities According to Telephones per 100 Population and Status as Developed or Underdeveloped[3]

Telephones per 100 Population	Developed	Under-developed	Total
−2	13	88	101
2+	30	15	45
Total	43	103	146

CINEMA SEATS

Another media of mass communication, the motion picture, is of perhaps even greater importance in underdeveloped areas than other media of mass communication. Since literacy is not essential to understanding the motion picture, it is particularly popular as a media of mass communication in underdeveloped areas. The range in this case is from no seats to almost 200 seats per 1000 population. The phi coefficient of correlation between development and cinema seats is .666. The data are shown in Table 16.

TABLE 16.   Distribution of Political Entities According to Cinema Seats per 1000 Population and Status as Developed or Underdeveloped[4]

Cinema Seats per 1000 Population	Developed	Under-developed	Total
−21	7	50	57
21+	29	27	56
Total	36	77	113

SCHOOL ATTENDANCE

The data on school attendance are not so adequate as desired, and the lack of comparability of school systems from one country to another leaves us with

[3] Data from *ibid.*, Table 145; and *Telephone Statistics of the World*, New York, American Telephone and Telegraph Co., 1950.

[4] Data from *World Communications Yearbook*, New York, United Nations, 1950.

little to present except the percent of the total population of each political entity that is classed as student. This, of course, says nothing about the varied quality and quantity of student life from one country to another. Nevertheless it is interesting to note that the percent classified as student ranges from less than 1 percent to more than 30 percent. The phi coefficient of correlation between percent of population student and development is .678 and the data are shown in Table 17.

TABLE 17.   Distribution of Political Entities According to Percent of Population Classified as Student and Status as Developed or Underdeveloped[5]

Percent of Population Student	Developed	Under-developed	Total
−10	2	70	72
10+	38	57	95
Total	40	127	167

The variation in quantity and quality of student life is readily seen by comparing student life as we know it in the United States with student life in Barpali, India, described in detail in an article to follow.

LITERACY

Definitions of literacy are quite varied but it may be that the demands of societies are so different that variations in definition are quite justifiable even when attempts at international comparison are being made. The percent of the population that is literate varies from 10 percent to more than 90 percent. The phi coefficient of correlation for the data shown in Table 18 is .824.

TABLE 18.   Distribution of Political Entities According to Literacy and Status as Developed or Underdeveloped[6]

Percent of Population Literate	Developed	Under-developed	Total
−50	0	28	28
50+	31	25	56
Total	31	53	84

As has been suggested, Nityananda Patnaik's article, "Education in the Area of Barpali," presents the reader with an intimate view of education in an underdeveloped area. This article describes the inadequate training of teachers in the Barpali area and the daily pattern of their lives. The vicissitudes of the teacher

[5] Data from *Statistical Yearbook*, 1952, New York, United Nations, 1953, Table 171.
[6] Data from *World Communications Yearbook*, New York, United Nations, 1950.

in an underdeveloped area are such that it might appear surprising that there are any persons willing to assume such a position. Not only do relatively few children attend school, but attendance is irregular for all students, particularly for the children of persons in certain occupations. It would seem that continuity in the learning process would be next to impossible in Barpali. The most important "causes" for poor attendance may all be related to the low level of living of people in the area and to the general lack of development.

On quite a different level, Hilda Hertz Golden, in her article "Literacy and Social Change in Underdeveloped Countries," shows that literacy is not only an index of socioeconomic development but that it plays a part in the transformation of underdeveloped political entities into modern urban-industrialized nations. This excellent research suggests that judicious application of education may facilitate development.

In order to sensitize the reader to some of the problems of higher education in an underdeveloped area, a short selection is presented from W. Ivor Jennings' much larger article, "Universities in the Colonies." This article brings the reader close to an underdeveloped area where the symbol of higher education, the degree, has become the sought-after object rather than education in itself. Is it possible that this behavior is not entirely restricted to underdeveloped areas?

EDUCATION IN THE AREA OF BARPALI*

NITYANANDA PATNAIK

INTRODUCTION

IN ORDER to build up the programme of education a need was expressed some time ago by the Project to carry out a survey in the schools. Therefore, a research was undertaken in nine schools situated in the area of the Project in order to collect factual data for determining the present educational condition.

A GENERAL PICTURE

All the schools sit in the morning as well as in the afternoon every day for about 5½

* Adapted and reprinted by permission from *Man in India*, Vol. No. 34. No. 1, January–March 1954, pp. 20–38.

hours in the maximum, except for those attached to the Middle English schools which sit from 10 A.M. to 4 P.M. in the rainy and winter season, and 6 A.M. to 11 A.M. in the summer. It has been found on many occasions that the teachers come late to work in all schools. Where there is more than one teacher, one who lives nearer to the school, comes earlier and opens the school and takes the roll of the pupils. Then he conducts one class whereas the other classes remain unattended until the other teacher comes. In case of teachers who live in the village where there is a school they both come to school in time. As soon as the school closes the teachers as well as the students leave the school for their respective homes. In no school is there provision for boarding the boys. There is no necessity of hostels as the children come from villages which are, so to say, situated at a calling distance from the school.

The schools are situated at the outskirts of the villages and are named after the villages in which they are situated. In almost all cases the school building consists of one room. Where there are two rooms in a school there is only a thin partition wall separating one part from another. In two cases the District Board has constructed the school building and is also responsible for their annual repair. In the rest of the cases the villagers have constructed the schools and maintain them. The salaries of all the teachers in all the schools are paid by the District Board. There is a compound in each school. Pupils have desks and sit on the mats which they bring with them. There are one or two dilapidated blackboards in each school. In some schools a portion of the wall is cemented and blackened to serve as a board. There is no latrine or urinal in the compound of the school. The pupils as well as the teachers ease themselves here and there in or near about the compound. Few schools have a fence all round and the compounds remain barren except during the rainy season when the teachers raise some seasonal vegetables. Except in three cases there is no well in any school compound. At the time of leisure if there is a tank near the school the children go to quench their thirst. The children are accustomed to read at the top of their voice until they learn the subject by heart. The children, by turn, cleanse the floor of the school room, which is constructed from beaten earth, by cow dung once in a week. But the cleaning of the floor once a week is not sufficient, as the latter becomes awfully dirty and dusty within two or three

days. The boys sweep the floor everyday.

The repairing of the school building depends upon the villagers where the school lies. They raise subscriptions from each resident of the village and spend them in repairs. The schools in general are so narrow that the boys sit closely and uncomfortably.

Besides study the children play different games and do gardening and compost making in the school compound. But these activities are not sincerely and regularly done. The teachers do not play with the boys always and everyday. Ordinarily they let the children play of their own accord. Except in the rainy season they do not try to grow plants in the compound in dry seasons because of the non-availability of water in the compound and the absence of a fence around it and also due to lack of zeal and scientific knowledge. In one or two schools where the teachers teach the pupil about compost-making they do it in a mock manner. In all the schools the teacher gives more stress on book learning than on field work. The vegetable plants, which are grown in the compound in the rainy season, are cared for by both the teacher and the pupils. The idea is that all vegetables raised will be sold and the money thus earned will be spent in supplying the pupils with tiffin in the school. But in practice this is not done. All the vegetables are consumed by the teachers without giving any benefit to the pupils. This method of raising a garden does not teach anything to the boys and will never enthuse them about fruit and vegetable gardening. In the schools where there are wells in the compound a garden can easily be raised. But due to want of fence or a protection around the compound the teachers do not attempt to grow plants. A good garden needs regular watering and taking care of the plants and a good fencing lest the animals who wander about will destroy the plants. Fencing costs nothing but requires a sincere attempt at collecting fencing materials and putting them around the compound. All these activities can be done if the teachers want to undertake them. But the teachers who stay away from the schools have other heavy work to do at home and fail to devote most of their time in developing the school and its compound, although there is a desire among some of them to do so.

Except teaching the students in class the teachers have no other relationship with them or with their parents. The teachers do not take any interest in the home condition of the pupils. On some occasions they help their parents in writing letters or petitions. Whenever the pupils do not attend school in large numbers and the teacher apprehends that he might lose his job and be transferred to some other place, he approaches the parents of the boys individually and cajoles them in many ways to send their children to school. Only on such occasions do the teachers and parents of the children happen to meet and talk.

There is a great hue and cry among the primary teachers that they are never looked upon with a sympathetic eye. They are meagrely remunerated and that too does not come to them regularly at the end of every month. There are many teachers whose salaries are in arrears. This sort of irregular payment of salaries and unjust treatment of the teachers is extremely prejudicial to the progress of education in the rural area.

BACKGROUND LIFE HISTORY OF THE TEACHERS

All the teachers of the schools concerned are village-born and are local district people. They are teachers of schools in their own villages which are not far from their birthplace. There are generally two teachers in each school except for a few, such as Teleimal, Kusanpuri etc.

where there is one teacher in each because of the small size of the school. The head teachers have generally seven years of schooling and training whereas the co-teachers have only seven years schooling and no training. In one-teacher schools the teacher is generally untrained. Most of the teachers have land and this is their main source of livelihood. The income from the school supplements their principal source of living. The monthly salary which they get in return for their services is scanty and not enough for a man and his family to manage for a month. The teachers who have land and work in their village schools, carry on their agricultural duties at home even during school hours. A few of them also spend some of the school hours in astrology, calculating and predicting the horoscope of their clients. The teachers who work in schools of other villages try to get away from school as soon as it closes and are regularly late at school. The teachers whose villages are far away from their place of working find difficulty in attending school daily because of the distance. They usually make arrangements for their board and lodging in the village where they work. They cook their own meals. They teach the pupils in the village school as well as serve as private tutors. In the case of two-teacher schools both the teachers do not stay in the same village. One stays in the school village and the other in some nearby village from which some of the pupils also come. The teacher who stays in the non-school village collects all the pupils and guides them to the school every day. There is a general feeling, which all the teachers have expressed in their reports, that they are poor and their salaries are low. They are not regularly paid at the end of every month. Sometimes all payments are suspended for more than a month due to some official technical difficulties. Some of the teachers have expressed that they had taken up schooling with a concept not merely of teaching to read and write but also of imparting education in good manners, discipline in life and decent behaviour, etc. But they lack interest in teaching things to their pupils because of want of time to devote wholeheartedly for the wellbeing of their students.

STATISTICAL INFORMATION

This survey was carried out in nine schools. They are Raksa, Kumhari, Kainsir, Tulandi, Sikirdi, Satlama, Agalpur, Tehimal and Kusanpuri. The total strength of the students according to attendance register is 501. But the total figure of the number of pupils present on the day of visit was 329.

The following chart gives an idea regarding the total number of children between the ages of 5 and 15 of each caste in the above villages. It also shows caste by caste the proportion of those who attend school.

The table below shows that the maximum percentage is 60.0 and the minimum 11.43. The former relates to Sundi, a business caste and the latter to Kumbhar (potter). If a comparison is made among the castes given in the chart it is found that the children belonging to Tiar (fishermen), Brahmin, Bairagi (a religious caste) and Sundi castes are attending school in large numbers.

The following table gives the attendance figure in percentage on caste basis.

(1) The number of children belonging to Bhulia caste (expert weavers of Barpali) who are enrolled in the school varies from 30 to 40 per hundred. But they attend school less than 10 days in a period of 100 days (i.e., only 4.5%).

(2) The number of children of Ganda, Kumbhar, Sahara, Gond, Dhoba, Keut and Khadra, who read in the school varies from 11 to 20 per hundred. But they attend

TABLE 1

| Caste Names | Of School-Going Age | | Attending School | | % |
	Boys (5–15)	Girls (5–15)	Boys	Girls	Boys + Girls Attending
Ganda	139	134	30	6	13.18
Mali	33	33	13	4	30.30
Gour	219	197	52	2	25.62
Kulta	72	76	27	6	22.29
Pandra	57	47	24	2	25.55
Kumbhar	20	15	2	2	11.43
Sundi	—	5	—	3	60.0
Sahara	59	44	7	—	14.09
Gond	54	26	11	1	15.0
Binjhal	29	34	3	1	27.77
Teli	33	29	14	2	25.80
Dhoba	30	19	7	—	14.28
Keut	41	50	18	3	13.07
Thanapati	7	16	4	2	26.09
Bairagi	3	6	3	—	42.85
Bhandari	7	5	4	—	33.33
Brahmin	41	30	29	12	57.74
Tiar	1	1	1	—	50.0
Bania	4	6	3	1	40.0
Khadra	9	17	2	2	15.38
Bhutia	14	8	9	—	40.90

TABLE 2

Caste Names	Occupation	Average Attendance %
Ganda	} Weaving	37.0
Bhulia		4.5
Mali	Gardening	63.3
Gour	} Agriculture	37.5
Kulta		56.6
Pandra		40.1
Kumbhar	Pottery making	45.0
Sundi	Business	69.7
Sahara	} Hinduized tribal people	60.2
Gond		39.2
Binjhal		79.5
Teli	Oil-pressing	49.3
Dhoba	Washing	32.1
Keut	Fishing and parching rice	46.4
Thanapati	} Religious	65.1
Bairagi		55.3
Bhandari	Shaving and hair-dressing	61.0
Brahmin	Religious service	61.7
Tiar	Fishing	60.8
Bania	Smithery	55.3
Khadra	Business in bell-metal etc.	80.4

the school in the following order of days in a period of 100 days.

Ganda	
Gond	} 31–40 days.
Dhoba	
Kumbhar	} 41–50 days.
Keut	
Sahara	} 51 + above days.
Khadra	

Fewer Sahara and Khadra children are enrolled in school but they attend it regularly.

(3) Sundi and Brahmin children read in the school in large numbers, i.e., above 57 per hundred children and they also attend the school regularly, i.e., above 51 days in 100 days.

The children of the above three categories may be described in the following way:—

1. There are children belonging to some caste (Sahara and Khadra) who read in school in lesser numbers, i.e., 10 to 20 per hundred but attend it more than 50 days in a period of 100 days.

2. There are children belonging to some castes who read in the school more or less in large numbers, that is, 30 to 40 per hundred but attend it less than 10 days in a period of 100 days.

3. There are children belonging to some castes (Brahmin, Sundi) who read in the school in larger numbers and attend it also more days in a period of 100 days.

The reason of irregular attendance in case of those castes who send their children more or less in large numbers is because there is more work at home for the children to do. The children belonging to the first category have to work at home and their parents prefer apprenticing them in their caste occupation. That is why the children of such castes do not go to school. The castes of this category are, as a matter of fact, poor and live on a subsistence level. Therefore, in view of poverty and work at home, their parents do not like their boys to go to school. Those living above subsistence level do not require their children to work. Lastly, the castes who send their children in larger numbers to the schools and attend them regularly can afford to give their children primary education. Moreover, they have a desire for schooling their children because it helps a great deal in their caste occupation.

We shall now try to find out the causes of a low rate of attendance.

Amongst these causes the following are the important ones:

(a) Work at home.
(b) Lack of interest.
(c) Endemic disease and malnutrition.
(d) Distance from village to school.

A. WORK AT HOME

Work at home, which is a serious obstacle to regular attendance, plays an important part in the seasonal variation of attendance in the school. The following chart shows clearly that there is a variation in attendance seasonally.

TABLE 3

Attendance in Percentage

Name of school	Summer	Rains	Winter
Raksa	16.85	24.2	18.37
Kumbhari	29.2	63.2	66.2
Kainsir	52.9	63.2	67.02
Tulandi	59.75	70.36	68.44
Agalpur	34.53	49.63	55.29
Satalma	44.72	56.47	59.45
Sikridi	55.98	78.71	81.14
Mean	41.85	57.89	59.39

There is less attendance in summer season which includes the months of February, March, April and May and half of June (Falgun, Chait, Baisakh and Jesta). After the summer season the percentage of attendance increases until winter when it is highest. The attendance during the rainy season falls between the summer and winter attendances. The seasonal variation in attendance has a great bearing on the seasonal activities round about this area.

The weavers, such as Bhulia and Ganda, find a very good market during marriage ceremonies and after harvest. After harvest everybody has his paddy bins full with paddy. He is now happy because the toil of the year in the fields is over and he has plenty of food to eat. Naturally he tries to finish up his most expensive duties such as marrying his children and inviting fresh negotiations for marriage etc. In all these works a lot of new clothes and gold ornaments and iron materials used for domestic purposes are necessary. Ordinarily the people in general try to purchase new clothes in place of the old ones after the harvest is over. Therefore, a great deal of buying and selling of clothes and ornaments takes place for about three to four months after harvest until the accumulated wealth is nearly spent up. This sort of thing goes on every year. The weavers wait for this time. As soon as it sets in they flood the local markets with clothes of various colours and designs. During this period all hands in the family are set to weaving and even sometimes extra hands are required and plenty of clothes are turned out. This time of heavy work comes after the middle of January–February (Magh) and continues until the end of May–June (Jesta). Then comes a slack in the cloth market. Nevertheless the weavers do not on any account stop their looms. They carry on their business, however, from hand to mouth. In weaving complicated designs a weaver always needs a boy at his side to weave the side borders and that boy is generally paid Rs. 60/- per month. If the weaver has no son of tender age he employs a boy for the purpose. A boy in a weaver's family begins his work on the loom from the age of nine.

Regarding the work of bell metal and other metals done by Khadra, Kansari and Bania, the little children and specially girls are employed in washing and brushing ornaments and utensils, etc. In the case of Keut, Bhulia and Dhoba castes, the women have major works to do at home. A woman of the Keut caste fries rice which is called *muri*, and sells it either in the village or in the market. A Bhulia woman does all preliminaries connected with weaving and prepares the yarn for weaving. In case of the Dhoba caste the man collects clothes from house to house and the woman washes them. Therefore in order to allow the mother or both the parents to work, the elder children from a very early age are put in charge of the young ones and have full responsibility for them either in the absence of the parents or while they are busy at work. As the children in agricultural families are put in charge of tending and generally looking after the cattle and helping their parents in the sugarcane or paddy fields and vegetable gardens, so also the children in the Bhulia and other artisan families have enough work to do which keeps them out of school during these months.

B. LACK OF INTEREST

If a book reads well and is interesting the reader continues till he finishes it. The children use a most incongruous set of text books, most uninteresting to the boys. The books are written in Oriya script and in literary Oriya which is not spoken in this area. The contents of the books are such that the boys do not appreciate them. The descriptions of scenery or techniques in these books often transport them into a world entirely foreign to their own. This is purely mechanical education and the method of teaching is primitive. A boy reads a subject at the top of his voice over

and over again until he learns it by heart, without understanding the meaning of it. The teachers do not try to arouse the children's curiosity and broaden their understanding. This mechanical study is not even assisted by a blackboard or picture books, charts or illustrations. Under the circumstances, the question of aiding the children with visual materials in their schooling sounds ridiculous. The children do not learn anything in the school that will help them in their own caste occupation or trade or make their daily life easier and more varied. This is not done because of the lack of two things, namely, lack of equipment in the school and proper books, and secondly, lack of technical knowledge and training on the part of the teachers. If a syllabus were prepared on the subject matters of local geography, history and literature and general science it should certainly be interesting to the children of this locality. There is an express lack of interest among the parents in sending their children to school. They aim at only one thing which school training gives to their children, that is covered by the word 'Babu.' A farmer's child or a carpenter's or weaver's child, after a long period of schooling will become a babu or an officer or a white-collared lawyer, which are considered to be the real and great achievements in the life of a man. The change from plough to pen in the life of a farmer's son is the great ambition of his parents. But this change involves a lot of years and money which a farmer cannot afford to spend. Therefore, he says, 'What is the use of schooling my son? We have no resources to educate him till he becomes a babu.'

C. ENDEMIC DISEASE AND MALNUTRITION

Our enquiries have revealed that though sickness is not a serious cause of low rate of attendance, it still is an obstacle to regular attendance.

According to the parents the common sicknesses from which the children suffer are headache, colic, fever and small pox. To the obstacle caused by sickness, the problem of malnutrition, can also be added. When the school sits from 10 o'clock to 4 o'clock, the children eat their midday meal before coming to school and have nothing further to eat until they reach home. Although the children eat a little tiffin such as *muri* (puffed rice) at midday during the leisure hour, this is only for the few. In case of morning schools the children hardly find any substantial food to eat before they come to school. Generally speaking the people of this area eat their chief meal round about midday. The housewife begins preparing the meal nearly one hour before meal-time. Therefore school-going children who leave for school at 10 o'clock miss this meal and get their first and only substantial meal in the evening. In the case of morning school, the child goes, so to say, unfed but gets two substantial meals daily. Thus they are accustomed to a very limited diet which tells upon their health, and this makes the children at school inattentive and sleepy.

D. DISTANCE AS AN OBSTACLE

Distance is an obstacle in this area. Where there is a school in a village the children of that village read there. Very few children from other villages where there are no schools attend, because of distance between the villages and inter-village animosities. Every village likes to have a school of its own. But in many, as soon as it is started, enthusiasm dies out and the school begins to fail.

OPINION STUDY AMONG TEACHERS AND STUDENTS

The teachers of all the schools surveyed feel that the present educational situation in the country is very unsatisfactory. They suggest that there should be a *good garden* attached to the school. Flowering and vegetable plants will be grown and reared and watered by the pupils and teachers in co-operation with each other. The boys will be taught from the garden how plants are grown and under what conditions the plants thrive and fruit. A good school must have a neat and clean and a well-built building in the outskirts of the village. It must have all teaching materials such as maps, a library, good black-boards and a clock, gardening implements and other necessary tools. Children should be provided with seats. Education ought to be compulsory. In primary education the teachers must lead an exemplary life and bear a good moral character. There should be co-operation and better understanding and fellow-feeling between the teachers and the village people. The teachers must have a knowledge of games and ability to be pleasant and cheerful in the company of the students.

There should be sports and prize distribution once annually in the schools. The teachers feel a reshuffling of the subject matters included in the present curriculum of study is necessary. The teachers will try to make the pupils village-minded and train them to be good social workers. The teachers must have good health and training in a variety of subjects which they can teach the boys with a view to their applying this knowledge in the practical field of life.

Some of the leading students of each school were asked as to how they feel about the present educational system and what improvements they suggest in order that they might be happy and feel attracted to come to school regularly. The majority of the boys interviewed said that the teachers cane them severely, they are beaten like beasts; therefore they are afraid of the teachers. The second thing which the boys pointed out is this. They said they would feel happy if there were a strong fencing round the school compound with a beautiful flower garden in it. The next thing which they suggested was that plays and games should be given some important place like book-learning in the curriculum. Reading and playing should go side by side. They felt the school needs building repairs every year and it should be furnished with pictures, diagrams and illustrations in various subjects. The school and its surroundings must be kept neat and clean always. The school building needs extension as the present accommodation is too restricted. They said that if the school building is extended there will be more room and they can sit comfortably and openly. The boys say that whatever vegetables are grown in the school are consumed by the teachers. The boys feel extremely unhappy about this. They said that the vegetables should be shared with them. The boys have marked that the teachers do not come to school regularly everyday and also in time. They say that teachers come to the school late and long after the boys. The boys said that there is no teaching of handiwork or clay modelling etc. in the school. They have marked

that the school building serves as a place at night for secret love-making by men and women of the village. They said that the school building which is a holy institution should be protected against this sort of clandestine use.

CONCLUSION

By and large the educational process existing at present in our country for the young children inculcates only the knowledge of reading and writing to them. This is without doubt a good thing, but how far this helps one in making a living in a society which stands below the level of subsistence is the question. In a society which lies below the level of subsistence and where not enough food is produced to provide for basic physiological needs, teaching the children simply to read and write or to be expert in some handicrafts is not enough unless a sufficient number of pupils are trained in improved agricultural techniques and food production. The school should include teaching of both agriculture and non-agricultural techniques simultaneously.

LITERACY AND SOCIAL CHANGE IN UNDERDEVELOPED COUNTRIES*

HILDA HERTZ GOLDEN

DEFINITION AND MEASUREMENT

EDUCATORS have long debated the question of where, on the continuum of edu-

* Adapted and reprinted by permission from *Rural Sociology*, Volume 20, No. 1, March, 1955, pp. 1–6.

cational achievement, to draw the line dividing literacy from illiteracy; they are still far from a unanimous answer. Fortunately, almost any point would do for present purposes, since all that is needed is an accurate *indicator* of educational achievement, not a final definition of literacy.

The dividing line used here is the one drawn by most governments, particularly governments of underdeveloped countries, for purposes of census enumeration—the ability to read and write one's name. On this basis literacy rates can be readily calculated, and these rates correlate highly with other indices of educational achievement.[1]

TABLE 1. Illiteracy in Developed and Underdeveloped Countries, 1950[a]

Geographical Division	Percentage of Illiterates in the Population Aged 10 and Over		
	All Countries	Developed Countries	Underdeveloped Countries
World	47	6	70
North America[c]	2	2	[b]
Europe	8	3	20
Oceania	11	1	88
U.S.S.R.[d]	11	11	[b]
South America	42	17	51
Middle America[e]	48	20	52
Asia	70	2	75
Africa	88	55	91

[a] Developed countries are those with less than 50 per cent of their economically active males in agricultural pursuits, including hunting, fishing, and forestry; underdeveloped countries are those with 50 per cent or more of their economically active males in these pursuits.
[b] No country in this category.
[c] U.S.A., Canada, and Alaska.
[d] The U.S.S.R. is a borderline case but has been classed here among the developed countries, since today its agricultural labor force is probably slightly below 50 per cent.
[e] The Central American republics and the islands of the Caribbean.

The data have been taken mostly from national censuses. Because definitions differ slightly from country to country, census data occasionally have had to be ad-

[1] The proportion of the population aged 10 years and over that is literate correlates highly with the proportion of the population aged 5 to 14 years that is enrolled in school. The coefficient of correlation, based on data for a third of the world's countries including about 42 per cent of the world's total population, is .92.

justed to conform to one definition and to refer to one date—1950.[2] To achieve world coverage, however, other educational statistics have been converted into estimates of literacy rates whenever census data were lacking.[3] Even though the estimates may be quite rough and the census data not strictly comparable, the information is sufficiently accurate to place all countries, except borderline cases, within broad categories and to provide a basis for exploring the problem in a world-wide context.

THE RELATION OF LITERACY AND INDUSTRIALIZATION

If those countries in which 50 per cent or more of the gainfully occupied males are engaged in agriculture are regarded as underdeveloped,[4] we find, as expected, that the underdeveloped countries are highly illiterate, with the striking exception of those in Europe (Table 1). But even the latter are far more illiterate than the industrial nations. Despite exceptions, then, Table 1 demonstrates the close association between the levels of educational achievement and of industrialization.

The application of correlation analysis to the data provides both a measure of the degree of correspondence of the variables

[2] For an excellent discussion of the criteria of literacy used in census enumeration, see UNESCO, *Progress of Literacy in Various Countries*, Monograph on Fundamental Education, No. VI (Paris: UNESCO, 1953), *passim*.
[3] Whenever statistics are given here for the entire world, they are composed, in part, of estimates. In some cases these are official estimates prepared by the statistical offices of the countries concerned; mostly they have been calculated by the staff of the Population Division of the Bureau of Applied Social Research, Columbia University.
[4] For a rationale of this division, see K. Davis, "Population and the Further Spread of Industrial Society," *Proceedings of the American Philosophical Society*, Vol. 95 (Feb. 13, 1951), p. 8; and K. Davis and H. Hertz, *The Pattern of World Urbanization* (New York: Macmillan forthcoming).

and a regression equation through which deviant cases can be isolated. Literacy and industrialization in 1950 correlate closely: the coefficient of correlation is .87 when industrialization is measured by the proportion of gainfully occupied males in non-agricultural pursuits, and .84 when measured by per-capita income.[5] The closeness of these relationships is further substantiated by historical data for individual countries. In England and Wales, for example, the growth of literacy has been closely associated with that of industrialism, as is confirmed here by a coefficient of correlation of .98.

Establishing the close interrelation of the diffusion of literacy and industrialization invites speculation on why it should exist: Literacy is not essential in the training for or the practice of traditional agriculture and its related handicraft occupations. These occupations can be learned through apprenticeship, by watching an experienced person, by attempting to imitate him by trial and error. The knowledge required for such work can be stored in a person's memory; the principles can be transmitted verbally as part of the apprenticeship process. Since neither business documents nor accounts need be kept, and since the work requires no blueprints, reading and writing are not essential to everyday life.

When most parents follow these traditional occupations, they feel no strong incentive to send their children to school or to arrange somehow that the children acquire literacy skills; they view with indifferent skepticism the practical benefits to be derived from literacy and education.

They are easily discouraged by lack of funds, by long distances from school, by their need for their children's labor.[6] Therefore, unless local governments or outside agents push a program of formal education with unusual vigor or attempt with great persistence to diffuse literacy skills, their prospects of success are slight.

Besides the agriculturalist's apathy toward formal education and his poverty, lack of government funds is an additional obstacle to the diffusion of literacy, since governments of underdeveloped countries cannot provide adequate educational facilities even when they want to. Many impoverished governments, for example, exempt rural children from school attendance because providing school facilities for them is too costly.[7]

In peasant-agricultural countries, literacy begins to diffuse beyond a few traditional occupations (such as the scribe's) and beyond the confines of a literate élite when the society is starting to change in its occupational structure. Since urban-industrial occupations require reading and writing for their acquisition and practice, literacy appears as a skill that leads the individual out of traditional agriculturalism. Education begins to be regarded as a passport from the hard and primitive life of the subsistence farmer to the haven of nonagricultural employment.[8] When parents are no longer employed in traditional agriculture but instead have become unskilled industrial laborers, occupational

[5] The second coefficient of correlation is based on data for only 70 countries, but these include more than 85 per cent of the world's population. See Statistical Office of the United Nations, National and Per Capita Incomes, Seventy Countries: 1949 (New York: United Nations, 1950).

[6] Cf. United Nations, Department of Social Affairs, Preliminary Report on the World Social Situation (New York: United Nations, 1952), pp. 60–98.

[7] UNESCO, Basic Facts and Figures (Paris: UNESCO, 1952), pp. 13–17.

[8] For an illuminating discussion of the role of education in Africa, see Nuffield Foundation and Colonial Office, African Education: A Study of Educational Policy and Practice in Tropical Africa (Oxford: The University Press, 1953).

training of children requires time and
skills beyond the power of parents to provide. Parents thus acquire incentives to
send their children to school; they acquire
some notion of the usefulness of primary
education and are less likely to demand
their children's services at an early age.
They may view education as a channel of
mobility from unskilled to skilled occupations, from agriculture to industry. Furthermore, with increasing industrialization
governments become more able to provide educational facilities and to enforce
school attendance. In brief, the growth
and diffusion of literacy in underdeveloped
countries is closely tied to the growth and
diffusion of an urban-industrial civilization.

LITERACY AS A FACTOR IN SOCIAL CHANGE

Although all underdeveloped countries
show a glaring lack of trained manpower,
some are far more deficient in this respect
than are others at the same stage. The
skills of a population are, within limits,
subject to manipulation, and a few peasant-agricultural countries have diverted an
unusually large share of their means toward the diffusion of literacy, others only
a small share. As a result, educational progress when compared with industrial advance may be retarded or advanced. Sin-
gling out the deviant countries by using
the regression equations mentioned earlier
serves a twofold purpose: An analysis of
the deviant countries may indicate the factors that account for the differential support of education, and it may also suggest
the role of educational achievement in future economic development.

Among the underdeveloped nations, the
following are noteworthy for their deviation:[9]

More Literate than Industrial	
Bulgaria	Panama
Colombia	Philippines
Costa Rica	Poland
Ecuador	Rumania
Finland	Thailand

Less Literate than Industrial	
Egypt	Libya
India	Malaya
Indonesia	Nepal
Iran	Union of South
Iraq	Africa

The information available about these
countries suggests that two kinds of factors
largely account for the retardation or advance of educational vis-à-vis industrial development. The first set of factors are
those determining the relative claim that
a nation's goals, such as mass literacy or
the support of religion or an army, have
upon a nation's wealth; second, there are
those determining the cost of achieving
widespread literacy and education, such as
linguistic diversity or the esoteric nature
of the literary language.

In a few countries the literate and educated class has been particularly narrow
in its interests and pursuits; its learning
has been oriented away from the everyday
life of the community and toward traditionalism, abstruse religious scholarship,
and magic. Conversely, in a few nations
the literate élite has conceived of education as a means to increased national
strength or national independence; the in-
telligentsia have taken an interest in scientific and technological knowledge, and
their scholarship has received the stimulus
of daily necessity and economic need. In
Bulgaria prior to independence, for example, wealthy persons conceived it their
duty to open and to maintain schools de-

[9] Those listed are the major countries in
which the actual rate deviates approximately 20 or more percentage points from the expected
rate.

spite the opposition of the Turkish state; the élite of the Arab areas of the Ottoman Empire showed no such interest.[10]

One result of a great emphasis on traditionalism by a small literate class in a generally illiterate population is the tendency of the written language to diverge from the spoken vernacular. This process may go so far that the written language becomes meaningless to the masses. If the educated class extols the virtues of the "classical" language instead of working toward reducing the vernacular to writing and toward simplifying the script, there is no chance for widespread diffusion of literacy.[11]

In addition, the great diversity of languages and scripts in some of the world's underdeveloped nations compounds the cost of achieving widespread literacy. Africa south of the Sahara is "a vast mosaic of vernacular languages, spoken by groups ranging in size from a few hundreds to several millions of persons," and this is one of the major difficulties encountered in the diffusion of literacy.[12] Furthermore, the controversy over the medium of instruction, so endemic to the efforts to diffuse literacy and education, is an ample tribute to the magnitude of the problem of linguistic diversity.

In brief, the diffusion of literacy and education in a country beyond the comparable point of economic development, or the retardation behind that point, derives from the factors just mentioned— and perhaps others. Next comes the question of the significance of such retardation or advance for future economic development.

The modernization of peasant-agricultural countries is usually conceived of as a moving equilibrium in which no one element can be for very long out of line with the others, because they are functionally interdependent. On this basis we would expect that countries in which educational retardation is considerable and has lasted for some time would now be making relatively greater headway educationally than economically. Conversely, countries in which the advance is considerable and has lasted for some time should now be making relatively greater progress economically than educationally. Despite the paucity of information, it can be shown that this is true for many countries.

Since about 1900, India has exhibited faster educational than economic progress. It has slowly narrowed the gap created by the more rapid economic development of the nineteenth century, although in 1951 the difference had not yet disappeared (Table 2).[13] Again, in nineteenth-century Egypt, economic development, though spasmodic, took place faster than educational change.[14] During the first three decades of this century, both industrial and educational advances were slight. Since about 1930, educational progress has been faster than economic development, despite the fact that during the period of World War II economic change was rapid. Egypt seems to have entered the phase in which for some time educational advance will remain faster than economic development. The examples of Egypt and India suggest that in countries like them educational progress is likely to accelerate.

[10] William F. Russell, *Schools in Bulgaria* (New York: Teachers College, Columbia University, 1924), pp. 7–11; Alfred Bonné, *State and Economics in the Middle East* (London: Kegan Paul, Trench, Trubner, 1948), pp. 46–48.

[11] Frank C. Laubach, *The Silent Million Speak* (New York: Friendship Press, 1943), p. 92.

[12] United Nations Department of Social Affairs, *op. cit.*, pp. 76–78.

[13] Kingsley Davis, "Social and Demographic Aspects of Economic Development in India," to be published soon as part of a symposium sponsored by the Social Science Research Council.

[14] Bonné, *op. cit.*, p. 238.

TABLE 2. Actual and Expected Decline in Illiteracy in Selected Countries

Country and Year	Percentage of Illiterates in the Population Aged 10 and Over		Difference (Actual Percentage Minus Expected)
	Actual	Expected[a]	
India:[b]			
1911	93	64	29
1921	92	65	27
1931	91	64	27
1941	85	67	18
1951	80	61	19
Egypt:			
1907	93	67	26
1917	91	62	29
1927	86	56	30
1937	85	61	24
1947	75	51	24
U.S.S.R.:			
1926	49	80	−31
1939	19	39	−20
Brazil:			
1940	57	61	− 4
1950	52	52	0
U.S.A.:			
1870	20	37	−17
1910	7	5	2

[a] By means of the regression equation, the expected percentages were calculated from the percentages of economically active males engaged in agricultural pursuits in each country (see text).
[b] Data on India's agricultural labor force have been taken from Kingsley Davis, "Social and Demographic Aspects of Economic Development in India," to be published soon as part of a symposium sponsored by the Social Science Research Council.

Among the underdeveloped countries that are more literate than industrial, there are none for which we have as adequate information as we have for India and Egypt. Nevertheless, the scanty information that is available corroborates the contention. For example, Brazil, which in 1950 had a level of literacy commensurate with its level of industrialization, achieved this condition after a decade of considerably more rapid economic than educational progress. Similarly, Puerto Rico's rapid economic expansion began when educational advance had caught up with economic development. Today, Puerto Rico is more literate than industrial—its actual illiteracy rate is 24 per cent, whereas the expected rate is 32 per cent—and it is also making rapid economic progress. Unfortunately, there is little information available on the Balkan countries; but what there is suggests that they are repeating the pattern characteristic of the U.S.S.R. between 1926 and 1939 and of the U.S.A. between 1870 and 1910 (Table 2).

The differential rates of economic advance for the educationally retarded and the educationally advanced countries point to the importance of the dissemination of literacy and education in the transformation of peasant-agricultural nations into urban-industrial nations. In the "bootstrap" operation in which all underdeveloped countries are engaged, training the population for urban-industrial occupations is crucial to the achievement of higher levels of industrialization. Clearly the countries that today are ahead educationally will find it easier to achieve this goal than those that are behind. The latter countries will find their lack of literate and trained manpower a major obstacle to rapid industrialization. Paradoxically, they will need to spend a great share of their wealth, even though they have almost none, for the long-neglected goal of mass education before they can aspire to become modern industrial states.

UNIVERSITIES IN THE COLONIES*

W. IVOR JENNINGS

It is probable that the problem of creating a university in Jamaica, or Nigeria, or Uganda, or Malaya, would not be fundamentally different from that of creating a university in Ceylon, because it is irrelevant that these territories are colonies, and what is relevant is that they have no universities already, that their educational systems are not fully developed, that (apart from Jamaica) the medium of higher education is not the ordinary language of the people, and that there is only a very small middle class.

II

The fundamental characteristic of the colonial university is that it has very little cultural background, except of course in Malta. This is true even in Ceylon, where both the Sinhalese and the Tamils had a high standard of civilization long before the University of Oxford was founded. There was, however, very little left when the Portuguese landed in 1505, and most of what culture there is has come from the west or from the revival of indigenous culture in India. There is, it is true, a tradition of learning expressed in the literatures of Buddhism and Hinduism, in the work of a few learned monks in the pirivenas, in the frescoes of Sigiriya, and in the ruins of Anuradhapura and Polonnaruwa. This tradition is extremely valuable, for though it does not provide a

* Adapted and reprinted by permission from *The Political Quarterly*, Vol. 17, No. 3, 1946, pp. 228–244.

foundation on which to build, it enables the university to realize as its task, not the creation of a pale imitation of western culture, but the revival of an ancient civilization which would, in the process of redevelopment, absorb the best that East and West could produce, and at the same time to associate a cultural renaissance with the nationalism of the politically-conscious classes. Elsewhere colonial universities are not likely to have this advantage and are therefore likely to find their task even more difficult. Still, it is a very small advantage; for what culture there is comes from Europe or from India. The art is almost entirely western, the music is either western or Indian, the general literature is almost entirely in English, the drama is mainly western, and the films are either western or Indian. The great mass of the people are in much the same cultural state as the peasants of Eastern Europe. The small middle class has been educated through the medium of English, but only a very small section of it can be said to be cultured in any real sense, and this culture comes almost entirely, directly or indirectly, from a few "England-returned men." It must be added that only a proportion of those who have studied at universities in Great Britain have managed to acquire much of the culture of the west. The Ceylonese is a very adaptable person and his background is more English than that of the average Indian. He therefore fits more easily into the university system of Great

Britain: but he carries something of his own environment with him and considers that his main task in England is to pass his examinations with distinction and to secure a place in the Ceylon Civil Service. Accordingly, he does not necessarily bring back from England much more than the elementary knowledge of his "subject" which he acquires by strict attention to it in his lectures and his reading. As the West Indian Committee of the Commission on Higher Education in the Colonies very truly remarks:[1]

It must not be assumed that a West Indian youth, living possibly upon very small means in lodgings in some large city and attending lectures, is necessarily laying up a rich store of culture or strengthening either his character or physique for his coming work in life.

The truth is that the proportion of "England-returned men" with a broad culture is lower than the proportion among English undergraduates, and that proportion is low enough.

It is therefore one of the tasks of the colonial university to act as a major culture centre. There is in London or other large cities a cultural nucleus—artists, musicians, authors, dramatists, and the rest— quite distinct from the local universities. No doubt the proportion of cultured men and women on the staff of the university is high, and they help to create a demand for intellectual food outside their "subjects": but culture is generally the concern of a wider class. In Ceylon the equivalent class is very small and much of the stimulus must come, when it comes, from the University. In other territories, no doubt, the nucleus does not exist at all. This characteristic extends, too, to branches of knowledge which are not generally classed as cultural—except so far as

[1] Cmd. 6654, p. 16.

they were dealt with by the Greeks—economics, politics, and sociology. Here there is a thin veneer which hides the yawning void beneath. The "England-returned man" is generally politically conscious, as the cant-phrase has it, but he is rarely politically informed; and the local product is even more ignorant. Probably ninety per cent of the students of the University of Ceylon call themselves "socialists"; it may be doubted, though, whether five per cent have read a book on socialism or any other "ism." What is more, their ignorance of the economic, social and political conditions of their own country is abysmal: though this has also other causes. For the moment the conclusion to be drawn is that those who establish universities in less fortunate territories, whether as administrators or as professors, should not merely be distinguished scholars, but also should have broad interests which they can pass on to their students and to the general population.

III

The school system in Ceylon was established not to provide education, but to train people to fill jobs. The administrators and commercial men were sent out from England, but they needed clerks and other assistants. Accordingly, "English education" was provided for the Burghers and Eurasians and afterwards the Sinhalese and the Tamils. It is true that the missionaries also provided education in all three languages as part of their duty to teach the Gospel to all nations. But what induced the Ceylonese parent to spend money on his son's education was the prospect of a Government job or, failing that, a lucrative position or practice in Colombo. As the Ceylonese replaced the Europeans, the attractions of Government jobs became ever greater. The villager who in normal times has an income equivalent to thirty shillings a month is comparatively prosperous; but there is one Ceylonese in the public service earning £3,000 a year with a right to a pension of £2,000 a year in a few years' time. He is certainly exceptional, but the ordinary Civil Servant expects in due course to earn £1,500 a year. Now the steps to this affluence are clear. First, the lad must attend an "English" school; secondly, he must matriculate; thirdly, he must get a degree; and, fourthly, he must pass an examination into the Civil Service. Only the exceptional boy goes the whole way, but the social gradation is marked by examinations; Matriculation, Intermediate, Final Examination, Civil Service Examination. Income and social status depend primarily on which of these one has passed. It is true that there are a few wealthy families whose wealth arises from coconuts, rubber, plumbago, or even tea (which is mainly in European hands). It is true also that the dowry system enables one to marry wealth; but a young man who wants a large dowry must have "prospects," and these depend mainly on his examinations—a civil servant has the highest dowry value. It is also true that a few, very few, have been able to achieve success in commerce or industry without examinations. For the ordinary parent, however, the problem is to make certain that the lad passes his examination.

There is, of course, much of this in England also, particularly with the extension of the scholarship system; but the universities and schools which set the tone were established long before there were examinations. Though Oxford and Cambridge seem to me—if a mere colonial may presume to criticize—to place too much emphasis on Schools and Triposes, the ordinary undergraduate does not prefer them because their teaching is better and their examinations are of higher standard. He chooses them because the middle classes converted Ox-

ford and Cambridge into centres of broad education. The preference of the employer for a graduate from Oxford or Cambridge is not due only to snobbishness, nor certainly to their examination standards, but to the presumption that he will get a more adaptable and educable employee, somebody who will learn to do the job efficiently. In Ceylon, on the other hand, the examination system was taken over ready-made from Great Britain. The examination was not merely an incident of education, it was its whole aim and object. No doubt the problem is equally great, if not worse, in other territories.

It is almost impossible to exaggerate this point in writing for English readers. After four years in Ceylon I still make the mistake of forgetting that, when a Ceylonese talks about education, he probably means preparation for an examination. Confusion creeps into a conversation when, for instance, a senior civil servant can be described as "first-class" not because his qualities as an administrator would place him at the top of any classification, but because he obtained a first-class in his Tripos twenty years ago. The Ceylon University College was deemed to become a University overnight because it started to hold its own examinations. The University is hindering the economic development of the Island, because it has not yet created a degree in commerce. In recommending that the student of economics should be awarded the degree of Bachelor of Arts instead of the degree of Bachelor of the Science of Economics, the vice-chancellor must be anxious to maintain the hegemony of European capital by stopping Ceylonese students from taking degrees in economics.[2] If the Head of a Department promotes a non-gradu-

[2] This allegation was actually made in public: a B.Sc. (Econ.) is an economist; a B.A. in Economics is not.

ate when he has a graduate in his Department, he must be influenced by race, religion, caste, or some even less worthy motive. A man with two degrees is better than a man with one. Some of the State Councillors are ignorant men; they did not even pass Matriculation. No, I have not read anything by Tagore; he was not set for the School Certificate. No, my son does not know much Sinhalese; he took English and Latin. Please may I enter the University to be coached for a degree in Physics? I do not know anything about birds: we did not take biology at our school. And so on.

It has further to be remembered that, until recently, the examinations were inevitably English examinations. To get into the civil service it was necessary to have a degree, and this meant, for those who could not go to England, a London degree. To get a degree one had to pass Intermediate. To pass Intermediate one had to pass Matriculation. To pass Matriculation it was necessary to study English, Latin, Mathematics and two other subjects. Therefore, any education outside English, Latin, Mathematics and two other subjects was "no use." Many schools fought hard against this tradition, but in others it was literally true that the student entered the school in order to pass Matriculation, that he did nothing there except study for Matriculation, and that he left as soon as he had passed Matriculation. In fact, the situation deteriorated after 1914, when the high price of rubber brought "English education" within the reach of a larger section of the population. The older schools had fairly broad traditions, and their final examination was the Cambridge Senior. Cambridge, unlike London, adapted its syllabuses to local conditions and it was common to take six or seven subjects. The post-war generation, however, wanted degrees and therefore either London Matriculation or

exemption from it. It was easier for the schools to prepare for London Matriculation than to prepare the students to get five credits in the right subjects in the Cambridge Senior. The newer schools, of which many were established in this period, were frankly preparing for London Matriculation and for that examination only. The result was that the youth of Ceylon—or rather the small middle-class section of it—had as preparation for life the five subjects of London Matriculation.

The whole Ceylon system of education was determined by syllabuses drafted in London for the benefit of English students. Latin was compulsory, and so nearly every educated Ceylonese has a vague recollection of the conjugation of *docere* but few know anything of Sanskrit and Pali. English was English for English students and that meant (in London) mainly Anglo-Saxon and linguistics, not English literature. I have no doubt that in "English Literature" the following colloquy was common:

TEACHER: "O daffodil we weep to see you fade away so soon."
PUPIL: What is a daffodil?
TEACHER: Just an English flower, but the examiners will not ask questions on that. Take this note: The imagery in this poem . . .

This kind of thing extended even to Mathematics. The pupil was not asked to work out the profit on a transaction in copra at so many rupees a candy, but the profit on a transaction in cotton at so many pence a pound. If a man cycled from London to Brighton . . . History was, of course, English history, and Ethelred the Unready was more important than Parakrama Bahu the Great. The student knew all about the English coalfields and had not the least notion where plumbago was found in Ceylon, still less why.

The consequence was not merely that

"English education" consisted in acquiring irrelevant knowledge. It was that education consisted in learning the substance of something in a text-book. Our Geography Department, which is able to check the consequences in field classes, has had some astounding results. For instance, there are students who can draw perfect isotherms, but who have never seen a thermometer. It is possible to take a class, every member of which could draw a picture of a particular type of land formation, to the edge of that kind of formation, to tell the class that that kind of formation is in sight, and to find not a single person recognize it. We have had students, to whom a type of vegetation has been described, deny that there was any in Ceylon, while literally they were standing on it.

Of course, this exhibits bad teaching; but why is teaching so bad? Evidently because education consists in learning something for an examination, and an irrelevant external examination at that. The teachers were teachers because they had passed London Matriculation, or London Intermediate, or even (though only the high and mighty ones) a London Final Examination. It is doubtful if there are more than a hundred people in Ceylon who really appreciate that University education is something more than study for an examination.

IV

The solution was plain, though it would take a generation to accomplish. First, a University of Ceylon should be created. Secondly, it should be residential and concentrate heavily on providing a broad, general education through all available instruments. Thirdly, it should so orientate its courses as to compel the student to relate his academic knowledge to his practical experience, and for this purpose should engage in the research

necessary to enable books having a Ceylon orientation to be produced. Fourthly, it should sweep away London Matriculation as its entrance qualification and have an entrance standard which would compel the schools to establish sixth forms. Fifthly, it should incorporate Faculties having a professional and technical bias —especially Medicine, Agriculture and Engineering—so as to have a substantial body of students in direct contact with reality. Finally, it should have a Department for the training of teachers which would gradually create a body of teachers having an entirely different approach to education.

This was a large and ambitious programme, but fortunately all the decisions taken before 1942 were on the right lines. A site for a residential university had been acquired in proximity to a School of Agriculture with a large experimimental farm, which could be converted into a Faculty, though space had not been provided for a teaching hospital or a Faculty of Medicine. An entrance examination at higher level than London Matriculation had been established. A Bill had been drafted which compelled an entrance examination and residence for three years, and forbade external examinations. It had been intended to create the University on its movement to its residential site, but it was readily agreed that it should be created at once in order that a Ceylon orientation might be given immediately and the courses changed pending the removal. The Ceylon Medical College was brought in as the Faculty of Medicine, though its physical separation prevented the full benefit from being obtained for the time being. The Government readily agreed to abolish London Matriculation and the Cambridge Senior Examination. In other respects, however, the London examinations continue and indeed the State Council has resolved that the University of Ceylon itself confer external degrees. Obviously, the notion that university education consists in passing an examination will die hard, and it will take years to overcome the handicap of the London external system.

Sir Ivor Jennings is Master of Trinity Hall and Hon. Fellow of St. Catherine's College at Cambridge. He was formerly Vice-Chancellor of the University of Ceylon and Constitutional Advisor to the Government of Pakistan. He is the author of *Cabinet Government; Parliament;* and other scholarly works.

Dr. Hilda H. Golden was a Research Associate in the Population division of the Bureau of Applied Social Research, Columbia University, from 1949 to 1955. In addition to being an author of articles in various professional journals, she is coauthor with Kingsley Davis of a forthcoming book, *The Pattern of World Urbanization.* She has also taught at Georgia State College for Women and Randolph-Macon Woman's College.

Mr. Nityananda Patnaik holds a master's degree in anthropology from the University of Calcutta. He has been serving as a Rural Life Analyst since 1952 with the American Friends Service Committee on their project at Barpali Village. His village studies have been published in *Man in India* and *Economic Weekly.* He is a member of the Tribal Research Bureau, Tribal and Rural Welfare Department, Government of Orissa, India.

V

ECONOMIC DEVELOPMENT
AND FINANCE PROBLEMS
IN UNDERDEVELOPED AREAS

IN THE first chapter of this volume we discussed at some length the difficulty in defining underdeveloped areas and pointed out that the information available for use in classifying political entities on a basis of their development was rather inadequate. The necessity of moving from the ideal type of information, found unavailable, to the type of data that are currently being collected, was emphasized. In this chapter, as an introduction to the various readings on economic development and finance problems in underdeveloped areas, we shall discuss the relation of numerous economic data to the dichotomy of political entities as we have previously classified them, developed or underdeveloped. Assuming that our division of the political entities of the world into developed and underdeveloped areas, following broad geographical lines, was a division closely related to economic development, we would expect the variables presented on the next few pages to have a very high correlation with our dichotomy of developed or underdeveloped political entities. It is possible, however, that either our original division of political entities into developed and underdeveloped areas has certain shortcomings, or that the political entities for which we will find data available are not representative of the universe of 195 political entities, or that the data are so inaccurate that a true picture of the relationship of these variables to the development dichotomy cannot be presented. Since the latter two possibilities are present, at least to some extent, we shall not expect to obtain one-to-one relationships between the various indices of economic development to be presented and the development dichotomy that we set up in the first chapter.

In order to represent parsimoniously the relationship of a number of variables to the development dichotomy, we shall, as in the past, present the data in a series of 2-by-2 tables, commencing with Table 19. The data contained in these tables are in every case for the year 1950 or thereabouts.

IRON ORE RESOURCES AND THEIR DEVELOPMENT

Table 19 deals with known reserves of iron ore. New iron ore reserves may be discovered in years to come or techniques may be developed that will permit the use of lower-grade ores, but the distribution of known iron ore reserves as of about 1950 is pertinent to the present research. The presence of iron ore in a country provides a basis for industrial development if other necessary resources, natural and capital, are present. The phi coefficient of correlation is .555. The cutting point and results would be the same if this variable was presented on a *per capita* basis. Thus we see that it cannot be said that the existence of a re-

TABLE 19. Distribution of Political Entities According to Probable Reserves of Iron Ore in Millions of Tons of Iron Content and Status as Developed or Underdeveloped[1]

	Developed	Under-developed	Total
No recorded reserves	20	119	139
Iron ore reserves	22	23	45
Total	42	142	184

source such as iron ore has been any assurance of development. But neither can it be said that the absence of reserves of iron ore has been an insurmountable obstacle to development.

The relation of a country's classification as developed or underdeveloped to iron ore production should be considerably greater. This correlation presents some indication of the extent to which available resources have been developed. The data are presented in Table 20, and the phi coefficient of correlation is .731.

TABLE 20. Distribution of Political Entities According to Iron Ore Production in Millions of Metric Tons and Status as Developed or Underdeveloped[2]

	Developed	Under-developed	Total
No iron ore production	23	135	158
Iron ore production	21	10	31
Total	44	145	189

As we would hypothesize, only a small proportion of the underdeveloped areas are iron ore producers. Another index of production that should be related to our development dichotomy is *per capita* production of steel. As in the case of other data on iron, the relation between production and development is not surprising. The phi coefficient of correlation for the data in Table 21 is .888.

It is seen then, that our dichotomy of developed and underdeveloped areas is correlated with the presence and development of iron ore, but not in a 1-to-1 fashion. We shall now turn to a less specialized indicator of development and observe its relationship to the development dichotomy.

[1] *World Iron Ore Resources and Their Utilization*, Table A, Lake Success, United Nations Department of Economic Affairs, 1950, pp. 66–67.
[2] *Ibid.*, Table B.

TABLE 21.   Distribution of Political Entities According to the Production of Steel in Kilograms *Per Capita* and Status as Developed or Underdeveloped[3]

	Developed	Under-developed	Total
No steel production	22	141	163
Steel production	24	6	30
Total	46	147	193

PRODUCTION AND CONSUMPTION OF COMMERCIAL ENERGY

We would expect that a series of indices on the production and consumption of commercial energy should sharply differentiate developed from underdeveloped areas. These indices, like steel production, are a measure of economic processes. In Table 22 we see the relation of *per capita* production of commercial energy

TABLE 22.   Distribution of Political Entities According to *Per Capita* Production of Commercial Energy and Status as Developed or Underdeveloped[4]

Per Capita Production in 1000 Metric Tons	Developed	Under-developed	Total
−.3	11	91	102
.3+	27	16	43
Total	38	107	145

in thousands of metric tons of coal equivalent to the development dichotomy. The political entity that is a coal or oil producer, albeit not for its own consumption, will score highly on such an index. The phi coefficient of correlation between *per capita* production of commercial energy and political status is .848. The inability to consume any large proportion of its produced commercial energy is, of course, one of the characteristics of many underdeveloped areas, particularly those that are non-self-governing or those in which there are heavy investments by large, developed countries. But, on the other hand, considerable amounts of commercial energy may be brought into an underdeveloped area and consumed in the course of mining and processing raw materials, thus resulting in a high index of commercial energy consumption for an area which is not a high producer of commercial energy.

In Table 23 we have an index of commercial energy consumption in thousands of metric tons of coal equivalent. This index has a phi coefficient of correlation with our development dichotomy of 1.122. We see that an index of

[3] *Ibid.*, Table B.

[4] *World Energy Supplies in Selected Years, 1929–1950*, Statistical Papers, Series J, No, 1, New York, Statistical Office of the United Nations, 1952, Table 13.

commercial energy consumption differentiates between the developed and underdeveloped areas more sharply than the other variables that we have examined.

TABLE 23.   Distribution of Political Entities According to
Per Capita Consumption of Commercial Energy and Status
as Developed or Underdeveloped[5]

Per Capita Con- sumption in 1000 Metric Tons	Developed	Under- developed	Total
−.5	7	91	98
.5+	31	9	40
Total	38	100	138

In Table 24 an index of the *per capita* production and consumption of noncommercial fuels is presented. This index has a phi coefficient of correlation
with development of .596.

TABLE 24.   Distribution of Political Entities According to
Per Capita Production and Consumption of Noncommercial
Fuels and Status as Developed or Underdeveloped[6]

Per Capita Pro- duction and Con- sumption in 1000 Metric Tons	Developed	Under- developed	Total
−.2	17	84	101
.2+	15	11	26
Total	32	95	127

When the *per capita* production of commercial and noncommercial energy
are combined, the relation between total energy production and development
has a phi coefficient of correlation of .926.[7] This coefficient is probably more
indicative of overall development of available energy resources than those previously presented. The various indices of production and consumption of energy
indicate a relatively greater development of the areas classified as developed than
those classified as underdeveloped, following the dichotomy that we established

[5] *Ibid.*, Table 4, and *Statistical Yearbook, 1952*, New York, United Nations, 1953, Table
123. The figures given here refer to the gross inland consumption of commercial fuels and
water power, expressed in terms of coal equivalent. The production data include coal and lig-
nite, petroleum, shale oil and natural gasolines, natural gas and hydro-electric power, the consumption of briquettes, coke, gasoline, kerosene, fuel oils, benzol, manufactured and bottled
gases, and electric power. Fuelwood and other vegetable fuels have been omitted because of
the absence of adequate data.
[6] *World Energy Supplies in Selected Years, 1929–1950*, Statistical Papers, Series J, No. 1,
New York, Statistical Office of the United Nations, 1952, Table 14.
[7] *Ibid.*, Tables 1, 15.

on a broad geographical basis. Quite a different series of indices of production will now be presented, dealing with the production of food.

FOOD PRODUCTION

One index of development that is not essentially an index of industrial development, i.e., food production, reveals that our development dichotomy is highly correlated with agricultural development. Table 25 shows the relationship

TABLE 25.   Distribution of Political Entities According to
Per Capita Production of Grains and Foods and Status as
Developed or Underdeveloped[8]

Per Capita Production in 1000 Metric Tons	Developed	Underdeveloped	Total
−.25	6	63	69
.25+	30	7	37
Total	36	70	106

between our development dichotomy and tons of grains and foods produced *per capita*. The phi coefficient of correlation between the production of grains and foods *per capita* and the development dichotomy is 1.144.

Another index of agricultural production is *per capita* livestock production. This is shown in Table 26; the phi coefficient of correlation between the development dichotomy and this index is .136. A high index of food production may be related to mechanization of agriculture, while a high index of livestock production may be indicative of a herding economy; a high score on the first index may be related to economic development, and a high score on the second index may be related to underdevelopment.

TABLE 26.   Distribution of Political Entities According to
Per Capita Livestock Production and Status as Developed
or Underdeveloped[9]

Livestock *Per Capita*	Developed	Underdeveloped	Total
−.8	14	41	55
.8+	16	32	48
Total	30	73	103

Another variable of interest is the percent of the total area of a country consisting of arable land, including fallow land and orchards. This variable has a

[8] *Statistical Yearbook, 1952*, New York, United Nations, 1953, Tables 10 through 26.
[9] *Ibid.*, Table 27.

phi coefficient of correlation with the development dichotomy of .181.[10] If permanent meadows and pastures are also included, the phi coefficient of correlation becomes .561.[11] This indicates that the percent of the land that is arable has a positive relationship, although not great, to the classification of political entities as developed or underdeveloped. The next series of data is quite different, and may, to some persons, reveal unexpected relationships to development.

FOREIGN TRADE

The data on foreign trade give us some indication of the amount of economic activity of a different type, i.e., activity involving interaction with other political entities. In Table 27 we have related *per capita* foreign trade to the development dichotomy. The phi coefficient of correlation is .155. This means that developed political entities have relatively little more foreign trade than the underdeveloped areas when the data are on a *per capita* basis. This should not be surprising, since some of the underdeveloped areas are exporters of large quantities of raw materials. This correlation does not have any implications about the relative benefit from foreign trade to the indigenous inhabitants of an underdeveloped area as contrasted to the benefit to outside investors from more developed areas. The activity takes place and at this point no statement is made about the relative benefits to either persons or political entities. If we break down the data in Table 27 on a basis of imports and exports the results are somewhat different. Im-

TABLE 27.   Distribution of Political Entities According to *Per Capita* Foreign Trade in U.S. Dollars and Status as Developed or Underdeveloped[12]

Dollars Per Capita	Developed	Under- developed	Total
70+	16	59	75
−70	24	56	80
Total	40	115	155

ports have a phi coefficient of correlation with the development dichotomy of .356 and exports have a correlation of .209.[13] If each political entity is arranged on a continuum on a basis of the dollar value and direction of its *per capita* balance of foreign trade, we find that developed countries tend to have import balances rather than export balances, to a somewhat greater extent than do the underdeveloped countries; the phi coefficient of correlation between foreign trade balance and the development dichotomy is .122.[14] The foreign trade

[10] *Yearbook of Food and Agricultural Statistics*, 1952, Rome, Food and Agricultural Organization, 1952, Table 1.
[11] *Ibid.*
[12] *Statistical Yearbook*, 1952, New York, United Nations, 1953, Table 148.
[13] *Ibid.*
[14] *Ibid.*

data presented in this chapter must, however, be considered as descriptive of the situation at a particular time. While the relationship of foreign trade to our development dichotomy may be essentially the same over a period of years, there are variations from time to time in relation to war, armaments races, and the like. The findings on foreign trade data will be surprising to persons whose preconceptions have led them to predict that developed countries have much larger dollar values of foreign trade than underdeveloped countries. We shall now turn to a brief analysis of the relation of several indices of transportation development to our development dichotomy.

TRANSPORTATION

The transportation indices are limited to those on which extensive data have traditionally been collected; we lack data on river and air transportation as well as camel caravans, wheelbarrows, and horse-drawn or ox-drawn vehicles, or human bearers for that matter. We are showing only the relationship of certain types of very efficient transportation to the development dichotomy. But, if we were to inquire whether or not the transportation system of an entity meets the needs of that particular economic system we might find a different answer. In Africa, for example, there are 5 different economies.[15] The transportation necessary for the normal functioning of an economic system can be conducted in some cases without railroads and airlines. It can probably be shown that under certain conditions the "primitive" methods of transportation are more suitable than the modern types that we discuss below. In Table 28 we see the relation of one measure of railway development, *per capita* rolling stock, to the development dichotomy. The phi coefficient of correlation is 1.202.

TABLE 28. Distribution of Political Entities According to *Per Capita* Amount of Rolling Stock, Freight and Passenger, and Status as Developed or Underdeveloped[16]

Rolling Stock *Per Capita*	Developed	Under-developed	Total
−1.1	1	34	35
1.1+	29	8	37
Total	30	42	72

Table 29 shows the relationship of railway freight in net ton-kilometers to the development dichotomy; the phi coefficient of correlation is 1.228.

Another index of transportation development is the number of motor vehicles

[15] See Lord Hailey, *An African Survey*, London, Oxford University Press, 1938, Chap. 20; Melville J. Herskovits, *The Economic Life of Primitive People*, New York, Alfred Knopf, 1940; Raymond Firth, *Malay Fishermen: Their Peasant Economy*, London, Kegan, Paul, Tench Trubner & Co., 1946.
[16] *Statistical Yearbook, 1952*, New York, United Nations, 1953, Table 132.

TABLE 29. Distribution of Political Entities According to Railway Freight in Net-Ton Kilometers and Status as Developed or Underdeveloped[17]

Millions of Tons Per 1000 Population	Developed	Under- developed	Total
−.16	3	37	40
.16+	29	5	34
Total	32	42	74

in use per 1000 population. These data are presented in Table 30, and the phi coefficient of correlation is .791.

TABLE 30. Distribution of Political Entities According to Motor Vehicles in Use per 1000 Population and Status as Developed or Underdeveloped[18]

Motor Vehicles Per 1000 Population	Developed	Under- developed	Total
−10	8	58	66
10+	24	22	46
Total	32	80	112

One final economic index will be related to the development dichotomy—*per capita* income. As we have previously said, *per capita* income estimates have been used as a single index in defining areas as underdeveloped. These data are unavailable for even half of our political entities, but nevertheless are presented here in order to demonstrate that a development dichotomy based on this item would be considerably different than the development dichotomy that we have accepted. The data are shown in Table 31; the phi coefficient of correlation is 1.002.

The $100 *per capita* cutting point frequently mentioned in the literature on

TABLE 31. Distribution of Political Entities According to *Per Capita* Income in U.S. Dollars and Status as Developed or Underdeveloped[19]

Per Capita Income in Dollars	Developed	Under- developed	Total
−100	0	27	27
100+	33	16	49
Total	33	43	76

[17] *Ibid.*, Table 134.
[18] *Ibid.*, Table 135.
[19] *National Income and Its Distribution in Underdeveloped Countries*, Statistical Papers, Series E-1 and E-3, New York, Statistical Office of the United Nations, 1951, Table 1.

underdeveloped areas appears to be a point below which we do not find developed areas but above which we find some of the underdeveloped areas. Although it is possible to combine the various indices of economic development into a scale in order to obtain some measure of overall development, that will not be done at this point but in a later chapter of this volume.

The data that we have just presented give us some notion of the relative lack of development in certain specified directions in underdeveloped areas. These data are only skeletal. They enable us to contrast the areas that we have labeled developed with those which we have labeled underdeveloped. The contrast is generally unfavorable to the underdeveloped areas. We have not expected that the relationships obtained would be of a one to one order—for several reasons given at the outset. Since these empirical data present only an introduction to the topic—the bare empirical basis for discussion of conditions in underdeveloped areas—the articles selected for the remainder of this chapter are of quite a different nature. They offer little in the way of statistics but describe and explain in detailed fashion, in several instances using the case approach, the conditions to be found in underdeveloped areas. Having read these articles, the reader will have a better understanding of the meaning of the statistical materials, the empirical data presented in these introductory pages.

The first selection in this chapter, "Principle Factors of 'Per Capita' Output," emphasizes the great variety of factors that are determinants of the level of living that may be found in a given area.

Morton R. Solomon's article, "The Structure of the Market in Underdeveloped Economies," sensitizes the reader to the details of the market in underdeveloped areas at 5 different levels. This article brings the reader close to the actual working of the market in these areas and is of particular importance to us because the sociological factors are implicitly recognized as determinants of price in addition to factors usually mentioned as determinants of behavior in similar analyses. A grasp of this article prepares the reader for additional readings on the economic characteristics of underdeveloped areas.

Since it is frequently argued that the percent of the gainfully occupied that are in tertiary production is a good index of the stage of economic development of a political entity, the article "Problems in Classifying Economic Activity in Underdeveloped Areas" by Peter T. Bauer and B. S. Yamey becomes highly relevant to the content of this chapter. Not only does this article present an excellent argument against this contention, but it likewise gives us another detailed view of an aspect of the underdeveloped economy.

"Income and Leisure in an Underdeveloped Economy" by Simon Rottenberg emphasizes the importance of values as determinants of the available supply of labor. This article points out, perhaps even more explicitly than the Solomon article and the Bauer and Yamey article, the importance of considering sociological factors in order to gain a complete understanding of the functioning of the economic institution.

PRINCIPAL FACTORS OF "PER CAPITA" OUTPUT*

LIST OF FACTORS

THE factors which govern the levels and trends of the *per capita* output of national economies are only imperfectly known. Data needed for measuring the effects of various factors are largely missing, and social and economic theory is not sufficiently developed to exploit fully the available data. In particular, the extent to which apparent effects of certain factors may really be due to other prior determinants shaping these factors has not been adequately explored. As a result, considerable differences of opinion exist among scholars in this field.

The attempts which have been made to isolate the main factors governing output vary in scope and value. In some cases, only one or a few factors have been stressed, while in others a complete inventory has been attempted. For the purpose of analysing the relative importance of demographic and other factors bearing on output, a nearly complete list of them is required. Otherwise the partial and the current influence of some factors may not adequately be taken into account. Such a list guards against the neglect of significant variables especially when the factors are many and somewhat interdependent.

A list of factors based on the work of Spengler but considerably re-arranged, is

given below.[1] For the present discussion, the list has been arranged with reference to the degree to which each factor may be influenced by population trends. Thus, the order of presentation is not intended to represent the relative importance of the various factors.

HUMAN RESOURCES

I. The ratio of the labour force to the total population.

II. The geographical and occupational distributions of the labour force, and the degree to which these distributions correspond to the requirements of demand and production.

III. The skill and efficiency of the labour force, considered independently of the non-human productive assets. This determinant reflects immediately (a) "the state of the industrial arts" and, in the long run, (b) the educational, scientific and cultural attainments of the population."

MATERIAL RESOURCES

IV. The amount of productive assets (e.g., land, machinery, buildings, and

* From "Effects of Population Growth on 'Per Capita' Output," Chapter XIII, *The Determinants and Consequences of Population Trends*, Population Studies No. 17, Population Division, Department of Social Affairs, United Nations, New York, 1953, pp. 220–222.

[1] These factors, based upon economic and non-economic literature relating to economic growth, were utilized by Spengler with respect to income movements in: "Theories of Socio-economic Growth," *Problems in the Study of Economic Growth*, National Bureau of Economic Research, New York, 1949, pp. 46–115, and with respect to industrialization in: Spengler, "Economic Factors in the Development of Densely Populated Areas," *Proceedings of the American Philosophical Society* (U.S.A.) Vol. 95, No. 1, February 1951, pp. 20–53.

other forms of capital) in use per employed member of the labour force.

V. The geographical location of productive assets and their distribution among types of employment.

ECONOMIC ORGANIZATION AND TECHNOLOGY

VI. The effectiveness with which economic activities are organized, which depends upon:

(a) The degree of specialization and division of labour in effect;

(b) The extent to which economies of scale, as distinguished from economies included under (a), are attained;

(c) The manner in which the activities of firms composing given industries are adjusted to those of firms composing other industries.

VII. The efficiency of the techniques by which productive assets are utilized.

VIII. The degree to which the labour force and the stock of non-human factors of production are employed, in terms of some stipulated normal rate per annum.

SOCIAL AND CULTURAL FACTORS

IX. The family and caste system.

X. The political elements of the social structure, including:

(a) The powers of direction and regulation in regard to economic activities exercised by the State;

(b) The class composition of society;

(c) The relations between classes and between other economically significant social groups.

XI. The economic elements of the social structure, including:

(a) The system of allocating resources (which may vary from an unregulated price system to one of complete planning);

(b) The system of property relations;

(c) The system of incentives;

(d) The system of institutions designed to facilitate the functioning of the economy, such as monetary, banking, fiscal and other financial institutions;

(e) The conditions surrounding the activities of persons performing entrepreneurial functions and making innovations;

(f) The extent to which prevailing habits of consumption are adjusted to the productive assets at the disposal of the population.

XII. Those elements in the prevailing value system which affect human behaviour with respect to economic goals and permissible ways of achieving these goals.

EXTERNAL ECONOMIC RELATIONS

XIII. The exchange relations obtaining between the economic society under analysis and other economic societies, especially terms of trade.

THE STRUCTURE OF THE MARKET IN UNDEVELOPED ECONOMIES*

MORTON R. SOLOMON

THIS paper attempts an examination of the market structure in the economically backward countries of the world today.

The dearth of written material on the market structure of undeveloped economies has compelled the writer to draw primarily upon his personal observations over a period of four years in the Middle East, but he has been encouraged and justified by two considerations into extending his analysis to the entire belt of densely populated undeveloped economies stretching from Southeastern Europe through the Middle East and India to China. First, the few empirical studies of the economies of Southeastern Europe, India and China yield data regarding the size and organization of production units (both agricultural and nonagricultural), customary marketing practices, distributive margins, spatial and temporal price differentials, etc., which are remarkably similar to the writer's observations in the Middle East, and therefore a theoretical analysis of market structure based on these observations appears to be valid for this entire geographical belt. Second, a preliminary theoretical consideration of the over-all problem makes one realize that the organization and structure of the market are probably a function of certain economic variables like the size of the

market, the nature of the goods, the size of the production units, the degree of specialization, etc. And these are the variables which show a basically similar pattern throughout the densely populated undeveloped economies, because they, in turn, are the products of a certain stage of economic development and technological advancement and relative factor supplies expressing itself in a production function varying little throughout this area. Expressed more concretely, it is the writer's belief that a definite type of market structure is to be found throughout this area, whose basic uniformity is eventually ascribable to a certain relationship of factor supplies—i.e. low capital *and* low natural resources per capita. In contrast, those undeveloped economies possessing large natural resources per capita —the sparsely populated undeveloped economies—have a market structure distinctly different, and are not treated in this paper. The sparsely populated undeveloped economies are characterized by specialized plantation farming, primarily for export to industrialized economies, with very little development of industry, urban life or local markets, while the densely populated economies—the subject matter of this study—reveal a peasant system of agriculture, nonspecialized farming, a large measure of foreign trade among themselves, and a considerable development of secondary industry, town and local markets.

* Adapted and reprinted by permission from *The Quarterly Journal of Economics*, Vol. LXII, August, 1948, pp. 519–537.

THE PERSONAL SERVICES MARKET

The problem of market structure is, in the first instance, a problem in classification. Sharply different marketing methods and market structures suggest the following five-fold classification for goods and services: personal services, perishable produce, agricultural staples, manufactured consumers' goods, and capital goods.

The personal services market occupies a much more minor rôle in an undeveloped than in an advanced economy. In rural areas it is largely non-existent, for each peasant family, through a household division of labor, itself satisfies in a crude fashion the bulk of its limited service requirements. The remaining and usually more skilled requirements (such as the blacksmith's and religious elder's services) that cannot be rendered within the family grouping are supplied within the village grouping. In these cases, the supplier of the service has a nominal monopoly within the village; other members of the village may be equally capable, but tradition and custom tend to dictate the choice of a particular person for each type of service. However, our village monopolist can rarely maximize his earnings, since just as tradition and custom give him his monopoly, so do they limit his fees to a narrow range. This conventional limitation of fees does not exclude, however, a certain amount of price discrimination based more upon the social than upon the financial status of the buyer.

In the towns and cities the subsistence existence of the bulk of the population does not permit them to resort to the personal services market; their needs are either met within the family, or very infrequently by charitable institutions, or—the usual case—ignored. Only the members of the middle and upper classes—probably less than 10 per cent of the population—resort to the organized personal services market. This market typically consists of a few artisans who occupy small shops but who also frequently work in the homes of their more important customers. They are often organized in sime sort of guild or association, but the functions and strengths of these vary enormously. It can be safely stated, however, that these associations are just as much concerned, if not more so, with political lobbying on a municipal level to protect themselves against what they consider excessive police and tax burdens as they are with wage and price policy.

The degree or generality of collusive wage and price fixing is unknown; that there is a remarkable uniformity of wages and prices in each local area is undeniable, but it may be explainable on two other grounds: (1) a strong wage and price rigidity through time is the tradition of this market; it encourages price conformity among suppliers, which in turn tends to reënforce the tradition-created rather than policy-created rigidity; (2) a preference for non-price forms of competition that is only natural in personal service oligopolies, and that is also present in the more developed economies of the world. However, the non-price forms of competition among personal service suppliers typical in undeveloped economies are not as much manifested in giving additional or better quality services as they are in creating psychological relationships with customers which will attract and maintain their patronage. An illustration of this phenomenon is the very prevalent custom of competitive flattery of one's patrons, an understandable tradition in a society where personal status in the local community is all-important. Price discrimination similar to that in the rural areas is prevalent in the towns, although it should be noted that in the towns it is even more of a conventional price discrimination than that which arises from a monopolistic position. Entry into the personal services trades is very difficult for outsiders, since the business units are invariably small and, therefore, selection of apprentices tends to be confined to family circles.

The structural rigidity and price inflexibility of the personal services market is reënforced by a surprising degree of government regulation. Government, on the municipal level, generally exercises more control over the personal services market than over any other type of market. Licensing, excise taxation, and even price fixing by government are prevalent in this sector of the economy to an extent unapproached in the other sectors. Government price fixing in this area is not an emergency device to combat inflationary pressures, but a permanent practice which seems to serve no real function, since the municipal price-list simply recognizes the *de facto* situation when the infrequent changes do occur.

THE PERISHABLE PRODUCE MARKET

The perishable produce market (fruits, vegetables, meat and dairy products) also occupies a considerably less important place in the undeveloped than in the developed economy. Perishable produce farming is rarely specialized in the undeveloped economy; typically it represents a part, usually a small part, of each peasant farmer's total output. Produce, unlike cereals and other staples, belongs entirely to the peasant, since even tenant peasants do not share their perishable produce production with landlords. On a rough average, less than half is consumed by the peasant producer, even though his output is very small; the bulk is marketed, since perishable produce is considered a semi-luxury. Marketing is direct by the peasant farmer to the retailer, or to the final consumer in his home or at the market-place. There is no wholesaling or jobber class in perishable produce. Nor is there any speculation in this market for the same reason— the impossibility of inventory holding due to the lack of suitable storage facilities.

Prices are determined by individual bargaining, whether with the retailer or the consumer; they are extremely flexible, since the daily supply is inelastic, the farmer being unwilling to cart his produce back to the farm. Seasonal price variations are, of course, very wide, owing to the lack of storage facilities and feasible transportation from climatically different areas. These individual bargaining transactions between peasant and retailer, or peasant and consumer, approach the nature of isolated exchange, with the exact location of each transaction's price depending upon the two parties' indifference curves and bluffing abilities; but this is only within a narrow range limited by a knowledge of probable competitive offers if either party waits a while.

Analysis of the elasticity conditions of demand and supply in this market give these results. The fairly elastic nature of consumer demand schedules and the slight tendency of the peasant producers to vary somewhat their own consumption of produce inversely to price are price stabilizing factors; but the purely local nature of the market, which prevents supply movements to and from other areas in response to price, the variations in the quantity of produce transported to the market from day to day, and the necessity of disposing of the entire day's supply, once it has been transported, are factors of greater weight making for extreme short-run price variations. The individual peasant producer is confronted by a horizontal demand curve, in that variation in his output will not affect market prices, but it is important to note that owing to his unquestioning submission to custom, he does not vary his output (i.e. re-allocate his resources) in response to market price movements. If the function of a price system is the proper allocation of productive resources, as well as the rationing of goods, it is apparently not performing that function in the perishable produce market of the undeveloped economies. This relative constancy from year to year in the proportion of the peasant producer's resources allocated to perishable produce production implies that long-run or secular price trends in this market of the undeveloped economy must be explained primarily through studies of shifting demand conditions.

The regional pattern of supply flows in this market is extremely well defined and invariant. Unless situated more or less centrally between two towns, the peasant farmer almost invariably transports his perishable produce to the nearest town, which is usually serviced from a 10 to 30-mile radius. Although the lack of any marketing organization here is wasteful, in that each farmer has to act as transporter, it seems probable that the elimination of the generally very large profits of wholesaling merchants probably results in lower priced produce for the consumer. Given the exclusively local nature of this market, the price differentials among the local market areas are, naturally, extremely wide. Wide spatial price differentials are, of course, an outstanding feature in all markets of an undeveloped economy, but they are greatest in the perishable produce market. Only high-priced produce, such as some fruits, will ever be reshipped from a local market (i.e. the town that is the center for the surrounding peasant villages in a 10 to 30-mile radius). The tendency in these low-standard-of-living undeveloped economies to consider all perishable produce a semi-luxury, plus the relative unimportance of the market, probably explain the lack of

government intervention. Municipal price control has been applied in some areas, but apparently for formal reasons of consistency with price control in other types of markets, since enforcement in this sector is rarely attempted.

THE AGRICULTURAL STAPLES MARKET

The third in our category of markets, that of agricultural staples, consisting primarily of cereals and rice, is not only relatively more important in the undeveloped than the developed economy, unlike the two preceding markets, but is overwhelmingly the most important market judged by any economic criterion. In a sense, it is the most typical in market organization and structure, for these directly reflect the essential features of an undeveloped economy qua undeveloped—little real capital formation, subsistence standard of living, importance of the middleman, network of local market areas, etc.

The most significant fact for the agricultural staples market is that the individual peasant, whether he be tenant or proprietor, cultivates such a small acreage that after meeting his needs and obligations he has little or no crop to dispose of on the market. Home consumption (since staples supply the main diet), seed required for next year's sowing, and, if a tenant, the landlord's share of the crop account for 70 to 100 per cent of the peasant's output. The result is that the bulk of the staples reaching the market is owned and disposed of by large landlords, whether share-receiving landlords or large-scale active agricultural entrepreneurs. Since the large landlords' holdings are customarily contiguous, or at least tend to be in the same locality, the number of important market suppliers in each local producing-marketing area is very small. The local market is thus characterized in the producer-middleman transaction by a small group of big sellers (landlords) and a large varying number of unimportant sellers (peasants). The large landlords may sell on a fixed-price contract basis to merchants or wholesalers at harvest time, or they may gradually sell their stocks at the currently quoted local market prices over the course of the year to the same or other wholesalers, all of whom are located in the local town market of the producing area. The small peasant producers having surpluses usually sell to the wholesalers at the local market quotation, rather than on fixed-price contract. Neither landowners nor peasants sell staple crops directly to retailers, primarily because landowners are reluctant to engage in commercial activity, and because neither peasant nor retailer has the capital to enable him to carry the stocks required to maintain a regular flow of trade.

Each large landlord is very conscious of the size of his large competitors' crops, any contractual sales they may have made, the rate at which they are offering supplies to the market, and of the effect on the price quotations in the local town market of any large amounts he may offer. He does not react by curtailing his output, either independently or in collusion, and therefore his sales over a long period of time are not curtailed either, partly because he may have no control over the total quantities grown by his peasant tenants. Instead, he attempts to maximize his profits by creating favorable local market price movements through variations in the supply flows that he controls. Although collusion among landlords in this type of control would certainly pay, there is apparently very little—probably due to an even greater degree of the same type of mutual distrust that often breaks up an industrial cartel. Peasants also go in for hoarding when they see an upward price movement and their landlords withholding supplies from the market, but their reactions are usually constrained by the pressure of debts and the immediate need for cash. This local market manipulation, which is reënforced by the interests and activities of the speculative middlemen, results in relatively wide swings in the price quotations of the very thin local market. The meagreness of the market naturally facilitates manipulation, but makes the sudden disposal of large inventories very difficult.

The output of agricultural staples in undeveloped economies is very inelastic with respect to price, especially in an upward direction. The peasant producer has severely limited land and labor resources, cannot increase his productivity because he lacks capital equipment, and lives so close to the subsistence level that the amount of seed he can sow is a direct function of the size of last year's crop. A good crop the preceding year may have meant a lower price but, more important, it also provided for a large quantity of seed to be sown the following year. It is interesting to note that just as the competitively determined prices in the perishable produce market do not seem to influence the allocation of resources, so the locally manipulated prices in the agricultural staples market do not seem to influence the allocation of resources. The heavy hand of peasant tradition creates a price inelasticity of output that is apparent even in the long run, for long-run shifts over the decades in the agricultural allocation of resources appear, on specific examination, to be due to non-price factors.

The merchants, like the landlords, are very conscious of each other's buying and selling policies. This could conceivably result in intense rivalry, but in practice there seems to be a recognition of their common interests in manipulating the local market. If a leading merchant begins large-scale hoarding, other merchants find it to their advantage to help the price movement along by withholding also, for it is the size of the profit margin on a given inventory rather than the expansion of business that means profit maximization under these conditions.

In their routine distribution to retailers (and, in the case of the few inedible staples, to secondary industry), the wholesalers' margins are markedly high, even though here increased selling volume is presumably an objective and thus the competitive process might be expected to reduce these extremely high margins.

The middleman stands at the crossroads of economic life in the undeveloped economy, and thereby occupies an unusually powerful position. The theoretical justification for the middleman is that through specialization he performs more efficiently and cheaply the function of linking the producer with a market demand increasingly distant in time and space. But the middleman in the undeveloped economy does not appear to service a large enough market, either in time or space, to derive these economies. It seems unquestionable that his exaggerated position arises primarily from his control of the only capital available to carry inventories.

Considered in its spatial and temporal framework the agricultural staples market, like the perishable produce market, reveals a network of price differentials through space and time. But although the costs and risks of transportation through space and the costs and risks of storage through time are sufficiently large to create an essentially local and manipulable market in each area, they are nowhere as large as the price differentials in perishable produce.

THE MANUFACTURED CONSUMERS' GOODS MARKET

The manufactured consumers' goods market is supplied in undeveloped econo-mies by all of the following: rural industries, urban handicrafts, the putting-out or domestic system, factories, and imports. The evolutionary development of the first four of the "stages" which the advanced industrialized economies experienced has been varied in the undeveloped economies through imitation of the factory mode of production. This early adoption of factory production, plus an increasing reliance upon imports, may account for the less important rôle that the putting-out or domestic system is playing today in the undeveloped economies than it did in the historical evolution of the industrialized economy, and certainly explain the decline of rural industries and handicrafts. To a large extent, rural industries, such as weaving, have become a factor in the market on the initiative of the merchant who commissions the work, and thus they are identified to some extent with the domestic putting-out system. The merchant operating a domestic system in either rural or urban areas does not appear to possess any particular control over the market, because even if he is the sole employer in the area he must compete with local handicrafts and the imports and domestic factory goods that find their way into the most remote areas. However, he receives a large return on his capital—even larger than that customarily received by the merchant wholesaler in agricultural staples—which, judged by an advanced economy, might misleadingly indicate some control over the market.

Urban handicrafts are largely sold by the craftsmen themselves, who operate under conditions of fairly constant costs and very little overhead. Total unit costs vary little from area to area within an undeveloped economy, as a result of the generally equalized distribution of the production factors needed for this output, and thus there is little area specialization. Given constant costs more or less similar in the various market areas of an un-developed economy, an improvement in transportation facilities would not widen the essentially local nature of the handi-craft market. It would simply abolish it, once production units were established capable of achieving large-scale economies through extension of the market. Handi-craftsmen in the undeveloped economies are frequently organized in guilds, but the price fixing abilities of the guilds are limited by the competition of imports and domestic factory output.

Factory production of manufactured consumers' goods is found to some extent in all the undeveloped economies, custom-arily beginning with textiles, whose suc-cessful development is primarily due to the use of the inexpensive unskilled labor made available by the low labor produc-tivity in densely populated undeveloped economies. Factory units vary considera-bly in size, the smaller plants servicing only their local markets, while the few large plants enter many local markets. But whether small or large, the factory plants are predominantly located in or near urban market centers; there they have direct access to markets, a larger labor sup-ply (since there is little labor mobility in these countries), and less risk of dam-age or pilferage in transporting the fin-ished goods (the risks of transporting their raw materials being less, and usually rest-ing on the raw material sellers). Further-more, the types of raw materials used in the light consumers' goods manufacturing of undeveloped economies are neither bulky nor limited to special areas. Fi-nally, and possibly most important, there is the greater security of an urban center for the protection of physical property. This concentration of factories, like hand-icrafts, near urban markets increases price differentials among local markets; they are still not as large as in perishable produce or agricultural staples markets.

There seems to be little or no vertical integration or horizontal combination among factories manufacturing consumer goods, vertical integration not being very meaningful in this type of simple consum-ers' goods manufacturing, and horizontal combination of little use where a factory rarely has other factory competitors in the same local market and competition comes chiefly from imports and handicrafts. As far as other local market areas are con-cerned, factory owners tend to be re-luctant to make investments where they are not residents and cannot watch those investments.

Considerable differences appear in the crudity and quality of the products of dif-ferent factories, but little product differen-tiation is attempted. Advertising and other non-price forms of competition designed to obtain a larger share of the market are negligible. Although the lone factory pro-ducer in a local market is sometimes loosely referred to as a local monopolist, the competition of imports in most mar-ket areas and the luxury nature of manu-factured consumers' goods in a subsistence economy confronts him with a more or less horizontal and elastic demand curve. Even in the more inaccessible areas where large transportation costs give the small local producer control over the mar-ket within certain price limits, he cus-tomarily will not curtail output in order to raise price, because he can usually dis-pose of his entire output at the maximum price—that is, the local price of the im-port. The great importance of imports on the operations of domestic factory pro-ducers of consumers' goods is indicated by the fact that in the period before the war those undeveloped economies geo-graphically nearer to the industrialized ex-porting countries operated their consum-ers' goods factories at lower percentages of capacity.

The manufactured consumers' goods

market, unlike the perishable produce and agriculture staples markets, is characterized by a considerable degree of price stability, due to very rigid wage rates, the constant cost conditions in the handicrafts trades, and the practice of fixing prices to meet the competition of industrial imports subject to administered pricing in industrialized countries. This price stability, as is evident, is not a manifestation of monopolistic rigidity.

On the retailing end, price competition is dominant. In fact, the tendency to vary prices within a certain range as a result of individual bargaining between the consumer and the retailer intensifies the importance of price to the average consumer, who tends to do more comparative shopping as a result.

Government intervention in the manufactured consumers' goods market frequently takes the form of direct investment—i.e. the building and operation of large factories—and infrequently the sponsoring of coöperatives. Operation of the government factories has been on a commercial basis, prices conforming to the market, but has generally not been profitable, due to a more than customary degree of nepotism and inefficiency. Profit-margin fixing on mass consumption articles, especially imports such as sugar and tea, is not uncommon but rarely effective.

Perhaps the most significant type of government intervention—and one I believe peculiar to the undeveloped economies—is the unwitting creation of uncertainty and risk for the factory owner and importer through the government's willingness to legislate and act, inconsistently and haphazardly, on any and all matters. Government has no laissez-faire conception of a clearly defined free economic sphere distinct from its own province, nor on the other hand does it have a planned economy conception of its responsibilities.

Therefore, its intervention takes the form of spasmodic and inconsistent sallies into various sectors of the economy. Without warning, and depending upon the ideas of whoever is in power, the free import of a particular commodity may be succeeded by a total ban which may then be replaced by a succession of tariff rates, or by the active encouragement of private capital investment to manufacture the commodity, which may then give way to the granting of a private monopoly and/or the construction and operation of government factories. Price fixing often *alternates* with a free market, and the increasing necessity of adopting import quotas permits even greater scope to the arbitrariness and unpredictability of government policy. The undeveloped economies have thus contrived to obtain all the disadvantages of an economy lacking both vigorous enterprise and central planning. The facetious expression, "neither free nor enterprise," is a correct description of the undeveloped economy.

THE CAPITAL GOODS MARKET

The capital goods market, the fifth and last of our market classifications, is naturally the least developed in the undeveloped economies, but its structure and future development will have important directional effects upon the economic development of these countries. At present, these countries find it necessary to import the bulk of their relatively small capital goods requirements, partly because of the economic handicaps (unskilled labor, lack of know-how, etc.) that were also present in the early stages of the development of Western economies, but also partly because of the insecurity generated by a political philosophy of economic life that is neither laissez-faire nor paternalistic, and has no discernible principles of what is a proper rôle for government and what is not. So great, for this reason, has been the reluctance of capital-possessing merchants and landowners to immobilize their liquid and semi-liquid assets (paper money, precious metals, stocks of goods, etc.) through real capital formation that an increasing proportion of the relatively small capital goods importation and production is being undertaken by the governments themselves, who are also tending to replace foreigners' direct investments in this field. The latter are finding that, except where direct political ties and therefore control exist, their investments are increasingly threatened by rising nationalistic feeling and political insecurity. The extent of direct government importation of capital goods for public projects and for the construction of government-owned consumers' goods and capital goods factories is startling to the Western observer, who tends to assume that government ownership and administration of factories is a concomitant of very advanced economies and sophisticated governments. Governmental dominance in the field of capital goods production is particularly evident when a rapid rate of industrialization is being forced on the population, which typically wants industrialization but is not prepared to reduce immediate consumption or do anything else to help obtain it.

Whatever *private* capital goods production there is (e.g. some iron and steel, some cement, etc.) definitely enjoys positions of monopoly and is usually not controlled as to price, in spite of similar governmental intervention in other markets. Its only competition comes from very expensive imports (due to transport costs), or to the equally expensive output of government operated factories.

Before closing the analysis of the market structure in undeveloped economies a few words about the nature of the money market seem advisable, since its peculiarities help to explain the business behavior and market structure we have been examining. First, there is no long-term money market to speak of in these countries; the general desire for liquidity is so strong that neither individuals nor private banks will lend money for more than a year or two, not even to the government. This inability of government to sell securities to its own people is the primary reason for the establishment of national central banks in virtually all of the undeveloped economies, for it is only from this source that governments can obtain credits. Governments are increasingly trying to improve the long-term agricultural credit situation by setting up special farm banks and sponsoring rural credit coöperatives designed to supply credit at lower rates, but to date they service very few of the farmers. Second, private banks, frequently branches of large European banks, concentrate on short-term lending to merchants at interest rates of 10–15 per cent a year. Those merchants and farmers unable to establish credit lines with the banks are forced to obtain short-term loans from the numerous individual money lenders at interest rates of 25 to 35 per cent a year, and sometimes higher. Third, there is no evidence of collusive control or monopoly over the money market. However, the existence of competitive conditions in the money market has apparently not been a sufficient condition for restraining interest rates from exceeding even those high levels understandable in an economy characterized by capital scarcity; the competitive process offers no solution for the problem of a "liquidity complex."

It is this reluctance to sacrifice liquidity or, if you prefer, it is the high productivity of capital that explains huge profit margins, even in those few sectors of the economy not characterized by any apparent market control. It also explains, along with what I have called the "government generated insecurity," the paradoxical failure to meet the crying need for real capital formation for the production of consumers' goods and capital goods when there *are* available considerable quantities of liquid capital and other resources. For the merchant-capitalists can play safer by lending out their money, or engaging in the agricultural staples trade, or in the importation of consumers' goods,

all at rates of return which they would have difficulty in obtaining as manufacturers of consumer and capital goods. They are behaving like true economic men and applying their resources in the "best" (i.e. most productive) of the possible uses for their capital—but the result is by no means best for the economy as a whole.

PROBLEMS OF CLASSIFYING ECONOMIC ACTIVITY IN UNDERDEVELOPED AREAS*

P. T. BAUER AND B. S. YAMEY

THE principal purpose of this article is to examine the validity and significance of the widely held view that economic progress is generally associated with certain distinct, necessary and predictable changes in occupational distribution, in particular with a relative increase in the numbers engaged in tertiary activities.[1] Our method is

largely analytical; but since a strong empirical basis is claimed for the generalisation we are examining, we have found it necessary to make frequent descriptive reference to the composition of economic activity in economies at different stages of development. Most of the description is concentrated in the first section of the article, which describes and analyses the volume and significance of trading activity in British West Africa. The remaining sections of the article examine the analytical and statistical foundations of the generalisation and suggest that these are defective.

I

The few available occupational statistics of backward economies, especially in the

* Revised and reprinted by permission from "Economic Progress and Occupational Distribution," *The Economic Journal*, No. 244, Vol. LXI, December 1951, pp. 741–755.
[1] "For convenience in international comparisons production may be defined as primary, secondary and tertiary. Under the former we include agricultural and pastoral production, fishing, forestry and hunting. Mining is more properly included with secondary production, covering manufacture, building construction and public works, gas and electricity supply. Tertiary production is defined by difference as consisting of all other economic activities, the principal of which are distribution, transport, public administration, domestic service and all other activities producing a non-material output." Colin Clark, *The Conditions of Economic Progress*, 1st edition, p. 182.

See also, Professor, A. G. B. Fisher, *Economic Progress and Social Security*, pp. 5 and 6.

colonies, purport to show that the great bulk of the population is occupied in agriculture. This impression is also often conveyed in official statements on economic activity in these territories. An example may be taken from *An African Survey*:

"In the Northern Province of Nigeria, at the census of 1931, about 84% of occupied males whose returns permitted them to be classified were shown as engaged in agriculture and fishing, about 9% in manufacture, and under 3% in commerce and finance. . . . For Southern Nigeria less detailed information is available. The returns, which are less reliable than those for Northern Nigeria, would suggest that the proportion of males engaged in agriculture is about 82% and that concerned with handicrafts about 4.7%."[2]

Trade and transport are not mentioned. No attempt is made to reconcile this with another statement (on the same page) that almost 30% of the population of Nigeria lived in towns of over 5,000 inhabitants. In the same vein the official *Annual Report on Nigeria* states year after year that the great majority of the population is occupied in agriculture: trade is not among the other occupations listed.

In contrast to these statements and statistics a remarkable multitude of traders, especially of small-scale sellers of both local produce and of imported merchandise, is a most conspicuous feature of West Africa. This is so apparent that it has not escaped attention. It is freely said by responsible administrators that in the southern parts of Nigeria and the Gold Coast everybody is engaged in trade, and this is hardly an exaggeration.

For reasons to be explained it is not possible to give specific quantitative information about the volume of trade or of the numbers engaged in it. Certain sporadic but conservative data, relating, for example, to numbers of market stallholders' and hawkers' licenses, indicate that the number of selling points, including children hawking very small quantities of goods, is very large in the principal markets. But the figures give an imperfect idea of the multitude of people engaged either part-time or whole-time in selling small quantities of goods or conveying them to dispersed points of sale. In the aggregate there is an enormous amount of activity the quantitative significance of which is obvious to the observer.

The seriously misleading impression created by official statistics and statements derives from the inappropriateness of classification by distinct occupational categories in an economy in which occupational specialization is imperfect. The economic activity of a large proportion of the population of West Africa is better described as the performance of a number of different things rather than as the pursuit of a definite occupation. In many of the so-called agricultural households the head of the household trades part-time even during the normally short farming season, and more actively outside the season, whilst members of the family trade intermittently throughout the year. Even if only main activities are considered, it is doubtful whether five-sixths of the population is engaged in agriculture; when it is realised that even the head of the family is likely to have part-time economic activities and that many of his dependents (including children) are engaged at least periodically in trade, it becomes clear that the official statistics in their present form are apt to mislead.

The imperfect specialisation of economic activity is not confined to the agricultural community. Many African doctors and lawyers and almost all the leading chiefs have extensive trading interests. Government employees and servants of

[2] *An African Survey*, 2nd edition, pp. 1425–1426.

the European population trade part-time, either importing merchandise or dealing in merchandise and foodstuffs bought locally. The fluidity of activity extends to personal relations where they bear closely on economic life. A prominent African trader in Lagos whose children are being educated at expensive universities and schools in England includes his wife among his principal retailer customers. Similar commercial relations exist between other prominent Africans and their wives and children.

Even where the conceptual and statistical difficulties arising from imperfect occupational specialisation are fully appreciated[3] it is difficult to collect the required information on subsidiary activities of individuals, particularly on part-time trade. Africans frequently do not regard trade as an occupation, especially when carried on by dependents, and would not refer to it as such when questioned, because they regard it as part of existence and not as a distinct occupation. In many cases it may not be possible to draw the line between the social and commercial activities of, say, a group of women traders in the market. There is, however, no doubt that the commercial element is generally substantial.

Once the level of economic activity has risen from that of a subsistence economy to that of an emerging exchange economy —a process which is encouraged and promoted by the activities of traders—the task of distribution may require a substantial volume of resources. Much depends upon physical and climatic conditions. But the circumstances of West Africa are certainly not exceptional in requiring a large volume of distributive activity. The large

[3] It is not suggested that those responsible for census work in the colonies are unaware of these difficulties. But they are not appreciated by many of those who publish and use the results of their work.

number of dispersed farmers and holdings, poor natural communications and long distances and the difficulties of prolonged storage in the open, together postulate a substantial volume of resources in distribution and transport for raising and maintaining the economy above the subsistence level even at an early stage in economic development. In this type of economy the indispensable tasks of assembly, bulking, transport, breaking of bulk and dispersal may require a large proportion of available resources. Moreover, in an economy which has recently emerged from the subsistence level, some transactions are still likely to be on a barter basis. Barter tends to use more resources, especially labour, than a fully developed money economy to transact a given volume of trade.

There is in West Africa widespread involuntary idleness of unskilled labour, resulting from lack of other co-operant resources, especially capital, to set it to work. This lack of employment is a major feature of comparatively underdeveloped economies which in the aggregate comprise probably over half of the population of the world, including India, China, Java, large parts of Eastern and Southern Europe and much of Africa. The dependence of the volume of employment on the amount of the stock of capital used to be a major topic of political economy. The subject gradually receded from economic discussion as economists became preoccupied mainly with unemployment in advanced industrial economies, resulting not so much from lack of co-operant resources as from fluctuations in aggregate demand or various other influences discouraging investment and enterprise.

The missing co-operant factor (or factors) of production can be capital, land or technical and administrative skill. The type of scarcity or its incidence varies greatly in different regions and even districts in West Africa as elsewhere. But in many regions the low level of capital and of suitable administrative and technical skills constitutes the principal shortage.

Entry into small-scale trade is easy, as at this level no technical or administrative skill is required and only very little capital. Trade is attractive even for very low rewards in view of the absence of more profitable alternatives. Women and children are also available for trade, partly for social reasons; for example, in some areas the wife is expected to make a contribution to the family's income; also there is little for women to do in the house and there are few schools for children.[4]

The type of resources to be found in trade and transport depends, given the state of technique, upon the relative terms at which different productive resources are available. In an economy such as West Africa, where capital is scarce and expensive and unskilled labour abundant and cheap, the large volume of resources in distribution and transport consists very largely of labour. As compared with more advanced economies there is a mass emphasis on labour rather than on capital. This tendency, which may proceed very far and reveal unsuspected possibilities, permeates West African trading arrangements; a few examples will illustrate it.

In West Africa there is an extensive trade in empty containers such as kerosene, cigarette and soup tins, flour, salt, sugar and cement bags and beer bottles. Some types of container are turned into household articles or other commodities. Small oil-lamps are made from cigarette

[4] It is possible that the numbers attracted into trade in West Africa are increased because of a largely institutional rigidity in money wages. But even if money wages were to fall to the equilibrium level the number who would find trade attractive would still be very large as long as the underlying economic factors remained broadly unchanged.

and soup tins, whilst salt bags are made into shirts or tunics. But more usually the containers are used again in the storage and movement of goods. Those who seek out, purchase, carry and distribute second-hand containers maintain the stock of capital. They prevent the destruction of the containers, usually improve their condition, distribute them to where they can best be used, and so extend their usefulness, the intensity of their use and their effective life. The activities of the traders represent a substitution of labour for capital. Most of the entrepreneurs in the container trade are women or children. The substitution is economic as long as six or eight hours of their time are less valuable (in view of the lack of alternatives) than the small profit to be made from the sale of a few empty containers. So far from the system being wasteful it is highly economic in substituting superabundant for scarce resources; within the limits of available technical skill nothing is wasted in West Africa.

For various reasons, of which the low level of capital is one, the individual agriculturalist produces on a very small scale. Moreover, the same lack of capital is reflected in the absence of suitable storage facilities and of cash reserves. As a result each producer has to dispose of small quantities of produce at frequent intervals as they become available during and immediately after the harvesting season. This postulates a large number of intermediaries, who, because of the high cost of capital, employ methods of transportation using relatively little capital and much labour. Donkey and bicycle transport are examples, while in some cases there is still head loading and human porterage, especially in the short-distance movement of local crops. The available transport equipment is used continuously with the assistance of large quantities of labour (subject to frequent breakdowns owing to poor roads and low technical skill).

The same phenomenon of the more intensive use of capital, that is its more rapid turnover, can be observed in the breaking of bulk into the minute quantities in which imported merchandise is bought by the ultimate consumer. The purchase of a box of matches is often still a wholesale transaction as the buyer frequently breaks bulk and re-sells the contents to the final consumer in small bundles of ten to fifteen matches. Similarly, at the petty retail stage sugar is sold in lots of three cubes, trade perfume by the drop, salt by the cigarette tin and cheap biscuits by the small heap of three or six. The small purchases are the result of low incomes and low capital, and the activities of the numerous petty retailers represent a substitution of labour for capital.

In Nigeria the small number of telephones and the low rate of literacy render it necessary for the importing firms and the larger distributors to use the services of numerous intermediaries to keep contact with smaller traders and to distribute their goods to them at an economic rate of turnover. The intermediaries reduce the size of stocks which need to be held. This is of particular importance, since the low level of fixed capital tends to enhance the economy's requirements of working capital. The large accumulation of unrailed groundnuts in the producing region of Nigeria is a familiar instance of a general problem.

The narrowness of markets and the backwardness of communications are reflected in inter-regional price differences which provide profitable opportunities for successful arbitrage (particularly in locally produced goods), from region to region. This attracts traders and intermediaries, and also makes it profitable for non-trading travellers to take part in trade, which they frequently do on a casual basis.

The foregoing may be summarized as follows: in West Africa, as in other emerging economies, the indispensable task of commodity distribution is expensive relatively to available resources; of the available resources, capital is scarce and unskilled labour is abundant; the multiplicity of traders is the result of the mass use of unskilled labour instead of capital in the performance of the task of distribution. There is an extensive demand for the services of intermediaries, and there is a large section of the population available to perform these services at a low supply price in terms of daily earnings.

II

The description and analysis of Section I show that there are severe limitations and qualifications to the generalisation that a high proportion of labour in tertiary production is both a consequence of and a pointer to a high standard of living.

The analytical reasoning purporting to sustain this generalisation seems to be based on the view that tertiary production is less essential than primary or secondary production; and that its products are in the nature of luxuries which cannot be afforded in economies with low real incomes. In essence the argument is that the income elasticity of demand for tertiary products is higher than that for the products of primary and secondary activities; and that therefore the demand for tertiary products increases relatively more rapidly with economic progress. Moreover, it is argued that technical progress is relatively slower in tertiary production. For both reasons taken together the proportion of occupied labour in tertiary production is supposed to rise with economic progress.

This viewpoint is open to criticism on several independent grounds of which the following are the most important. First, a substantial proportion of tertiary products are not luxuries with a relatively high income elasticity of demand; conversely, some products of primary and secondary production, possibly on a large scale in their aggregate, are such luxuries. Secondly, there may be large-scale substitution of capital for labour in tertiary production in the course of economic progress. Thirdly, the concept of the income elasticity of demand applied to a whole economy raises problems of aggregation which render doubtful any universal proposition about changes in its average value in conditions of change and economic growth; and this is particularly doubtful when relative factor prices and the distribution of incomes change.

For reasons already mentioned in Section I the distributive task in the early stages of economic development is likely to be expensive in terms of *all* resources. A considerable volume of trading and transport is necessary to develop and sustain an exchange economy at an early stage of its development; it is an essential prerequisite for the development of specialisation and thus to the raising of productivity in primary production. Thus the proportion of resources engaged in tertiary production, notably in trade and transport, is likely to be high. It is possible that this proportion may fall at certain stages because the distributive task becomes relatively easier and less expensive in resources as the economy develops. The task may become lighter with the growth of internal security, the development and improvement of communications and the growth and stabilisation of markets, all of which contribute towards more regular and continuous commercial contacts, more intensive use of available resources in distribution and an increase in the size of trading units. These improvements are likely to have differential effects on productivity in various types of economic activity. It is not unlikely that trade and transport may be

particularly favourably affected, and thus that the proportion of resources engaged in them may decline. This decline may continue until the fall is arrested by the possibly increasing volume of other kinds of tertiary products (including more elaborate distributive services) which may be called for at higher levels of real income.

Tertiary production, as it is usually understood, comprises a heteregeneous collection of different services. Some of these are qualitatively indispensable throughout economic development and quantitatively important at an early stage; others are not indispensable at all stages and are quantitatively important only in more advanced economies. The term "tertiary" carries the misleading suggestion that all these services belong to the latter category of luxuries.

There is no *a priori* reason to believe that as wealth increases a greater proportion of the luxuries consumed must be products of tertiary activities. The durable consumer goods of the North American economies provide numerous examples on a large scale of heavy expenditure on the products of secondary activities with growing wealth. Expensive motor cars, jewellery, works of art, mass produced but high-grade textiles and hand-made bespoke clothes and shoes are products of secondary activities.

The proportion of all resources in tertiary production will not provide an index of economic progress. Moreover, even if it did it would not follow that the proportion of occupied labour engaged in tertiary production must rise with economic progress. This proposition would be valid only if additionally it were legitimate to assume that labour and other productive resources were employed in tertiary production in fixed proportions. This would be true only if substitution were not possible in the whole range of tertiary production, or if the relative terms upon which labour and other factors of production could be obtained remained unchanged throughout the whole course of economic progress. These assumptions are inadmissible. Technical possibilities of substitution between productive resources are obviously possible in tertiary production; and clearly the terms on which labour and capital are available are certain to change in a growing economy.

In Section I examples have been given to show the emphasis in the use of labour rather than capital in tertiary production in an under-developed economy. An example has also been given (the trade in used containers) to show how a tertiary activity expands with a lavish use of labour to make good a shortage in the products of secondary production. Conversely, examples abound in more advanced industrialised economies where capital replaces labour in tertiary activities and where secondary production expands to economise on labour-intensive tertiary activities. There are familiar examples on a large scale in domestic services, laundry and repair services, and restaurant and retailing services, where capital equipment is now used instead of labour. The purchase of pre-cooked or prepared canned or processed food, or of paper cups and plates intended for one use only, represents an extension of secondary production to replace the tertiary activities in the kitchen. The mass substitution of capital for labour in tertiary activity in North America is as striking as the reverse substitution in West Africa.[5]

The neglect of the "substitution effect" destroys the general validity of the quantitative law connecting society's real income and the proportion of occupied population in tertiary production. Technical prog-

ress may greatly affect the demand for labour in primary, secondary and tertiary production, the possibilities of substitution between labour and other resources and the relative supply prices of productive resources.

Changes in relative factor prices and differential rates of technical progress in different branches of production will also affect the relative prices at which different luxuries (that is, goods or services with relatively high income elasticities of demand whether the products of primary, secondary or tertiary production) are available to consumers. This need not necessarily favour the luxuries which are the products of tertiary activities. If it were true, as is sometimes assumed, that productivity increases faster in secondary than in tertiary production, there would be a tendency for consumers to substitute luxuries which are produced by secondary production to those produced by tertiary production.

In any society it is unlikely that all members spend the same proportion of their incomes on tertiary products. Differences may arise either because of differences in incomes or because of differences in tastes and individual circumstances. The share of the total national expenditure on tertiary products is obviously an average for the population as a whole. There is no ground for assuming a unique relationship between changes in this average and changes in national income. Indeed, this average may well fall if the bulk of any increase in the national income accrues to members whose relative expenditure on tertiary products is below the average. In these circumstances the average can be pulled down, even though the income elasticity of demand of each member for tertiary products exceeds unity (which, of course, is by no means necessary). This is a very likely contingency in societies such as India and China, where a large proportion of the

[5] Of course even in West Africa the time may come when eight hours of a woman's time may be more valuable than the profit margin on the sale of three beer bottles.

population live near starvation levels and where there are great differences in the proportion of individual incomes spent on tertiary products. If in such communities there is a general increase in productivity the proportion of the total national expenditure devoted to the products of primary and secondary activity is almost certain to increase. The same increase in productivity is likely to reduce the superfluity of very cheap labor formerly available for employment in certain types of tertiary activity, notably domestic service, petty trade and menial tasks generally, and may thus accentuate the relative decline in tertiary activity.

A reduction in the national average expenditure on teritary products may also be brought about as a result of other causes not necessarily connected with increasing productivity. Thus graduated taxation and social-security payments may reduce the share of national expenditure on tertiary products through their effects on the pattern of demand and on the supply price of labour.

An important practical conclusion follows from the possibility that there may be a fall in the average proportion of expenditure on products of a relatively high income elasticity of demand with an increase in income if this proposition is extended internationally. If a large proportion of an increase in world income accrues to countries or to individuals who spend a smaller proportion than the world average on products of a luxury type it follows that the demand for luxuries would suffer a relative decline. This would tend to turn the terms of trade in favour of the producers of relative necessities and against the producers of relative luxuries. On an international scale the luxuries would be mainly the products of industrialised countries. There is implicit in this possibility a threat to the standard of living of some of these countries. It reinforces the more familiar argument based on population increase, especially in the primary producing countries. The relative demand for the essentials of life can clearly increase either because there are more mouths to feed or because an increase in incomes accrues largely to the relatively poor.[6]

The foregoing analysis may now be summarised. Even if acceptable statistics were found which should show that the proportion of tertiary activities has increased in particular countries with economic progress the findings would not be evidence of any necessary or predictable tendency. Tertiary production is an aggregation of many dissimilar activities, including domestic service, government service, transport, retail and wholesale distribution, entertainment, education and others. There is no reason why the demand for every one of these should follow a common trend. The only feature common to all tertiary production is that the output is non-material. This does not appear to provide a logical category of significance in the analysis of demand or of economic progress. Moreover, on the supply side the proportion of the labour force in tertiary production depends upon a number of different forces, the individual and total effect of which is in no way unambiguously determined by secular changes in the national income. Thus any observed correlation between economic progress and occupational distribution should be regarded as more in the nature of a statistical accident than as an indication or proof of a significant economic law.

III

Clear-cut occupational classifications are inappropriate in underdeveloped countries

[6] The two cases differ in their effects. Thus where there is a mere increase in numbers average income per head must fall, and those whose terms of trade are adversely affected are necessarily worse off absolutely. In the other case av-

where specialisation is imperfect. We are not concerned with possible inadequacies in the coverage and the arithmetical accuracy of the statistics but with their significance as a picture of economic activities. As has already been stated in Section I above, in these economies statistics convey a false impression of activities by concentrating on one activity of the head of the household to the exclusion of his other activities and those of the other members of his household.[7] Over a considerable period of development many activities, especially trading, porterage and domestic service, would not be regarded as separate occupations either by official enumerators or by the subjects themselves. This applies particularly where occupations are carried on by part-time workers or dependents. As specialisation becomes more definite and pronounced and as these activities are carried out by specialists, the performers and their performance are more easily identified and recognized and their quantitative extent looms larger, possibly much larger, in occupational statistics, even though in total the volume of these activities may be unchanged or even reduced.

It would seem that the classification of economic activities into three types, while superficially convenient and clear, conceals large arbitrary elements which greatly reduce its value. The activities of the agricultural producer selling his crops can be regarded partly as primary and partly as tertiary; this is particularly evident where he sells to the final consumer. Yet until they are taken over by an intermediary his activities will be regarded as primary. Where the intermediary is a member of the family the activity may continue to be

classed as primary. Its tertiary character is likely to be recognized only when the intermediary is an independent middleman. Since the emergence of an intermediary is likely to reduce the total effort in marketing a given volume of produce, tertiary activity may appear to be increasing at a time when it is actually decreasing.

It should not be thought that these difficulties of classification disappear entirely in more advanced economies. On a smaller scale similar difficulties appear in the classification of the activities of different departments of a manufacturing firm or of most forms of large-scale enterprise. Again, the activities of the cobbler and the milliner are likely to be classified as tertiary when these are carried out in establishments (shops) dealing with the public. Yet under factory conditions the activities would be treated as secondary production. A classification of economic activity which is tacitly based on a particular assumed but undefined degree of specialisation and disintegration of functions appears to have little value for economic analysis or statistics. When census material is used it is more than likely that the assumed degree of specialisation differs between countries and periods.

The difficulty of classifying and comparing economic activity where there are differences in the degree of occupational specialisation largely undermines the statistical approach to the study of the relationship between occupational distribution and economic progress. There is much scattered evidence of the importance of some of the main tertiary activities in underdeveloped societies to-day,[8] as well as in earlier periods in the history of Great Britain and Western Europe, especially

erage income per head must rise, and those whose terms of trade are adversely affected need not necessarily be worse off absolutely.

[7] It is not even certain on what criteria the principal activity of the head of the household is chosen for statistical purposes.

[8] In this respect conditions in West Africa are not exceptional. The large number of full-time or part-time domestic and menial servants in India and the Middle East is another obvious example.

when the services of part-time workers and dependants are also considered.[9]

The substitution of unpaid labour, with or without capital, for paid labour (or vice versa) is a form of substitution which affects the proportion of occupied labour in tertiary production and which illustrates and emphasises a conceptual difficulty present in a wide range of problems of economic statistics, particularly of indices of economic welfare. Such substitution takes place at all levels of economic progress, and not necessarily in the same direction at any given level. An obvious example in an advanced economy is the substitution of the activities of the household for those of the paid domestic servant; conversely, the household may frequently purchase the services of restaurants, laundries and repair agencies. Economic progress provides no general indication of the direction in which the shift between paid and unpaid labour will take place. Retail

[9] Thus there may have been a declining proportion of labour in tertiary activity in the early part of the industrial revolution with a rapid growth in factory production, particularly when allowance is made for paid domestic service performed by dependent members of agricultural households.

trade provides examples. In a poor economy the poverty of consumers does not allow them to buy in advance of requirements and to store their purchases. The tasks of holding stocks and of breaking bulk into the small quantities required for almost daily consumption devolve upon the paid intermediary. In these instances the activities of middlemen arise in response to the needs of poor consumers, to whom they secure access to commodities which would otherwise be outside their reach. By contrast, in advanced economies to-day housewives may store substantial quantities of consumer goods, especially of food, and may actually break bulk themselves. This development has gone far in North America. The tertiary activity remains, but unpaid labour of consumers and their own capital are being substituted for the services of the intermediary.

The examples in the preceding paragraph underline the arbitrariness of certain distinctions which are fundamental to national income and employment statistics. The shifting lines of demarcation suggest the advisability of caution in the use of such statistics as indices of economic welfare or as the basis of extrapolation.

INCOME AND LEISURE IN AN UNDERDEVELOPED ECONOMY*

SIMON ROTTENBERG

In the literature of economics the price of labor of a particular class affects the sup-

* Reprinted by permission from *The Journal of Political Economy*, Volume LX, No. 2, April 1952, pp. 95–101.

ply of labor of that class in two ways: first, by influencing the number of workers entering the trade; and, second, by influencing the amount of effort (usually measured in hours) which the worker will exert.

There is general agreement about the character of the first function. A rise in the price of labor in one trade, relative to others, tends to move workers to the trade in which the price has risen. However, there is less agreement about the shape of the second function.[1] Adam Smith apparently thought that it was positively sloped throughout its full length. He said in *The Wealth of Nations:*

> The liberal reward of labour . . . increases the industry of the common people. The wages of labour are the encouragement of industry, which, like every other human quality, improves in proportion to the encouragement it receives. A plentiful subsistence increases the bodily strength of the labourer, and the comfortable hope of bettering his condition, and of ending his days perhaps in ease and plenty, animates him to exert that strength to the utmost. Where wages are high, accordingly, we shall always find the workmen more active, diligent, and expeditious, than where they are low.[2]

This passage reflects Smith's general position of sympathetic partisanship toward labor at a time in history when employer-oriented writers and polemicists were contending that the worker, being naturally indolent, would offer services in inverse proportion to his wage.[3]

[1] See J. R. Hicks (*The Theory of Wages* [New York, 1948], pp. 97–98): "The other way in which wage-changes may react upon the productivity of labour is by affecting . . . his willingness to work. . . . It has sometimes been thought that a change in wages will always change the willingness to work in an opposite direction; but there is no logical justification for this view."

[2] Adam Smith, *The Wealth of Nations* ("Modern Library" ed.; New York: Random House, 1937), p. 81.

[3] Cf. E. S. Furniss, *The Position of the Laborer in a System of Nationalism* (Boston and New York, 1920), pp. 117–156. Smith did agree that "some workmen, . . . when they can earn in four days what will maintain them through the week, will be idle in the other

A more insightful and sophisticated treatment than Smith's appears in the neoclassical theoretical system. This system takes into account the worker's desire for leisure in the present, while Smith's formulation assumes only a desire for leisure in the future at the "ending [of] his days." The individual supply curve of labor of the neoclassicists has a backward slope for part of its length. At some point in the scale of prices for labor, the utility derived from additional increments of income is assumed to be disproportionately smaller than the disutility incurred from additional increments of work. At that point, and for a range of prices beyond it, the neoclassical doctrine tells us that the worker has a preference for leisure over income and that each successive rise in the price offered for his services will bring forth successively less effort.

The point at which the curve takes its negative slope is not the same for all persons; it must be somehow related to the aspirations which the worker has for income and to the intensity of his desire for leisure. If his income aspirations are strong or his desire for leisure weak, the point of backward turning is high on the price scale. Contrariwise, if his income aspirations are weak or his desire for leisure strong, the point of backward turning is low.

The logic of the doctrine thus requires that each person have a maximum aspiration, which he fixes for himself, for income acquired through effort. For, if the desire for income were without limit, the curve would have a positive slope for its

three." He argued, however, that "this . . . is by no means the case of the greater part"; and, in any event, for the minority of whom it is true, it may be necessary, since "excessive application during the four days of the week is frequently the real cause of the idleness of the other three, so much and so loudly complained of" (Adam Smith, *op. cit.*, pp. 81–82).

full length to the point where effort is limited by sheer physical capacity and would, thereafter, be vertical to the base, where the graph is plotted according to the traditional schema, with the price of labor on the y-axis and the supply offered on the x-axis.[4] The aspiration for income, however, need not be constant over time for the same person, nor need it be uniform among different persons.

The point at which an individual begins to be insensitive to income incentives will be partly affected by the cultural influences that play upon his character. A man who had been brought up in a community which places a high value on work, which is "consumption conscious," and which attaches prestige to the possession of material goods will not begin to offer less labor until there is a large increase in the price for his services or until the price is very high. On the other hand, a man who lives in a society which values leisure and which attaches no social stigma to living at a close-to-subsistence level will begin to offer less labor when small increases occur and when the price is very low.[5]

These conditions of quick backward turning are said to be particularly characteristic of the people of the underdeveloped economies. It has long been believed to be true of the people of the British West Indies. The ideas that the British West Indian has a large preference for leisure over work and that his wants are small have been advanced by the planter communities of the islands for many years and have been written into Royal Commission and other public reports. In this system of beliefs, the West Indian worker does not respond to income incentives. A small rise in the wage rate, it is said, induces him to exert less energy at work and to reallocate his time between leisure and work in favor of leisure. Similarly, an increase in the wages of some trades, others remaining unchanged, does not cause workers to transfer to the advantaged trades. The report of the Economic Policy Committee of Jamaica, published in 1945, for example, has been paraphrased as saying: "Many [West Indian] workers [do] not

---

[4] "Suppose, for instance, that an individual did not wish to earn more than a given money income. If his wage was such that he could obtain this money income without an unreasonable effort, any increase in his wage would result in a decline in the number of hours for which the worker would work. At the higher wage, he could obtain the income of his heart's desire by working fewer hours than at a lower wage" (Kenneth E. Boulding, *Economic Analysis* [New York and London, 1941], p. 227).

[5] Marshall's position was that the individual supply curve of labor is generally positively sloped and that the backward turn is "the exception to the rule." "The longer a man works, or even is on duty, the greater is his desire for a respite . . . while every hour's additional work gives him more pay, and brings him nearer to the stage at which his most urgent wants are satisfied; and the higher the pay, the sooner this stage is reached. It depends then on the individual, whether with growing pay new wants arise . . . or he is soon satiated with

those enjoyments that can be gained only by work, and then craves more rest, and more opportunities for activities that are themselves pleasurable. No universal rule can be laid down; but experience seems to show that the more ignorant and phlegmatic of races and of individuals, especially if they live in a southern clime, will stay at their work a shorter time, and will exert themselves less while at it, if the rate of pay rises so as to give them their accustomed enjoyment in return for less work than before. But those whose mental horizon is wider, and who have more firmness and elasticity of character, will work the harder and the longer the higher the rate of pay which is open to them: unless indeed they prefer to divert their activities to higher aims than work for material gain. . . . We may conclude that increased remuneration causes an immediate increase in the supply of efficient work, as a rule; and that the exceptions to this rule, just noticed, are seldom on a large scale, though they are not devoid of significance" (Alfred Marshall, *Principles of Economics* [8th ed.; London, 1938], pp. 528–529).

want to work for wages regularly five or six days a week all the year round. . . . 'They prefer to have a lower standard of living and more leisure; they are not educated to appreciate a higher standard of living, and would rather take life more easily than add to their material comforts.' "[6]

If the doctrine is correct that West Indian labor is indolent and incapable of being moved by earning opportunities to exert energy at work beyond what is necessary to achieve income for support of life at very low levels, the likelihood of successful development of the Caribbean economy is small. If the doctrine is true, an important objective of public policy ought to be to raise the level of aspiration for income and for the goods and services for which income exchanges.[7] An attempt to assess the correctness of the thesis that leisure is preferred to work at low standards of acquired income was made in the island of Antigua, one of the Leeward Islands of the British West Indies.

[6] T. S. Simey, Welfare and Planning in the West Indies (London, 1946), pp. 133–134.
[7] Any public policy which is calculated to sharpen the aspirations of backward peoples for goods, to make income-earning a more powerful lever, to introduce the competitive spirit, and to make them over in our puritan image, so that they, too, will look upon the leisurely as social pariahs, is fraught with danger. The backward peoples may very well be socially more stable as they are. To make a revolution among them, destroying value-systems which are ancient and rooted, may do enormous harm. But this is the risk to be run and, possibly, the price to be paid for economic development. In the backward areas, now, people live badly; they are malnourished, badly housed, ill and diseased. To improve their conditions of life, either more of them must work, they must work more hours, and they must produce more in each hour of work; or they must be a charge on the people of the developed areas. Our traditions must become theirs, or they must remain poverty-stricken, or the world's well-to-do must move a never ending flow of gifts to them. There is no other way out.

Antigua is a small island of 108 square miles (69,000 acres). Its population is now estimated to be about forty-five thousand, almost all of whom are of Negro descent. The conjunction of a high and stable birth rate and a constantly falling death rate has resulted in a high rate of natural increase of over twenty per thousand of population, so that, with opportunities for emigration now virtually shut off, the population increases by about one thousand per year. The people live at levels of extreme poverty, measured by the standards of the developed areas of the world. At current prices (1951), roughly estimated calculations of national income indicate that per capita income is less than $100 (United States) per annum.

The economy of Antigua is dominated by sugar, and has been throughout the three centuries of its history, although, from time to time, Sea Island cotton has played an important role. These two commodities now constitute close to 100 per cent of all exports. Other exports, principally rum, are of negligible importance. With the exception of ground provisions grown for local consumption, gravel taken from local quarries, charcoal used for fuel, and fish taken from the sea, almost all things consumed in Antigua are brought from abroad, either in finished form or as raw materials for such small-scale, or cottage, industries as furniture-making and tailoring or for the construction industry. For a community such as Antigua, therefore, which, in general, consumes things which it does not produce and produces things which it does not consume, the volume and value of exports are of enormous importance in determining the standard of living. Since agriculture is overwhelmingly the island's most important activity, the value of the sugar crop greatly affects the level of consumption in the island.

The history of the land-tenure pattern of Antigua shows a trend in the direction of concentration at one end and dispersion at the other. In the early years of the sugar industry's history, most cane in Antigua was cultivated on a considerable number of owner-operated estates, many of which ground their cane in small mills located on the estate. The difficulties occasioned by the falling price of sugar, emancipation of the slaves, severance of natural trade relations with the Americans at the opening of the Revolutionary War, removal of the preference enjoyed by the West Indies against East Indian sugar, and protection of the beet-sugar industries of Europe from the competition of lower-cost sugar cane producing areas led to the abandonment of land, the sale and resale of land at losses, the foreclosure by banks, merchants, or other forms of moneylenders of mortgages encumbering the estates, and the splitting of large estates into small plots which were rented to peasant operators. In 1943 a corporation was formed to amalgamate most of the remaining private estates still engaged in cultivating cane. This corporation now owns about 18,000 of the island's 69,000 acres, of which 9,000 acres are arable. Of this, 7,800 acres are worked by the corporation itself and 1,200 acres are rented to peasants on small farms. Peasants also work plots rented from the few private estates which remain and plots on government land settlements. The "Census of Agriculture of the Leeward Islands" of 1946 counted in Antigua 3,196 farms of one acre or more and 2,285 small plots of less than one acre.[8] A large proportion of these are devoted to the growing of sugar cane. In 1947, which was a typical recent year, the corporation delivered 110,000 tons of cane; other (private, non-corporation) estates, 15,000 tons; and peasants, 45,000 tons, to the single cane-grinding mill which is closely associated with the corporation through common shareholders.[9]

The planter thesis that the Antiguan worker is voluntarily underemployed because he prefers leisure to income at low living levels can now be discussed more meaningfully within this framework of the fundamental characteristics of the Antiguan economy. Planters of the community lament their inability to find sufficient workers to take the cane crop off the fields within an optimum time period and the unwillingness of workers to perform certain classes of tasks at all. Workers who do accept employment, according to the planters, refuse to work full work weeks but prefer to work relatively few days each week. This has been the traditional opinion of the planter community for many years. A report of 1891, for example, says:

The number of people is, on the whole, quite sufficient for the sugar estates, but the difficulty is for the planter to obtain that regular labor upon which his operations depend. The labor difficulty was the cause of the abandonment of estates in the past years. . . . All evidence shows that there is plenty of work and wages for the Antiguan laborer, if he would, more largely than he does, take advantage of the opportunity.[10]

The belief, thus, that Antiguan workers have small fixed wants which are capable of being satisfied with relatively few hours of work is inferred in part from the fact that many wage workers in the cane fields of the island work less than full work weeks. This is taken to prove that the West Indian puts a high premium on leisure. Workers are able to do this because field

---

[8] "Census of Agriculture of the Leeward Islands, 1946" (unpublished).

[9] *Report of the Commission Appointed To Enquire into the Organization of the Sugar Industry of Antigua* (London, 1949), p. 14.

[10] Vere Langford Oliver, *The History of the Island of Antigua* (London, 1894), p. clviii, quoting C.W.E. Eves, *The West Indies* (London, 1891).

workers in the cane industry assimilate the situations of contractors rather than of wage workers. For most occupational classes payment is by the task rather than by the hour. Workers report for work when they please, work the number of hours that suits their convenience, work at a pace set by themselves, and are paid for the tasks they perform. In part, also, the inference is drawn from the fact that workers prefer work of some kinds for which wages are low to work of other kinds which pay higher wages. This is taken to prove that the West Indian's desire for income is weak.

The facts from which the thesis is drawn are correct. It is true that wage workers in the cane fields put in short work weeks. Examination of the pay lists of four randomly selected estates for one out-of-crop week of 1949 and one in-crop week of 1950 revealed that, in both weeks, about 40 per cent of all workers worked for three days or less during the week and about 70 per cent worked for four days or less. A survey of employment in Antigua for a week of July, 1950, showed that almost 40 per cent of all wage workers in the cane fields worked less than thirty hours during the week.[11] It is also true that workers frequently reject high-earning trades in favor of others with less earning power. Some unskilled occupational categories in the

[11] Simon Rottenberg, "Report on Unemployment in the Presidency of Antigua" (unpublished, 1951). The short work week in the cane fields is not exclusively occasioned by the free decisions of workers about the allocation of time between work and leisure. In some cases it results from the assignment of short-work-week tasks by the estate managers and in other cases from the stoppage of reaping operations by the managers when the cutting of cane exceeds the capacity of the available railway cars used for transporting cane to the mill or when cutting exceeds the grinding capacity of the mill. It is true, however, that, these cases aside, workers also frequently choose a short week.

agricultural phase of the sugar industry, for which payment is by results, give higher average hourly earnings than most other unskilled classes of work. In spite of this, there is a tendency in the community for workers to eschew this work. Only 6 per cent of the unemployed surveyed in mid-1950 said they were seeking work in agriculture, although about 45 per cent of all employed persons are in agriculture and a high proportion of all opportunities for work is in this sector of the economy.

Yet, although the facts of the short work week and the rejection of higher-earning employments are true, there are ways in which they can be interpreted other than as evidence of a strong desire for leisure and a weak desire for income. It seems to be clear that the unwillingness of workers to spend the full weeks at work is confined, generally speaking, to the cane industry. In sugar-milling, in construction, and in the trades and services, workers turn up for work regularly and do not absent themselves without cause. There are no discernible qualitative differences between cane-field workers and wage workers in other industries. All have felt the same cultural influences, and there does not seem to be any reason to conclude that there is a diffential among them with respect to aspirations or incentive effects. Similarly, the higher-wage work which is rejected is always cane-field work or work in agriculture on other crops. The explanation for the difference in willingness to work between sugar-cane-estate workers and other wage workers must therefore be sought in some factor other than aspiration for income and the goods for which income exchanges or intensity of desire for leisure. Other causes do, in fact, suggest themselves.

Cane-field work for wages in Antigua (and elsewhere in the West Indies) ranks low in the occupational prestige scale of the community. This was quantitatively verified by asking one thousand adult persons to express an occupational preference for their male and female children (real or hypothetical) in a list of nine occupations for each sex. In an economy in which sugar-cane field labor offers an enormously high proportion of the total number of job opportunities, only 1.5 per cent of the interviewed persons chose cane-field jobs for male children and less than 1 per cent chose this work for female children. Four out of every five unemployed persons told interviewers that they were looking for work outside of agriculture.

The flight from the cane fields is not new in the West Indies. A St. Croix (American Virgin Islands) newspaper, for example, reported in 1883:

From the time of slavery it was the habit, when a fairskinned slave was born and reared, to bring up the same as house-servant or tradesman. Among the owners themselves the saying was current, "Too light to work in the field"; the result of this peculiar notion has been that our field hands, up to this day [1882] are almost exclusively blacks, that field-work is considered a disgrace, an imposition on the black race and the parents consequently do all they can to withhold their children from this occupation. . . . Poor whites here would rather starve than work in the field, such occupation being considered beneath them.[12]

The desire to escape from the cane fields and the search for prestige exert a powerful and pervasive influence in the Antiguan community. They create labor-force immobilities by causing workers to have occupational reservations which dampen the influence of relative wages as a regulator of resource allocation. The short work week in the cane fields and the re-

jection of cane-field work are more rationally explicable in these terms than in terms of low-level-income aspirations or preferences for leisure.

Other forms of occupational reservations in Antigua also depress the effects of differential prices in inducing movement of labor between jobs. Within the cane industry, male workers are known to be cutters or cartmen or loaders (all reaping crafts), and they will hold out for work in their own occupational classification. Sometimes a worker will refuse to perform some classes of work for wages, but he will be willing to do the same kind of work to assist, without wages, a peasant neighbor in harvesting his crop. Some kinds of cane-field work are recognized to belong to women or children. Such work is considered to be unfit for men; men performing these tasks are so ridiculed by others that they are unwilling to accept these jobs. Outside the cane fields, men will frequently consider that they are of a particular artisan's trade and they will reject work in other categories, sometimes holding so strongly to their reservations that they are willing to pay the price of unemployment.

That Antiguan workers sometimes reject classes of employment cannot be taken as clear evidence that they are satisfied with little income and that they have a high propensity to allocate time to leisure instead of to work. The refusal of employment ought rather to be interpreted as evidence of occupational immobility created by compartmentalization of the labor force and by custom, tradition, and community values. The facts of West Indian experience from which the conclusion has been drawn that the individual supply curve of labor turns backward when the price of labor is low do not seem to confirm that conclusion at all.

The Antigua inquiry raises a fundamental question about the meaningfulness of

---

[12] St. Croix Avis, July 19, 1882, quoted in Albert A. Campbell, St. Thomas Negroes (Evanston, Ill., 1943), p. 24.

the price-labor supply function for communities, such as this one, in which occupational immobilities are enforced by intrenched cultural traditions. The degree of influence exerted by earnings in bringing forth a supply of labor, either in the form of additional workers or in the form of additional hours of work from the individual worker, will vary from one place to another and from one time to another in the same place and will be affected by cultural and psychological factors operative in a community. Marshall, with his characteristic perceptive understanding, saw this, when he said:

The attractiveness of a trade depends on many other causes besides the difficulty and strain of the work to be done in it on the one hand, and the money earnings to be got in it on the other. . . . We must take account of the facts that one trade is healthier or cleanlier than another, that it is carried on in a more wholesome or pleasant locality, *or that it involves a better social position.*[13]

Despite this parenthetical note, most writers treat both the aggregate supply of labor in a particular trade and the supply of labor offered by an individual as though they were mainly functions of price. Where social-prestige factors intensify occupational reservations, however, price changes and relative prices may have a negligible influence on labor supply.

In these circumstances, movement between jobs and the number of hours worked or energy exerted at work may be more powerfuly affected by the value-system of the community than by the price of labor in different trades. Where this is true, the expression of labor supply as a function solely of price gives the economist a dull analytical tool which obscures perception of the really significant relationship.

[13] Marshall, *op. cit.*, pp. 556–557 (italics added).

Mr. Morton R. Solomon was Director-General of Finance of Southwest Persia from 1943 to 1946. At present he is in industry and business in Mexico, and is preparing A *General Theory of Economic Underdevelopment* for publication.

Dr. Peter T. Bauer is Smuts Reader in Commonwealth Studies and a Fellow of Gonville and Caius College, Cambridge University. He is author of *The Rubber Industry*, 1948; *West African Trade*, 1954; and with B. S. Yamey, *The Economics of Underdeveloped Countries*, now in the press. He has also authored numerous articles on economic theory, agricultural marketing, and problems of underdeveloped countries.

Dr. B. S. Yamey is Reader in Economics (with special reference to distribution) in the London School of Economics and Political Science, University of London. He is the author of *The Economics of Resale Price Maintenance*, 1954; and with P. T. Bauer, *The Economics of Underdeveloped Countries*, now in the press; and of articles on commodity distribution, monopoly, and problems of underdeveloped countries.

Dr. Simon Rottenberg is a Professor of Economics in the Department of Economics, University of Chicago.

VI

| SOME OTHER CHARACTERISTICS AND |
| PROBLEMS OF UNDERDEVELOPED |
| AREAS |

As MIGHT be presumed from the title of this chapter, its contents cover a variety of characteristics of underdeveloped areas that would seem to differentiate them from developed areas. The articles in this chapter also deal with problems that could not have been taken up so well within the framework of earlier chapters. And, in addition, they deal with some behaviors that may be characteristic of both developed and underdeveloped areas but which are of particular interest at this time in reference to underdeveloped areas.

URBAN AND RURAL LIFE CONTRASTED

The relation of population density to the development dichotomy is in itself small. Density of population is also unrelated to urbanization in a 1–to–1 fashion; furthermore it can be shown that agricultural density is inversely related to urbanization.[1] On the other hand, development and urbanization are closely related. The relation of urbanization to the development dichotomy is shown in Table 32; the phi coefficient of correlation is .787.

TABLE 32. Distribution of Political Entities According to Percent of Population in Urban Areas and Status as Developed or Underdeveloped[2]

Percent of Population in Urban Areas	Developed	Under- developed	Total
−35	7	42	49
35+	27	16	43
Total	34	58	92

[1] See Kingsley Davis and Hilda Hertz Golden, "Urbanization and the Development of Pre-Industrial Areas," *Economic Development and Cultural Change*, Vol. III, No. 1, October 1954, pp. 6–24.
[2] *Demographic Yearbook, 1952*, United Nations, New York, 1953, Table 6.

The first selection in this chapter, "Technology and Village Life in Mexico" by Frank Tannenbaum, describes life in the rural villages of Mexico. Not only has Tannenbaum shown the dire poverty of the Mexican village dweller but he has also carefully contrasted the Mestizo village with the "white" village in order to indicate the racial element in underdevelopment. This, it could be shown, is not an unusual situation but one generalizable to other underdeveloped areas. "Subcultural Groups in an Underdeveloped Area" by Robert A Manners and Julian H. Steward not only emphasizes the importance of observing the larger culture of an area in relation to problems of underdeveloped areas but also makes it clear that subcultural variation must be considered. This article serves to reinforce a point made in the first chapter of this volume; variation within a political entity makes the use of national aggregate data somewhat less desirable and useful than it would otherwise be. One further contribution of this article is its description of the variation in motivations of the Puerto Rican worker, variation related to the system of production, crop produced, and the worker's estimate of his life chances of reaching long-range rather than short-range goals.

HEALTH PROBLEMS OF UNDERDEVELOPED AREAS

A facet of life in underdeveloped areas which we have previously touched upon is again presented, but in a different way, in "Health Needs and Symptomatic Variation in Potential Colonization Areas of Peru" by Wilson Longmore and Charles P. Loomis. This article is based on an extensive survey in an underdeveloped area of Peru, an area considered available for colonists at the time of the survey. This research is not only a contribution to the volume in that it describes health conditions in an underdeveloped area, but it also shows that, in underdeveloped areas as well as others, a certain proportion of the medical symptoms reported are culturally derived and related to the subcultural social-class group. At this juncture we shall introduce some additional information on the relationship of medical facilities to the underdevelopment dichotomy. Table 33 reveals that the number of inhabitants per physician sharply differentiates developed and underdeveloped areas. The phi coefficient of correlation is 1.123.

TABLE 33.   Distribution of Political Entities According to Number of Persons per Physician and Status as Developed or Underdeveloped[3]

Inhabitants per Physician	Developed	Under-developed	Total
−2000	29	12	41
2000+	4	100	104
Total	33	112	145

The relation of persons per hospital bed to the development dichotomy is not very large by contrast. It is possible, and this has been suggested by the literature,

[3] *Statistical Yearbook, 1952*, New York, United Nations, 1953, Table 170.

that there is less variation from country to country in what is defined as a physician than in what is defined as a hospital bed. Assuming that this is correct we
must assume that hospital beds in many countries, particularly the underdeveloped,
would not be too impressive as hospital beds. The data on hospital beds appear
in Table 34 and the phi coefficient of correlation is .436.

TABLE 34.   Distribution of Political Entities According to
Number of Persons per Hospital Bed and Status as Developed or Underdeveloped[4]

Inhabitants per Hospital Bed	Developed	Under-developed	Total
−300	27	46	73
300+	9	61	70
Total	36	107	143

While these empirical data do present us with some idea of the relationship
of physicians and hospital beds to development, we have no knowledge of their
actual availability to all subgroups in the larger population. This national aggregate data on physicians and hospitals likewise gives us no information about their
geographical location and availability.

SOME OTHER CHARACTERISTICS OF UNDERDEVELOPED AREAS

The values and institutions of underdeveloped areas as they relate to the creation of competent white-collar workers for both private and public bureaucracies
are described in Hoselitz's, "The Recruitment of White-Collar Workers in Underdeveloped Countries." The supply of persons desiring such positions, it is found,
is relatively great in underdeveloped countries in comparison with the number
who are actually qualified. In such a situation, qualifications unfortunately have
relatively less importance than primary group or family relations. The consequences of this behavior and probable future outcome are described by Hoselitz
with special reference to the development of an educational system capable of
supplying workers with not only skills but, in addition, traditions of responsibility
and of loyalty to the service.

Professor Belshaw's article, "Some Social Aspects of Economic Development
in Under-developed Countries in Asia," concludes the chapter. It is unique in its
approach to economic development, at least unique in the sense that we do not
usually expect an economist to emphasize the importance of social factors. Belshaw
points out that economists are likely to overlook some of the noncapital, nonlabor, and nontechnological factors because they are not used to dealing with
such variables as attitudes. Belshaw also presents an excellent discussion of social
and cultural costs of economic development, a subject upon which we shall touch
again.

[4] *Ibid.*

TECHNOLOGY AND RACE IN MEXICO*

FRANK TANNENBAUM

MEXICO is a nation of villages. We know that they are small, isolated and poor. But what do we mean by poverty and isolation? How wide is the cultural gap between the Indian and the rest of the rural population, and how can it be described? A wide area of human competencies, possessions and beliefs lies beyond the easy reach of the sociologist and economist. But there remain numerous observable and countable "things" which can be used to give substance to the definition of "poverty," "isolation," and cultural differentiation in rural Mexico. That is what we shall try to do in the pages that follow, without overburdening the reader with too many figures.

It is difficult, however, to answer simple questions about the number of doctors or the kind of tools the villages have without some specific counting. In the attempt to secure some sense of the structure and pattern of the rural community, the author had the coöperation of the Mexican Department of Education and of the Federal Census Office (*Estadistica Nacional*) and with their help secured a description in considerable detail of 3,611 rural villages, representing every state and territory, and one half of all the counties (*municipios*) of Mexico. Before being sent out, the questionnaire was gone over and coded by the Census Office and when the returns came in they were tabulated and checked by that

office. It required over two years to complete the job.

These 3,611 villages had a population of 1,877,313, or 17 per cent of the total rural population of Mexico in 1930. As they stand, these villages are not typical in two important respects. They are larger, having an average of 520 people per village, whereas for the country it is much closer to 300. We are, therefore, describing communities that have greater material resources. They are also unusual in that all of these communities have the services of a teacher. Most of the Mexican villages have no teacher and no school. These communities are, therefore, closer to the larger world, are more in contact with it, are nearer to the urban centers, and have a greater measure of identity with modern Mexico. They are the richer and more "modern" rural towns in the country.

This study was commenced in 1931 and completed in 1933; but the rural picture drawn here is substantially unchanged, has remained so for the last century, and will, in the nature of the case, change but slowly in the future. Rural ways and traditions yield very slowly. What we have is a description of the Mexico the Revolution was fought to improve and modernize; how great and how difficult the task the reader will discover for himself.

The Mexican census of 1930 abandoned the effort to count the Indians of Mexico, and confined itself to enumerating the number of people who spoke Indian languages. In this study each teacher was

* Adapted and reprinted by permission from *Political Science Quarterly*, Vol. LXI, No. 3, September 1946, pp. 365–383.

asked to state whether the population of his village was predominantly Indian or mestizo or white. No teacher in a Miji, Zapotec, or Maya community could possibly miss the point. It is therefore of considerable interest to see the result of this report on the 3,611 villages, and, it ought to be repeated, these are the larger communities of Mexico. The returns may be compared with the census figures for 1921. The following table shows that in 1931, on the basis of the personal testimony of the resident teachers, 36.2 per cent of the communities were Indian.

TABLE 1.   Racial Distribution

Race	1921 Census Per Cent of Population	Villages in 1931 Number	Per Cent
Mestizo (mixed)	59.33	2,035	56.3
Indian	29.16	1,306	36.2
White	9.80	270	7.5
Others	1.71	. . .	. . .
	100.00	3,611	100.00

If we remember that the census figures refer to the total population and the questionnaire to the rural villages, the slightly higher proportion of Indian communities is not surprising.

When we turn from race to language, our villages show 77.1 per cent of the villages as Spanish-speaking, and 22.9 per cent speaking Indian languages. That is considerably higher than the record shown by the census of 1930, but the census figures are in all likelihood an understatement.

The rental systems reveal how small a part money plays in the village economy. Only 18 per cent of the villages, 649 out of 3,611, pay cash for their land. The Mexican renter is known widely as an *aparcero*, or renter on shares, usually by halves. The contracts differ greatly and depend on the relative contribution made by the land-

owner and the cropper—especially whether the landowner provides, in addition to the land, animals, seed and tools. Nearly 40 per cent of the villages report "halves," only 6.8 per cent report "thirds," and 3.6 report "fourths." Money rentals are, therefore, much less general than crop-sharing systems; and rental by "halves," the *mediero*, is by far the most widely spread practice in land rentals in the villages. The ordinary share cropper who has to depend upon his patch of corn for an income for the year must raise double what he requires for his own needs, one half for himself, the other for the landowner.

Mexican agriculture is still in many places a hoe agriculture. The greater part of the Mexican crop is raised with primitive tools. These tools are often hand tools, or wooden plows drawn by oxen. In these circumstances each family could till but a small acreage. If we classify our 3,611 villages according to the average number of acres tilled by an individual peasant (including his family), we find that 20 per cent report one hectare (2.47 acres) as the average area tilled. Another 20 per cent report two hectares, while 14 per cent report three hectares. That is, 55.6 per cent, or well over half, of all the larger villages report three hectares or less as the average area tilled by each individual farmer. Only 16.2 per cent report a tillage of six hectares.

The tilling of these small fields still depends upon direct human energy. In many places the use of the plow—even a wooden plow—is not customary. In part this may be attributed to the nature of the terrain; it may be very rocky, as in Yucatan, it may be so steep, as in parts of Guerrero, that a plow is difficult if not impossible to manage, or, as is the case along the coasts, the heavy forests make it easier to burn down the trees and to plant between the stumps with the use of a pointed stick. That is, "fire agriculture" is still prevalent in many parts of the country. All of these factors, and many others, tend to explain why the use of modern tools in the agriculture of Mexico has been so limited.

Of our 3,611 communities, more than 96 per cent have no tractors. What is true of tractors is true of cultivators and of planting, threshing and shelling machines. Only 5.8 per cent of the communities have sowing machines, only 7.9 per cent use cultivators, only 4 villages out of every hundred have a threshing machine, and only 9.5 out of a hundred have shelling machines, this somewhat larger percentage being accounted for by the fact that corn (*maiz*) is grown everywhere. In recent years there has been an obvious increase in the use of steel plows, and 45.7 per cent of the communities report their use, while the wooden plow with one handle, drawn by oxen, is reported for 70 per cent of the villages. There are many communities using both wooden and iron plows, but 30 per cent use no plows at all. The following table gives a summary of the distribution of agricultural implements in the communities under discussion:

TABLE 2. Agricultural Implements in 3,611 Villages

Villages Having No	Number of Villages	Per Cent of Villages
Tractors	3,484	96.5
Planting machines	3,303	94.2
Cultivators	3,323	92.1
Threshing machines	3,465	96.0
Shelling machines	3,267	90.5
Steel plows	1,962	54.3
Wooden plows	1,070	29.6

What proportions of the villages in Mexico lack certain kinds of domestic animals? For the 3,611 villages, 5.4 out of every hundred have no cows, 13.5 have no oxen, 7.3 have no horses, 26.4 have no mules, 10.7 have no burros, nearly one third or 31.0 have no goats, 38.1 out of every hun-

dred have no sheep. When it comes to pigs and chickens, the number of the villages that have them rises markedly. All but 2.1 out of every hundred of the villages have pigs and all but 1.1 out of a hundred have chickens. Taking the villages separately and by areas, we find marked differences: differences between villages that are Indian and non-Indian, differences between those that have *ejidos* and those that have not, and especially marked differences between regions. There are villages so poor that they have neither horses, nor mules, nor burros, nor cows, nor oxen. There are some that have considerable numbers of one and none of others. But it may be said that, on the average, meat and draft animals are to be found in most, even if not in all, of the villages of rural Mexico.

This description of the rural Mexican community must, for the purposes of drawing the picture in fuller detail, be further itemized. Out of 3,611 villages, 765, or 21.2 per cent, are reported as still using barter, and only 260, or 7.2 per cent, have a local market. That means that 3,-351 must market their goods and do their purchasing outside of their own borders. The distance between the town and the market is therefore an important consideration. Over 116 villages report that their nearest market is 80 kilometers distant, 237 villages are 20 kilometers from their market, and nearly 500 are 15 kilometers from their market town.

Of the villages under consideration, 1,964, or 54.4 per cent, had no stores (*tiendas*).

Furthermore, the Mexican village lacks easy communication. It generally has neither train nor automobile. It has neither telegraph nor telephone; it has no post office. In addition to having—as is frequently the case—a different language, it has, even where Spanish is a common bond, no means of keeping in touch with the world beyond its own borders. The people read no newspapers, and live dependent upon the stray rumors that come from irregular contacts, through visits to markets or from itinerant passers-by. But the mere fact that the 3,611 villages we are describing have a school gives them a contact with the world that smaller communities lack. The school community is in closer contact with the world abroad than the one that has no school. In spite of that, 93.1 per cent of all our villages have no train communication.

It has frequently been said that the Mexican railroads have not opened up the country, that they were built for communication with the outside world rather than to satisfy internal needs. Whatever the reasons that justified the construction of the railroads through the northern and less populated areas, it is obvious that the great majority of even the larger rural communities are not served by the existing railroads.

This lack of railroad contact is partially made up by other means of communication. Since 1924 a vigorous program of road building has been pushed by the federal and state governments. That program, as measured by the school communities in 1931, has been successful to the extent of placing automobiles in 8.2 per cent of the school villages. In other words, 91.8 per cent of the communities under discussion are without automobiles. In part, this is an overstatement, as some 5 per cent more of the villages report bus travel. But anyone who knows Mexico knows that buses in Mexico travel almost where no roads exist. No driver from the United States would venture his bus on roads, at least during the rainy season, that are utilized in Mexico. But even so, over 86 per cent of all villages have neither bus nor automobile transportation. Over 28 per cent of the villages report the use of ox-carts as a means of carrying their products

to market. A great majority of the villages (72 per cent) still depend upon mule and horse for their means of conveyance.

These figures are partially overlapping. A village that has a good road may still use the older and more traditional mode of transport, at least in part. The old method may seem less expensive, as no money value is placed upon time in the rural community. A man who has pottery to take to the market loads it on his little horse, burro, or mule, and leads it for days down mountain paths to the market, as has been the custom for centuries. He may continue doing that even if the tourist or outside merchant has found a way of reaching that particular village by automobile or by bus. With the use of the horse, burro and mule has gone the habit of carrying one's wares on one's shoulders. Anyone who has made the trip from Mexico City to Toluca over a new and excellent road will recall seeing numerous Indians plodding along with heavy loads on their backs, carrying pottery, baskets, blankets, all of the wares which they manufacture in their little villages. The road has only made travel a little more difficult because macadam roads are hard on one's feet, and because speeding automobiles are dangerous. Nearly one half of all the villages (45.8 per cent) report that the system of people carrying goods to the markets on their own backs is still the common practice.

Here we have a Mexico in which a few of the villages have trains, a few have automobiles, a few more are reached by buses, 70 per cent enjoy the privilege of carrying their goods by cart, horse, mule and burro, and nearly one half still practice the precolonial system, reminiscent of the days when there were no draft animals in the country, of people carrying their burdens upon their backs, and doing ten, fifteen and twenty miles a day with them.

What is true of transportation methods

is equally true of communication by telephone, telegraph and post office. These communities report that 11.6 per cent are served by telephones. But to some extent the telephones are directly a result of the activities of the schools. The schools have often been responsible for bringing telephones to communities. There are such regions as the Miji area in Oaxaca where through the coöperation of the federal school directors telephones have been brought into the region, connected with the schools, the teachers acting as the telephone operators. Even so, more than 80 per cent of the rural villages are without telephone communication with the outside world. What is true of telephone communication is still more obvious with the telegraph. In spite of the fact that the schools have on their own initiative organized post offices, 80 per cent of even the larger communities have no postal connections. This gives us a picture of the isolation in statistical terms that confirms the impressions of travelers and observers in Mexico, and makes realistic the fact that all of the modern means of communication—train, automobile, telephone, telegraph and post office—are items of minor significance in the lives of the rural folk of Mexico.

TABLE 3. Means of Communication of 3,611 Communities

Villages Having No	Number of Villages	Per Cent of Villages
Trains	3,363	93.1
Automobiles	3,305	91.8
Buses	3,123	86.5
Oxcarts	2,585	71.6
Animals	996	27.6
Human carriers	1,958	54.2
Telephones	3,192	88.4
Telegraph	3,451	95.8
Post Offices	2,923	80.9

This general isolation physically is even more marked professionally. The following table gives the number of villages that had no doctor, lawyer, engineer, druggist, midwife, herb doctor, or priest. They all had teachers.

TABLE 4. Specified Professionals in 3,611 Villages

Villages Having No	Number of Villages	Per Cent of Villages
Doctor	3,530	97.8
Lawyer	3,581	99.2
Engineer	3,570	98.9
Druggist	3,501	97.0
Midwife	3,011	85.4
Herb doctor	2,622	72.6
Priest	3,384	93.7

Striking as is this lack of professional service in the rural community, it is even more surprising to find how poor the rural community is in terms of skilled artisans. The following table will tell its own story:

TABLE 5. Skilled Artisans in 3,611 Villages

Villages Having No	Number of Villages	Per Cent of Villages
Carpenter	1,845	49.9
Mason	1,892	52.4
Plumber	3,477	96.3
Horse shoer	2,854	79.0
Tinsmith	3,254	90.1
Shoemaker	3,012	83.4
Harness maker	3,241	89.7
Tanner	3,082	85.4
Tailor	3,224	89.3
Weaver	3,039	84.2
Potter	3,007	83.3

There is one item of modern equipment which most of the villages can almost always boast of, and that is the sewing machine. Of all the villages, 3,286, or 90.5 per cent, had one. It would be possible and interesting to follow this story in even greater detail and show the differences between various parts of Mexico, but space will not permit.

There is, however, one feature which

must be included, and that is the differ-ence between the Indian and the mestizo and white communities. It is an important fact that in all items here considered—in wages, distance from town, the amount of land an individual can work, the possession of tools, the presence of professionals or skilled artisans—the Indian communities are visibly poorer than the others. There is, in fact, a striking difference in cultural equipment and possessions between these two elements in the population that helps reveal the two Mexicos; and the record here is of things symbolic of the greater spiritual and moral difference that cannot be measured.

We may now compare the position of the Indian with that of the mestizo and white communities. While about the same proportions of Indian and mestizo com-munities report persons seeking work on neighboring plantations (40.7 per cent as against 41.1 per cent), as many as 25.9 per cent of the mestizo villages have resi-dents seeking work in the mines, and only 5.7 per cent of the Indian villages. Even more notable is the Indian tendency to stay at home, only 5.2 per cent of the In-dian villages reporting that their inhabit-ants migrate abroad, as against 33.7 per cent of the mestizo communities. This sharp divergence is reflected in the fact that many of the mestizo communities are located in the North.

Of the villages that report maximum wages of 1.25 pesos per day or over, only 8.7 per cent are Indian, 29.4 per cent mestizo. In the case of minimum wages of between 10 centavos and one peso, 2.0 per cent Indian as against .05 per cent mestizo report 10 centavos, 2.3 per cent Indian as against .4 per cent mestizo report 20 cen-tavos. Exactly 20 per cent of the Indian villages report 25 centavos per day as against 6.8 per cent mestizo. All together, 77.4 per cent of the Indian communities report up to 50 centavos as against 57.3

per cent mestizo communities. When we come up to 80 centavos and one peso, then there is a sharp reversal. In the first case, the figures stand 9.4 per cent as against 19.4 per cent, and in the second, 7.9 per cent as against 20.5 per cent for Indian and mestizo. The over-all figures for wages between 50 centavos and one peso show 22.6 per cent for Indians and 47.7 per cent for mestizos.

This contrast in wages is substantiated by another revealing economic measure-ment: "How many hectares can one indi-vidual work with the customary tools used in your village?" With a tillage of one hec-tare, the villages are Indian, 30.8 per cent, mestizo, 14.8 per cent; two hectares, In-dian, 26.7 per cent, mestizo, 16.8 per cent. When it comes to an acreage between four, five and six hectares, then one gets 22.5 per cent for Indian villages, and 45.1 per cent for mestizo communities.

In the distribution of professional serv-ices the contrast is sharp indeed. The rural districts in their entirety are poor in pro-fessional services, but poorest of all are the Indian communities.

The following table will summarize and illustrate the characteristics of Mestizo vil-lages as compared to "White" villages:

TABLE 6. 1,306 Indian Villages Compared with 2,305 Mestizo and "White" Villages, Ac-cording to Specified Cultural Attributes

Villages Having No	Indian		Mestizo and "White"	
	Num-ber of Vil-lages	Per Cent of Vil-lages	Num-ber of Vil-lages	Per Cent of Vil-lages
Workers on haci-endas	775	59.1	1,358	58.9
Workers in mines	1,231	94.3	1,709	74.1
Workers migrating out of the country	1,238	94.8	1,528	66.3
Train connections	1,253	95.9	2,110	91.7
Automobiles	1,266	96.9	2,049	88.9

TABLE 6. 1,306 Indian Villages Compared with 2,305 Mestizo and "White" Villages, According to Specified Cultural Attributes

Villages Having No	Indian		Mestizo and "White"	
	Number of Villages	Per Cent of Villages	Number of Villages	Per Cent of Villages
Oxcarts	1,077	82.5	1,508	65.4
Telephones	1,188	91.0	2,005	86.9
Telegraph	1,280	98.0	2,181	94.6
Post Offices	1,097	84.0	1,826	79.2
Tractors	1,286	98.5	2,198	95.4
Iron Plows	930	71.2	1,032	44.8
Planting machines	1,284	98.3	2,119	91.9
Cultivators	1,262	96.6	2,064	89.5
Threshing machines	1,287	98.5	2,178	94.5
Corn-huskers	1,265	96.9	2,002	86.9
Cows	129	9.9	67	2.9
Oxen	244	18.7	245	10.6
Horses	161	12.3	104	4.5
Mules	465	35.6	489	21.2
Burros	248	19.0	137	5.9
Goats	509	39.0	609	26.4
Sheep	526	40.3	851	36.9
Pigs	36	2.8	40	1.7
Chickens	18	1.4	20	0.9

Villages Having No	Indian		Mestizo and "White"	
	Number of Villages	Per Cent of Villages	Number of Villages	Per Cent of Villages
Markets	1,204	92.2	2,147	93.1
Stores	804	61.6	1,176	51.0
Roads	818	62.6	867	36.1
Doctor	1,295	99.2	2,235	97.0
Lawyer	1,300	99.5	2,281	99.0
Engineer	1,302	99.7	2,268	98.4
Druggist	1,289	98.7	2,215	96.0
Midwife	1,133	86.8	1,878	81.5
Herb Doctor	965	73.9	1,657	71.9
Priest	1,239	94.9	2,145	93.1
Carpenter	707	54.9	1,059	45.9
Mason	749	57.4	1,143	49.5
Plumber	1,275	97.6	2,202	94.5
Horse Shoer	1,125	86.1	1,729	75.0
Tinsmith	1,226	93.9	2,028	88.0
Shoemaker	1,186	91.8	1,827	79.3
Harness maker	1,230	94.2	2,011	87.2
Tanner	1,141	87.4	1,941	84.2
Tailor	1,190	91.1	2,034	88.2
Weaver	1,046	80.1	1,993	86.5
Potter	1,116	85.5	1,891	82.0
Sewing machine	228	17.5	115	5.0
Phonograph	703	53.8	956	41.5

THE CULTURAL STUDY OF CONTEMPORARY SOCIETIES: PUERTO RICO*

ROBERT A. MANNERS AND JULIAN H. STEWARD

THE traditional holistic or cultural approach employed by anthropologists in their studies of relatively undifferentiated primitive societies seemed, to the investigators involved in this study, to be entirely inadequate to the examination of a heterogeneous society like that of Puerto Rico, with its population of well over 2,000,000 people.[1] And although several anthropolo-

* Adapted and reprinted by permission from *The American Journal of Sociology*, Vol. LIX, No. 2, September 1953, pp. 123–130.

[1] The participants were Drs. Sidney Mintz, Elena Padilla, Raymond Scheele, Eric Wolf, and Robert Manners. The study, which was conducted at the invitation of the Puerto Rican

gists have, with little or no modification, attempted to transfer methods suitable for analysis at one sociocultural level of complexity to analysis at a much higher level of complexity, their conclusions have been called in question by many social scientists.[2] For the most part, the mechanical transfer of method leads these investigators to construct an image of cultural homogeneity that is false for these complex contemporary societies, or to conclusions about "national character" and nationally shared traits which are, to say the least, of doubtful heuristic value. Bearing these considerations in mind, our first need in the Puerto Rican study was to define and delimit the scope of inquiry so that the traditional methods of anthropology could be utilized most effectively. Second, we had to be certain that this very definition and delimitation would not be so narrow as to lead us to overlook or obscure the sociocultural distinctions which we believed existed on the island. And, third, we concluded that we needed as much documentary, historical, and institutional study at the insular and supra-insular level as was practicable and necessary to illuminate and to frame the findings of the community research.

As our primary objects of investigation, we selected certain subcultures which we believed, on the basis of a preliminary survey, to be of major practical importance either because of the sheer numbers of individuals represented or because of significant trends of social and cultural change.

The subcultures themselves were studied by the usual methods of the ethnologist.

government and with the co-operation of Puerto Rican social scientists, was under the direction of Dr. Julian Steward.

[2] Cf. J. H. Steward, "Levels of Sociocultural Integration: An Operational Concept," *Southwestern Journal of Anthropology*, VII, No. 4 (1951), 374–390, for a detailed discussion of the problems of cultural research at various levels of integration.

Although the community inquiries led into analyses of all socioeconomic segments in their interrelatedness, we devoted our major efforts to half a dozen of these groupings: landless workers on a corporate, American-owned sugar plantation on the south coast; landless and near-landless workers on a Land Authority (project of the insular government), proportional-profit sugar plantation on the north coast; hacienda owners and laborers engaged in coffee production in a west-central highlands community; and the small farmers and landless workers of a tobacco and minor cash-crop adaptation in the eastern highlands. In each community there were perhaps 200–300 representatives of the subcultural types, with whose way of life each major field worker and his assistant became comparatively well acquainted in the course of a year and a half. The larger insular and extra-insular institutional framework within which these subcultures emerged and are today functioning demanded additional methods of analysis. It required that the staff spend considerable time studying published documents and consulting with island authorities in order to understand the basic trends in local land use, internal specialization and trade, overseas commerce, the manipulation of credit, political patterns, religious institutions, and other factors which have originated outside, yet strongly affected, the way of life within each community and which have helped to create the sociocultural differences found within and among the communities. That is, the analyses of the contemporary subcultural groups were made against a background of general change on the island.

In the following account we deal only with those subcultural distinctions which clearly appear to be related to the differing crop emphases developed within the confines of this small island. Lengthy descriptions and detailed ethnographic accounts of each of the four communities studied are, of course, precluded by the required brevity of this report.[3]

THE SUGAR COMMUNITIES

Under present conditions of the world market, sugar cane is believed to be the crop that can be cultivated most profitably on the land of certain areas. Since the cane is harvested from about February to June, the rest of the year is a time of serious underemployment; hence is locally designated the *tiempo muerto* or "dead period."[4] Among the more important consequences of this seasonality is the elaboration of subsidiary economic activities to insure survival during the six to seven months of scarcity. Another effect of considerable cultural significance is that the wage labor of women and children has become a vital factor in family survival and has given to the former a relatively high status and a position of some authority in the family which is not encountered in either of the mountain communities.

The concentration of land in large, stable holdings—which is required for the most economical use of the expensive and essential processing equipment—discourages ideas and chances of upward economic mobility and promotes cynical attitudes toward the ultimate value of savings, while substituting a hope for advancement

[3] The full report of the Puerto Rico study is now in press.

[4] Although cane could presumably be planted to ripen throughout the year—especially in the irrigated areas—the sugar content would be adversely affected. But an even more important consideration dictating the present pattern of production is that it is most economical to keep the existing processing equipment operating continuously during the harvest. Consequently, there is currently a trend —especially on the south coast—toward *lengthening* the dead season and shortening the total harvest time, in order to reduce even further the overhead costs of processing.

through sudden accessions of money, such as gambling.

There are a number of ways in which the sugar workers try to meet the problem of getting enough to eat during the dead season. Those in the Land Authority community who live on small plots donated by the government sometimes cultivate subsistence crops to see them through the dead time. But the generally low fertility of their land—as well as several other factors which we do not have the space to discuss—tends to discourage careful or adequate use of these plots by most of the *parceleros*. Some workers from these communities commute daily during the dead season to one of the large cities in search of work, for example on the docks. Others fish or hunt crabs. Still others carry sand for a local contractor. The making or sale of illegal rum for a commission; acting as agent for the illegal lottery; washing clothes and doing home needlework; part-time artisanry and so on are some of the other devices for surviving the dead period. Thus, the so-called "subsidiary" activities in these communities are numerous and diversified and have developed, under these conditions of monocrop, seasonal agriculture, an importance frequently equal to that of the prime source of income.

Strong kin, ritual kin, neighbor, and class ties arise or persist in the needs and exchanges of the dead season; while there has been a concomitant decline in face-to-face relationships between owner and worker, accompanied by a breakdown of the older patterns of respect and other traditional paternalistic ways. Collective activity through labor unions and political organizations has replaced personal appeals to the landowner as a device to gain economic and political objectives. Among the landless proletariat in the south-coast sugar community the family is bilateral and nuclear rather than extended, and the wife tends to be the stable member. Common-law marriage is just as prevalent among this group as it has always been. There are no new considerations of property, status, or religious orthodoxy to induce civil or religious marriage. Religion is individualized, the state church being weak. Various denominations, especially the evangelical sects, which afford common emotional outlets, are increasingly popular and important. Good roads and generally flat country reduce isolation, make electricity and radios available, and raise the general level of sophistication of the rural working class.

The opportunities for upward movement in the socioeconomic scale are so limited that many of the devices which in other localities may be looked upon as offering a way up are generally not so envisaged by the landless of these communities. This is particularly striking in the attitude toward education. There is little interest in education per se, less in the hope that it is the device which will lift an individual or his children out of a depressed position. Besides, to keep a pair of employable hands in school in the hope of creating a better provider later on is too great a sacrifice, too problematic, and too remote.

Despite some distinctive features, the culture of the laboring class on the profit-sharing plantations of the government community is strikingly similar to that of the equivalent group on the south coast. Although conditions and tenure of work are secured by the government and although many of the workers receive subsistence plots donated by the government, the incentives which are implied in these arrangements are, as we have suggested, more apparent than real at present. New attitudes and patterns of behavior appropriate to having a stake in management and being owners as well as employees seem not yet to have developed to any marked degree, according to the findings of the field workers.

The similarities between these two communities are more striking than the differences, despite the contrasting type of ownership. Thus it seems that the nature of the crop and the techniques required for its optimum exploitation under existing economic arrangements have a more profound effect on the way of life of the vast majority of the workers engaged in its production than does the nominal ownership situation. In both kinds of ownership, efficient production demands land concentration and seasonality, encourages the owning of the processing mill by the grower, and requires a large and settled labor supply for at least six months of the year.

In both cases, a group of landless or near-landless wage workers is to be found who have no hope or expectation of moving upward in the community—who see opportunities, if they see them at all, in sudden accessions of wealth or in escape to another part of the island or the world.

Both sugar communities have functioning unions of sugar workers. The presence of unions, in turn, seems to stimulate group consciousness and the power of the working groups. Thus the representative to the Insular House of Representatives of one community and the mayor of the other were, during the period of our study, leaders of their respective locals. This is in contrast with the complete absence of unions, agricultural or other, in the mountain communities, where proletarization of the workers has not proceeded so far, where the nature of the crops and the methods used in their cultivation in the natural environment permit a lower degree of land concentration, dispersed settlement, subsistence crop cultivation, retention of some of the older paternalistic arrangements, and, particularly in the tobacco-minor crops community, the prospect of upward mobility.

THE COFFEE COMMUNITY

The coffee community shows a much larger spread of landownership than either of the sugar communities. There are more than 1,300 farms in the municipality. Of these, about 90 are larger than 100 acres. The general tendency within recent times has been for the larger farms to grow larger, the smaller to grow smaller. Because coffee production is most economical in large units, where processing operations may be conducted by the producer, the smaller units are at a competitive disadvantage. They compensate for this in part by the high proportion of family to hired labor, the smallest farmers using family labor exclusively.

Because coffee is a perennial, land devoted to it cannot be used for the cultivation of subsistence crops as in the case of tobacco. Therefore, the land devoted to coffee must be extensive enough to provide cash income for all needs, or the farm itself must be large enough to permit a combination of coffee and subsistence crops, which insures subsistence plus the income to purchase supplementary food and other commodities. Owing to this nature of the crop and the average market price of coffee, the amount of land required per family is greater in the coffee region than in the region of tobacco-minor crops. For example, the gross return on an average acre of coffee would be about $25 at the highest market price per pound during the ten years from 1937 to 1946. The gross return on an average acre of tobacco at the highest market price during this same period would be about $342. And, while labor and fertilizer costs in tobacco would account for a little more than half the gross, the net return per acre of tobacco is likely to be many times higher than in coffee. Add to this the fact that corn generally follows the tobacco and that beans may follow the corn before it is time for the next tobacco planting, and the much higher value of an acre of land devoted to tobacco becomes even more apparent.

Because coffee is a perennial, it is never worked by sharecroppers, always by daywork or piecework. Thus, unlike the tobacco sharecropper, who participates in any profit made from the sale of the crop, the landless coffee worker depends upon his wages, much as does the worker in the cane fields. Like the latter, the day worker of the coffee community has little hope of accumulating any excess—especially since his weekly wage when he does work is considerably less than that of the cane-field worker.

Often the landless worker is permitted the use of one or two acres of generally inferior land for the cultivation of subsistence crops for his own use. This insures the landlord a dependable labor supply and provides the worker with part of his annual subsistence needs. The effort devoted to the care of these plots here contrasts sharply with the careless handling of their plots found among the *parceleros* of the Land Authority community. This difference is related at least in part to the wages paid in the two regions. The sugar worker earns from two and a half to three and a half times the daily wage of the coffee worker. Even a solid week's work in coffee may provide little more than the family requirement for food alone. Thus the scrounging which becomes so acute during the dead period in cane is an almost permanent condition of the landless agriculturist in the coffee region. And a plot of one's own is likely to seem more precious to the coffee worker than to the cane worker, who contrasts the meager returns from the work on his own plot with the much greater return from work for wages.

Off-season subsidiary activities of the coffee worker are generally agricultural. He may migrate to the cane fields to compete with the coastal cane cutters, or he may find some work in the preparation of the tobacco seed beds on farms in the highlands. Nonagricultural activities are more restricted here than on the coast, some of the more important being the making and peddling of illegal rum and the selling of illegal lottery tickets. But the main difference in dead-season patterns between this and the coastal areas is the presence in the coffee community of some subsistence crops, either on the field loaned by the landlord or on the field of a friend, neighbor, or ritual kinsman. Often, therefore, there is a way to stretch small favors or obligations into enough vegetables to keep one's family going until the next season.

Because accumulation is difficult, land prices relatively high, and credit hard to come by, saving is not here looked upon as a "way out." Here, too, the illegal lottery is popular. As in the coastal communities, the illusion of upward mobility is not very strong, and education is not looked upon as a way of climbing from landlessness to land-ownership.

Differences in the size and nature of the operations here promote stronger face-to-face relationships between producer-owner and worker than can be found in the coastal communities. The owner or his surrogate knows all tenants by name. And although the paternalistic patterns which flourished under these productive arrangements are reportedly much weaker than in former times, the landlord may still count on the support of the tenant in such matters as, for example, political allegiance. These strong face-to-face relationships and their concomitant paternalism seem further to have preserved social class distinctions and attitudes of respect more rigidly than in the cane regions, where the higher degree of proletarization and the disappearance of the old face-to-face arrangements have been accompanied by declining respect forms and increasing formal assumptions of equality or democracy.

Catholicism in the isolated rural areas of this region is strong, in contrast with the growing importance of the evangelical sects on the coast, and tends to emphasize the cult of the saints. These are manipulated for practical purposes. Among the landless and the submarginal landowners, the family pattern is strongly patrilineal, with the father controlling the family labor, either on or off the farm. He determines inheritance and disposal of any land, and he dictates the social relationships of his wife and children. Marriage in this community is usually ritual, even among the landless, and may thus reflect the importance of property as well as of the traditional religion.

The rugged terrain of this area, as contrasted with the coastal plains of sugar production, has prevented the development of good roads. And the crop itself has not demanded good roads, as does the cultivation of sugar. Transportation of sugar cane is too costly when performed by mule or human carrier. This is not the case with coffee. Proof of this relationship between good means of communication and the crop may be seen in the island-wide tendency for new roads to follow the spread of sugar cultivation into the more hilly regions.

Thus the isolation fostered by the nature of the landscape is heightened, in contrast to the coast, by the lack of good communication. The implications of this contrast in terms of mobility, conservatism, general slowness of change, and so on, are profound.

THE TOBACCO–MINOR CROPS COMMUNITY

In contrast with the coffee community, where over 90 of about 1,300 farms consist of more than 100 acres, in the tobacco–minor crop municipality, only 21 of almost 1,100 farms are larger than 100 acres. On the other hand, the number of

farms here with less than 15 acres numbers 875, and no single farm is as large as
500 acres. There is a rapid turnover in
landownership from generation to generation, the dominant pattern being one of
inheritance fragmentation, with holdings
re-formed under different families. The
sucesión or other managerial types of inheritance are much less common here than
in the coffee region, where heavy investment in processing machinery on the large
farms acts as a deterrent to fragmentation.

Tobacco is the principal cash crop in
this community, with minor crops a
strong contributor to cash income. The
combination of a cash crop requiring little
acreage and a subsistence-plus-cash crop
makes survival on small holdings more
feasible here than in any of the other
communities. Nobody in this community
devotes himself exclusively to the cultivation of the major cash crop, as in sugar-
cane or, to a lesser extent, in the coffee
community.

Because tobacco may be cultivated
profitably on small plots, requires no machinery, and calls for no long wait to realize a return on investment; because production credit is readily available and
family labor may supply all the labor for
an average-sized plot; because tobacco occupies the land for only four months of
the year and important food crops may be
sequentially intercropped; because a natural catastrophe, which may wipe out the
cash crop, does not necessarily condemn
the grower to total loss of annual income
—for all these reasons, tobacco has been
called the "poor man's cash crop."

In this community the sharecropper
segment of the landless workers hopes for
betterment in a way not found among the
landless of other areas. The sharecropper
may accumulate enough money in a single year of good crops and prices to buy a
small piece of land. This is the ideal, the
dream. And to the extent that low-priced,

small parcels of land are often available
through the usual breakup of farms upon
the death of the owner, the dream is
often realizable. Each year of good tobacco prices has witnessed at least a few
such conversions of the dream into reality.

As a matter of fact, the largest proportion of the big landowners of this municipality were found to have reached their
present status from poverty or nonowner-
ship. The example of their success makes
the goal real to today's landless workers.
Thus, economizing and saving through
thrift are found more commonly here
than among the landless of the other
communities. And gambling, instead of
appearing to them as the most likely road
to betterment, looks more like a means of
losing one's way on the road. That is not
to say that there is no gambling in the
municipality. There is, but there is significantly less of it; and the illegal lottery,
which flourishes in other areas, has virtually disappeared here.

Subsidiary economic activities are
strongest among the landless of the one
barrio which is almost completely devoted to the production of tobacco. But
landlord credit to sharecroppers during
the dead season reduces the burden of
that period for them. In the other barrios
minor crops are produced throughout the
year and provide a steady, if small, subsistence and salary for most of the landless. Some of the landless workers who
are not sharecroppers migrate to the
coastal towns for part of the sugar harvest,
but most remain within the municipality,
working at odd jobs, borrowing, or exploiting kin and neighbor relationships. Peddling or making illegal rum is of no importance in the tobacco barrio; there is
only one still in operation, and that is run
by an independent large landholder who
takes care of most of his own marketing
of the product as well.

Despite the dependency relationships

of many of the landless, who have neither tobacco, fields for subsistence, nor easy access to food crops, ritual kin relationships are here treated more lightly than in any of the other communities studied. It may be that the lesser severity of the dead season weakens these relationships which were reportedly stronger at one time. Also, the greater fluidity and the possibilities and the facts of upward mobility tend to minimize the importance of the *compadre* ties.

While demands for their labor may often interfere with education of the children, the general tendency is to view education as a device for upward mobility. Parents will frequently educate their children at some sacrifice. And the town supports two private high schools, a Catholic and a Baptist academy, in contrast to the other communities, where no private high schools are found.

Face-to-face relationships are perhaps stronger here than in any of the other communities. Upward mobility and the almost universal direct supervision of farming activities by the owner insure them. And while it is well known that many of the wealthy farmers were once poor men, that does not lead to an informal backslapping relationship; but it does promote an easier accord that is rare in the near-caste rigidity of areas where land, wealth, and power have come down for a number of generations.

The importance of minor crops and the greater bulk of these have stimulated the building of roads. Transportation of tobacco, like that of coffee, may be accomplished by mule or by human carrier, but this is not ordinarily the case with bananas, plaintains, yams, tanniers, and the like. Thus in those areas where minor crops have become important, new roads have been built, despite the unevenness of the terrain. There has been an attendant decrease in isolation, until now there

is no place in the entire municipality that is more than forty minutes' walk from a hard-surface road.

Among the landless and the small farmers of this region the family is bilateral, emphasizing descent on the side where most property lies. Authority for social relations in the family lies generally —but not always and not so strongly as in the coffee region—with the father. Marriage is consensual only where property is not now or is not likely ever to be a consideration, otherwise it is most often civil or religious. The traditional religion appears weaker here than in the coffee region, with no saint cults and with a minor penetration of evangelicism into the nominally universal Catholicism of the rural areas.

Some of these data will strike students of other world areas as familiar. The homogeneity of agrarian ways of life, which is often assumed to exist in countries as small as Puerto Rico, may, upon examination, turn out to be a fiction. The modes of life may instead be discovered to be heterogeneous, not only in horizontal or class terms but in terms of regional and crop adaptation as well. These data suggest that under a system of production for profit and in the multiple context of a dependent, class-structured society, which participates in the world market, certain cultural forms and productive arrangements tend to be associated in special ways with the crops cultivated. Thus the nature of the crop—under the above conditions—may favor the predominance of holdings within a certain range in size; may dictate the general patterns of inheritance and the rate of turnover in landholdings; fix the seasonality of employment; determine the proportion of land devoted to producing subsistence crops; and affect the family, the local class structure, and the religious and political attitudes of the people.

HEALTH NEEDS AND POTENTIAL
COLONIZATION AREAS OF PERU*

WILSON LONGMORE AND CHARLES P. LOOMIS

THE PROBLEM

THE problem, stated in a general way, is to assess the potentialities of the Huallaga Valley as a site for extensive agricultural colonization. It is the purpose of this paper to analyze some of the significant health aspects of the valley. Other aspects of the problem, such as housing, capital investment, settlement patterns, etc., are dealt with in other reports. It is recognized at the outset, however, that any scheme for colonizing must give careful consideration to the factor of health if it is to succeed.

METHOD OF STUDY

The method employed in the analysis of health conditions of the Middle Huallaga Valley consists essentially in the application of the community survey techniques as developed by rural sociologists in the United States. Two approaches were made: The first may be referred to as an adaptation of the "medical symptoms approach" as developed principally by Schuler. Using a carefully designed schedule that covers a selected number of medical symptoms, the field interviewer asks the family to report all members with positive symptoms on the day of visitation and simultaneously to inquire as to the method of treatment of each symp-

tom.[1] The second approach consists in the application of statistical techniques of community surveys as developed by Smith in Colombia, Loomis in Peru, Leonard in Ecuador and Bolivia and Longmore in New Mexico.[2] The community data gathered in this way provide the basis for interpreting and analyzing results of the medical symtoms schedule.

The original symptoms schedule was designed by Schuler for use under conditions found in the United States and was revised later to fit Latin American conditions in consultation with medical doctors of the Pan-American Sanitary Bureau and the United States Public Health Service. The Spanish schedule was pretested by Lewis in Cuba and by Longmore in

[1] Edgar A. Schuler, "Development of a Method of Measuring Unmet Needs for Medical Care," (unpublished manuscript).

[2] T. Lynn Smith, Justo Diaz Rodriguez and Luis Roberta Garcia, *Tabio: A Study in Rural Social Organization*, United States Department of Agriculture, Washington, November 1945; Olen E. Leonard, *Pichilingue: A Study of Rural Life in Coastal Ecuador*, United States Department of Agriculture, Washington, March 1947; also *Canton Chullpas: Estudio Economico Social en el Valle de Cochabamba*, Ministerio de Agricultura Ganaderia y Colonizacion, La Paz, Bolivia, 1947; Charles P. Loomis, *Studies of Rural Social Organization in United States, South America and Germany*, Chapter 15; T. Wilson Longmore and Theo L. Vaughan, *Taos County Cooperative Health Association*, 1942–43, Little Rock, Ark., November 1944.

* Adapted and reprinted by permission from *Inter-American Economic Affairs*, Vol. 3, No. 1, 1949, pp. 71–93.

Puerto Rico in 1946. But it should be noted that the medical symptoms instrument has not been validated for accuracy of information obtained with it under South American conditions. For this reason it seemed desirable to supplement the symptoms schedule with material that might allow checks and thus provide some basis of confirmation as to its accuracy. Therefore, additional questions were included in the survey schedule concerning the prevalence of disease, the pattern of medical treatment, and the general awareness of need.

The family schedule used in the community survey was based primarily upon the schedule used by Smith in Ecuador and Leonard in Bolivia. It was adapted to the Huallaga Valley Region in consultation with specialists of the Peruvian Census, the Agricultural Experiment Station of Tingo Maria, and the University of San Marcos.

A field party consisting of one party chief and four interviewers, all native Peruvians, interviewed all families in the communities between March 6, 1947 and May 26, 1947. In the three communities, 1,140 family schedules were secured covering 5,853 individuals.

FINDINGS OF THE STUDY

In Tingo Maria, the center of recent colonization, 36 per cent of the population reported one or more medical symptoms compared with 28 per cent in Juanjui. On the other hand, in Panao, the highland community, only 16 per cent of the population reported symptoms.

Not only do relatively more individuals have medical symptoms in Tingo Maria than in the other two communities but the number of medical symptoms per 1,000 population, which we will hereafter call the "symptom rate," is more than 80 per cent higher in Tingo Maria than in Juanjui, and almost 170 per cent higher

than in Panao. That is to say, Tingo Maria has a symptom rate of 609 per 1,000 population compared with 333 in Juanjui and only 225 in Panao.

Assuming that positive symptoms constitute a measure of need for medical attention, it is clear that Tingo Maria has a much greater burden of medical needs than either Panao or Juanjui. These data may be summarized as follows:

TABLE 1

	Total Population 1947	Percent of Total Population Reporting One or More Symptoms	Number of Symptoms per 1,000 Population
Juanjui	1,854	28.1	333
Panao	877	16.2	225
Tingo Maria	3,122	36.0	609

CLIMATE AND MEDICAL SYMPTOMS

It is to be noted that the three communities are all within 10° of the Equator and are therefore subject to rain and cloud, because the heated air is full of water vapor brought by winds crossing the warm, moist Amazon Plain. The entire area is subject to alternate seasons of wind and calm, and rain comes in the months from October to April, while the so-called "dry" season lasts for the rest of the year. Altitude, however, has the effect of lowering the temperature and alone accounts for the climatic differences that are peculiar to each community. The weather station at Tingo Maria (altitude 2,211 feet) reports relatively uniform temperatures throughout the year averaging from 64° to 88°F. compared with temperatures in Panao (altitude 7,500 feet) ranging from 50° to 72°F. in the summer and 41° to 50°F. during the winter. Thus for every 500 feet of increase in altitude there is a corresponding decrease of about 1°F. in temperature.

In the absence of any weather record for Juanjui, about all we can say is that if the effect of altitude on temperature maintains throughout the Valley, as suggested above, average temperatures at Juanjui (altitude 1,048 feet) may be from 2° to 3° higher than at Tingo Maria. Effects of the higher temperature are readily seen in the landscape as the tall hardwood trees of the Tingo Maria area give way to the palms and shorter hardwoods at Juanjui. Early morning fogs so characteristic in Tingo Maria are not so prevalent around Juanjui and humidity seems to be lower.

But lands around Juanjui are lower than at Tingo Maria and less well drained so that the virulence of malarial infection among the people is enhanced. The general environment in and around Tingo Maria should be as salubrious as that around Juanjui, and most observers seem to feel that the "cabecera de la Montana" of which Tingo Maria is typical provides more healthful conditions than the lower jungle. It appears therefore that the greater medical needs of Tingo Maria cannot be explained by the climatic factor. If climate were the crucial factor, certainly Juanjui would have a higher symptom rate than Tingo Maria. The lower medical symptom rates in Panao may be explained to a large extent by its more healthful highland climate.

ANALYSIS OF INDIVIDUAL SYMPTOMS

Taking up the symptoms one by one, it is clear that each community displays a unique pattern of medical symptoms. For example, the five most prevalent symptoms in Tingo Maria are chills and fevers, toothache, headache, diarrhea, and defective vision, whereas in Juanjui the most

important are pains in joints, chills and fevers, persistent cough, abdominal pains, and defective vision. Thus only two symptoms—chills and fevers and defective vision—were ranked among the most prevalent symptoms in both communities. Yet the rates for both these common symptoms are more than twice as high in Tingo Maria as they are in Juanjui.

Tingo Maria has the highest symptom rates in 17 of the 24 symptoms reported upon, including diarrhea, chills and fevers, loss of weight, loss of appetite, unexplained tiredness, running of the ear, nosebleed, headaches, toothache, defective vision, skin rash, pains in chest, persistent cough, vomiting, abdominal pains, and hernia. Juanjui has the highest rates for the following symptoms: spitting blood, pains in back, pains in joints, running sores, and nervous disorders.

In only three symptoms, and they are minor ones, the families of highland Panao report higher rates than the jungle communities; namely, accidental injuries, difficult breathing, and swelling of the ankles.

INCIDENCE OF DISEASE

In addition to symptoms all families were asked to specify what diseases, in their estimation, were most prevalent in the community. Malaria was reported most commonly in Tingo Maria and Juanjui, thereby confirming their high symptom rates for chills and fevers (see Table 2).

In sharp contrast to the warmer and more humid climate of Tingo Maria and Juanjui, only 3 per cent of the families in the highland community of Panao reported malaria, undoubtedly resulting from the inhibiting influence of climate and altitude on the vectors of the disease. Grippe (influenza) was the most prevalent disease reported in Panao (79 per cent of all families). Grippe should nec-

TABLE 2. Percent of All Families in Each Community Reporting Most Prevalent Diseases in Juanjui, Panao, and Tingo Maria, Peru, 1947

	Juanjui	Panao	Tingo Maria
Malaria	86.7	3.1	79.0
Mal de ojos	7.3	2.5	24.8
Grippe	54.0	78.9	22.3
Rheumatism	36.3	3.7	4.4
Intestinal troubles[a]	7.3	8.1	18.0
Pneumonia	4.7	34.8	1.9
Anemia	.0	.0	5.9
Bronchitis	.0	16.1	0.1
Whooping cough	14.3	7.5	9.7
Typhoid fever	.0	42.9	1.6
Measles	10.3	0.6	2.8
Small pox	.0	9.3	1.0
Tuberculosis	3.0	1.2	0.3
Uta (probably leishmaniasis espundia)	.0	.0	1.3
Yaws (probably framboesia)	11.7	.0	.0
Venereal disease	1.7	10.6	.0

[a] Includes parasites, colic, vomiting.

essarily be associated with the colder and more variable climatic conditions prevailing in the highland Sierra of which Panao is representative.

The other diseases reported most often in Panao were typhoid, pneumonia and bronchitis. The latter two diseases are associated understandably with the high incidence of grippe and influenza; but such general awareness of typhoid fever is due, no doubt, to its epidemic character.

Whooping cough is recognized as an important disease in all three communities as reported by 14 per cent of the families in Juanjui, 10 per cent in Tingo Maria, and 8 per cent in Panao. The people's awareness of the prevalence of measles seems to be greatest in Juanjui (10 per cent reporting it), while small pox is reported to be prevalent in Panao.

Relatively more families reported the prevalence of tuberculosis in Juanjui than in either Panao or Tingo Maria, but rec-

ognition of this disease is not general in any of the communities. The same comment might be made with reference to hookworm, which was reported by only one family. Both of these diseases undoubtedly require more widespread recognition of their incidence in the community if they are to be accorded proper treatment.

Uta was reported by slightly over 1 per cent of the families in Tingo Maria. This disease is a form of cutaneous leishmaniasis which is frequently followed by horrible, spreading ulcers of the mucous membranes of the nose and pharynx and occurs endemically in areas where the climate is hot and moist. However, *uta* also occurs in certain mountain valleys of Peru. Unfortunately little is definitely known about the transmission of the disease.

Yaws (or framboesia) is reported as prevalent by 12 per cent of all families in Juanjui. It is caused by a spirochete morphologically indistinguishable from that of syphillis. To some extent, at least, the two diseases produce immunity to each other, and the general nature of the infections to which they give rise is strikingly similar. The fact that both yaws and venereal disease are not reported together in Juanjui or Panao may be due to the reciprocal immunity conferred by these diseases on each other.

Relating the results on symptoms with the diseases reported we find that approximately 1 in 7 of all positive symptoms reported in Tingo Maria and Juanjui were chills and fevers, thus diagnostically related to malarial infections. Since temperatures below 60°F. inhibit the cycle of development in mosquitoes, Panao, where such temperatures are not uncommon, reported chills and fevers only 1 symptom in 20. Other symptoms each making up at least 10 per cent of all symptoms in Tingo Maria were toothache, headaches, and defective vision; in Juanjui, only pains in the joints. Panao reported only 3 symptoms with at least 10 per cent of the total volume of symptoms each; namely, abdominal pains, toothache, and pains in joints.

The first conclusions drawn on the basis of the preceding discussion may be stated in tentative form as follows: (1) The highland region typified by Panao is relatively more free of medical need than the jungle, and the generally prevailing folk attitude that migration into the jungle presents the individual with greater health hazards seems to be justified. (2) People of a colonization community (Tingo Maria) tend to have greater medical need than families of a stabilized community (Juanjui) in the same general environment. (3) Health hazards as measured by symptom rates are more faorable in the Juanjui area than in the present colonization area around Tingo Maria, yet the latter colonization effort has been highly successful.

Further confirmation of these conclusions, however, must wait now on the analysis of the relation between social stratification and medical needs. Such analysis allows some control over the socio-economic factor and thus demonstrates just how influential socio-economic status is.

SOCIO-ECONOMIC CLASSES AND HEALTH NEEDS

Using economic status (income) and social interaction (visiting behavior) as quantitative variables of measurement, the families were grouped into three socio-economic classes, as follows: "High Status," "Medium Status," "Low Status."[3] The meaning in sociological and

[3] For a detailed description of the method used to delineate these classes see T. Wilson Longmore, "A Matrix Approach to the Analysis of Rank and Status in a Community," *Sociometry*, August, 1948.

economic terms can best be illustrated by analyzing briefly how these status classes correlate with selected items in the standard of living.

For example, the percentage of families reporting possession of radio, clock, eating forks, sewing machine, bedstead, wardrobe, and iron increased with socio-economic status. The same direct relationship that exists between status and material possessions persists in respect to certain cultural practices which may contribute directly to health such as the proportions of families who boil their water for drinking, or who wear shoes. Families reporting mosquito nets and toilet facilities constitute indirect evidence of certain crucial health practices; the proportion of families reporting these facilities is, as might be expected, correlated directly with ascending status.

Inverse relationships exist between socio-economic status and the proportion of families reporting over-crowding (2 or more persons per room), or who report that they habitually sleep on the ground, or walk barefoot.

In the subsequent part of the report we will analyze, to what extent socio-economic status of families as defined correlates with the health experience of the same families using medical symptom rates as an index.

High-status families in Tingo Maria have a rate of 492 symptoms per 1,000 population compared with 737 for the medium-status families and 735 for the low-status families. Thus, high-status families in Tingo Maria enjoy a symptom rate approximately one-third less than the other two classes of families.

On the other hand, socio-economic status in Juanjui appears to have less influence upon medical need than in Tingo Maria; the overall symptom rates vary only from 315 to 365 per 1,000 population. Furthermore, the variation is not entirely consistent for the lowest rate is associated with medium-status and the highest rate with high-status families.

Only in the community of Panao is the total symptom rate clearly correlated with socio-economic status. In fact, in Panao low-status families are burdened with two and one-fourth times the volume of symptoms as found in high-status families.

Chills and fevers, pains in the back, and pains in the joints are inversely related to socio-economic status in each community. Since these three symptoms comprise more than a fourth of all positive symptoms reported (ranging from 12 per cent in Panao to 36 per cent in Juanjui) it seems clear that socio-economic status is an important contributing factor to the burden of medical need. However, it does not appear to account to any great extent for 10 of the symptoms in Juanjui, 7 in Panao and 3 in Tingo Maria. Clearly there appears to be little uniformity between the three communities in the way that symptom rates are related to socio-economic status. To give one example, the symptom rates for "unexplained tiredness" bear an inverse relationship to status in Panao, a direct relationship in Tingo Maria, while in Juanjui they are not related.

Socio-economic status, therefore, appears to have an inconsistent, albeit significant effect upon specific symptom rates. Furthermore, the detailed analysis serves to confirm what was already seen in the total over-all symptom rates; namely, that socio-economic status seems to be of lesser importance as a determinant of medical need in Juanjui and Tingo Maria than in Panao. The latter community, on the other hand, reveals more consistency between socio-economic status and medical symptom rates. The excess of medical symptoms in Tingo Maria over those of Juanjui and Panao are therefore not due entirely to the contributory effects of socio-economic status.

The average age of the family head in Tingo Maria was 35 years, or 5 years less than in Juanjui, and 9 years less than in Panao. Thus Tingo Maria with a larger proportion of adults in the prime of life, which might anticipate less medical need than in the other two communities, still reports the highest symptom rates.

There is much evidence, however, to support a hypothesis that the population of Tingo Maria is less healthy than the population of Juanjui because of its recency of settlement and consequent high social mobility. It seems of crucial importance that almost 100 per cent of the population of Tingo Maria has migrated into the community since 1938, the first year of colonization. Panao undoubtedly has the most stable population since only 18 per cent of the heads of families have resided less than ten years in the community. The families of Juanjui reported only 34 per cent of the family heads as resident less than 10 years.

It is generally known that after a man has recovered from certain diseases he is thereafter immune to those diseases. It appears that the fundamental principles of immunity are the same for parasites as they are for bacteria and proteins. Most of the people who make up the population of Tingo Maria have migrated from the Highland and Central Regions of Peru. They have had to adapt themselves to a new and what to them must be an extremely hostile environment.

At first the family must bear the main burden of coping with the new environment. As a consequence its adequacy as a functional unit in health protection must certainly be of paramount importance.

Tingo Maria has approximately the same proportion of normal families, that is families with mother, father and one or more children, as are found in Juanjui and Panao. But it also has about three times as many husband-wife families and twice as many single person units. On the other hand Tingo Maria has only about half as many "broken" families as are found in either of the other communities. All in all it would appear that Tingo Maria should be as well equipped, insofar as the family institution is concerned, to cope with health needs.

It appears that symptoms of disease are not clearly a result of any one factor, such as climatic conditions, socio-economic status, family structure, or age composition. Thus it would seem that causes of differential morbidity evidenced by the symptom data are complex and are incapable of being explained by any single factor.

CONCLUSIONS

Certain practical conclusions may be drawn from the preceding analysis. The pattern of sickness is characterized by high incidence of parasitic diseases that are normal in the area.

The study suggests rather clearly that a new colonization community may expect a greater volume of medical need than a long-established community.

A tentative conclusion may be ad-

vanced: On the basis of the evidence presented in this paper social mobility seems to have a decidedly adverse effect upon the incidence of medical symptoms. On the other hand it is not clear whether in the process of resettling, with its consequent increased social mobility, there does not arise an increased awareness on the part of the population of health needs and perhaps even a lowering of the "pain" threshhold so that individuals tend to report more and varied symptoms. Mayo and Fullerton in a study of a southern county suggest that the explanation for their finding that the probable under-representation of positive symptoms in the Negro population was due in part to the "pain endurance" attitude developed by the Negro.[4]

The possibility that the number of medical symptoms reported by any community might be culturally determined must not be overlooked, and it must be readily acknowledged that as yet there is no test of validity under Peruvian conditions.

[4] Selz C. Mayo and Kie Sebastian Fullerton, *Medical Care in Greene County,* A. E. S., Bull. 364, North Carolina State College, Raleigh, November 1948.

THE RECRUITMENT OF WHITE-COLLAR
WORKERS IN UNDERDEVELOPED COUNTRIES*

B. F. HOSELITZ

IN THE discussion of the human problems arising in underdeveloped countries undergoing a process of technological change, the question of the formation and training of an industrial labour force stands in the foreground. It is, indeed, a most important problem, especially if a process of relatively rapid industrialization is envisaged, and if not merely the acquisition of new manual and technical skills, but the entire alteration of the way of life of large masses of the population takes place. Most of the past discussions of the development of an industrial labour force have concentrated on two groups within the new industries: the industrial labourers at the bottom of the scale, and the technical elite, the engineers. Some attention has also been given to the problem of how managers concerned with the organizational and 'business' problems of the new industries can be trained and, in some underdeveloped countries, what steps could be taken to induce the development of a class of private entrepreneurs in industry.

The problems which arise in all these areas are complex and differ from one another considerably. The transformation of 'peasants and primitives' into industrial labourers is a task involving masses of people, and which affects not merely the place and manner of their daily activ-

ity, but their entire social existence.[1] The training of engineers and top managers involves fewer individuals, but because of the strategic positions which these obtain in an industrializing economy, their selection and their most appropriate employment also involve, from the viewpoint of the economy as a whole, various difficult problems.[2]

With all the attention which has been given to the incentives and motivations which may exist for industrial workers on the one hand and managers, entrepreneurs, technical leaders, and engineers on the other, one group has received little attention, though, in the last resort, their successful recruitment and effective co-operation is indispensable for a process of industrialization. This group is that of the white-collar workers. In the subsequent paragraphs I propose to suggest a few thoughts on the role which this group may play in a process of industrialization and on some problems which arise. When we speak of white-collar workers we deal with a group of people who, in terms of economic position and social ranking, exhibit great heterogeneity. In most of the theoretical treatments, white-collar workers, as a group, are counted among the

[1] On this problem, see Wilbert E. Moore. *Industrialization and Labor*, New York, 1951.
[2] See on some aspects of this point my article 'Entrepreneurship and Economic Growth,' *The American Journal of Economics and Sociology*, vol. XII, no. 1 (October 1952).

* Adapted and reprinted by permission from *International Social Science Bulletin*, Vol. VI, No. 3, 1954, pp. 3–11.

middle class, and I will follow this practice by making use of the classification of the middle class presented by Professor F. Marbach.[3] Marbach distinguishes between the 'old' and the 'new' middle class, and further between the 'self-employed' and the 'non-self-employed' members of the middle class. Although, on the whole, there is some overlapping between the 'old' and the 'self-employed,' on the one hand, and the 'new' and the 'non-self-employed,' on the other, the two principles of classification yield four easily distinguishable categories. In this paper we are concerned only with white-collar workers, i.e., with members of the non-self-employed sector of the middle class. And here, we may distinguish two groups again, one of which corresponds, on the whole, with Marbach's old, and the other with his new middle class.

The new non-self-employed middle class is made up of white-collar workers who perform relatively unskilled labour. Although they do not work with their hands, their real income, in the advanced countries, is normally not above, and frequently even below that of semi-skilled and skilled manual workers. In this group belong the typists, bookkeepers, shipping clerks, filing clerks, and other persons engaged in commercial and industrial establishments and in public service. This group will be designated in this paper as 'employees.'

The old non-self-supporting middle class is made up almost entirely of public officials, normally in the higher ranks of the public service. To this group should be added persons engaged in occupations of similar complexity in the service of private firms or individuals. We will designate this group hereinafter as 'officials.'

The 'employees' are distinguished from the manual labourers in that they work in

[3] Fritz Marbach, *Theorie des Mittelstandes*, Berne, 1942, esp. p. 188 ff.

an office rather than a workshop or a factory, and that their work requires, in general, a higher degree of literacy than most manual jobs. A typist must know how to spell, and a bookkeeper must have, on the whole, a greater ability for arithmetic than most manual workers. The 'employees' are distinguished on the other hand from the 'officials' in that their jobs usually do not involve, nor permit them to make, decisions of any significance. The work of employees is mostly routine work, it requires, apart from certain relatively non-complex skills, chiefly the ability to be attentive, patient, and careful. Moreover, as a rule, the incomes and also the social position of officials is considerably higher than that of employees, as also of skilled manual workers.

The most characteristic aspect of the economic role of officials is their intermediary position in a bureaucratic hierarchy.[4] This means that they are normally in a position in which they receive general directives from the persons in elite positions within their bureaucratic hierarchy, and it is their task to translate these general directives for their subordinates. In addition they are usually called upon to make decisions within a rigorously prescribed field, to iron out differences between their subordinates, and to maintain channels of communication with co-ordinated portions of their bureaucratic hierarchy. The most significant difference between officials and the members of the 'elite' is that only the latter make policy decisions, and occupy, in governmental hierarchies or in business organizations, the positions of ultimate re-

[4] I shall not distinguish in what follows always between public, i.e., governmental, and private, i.e., business bureaucracies. Although I shall be concerned mostly with public bureaucracies, most of what applies to them also applies, *mutatis mutandis*, to business bureaucracies.

sponsibility. As a rule, there is also some difference in the level of income and general social ranking between members of the elite and even the highest-placed officials.

From the distinctions made, it is clear that there exist important differences in the incentives and motivations of employees, on the one hand, and officials, on the other. I shall first briefly consider the former group.

The employees are, in the advanced countries, the 'proletarianized' portion of the middle class. Their income often remains below that of manual workers, and this appears to be a correct reflection of the overall social value of their economic contribution. The particular jobs which they perform require few specialized skills, apart from those acquired by almost all children in school. Whatever skills are needed in addition can usually be learned by a very short training or by some process of on-the-job training. Moreover, since many of the jobs performed by employees are on a low level of technical complexity, the human factor can be replaced relatively easily by machines. In other words, machines plus high-grade engineers can often be substituted for employees—the various types of office equipment from the simple typewriter to the most complex Hollerith machine are examples of this. Whether or not, and under what conditions such substitutions will take place is a question of relative prices. But the ease with which such substitution can be accomplished is another factor pressing the incomes of employees to a low level.

Compared with this situation in the advanced countries, a different situation is likely to persist in many underdeveloped countries, at least during the early period of the industrialization process. The differences are due mainly to two factors: the much greater illiteracy rates

in underdeveloped countries and the very low prestige that in many of these societies is attributed to manual work which 'dirties one's hands.' (This last factor plays a certain role too in advanced countries.) Some employees endure their economically unenviable position, because being a white-collar worker gives the illusion to the outside world—and sometimes even to oneself—that one is above the ordinary crowd of common labourers. This has the consequence, as Marbach has shown, that employees in advanced countries are recruited, on the whole, from a higher social layer than manual labourers, even though the amount and quality of education required for the two types of position are not very different.

In many underdeveloped countries the relative social prestige which attaches to white-collar jobs is even greater, and that is in close correlation with the relatively greater scarcity of literate persons. For this reason white-collar jobs which require few or no advanced skills are in great demand, often by people who do not even possess these skills—although they only know how to read and write. This makes the problem of selection difficult and here another characteristic of many developing countries comes in: the partial absence of impersonal market relations and the much greater weight of family and other primary group relationships in these countries.

In practice these factors have the following consequence: lower-rank employee positions become available to persons with a minimum degree of literacy. In view of the social prestige of white-collar positions as compared with manual labour, and because of the relatively greater scarcity of individuals even with a minimum degree of literacy, such positions will normally pay higher wages then these of manual workers and most occupations in agriculture. Hence, with an increase of the rudiments of literacy there will be a race for these jobs and selection for them will depend, to a large extent, on personal connections and friendships between applicants and persons in the higher echelons of an administrative organization. It is no secret that, in many underdeveloped countries, the staffs of certain government offices are composed of relatives or co-villagers and other personal friends of one or several heads of a department or division. It is not necessary to point out that this method of recruitment of even the lowest ranks of a public bureaucracy has many undesirable aspects. It tends to keep out many qualified persons; it places professional relationships within the bureaucratic hierarchy on a non-rational basis; it produces vested, almost clannish, interests within the public service; and it endangers the principle of promotion within the bureaucracy from the ranks, since not effective performance but personal friendship is the decisive criterion. At the same time, this system bears the seeds of producing corrupt administrations, since every applicant for a position will find it desirable to 'become a friend' of persons with the power of appointment—if necessary by means of gifts or bribes.

It is, of course, not suggested that this must be the rule in all public administrations in underdeveloped countries. But we must consider that even its sporadic occurrence may have serious adverse consequences, and we must moreover bear in mind that with progressive industrialization, the expansion of public and semi-public bureaucracies of various kinds is inevitable. Industrialization leads to great population shifts. New cities arise, villages become towns. New administrative functions become necessary, called forth by the increased need for speedy and accurate communication and transportation and by the new functions which national,

provincial, and local governments are forced to adopt.

Moreover, the drafting into industry of peasants and other persons without urban background requires the increase of various welfare, educational, and other administrative agencies which normally only central or local governments can provide. All these trends make necessary a large increase of bureaucracy and thus pose a problem in the recruitment of employees, as well as officials. In view of the pressures which are likely to arise, it is most desirable to found effective 'community-oriented' administrations, and the ambiguity in the social and economic position of lower-rank employees may operate against this objective.

An alternative would be the attempt to substitute, wherever possible, machines for employees. But this would lead to the contradictory result that in countries in which labour is cheap, labour-saving machinery would be employed in occupations where a number of new career opportunities could be created which, in the long run, would have an important beneficial effect on the economic growth potential of the country. It would have the other unfavorable result that the scarce foreign exchange would have to be used for the purchase of expensive equipment and that the middle and upper ranks of the bureaucracy would be even more heavily overburdened with work and responsibility. And these persons, who are in crucial positions, are already in short supply. Whatever dangers and inadequacies may lie in the recruitment of employees, the chief bottleneck in the building up of administrative bureaucracies in underdeveloped countries is in fact in the lack of trained officials.

Many of the problems which we observe in the recruitment of employees are also encountered in the building up of a staff of officials, and *vice versa*. Some of the points which will be discussed below apply also to the expansion of the lower ranks of an administrative organization. The constitution of a bureaucracy is fraught, on all levels, with analogous problems. But the important difference between inducting employees and officials is that because of the differences in the nature of their respective roles different factors are of chief importance in the case of each of the two groups.

As has been pointed out, the peculiarity of the role of officials consists in that they make decisions. They cannot, therefore, be replaced by machines. But in a well-functioning bureaucracy their decisions are not arbitrary, however independently they may be made. I do not refer to the fact that the decisions made by any official are limited by the competence of his department, division, or section, but rather that however free he may be, and may need to be, in some respects, he is merely an instrument implementing policies which were not designed by him, but imposed upon him. To fill the position of an official properly, it is, therefore, necessary that the holder of such an office be ready to place himself fully at the service of the bureaucratic hierarchy he serves and that he ask himself at every juncture whether his activity is in pursuit of the general policy directives under which he functions. In addition he is charged with doing his work in the most efficient manner possible. Efficiency in this context means something very similar to what economists have in mind when they speak of 'economizing': the attainment of a given goal with a minimum of means.

These limitations ideally impose upon an official a perfectly 'rational' method of action. There is a close analogy between an ideal-typical official and an ideal-typical entrepreneur. The latter 'economizes' means in order to maximize profit, the former in order to maximize the imple-

mentation of whatever policy he is charged to execute. It is no wonder, therefore, that really efficient bureaucracies exist only in a social framework in which rationality (in Max Weber's sense) has become a widely generalized principle of social action. Weber sums up thus his penetrating discussion of the bureaucracy.

'Bureaucratic structure is everywhere a late product of development. The farther we go back in historical development, the more typical become forms of government which lack a bureaucracy and officialdom altogether. Bureaucracy has a "rational" character: it is dominated by rules, purposiveness, means, "objective" impersonality. Its origin and growth has had everywhere a "revolutionary" effect, in a special sense; an effect which the advance of rationalism usually produces wherever it occurs. In this process structural forms of government became annihilated which did not have a rational character, in this special sense.'[5]

The specific conditions which are associated with this kind of rational action, and without which it cannot function properly as a generalized principle of social action, include at least the following: tasks in a society must be distributed on the basis of achievement, rather than on the basis of a person's status. That is, in order to implement his job effectively, an official must select those persons and other means which, on the basis of known scientific and technological relations, are most efficient. This demands, moreover, that the exercise of the functions of an official must be 'democratic,' in that he disregards, in a formal sense, special claims of individuals which are not based on objective criteria of achievement or on clearly established legal claims. Moreover, this rationality of an official's actions will normally lead to his making use of whatever specialized

[5] Max Weber, *Wirtschaft und Gesellschaft*, Tuebingen, 1947, vol. II, pp. 677–678.

skills exist, in order to achieve an end. Hence rational bureaucratic activity tends to support and sometimes even to initiate division of labour and specialization. Finally, the impersonal quality of the official's purpose requires that he be 'community-oriented,' i.e., that he regards his office as a trust which he administers in the interest of the community as a whole, rather than as a benefice which leads to his own enrichment or the accumulation of power.[6]

Many of these principles of social action are foreign to the value systems dominant in some underdeveloped countries. Moreover, in some countries the social structure and its maintenance work against the introduction of these principles. Hence the development of effective bureaucracies encounters great obstacles. Indeed, really efficient administrative organizations have been created only in economically advanced countries; the governmental and administrative apparatuses of most underdeveloped countries were, until recently, either manned in their higher positions by non-natives, or experienced periodic breakdowns.[7] In other words, the admin-

istrations of native governments or enterprises in many countries of, say Latin America or the Middle East, exhibited a degree of inefficiency and instability which was one of the factors accountable for the relative economic backwardness of these countries. The administrations of colonies and foreign-owned enterprises in underdeveloped countries were manned, at least, in their higher positions by citizens of the metropolitan country, who transplanted their own organizational and administrative procedures. With the attainment of independence by many former colonies, and the increasing trend to place foreign investments in all underdeveloped countries under the supervision of the national government, the growth and extension of native bureaucracies is necessary. These must take over the functions exercised until recently by non-natives. In other instances they must modernize themselves and replace their often inefficient and non-rational methods of operation by the introduction of the principle of rational action on an impersonal, formally egalitarian, basis. This process of innovation makes great demands on a new type of manpower, and it is not surprising that the recruitment of officials equal to the tasks demanded of them forms a serious bottleneck in the economic development of underdeveloped countries.

In the subsequent paragraphs I shall try to analyse some of the factors which exert an influence on the number and types of persons who become officials in the bureaucracies of underdeveloped countries. This may explain why the shortages exist and how they might be overcome. One important factor is the absence, in most underdeveloped countries, of well-

[6] A more extensive discussion of these inter-relations can be found in my essay, 'Social Structure and Economic Growth,' *Economia Internazionale*, vol. VI, no. 3 (August 1953). See also Marion J. Levy, Jr., 'Some Sources of the Vulnerability of the Structures of Relatively Non-Industrialized Societies to Those of Highly Industrialized Societies' in B. F. Hoselitz, ed., *The Progress of Underdeveloped Areas*, Chicago, 1952.

[7] On some of the bureaucracies in antiquity and the middle ages and their differences with the modern type of governmental and business bureaucracies, see Weber, *op. cit.*, p. 655 ff. One of the outstanding examples of a bureaucracy in a country which did not belong to the group of economically advanced areas was imperial China. But whatever may be said about the merits of the Chinese imperial bureaucracy, one of its main features was its instability which made it incapable of functioning in a period of social and economic transi-

tion imposing increased stresses. See on this point, Marion J. Levy, Jr., 'Contrasting Factors in the Modernization of China and Japan,' *Economic Development and Cultural Change*, vol. II, no. 3 (October 1953), esp. pp. 165 ff.

ordered administrative procedures. Existing bureaucratic procedures are outdated and often derived from the practice of some more advanced country with entirely different conditions. The previous colonial status of some countries and the fact that others, though politically independent, were culturally dependent on an advanced country have caused the adoption of certain European systems of administration which sometimes were altered a little to suit local conditions better, but which in general need considerable overhauling. These very procedures often make public, as well as business, bureaucracies in underdeveloped countries top-heavy, cumbersome and ill-adapted to the needs of the country. Examples of this can be found in the tax and fiscal administrations of many underdeveloped countries, but they exist also in other fields.[8] The most appropriate method to deal with this situation is the substitution of existing administrative procedures by more suitable ones, a task in which the United Nations and its specialized agencies may provide considerable assistance.

In addition to the external cumbersomeness of administrative structures which could be relatively easily removed, if it were not for a multitude of vested interests of office holders or other beneficiaries of the system, there are factors in the social structure of some countries which make the formation of rationally operating bureaucracies difficult. I refer to the excessive inequalities in social position and, resulting from it, the quasi-feudal character of some underdeveloped societies. At the top of the social pyramid is a small group which has a virtual monopoly of wealth, political power, and education—the three main status-conferring variables. The officials who are appointed under such a system usually stand in a relation to the political power holders which resembles that of the medieval *ministeriales* to their clerical or secular overlords. In other words, the officials do not serve the community as a whole, but the special interests of a politically powerful group. This has the consequence that not only excessive emphasis is placed on the preservation of the *status quo*, at least as far as the distribution of political power and social prestige is concerned, but it also tends to keep out of the administration persons who have undoubted objective qualifications, but who do not stand in a quasi-retainer position to the members of the community's elite. Quite apart from the fact that such bureaucracies are in any case unsatisfactory because recruitment is based not on the principle of achievement, but on that of personal status, a class of discontented intellectuals is created, who often turn to various radical movements in order to attain positions in which their capacity for political leadership can find some expression. But in the shadow of the division of the world into two great camps, the formation of political opposition groups often leads to a repetition of the world conflict between communism and democracy within the underdeveloped country. Although the radical groups are sometimes illegal and may exist only underground, they are present nevertheless, and impose serious difficulties on the smooth economic progress of the country. Furthermore, this very situation makes the introduction of more rational community-oriented bureaucracies even more difficult. For, as Weber has pointed out, this process of rationalization is 'revolutionary' in a certain sense. It has the tendency of reshaping social relations and introducing a

[8] On this point, see Henry S. Bloch, 'Economic Development and Public Finance,' in B. F. Hoselitz, *op. cit.* I was able to observe personally the extreme clumsiness of the customs administration of a Latin American country in which I served on a United Nations Technical Assistance Mission.

principle of formal egalitarianism which the political elite may regard as dangerous to its interests and whose introduction it will therefore attempt to resist. In such countries—and some of the Middle Eastern and Latin American nations belong to this group—the introduction of modern bureaucracies may encounter great difficulties. This will, at the same time, affect the speed and ease with which an overall process of economic development can be accomplished.

Fortunately, the majority of the larger and more important underdeveloped countries do not have quite such rigid social structures. Some rigidities exist there also, and they impede the extension of rational, impersonally operating administrations. For example, Daniel Thorner recently surveyed the prospects of reshaping the village administrations in India through the establishment of village *panchayats*. He found that in most parts of India the *panchayats* have no power whatever and are not likely to obtain it, and that in those parts where they are effective they have been built into old-established power and social structures reinforcing the caste system where it still exists, and a class system based on differential land-ownership and wealth, where the caste system is weaker. Thorner sums up his observations with the remark that 'to rebuild village life would require far greater vision, authority and popular support than is commanded by the *panchayats* anywhere in India. To approach the goal of rural economic development through the agency of the existing village *panchayats* would appear to be an exercise in frustration.'[9]

But although such impediments to the formation of modern rational bureaucracies exist probably in all underdeveloped

[9] Daniel Thorner, 'The Village *Panchayat* as a Vehicle of Change,' *Economic Development and Cultural Change*, vol. II, no. 3 (October 1953), p. 215.

countries, they have become relatively subordinated in some, especially in the formation of governmental bureaucracies in the larger administrative units and, above all, also in the business bureaucracies. Yet even there some obstacles still exist, which are due partly to the lack of adequate training facilities for officials, and partly to the absence of traditions of officialdom which prescribe a strong ethic for the profession and produce the sentiment of responsibility and loyalty to one's task so characteristic of bureaucracies in advanced countries.

Although the systems of professional and higher education are being re-examined in almost all underdeveloped countries, there is still too great an emphasis on literary-historical and narrowly legal training. This is also the case with requirements for positions in the higher ranks of the bureaucracy. The notion that an official is often, even predominantly, not a 'generalist,' but a specialist in a particular field of knowledge has not yet fully penetrated the public administrations of advanced countries and lags badly behind in underdeveloped countries. One consequence of this fact is that in advanced countries, as well as in underdeveloped countries, private bureaucracies are often staffed with better qualified and sometimes better educated men than public bureaucracies. In underdeveloped countries where specialized technical and professional skills are relatively scarce, the loss of many qualified individuals who might have performed valuable public service to private enterprises is a serious blow to government administration. Again, many officials who go abroad on government fellowships in order to acquire special skills soon after their return drift into better paid or more honorific positions in private business administration.

A sufficiently large supply of adequately trained persons for higher positions in public bureaucracies will only be forthcoming when educational facilities are increased and improved. But here, as in so many other instances, the intermediate schools are in the greatest need of improvement. In some underdeveloped countries there exist excellent universities, and a small number of persons may even receive a university education abroad. The extension and improvement of elementary education is also given high priority in all development plans, and this is quite appropriate in view of the still high illiteracy rates. But it is of almost equal importance to modernize and improve secondary education and technical training. Here is a great field of development in which Unesco can be of inestimable service.

Even the provision of more adequate educational facilities on the secondary level and in special technical fields will have only limited results if traditions of loyalty in service and responsibility are not developed. There are many factors which operate against the rapid and easy introduction of these values. As already stated, in some underdeveloped countries, public officials—and within a somewhat different context officials in business enterprises—often occupy positions similar to those of personal retainers of their superiors. Although this may be acceptable in business bureaucracies, in the long run, it defeats the effective operation of a public administration. But the replacement of this personal tie of service to one's superior by the integration of an official into an impersonal hierarchy is a most difficult process, requiring a total re-adaptation in thinking and values. It is clear that in order to achieve such a transformation powerful incentives must be present. I can

think of only two developments in the societies of underdeveloped countries which may support it. One is the elevation of the prestige and power of officials and the other is the persistence of nationalist sentiments. Neither of these alternatives appears attractive to a person educated in and adhering to the values of Western society. The first tendency seems to increase greatly the danger of creating a managerial class, possibly with totalitarian predilections, and the second to contribute to a growth of ethnocentrism and rejection of cultural and other influences from abroad which may ultimately endanger the peaceful development of international relations.

But the dilemma may appear greater than it really is. The growth of managerial tendencies in public administrations may be tempered with an enhanced emphasis on popular democratic processes, and nationalism may perform a positive function in destroying primary loyalties to a family, tribe, or local village group, and replacing them by loyalties to the nation as a whole. We should not forget that also in Europe nationalism passed through this positive constructive phase, and is responsible, in part, for the consolidation of the great nations of contemporary Europe. If the underdeveloped countries can achieve the creation of smoothly functioning bureaucracies without giving way to the excesses of managerialism or nationalism—both of which contain the seeds of political and social totalitarianism—they will have made a contribution to socio-political practice in this matter equivalent to any achievement of the already advanced countries.

SOME SOCIAL ASPECTS OF ECONOMIC DEVELOPMENT IN UNDER-DEVELOPED COUNTRIES IN ASIA*

H. BELSHAW

ECONOMIC DEVELOPMENT AND MORALS

WHAT people mean by economic development is by and large a moral question. This was brought home to me very forcibly a little over a year ago, when I attended a conference of village workers at Gandhi's headquarters at Sevagram in the Central Provinces of India. The Gandhian members of the conference thought of economic development in terms of progress towards a society in which people were healthy, had sufficient food, and adequate clothing and conditions of housing. But it was predominantly a village society in which levels of consumption were modest and standards were simple. Consumption levels must be sufficient for a rich and full life, but this was interpreted primarily in spiritual terms. Spiritual values must not be sacrificed for higher consumption.

IMMEDIATE DETERMINANTS OF ECONOMIC DEVELOPMENT

Economists, not being well up in attitudes, are prone to express the requirements for economic development in terms of changes in capital, labour or technology. These are the immediate determinants of economic growth. The economist is well aware that behind them are complex

*Adapted and reprinted by permission from *Civilizations*, Vol. 4, No. 4, 1954, pp. 525–538.

changes in human behaviour, relationships and organizations, but he normally shrinks from the task of exposing these to view, and concentrates on the variables mentioned, often abstracting them rather ruthlessly for convenience in manipulation. It is legitimate enough to do this, but we must occasionally look at the untidy pattern from which the immediate determinants emerge.

For economic development in our sense to occur, the combined effects of changes in capital, labour and technology must increase output more than population growth. I am not over-fond of the term technology, because it usually connotes machines and processes, which is too narrow. I prefer to speak of *innovations*. In our context these are ideas which become embodied in improvements in the quality of labour, capital, processes or organizations. But they may also be expressed in the *quantity* of labour, since improved health measures, or changes in the practice of family limitation would be innovations of first rate importance; or in the *amount* of capital through changes in the practice of conspicuous consumption, or putting savings in a bank instead of hoarding them, or investing in small industries or better ploughs instead of buying jewellery or land (which is already in use by somebody else).

Apart from innovations, capital must

normally grow faster than population for a cumulative increase in output per head to occur. But it would be possible to demonstrate that in the same circumstances growth in income per head would eventually peter out. This throws the main responsibility for economic development on innovations, the nature and role of which are our main concern in what follows. Even if the above thesis is not accepted, there should be no disagreement that economic innovations profoundly affect productive efficiency.

SOME GENERAL OBSERVATIONS ABOUT INNOVATIONS

If economic development is to proceed, value systems, attitudes and economic institutions, relations and organizations must correspond more closely to those of the West with their greater emphasis on material gain. But future societies will grow out of those which exist so that they need not be indentical, indeed cannot be identical, with those of the West. This means, inter alia, that our stereotype of democracy may be even less appropriate to Oriental societies than it is to our own. Moreover, the mistakes as well as the achievements of the West can be used as a warning or a guide. There is no necessity to follow entirely either the individualism of the United States—a tradition in any case rapidly being dissolved in a different matrix—or adopt the Russian totalitarian monolith as a pattern, but rather the need to evolve indigenous forms.

Perhaps the most significant development programmes anywhere are the community projects in Ceylon and India.[1] These coordinate the various "nation building" services in an integrated approach to rural betterment which stresses

[1] For an account of these cf. *Report of the Mission on Community Organization and Development in South and South-East Asia.* United Nations, December 1953.

voluntary participation of the people, both in making and implementing decisions and in self-help and mutual help. In these elements at least they express the essence of democracy as I understand it. They draw on the principles of agricultural extension, and the techniques of the West, but aim to apply them through agencies and types of organizations designed to fit agrarian needs and culture within Oriental societies.

One of the dangers of international technical assistance, be it added, is sometimes the ethnocentrism of experts and contributing governments and their disillusionment when their pupils and beneficiaries do not see the light, or seem grateful enough.

A further consideration is that existing culture presents obstacles to economic development, and another that economic development involves a social cost, as well as an economic cost in the form of deferred consumption.

SOME OBSTACLES TO ECONOMIC DEVELOPMENT

Despite the changes which have occurred there remain important cultural obstacles to economic development. People in a society must want economic development sufficiently to pay the price needed in terms of the modification in existing attitudes, institutions and relationships. The sort of changes just exemplified may to some extent have prepared the way even at heavy cost, by loosening the fabric of convention; but they have not necessarily changed the right things, and may have substituted one impediment for another. In any case, it is clear that some important obstacles to necessary changes in attitudes and their positive expression in innovations still remain. We touch briefly on one or two.

The first of these is existing poverty. As is argued later poverty and its concomitants of disease and under-nourishment lower the quality of labour and are conductive to inertia. Poverty also reduces the capacity to invest. This has a direct bearing on innovations because new ideas are embodied in capital. New processes may not be possible because resources are insufficient to apply them. Moreover, where incomes are small and precarious, the risks involved in failure are a serious deterrent to trying new ways until their success has been amply demonstrated.

Beyond this, in societies which are still mainly agrarian, there are cultural characteristics which inhibit growth. In them the family is still the primary economic and social unit. Its welfare and perpetuation become primary responsibilities; and loyalty to the extended family and the village is stronger than in the West. Familial attitudes have an important bearing on the population problem through their effects on attitudes toward family limitation. They also circumscribe the range of individual freedom in economic decisions and influence the motives for saving and investment. Hoarding provides a security reserve or a means to finance the ceremonial expenditure necessary for status. Failing such a security reserve, the hazards of nature or of life, or the pressure to meet social obligations on ceremonial occasions, mean debt under such onerous conditions that recovery is difficult or impossible. Investment in land purchase which will not normally increase aggregate productive power, appears to provide a better foundation for security and family perpetuation than other investments bringing in a financial return. But in any case the facilities for the latter are inadequate, or not understood. Ostentatious expenditure among wealthier classes, and a preference for investment in real estate or financial enterprise and trade, rather than physical production, also limit the influence of saving and investment on economic growth.

In such a society relations are personal or particularist rather than universalist. They are affected by kinship, friendship, or status as determined by caste or other institutions, and dependant on who a person is rather than what he can do. On peasant holdings or other small scale enterprises, relationships based on these desiderata may work enough: but they are unsuited to the requirements of modern government, public administration or large scale enterprise. In the two latter bureaucratic forms of organization are necessary. By these we mean organizations characterized by the professional performance of functions in an impersonal way, with primary loyalty given to the enterprise and its purposes.

Within the village, the compulsion of public opinion is substantially directed towards conformity with a conservative tradition, often with leadership also vested among elders who are conservative and traditional.

By comparison with Christianity, Oriental religions give less positive inducements to the "virtues" of thrift and hard work. Many writers comment on acceptance of work as a necessary evil, rather than a virtue—which does not mean that peasants do not work hard—and on the high value placed on leisure, contentment, and participation in the recreation and ceremonies of the village. Such attitudes must be weighed against the desire for more goods and willingness to accept greater continuity of labour (especially under conditions controlled by the machine), as a means of earning more income. They must be considered within the framework of institutions such as land tenure and caste which reduce economic means and incentives, or the freedom of economic manoeuvre. In urban areas, the forces making for change are more powerful and more disruptive. But Asian societies are still predominantly agrarian.

Because of the social dislocation which has occurred and is still to be expected there are important concealed assumptions in the belief that economic development will lead to internal harmony and be conducive to world peace. It is not so much poverty, as relative poverty associated with exploitation and mistrust of leaders, and change which disturbs and does not satisfy, which breed revolution.

Economic development as a peace programme requires attention to the process as much as to the end result; for it is not merely higher consumption to which people aspire, but also satisfying conditions of work, and positive opportunities for self expression.[2] It requires, for example, minimum labour standards in factory employment, reform of land tenure and usury in the villages, and provision through credit of the means for an approach through self-effort to the higher consumption levels and satisfying conditions of work aspired to, as well as more capital and better technology. Equally, it requires integrity and stability in government, and agencies directed to enabling the people, especially the villagers, to participate actively in making decisions on programmes directed to their own benefit and in implementing them.

SOCIAL WELFARE A MEANS AS WELL AS AN END

More capital and improved technology are necessary requirements for economic development; but it is a profound mistake to look on these as the means while regarding improved social welfare simply as an end. Together with institutional changes, such as expressed in land reform,

[2] As one facet of this problem Riesman draws attention to the shift from "conspicuous consumption" to "conspicuous production" in American life. "Some Relationships Between Technical Progress and Social Progress," *Explorations in Entrepreneurial History*, Vol. VI, No. 3, 1953–4, p. 136.

improved social welfare is important among the means. Whatever may be the nature and validity of the mystical concept of the "social will," a concept which I do not understand, a certain elan and confidence among members of society are necessary elements in economic development. Emergent nationalism may help, but is not enough; for these elements cannot gather strength in a society where people are under-fed, malaria ridden, exploited, unorganized or cynically mistrustful of their leaders.

But social reform is necessary as a means because of its more direct economic impacts. Better nutrition and health improve the efficiency and energy of the workers and their propensity to innovate or accept innovations. Literacy education extends the horizons of knowledge and facilitates receptivity to new ideas. Training and "extension" education of skills and the latter can embody effective arts of demonstration and persuasion. Land reform and other institutional changes may improve both the incentive and the resources available for the fuller expression of individual potentialities.

We may interpolate that the question of incentives just touched upon has a bearing on investment criteria. While massive public works and other capital intensive types of investment with deferred results in consumption may be necessary, adequate emphasis on investment yielding an early return in consumption goods is needed so that the fruits of additional effort can be seen and enjoyed. The balance of growth must be consistent with consumption functions; with the proportion of additional incomes spent on different classes of goods. These functions we have pointed out, emerge out of existing consumption patterns culturally determined.

The approach must be integrated—or "multipurpose" to use the jargon which is becoming fashionable—if it is to succeed. This does not mean that everything can be attempted at once, but rather that the minimum necessary supporting or complementary measures must be undertaken for the success of any given approach. It will be futile to attempt to improve agricultural techniques if the malaria ridden population cannot apply them. On the other hand improved agriculture is necessary so that further health measures can be afforded. It is necessary to awaken new wants, but dangerous to do so unless the means to satisfy them are made available.

SIGNIFICANCE OF SOCIAL SERVICES

These observations lead to the important conclusion, that governments must extend *services which compete with capital formation in their demands on the small surplus above current consumption.* Failing adequate services designed to accelerate the process of innovations, investment is likely to go to waste, and productive power will fail to outstrip population increase.

This puts the case for international capital aid in somewhat different terms from those commonly used, especially if it be considered with the necessity for capital investments in social overhead which *directly* may have a low output: capital ratio. On the average for new investment as a whole, even on the most optimistic assumptions as to this ratio, current savings in most under-developed countries in Asia are barely sufficient to maintain output per head at current rates of population growth. If population growth is accelerated because of the extension of cheap health measures the prospects are even less bright. But the sparse savings must be trenched upon by the extension of services. The necessity for international capital aid then becomes all the more urgent, and the case for grants-in-aid all the stronger, so that sufficient social overhead and services can be developed to promote a break through. These are also necessary to increase absorptive capacity for capital imports: but as in other aspects the problem is again one of balance between the use of scarce resources for capital formation and for services.

PUBLIC ADMINISTRATION

The above analysis brings us back to the importance of integrity, stability and continuity in government so that social overhead and services are in fact extended and reforms instituted. But however well intentioned a government may be, the establishment of an efficient public administration in which the people have confidence becomes a key requirement. It is also one of the most difficult to bring about. In some countries there is a competent cadre of civil servants at the centre. In others even this is lacking, and necessary government departments are nonexistent, or embryo. In most there is the need for extension of the civil service and especially for more public servants of the lower ranks concerned with action programmes rather than regulatory functions. An elaboration of the problem would carry us too far afield into aspects of recruitment and training, and especially into questions of status and attitudes. For example, as long as a desk strewn with files is the hall-mark of status, and field work with its dirty hands and dirty boots has low prestige value, success in implementing development plans will be limited.

Dr. Frank Tannenbaum is a Professor of Latin American History at Columbia University. His most recent books are *Slave and Citizen*, 1947; *Mexico: The*

Struggle for Peace and Bread, 1950; *A Philosophy of Labor*, 1951; and *The American Tradition in Foreign Policy*, 1955.

Dr. Julian H. Steward is a Graduate Research Professor, Department of Sociology and Anthropology, University of Illinois. He is editor and part author of the *Handbook of South American Indians*, 6 volumes, B.A.E. Bulletin 145, and author of *Theory of Cultural Change*, 1945.

Dr. Robert A. Manners is an Assistant Professor of Anthropology at Brandeis University.

Dr. Charles P. Loomis is Head of the Department of Sociology and Anthropology, Michigan State University. He was formerly Director, Extension and Training Office of Foreign Agricultural Relations, U.S. Department of Agriculture, and is now Head of the Inter-Governmental Commission on Refugees, Mission to the Andean Countries. He is coauthor of *Rural Social Systems, Rural Sociology, Turrialba-Social Systems and the Introduction of Change*, and translator of Ferdinand Toennies' *Gemeinschaft vs. Gesellschaft*. Dr. Loomis has, in addition, published numerous articles in professional journals.

Dr. Wilson Longmore is with the Agricultural Institute in Allahabad, India. He was formerly Housing Economist with the Division of Health, Welfare and Housing, Institute of Inter-American Affairs, Bogota, Colombia.

Dr. Bert F. Hoselitz is a Professor of Social Sciences at the University of Chicago, Editor of *Economic Development and Cultural Change*, and Executive Secretary of the Norman Wait Harris Memorial Foundation in International Relations. He is a coauthor of *The Progress of Underdeveloped Areas*, 1952, and of *Capital Formation and Economic Growth*, 1955, and of numerous articles in professional journals.

Dr. H. Belshaw is Macarthy Professor of Economics, Victoria College, Wellington, New Zealand. He has in recent years been the author of numerous articles showing the complex interrelationships of variables usually studied in separate disciplines.

VII

THE PROCESS OF DEVELOPING UNDERDEVELOPED ECONOMIES AND INCREASING PRODUCTION

Up to this juncture we have been concerned only indirectly with
what ought to be done about underdeveloped areas. The descriptive material
included thus far has indicated to the reader the nature of the problems in underdeveloped areas and has suggested numerous tasks that should be undertaken. But
how should we go about developing underdeveloped areas and what processes are
involved? We will attempt to answer this question in part in the present chapter.

In an address presented to the Auckland Branch of the Economic Society of
Australia and New Zealand, Prof. H. Belshaw has stated,

Economists no doubt would accept the obvious view that economic development is a
social process, but this process involves much more than the response of individuals to
material incentives and is of such a nature that the usual equilibrium analysis offers little help. There is the need for a wider, if less tidy approach by economists, which draws
on the resources of other social sciences or applied arts—anthropology, sociology, political science, education, law or public administration—and sets economic motivation,
not austerely apart but in its proper place in complex systems of responses, beliefs,
organizations and institutions. If we begin with acceptance of economic development as
a social process, and bear this consistently in mind, and not, as is common, think of it
primarily as a set of requirements such as more land and capital, and better techniques,
it should make a profound difference to our assumptions, our time perspective and systems of priorities, judgments on the relative importance of various requirements at different times, and procedures.[1]

Belshaw continues his basic approach, an approach to economic development
that emphasizes an understanding of human behavior as crucial to success, when
he says,

If we consider economic development as an operational problem the keys to success
are: participation of ordinary people in development programmes and the sharing by
ordinary people in the benefits.

[1] "Economic Development as an Operational Problem," H. Belshaw, *Civilizations*, Vol. II,
No. 2, 1952, pp. 159–160.

This approach goes much beyond economics as usually conceived or the calculated superiority of one practical technique over another on the *assumption* that it can be applied; for it *begins* with the notion of changing the willingness and ability of individuals to respond, now inhibited not only by the pressure of poverty but also by cultural, institutional, political and administrative conditions.[2]

Consistent with this approach, Belshaw, as a first interest, has presented the development of the capacities of people—improved health and education.

The first need here is improved health, especially by the attack on major endemic diseases such as malaria and intestinal parasites. If it succeeds, economic development should bring better health; but a vigorous forward movement is scarcely conceivable among a people decimated by disease so that they lack initiative and energy and so that a large proportion of national income is wasted through early deaths. In Guatemala the diet of the Indian populations is said to be adequate except for minor deficiencies; but the masses suffer almost universally from intestinal parasites. There seems little point in providing more food for worms; but to get rid of them is the equivalent to a substantial increase in food supply and so would be an important direct contribution to development, as well as an indirect contribution in preparing a healthier population for further advances.

The second necessity for improving individual capacities is education, both to persuade people to make changes and show them how. Persuasion leads us into the whole question of cultural and institutional obstacles. The types of education and the methods must be suited to the culture—what is called extension in the United States, but patterned to suit local requirements.[3]

But even more difficult of accomplishment is the change in social environment suggested by Belshaw. As he points out,

Some social attitudes involve an allocation of resources of time, effort and material things which is not consistent with economic progress, and this must be changed by education or providing the right incentives. As long as debts equivalent to several years' income are incurred to spend on feasts on the occasion of funerals or marriages, the load of unproductive debt will be an obstacle to agricultural improvement. As long as cows are sacred in India, there will be a huge excess of cattle population which exhausts the soil and reduces the area for food production. The low elasticity of demand for income in terms of work, for example among peasants working on plantations in Indonesia, discourages that expansion of demand which is implicit in economic development and requires special attention to discovering and offering the appropriate incentives.

We may illustrate institutional impediments by systems of land tenure associated with excessive fragmentation and rack renting. Often as much as two-thirds of the crops goes to landlords, and even the small holdings are subdivided into numerous tiny patches. The reform of land tenure is admittedly full of difficulties, but it is necessary to improve both the incentives and the capacity to use improved techniques and methods of farm organization. Similarly stratification based on caste or other institutions, limits effective demand and the distribution of labour and so creates impediments to change.[4]

[2] *Ibid.*, p. 163.
[3] *Ibid.*, pp. 163–164.
[4] *Ibid.*, pp. 165–166.

A third major requirement involves greater use of existing resources. It is this requirement that is so often cited as the primary requirement or only factor in economic development. It is here that we are concerned with maximum efficiency in land use and the application of additional capital in order to facilitate the development of resources. Other questions with which one becomes involved at this point, and which will be answered more fully in later chapters, concern the desirability of local capital as contrasted to foreign capital, taking into consideration not only availability and interest rates but, in addition, public attitudes toward each. Another question concerns the size of development units, not only in terms of maximizing mechanical efficiency but also in terms of maximizing output with people whose existing work patterns and attitudes may militate against machinery and equipment.

There is much scope for developing units, even of unfamiliar types which can operate economically on a small scale. For example the small industries unit of UNRRA in China, developed a forty-bag-a-day cement plant in Shaoyang in Hunan Province. When I saw this in 1947 it was producing cement more cheaply than it could be delivered from the large cement plant on the coast. The designing and making of simple tools and machines for agriculture also present opportunities, especially if mass produced parts can be made available to local blacksmiths and other artisans. One expert from FAO gave it as his considered opinion that an amount equivalent to the cost of imported tractors into India would have made a substantial, much larger contribution to improved agriculture, had it been used to produce and distribute a simple improved plough as designed by one of the Indian Agricultural Colleges; and again, UNRRA in China was doing a potentially significant job in improving hoes, cotton gins, threshers, oil presses and other implements and machines, and even a tiny internal combustion engine not beyond the co-operative ownership of a small group of farmers for pumping, hauling and other farm operations.[5]

In concluding his address, Prof. Belshaw cautions,

The whole problem of development is one of great complexity and difficulty so that one cannot regard it with easy optimism. But provided we take a long view we need not lapse into defeatism. If we are in a hurry and set our sight for five years hence, the gap between targets and achievements will be so great that we cannot fail to be despondent; but if we set progressive achievements against a goal which is twenty or thirty years hence, we shall have a better perspective, and interim progress may be gratifying; especially if we regard this present period as one of *experimentation* in organized international collaboration for economic development primarily in the interests of underdeveloped countries themselves.

Already scattered throughout the world are experiments which have succeeded or have great potentialities; the Jamaica Welfare Commission in the Caribbean; the Near East Foundation in Greece, Syria, and Lebanon; co-operatives in a score of countries; many experiments in mass education in British Dependencies; medical training in Fiji; social centres in Egypt, India and Mexico; the Panchayats in India; supervised credit in Paraguay; nuclear schools in Guatemala; the Shantan Baillie School; the work of Cath-

[5] *Ibid.*, pp. 169–170.

olic and Protestant missions in many parts of the world; the co-operative programmes of the United States in Latin America. These and a host of other activities are providing a leaven in widely separated places, or spinning threads out of which patterns of development may be woven. From them much can be learned of the processes by which people may be persuaded, taught and organized. All the examples mentioned have this first premise in common; that for programmes to succeed, for body to be given to blueprints, an answer must be found to two questions: How can ordinary people be encouraged to participate? How can ordinary people benefit? And all have in common the spirit of experimental exploration as a means of discovering the route to economic and social improvement.[6]

The selections in this chapter provide a rather detailed approach to the problem of developing underdeveloped areas, following the approach suggested by Belshaw. They have been arranged so as to provide an orderly and systematic introduction to the process of developing underdeveloped areas.

"What the Underdeveloped Countries Have to Do" by Maurice Zinkin consists of a straightforward list of steps that must be taken by the underdeveloped country if it wishes to have the benefits of an industrial economy. This is a businessman's viewpoint. The items on this list involve not only short-run sacrifices, but they also involve fundamental changes in attitudes, values, and specifically, definitions of desirable human behavior, i.e., behavior that must be oriented toward long-term goals. The importance of savings as a technique for the internal acquisition of capital is an example of behavior which must be defined as desirable rather than undesirable. After reading this article one may well ask whether all underdeveloped areas would ask for help in developing their economies if they realized what the costs and consequences might be.

The article which follows, "Mobilization of Domestic Resources for Economic Development" by I. G. Patel, continues in the same vein by emphasizing the importance of the acquisition of capital. In this contribution private and government approaches are described and the different role of each is made clearer for the reader.

Following the more general articles on economic development that we have just mentioned is a selection from Henry G. Aubrey's lengthy paper, "Small Industry in Economic Development." This paper makes the important point that presently developing countries will not necessarily evolve through all the stages that typical western nations have evolved. The pattern in underdeveloped areas may be somewhat different in that large industrial plants may not be appropriate; in their place will be found a multitude of smaller industries. The appropriateness of small industry is then discussed in the original article, we should add, in excellent detail with numerous examples. The advantage of small industry, of course, lies in the fact that it may not be nearly so capital intensive as the larger plant and in addition may make better use of the available labor supply. For a variety of reasons it is shown that the process of development may call for the

---

[6] *Ibid.*, p. 173.

small plant approach already familiar in part of Asia, notably Japan. It should not go without mention that the original article by Aubrey contains perhaps the best available selected bibliography on the subject to date, one close to 200 items.

An even more specialized article by Kenneth A. Bohr follows, "Investment Criteria for Manufacturing Industries in Underdeveloped Countries." This carefully executed research analyzes the characteristics of selected industrial plants in order to classify them on a basis of capital intensiveness, labor intensiveness, locational factor, and size. These data facilitate the decision as to which kind and under which conditions industrial plants should be established in underdeveloped areas.

Although automatism might be thought of little use in underdeveloped areas, Richard L. Meier, in "Automatism and Economic Development," presents a cogent argument for its usefulness under certain circumstances. The contention is that at times the pace of economic development may be hastened by using efficient nonlabor intensive techniques and that in these cases automatism may be the best approach; capital may then be devoted almost entirely to productive facilities without the diversion necessary if additional facilities must be provided for a work force.

These articles present a picture of the process of economic development in underdeveloped areas: first, a description of the problems of these areas and the general processes of economic development; second, more specialized articles showing how specific approaches may or may not be efficient in a given situation.

WHAT THE UNDERDEVELOPED COUNTRIES HAVE TO DO*

MAURICE ZINKIN

IF THE underdeveloped countries are to achieve their objective of economic development, they not only have to acquire capital and to invest it, though these by themselves are formidable enough tasks. They also have to make all the changes which are required to produce a population which

*Adapted and Reprinted by permission from *India Quarterly*, Vol. VIII, No. 2, April–June, 1952, pp. 132–141.

is saving-minded and an economy in which investment is attractive. And beyond that again they have to make all the changes in the attitude of their people and the structure of their society which are necessary if their economic life is to become dynamic instead of static. In all their habits and customs and training there will have to be an emphasis on economic initiative and material welfare without which their best talents will continue to go, as in the past, to the intellectually often more satisfying pursuits, of culture and saintliness.

Many estimates have been made of the investment which is necessary in the underdeveloped world. The most recent United Nations guess ran into billions of dollars over a few years, and indeed the value of such estimates is mainly to reveal the magnitude of the problem. Even the U.S. still has its poor. And to give the rest of the world the investment required to produce an American standard of life would involve a sum beyond practical imagining. It is more useful, if one wishes to generalize, to start from the fact that roughly one Rupee of investment will produce rather under a Rupee of extra production. The exact amount of production will vary according to the type of investment which is made. Thus, to take a concrete case: in order to provide for India's annual increase of population, at India's existing standard of life, perhaps Rs. 150 crores (Rs. 1,500 millions) of investment annually is required and to increase the standard of life by 1 per cent or so would probably require something approaching another Rs. 150 crores. This 300 crores per year is roughly the rate envisaged in the Draft Five Year Plan, and, were India in fact to invest at this pace, it is likely that at the end of the five year period there would be a small but definite improvement in the standard of life, though some allowance must be made for the fact that there is a certain bias in the plan towards projects, notably the multi-purpose schemes, which are capital-intensive.

Requirements and programmes in the underdeveloped countries are on a similar modest scale. The United States, by contrast, invests some twenty times as much as is proposed for India; but then U.S. industry in 1951 achieved an increase in production of 8 per cent in one year. The underdeveloped countries are, therefore,

after straining every nerve, not catching up; on the contrary, they are not always even improving their standards absolutely; and they are almost never—the only exceptions are places like Venezuela and Kuwait and Malaya in their most expansive periods—improving their position relatively to the most advanced Western countries. Yet it is relatively, quite as much as absolutely, that their populations judge. Nothing makes one feel so poor as the comparison with someone else's riches and no one feels the comparison more bitterly than those who are themselves comfortably off, and therefore have the leisure and the intellectual energy to be affected by their country's poverty.

If, therefore, the poorer countries are to give contentment to their people, investment on some scale larger than any hitherto known must take place. That is generally accepted, though everywhere there are those who hearken back to the old simple life of the self-sufficient village of peasants and craftsmen. For their values, notably when they are Gandhians, one must have respect; but their policy would be possible of achievement only in a world of static population, where the bounds of self-sufficiency were not perpetually burst by an unceasing increase in numbers. In underdeveloped countries where there is a large increase of population to provide for, and that is virtually all of them, the Gandhian ideal must remain a dream. Industry and machines, power for the craftsmen and science for the farmer, are an inevitability if poverty is not to become ever more grinding, high though the price may be in slums and ever deepening dependence upon the market, a dependence all too liable to bring into the village the low moral standard of the bazaar.

Once it is accepted that investment on the maximum possible scale is a necessity, the first problem is where to find the savings. There can be no investment unless somebody first makes a corresponding saving, though that saving need not necessarily be in money. It can be in kind. The farmer who builds a bund in his own time with the help of his own bullocks saves just as surely as the Government which taxes for a surplus in order to permit its Public Works Department to pay for a bund to be built for it. The man who brings bamboos from the jungle to build a hut is saving just as much as the man who puts money in the post-office in the hope of one day being able to buy a house.

Of this second type of saving, saving in kind, most underdeveloped societies do a certain amount, though usually very much less than is possible. Of saving in actual money, almost all do very little. Much has been said, notably in the recent U. N. Report 'Domestic Financing of Economic Development' on the institutional improvements required in order to increase savings, and to see that, when they are made, they are put to the most advantageous use; and what has been said is true. If Governments issue bonds in denominations and of maturities to appeal to every class of savers; if savings institutions are decentralized by the use of post-offices and the spread of branch banks; if the banking system is organized to direct town savings into the financing of the peasantry, rather than rural savings into town real-estate, as happens notably in Latin America; if a sound co-operative system is built up with real local control, and a keen eye for a good borrower; if banks and insurance companies are enabled to invest a part of their funds in providing certainly working capital, and possibly longer-term capital also, for industry; if Stock Exchanges were developed; above all, at the present moment, if Governments would resist the temptation to evade their problems by inflation, so that the saver does not always find that his present sacrifice gives him not a greater, but a smaller, future gain; if all these

things were done, savings could doubtless be larger and better used.

But neither that, nor such dubious expedients as gold certificates, would solve the real problem, which is the very low propensity to save at all of underdeveloped societies. All their social values are against saving, particularly saving in an economically advantageous form; and men act far more in accordance with their social values, in order to be approved of by their neighbours, than they do on any cold calculation of profit and loss. Much money, for example, is spent on jewellery, especially at weddings. Both the newly-weds and the country would be better off if this money went into saving-certificates instead; but anyone who has tried, as I have, to persuade Bhil parents to change over to saving-certificates, will be aware of how profound is the urge to keep up with the neighbours in the most primitive of societies. A saint, or the draconic punishments of the totalitarian state, might change the ways of spending money at weddings; little less will do. Yet these are probably the main savings of most underdeveloped countrysides; savings to buy land do not really count, since, in any country, where all the useful land is occupied, and this is true of most underdeveloped countries, for every purchaser there must be a seller, for every saver a dis-saver.

The whole atmosphere of most underdeveloped societies is hostile to saving. Compared with hospitality, generosity or even ostentation, thrift is not a virtue, but a vice, fit only for a merchant. The man who saves is, of necessity, very often also the man who does not pay his fair share for village ceremonies or village amusements, the man who marries his daughter meanly or buries his mother shabbily. The West owes more of its advance than is commonly realized to the Puritan doctrine which made of thrift and quiet living a moral virtue pleasing to God. There is no corresponding belief in any underdeveloped society. The man who gets on, who rises above his fellows, is not emulated, but cut off; his eminence is a lonely one to which others are rarely tempted.

Nor are the other incentives to save of a Western society available in anything like comparable strength in the underdeveloped countries. Family obligations are usually strong, so that the need to save for old age is relatively slight, especially in the countryside where formal ownership, or the formal tenancy agreement of the family plot will probably remain in the old man's name. The scope of insurance companies, except amongst the gradually growing, Westernized urban middle class, is, therefore, limited. The industrial corporation, whose undistributed profits are so important a part of the savings of all advanced economies, exists only on the fringes of underdeveloped societies. Taxation is needed so urgently for the most elementary requirements of defence, education, health and order that none of the underdeveloped countries is able to obtain a regular surplus of even as much as Rs. 50 crores a year. Of all the stimulants to saving which work in England or America, indeed, probably only the desire to own one's own house has anything like comparable importance; and probably the lack of building societies and speculative builders of small houses is in many countries one of the few institutional defects which are of real importance. The difficulty is not, however, only that people in the underdeveloped countries are unwilling to save. It is also that they cannot. Those whose incomes barely provide subsistence, who are driven into debt by every family calamity or bout of unemployment, nowhere provide any substantial portion of the national savings. The difference in the underdeveloped countries is that these poverty-stricken sections of the population are not a mere fringe, proper objects of the solicitude of a motherly Welfare State, but the vast majority, the great mass from whom savings must come—or be squeezed—and for whom the investment is required. Savings one-twentieth the size Americans make every year of their own free will are for Indians, or Chinese, or Indonesians an almost impossible burden.

It is made even more impossible by the modern social conscience. Most underdeveloped countries have a wide range of incomes. There are many poor, but there are also a few who are rich, even on European or American standards. Social custom prevents these rich saving as they did in Victorian England; much of the ostentation of a Maharaja was obligatory—the expected 'Circensis' of his people. Nor have the rich of underdeveloped socieites had the habit of lavish and imaginative giving which is so notable in the United States or England; the Nuffield and the Rockefeller are almost unknown. Yet, with all these handicaps, much of the indigenous savings of these communities has in fact come from the few rich, the Indian Maharaja, the Egyptian Pasha, even the Chinese Warlord. This type of saving is now being cut down, in a way that is quite irreversible, by taxation. Conscience combines with fear of Communism to make intolerable the spectacle of extreme luxury side by side with starvation, of the rich growing richer next door to the poor growing poorer. It does not matter that economically it may be argued that the poor grow poorer because they have too many children, and that for the rich to get richer is the inevitable result of their performing their duty of saving. So everywhere taxation on the rich has gone up, and it is more likely that the loopholes of evasion will be closed, and that the few countries, like Egypt, whose super-taxes are still not really high, will raise them, than that there will be any appreciable reduction of taxation in countries like India. The rich can no longer be relied upon as a major source of savings, though sometimes the State which taxes them may use their taxes for economic development itself. This has happened in Mexico, for example, and is happening to some extent in India. It needs to be more widespread, bitter though it is to have to use the meagre revenues of these States for bridges and dams and power-stations, when there are sick needing doctors and children waiting to be taught.

To some extent the rising middle-class, and the growing undistributed profits of industry, may help budget surpluses to fill the gap resulting from increased taxation of the rich. They cannot do more. The rest, probably a very large percentage, of what is needed, will have to come from abroad, from those countries whose savings exceed their own most necessary demands; which means today in effect the United States, though, in special cases, like India, something may come also from Great Britain and the Commonwealth.

In these circumstances, it is natural that much has been made recently of the need for special inducements to attract the foreign investor. Yet these are, in fact, little different from those needed to attract the domestic investor. The same circumstances which will keep the foreign investor away will cause the domestic investor to hoard or to try to export his capital; so universal is this truth that the best recent examples come not from the underdeveloped countries at all, but from Western Europe, from countries like France and Germany and Italy. The only special inducement the foreign investor needs is the promise that he will not be discriminated against, that if he is more efficient and cheaper than his native competitor, neither he nor his customer will be artificially prevented from reaping the reward of his superior ability.

The conditions required to make investment possible, whether domestic or foreign, are quite simple to state, though not easy to attain. The business man must be a reasonably respected member of society, or business will not attract its fair share of talent. Standards of business integrity must be high, or the local entrepreneur will find it difficult to persuade investors to trust him, and the foreign entrepreneur will find himself under-cut by competitors whose favourite weapons are the evasion of sales tax or income-tax. There should be a minimum of Government interference, though what constitutes the minimum may reasonably vary from society to society in accordance with the standards, or lack of them, of the local business man. Such measures as Compulsory Provident Funds, or Factory Acts, or Minimum Wages, may indeed, if industry can afford them, and if they result in a more contented labour force, be economically, as well as socially, advantageous. What is damaging is the attempt to take out of the business man's hands his major business decisions, from the location of his plant, to the qualities he will sell, from the destination of his exports to the methods of his rationalization. It is the investor who has to bear the loss if the decisions are wrong, and he carries a severe enough risk if he, or his managers for him, makes the decisions himself. To bring in also an administrator who, however, skilled in his own line, is necessarily an amateur in the manufacture of cloth or confectionery, or whatever it is, is to very much more than double the risk. It is also, and correspondingly, to very much more than double the difficulty of getting new capital. And this difficulty is greatly increased by the delays inherent in any system of Government control. When a permit is required to issue capital, to locate one's plant, to get the steel and cement to build it, perhaps to expand at all, when one's profit, the customer to whom one sells, perhaps even one's specifications, are all rigidly controlled, the delays at every stage are such that it is only the most persevering of entrepreneurs who ever comes into production at all; but once he is in production, Government controls nearly always protect him against the consequences of his own inefficiency, and thus again reduce investment by slowing down the expansion of the more efficient firms.

This is not an argument for no Government controls. In today's inflation they are often a necessity; but Governments should at least recognize how severe a discouragement to investment they can be, and approach those on production, if not always those on prices, with a corresponding bias against their continuance. Moreover, in the underdeveloped countries their discouraging effect is greatly exaggerated by the relative corruption and incompetence of most underdeveloped Governments, and by the growth of the black market. Once any large proportion of the production of any community goes through the black market, business passes more and more to rascals. Government reacts with stiffer and stiffer controls, making life more and more difficult for the honest man; prices are fixed so low that real profits, after allowing for true depreciation, are cut to very low figures; and the community's respect for the business man, never, in these countries, very high, descends to a new nadir. The honest entrepreneur is stifled; the savings are made in the black market, and black marketeers are neither very good judges of the best investments to make, nor in a position to make their investments very openly. They are more likely to buy gold than to build workers' houses.

The effect of governmental incompetence and corruption is extremely serious. Every time a decision is sold, not only do the costs of industry go up, but its control passes further into the hands of scoundrels; and the building-up of modern industry, if it is to be done really successfully, requires the highest standards of integrity. Mass-production does not depend only on a large and standardized market; it depends also on the unquestioning trust that the public places in the manufacturer's brand name, in the knowledge that something made by General Motors, or I.C.I. or Bombay Dyeing will be all that it claimed to be; for great businesses are not built on short measure and skimped quality.

More important even than Governmental corruption, however, is Governmental incompetence. Business decisions have to be made quickly; otherwise goods will rot, or demurrage be incurred, or machines stand idle. The file which stays in the 'Pending' tray, the case which peregrinates from 'Department to Department,' are, to the business man, so much lost money; and economies which are already short of savings cannot afford such wastes.

One more possible source of money for investment must be mentioned, and that is the foreign loan or grant. The great method of developing in the 19th century, on which the U.S. itself partly grew, was the loan raised in London, or Paris, or, later, Berlin. But these markets no longer have the money to lend, and the misfortune of the underdeveloped countries is that they, and particularly their Governments, have so far found no substitute. The World Bank tends to lend only the foreign exchange required for specific projects, where a Government may need much more than a general development loan, or be unable to undertake the project at all without inflation, unless it can borrow to cover its expenditure in its own currency as well. The American investor is simply not interested in loans to foreign Governments. The Export-Import Bank, though it has done useful work, is only for American Allies, or immediately potential Allies. So Governments get driven back on American Government loans or, more often still, since the loans are not always easy to repay, on American Government grants; and these are not an altogether satisfactory basis for development either, for even the American taxpayer's generosity must be exhaustible eventually. He has many other responsibilities, and those who he is helping are very far away.

It may, however, be assumed that, in combination—from their own private investors, foreign private investors, and American loans and grants—the underdeveloped economies will have available for investment very considerable sums, adequate to enable them to provide for their increasing population with perhaps a margin to spare. Many conditions will still have to be fulfilled, however, if this investment is to be effective.

The first is that underdeveloped countries have generally to accept a very large prior, and mainly governmental, investment on items which yield only a small return before private enterprise of the ordinary industrial sort can undertake its, usually much rapider, forms of development. Before an industry, or, for that matter, modern farming, can develop, there must be a certain minimum modern substructure in the society. Without some railways, a few roads which are at least metalled, a port, electric power and anyway elementary education, no development at all is possible. That is why, whether one is considering the plans of the Colombo Plan countries or those of the Rhodesias, there is always a heavy emphasis on power and communications. The machines have to be turned, the raw materials and the finished products have to be moved in and out, if factories are to make a profit.

The need for electric power-stations and railway lines, roads and docks, is thus fairly obvious. Not quite so obvious is the need for an adequate educational standard. All development requires certain sorts of skill; and many of the underdeveloped countries are either almost totally lacking in modern skills, like much of Africa, or so set in certain ancient ways, like most of Asia, that even persuading road-menders to use wheelbarrows is a major educational task. It is not that the Asian peasant or African tribesman is ignorant, though he is usually illiterate. It is rather that his education, based as it is on traditional lore and magical formulae, is becoming as inappropriate to a modern society as the knowledge of a Roman Augur. If, therefore, these countries are to create a population which can drive tractors, go into factories, or use fertilizers, their educational system has to be both extended and transformed. Everybody must be able to read, for a farmer who cannot read a leaflet can only be shown how to change his ways orally, and therefore very slowly, and an industrial worker who cannot read a warning notice is a positive menace; but that is only the beginning. Education must change a whole series of attitudes, as well as import a whole range of new forms of knowledge. Factory workers must be punctual, a virtue of no meaning to the peasant, they must be disciplined, for the life of others may depend on their doing what they have been told in exactly the way they have been told to do it. They must have a feel for machinery, for bad treatment will wear out a machine more quickly than a bullock. They must not be too attached to routine, for every new method changes routine in order to increase productivity.

In the countryside re-education is even more difficult. The factory worker is at least in a new environment, and cannot therefore but be aware that some changes, some adaptations are necessary. The peasant is still in his old environment. Everything appears as it did in grandfather's day, yet he must now be prepared to substitute at every stage some new-fangled method, demonstrated perhaps by a young Jackanapes, fresh out of college, for grandfather's tried ways. He needs in fact to change from a peasant, shrewd in his centuries of experience with the same land, to a farmer, governing his operations by botany, biology, and relative market prices. Otherwise, improvement will be beset by setbacks. The use of fertilizer is often a delicate balance between too much and too little; the improved breed of cattle may need much more fodder than the peasant is accustomed to give; the new strain of cotton may not grow on his soil.

Compared with this general problem of re-education, the difficulty of getting technicians is not great. Experts can be hired, good students can be sent abroad. The difficulty is rather one of getting good foremen and adequate skilled workmen, for it is too expensive to bring in all one's foremen from outside, and impracticable to send every foreman, and still more every skilled workman, to the West to learn his job. So the task of producing them has to be left to managements who do not always realize that they have to create a new attitude and not merely teach specific skill.

In the countryside, education, though perhaps more important than any other single factor, can nevertheless only take full effect if land tenures themselves are changed in a way which will permit investment. No one will build a well if his land is scattered over a dozen tiny fragments and the well can only serve one. No farm will remain large enough to justify mechanization if on every death it has to be divided amongst many heirs. Above all, no tenant is going to be able to find the money for improvement so long as he has to pay his landlord one half of the crop; and even if he could, he would not, so long as he has no security that he will be the tenant again next year, or any guarantee that he will be reimbursed for his improvements if his tenancy is terminated. Moreover, where the landlord is an absentee and, as so often happens, an improvident one at that, and the tenant holds at

will, there is nobody who has at the same time the knowledge of what improvements to the land will be profitable and an interest in the land which can be pledged in order to raise the money to effect the improvements. Even amongst peasant-owners, who have a mortgageable interest, the history of the last hundred years, in India, or Burma, or China, or even Japan, suggests that it is unwise to make the interest absolute; the peasant who can mortgage without restriction does so far more often to dower a daughter or finance a son than to buy a pedigree bull or build a contour-bund. Until in the countryside there is either a protected tenantry or an owning peasantry, unable to mortgage except for productive improvements, and whose holdings can neither be fragmented nor reduced below a certain size, it is unlikely that there will be extensive improvement, however much money may be made available from domestic or foreign sources. This has, indeed, already been realized by many underdeveloped countries, as is shown by the extensive reforms undertaken in, for example, India and Mexico.

It would be possible to continue with an ever-lengthening list of detailed reforms, each of which, if carried out, would contribute something to the capacity of the underdeveloped country for economic development. But the issue is not really one of this detailed change or that. What is needed is a complete change of attitude.

Every country in the world which is poorer than America, even England, would like to have America's riches; and all of them, more or less, would like to have these riches without having to accept the American attitudes which have made them possible, but to which they are, in different degrees and for various reasons, allergic. These American attitudes may indeed have their weaknesses. The underdeveloped countries may argue that they do not produce the culture of France, or the high thinking of Scotland, or the mystic experience of India, or the feudal devotion of old Japan. But they do produce wealth, and if what the underdeveloped countries want is wealth, if without a rise in the standard of living their whole stability will be undermined, then they will have to sacrifice some of their traditional, and possibly absolutely more valuable values, in order to attain it. Sales-managers and production-engineers are perhaps less admirable than lawyers and minor civil servants (though there seems no real reason for this general underdeveloped belief); but countries which continue to believe so will also continue to have poor sales-managers and poor production-engineers; and lawyers do not increase productivity or create mass-markets. So again, it may be that speculation, black marketing, ostentatious expenditure and evasion of tax may be more exciting, and a quicker way of getting rich than the slow slog of building up a busi-

ness, soundly rooted in the goodwill of its customers; but countries whose business men continue to think so will neither have adequate savings, nor a sound Stock Exchange, nor that respect for business achievement without which capitalism cannot flourish. Yet a third example is the attitude to work. Contemplating under a coconut tree is a better way of developing the soul than carrying the stones for a new railway embankment, but societies where all the emphasis is on leisure, where work is merely an unpleasant necessity to be slopped through as quickly as possible, may be high-souled, they will never be rich.

If what the underdeveloped countries now want is to get richer, then it is upon getting richer that they must concentrate; if, in the process, they lose some of the graciousness and attractiveness of their lives, that is a sacrifice which must be accepted.

MOBILIZATION OF DOMESTIC RESOURCES FOR ECONOMIC DEVELOPMENT*

I. G. PATEL

INTRODUCTION

THERE is one central problem which is common to all the underdeveloped regions. The essence of economic development everywhere is the building up of capital equipment on a large enough scale in order to increase productivity in industry, mining, agriculture, etc. Capital in the form

*Adapted and reprinted by permission from *Civilizations*, Vol. II, No. 4, December 1952, pp. 487–495.

of schools and laboratories is required for raising the general standard of technical know-how in the people, and equipment in the form of up-to-date machines, ploughs, etc. is essential if people are to eke out more than the bare necessities of life from their farms and factories. At any given time, a society can produce only a limited amount of goods and services from its available resources for current consumption in the form of food, clothing, etc. or for the formation of capital goods for increasing its productivity in the future. If it wants more of capital formation, it must devote a smaller proportion of its current income or output to consumption and save the rest and invest it in productive equipment. A rapid accumulation of capital requires, therefore, a high rate of savings on the part of the people and a proper use of the savings for productive purposes.

There are three main reasons why the process of capital formation needs conscious direction in underdeveloped countries. Left to himself, a poor man necessarily saves a smaller part of his income than a rich man. That is why countries already prosperous are able to increase their capital equipment more rapidly than poorer nations. But if the vicious circle of the rich getting richer and the poor becoming poorer is to be broken, the rate of savings in underdeveloped countries has to be raised by suitable measures. The low rate of savings in these countries becomes even more disturbing when viewed in the light of the rapid growth of population. If the current rate of savings and capital formation is such as to lead to some improvement in the standard of living from year to year, one can hope that with the passage of time there would be a cumulative rise in the rate of savings as these nations become more and more prosperous. But in most underdeveloped countries, current savings are so low that productivity is barely able to keep pace with the growth of population. If this initial hurdle is to be crossed and savings and capital formation are to be pushed ahead of population, some steps have to be taken to give a spurt to the current rate of savings. Again, in a predominantly private enterprise economy, no individual can be induced to acquire capital equipment unless he finds it worth his while to do so. But if a farmer is to find it worthwhile to use a modern plough, he must have a regular supply of water to ir-

rigate his land and an efficient system of transportation to market his products. It is only when a society has acquired sufficient basic capital in the form of transportation, electric supply, irrigation projects, etc. that private capital formation can gather momentum. There is an urgent need, therefore, to cross the initial hump of capital formation in underdeveloped countries if the process of accumulating capital is not to prove abortive for want of proper incentive and opportunities.

MEASURES FOR INCREASING THE RATE OF CAPITAL FORMATION

Given the need for rapid capital formation in the initial stages, how is this to be done? The responsibility for capital formation in a free society rests both with the government and private individual; but the means available to each of them for acquiring capital assets are different. Even among private individuals, some distinctions must be drawn between different types of capital formation.

The basic capital needs of a society in the form of irrigation facilities, transportation, schools, etc. are such that no private individual can find it profitable to provide them. The responsibility for creating such capital is the government's, and the provision for such capital formation is made through normal budgetary channels—i.e., through the proceeds of government taxes and loans. In recent years, governments in a large number of underdeveloped countries have devoted an increasing share of their budgets to expenditure on capital projects. Indeed, the capital expenditure undertaken by governments is perhaps of the most urgent type, and the proper financing of such expenditure holds the key to the success of capital formation in other sectors.

In the private sector, capital is formed first by self-employed farmers and artisans

owning their means of production and re-
lying on their own labor and savings for
the most part. Such persons form the
largest sector of productive agents in most
underdeveloped countries, and perhaps the
most intractable part of the problem of
capital formation in these countries arises
in this sector.

Second, capital is formed by the entrepreneurs in business, mining, plantations
or industry on the basis mainly of money
borrowed from other people. In this sector,
production is generally on a large scale
and is undertaken by hired labor. The
formation of capital in this sector requires
an elaborate institutional and legal set up
for mobilizing the petty savings of myriads
of people and channelling them for use
by a few enterprising persons.

A society can also acquire capital
through the spontaneous efforts of people
cooperating to create useful assets for the
joint benefit and ownership of a group or
a community. If the residents of a village
contribute their labor or savings freely to
build wells, schools, roads, etc. for the
benefit of all, they add to the capital equipment of the country just as much as they
would have done if they had paid more
taxes to the government to enable it to
build these things for them.

Each of these types of capital formation
have their own part to play in a properly
conceived scheme of economic progress.
The spirit of voluntary cooperation among
citizens and the paternal care of the government, the growth of large-scale private
enterprise and the rejuvenation of small-
scale peasants and artisans have all their
unique contribution to make in a free society; and care has be taken to avoid the
starvation of any of these sectors by undue concentration of resources in others.

CAPITAL FORMATION BY THE GOVERNMENT

Capital formation by the government

can be increased by raising taxes or by borrowing more from the public. In most underdeveloped countries, the tax system re-
lies heavily on indirect taxes rather than on
direct taxes, and as such, is somewhat re-
gressive in character. In a country where
most people are poor and the need for en-
forcing sacrifices from as wide a part of
the population as possible is very urgent,
it is unavoidable that most of the taxes
should be borne by the poor. But there is
some scope for increasing direct taxation
in a number of underdeveloped countries.
The principal difficulty here is an administrative one—viz.: overcoming widespread
tax-evasion. There is also the danger that
after a point, taxation tends to discourage
investment by private entrepreneurs, so
that the gain to capital formation in the
government sector is offset by the loss in
the private sector.

There is one type of tax which has not
received adequate consideration in underdeveloped countries. The capital expenditure by the government, say for irrigation
or electric power, necessarily tends to be
concentrated in certain areas which also
get most of the benefit of such development. If part of the cost of such projects is
defrayed by special ad hoc taxes levied on
the people in the area rather than be met
from the general exchequer, it is conceivable that the resistance of people to higher
taxes may be diminished. They may even
be encouraged to take more interest in
such projects out of local patriotism.

A similar problem arises in connection
with the charges the state should levy for
the services of the capital projects already
completed. Should the state charge sufficiently high rates for water supply to farmers so as to extract sufficient purchasing
power from the people for extending irrigation facilities in other areas, or should it
charge very low rates in order to encourage
farmers to buy better ploughs and make
more use of the water newly available?

The problem of pricing public utility services has received a great deal of attention in economic literature; but the solution of the problem from the stand-point of expediting capital formation in the community can perhaps only be found by trial and error.

The Government can also acquire the resources needed for its capital expenditure by borrowing from the general public. The extent of such borrowing can be increased in three main ways. First, efforts should be made to encourage people to save more and to discourage unproductive expenditure on say, gold or ostentatious residential construction. The pattern of people's tastes is the product of tradition and social custom, and it would take years of persuasion and education to induce people to give up the prevalent forms of wasteful consumption. In some countries, this task is complicated by the need to dispel the existing disregard for the material well-being which inhibits any conscious drive for economic progress. Proper incentives have to be developed for inducing people to produce more. But once the extra production becomes available, people have to be persuaded to devote a large part of it to accumulation rather than consumption. The incentives to foster are property incentives rather than income incentives; and even then, the traditional urge for certain types of property has to be eschewed.

The response to the government's borrowing program would also depend on the degree of popular confidence in the financial and political stability of the country and on the ingenuity of the government in adapting its loan program to suit the needs of the people. A variety of technical problems arise in this connection. Should the government pay high rates of interest on its bonds to attract more savings or should it keep interest rates low so as not to discourage capital formation in the private sector? The expectation of life in poor countries is short, and the emergency needs for drawing on one's savings are more frequent for people with low and perhaps unsteady incomes. Should the government, therefore, float only medium-term or short-term bonds, and keep interest rates stable or guarantee capital values of bonds by other devices? Should any special facilities be devised for small contributors and for simpler and speedier encashment of bonds?

Third, the success of the government borrowing program depends on the establishment of suitable intermediate agencies which can attract savings from the people more easily and loan them on to the government. A complex structure of savings banks, commercial banks, insurance companies, social security institutions, etc. can provide a more varied incentive to save to people and relieve them of many difficult decisions about how and where to invest. Such an institutional framework is also essential for channelling private savings to private investors. Much remains to be done in this field in many underdeveloped countries. To give only one example, people are more likely to contribute to pension funds, death and accident benefit schemes, etc. than to invest directly in government bonds or company shares. But if such social security schemes are set up and expanded, additional funds can accrue to their accounts from year to year (at least in response to the growth of population) and these could be invested in the private or the public sector. Whether the government itself is able to increase its command over the nation's resources by setting up social security funds would depend, of course, on whether its own contributions to such funds are smaller or larger than the amounts it is able to borrow from the funds from year to year. But for the society, as a whole, it is possible to collect additional savings through the establishment of suitable social security schemes, and it would be interesting to assess the actual experience of countries in this field.[1]

In addition to taxation and borrowing from the public, the government can also resort to inflationary financing for its capital expenditure. It is sometimes contended that a deliberately sponsored inflation would expedite capital formation and economic development.

So far, we have only suggested the ways and means of raising adequate revenue for government capital expenditure. But if capital formation by the government is to proceed on efficient lines and to a maximum extent, a prudent management of government expenditure must also be ensured. There is not much one can say about how this is to be done. The avoidance of wasteful or ill-conceived or grandiose schemes for development presents one of the most difficult problems in this field—it is necessary to complete much needed projects as quickly as possible, and there are no strict criteria to determine the relative usefulness of different projects in a rapidly changing environment. It is of the essence of basic social expenditure on irrigation, transportation, etc. that they should not be governed strictly by profit and loss calculations, and they are liable to be determined, therefore, by local jealousies and pressure groups in democratic countries. To some extent waste can be avoided by suitable administrative arrangements. But whether such capital projects should be managed centrally by the government or by separate corporations created for the purpose, and whether the people directly affected by such projects

should be given a share in their management are questions to which no simple answers can be given—an arrangement which is likely to be most economical may not enlist enough popular cooperation or enthusiasm, and a compromise has to be devised.

PRIVATE CAPITAL FORMATION

Private individuals or agencies are responsible for most of the capital accumulated in a free society. It has already been suggested that the process of building up capital in a society on private initiative takes three rather distinct forms—by thousands of small peasants and artisans whose resources consist mainly of their own labor and savings, by large-scale capitalistic enterprises that draw to a large extent on the savings of other people, and by the cooperative effort of individuals who create capital assets for joint use.

The basic reason for the low standard of living in underdeveloped countries is the primitive condition of the tools and techniques used by the thousands of self-employed peasants and artisans who account for the largest share of production. In recent years, the need for expediting capital formation in this sector has become even more urgent. The spread of democratic institutions has encouraged egalitarian ideas in many of these countries, and one of the manifestations of this new spirit is the gradual distribution of land held by big land-owners to small peasants. It is inevitable that this process would retard capital formation on land unless some steps are taken to encourage the new owners of small parcels of land to save and invest in better implements.

To some extent, the general spread of education and the completion of some of the basic capital projects such as irrigation works started by the government would naturally lead to more capital formation

---

[1] It is, of course, conceivable that social security schemes can act as a drag on the nation's savings rather than contribute to them. It is only when the current receipts of a social security fund exceed current expenditure from it that savings are created—and even then, it should be remembered that in the absence of such schemes, part of the contributions now made to such funds would be saved or spent on capital expenditure.

by this sector. But what is needed most is a type of leadership which is prepared to permeate down to the smallest village and to share in the day to day struggle of the masses. No amount of governmental propaganda and central direction can achieve what a group of selfless workers can. And trite as it may appear, it is by the example, advice and guidance of a few leaders that the mass of peasants can be induced to cast off superstitions, adopt newfangled ways and implements and accept privations with enthusiasm.

This becomes even more clear when one remembers that a great deal of capital needed in rural areas will have to be of the social or communal type. If each peasant and artisan were to try to own his means of production by himself, the process of modernization cannot go very far— he cannot afford to have a harvester and a tractor, and in any case, his tiny plot of land cannot utilize them fully. If efficiency is not to be sacrificed, a group of farmers and artisans have to be encouraged to own such implements jointly. There are a number of things a group of farmers can only do in cooperation with each other—e.g., plant trees to increase rainfall in the areas, build embankments to prevent land from being washed away, repair roads, tanks, etc., and it is only by the leadership of a few that the hidden energy and enthusiasm of the masses can be released for such joint activities. A good deal of useful capital can be created by free contributions of labor to the community. To rely on the government for such activities would be a total denial of the spirit of democracy and self-help. It may be necessary for the government to provide some technical advisers to the rural communities; but the technicians would have to be leaders too in order to be really useful. If the young democracies with the uphill task of economic development are to provide an adequate substitute for the totalitarian techniques of forced labor and complete abolition of private property, it would be largely by exploiting to the full their resources for leadership and voluntary cooperation.

There would always be some need for drawing on outside resources even in the rural sector. Some form of credit to peasants and artisans is always necessary, and the facilities for such credit have to be developed if capital formation in this sector is to be expedited. A variety of organizations are developed for this in several countries, e.g., cooperative or Land Banks, Rural Finance Corporations, etc. The essential problem here is to ensure that such institutions collect savings as well as distribute credit, and that such credit should increase capital formation rather than consumption. Otherwise, multiplication of credit facilities merely produces more indebtedness and inflation.

To turn to the financing of capital accumulation by large-scale capitalistic enterprises in mining, manufacturing, etc. Once such enterprises get established, they tend to finance further expansion out of their own profits. But in underdeveloped countries where the problem is to start new factories and open new mines, there is an obvious need for creating institutions to channel private savings to entrepreneurs. The problem here is similar to that of making the government's borrowing program more successful. But there are additional difficulties to be overcome also. For one thing, even the intermediate institutions such as savings banks, commercial banks, insurance companies, etc. would not have the same confidence in new producers as in the government. Some specialized institutions such as industrial banks or government sponsored Industrial Finance Corporations may be required. Again, some legal safeguards have to be erected to protect investors in private industry. The techniques or instruments employed by private companies for borrowing have also got to be adapted to the peculiar needs of an underdeveloped country. Thus, if most investors can invest only for comparatively short periods and if the emergency needs for realizing past savings is more frequent, some special type of private securities may have to be created to minimize the risk of capital loss. During the second World War, governments developed many new types of bonds to draw out savings from different types of investors. It would be interesting to examine if any of these experiments could be adopted by private borrowers.

One of the most obstinate problems that arises in an underdeveloped country is that of determining the proper rate of profit for the big enterprises. It is arguable that unless new enterprises are allowed to make large enough profits, they may not be able to start new industries and expand them. If profits are stimulated in the early stages of development, capital accumulation would be more rapid and as industries expand by reinvesting part of the profits and economies of growth develop, the initial artificial support to profits can be removed. In the ultimate analysis, such a stimulus to profits can only come at the expense of the rest of the society; but it is urged that some steps to influence the distribution of income in favor of the profit-earners are desirable. There are various ways of propping up profits—by subsidies, favorable treatment in taxation or government purchases, tariffs and import restrictions, control over wages or trade unionism, favorable exchange rates for raw materials and equipment requirements, or by allowing private industry to initiate an inflation. All these devices can lead to vested interests and mal-distribution of resources, and some of them have definitely an anti-democratic twist. But the problem posed by the use of such devices is a real one and arises in one form or another in most countries. A totalitarian society has no difficulty in appropriating much of the fruit of economic progress for capital accumulation rather than for increasing consumption standards of the masses. If a democratic society tries to achieve the same objective by taxation, it would soon find most of its productive capital in the hands of the state. But so long as some areas of capital formation are in the hands of large-scale entrepreneurs, some struggle between profit-earners and the rest of the society for appropriating a larger share of the national product is inevitable, and there is no simple way of resolving this struggle in the interest of both capital accumulation and a distribution of income desired by the majority of the population.

SMALL INDUSTRY
IN ECONOMIC DEVELOPMENT*

HENRY G. AUBREY

RURAL overpopulation and underemployment are characteristic of underdeveloped economies, and there is a fair amount of agreement among economists that progress requires the withdrawal of surplus population from the land and its integration into an expanding industrial organization. At this point agreement ends, however, and the proponents of mechanization of agriculture, and of heavy or light industry, follow diverging paths.

Agricultural productivity may indeed be heightened by the removal of partially idle labor, the assumption being that simultaneous progress of industrialization will supply better implements and fertilizer, which will more than compensate for the loss of labor. This implies, however, increased application to the land of that other factor of production—capital. At the same time, more capital is needed to build up industry, so that it can absorb the surplus labor. And this, in turn, requires an expansion of basic services—power, transportation and communication, education, health, and administrative units—all requiring further capital.

This cumulative need of capital was not fully understood by most postwar planners. Their aim was to duplicate by large-scale industrialization as quickly as possible the pattern established by the industrial na-

* Adapted and reprinted by permission from *Social Research*, Vol. XVIII, No. 3, September 1951, pp. 270–312.

tions. They did not realize that enough capital could not be rapidly created by the impoverished economies themselves; nor did they consider that foreign investment, even including international loans and grants, would not come forward in sufficient volume for *all* desirable projects.

The crux of the matter is not a theoretical decision which is the more important: improvements in agriculture, in industry, or "economic and social overhead expenditure." If there is not enough capital to take care of all these needs at once, as is quite clearly the case, the problem becomes one of allocation of that scarce factor. Its most efficient use must be the vital concern of underdeveloped countries, and is equally important to foreign investors, for the outcome of any single venture depends on the progress of the entire economy. But long-run efficiency alone cannot be the sole consideration when accelerating population growth is steadily depressing the standard of living. It is necessary to increase output rapidly enough to raise real per capita income, even if in the beginning only slightly. Clearly, only a wise combination of various economic measures can approach these objectives.

THE SETTING OF THE PROBLEM

Any realistic approach to the problem of capital allocation in industrialization must consider the balance to be established between small-scale and large-scale, light and heavy, labor-intensive and capital-intensive, industries. In determining the desirable and practical levels of technology in specific instances, it will be necessary to find a place for handicrafts for a considerable period. And finally, thought must be given to what weight should be accorded rural and urban industry.

It is, unfortunately, extremely difficult to achieve a sharp definition of what constitutes small-scale or large-scale industry, home or cottage industry. In some cases distinctions are made on the basis of the number of workers employed, with all plants employing fewer than 10 classified as small-scale. In others the use of machinery is regarded as the distinguishing feature of large-scale operations. And in still others it is the site of activity—home or workshop—that determines its category. Classification is also made according to the relationship existing between the producer and the market for his product or raw material. Actually, all such categories overlap to an extent that makes clear-cut definition difficult and perhaps not even fruitful. Moreover, there is an almost infinite number of intermediate types which defy clear-cut classification.

Actually, small enterprise has displayed a remarkable persistence. In Germany, France, Switzerland, and other continental countries there still exists an important core of home industries and small-scale workshops. True, some of these industries are gradually receding under the constant pressure of large-scale competition. But it is important to note that in our already industrialized countries the process took several centuries, and that for extended periods various stages of development existed side by side. In Japan, even after seventy years of industrial development, home industry, very small workshops, and modern, large-scale industry can still be found in close proximity. The transition

from one kind of industrial organization to another is effected by a slow shift in the relative importance of the various systems in the total output.

Thus far western industrialization has typically taken the form of large-scale urbanized industries, and the eventual application of this pattern to underdeveloped countries is regarded as inevitable by most economists and planners. In fact, the underdeveloped countries themselves frequently reject as unworthy of consideration the mere suggestion that anything less than the latest technology might be acceptable. And yet, it should be quite clear that a number of economic and technological factors will determine the optimum level of technology under specific conditions.

The operation of any modern plant presupposes not only a source of power, but transportation and communication facilities, the availability of skilled labor, and a large number of those related services that industrial countries take for granted. It is easy to see that even with identical cost relationships the absence of several or even of one essential link may impair the economy of operation in a modern plant to such a degree that its very existence would be jeopardized. The high level of technology implied by modern industrialism involves a much greater dependence upon these factors than was the case in the early stages of industrial development. As a consequence, the scope of large-scale operations which an underdeveloped country can master in any given period depends to some extent on factors quite outside the economic sphere—on a way of life that cannot be acquired overnight. The degree of social and cultural change implied by industrialization is perhaps more difficult to achieve than the creation of capital.

Since these considerations raise strong doubts whether currently developing countries must fully repeat the pattern we associate with western industrialization, the task of outlining other, and possibly more appropriate, patterns is legitimate. What are the determining factors—economic, technological, organizational—for size of plant and location? What is the minimum efficiency and what is the optimum efficiency under specific conditions? Which industries can operate efficiently in traditional rural surroundings? To what extent and under what conditions can small-scale industry compete with large plants? How can small firms complement large operations instead of merely competing with them?

These are some of the problems whose solution would go a long way toward determining economic policy aimed at the best use of restricted capital and other resources. This study does not pretend to offer answers to all the questions. Its chief purpose is to organize a representative section of the available material into a composite picture; to determine from these facts, so far as the material permits, the controlling factors; and finally, to analyze these factors in such a way as to indicate the framework within which further research would be fruitful.

Small Industry in the Far East

SPECIALIZATION

Characteristic of ancient handicraft methods is the completion of the finished product by any required number of operations performed in one workshop or by one person, whereas factory methods require that each worker perform, as a rule, only one or a few of the many operations into which the production process is broken down. The reorganization of handicraft procedures to fit modern industrial methods was a slow and gradual evolution. In England, as long ago as the first half of the nineteenth century, it was customary even for outweavers to receive the prepared warps. In China, however, weavers in specialized weaving communities still prepare their own warps, and this is true of many other countries as well.

But specialization alone, it should be noted, is not identical with modernization; in India, for example, warping and sizing are frequently done not by the weaver but by special castes of craftsmen, using the most antiquated methods and without benefit of modern machinery. A simple sizing machine would go a long way to improve the workers' productivity, but the capacity of such machines makes them suitable for centralized operation only, preferably on a cooperative basis, as is now being recommended in India.

Similar advantages can be achieved in finishing processes, like the bleaching and dyeing of textile piece goods. We have already referred to the success of finishing centers in Indonesia in other trades. Combined with inspection, grading, and packaging, and possibly even marketing, such establishments build a bridge between the individual craftsman and the modern market's requirements of standardized quality. In Japan this type of cooperative organization has reached an unusual degree of perfection; as a result, certain benefits of large-scale operation are conferred on a number of small-scale enterprises.

JAPAN: A CASE STUDY

One of the most interesting aspects of the Japanese development is the division of labor among separate manufacturing units.

The bicycle industry in Japan is an interesting example of a large western type of industry which has adopted a system of extreme specialization. It was started for the purpose of making spare parts for the repair of imported bicycles. But the Japanese soon found that standardization of parts permitted the manufacture of many components in very small manufacturing units, of which very few make more than two kinds of parts and many make only one. Sometimes even a single part is not completed in one shop or home, but is shaped in one and painted or plated in another. For instance, one manufacturer has four simple machines in the front room of his house; with his daughter and four employees he manufactures nuts, which he sells to the factory from which he gets the raw material. Next door, another home unit, with four machines operated by the owner and one employee, finishes hub castings received from a large factory.

The Japanese rubber industry illustrates another type of division of labor. Certain operations in the rubber industry, like mixing and curing, cannot be done without fairly large machinery, but the system of performing various operations in separate shops rather than under one roof has not been entirely abandoned. Small shops receive compounded rubber, mold and shape it, the curing is done by another shop, or possibly by a larger factory. Painting and other finishing processes are performed by still other units. We notice in the rubber industry, however, also a division of labor between units of different size: large and small industries produce different articles. Thus tires are made exclusively in large factories, boots or shoes in medium-size plants, toys and small rubber goods in the smallest shops or homes.

Another phenomenon that can be observed in Japan, and to an even greater degree in industrialized countries, is the complementarity between large-scale industries and smaller units. Some spinning mills in Japan have their own weaving departments, but they also farm out work to independent weavers. Such a system of integrated but decentralized production relieves the weaver of worries about his yarn supply, but it may in turn increase his dependence upon the larger unit to an extent which leaves him little more than subsistence wages.

Thus there is in Japan a system of minute subdivision of labor among small independent units, and also a system of part-time labor, to be found not only in rural districts but in the cities—labor during evening hours, or by housewives, and so forth. The undesirable social aspects of these practices should not be minimized; and on the other hand, such labor could not be attracted to factories under any conditions.

MARKET ORGANIZATION, MIDDLEMEN, AND COOPERATIVES

Special emphasis must be given to the importance of commercial organization for the survival of small-scale industry in Asia. The craftsman or owner of a small shop has to contend with many difficulties, which frequently prevent him from making the best use of his meager resources and abilities. His lack of capital makes him dependent on his supplier for credit, and upon his customer for quick cash. If his supplier, his customer, and his financier are one person—the traditional middleman or merchant—his position deteriorates to one of complete dependence.

The role of the middleman is rightly stressed as one of the most important problems in Far Eastern small-scale industry. It is necessary, however, to distinguish between the middleman's useful function and the excessive remuneration he is able to extort for it. The middleman or trader is indispensable as a link between the outside market and the multitude of local craftsmen. He not only knows where to sell their products but usually provides the raw materials and frequently the capital. It is in this function as a capitalist or money-lender that his power is most strongly felt. He is the man to whom the worker will turn for funds in case of death or sickness, or for the celebration of a marriage or for other festivities on which local prestige depends. He knows his debtors personally and he is usually their sole source of credit. For that very reason, however, an artisan may by-pass a better opportunity for trading or buying because he dares not endanger his connection with the employer to whom he is in debt.

The obvious way out is some sort of organization in which a number of individuals combine for joint action. Cooperatives are clearly the best remedy, and we have already noted several instances where their operation has been highly successful. In China, Indonesia, India, and Japan, such cooperatives have often come to life spontaneously. But the obstacles to practical operation are very great, and so is the number of failures. Lack of experience, private feuds, and petty graft are partly to blame. The chief reason, however, is the very dependence which the cooperative is supposed to remedy. The middleman opposes the cooperatives, of course, and will not fail to make this clear to the craftsman who is in debt to him. The latter realizes that he may lose the support of the middleman if he joins the cooperative, and will be helpless if it fails. Moreover, the cooperative may not be able to guarantee year-round employment to provide even the modest minimum for which he depends on the middleman.

Lack of space does not permit a detailed analysis, but the cooperative clearly needs a wide base of operations, which should include all the commercial functions of an entire industry: assuring a steady supply of raw materials at reasonable prices; obtaining improved tools and equipment; making supplies and equipment available to members on easy terms; instructing members in the use of improved methods and inducing them to make what the market demands in reliable quality; taking over from the members what they make and paying cash or part cash for it; if nec-essary, finishing, inspecting, and grading the goods for sale, building up a merchandising organization strong enough to sell all that the members make, and carrying buffer stocks for seasonal variations.

We propose now to analyze the factors that are today determining priorities and broader policy for the developing countries. The main consideration for the present and the foreseeable future, as has already been pointed out, is the limited availability of development capital. It is therefore worth while to take a look at the allocation of capital in the most recent and most realistic of postwar plans for the Far East: the Colombo Plan for British Commonwealth countries in south and southeast Asia. In developing this plan the Commonwealth nations intended to draft a program large enough to provide for essential development needs in the next six years. Thus the production of food and basic raw materials for the requirements of rapidly growing populations was given priority. Agricultural, transportation and communications, and electric-power projects had to be assigned more than 70 percent of total funds. Next comes expenditure for social capital, chiefly housing, health, and education. It is significant for our purposes that industry ranks next to last, with an average of only 10 percent of projected expenditures, public or private. The percentage distribution of the total planned expenditure of 1,868 million pounds sterling is as follows: transportation and communication 34; agriculture 32; social capital 18; industry and mining (excluding coal) 10; fuel and power 6.

This brings up the big question of development policy: how much industrialization can a country afford? The first practical answer is provided by the Colombo Plan. Of the countries included, only Pakistan plans more than 10 percent of her expenditure for industry, because her partition from India left her virtually without any modern industrial plant. Ceylon, still depending on export agriculture, plans only 6 percent.

The next issue to be decided is how to use most effectively the limited capital for industrial development. Two major areas of investigation present themselves: how much additional plant can be built; and how much capital should be allocated to the replacement or the improvement of old equipment. Each of these areas is, in turn, subject to various considerations.

If we consider the efficiency of new equipment and plant, it is very tempting to take the long view and to select a level of technology geared to future needs. In this manner, it may be argued, there will be a minimum of waste as the economy develops. This thinking stems typically from the perspective of capital-rich, technically fast-developing industrial regions. Clearly the obsolescence of a plant depends upon the rate of development of the economy as a whole, and upon competitive alternatives in the specific industry under consideration. From both angles the limitation of available development capital is of decisive importance in underdeveloped countries. If it is true that available capital is small compared with total needs, and that a rate of development faster than population growth is a hope rather than a definite prospect in most countries; if it is further true that the output of efficient and less efficient units alike will be required for the growing needs of the population; if it is finally true that under these conditions development can only be very slow in the economy as a whole and in most individual industries— then indeed obsolescence and waste seem to lose a great deal of their significance. Thus the problem at hand is one of short-term efficiency; simple equipment pays for itself quickly, and not much overall change need be expected within the period of amortization.

We shall not discuss here the general problem of how to allocate available capital resources to specific industries. This decision is as a rule dominated by the natural and social-political conditions in which an individual country finds itself. To take the most obvious example, the relative emphasis on heavy industry as against light industry is first of all a matter of available natural resources. In addition, considerations of national security or of political power and even dogmatic principles of planning enter into the picture. But even countries that plan to allocate a large share of their resources to basic projects whose output will be intangible, or at best very long delayed, will do well to devote their remaining capital resources to less capital-intensive types of production which yield output quickly. Within the latter field, too, decisions have to be made: the size and location of plant, and the level of technology. Is the prevalence of small-scale manufacturing units really only the result of general backwardness, as it appears to the historian, or are there economic, institutional, and social reasons for their continued existence in the future as well? To what extent do the limitations of capital resources affect the geographical and the size distribution of manufacturing activities?

DOMESTIC CAPITAL SUPPLY

In discussing the capital supply for industry, we treated it as if it were of a determinate and invariable size. In reality, however, the availability of capital for manufacturing is to some extent connected with size, type, and location of plant. Capital markets of underdeveloped areas are not highly organized; they are not usually suited to the raising of large blocks of capital for big industry; and personal control is frequently preferred to anonymous fractional holdings. Thus it may be easier to raise private capital for a number of small enterprises over a period of time than for a large plant.

Moreover, only a part of an underdeveloped country's wealth is located in the large cities. It is true that financial centers have some attraction for industry, especially where financial and managerial functions are combined. Accumulated trading capital will expand into industry in ports, which are in any case desirable centers for production and marketing. But there exist in rural areas and provincial trading centers sources of capital which have not been sufficiently tapped. Some economists believe that rural exceed urban savings. The merchants or middlemen who finance innumerable small manufacturers in Asia are located, for the most part, in small towns or villages. Peasants' and craftsmen's hoards, which would not be available for shares in remote impersonal ventures, might well be attracted to local enterprise which is a part of their daily experience. Small funds can also be accumulated to mutual advantage in local productive cooperatives which provide capital and work at the same time.

Thus more capital may be available for small industry than could ever be mobilized in underdeveloped countries for large industry alone. Furthermore, in small plants a larger share of whatever capital is available could be used for productive equipment. Large industry requires in addition to such equipment, capital-consuming installations like power plants, workers' housing, administrative offices, and other capital-intensive overhead expenditure. Large-scale manufacturing for indeterminate demand requires the erection of storage facilities and the carrying of inventories which a small manufacturer who sells in a well-defined local market does not need.

Concentration on small industries may be capital-saving also in other ways. We have noted that in the Colombo Plan only 10 percent of the funds was left over for industry after expenditure for basic projects. Social capital, which includes housing and health, averages 18 percent of total expenditure in the entire region, but it makes up more than 50 percent of the expenditure in Singapore. This illustrates vividly the large cost of urbanization. Housing is only the most obvious item; streets, sewers, water, light, public services and health, safety measures, and offices for all levels of government require huge initial amounts for construction, and periodic expenditures for upkeep and administration.

The great economic cost of urbanization was in part delayed during the industrial transformation of the western countries, and as a result the social cost in human misery, disease, and death was extremely high. Today, in Asia and elsewhere, slum conditions will not be tolerated much longer in industrial cities where they exist. And it is certainly not compatible with modern minimum standards to permit the spread of industrial slums with the progress of industrialization. Thus, under the pressure of unionism and general social awareness, urbanization will in the future tend to be even more capital-intensive than in the past. The conglomeration of large industry in the cities will therefore require social overhead capital expenditure a part of which could be deferred or even avoided by a wider use of smaller units scattered in rural areas.

Under conditions of capital scarcity it appears, therefore, that several factors combine to favor the greatest possible use of decentralized small-scale industry. In the first place, some capital may be available only for small local industries, its use thus increasing the total capital supply. Second, by using relatively labor-intensive technology, which requires less capital per unit of output, more total output can be achieved with a restricted amount of total investment capital. Third, in small plants a larger part of total investment can be used for the productive processes than in large industry, which requires additional capital-intensive overhead expenditure. And finally, small rural industry can do without a large part of urban services, and can save for productive purposes that part of capital expenditure which would otherwise be reflected in the cost of urbanization.

LABOR SUPPLY

In addition to the obstacle of limited capital supply, the introduction of large-scale urban industry encounters another in the scarcity of skills among labor and management alike. Traditional skills are of little use. Moreover, in a system of manufacturing in which the worker performs only one operation and has nothing to do with the beginning and the end of the entire process, the incentive of craftsmanship has to be replaced by a willingness to obey commands. Complex machinery means little to the worker without a protracted period of acquaintanceship. Similar difficulties of adaptation need to be overcome by management. Where the family has been the traditional productive unit, it is not easy to recruit a staff of responsible managers for modern enterprise; the evaluation of market trends requires greater skill and experience than are needed for manufacture that is conducted to consumers' orders.

Quite apart from skills there are definite local limits to the quantity of labor, which is widely distributed. Urban industry needs to attract labor from the adjacent countryside, or possibly from fairly remote regions. This may not be too difficult if urban industrialization does not proceed too fast. But we noted in regard to Japan how manufacturers were compelled to recruit labor from farming districts, sometimes at considerable cost. Underemployment in rural districts is not alone a sufficient incentive to migrate. Conservative social habits, strong family ties, poor living conditions in fast-growing cities, all restrict the mobility of labor.

This fairly general situation suggests an alternative to the historical pattern of shifting labor to urban capital. Japan and other countries have found it desirable to bring equipment and employment to rural labor, frequently at a saving of capital and cost. The total supply of local labor is sometimes more limited for large-scale plants on strict working schedules than it is for very small units. We have already pointed out the inclination of rural labor toward part-time and home work. Expensive equipment of large-scale industry cannot economically stand idle in accordance with fluctuations of labor supply, but small plants, which use but little and inexpensive equipment, are much more flexible in that respect; their operation at odd hours or slack seasons, notably in rural districts, can make a significant contribution to the total supply of goods in a growing economy.

EFFICIENCY OF OPERATION

We come now to the vast problem of the relative efficiency of large-scale and small-scale plants, of higher and lower levels of technology. There is, even in developed countries, no general agreement about the correlation between efficiency of operation and the size of the plant or the size of the industry. Investigations have shown a greater variation in efficiency among plants of similar scale than between large and small plants in general. In underdeveloped countries, however, there are specific factors which tend to decrease the relative efficiency of large-scale and modern technology.

Identical modern equipment often produces less in underdeveloped areas. The continuous operation of high-speed machinery is impeded by the operator's lack of skill, carelessness, or indifference; flaws in raw materials also cause repeated and long interruptions; breakdowns are more frequent and repairs take longer. Thus the output per unit of capital is drastically reduced, sometimes by as much as half. Moreover, the continuous and interlocking flow of raw materials and intermediate products all through the process of manufacture is one of the conditions of efficient large-scale operation. The effect of stoppages anywhere along the complicated path of manufacturing is not only felt at the specific trouble spot in question but is multiplied by the very size of the establishment. The degree of efficiency needed to keep such disturbances at a minimum is rarely obtained in less developed countries, even after considerable expenditure for training.

These facts demonstrate why the experience with modern technology in industrial countries cannot be transferred without question to underdeveloped areas. It is likely that the maximum size for efficient operation may be quite low in certain regions. The question arises, of course, whether there are not minima below which modern technology would not be economical at all. No doubt many engineers would place the minimum rather high, because their entire experience is based on a resource pattern in which capital is relatively plentiful as compared with labor. But evidence to the contrary was furnished by the Agricultural Industry Service of UNRRA, which found it possible to erect, at incredibly low cost, plants so small that they would have been rejected as uneconomical by most engineers of industrial countries. By way of example, we mention a cement plant with a weekly output of 400 bags, a brick kiln producing 20,000 bricks a week, and a sulphuric-acid plant with a weekly output of only 4 tons. It appears, therefore, that the possibilities of small-scale

technology are frequently underestimated; the "overdesigning" of plants for underdeveloped countries induced by this point of view results in waste of capital resources instead of the optimum technology for primitive conditions.

Clearly, the controlling factor in decisions on level of technology and size of plant is the relative supply and the price of the factors of production. In underdeveloped areas capital is scarce relative to labor. This is true not only in densely populated regions; it could be taken as the chief criterion in a definition of economic backwardness. If capital is scarce and expensive, and if labor is plentiful and cheap, it would seem natural to combine these two factors in a less capital-intensive technology than in industrial countries where the relationship is reversed. This judgment should be reinforced by the fact that heavy and bulky imported equipment entails heavy shipping costs and incidental expenses, which widen the discrepancy between the cost of capital and of labor.[1]

Hand-operated equipment in underdeveloped countries is frequently so primitive that there is much scope for technological improvement, even without the use of power. Still, in the long run, small industry cannot survive economically unless it assimilates the potentialities of power. We need not, however, regard steam and electricity as the only source of power, without which industry is doomed. Water wheels along rivers or irrigation ditches can be used to advantage. Wind wheels, ancient sources of power, can be used to drive small generators and store up electricity in batteries. Even large-scale generation of power, near the source of fuel or hydro-electrical energy, is feasible, as the power can be distributed over

[1] Possible savings in foreign-exchange outlay may also be worth considering in deciding the level of technology for new equipment.

wide areas by grids; it is no longer necessary to cluster industry at the site of coal.

Capital and labor are not the only determinants of industry's cost. Production overhead and the expenses of commercial management and distribution affect large and small units very differently. Labor needs relatively little supervision where the production process does not involve the complicated and continuous flow which we mentioned above as characteristic of large operations; the latter require large overhead expenditure for management, supervision, records, and staff, in addition to the amortization of capital-intensive overhead investment in storage and office buildings, office machinery, and supplies. It is easy to see that such overhead can be justified only if it is spread over a still larger continuous volume of output than the nature of modern large-scale equipment itself requires. Again these considerations point to a comparative advantage for small scale enterprise.

The costs of distribution account for a considerable part of the retail price of goods, even in developed countries. Small local manufacturers could dispense with many of these; packaging and shipping, financing of inventories and accounts receivable, sales commissions, and dealers' markups at the wholesale and retail level. Most underdeveloped countries have no large unified markets, but consist of any number of small market sections between which the flow of exchange is very restricted. The size of the market is further limited by transportation deficiencies. The cost of out-of-town transportation may provide a powerful element of protection to local industries against machine-made goods of lower production cost which have to be brought in over long distances with primitive equipment.

This same transportation factor may of course have also an adverse effect, in re-tarding the introduction of new machinery—a consideration that is very important in regard to agricultural machinery. But many simple tools for an interim improvement of agricultural productivity can easily be manufactured from local materials by scattered light industry. Regions closer to the main arteries of transportation could possibly afford some heavier equipment; thus different levels of technology may be economical and desirable at the same time in various parts of a region.

IMPROVEMENT OF EXISTING FACILITIES

The discussion so far has been concerned with various considerations regarding the size, technology, and location of new plants. Developing countries also have the alternative of capital expenditure on the improvement of existing facilities. As has been demonstrated in China, India, and other countries, a number of improvements can be achieved with very little capital by making changes in design, by the use of a little more metal, and in many other ways. Clearly the marginal increase of output per unit of the scarce factor, capital, will be very large if the primitive equipment of traditional industries is improved. Social policy and social considerations may weigh heavily in the allocation of resources to improvement of existing equipment. Whenever large numbers are employed in traditional industries, there is much to be said for the preservation of existing patterns. It may be sound procedure to improve technology step by step in many places at once, rather than to sink large portions of a limited capital supply in a few large ventures.

Improved equipment in small manufacturing can also become the nucleus of scattered light industry of a more advanced type. Acquaintanceship with machines will spread, and will even accelerate the training of a large reservoir of workers, some of whom will in time be attracted to urban industry as their skills and their tastes broaden. Thus the improvement of small-scale industry will conform to the slow rate of large-scale industrialization imposed by the limitations of capital and skills, of transportation and power facilities.

COMPLEMENTARITY OF LARGE- AND SMALL-SCALE INDUSTRY

Competition between the traditional and the modern sector of industry is sometimes cushioned by government regulation, in order to mitigate social disruption. We have seen in the preceding sections of this paper that small, decentralized industry has, under certain conditions, comparative advantages of size and location in competitive trade. There are also areas of cooperation, however, between large and small, urban and rural industries, as has been demonstrated in Japan. Small shops may make accessories for large factories, cheaply and efficiently, where machinery is standardized and parts are interchangeable. Thus operations that justify large-scale equipment can be done by big plants, while others are left to small shops which fit into certain stages of the production process. As an alternative, small enterprises can combine in cooperatives or associations to gain the benefits of large-scale industry in certain operations. By means of such lateral combinations and forward or backward integration, independent units can parallel advanced types of modern industrial organization.

INVESTMENT CRITERIA FOR MANUFACTURING INDUSTRIES IN UNDERDEVELOPED COUNTRIES*

KENNETH A. BOHR

THE very fact that an economy is underdeveloped implies that there are special limitations to the establishment of manufacturing industry. In the typical case the small size of the local market, the shortages of financial capital and skilled labor, and the availability of relatively inexpensive industrial products from abroad are among the factors that combine to se-

* Adapted and Reprinted by permission from *The Review of Economics and Statistics*, Vol. XXXVI, No. 2, May, 1954, pp. 157–166.

verely restrict the types of industry that can be economically justified.

Various criteria have been suggested by economists to assist in selecting industries under such conditions. They range from simple rules of thumb, such as those based on capital intensity and balance of payments effects, to elaborate applications of the principles of marginal productivity on the one hand and comparative costs on the other. This paper follows the latter approach in attempting to indicate by an analysis of industrial characteristics the extent to which various industries may be adapted to the conditions usually found in underdeveloped economies. This approach is particularly appropriate for a broad treatment of the subject.

The method used assumes a certain degree of constancy of industrial characteristics from country to country. This seems justified on technical grounds. The physical processes of production do impose certain characteristics upon each industry. The amount of capital required, the skills needed, and the presence or lack of significant economies of scale are all inherent in the processes themselves as are also, for all practical purposes, the relationships between the location of the industry, its market, and its source of materials.

The characteristics selected for study were the requirements of capital and skilled labor, plant size, and locational pattern. The importance of the first three is obvious. The lower they are, the more easily will an industry fit the conditions typical of underdeveloped areas. In the case of location, industries which are widely dispersed in developed countries or those oriented to sources of materials will tend to be in a strong position to compete with imports when established in underdeveloped countries. Material-oriented industries may also be successful in export trade.

MEASUREMENT OF CAPITAL REQUIREMENTS

Underdeveloped economies are typically short of capital in all forms, so that it is particularly important that available capital be allocated to its most productive uses. The fact that a basic need for development is investment in projects of a social overhead nature (transport, power, housing, etc.), which are not directly productive and which consume great quanti-

ties of capital, only serves to emphasize the importance of investing in manufacturing industries with low capital requirements where this is compatible with other investment criteria.

There are several ways to measure capital requirements. In this study the ratio of fixed capital to value added was used. The values of fixed capital available are generally those submitted by firms for tax purposes and have the usual shortcomings associated with variations in depreciation practices and age of equipment. But although these values may not be representative of replacement costs they may still be considered suitable measures of relative requirements among industries when many firms are involved. To eliminate some of the problems of evaluation a physical measure of capital such as horsepower has some merit. However, though useful in making international comparisons between similar industries, it is not suitable for the purpose of this study because of the poor correlation of horsepower with value of plant and equipment over any wide range of industries.

The value added by manufacture reflects more closely the output attributable to the capital investment than does total output, which includes the value of the materials processed. Number of workers employed is a measure similar to value added, since wages and salaries are a chief component of the latter; but it is a less useful measure when considering a range of industries where differences of skills (and wages) are important.

Some of the results of the investigation into industrial capital requirements may be presented briefly. The principal purpose in all cases was to establish the relative importance of capital among a representative group of industries and to determine the best sources of data for the general analysis.

Table 1 represents a first approxima-

TABLE 1. Frequency Distribution of Rankings of Industries in Five Countries,* 1936–37, in Order of Increasing Amounts of Capital Per Employed Person †

Industrial Category	Rank										
	1	2	3	4	5	6	7	8	9	10	11
1. Clothing & bedding	****c										
2. Furniture, woodwork, pottery, glass, and miscellaneous		c*	*	*							
3. Leather, fur, & rubber		***			*c						
4. Textiles			c	*	*	*	*				
5. Light metals & electrical products			*	*	*			c			
6. Semi-manufactured metals & engineering					*	*c	*				
7. Building materials			*	c				**			
8. Paper, stationery, & printing						*	**	*	c		
9. Metal extraction									***		c
10. Food, drink, and tobacco							c		***	*	
11. Chemicals										c*	***

* Australia, Canada, Hungary, Palestine and Rumania. Palestinian statistics are not comparable in all classifications.
† Capital is valued in various ways in the separate countries, e.g., total capital assets, fixed capital assets only, or fixed capital plus inventories.
c = Canada.
* = Other countries.
SOURCE: Adapted from K. Mandelbaum, *The Industrialization of Backward Areas* (Oxford, 1945).

tion of a ranking of industries in order of capital requirements in five countries—Australia, Canada, Hungary, Palestine, and Rumania. In this table the classifications are very broad so that the variations in the capital measure and the fact that it is related to employed persons instead of value added are not important. On the other hand, the use of such broad classifications accentuates the problem of structural differences among the countries. Consider the case of Canada. The ranking of its industries is considerably different from that of the other countries since the Canadian category of "light metals and electrical products" includes a great aluminum industry, and "paper, stationery, and printing" includes a huge

newsprint industry. Both require heavy capital investment and neither has any approximate counterpart in the other countries. The effects of the unusual capital requirements of these industries on the Canadian rankings naturally extend to other industries, as, for example, "food, drink and tobacco." But, if Canada is considered a special case, the similarity among the rankings in the table is quite general.

Clothing, electrical equipment, leather products, and furniture appear to have relatively low capital requirements in all the cases examined. The requirements for textiles vary but are relatively light in a number of cases. Chemicals, non-metallic minerals (bricks, cement, etc.), and paper appear relatively heavy in all cases, while food, drink, and tobacco appears heavy in most cases.

For a more detailed ranking one must turn to separate country studies. From the data presented here, and on the basis of further material collected in the course of this study, the Australian data appear to be the most suitable starting point for more detailed comparisons of industries.

Actually the usefulness of this type of data would be increased if the composition of the capital were known. It may make a difference whether capital goods must be purchased with foreign currencies or whether they can be produced by local effort. A very rough approximation of the foreign exchange component of industrial capital requirements may be made by breaking down the capital data into "plant and equipment" and "land and buildings," as is done in the Australian statistics. The proportion included in plant and equipment may then be considered a rough indication of the amount that may have to be imported.

SKILLS

A program of industrial investment in an underdeveloped country may be frustrated by a shortage of skilled labor just as it may by a shortage of capital. All industries require some skilled labor, and their ability to absorb unskilled labor is generally limited by the supply of skilled workers. The level and distribution of skills among a local population has an important effect upon the level of industrial development that can be attempted, at least in the short run. Labor can be trained, and skills acquired in one field may be adapted for other fields, but all this takes time and even if the importation of skilled labor is feasible it is expensive.

The requirements for skilled workers

vary considerably from industry to industry. A study of United States industry based on the 1930 Census presents considerable information on this subject.[1] The study divides gainful workers into six classes:

1. Professional persons
2. Proprietors, managers, and officials, including farmers (owners and tenants)
3. Clerks and kindred workers ("white-collar workers")
4. Skilled workers and foremen
5. Semi-skilled workers
6. Unskilled workers

The measure of skilled labor requirements used in this paper is that per cent of the total labor force employed by the industry which consists of professional persons and skilled workers and foremen (categories 1 and 4). This seems a reasonable measure for general purposes, although in the case of particular countries it might be preferable to adjust the measure to fit more precisely the available distribution of skills. For example, it is conceivable that in some areas clerks might be as scarce as skilled workers.

Table 2 lists a number of industries in order of increasing requirements of skilled labor.

LOCATION

The final test of the economic suitability of an industrial project is how cheaply it can deliver its products to the consumers. In the developing countries this frequently becomes a question of how well local producers can compete with imports. Although economic reasons can be advanced for protecting industries during

[1] A. M. Edwards, "A Social-Economic Grouping of the Gainful Workers of the United States—1930," U.S. Dept. of Commerce, Bureau of the Census, 1938.

TABLE 2.   Selected Industries in Order of Percentage of Skilled and Supervisory Workers to Total Gainfully Employed: U.S., 1930

Professional Persons, Foremen, and Skilled Workers as Per Cent of Total Gainfully Employed	Industry	
Less than 10%	Turpentine farms and distilleries Gloves Shirts, collars and cuffs Cigars and tobacco Hats Shoes Leather goods Knitting mills Fish-curing and packing Fertilizers	Pottery Tanning Silk Lace and embroidery Woolen and worsted Cotton Slaughter and packinghouses Buttons Brick, tile, and terra cotta
10 to 20%	Hemp, jute, and linen Paper boxes Paper and pulp Carpets Fruit and vegetable canning Ropes and cordage Textile dyeing, finishing, and printing Rubber	Paint and varnish Glass Soap Rayon Sawing and planing Quarrying Lime, cement and artificial stone
20 to 30%	Sugar and sugar-refining Charcoal and coke	Blast furnaces and steel rolling mills
30 to 40%	Electrical machinery and supplies Flour and grain Agricultural implements Jewelry	Tinware and enamelware Automobiles Furniture
Over 40%	Printing, publishing, and engraving Marble and stone	Suits, coats and overalls

SOURCE: National Resources Planning Board, *Industrial Location and National Resources* (Washington, 1942). Compiled from Edwards, *op. cit.*

the early period of adjustment, it is obvious that the more competitive the new industry, the greater the benefit to the country.

The total cost of delivering a manufactured product to the consumer consists of three elements: the cost of procuring the raw materials, the cost of manufacturing, and the cost of distributing the product. Costs of transportation may be an important part of both procurement and distribution costs. In cases where this is so, industries tend to choose among alternative locations those which minimize total transport costs. Where perishability of the raw material or the product is an important factor, location is also strongly influenced by transport considerations—in these cases the difficulty of transport may be considered equivalent to very high transport costs.

If materials must be processed where they originate to avoid spoilage (e.g., canning and meat-packing), or to reduce their bulk to make transport easier (e.g., sawmills and the reduction or smelting of nonferrous ores), plants are located close to raw material sources. Similarly, plants making products which are perishable, or which are more difficult to transport than the materials from which they are made, must be located close to their markets (e.g., bakeries, soft-drink bottling plants, sheetmetal fabricating shops).

above category, but which are oriented to raw material sources. In instances where the required raw materials exist in underdeveloped countries this type of industry may be particularly well adapted, especially when the material can be processed for export (e.g., sugar, tea, copper).

A coefficient of localization is used to

TABLE 3. Selected Industries in Order of Increasing Coefficients of Localization: U.S., 1939

	Industry	
Class 1 (.14 to .33)	Bread	Sheet metal work
	Concrete products	Beer
	Machine shop products	Mattresses and springs
	Foundries, grey iron & nonferrous metals	Bricks and tile
Class 2 (.34 to .42)	Household furniture	Cordage and twine
	Bookbinding	Stoves, ranges, and water heaters
	Clothing	Rubber products
	Iron and steel forging	Leather goods
Class 3 (.43 to .55)	Batteries	Steelworks and rolling mills
	Shoes	Woolen textiles
	Hardware	Dyeing and finishing textiles
	Cutlery and edged tools	Petroleum refining
Class 4 (.57 to .83)	Fertilizer	Motor vehicles
	Aircraft parts	Clocks, watches, etc.
	Office & store machinery	Textile machinery
	Synthetic textiles	Cotton textiles

SOURCE: Adapted from National Resources Planning Board, *Industrial Location and National Resources* (Washington, 1942).

Developing countries are particularly interested in industries whose transport costs give some natural protection to local producers. Such industries may be identified by their pattern of location in the developed countries. In general they comprise two categories:

1. Industries which appear widely scattered (low coefficient of localization). In the case of industries with this type of location pattern, any particular plant need not fear the competition of a neighboring plant located beyond a limited distance. This includes industries whose location is oriented to markets, or to widely scattered raw material sources, or to combinations of the two.

2. Industries which are not widely scattered and thus are not included in the

determine the degree of scatter of industries. This coefficient is determined by dividing a country into a number of regions (for this purpose, the United States was divided into 34 regions and the United Kingdom into ten), and then taking the sum of the plus differences between the regional percentage of workers in a given manufacturing industry and the regional percentage of workers in all manufacturing industry. This coefficient is a measure of the local concentration of a particular industry compared with the distribution of industry as a whole. A coefficient of zero would mean that the distribution of workers in that particular industry coincided completely with the distribution of industrial workers in general. The greater the coefficient the more localized (or geo-

TABLE 4.   Size Characteristics of Establishments in Selected Industries Located Primarily with Reference to Raw Materials: U.S., 1939

Industry	Median Size* (*Number of wage earners*)	Minimum Size † (*Number of wage earners*)	Coefficient‡ of Size Variation (*Per cent*)
Processing of minerals:			
Primary smelting and refining of nonferrous metals	750.0	202.8	56.2
Gypsum products	144.3	42.0	38.5
Salt	201.2	40.2	57.8
Lime	77.0	16.5	64.1
Bone black, carbon black, etc.	38.4	15.5	34.6
Minerals and earth, etc.	44.9	10.7	67.6
Monuments, tombstones, cutstone, etc.	43.0	5.7	74.1
Processing of forest products:			
Pulp mills	243.6	69.7	50.3
Wood naval stores	227.0	40.6	43.7
Wood preserving	85.4	29.3	47.6
Hardwood distillation and charcoal	119.7	18.2	62.8
Wood products, not elsewhere classified	60.8	10.8	69.2
Planing mills	48.9	8.8	79.5
Excelsior	26.5	7.8	44.7
Gum naval stores	3.7	1.1	43.2
Processing of vegetable products, etc.:			
Sugar refining, cane	765.0	290.3	33.1
Corn sirup, corn sugar, etc.	659.5	137.6	55.3
Beet sugar	153.2	72.3	31.8
Linseed oil, cake, and meal	134.4	51.8	41.0
Cane sugar, except refineries	70.3	27.0	43.4
Canned and dried fruit and vegetables, etc.	132.6	20.2	75.9
Rice cleaning and polishing	48.8	18.4	41.9
Cottonseed oil, cake, and meal	46.6	17.3	44.7
Malt	49.5	13.3	55.0
Prepared feeds for animal and fowl	32.5	4.4	73.7
Wines	17.1	3.4	68.0
Vinegar and cider	14.8	3.3	54.8
Processing of animal products:			
Poultry dressing & packing, wholesale	39.9	9.0	57.6
Condensed and evaporated milk	37.97	8.8	50.8
Butter, creamery	12.2	1.9	75.4
Cheese	4.6	1.3	69.6

* Half of wage earners in industry employed in smaller plants, half in larger plants.
† 90% of wage earners in industry employed in larger plants.
‡ 25% of wage earners in the industry employed in plants larger than the first quartile size and 25% in plants smaller than the third quartile size. The coefficient of size variation is the ratio of the difference of these two quartile sizes to their sum. The greater the coefficient the greater the variation in size.
SOURCE: National Resources Planning Board: *op. cit.*

graphically concentrated) is the industry. Although the data used in this paper were taken from studies of United States and British industry, a remarkable similarity has been observed between the location pattern for similar industries in different countries. This tends to substantiate the belief that location is essentially determined by basic technical factors which are related to each industry and which are generally unaltered by transfer from country to country. The coefficients for a group of United States industries are presented in Table 3.

SIZE OF PLANT

The level of the capital coefficient tells nothing about the economic size of producing units. An industry with low requirements of capital per unit of value added may be uneconomical to operate on the small scale required by the restricted demands of the local market typical of underdeveloped areas. Or an industry with high requirements may be operated efficiently on a very small scale. There is reason to expect some correlation between size and location, with the most widely scattered industries tending to be those with small producing units, but it is also useful to investigate the size aspect directly. This can be done by noting the size distribution of industrial units already existing in the more developed countries.

For this purpose industries have been classified according to prevalent size, with size being measured by employment. Where distribution of employment in an industry by size of plant shows a regular concentration in certain size groups, the prevalent size is given by the size of the median plant—such that half the wage earners in the industry are employed in smaller plants and half in larger ones. Where employment is fairly evenly distributed among all size groups or where there are several groups arising from the heterogeneity of the industries comprising the industrial class, there is not considered to be any prevalent size.

A marked tendency toward small plants, or wide variations in size with a small minimum size, are industrial characteristics of particular interest to underdeveloped countries. It makes little difference whether the small size is the result of limited economies of scale or of increasing costs of procurement and distribution, or any combination of the factors. Processes adaptable to small-scale operations will be better able to supply local markets economically and to withstand competition from abroad.

The classification of prevalent size might be further refined by data on minimum size. Some data of this type for raw material processing industries are presented in Table 4.

This table gives an idea of the range of sizes found in a group of industries which are generally located close to sources of raw materials. This type of industry is of obvious interest to underdeveloped countries which are able to produce these raw materials.

AUTOMATION AND ECONOMIC

DEVELOPMENT*

RICHARD L. MEIER

How should an appropriate set of tools and techniques for economic development be selected?

In none of the current plans are automatized industrial processes seriously considered as a tool which can aid economic development. It is true that hydro-

* Adapted and reprinted by permission from *Bulletin of the Atomic Scientists*, Vol. X, No. 4, April 1954, pp. 129–133.

electric power production is enthusiastically employed in some cases, but never with the recognition that it is the forerunner of a new stage in the industrial revolution. The principles of automatism, or automation, in their most insightful formulation, are almost entirely a product of postwar science. Many operations in industry, commerce, and services have very recently become susceptible to marked improvement in their efficiency by the application of these principles. The improvement is enhanced if the design does not have to be compromised by prior investments in older type equipment. The question to be discussed then is whether the countries coming late on the scene can shortcut the long, hard, and risk-laden path of classical economic development through using, among other things, the shiny new tools being created by the most modern science and technology.

FRAMEWORK

Two important concepts must be introduced at this point. The first is *pattern*, the sequence in which the respective tools and techniques are used and the degree to which they are applied at any given moment in the development. The second is *pace*, which is concerned with the amount of acceleration that can be achieved.

A common pattern in the past has been to extract the capital from the peasantry by taxation, price manipulation, or seizure, often in the form of produce which could be traded on the world market. With the stock of goods and materials so obtained, cities and the associated industrial establishments were built. Unskilled labor was disciplined first in construction, mining, and the service trades; industrial skills were introduced with textiles, transport equipment, crude metallurgy, and similar activities; succeeding

generations of workers became skilled machinists, high-level technicians, and precision craftsmen. These advances were associated with rapid increases in the amount of schooling and marked improvements in public health.

If the pace of economic development is slow, then the increases in income are easily absorbed by the natural increase in population or swamped by the periodic inclemency of both weather and world markets. A development which calls for sacrifices coupled with only very gradual improvements is likely to lead to unrest and political dissension; order can only be maintained by the use of continued force and threats of force. In a well-balanced economic development proceeding at a good pace, the society can deploy rapidly increasing capital and skills so as to meet the inevitable crises, as they come up. The rate of gain per capita has been 2–3 per cent per year in the United States, almost double that for long periods in prewar Japan, and is currently more than three times that in Puerto Rico. The pace with which unfulfilled needs can be met depends in part upon the effectiveness of the tools for manipulating resources and processes.

PRODUCTION FOR NEEDS

A country in the throes of development must initiate an array of efficient productive activities to meet its rapidly increasing needs. The most significant of these are listed in Table 1, according to the degree to which they appear to be able to use automation.

It may be concluded that, in the not so distant future, most kinds of industry could be built so as to require a very small labor force. Thus, migration to manufacturing centers could be reduced to much smaller numbers than were required in the United States, Japan, or the USSR during the period of most rapid in-

TABLE 1. Automation in Industry

1. **Industries where advanced design now aims at fully automatic facilities**
   Electric power generation
   Telecommunications
   Liquid fuels
   Chemicals
   Cement and bricks
   Paper products
   Containers
   Fertilizers (synthetic)
   Fermentation products (antibiotics, beer, etc.)
   Soaps and detergents
2. **Industries in which major units will become fully automatic but portions of the process may still utilize manual skills**
   Fibers and textiles
   Glass and ceramics
   Iron and steel
   Nonferrous metallurgy
   Printing
   Machine-building
   Processed foods
   Mining
3. **Industries tending to become mechanized in the traditional manner, thus depending upon skilled operators and semiskilled laborers**
   Transport
   Forestry and wood products
   Garments
   Shipbuilding

dustrialization. If such a policy were accepted, then less new housing and fewer social services need be provided to maintain the influx, and more capital could be allocated for the production facilities. It then follows that dislocation of the rural economy would be reduced when using automation. All this suggests that automation might be preferred over the better known alternatives for achieving the same ends, but a more quantitative analysis would be more convincing.

MODES OF INDUSTRIALIZATION

Alkali production was chosen as an example partly because it seems to be typical (one would get much the same picture if fibers, fertilizers, nonferrous metals, or paper were selected) but also because it is an essential industry rather neglected by the economists. Improved supplies of alkali in an economy would encourage such industries as soap, glass, leather, paper, cotton textiles, rayon, fertilizers, etc. The rather minor quantities used in the primitive economy were either obtained by commerce or by the treatment of wood ashes with lime.

A. RURAL INDUSTRY APPROACH

In areas of high evaporation and poor drainage, saline ponds are frequently found. In many places when the salt crust is recrystallized a crude sodium carbonate can be obtained. If this were treated with lime an impure solution of alkali results. A few thousands of dollars invested in kilns, tanks, sluices, and kettles made of wood or iron would probably be sufficient equipment. The ultimate return from labor would be highly variable, but could probably reach the neighborhood of 10–30 lbs. per man day. A by-product might also be manufactured for chalks and fertilizers but, even if this were sold, miscellaneous wastes are likely to accumulate to the point where they force abandonment of the site. Under the best circumstances quality would remain uncertain.

B. PRIMITIVE FACTORY APPROACH

Second-hand equipment could be collected from various parts of the world for a Solvay process plant employing limestone, salt, ammonia, and a fuel as raw materials. If labor were to be substituted for capital wherever feasible, the cost might be in the range of $50–$100,000, the labor force at least 50 persons, and their production might reach close to $100,000 per year at world market prices (100–300 lbs. per man shift). Coal or fuel oil would provide the heat source, and the ammonia requirements (small) would be imported. Thus rail or port connections are required but, since electric power requirements are self-contained, none of the standard urban utilities. The products should meet fairly consistently the lower grade commercial specifications for purity.

C. AUTOMATIC UNIT APPROACH

An electrolytic process requiring only brine and a supply of electric power can be made fully automatic and continuous. If one person were to be fully employed on each shift (4 jobs) the minimum size would cost around $300,000 and produce about 1,000 tons per year (assuming a few scheduled shutdowns for maintenance). The efficient use of by-products—chlorine and hydrogen—might require another half-dozen workers. The total annual output, including by-product values, would be in the neighborhood of $120–$150,000. The caustic soda[1] produced would be of the

[1] A plant slightly larger than this was constructed recently in the Philippines (see R. L. Murray, "The Chlor-Alkali Industry . . . ," In-

highest quality, salable anywhere in the world.

There are occasions when the first or second of these alternatives will have unique advantages and therefore will be preferred. This is quite likely in smaller countries or island economies which have scattered resources suitable for exploitation or may be handicapped by high transport costs. But for the major countries, such as China, India, Indonesia, Pakistan, etc., or those which depend upon the export of a mineral resource, such as Iraq, Chile, Jamaica, etc., the automatic unit has a marked superiority. The reasons for choosing automation stem not only from its greater efficiency but also from the smaller demands that are made upon the factors of production which are continuously in short supply during the period of rapid economic development. The effect of these scarcities upon the choice of the approach are worth closer investigation.

CAPITAL NEEDS

The scarcity of capital is one such problem. Most underdeveloped areas have neither the capacity to build their own capital equipment nor sufficient accumulated savings to buy it elsewhere. Thus, whatever capital is available must be carefully allocated to enterprises which yield the greatest returns.

When the capital required for a *dependable* ton of annual output is calculated, the figures for all of the approaches fall into the same general range—$70–$150 per annual ton of alkali. The qualification "dependable" must be emphasized, be-

dustrial & Engineering Chemistry, 41 (1949), 2155, but it did not yet have the automatic features embodied in the newest equipment designed for underdeveloped areas as described by C. D. Goderez, "An Engineer Looks at Point Four," *Chemical and Engineering News*, 29 (1951), 1928. A virtually automatic plant three times this scale was recently completed in the south of India, *ibid.*, 31 (1953), 687.

cause the product here is an industrial raw material and many factories essential to economic development are dependent upon the continuity of supply.

For the developing economy the indirect capital requirements associated with each approach must be included in any comparison. For a rural industry it is assumed that village life has already provided shelter and essential services with no charge to the treasury or to the enterprise, but the cost of providing specialized talent to spark the village development, as well as the considerable number of failures which must be balanced off against the successes,[2] will need to be borne by the central government. In a primitive factory failure is less probable (only 20–50 per cent within the first three years), but the capital costs of urbanizing at least fifty workers should be included—even at a most primitive level of living the barracks and services will amount to perhaps half the cost of the factory itself, while the construction of a "company town" could easily exceed the total plant cost. For the automatic solution the costs of urbanization are trivial, even if the standards of housing, education, and health were high. A prior investment in electric power generation is necessary, but this installation could be adjusted to use off-peak load and thus make very small demands upon the total capacity. The indirect capital requirements are much more nebulous than plant costs but they tend to equalize capital needs at around a total of $200 per annual ton of dependable capacity.

Equipment and technical services com-

[2] In the projects set up for China only a third succeeded, and the cost to the United States for training and dispatching experts was many times the amounts expended for equipment. For some illuminating comments upon the technique of industrialization described by Stepanek and Prien, see letters by C. D. Goderez and Lionel Benjamin, Chemical and Engineering News, 29 (1951), 538.

ing from outside the locale must be largely donated for A, the necessary capital is acquired at high interest rates from entrepreneurs for B, but it may be obtained from institutional sources (local and international) at medium to low rates of interest for C. Outside capital is much more easily obtained for C because it is modern, competitive, and likely to be well managed. In addition, it is probable that C would not need "infant industry" protection and therefore would not complicate international agreements.

An underdeveloped area tends to have trouble marshalling its financial resources for development. The larger the enterprise, and the more modern its records and technology, the more feasible is the directed translation of the profits into new industrial investments. Thus, the choice of automatism makes possible large net savings and re-investment from industrial income. The pace of development, as measured by increases in production, would naturally be more rapid when using automation. The tendency to attract international credit is probably as important a contribution to the acceleration of pace as that of re-investment; these are together rather powerful reasons for abandoning the more traditional approaches to industrialization at points where technology has advanced to the automatic stage.

LABOR NEEDS

Another critical problem during early stages of development is that of assembling and training a suitable work force. In the case of A, de-tribalization or separation from the pattern of subsistence agriculture need not be complete, and perhaps 10 per cent literacy may be all that is necessary for a successful enterprise. With approach B, a stabilized literate work force would be desirable but hardly to be expected under the primitive circumstances assumed. In the instance of C, virtually all the labor would be highly liter-ate, some of it skilled and semi-profes-sional; the total labor requirement, how-ever, would be less than the managerial complement of either A or B. Therefore even an acute shortage of technical and white collar personnel, such as exists in Indonesia, would still favor C against the other approaches. Thus labor conditions as a whole are not antithetical to automatism, and may occasionally favor it.[3]

For a government plagued with the po-litical demands of the unemployed, auto-matic factories may be an anathema. The government's basic problem is defined po-litically as one of producing as many jobs as possible at subsistence levels of pay or slightly above. Ordinarily one would think that automation would, almost by virtue of definition, be ruled out as an approach to industrialization, since the capital cost per new industrial job created would be very high. Yet this is not always the case. One can conceive of the stratagem of pro-ducing materials of construction, such as cement, ceramics, steel rod and sheet, aluminum sheet, and power, by contin-uous and fully instrumented processes which employ very few men; these ma-terials could permit very large numbers of workers to be employed quite productively in construction work. If the construction projects are carefully planned so as to make more resources available to the econ-omy as a whole then one could foresee an expansion which would provide not only

[3] The new fertilizer plant at Sindri, in In-dia's Damodar Valley, exemplifies many of the trends suggested here. This $50,000,000 instal-lation, well instrumented but only partly auto-matic in character, employs only 2,000 persons, 87 per cent of whom are in skilled and man-agerial capacities—The Economist (London), 163 (1952), 448. A synchronized, fully auto-matic plant, such as is now designable, would very likely employ only half this number, and reduce the $8–$10 millions allocated for housing and social services accordingly.

more jobs in construction but an increas-ing number in the service trades as well.

In this instance, also, automatism might be used to accelerate the pace of economic development, but it would also make rather basic modifications in the pattern of development. With a high intensity of construction the opportunities for employ-ment would be much greater in the hinter-land than in cities, a condition which might be expected to diminish the inunda-tion of the commercial and manufacturing centers by landless migrants. The cities would also have less use for unskilled la-bor, if they were to use the most advanced technology in important instances. There-fore measures to slow the migration would have both economic and political justifica-tion and there is some possibility they may work for a while.

The great advantage of automatism in dealing with the labor supply problem is that it opens up a new strategy for indus-trial development. This strategy brings to the heavily populated areas some of the advantages enjoyed by such countries as Australia, Canada, and Turkey which had quite thinly settled hinterlands. If applied boldly it might be effective enough to break a well-known vicious circle in the towns and cities which are unable to turn back the flow of landless peasants—low wages lead to tragically poor living condi-tions, which in turn engender poor health and cynical apathy, which are sufficient causes for low productivity and necessarily low wages.

MANAGEMENT AND TECHNI-CAL PERSONNEL

The scarcity of well-trained engineers and applied scientists in underdeveloped areas is much talked about but mislead-ing. Actually the shortage is most intense for the type that can make a primitive fac-tory work efficiently up to the limits of its equipment. The primitive factory requires a man who is broadly competent in engineering but is also very knowledgeable about the traditional society so that the best compromises can be found for the operation of the factory. It is preferable that he be a man who is willing "to get his hands dirty." In societies which have for ages decreed that persons who wielded authority should live almost as a race apart, never indulging in menial tasks, it is easy to see why engineers and managers, even if they were not born to the upper classes, would ordinarily be too isolated from the workers to perform their duties with maximum efficiency. Thus it is quite common to find many young men abandoning engineering as a profession, at a time when the apparent shortage is extreme.

It is much easier to find engineers, even native ones, who have excellent training for handling advanced technical processes. This can be achieved quite easily by sending a man to a Western engineering school for a higher degree. He may then either obtain a few years experience before going back home, or be trained on the site by the contractors who built the plant.

In the long run, some of these engineers will graduate to become the managers. In the initial stages managers would have to be sought who have already had some experience in the country where the installations are being made. These experienced men are often found in commerce, but in mining and in government service one may possibly turn up a few more. They would be broken in and advised by the contractors. On the whole, management for a prestige operation is not hard to find.

Some experienced people will point out that maintenance would be the biggest difficulty to overcome, particularly for small to medium size operations. Engineers report that more than half of the control instruments that have been imported into the underdeveloped areas in recent years already require major repairs or adjustment. Most are not being used. This rather discouraging situation is due to the lack of maintenance service. But such a service cannot exist if a dozen or so quite different kinds of plants have only two or three automatic control devices apiece. It would be preferable to have either many more or virtually none at all.

SOCIO-POLITICAL FORCES

At each critical phase in the larger economies the most highly automatic approach, whenever it was technically feasible, promised to yield greater efficiency in the allocation of scarce factors of production. At any rate, no basic objections were discovered. There are, however, some real, though less tangible, objections to a policy encouraging automatism. Some national movements, such as that sponsored by Gandhi in India, will prefer rural industries because they seem more readily adapted to local tradition and ideology. Others who would, or must, imitate the development of the USSR would ordinarily choose primitive factories as a first step because they have become familiar with the techniques of social organization required for this approach. Remarkably enough a government grounded in *laissez faire* principles and their applications in Western countries, would normally choose policies which also result in the building of primitive factories. It is only when the country gives free rein to its cadre of scientists and engineers trained in Western universities that automatic units would be consistently chosen.

The applied scientists and engineers are less encumbered with tradition than any other group in the society. They tend to choose the neatest possible solution for a production problem, partly from an inclination to eliminate as many complex nonmaterial factors as possible, but also because it is esthetically preferable to the designer and is a means of obtaining prestige in the profession. There is a tendency, too, to imitate the most advanced designs published in the internationally distributed technical journals from the United States, Great Britain, and Germany. The neatest solution nowadays almost always incorporates feedback controls, and is fully automatic whenever possible. Rather than carry out an assignment in a routine fashion, scientists and engineers will put in a great deal of overtime trying to find a "nicely automated operation" which would also be economic.

A carefully planned development of a poor country would have to be managed by a professional elite not much different in character from the crack research and development groups assembled by firms and governmental agencies. It would have to be competent, aggressive, versatile, and quick-acting. It would need political support from a majority group of politicians who were agile enough to exploit the results of rapid economic development in order to stay in power. There are a few places in the world where this vigorous approach to planning exists, such as Puerto Rico, Newfoundland, Turkey, and Israel, and a few others like Costa Rica, Jamaica, and Ceylon, where it might come into being. Virtually all these economies are too small to apply much of the automation that has been developed to date. But they do give some hints of what sociopolitical framework is necessary for starting a rapid economic development in a larger economy, and there are enough examples of automatic production units getting started to see the pattern.

The ascendancy of a new managing and governing elite in the later stages of economic development is a rather likely phenomenon. The difficulty is that it, too, unless some other measures are simultaneously taken, can become an entrenched aristocracy blindly dedicated to its own special advantage and hardly any more susceptible to suggestion than the land-owner-military cliques which now hold veto power in a great many of these countries. Engineers, lawyers, scientists, and managers show no evidence of being an exception—unless they have developed a sense of dedication to a mission, accept an austerity standard in their living conditions, and develop measures for co-option from the masses into their ranks. Otherwise the extensive use of automation and other productive techniques would promote diverging standards of living which could lead in the end to nothing but added social unrest. To restate the point in different words, the benefits which it has been argued should flow from the use of automatism will occur only within a special context, i.e., when the managing, operating, and technical classes are predominantly disciplined, forward-looking, and devoted to public service. When these qualities disappear, automation becomes a gimcrack, a showpiece which can only be misunderstood by barely literate people. Under such conditions it might contribute to the frustration and truncation of future developments.

Maurice Zinkin joined Unilever in 1948 and is now on the staff of Lever Brothers (India) Private Ltd. He was for some time personal assistant to Sir Geoffrey Heyworth, Chairman of Unilever Limited, in London. In 1938 he was appointed to the Indian Civil Service and served in the Districts, Bombay Secretariat, and in the Ministry of Finance, Delhi. Mr. Zinkin is the author of *Asia and the West* and the forthcoming volume, *Development for Free Asia*.

Dr. I. G. Patel, at present Deputy Economic Advisor to the Ministry of Finance of the Government of India, was educated at the University of Bombay, University of Cambridge, and Harvard University. He was for some time Professor of Economics at the University of Baroda in India and Assistant Chief in the Fiscal Problems and Policies Division of the Research Department of the International Monetary Fund. He is the author of numerous articles appearing in professional journals in the United States and abroad.

Dr. Henry G. Aubrey is research director of a project on "The Economics of Competitive Co-existence" for the National Planning Association, and a visiting professor in the Graduate Faculty of the New School for Social Research. Until August of 1956 he was an economist in the Balance of Payments Division of the Research Department of the Federal Reserve Bank of New York. He is the author of *United States Imports and World Trade*, 1956; "Investment Decisions in Underdeveloped Countries" in *Capital Formation and Economic Growth*, 1955; "Mexico" in *Economic Development, Principles and Patterns*, 1954; and numerous articles on foreign trade, national income, and economic development.

Dr. Kenneth A. Bohr has been an economist with the International Bank for Reconstruction and Development since 1950. He is also author of the article "Steel Industries in Underdeveloped Countries" appearing in *Economic Development and Cultural Change*, 1952.

Mr. Richard L. Meier is with the Program of Education and Research in Planning at the University of Chicago. He was trained as a chemist and worked for 5 years in petroleum and chemical industries both here and overseas. He is the author of *Science and Economic Development*, 1956, and of numerous articles on scientific applications to the solution of difficult social and economic problems.

VIII

PRIVATE INDUSTRY VS. GOVERN-
MENT IN UNDERDEVELOPED AREAS:
EARLY AND RECENT PERIODS

THIS chapter takes up a subject that has been controversial for many years—private industry vs. government in underdeveloped areas. The argument seems to hinge in part on the question of who benefited how much by such development plans or "exploitation" as it has so often been called. Private industry has justified its profit by citing the high risks of foreign investment; government has rationalized its behavior by calling attention to the public works that have been provided, and representatives of the indigenous inhabitants tend to derogate any benefits accruing to them by assailing the foreigner for his high profit and dislocation of the traditional social organization.

Historian J. Fred Rippy has made the point that although exploitation of indigenous people has sometimes taken place, many of the inhabitants of developed countries have been exploited, for example, investors have had some very poor investments palmed off on them and have lost heavily on occasion. Rippy further suggests that it might be well to approach the subject of foreign investment from the standpoint of group interests. The groups most likely to benefit from foreign investment are: (1) investment bankers and speculators; (2) managers and other technicians; (3) shipping companies; (4) manufacturers; and (5) officials and agents of recipient countries or underdeveloped areas.[1] To quote Rippy a bit further,

The bankers, of course, reap profits from the sale of securities, good or bad, although the exact size of the harvest is customarily not revealed unless and until disclosed by a parliamentary investigation, and the speculators profit by buying up securities from discouraged or hard-driven investors and gambling on a rise in price, which may result from the pressure they are able to exert upon the parties involved, from market manipulations, or from other cause. The shippers benefit from the increased international trade that foreign investments stimulate. Officials and agents (or attorneys) of debtor countries sometimes share in sales commissions or profit as open or concealed partners in

---

[1] "British Investments in Latin America: A Sample of Profitable Enterprises," J. Fred Rippy, *Inter-American Economic Affairs*, Vol. VII, No. 4, Spring 1953, pp. 3–17.

foreign enterprises, although, here again, the evidence is hard to ferret out. Manufacturers and managers and other technicians of the investing countries, by and large, probably benefit most of all. Certain manufacturers are not only provided with increased export outlets to prevent the sagging of prices; they are also supplied with additional raw materials and food for factory workers. Information on salaries and other remunerations of managers and technicians engaged in operating economic enterprises in foreign countries is not readily available to the historian, but one may reasonably conclude that the compensation is higher as a rule than the same individuals could obtain at home or else they would not venture out to distant lands. On the basis of rational expectations, shipping companies, bondsellers, and manufacturers producing for export, along with managers and technicians, should be, and probably are, the most enthusiastic advocates of foreign investments.[2]

Rippy has authored a series of articles on the profitability of foreign investments. The almost complete absence of studies on the dividend records of British overseas economic enterprises is noted by him in an article titled, "Background for Point Four: Samples of Profitable British Investments in Underdeveloped Countries."[3] As a preface to this article and again in conclusion Rippy points out that ". . . only the most profitable of the British overseas investments have been selected as exhibits; average rates of return on the total British investment in most of the regions dealt with, and even the aggregate investments themselves, have never been precisely determined, but it is likely that for every highly remunerative enterprise there were as many as twenty which yielded no better than moderate returns and a few that ended in loss of capital."[4]

Rippy then proceeds to unfold an amazing picture of success for British investments in Asia, Africa, and South America. Not only did these companies pay dividends, sometimes averaging between 200 and 300 percent per year for 5-year periods, but generous paper bonuses in shares were granted besides. In some instances, British investments in African gold and diamond mines paid average dividends of over 500 percent per year during the best 5 years of operation. By no means can it be said that these periods of success were of another generation for some highly successful periods were found as recently as from 1946 to 1950. In summarizing the data presented in the article to which we have just referred, Rippy states,

The facts presented may be summarized in a few words: (1) Of the more than 120 companies whose dividend records have been presented, only 10 failed to make average annual returns of more than 10 per cent over periods of from one to several decades on the face value of their ordinary shares, and only 17 failed during their most prosperous five years to pay aggregate dividends at least equivalent to their capital; (2) 70 companies made aggregate payments during their most flourishing half-decade amounting

---

[2] *Ibid.*, pp. 5–6.
[3] J. Fred Rippy, "Background for Point Four: Samples of Profitable British Investments in the Underdeveloped Countries," *Journal of Business of the University of Chicago*, Vol. XXVI, No. 2, April 1953, pp. 110–124.
[4] *Ibid.*, p. 124.

to more than twice their capital, and, although this was not brought out in the tabulations, more than a fourth of the group recouped their entire capital in a single year or less; (3) the returns for 1946–50 suggest that the years of lush dividends have not vanished; and (4) British investments within the Commonwealth and Empire have yielded larger profits than British investments in Latin America.[5]

In another article Rippy concludes his evaluation of British overseas investments by stating that

British investments within the Commonwealth and the Empire during the period 1939–48, in the aggregate, and with few exceptions, were more profitable than foreign investments. For investors residing in the United Kingdom, the most profitable segments of the Commonwealth and the Empire were South Africa, British Central Africa (the Rhodesias and Nyasaland), India and Pakistan, and Ceylon, while Australia, New Zealand, and Canada were among the least profitable. The most remunerative foreign investments were those in Egypt and Iran, which were the most profitable of all British overseas investments during the period. Also fairly profitable were British investments in the United States, Venezuela, and Bolivia.

Excepting the United States, which seems to depart from the norm, the conclusion seems to be warranted that rates of return tend to be higher from countries in which the masses are poorest. But this generalization is affected by another important factor, namely, the type of economic activity in which the capital is engaged. If the capital is in breweries, in banking or trading organizations, or in the manufacture of tobacco, chemicals, medicines, or cosmetics, it is likely to be profitable almost anywhere. If the investment is in tea plantations, it is apt to be profitable in India, Pakistan, Ceylon, and some parts of Africa where tea grows best. If it is in the production of petroleum, it probably will be most profitable in areas where the richest deposits of petroleum exist: in Burma, Iran, Iraq, Saudi Arabia, Venezuela, and Trinidad, for instance. If it is in mining, it is likely to bring high returns from British Malaya and certain parts of Africa, India, and Latin America where tin, copper, manganese, gold, and diamonds abound. And the masses are poor in all the countries and regions mentioned.

Aside from some organizations producing electric power and light (and, perhaps, also a number of enterprises operating wireless and radio systems), public services—broadly defined so as to include railways, docks, canals, tramways, gas plants, waterworks, telephones, and irrigation systems, along with public health, sanitation, and education —returned rather meager profits to the British overseas investor. But such public services will have to be included in any effective program intended to raise levels of living in retarded countries.

Granted that the recent British experience is typical, this poses a major problem, one of the most serious problems that the Point Four program is likely to encounter. Must these public services be subsidized by cheap loans and gifts from the more prosperous nations until the people of the underdeveloped regions attain sufficient prosperity to pay for them? If the burden of providing such services must be carried by the taxpayers of the more wealthy nations, should the governments of such nations attempt to set limits on the profits of private investors who engage in the more remunerative activities in the underdeveloped regions? Will private capital continue to migrate to these regions

[5] Ibid., pp. 122–124.

if public officials place limits on profits? To what extent are these higher profits made at the expense of native labor and to what extent are they extracted from consumers in the more intensively developed countries? Should such consumers be compelled to increase their contribution in order to stimulate the flow of private capital, paying higher prices as well as higher taxes?[6]

This chapter does not purport to present a complete story of private approaches in underdeveloped areas. If anything it presents the most favorable view possible in that the approach is positive. No effort is made to detail the reactions of indigenous inhabitants to past and present private efforts. It may be assumed, and correctly so, that their reaction has been varied, depending to some extent on the policy of the investor toward the indigenous inhabitants. Everyone is familiar with some of the reactions to foreign investment in recent years, the British difficulties in Iran being a notable example.

In order to illustrate more clearly the profitability of some British colonies we have included in this chapter one of Rippy's articles, "Trinidad and Ceylon: Two Profitable British Crown Colonies." Further introduction is unnecessary except to remark that a similar picture could be painted of foreign investments by other developed areas in underdeveloped areas; no attempt has been made to single out Britain as a predator or otherwise, but merely as a handy example of the point to be made.

The desirability of private foreign investments, both for the investor and the indigenous inhabitants of underdeveloped areas, is argued in "Private Foreign Investment: A Means of World Economic Development," by William Harvey Reeves and Paul D. Dickens. Dickens and Reeves argue that foreign investments not only permit earlier development of an area than would otherwise take place but without tremendous sacrifices by the people in the process of capital acquisition. Hindrances to foreign investment are discussed and suggestions for their elimination set forth.

However, the inevitable conclusion is that we might not be faced with the present problem if private approaches had been an adequate means of developing the underdeveloped areas of the world. If private corporations had been capable of developing underdeveloped areas more thoroughly or perhaps in a more balanced fashion, their welcome might have been more extended. That we are still faced with such startling contrasts in the level of living of the developed areas as contrasted to the underdeveloped areas is due, in part, to the outcome of private development efforts in certain areas and the lack of private development efforts in other areas. It is doubtful, however, that we should even have expected private efforts to have accomplished the task of developing underdeveloped areas when their motivation for entering the area was primarily private profits—dividends for investors. As has been suggested by others, the motivation of private developers

[6] J. Fred Rippy, "Point Four Background: A Decade of Income from British Overseas Investment," *Journal of Business of the University of Chicago*, Vol. XXVI, No. 4, October 1953, pp. 236–237.

almost precludes the kind of development that includes relatively expensive public works, projects of such a nature that profit, if it comes at all, appears only over a period of years rather than immediately. Unless the indigenous inhabitants of an area were able to tax profits on private development efforts and establish public works through government, public works could be expected only when a necessity to private development programmes.

Governmental approaches to the development of underdeveloped or undeveloped areas have taken numerous forms. Government approaches have unfortunately not been entirely free of some of the criticisms of private approaches to the development of underdeveloped areas. The various governmental development plans may be classified as: (1) those in which the role of the government is to give technical assistance to private individuals or corporations, this aid perhaps taking the form of scientific publications based on government research and development of an improved brand of seed; (2) those in which the sole role of the government is to finance private development projects that are believed desirable by the government, this aid taking the form of either long-term or short-term loans depending on the needs of the private developer; (3) those in which private corporations erect installations according to government plans and at government expense and which upon completion are operated by the same or other private individuals under contract to the government, this type of development perhaps being a power plant or communication system; (4) those in which private corporations erect installations or facilities according to government plans and at government expense and which upon completion are operated by government employees, this type of development likewise perhaps being a power plant or communication system; (5) those in which the facilities are constructed and operated from the beginning by a government corporation or authority, this again perhaps being a power plant or transportation system.

Another way of classifying governmental development approaches is based on the geographical location of the project and the political status of the countries involved. In this system of classification we have the following types: (1) projects carried out by an independent or self-governing country or political entity within its own geographical limits, i.e., within the so-called metropolitan area; (2) projects carried on outside the metropolitan area but in a non-self-governing area under its control such as a colony or trust territory; (3) projects carried on outside the metropolitan area and in another self-governing area, on one hand, a political entity that is perhaps closely allied and of the same general culture or, on the other hand, perhaps one that is not too closely allied and of quite a different cultural tradition; (4) projects outside the metropolitan area and in a non-self-governing area not under its own control, perhaps the colony of another friendly self-governing area; (5) projects that may fall into one of the above categories but are carried out with the coöperation of one or more other self-governing areas, such as a joint development project with the British in a Middle-Eastern area; (6) projects that are carried out with the assistance of an international agency within one's own boundaries; and (7) projects carried out with the assistance of an international agency within the boundaries of another political entity, self-governing or non-self-governing.

Still a different manner of classifying government development projects might be based on the extensiveness of the program, i.e., (1) piecemeal development as contrasted to (2) extensive planned development of an entire country, the planning taking place on all levels and in a variety of problem areas.

Other systems of classification are possible and perhaps these systems could be extended. However, the important point to be made is that some types of government development have a greater probability of success than others. Some types of development are frought with obstacles not encountered in other types. Rather than speak of government development plans as having certain characteristics and probabilities of success or failure we must speak of various types of government development and the specific risks and problems involved. Data bearing on this aspect of development are far from conclusive in showing which type is most efficient, most likely to succeed, or most likely to be well received by those whom it is intended to benefit. It will be necessary to observe carefully many development projects over a long period of time before we can specify which of the various types of projects or combinations of types of projects is most likely to succeed in a given situation.

In his article "Deliberate Industrialization," Henry G. Aubrey points out that industrialization has been initiated or assisted by governments for almost 200 years in Europe and America. Industrialization is a process in which government has frequently had an important role. A carefully drawn description (and well documented in the original article) of the Mexican case not only points out the role of government in economic development but also shows that it has been a successful role, even in instances when superficial examination of the results might have indicated failure on the part of government.

"Some Problems of Economic Development" by August Maffry, discusses the role of the United States in the economic development of underdeveloped areas as well as that of other governments. Particular attention is devoted to the problem of inflation, capital acquisition, and private versus public investment.

Since other chapters have touched on the role of government in developing underdeveloped areas these selections are included only as examples of the role that government has on occasion played in the past, is presently playing, or conceives of itself as playing in the near future.

TRINIDAD AND CEYLON: TWO PROFITABLE BRITISH CROWN COLONIES*

J. FRED RIPPY

I

NEAR the end of the nineteenth century, while one of Europe's major wars was in progress, the British government seized two islands that were destined to bring rich rewards to British investors: Trinidad, off the northeast coast of Venezuela, and Ceylon, adjacent to India on the other side of the world, the one taken from Spain and the other from the Dutch Netherlands. In proportion to their size —less than 2,000 square miles in the first case and around 25,000 in the second— they turned out to be among the richest prizes ever added to the British Empire in so short a period. The full economic potentialities of these acquisitions were not disclosed, however, until several decades after the acquisitions were made.

British investors tried for many years without pronounced success to win profits from plantations engaged in large-scale tropical agriculture in Trinidad.[1] Accessi-

ble records of the plantation companies indicate rather trifling returns. Caroni Sugar Estates, for instance, organized in 1924, paid almost no dividends on its ordinary shares until 1946, and no more than 7.9 per cent for the half-decade starting with that year. Trinidad Sugar Estates, founded in 1923, returned an annual average of only 6.6 per cent during the first 28 years of its existence, on ordinary shares running from £175,000 to £195,000.

Somewhat more profitable were two earlier companies engaged in other activities. Trinidad Shipping and Trading Company, established in 1895, sent its ordinary shareholders a per-annum average of 7.7 per cent for 24 years before it went into voluntary liquidation in 1920. The par value of their investment was £72,000 in 1896, raised to £90,000 shortly before the firm was dissolved. Angostura Bitters, with its factory and bottling works in Trinidad but collecting some of its raw materials from Venezuela, made still higher returns. This firm, which deals in cordials and "home remedies," was organized in 1909 with a capital of £85,000 in ordinary shares and the same amount in preference, the latter being 6 per cent cumulative and participating. During the 41 years starting in 1910, Angostura Bitters paid an annual

* Adapted and reprinted by permission from *Inter-American Economic Affairs*, Volume VIII, No. 2, Autumn 1954, pp. 84–93.

[1] Statistical data presented in this dicussion have been compiled from two investment manuals published in London: *Stock Exchange Year-Book* and *Stock Exchange Official Intelligence*, the first since 1875 and the second from 1882 until it was merged with the first in 1934 under the new title of *Stock Exchange Official Year-Book*. Both are annuals and it has been necessary to thumb the pages of many volumes and make many computations; but, since both have exhaustive indexes of company names, page references will not be given, for, once the name of a company is ascertained, it can easily be traced through each number of these publications.

average of 8.9 per cent on its ordinary and more than 9 on its preference, while for the five years beginning with 1946 ordinary shareholders received an annual average of 24 per cent and holders of preference shares a per annum of 10 per cent.

The big profits, as one might expect, came from oil wells. Large petroleum lakes underlie the entire southern portion of Trinidad and at least half of the British companies operating there have prospered. On ordinary shares with a par value running from approximately £285,000 up to £300,000, Trinidad Central Oilfields paid an annual average of 6.1 during the 32 years that began with 1919, and the per-annum dividend for the last five years of the period averaged 16.5 per cent. United British Oilfields of Trinidad rewarded its ordinary shareholders with an annual average of 7.2 per cent for the quarter of a century following 1925 on securities with a face value expanding from half a million to a million and a half; and for the years 1946–50, inclusive, the per-annum average rose to 9.5.

But the profits of these two companies were dwarfed by those of three others operating in the island. On ordinary shares ballooning from a par value of £100,000 to £1,000,000, Trinidad Petroleum Development Company returned a per-annum average of 14.7 per cent during the 19 years beginning with 1932, averaged 15.7 yearly for the last five years of the period, and paid a dividend of 16.5 in 1951. Trinidad Leaseholds, on ordinary shares with a par value rising from £429,-500 to £1,639,452, returned an annual average of 15.9 for the 33 years starting in 1918; and Apex (Trinidad) Oilfields was still more profitable, rewarding the holders of its ordinary shares—expanding from £400,000 to £550,000—with an annual average of 32.7 per cent for 29 years (1922–50).

These three were among the ten or fif-

teen most profitable petroleum companies British investors ever owned. In size of returns they compare favorably with Anglo Egyptian, Anglo-Iranian, Burmah Oil, Lobitos Oilfields (Peru), Mexican Eagle, Shell Transport and Trading Company, and Venezuelan Oil Concessions. In the case of Trinidad, empire was beginning to pay at least a few investors.[2]

II

Available information regarding the earnings of early British economic organizations in Ceylon, as in the case of Trinidad, is rather scarce.[3] Britishers are said to have made handsome profits from coffee plantations for several decades until a leaf blight interfered in the 1880's. Then they turned to tea and rubber and eventually prospered as in few other parts of the Empire. Their plantations covered a good part of the island and, at one time or another, most of them grew both rubber and tea, so that the names of the plantation companies give no reliable indication of which product was being emphasized.

Approximately 200 companies were registered in the British Isles between 1880 and 1950 for the purpose of growing tea and rubber in Ceylon, and very few of them failed to pay yearly average dividends of as much as 10 per cent for a decade or two. Table 1 sets forth the divi-

[2] Statistics on yields given in this summary take no account of capital losses, which were rare, or stock bonuses, which were fairly large in some instances, or of "watered stock." Trinidad also has considerable natural asphalt, but investors from the United States seem to have controlled the asphalt production there as well as in Venezuela.

[3] *Stock Exchange Year-Book* lists only 8 British plantation companies active in Ceylon for 1886 and no more than 12 for 1891, but it lists 53 for 1900, describes 149 for 1916, around 136 for 1920, and 115 for 1950. Capitalization, mostly in ordinary shares, had an aggregate par value of £9 to £16 million after 1900 and was near its peak in 1928.

TABLE 1.   A Sample of the Most Profitable British Plantation Companies in Ceylon

Company	No. of Years	Initial Year	Annual Average	Highest Five Years	Annual Average	Annual Average 1946–50
Balmoral Estates (1898)	47	1904	24.2%	1924–28	51.0%	27.6%
Bandarapola Ceylon (1892)	47	1904	16.7	1922–26	45.0	11.0
Battalgalla Estate (1889)	45	1906	22.6	1924–28	74.0	25.0
Ceylon Planters' Assoc. (1897)	44	1907	15.0	1923–27	42.0	11.8
Ceylon Land and Produce (1884)	59	1892	18.4	1922–26	35.0	19.0
Ceylon Tea Plantations (1886)	64	1887	23.6	1912–16	50.0	25.0
Consolidated Estates (1891)	44	1907	24.2	1915–19	53.0	18.0
Eastern Produce (1888)	47	1904	17.9	1924–28	42.0	19.3
Kelani Valley (1886)	58	1893	15.6	1912–16	46.0	16.5
Mooloya Estates (1897)	42	1909	22.1	1922–26	60.4	16.5
New Dimbula (1899)	52	1899	26.9	1923–27	53.0	32.0
Namunakula Tea Estate (1894)	44	1907	16.4	1923–27	56.0	13.1
Nuwara Eliya Estates (1895)	52	1899	17.2	1924–28	44.6	19.2
Panawal Tea (1893)	53	1898	16.1	1922–26	49.5	9.4
Pelmadulla Rubber (1905)	46	1905	19.5	1922–26	39.0	27.6
Scottish Ceylon Tea (1889)	61	1890	16.4	1924–28	50.0	21.8
Spring Valley Ceylon (1865)	45	1906	17.2	1922–26	47.0	14.0
Standard Tea (1891)	59	1892	24.3	1923–27	60.0	34.0
Sunnygama (1893)	47	1904	21.7	1912–16	63.0	16.0
Ukuwela Estates (1899)	48	1903	38.1	1924–29	128.0	25.0

dend records of twenty tea companies which yielded annual averages of 15 to slightly more than 38 per cent for time spans running from 42 to 64 years. Dates of company organization are given in parentheses.

These were remarkably profitable companies. Nine of the group rewarded their shareholders with annual averages of more than 20 per cent, not including share bonuses, amounting to from 25 to 200 per cent, which twelve of the twenty corporations distributed (between 1919 and 1928, as a rule). Moreover, returns in recent years were still high, as indicated by the last column in this table, which shows that only one of the twenty dropped below a per-annum average of 11 per cent for the lustrum starting with 1946. In fact, the majority paid yearly averages running from 19 per cent up to 34 per cent during this recent half-decade.

The most fantastic statistics appear in column six, which contains the annual av-erage for each company during its most flourishing consecutive five years, usually in the middle 1920's, but earlier in three instances. Not one of the twenty companies yielded an annual average of less than 35 per cent during its most prosperous half-decade. Eighteen averaged above 42, two averaged exactly 50, and the per-annum averages of nine ran from 51 up to 128! In other words, the ordinary shareholders of the majority of these twenty tea corporations recovered twice their investment during a single lustrum and received handsome dividends besides. And let it be remembered that these twenty corporations are about a tenth of all the corporate enterprises registered in Great Britain during the seven decades following 1880 for the purpose of operating plantations in Ceylon and around a sixth of those operating there in any decade since 1900.

But these were by no means the only profitable tea corporations owned by Brit-

TABLE 2.   Other Profitable British Plantation Companies in Ceylon

Company	Annual 1911–50	Average 1946–50	Highest Five Years	Annual Average	Yield 1950
Anglo-Ceylon	15.6%	24.5%	1917–21	26.0%	30.0%
Bogawantalawa	15.4	9.8	1923–27	35.5	15.0ʲ
Carolina	13.3	9.5	1923–27	47.0	17.5
Central Province	11.2	13.8	1926–30	17.3	15.0
Ceylon Estates Investment	15.1ᵃ		1924–28	37.0	
Ceylon Para Rubber	19.7	23.0	1923–27	52.0	60.0
Ceylon Proprietary Estates	12.8	12.2	1923–27	30.0	22.5
Craighead Tea	15.0	9.6	1923–27	35.0	12.0
Demodera Tea	20.2ᵇ	24.1	1922–26	41.0	30.0
Dickella Rubber Estate	14.4ᶜ		1923–27	30.0	
Dimbula Valley Tea	16.2	10.0	1923–27	32.0	12.5
Duckwari Tea and Rubber	21.5	34.0	1924–28	65.0	37.5
East India and Ceylon Tea	11.0	11.8	1923–27	31.0	25.0
Ederapolla Tea	13.8	13.5	1922–26	38.5	32.5
Ellawatte Ceylon Estates	16.5	12.7	1923–27	26.2	20.0
Elmhurst Tea and Rubber	11.4	18.2	1925–29	35.0	25.0
Galaha Ceylon Tea	12.8	12.0	1924–29	25.5	15.0
General Ceylon Rubber	11.2ᵈ		1912–16	25.5	
Hanipha Tea and Rubber	14.6	10.6	1924–28	44.0	15.0
Hattangalla Tea and Rubber	11.7ᵉ	5.2	1915–19	21.0	10.0
Highland Tea	12.6	12.8	1924–28	27.0	16.0
Hornsey Tea Estates	15.2	16.0	1926–30	37.0	20.0
Kandapolla Tea	14.2ᶠ		1924–28	42.0	
Kintyre Tea Estates	13.7	13.0	1925–29	26.5	15.0
Lindoola Tea	10.0	10.0	1926–30	34.0	10.0
Lunuva Tea and Rubber	12.2	16.0	1923–27	23.5	20.0
Maturata Tea and Rubber	15.9ᵍ	18.7	1922–26	28.0	12.5
Mayfield Dimbula Tea	16.3	16.1	1924–28	37.0	15.0
Mount Vernon Tea	16.1	15.0	1923–27	34.0	20.0
Ouvah Ceylon Estates	14.9	17.9	1924–28	32.5	25.0
Pantiya Tea and Rubber	12.9	7.5	1924–28	29.0	25.0
Parambe Rubber and Tea	10.7	13.7	1922–26	23.5	40.0
Portmore Tea	16.6ʰ		1925–29	37.4	
Pundaloya Tea	16.4	13.0	1925–29	39.0	17.0
Ragalla Tea Estates	15.4	12.2	1925–29	28.0	15.0
St. George Rubber Estates	14.3	17.0	1915–19	38.0	45.0
Scottish Tea and Lands	17.4	21.8	1923–27	43.2	30.0
South Wanaraja Tea	13.8	13.5	1921–25	30.0	25.0
Talawakelle Estates	18.2ⁱ		1925–29	31.0	
Telbedde Ceylon Estates	25.8	16.5	1923–27	77.0	25.0
United Planters' Co.	15.4	10.8	1924–28	49.5	20.0
Vellikellie Tea	13.8	11.0	1924–28	28.0	15.0

ᵃ For 1911–45.   ᵈ For 1910–50.   ᵍ For 1912–50.
ᵇ For 1918–50.   ᵉ For 1912–50.   ʰ For 1905–38.
ᶜ For 1910–45.   ᶠ For 1911–46.   ⁱ For 1909–48.
ʲ For 1950; blanks in this column indicate incomplete returns or extinct companies.

ishers in Ceylon. They were, and are, merely those with the highest dividend records for time spans running above 40 years. Table 2 exhibits more than twice as many with yearly average yields of from 10 to 25.8 per cent for slightly shorter periods. Of the forty-two corporations included in this table, twenty struck medians of 15 per cent and above for a period of some four decades following 1910. Only one of them fell below an annual average of 21 per cent for its most prosperous consecutive five years, and even this one dropped no lower than 17.3. Thirty-one of the group averaged from 30 per cent up to 77 annually during this half-decade, thus recouping their entire capital after subtracting a fairly good dividend. And note, again, that these figures make no allowance for paper bonuses sent to shareholders, usually in the 1920's, by at least a third of the group, bonuses running from 20 to 200 per cent.

Table 2, like Table 1, also shows good returns for recent years. Thirty-six of the forty-two corporations listed—five had been dissolved and complete returns are lacking for one—sent their ordinary shareholders annual averages ranging (with two exceptions) from 9.5 to 34 per cent for the lustrum beginning with 1946 and dividends of from 10 to 60 per cent in 1950, the majority of them paying 20 per cent and above for that year.

The sixty-two companies dealt with in these two tables represent nearly a third of all the corporate enterprises organized in the British Isles since 1880 for the purpose of engaging in tropical agriculture in Ceylon and fully half of the average number operating there since 1900. Most of the others returned average dividends of 5 to 9 per cent annually during the forty years terminating in 1950. The median for the entire group, taking no account of stock bonuses, must have been around 15 per cent for the four decades, even including small issues of debentures and preference shares, which customarily paid only 5.5 to 7.5 per cent.

III

Such were the profits garnered by British investors from two very profitable crown colonies. This summary will now be concluded with a contrast, in order to present a more balanced view of the size of the returns from these smaller segments of the Empire. British North Borneo will serve this purpose as well as any other British possession.

British North Borneo was ruled by the British North Borneo Company, created by royal charter late in 1881, from the early 1880's until 1946, when the company's assets and sovereign rights were acquired by the British crown for the sum of £1,400,000. Among its original directors were a lord, two knights, and a rear admiral. A proprietary company, it was probably primarily interested in profits, but returns to its stockholders were very meager. During the 67 years following 1881 the average annual dividend on paid-up ordinary shares, ranging from approximately £400,000 at the outset to £1,852,385 in 1948, was less than 2 per cent. At certain periods debenture issues were as large as the share capital; but these paid only 4.5 and 5 per cent annually. When the company was liquidated in 1949 the holders of its ordinary shares suffered a loss of about 60 per cent of the par value of their investment. The best per-annum average for any five years in succession was only 4.8 per cent (from 1908 through 1912).

The British North Borneo Company tried to exploit the resources of its domain by sponsoring several economic organizations, more than 30 all told; but the majority of these were likewise unprofitable. Table 3 exhibits the records of 18 of the most remunerating, the majority of them plantation companies, all of which, with one exception, were growing rubber.

Compared with the returns from enterprises operating in Trinidad and Ceylon, dividends paid by these North Borneo companies seem insignificant. Only four of the 18 companies dealt with yielded annual averages of more than 5 per cent for the periods covered; and two of these four

TABLE 3. A Sample of the Most Profitable British Enterprises in North Borneo

Company	No. of Years	Initial Year	Annual Average	Highest Five Years	Annual Average	Yield in 1950
Bangawan Rubber	41	1910	2.8%	1924–28	7.3%	6.0%
Beaufort Borneo Rubber	44	1907	3.5	1925–29	12.0	5.0
British Borneo Para Rubber	45	1906	4.9	1925–29	17.0	nil
Kimanis Rubber	41	1910	3.9	1923–27	9.5	15.0
Lok Kawi Rubber	42	1909	4.4	1924–28	23.5	5.0
Manchester N. Borneo Rubber	45	1906	4.5	1924–28	27.0	nil
Marudu Rubber	35	1916	3.7	1936–40	12.2	10.0
Membakut Estates	42	1909	3.6	1916–20	8.2	10.0
New London Borneo Tobacco	34	1893	7.6	1899–1903	20.7	
Sablas Rubber	27	1910	3.7	1917–21	6.4	
Sapong Rubber Estates	40	1911	7.6	1923–27	28.6	25.0
Sekong Rubber	41	1910	2.0	1923–27	6.6	nil
Tenom Rubber Estates	45	1906	5.0	1915–19	16.5	10.0
Tuaran Rubber Estates	31	1920	6.8	1923–27	31.0	nil
British Borneo Timber	31	1920	3.6	1936–40	7.6	20.0
Borneo (trading)	37	1914	6.5	1914–19	24.0	10.0
North Borneo Trading	41	1910	3.0	1946–50	8.0	10.0
British Borneo Petroleum	28	1923	11.4	1946–50	12.3	14.0

—Borneo Company and British Borneo Petroleum Company—did not limit their business to North Borneo. It should be observed, however, that six of the 18 more than recouped their original investment during their most prosperous five years; that the majority of the group (two had been absorbed by other corporations) paid good dividends in 1950; and that, while three of them suffered capital losses, some seven or eight expanded their capital con-

siderably by distributing share bonuses. And it should also be noted that these and other British companies in North Borneo might have treated their shareholders somewhat better if the vicissitudes of the second World War had not deprived them of from five to eight years of profits. Nevertheless, it must be concluded that investments in this segment of the British Empire were not very profitable.

PRIVATE FOREIGN INVESTMENTS: A MEANS OF WORLD ECONOMIC DEVELOPMENT*

WILLIAM HARVEY REEVES
AND
PAUL D. DICKENS

THE post-war pattern, that is the concentration of private investments in extractive industries and in underdeveloped areas, differs from that of pre-war years. Then private American-owned foreign investments were normally concentrated to a considerable extent in the industrially advanced areas of the world. Two thirds of such assets were located in Europe and Canada in about equal amounts. The highly industrialized countries of the United Kingdom and Germany had, before World War II, attracted more American capital than any other country except one, our neighbor, Canada.

While, in absolute terms, investments were concentrated in the developed areas, American investments in the less well-developed areas were far greater than in Europe, proportionally to total capital investments .(the capital equipment of the country—domestic and foreign-owned). At the same time it is apparent from the available data that American holdings of noncontrolling interests in the securities of European and Canadian corporations were much larger than in those of Latin American corporations or those of Asia and

* Adapted and reprinted by permission from *Political Science Quarterly*, Vol. LXIV, No. 2, June 1949, pp. 217–244.

other underdeveloped countries, both in terms of value and proportionally to total American-owned assets in those areas. The significance of these facts will be alluded to in a later section.

WHY FOREIGN INVESTMENTS?

The motivation of these post-war foreign investments, as well as their character, differs greatly today from what it was fifty, twenty-five or even ten years ago. The reason is the vastly increased volume of intergovernmental loans made primarily for reasons other than financial returns. At earlier periods the generalization could be made with considerable accuracy that foreign investments were made because there was the reasonable expectation of greater profits from foreign than from domestic investments. That statement is still generally true with respect to private investments, although it has always needed some qualification and still does. Other motives than larger returns, for example protection of an already operating business in sources of raw-material supply, even noneconomic reasons, such as sentiment and prestige, sometimes are influential in causing foreign investments.

Governmental investments in foreign

countries have a different motivation. They have a superficial appearance of monetary return by specifying an interest rate, but interest is charged on intergovernmental loans not so as to make them profitable but to make the loan more palatable, politically, in the home country of the lender. The oft-used phrase "United States government investment" or "loan" is an euphemism. We never have had any federal policy of "investing" taxpayers' money for the sake of future return. From the taxpayers' standpoint the sounder public finance would be to lower taxes or reduce the national debt. We recognize the moral responsibilities of a more fortunate position in a post-war world and are moved by enlightened self-interest; we have legitimate economic ends in creating demands for American exports, which may be served initially by a foreign governmental loan. We should face the fact that most governmental loans and grants-in-aid since World War II were for some object, to achieve which we have been willing to make an expenditure of government funds; that the commercial terms attached have been with hope that they may be met in whole or in part, and that the taxpayer may be offered that much relief.

There are various types of governmental investments but the motivation is usually the same. The investments of the British government in the Near East oil fields have been made to further political ends —to control sources of fuel needed by the Royal Navy. The fact that the investments have been profitable has been fortunate but not determining. The United States government invested heavily in manganese production in Cuba, not because of any chances of profits, but because supplies of that metal were needed during the war, regardless of cost.

From the foreign country's standpoint, there are two major reasons for favoring foreign investment within the country.

Both are primarily economic and social. First, foreign investments permit the development of the resources and industries of a country earlier than would otherwise be the case. New and underdeveloped countries are lacking in both capital and skills. Both can be developed slowly through the gradual accumulations of the years, but in some areas it is conceivable that such development would take centuries. Private foreign investments bring the capital and the skills and, by creating larger local income and a broader range of activity in the country, can hasten the process of local accumulation of both capital and skills.

Second, foreign investments permit the development of the resources and industries of a country without tremendous sacrifices by the people. Totalitarian governments have frequently expanded the production of their countries greatly, with almost no assistance from foreign capital, but only on the basis of unnecessary suffering by their citizenry. In other words, goods for export to secure foreign exchange and capital goods that could have been purchased with foreign capital were produced instead of goods for domestic consumption.

We are now concerned with the future and must here consider what part private American capital should play in financing capital projects and the reasons why it is not presently filling that rôle. This question may be divided into two parts. First are private loans, or the flotation of foreign securities in the capital markets of the world. Since these offerings are usually issued in relatively small denominations, and the units are bought and sold freely, frequently listed on organized exchanges, they are called portfolio investments. Such loans by large numbers of persons, each by his purchase of bonds supplying a relatively small amount, presupposes that funds invested will be managed in the foreign country and usually by foreign managers. The American bond-holders are merely the lienors of a foreign enterprise or creditors of a government and more often than not are without the ability to enforce their rights as such, in case of financial necessity. Second are private direct investments, or investments by private capital involving control of business enterprises in foreign countries. This type of foreign investment usually presupposes a large unit investment by one company or syndicate.

PRIVATE FOREIGN LOANS— PORTFOLIO INVESTMENTS

There has been virtually a complete stoppage of private foreign loans in the United States since 1931. The very few loans which have been made were by the large commercial banks and insurance companies. There have been no public flotations of foreign securities of any magnitude since the end of World War II.

Several factors are responsible for the absence of new portfolio investments abroad. First, there is a general distrust of foreign bonds, with many selling at substantial discounts in the United States.

This distrust of foreign bonds is based partly on experience and partly on the failure of investors to appraise intelligently the inherent worth of individual issues. At one time more than 50 per cent of all outstanding foreign dollar bonds were in default; and about 48 per cent are in default at present, despite the adjustments that have been made. When all non-Canadian foreign dollar bonds are considered, the losses suffered by investors have been substantial, although there are a number of issues whose records merit considerable confidence.

A second reason for the absence of new private foreign loans is the international political tension, based partly upon differences in ideologies and partly upon do-mestic political instability. Conflicts of these kinds have made the effective administration of government difficult and have contributed to a lack of balance between governmental revenues and expenditures. This has helped cause exchange controls and defaults on bond service to remain longer than they otherwise would have.

Foreign countries have insisted on low rates of interest on their borrowings and have succeeded to a considerable degree because the United States government, and other governments able to lend, have charged only 2½ to 3½ per cent on loans. The International Bank has charged 4¼ per cent. Furthermore, since the war there have been ample opportunities for investments at home, yielding returns too high to make the rates foreign countries are willing to pay seem attractive.

PRIVATE FOREIGN DIRECT INVESTMENTS

Direct investments in foreign countries, in the past, have attracted less general attention than publicly offered foreign loans. Yet, they have been a more effective means of developing the industries of foreign countries and have generally resulted in large aggregate foreign investments in underdeveloped countries. They are not, for example, subject to automatic repayment provisions; when successful, they generate some of the means of financing their own expansion. In fact they normally are made with the expectation of developing industry by internal expansion as conditions warrant. Foreign direct investments embrace such outstanding developments as the nitrate and copper mines of Chile, the petroleum industry of Venezuela and the Near East, manufacturing plants of wide variety in Europe and Latin America, hydroelectric installations and nickel mines in Canada, and the sugar and banana plantations of Cuba and Central America.

They constitute a substantial part of the total invested capital of many countries, including, for example, Canada, Peru and India.

Unfavorable attitude of some countries toward foreign investment. Certain foreign countries, and in particular those relatively underdeveloped ones in greatest need of assistance through foreign investment, have assumed attitudes and adopted measures which are serious obstacles to new private investments. However lacking in enlightened self-interest these attitudes may be, they have some historical basis and should be considered.

Perhaps chief among the reasons are unfortunate experiences with foreign investments in the past. These cannot be lightly waved aside as only "events in history." The Near and the Middle East associate, with foreign investment, the system of "capitulations," and the Far East, particularly China, the system of "extraterritoriality." These systems were once undoubtedly economic measures. Furthermore, they grew from small beginnings and their power enlarged as the amount of the capital invested and the number of foreign persons within those countries increased, and in a later period their principal usefulness was to insure political controls which tended toward maintenance of monopolies. These systems may have been only indirectly related to economic matters for the protection of the instruments of private capital and of the foreigners, living outside of their own country, concerned with the operation of that private capital. In general, these arrangements as complete governmental units are disappearing. There are remnants of these practices, however, which still require governmental alertness. Some of the old concession contracts still remain in force; and wherever they exist, they contain certain elements of extraterritoriality. For exam-

ple, they often include provisions for police or security forces, under the control of the concessionaire. Furthermore, these concession contracts usually call for rights over land equivalent to "eminent domain," in order that lands may be taken whenever they are needed for the purpose of the concession.

Backward countries in need of capital usually must concentrate at the beginning of industrial development in the extractive industries; and here can be found a strong national prejudice. There is a feeling that manufacturing establishments bring something new to the country, while mining and other extractive industries take something away. The facts are contrary: first, the investment of mineral and petroleum companies in building and equipment is sometimes larger, in relation to gross income and operating income, than that of manufacturing companies; and, second, the companies in the extractive industries generally supply foreign exchange in greater amount than that needed for their dividends, whereas manufacturing companies are usually net users of the foreign exchange resources of a country. This preference for manufacturing industries may arise partly from the idea that their profits are not as large as those of the extractive industries and that the large-profit organizations should be reserved for domestic capital. The difference is not as great as supposed, although the amount of profits does favor the extractive industries. By way of example, it may be pointed out that, in 1943, the average yield on American manufacturing, mining and smelting, and petroleum investments abroad was 4.5, 8.5, and 5.6 per cent, respectively.[1]

[1] The Department of Commerce, Economic Series, No. 65, *International Transactions of the U.S. during the War, 1940–1945*, prepared under the direction of Robert L. Semmons, Table 17, page 211.

The higher earnings are partly offset by greater risks and difficulties connected with extractive enterprises. The certainty of larger profits probably is based on the fact that the extractive enterprises are usually primarily engaged in exporting their products for payment in foreign currency, which often makes it possible for them to retain their profits without the necessity of applying for foreign exchange to the local exchange authorities.

The more flagrant illustrations of capital exploiting a government are drawn from experiences of years ago. But whenever such an incident occurs, the results of prejudice lie heavy on both the foreign government and its population, and the frequently violent efforts by the country or populace to change such conditions are not forgotten by the capital investor.

The desire to prevent conditions which have existed in the past and cannot exist in the future, save as manifestations of invasion and political domination, has resulted practically in the expulsion of foreign capital and in repelling new investment, except on a government to government basis.

MAJOR HINDRANCES TO NEW FOREIGN INVESTMENT

There is no hard and fast classification of legal or administrative obstacles which have been placed by foreign countries in the way of foreign investment. If the intent is to drive out foreign capital or private enterprise, the obstacle is fundamental; it is minor when it results from protection of some phase of local economy or from temporary dislocation.

Perhaps the greatest immediate obstacle to private foreign investment is the present conflict in ideologies between the East and the West. Not only does this preclude any investments within Soviet Russia, and in the countries dominated by Soviet Russia, in many of which foreign investments have previously been made, but it is an obstacle to new investments in continental Europe.

Objection to foreign investment may lie in an antiforeign nationalism. Nationalism, with its basis in patriotism, is the ready tool of the local politician who can always make an appeal to the unthinking and arouse their hatred against people they have never seen and about whom they know nothing. Many extreme nationalists would rather see an economic resource remain undeveloped, and workers living in poverty, than see it developed by private foreign capital, with greater advantage to the country itself and higher living standards for its people. Unthinkingly, the laboring class within that country is led to favor such perverted policy, because workers are taught to believe that in this manner they are somehow defending their self-respect and their liberties.

There are varying degrees of nationalism, and it takes many forms. In some countries it has gone only so far as to limit foreign capital's entrance into certain fields; and here it is hard to say whether any particular industry should, as a matter of sovereignty and for protection of the national interest, be reserved to domestic capital and operation. Thus, in some countries, strategic and military industries are so reserved; and it would seem that this may be entirely proper. Added to the list, however, are found public utilities for which there is less reason for local ownership. In other countries, raw-material production is not permitted to foreign capital, although this prohibition has no reference to any local conservation laws.

The more extreme nationalism manifests itself in nationalization of industry. In underdeveloped countries nationalization programs usually affect foreign investors and immediately give rise to considerations with respect to compensation. Even where the foreign investor receives compensation, such payment is often ineffective since it cannot be converted into currency of his own country. Frequently these nationalizations have been of sufficient political significance to divert the attention of an unfortunate populace away from the basic inefficiency of its own government.

It should be remembered that most large installations of capital in foreign countries are made under solemn agreements, as to the length of time and the nature of the concessions of land and the like. Such agreements are abrogated wholly when expropriation takes place. Although it is recognized that differences exist as to concepts of eminent domain and judicial enforcement, these are not sufficient to explain such acts of expropriation.

MINOR HINDRANCES TO NEW INVESTMENTS

In addition to what may be called the major impediments already considered, certain minor impediments must be removed if foreign investment is to be encouraged. Antiforeign propaganda is one of these minor impediments. The demagogue seeking political power can always create in imagination a "foreign devil"; and calling upon unfortunate events of the past, with the aid of unrestrained imagination, can create antagonism which is destructive of good economic, particularly labor, relationships. Minor violations of property rights by local governments can become sufficiently annoying to be a real drain upon the effective operation of a business. Sometimes this antiforeign attitude leads to requirements that foreign investors relinquish the right to appeal to their own governments for diplomatic protection. This latter requirement is common in Latin America. It is right and proper that foreign capital should be gov-

erned by local law, where not inconsistent with property rights; and it should know what this is before it takes the business risk. But what is here referred to is the abrogation of recognized amenities between countries.

Foreign capital frequently encounters the requirement that local capital participate with it. This may be based upon the fear that local capital will be excluded from the best investment opportunities; but usually, depending upon the attitude of the government and people, this makes an uneasy partnership. Laws of this kind, however, are common. The government of India in a statement of industrial policy[2] says that foreign capital may participate in certain phases of the industrialization of India, but that as a rule the major interest in ownership and effective control should always be in Indian hands. The government of Pakistan, through a statement to the press made by the Minister of Commerce on April 2, 1948, ruled that nationals of Pakistan should ordinarily be given the option to subscribe to 51 per cent of all classes of share capital and debentures in major industries and to 30 per cent in other industries. If the government is satisfied that the requisite amount of indigenous capital is not forthcoming, the balance may be subscribed by foreign investors. Similar requirements can be found in Egyptian law and relate to issues of security at the founding of the company or when increasing its capital.

Obviously all this tends to reduce the amount of available capital and to confirm the suspicion that foreign capital is not wanted and will be taken only if there is no other source. Local capital and foreign capital may differ not only as to management but also as to fundamental policy.

[2] "Industrial Policy of India," resolution appearing in the *Gazette of India*, April 6, 1948, reissued in mimeographed form by U.S. Department of Commerce, June 22, 1948.

Foreign capital may anticipate a long-time investment; local capital may wish quick profits and object to reinvestment of earnings at the expense of higher dividends. At times such legislation is used as a means of driving out foreign capital by requiring that, in reorganization or expansion, local capital be permitted to acquire control. Foreign capital is apt to be unwilling to be managed wholly by local executives. American investors feel they cannot jeopardize their capital by a management over whom they have no control and in whose business judgment they may have little confidence.

In some countries labor laws require that a certain specified and large proportion of the workers be citizens of the country. The purpose is to make sure that local labor shall have an opportunity not only to secure employment but also to acquire industrial skills and to advance in salary and responsibility. The statement of the government of India is an example on this point. It specifies: "In all cases, the training of suitable Indian personnel for the purpose of eventually replacing foreign experts will be insisted upon."[3] In general if the laws go no farther, they merely create a norm which would be more than met in any event. Most United States corporations operating abroad state that their policy is to train personnel in the foreign country to as large an extent as possible, reserving to Americans only a few of the higher positions of responsibility. But such legislation sometimes goes farther and provides that the right to hire and fire employees, to promote or demote them, can be exercised only with the concurrence of labor unions and in accordance with seniority rules.

Occasionally labor laws, which ostensibly aim to give to the workers of the country a fair share in industry, merge into so-cial legislation. This is not bad in itself; in fact it can be commended as a goal, and many of the provisions in the foreign countries are modeled on our own laws or upon customary rules between labor and management here. Among them may be listed vacations with pay, separation allowances —frequently larger than is customary in the United States—maternity leave with benefits, insurance, health, and educational facilities. These are good in their basic intention; but countries desiring for their populations a standard of living comparable to that of the United States have felt that they could achieve it merely by legislating that it be so. The means of accomplishment are lacking. Production within a country, whether it be by local or foreign capital, is burdened to the point where the product can be sold only at a price beyond the reach of potential buyers. In such an instance foreign capital should beware; it would be welcomed as the goose which lays the golden egg and is likely to meet the fate of that fabulous bird.

Vested interests in foreign countries should be considered separately, although the difficulties which arise are often a combination of some of the factors already considered. In certain underdeveloped countries discrimination by race or caste exists. In others an almost feudal system of industry prevails. Agriculture and much of the industrial production are under the control of a few families.

In many countries business men having vested interests want neither competition with their business nor any changes which affect their labor supply. One hopeful sign is that these feudal lords are entering the manufacturing field more and more, are retreading unconsciously the path of the industrial revolution.

To the extent that government competition develops out of the idea of nationalization, it is an effective obstacle to new investments. Public utility enterprises have

[3] Industrial policy. See footnote 2, *supra*.

been recognized in many countries as a field for government investments. The social importance of an industry and its non-competitive nature are considerations in determining governmental regulation, control or ownership. The limitation of public utility profits is common in most countries and often results in profits so low that new private investments are not forthcoming.

Recently Latin American governments have been organizing development corporations, partly to stimulate industrial growth and partly to get the government in business. Some of them, such as the Chilean and Venezuelan, are supposed to assist, by loans or by participations, private capital to establish industries. Furthermore, they are expected to sell their interests in these enterprises to private capital whenever possible.

Limitation on the percentage of profits is another hindrance to foreign investment. This may take either of two forms, and both may be applied simultaneously: an actual limit upon the amount of profits which will be permitted to foreign capital or a limit on that which can be remitted abroad to the country from which the investment comes. This latter is a feature of foreign exchange limitation. Sometimes it is in an absolute guarantee or permission, but is hedged about with further restrictions. No matter how great the maximum, if there is not at least a minimum permitted absolutely and without qualification, the limitations are very unattractive to capital. If foreign investors could be sure that the profits they make, within the limitation, could be remitted, they might be willing to invest.

Other regulations have similar tendencies. In Argentina regulations exist to the effect that earnings of more than the maximum permitted (without reference to how much may be remitted through foreign exchanges) have to be reinvested. Such rein-

vested income, however, may not be considered as capital upon which to calculate percentage of earnings which could be remitted in subsequent years. Profit limitation, while not approved of by business men, is in general not the essence of the problem and, except for exchange control, is probably not a basic obstacle to investment. But it may and probably does have the effect of lessening the flow of more speculative risk capital.

There are additional types of control over profits and earnings exercised in other countries. Some legislation requires the reinvestment of earnings. An investor does not want to be bound by law to continue to reinvest in his business. He prefers to determine for himself whether he wishes to expand or, if the business be not profitable, to withdraw his earnings.

The necessity of foreign exchange in all international trade has been a recurring problem, and the effort to control it for the benefit of one country or another has become a great impediment to foreign investment. The problem itself is simple. The mechanics of foreign exchange, however, are complex; and the efforts to manage them have led not only to stagnation of foreign trade but to preventing the only ultimate remedy, namely greater unrestricted international trade.

Should a foreign investor loan money to a country having exchange controls, it would be relatively easy to have the loan expended, in the first instance, for materials, machines, and the like to be set up in the borrowing country and there put to productive use. But when interest became due on the loan, or profits were made on the business, the foreign investor would have no means of securing these in his own country for his use at home. It is of no advantage to him to know that his foreign investment is a profitable one, if he can receive neither income from it nor the return of his capital. He cannot withdraw his capital; for, even should he liquidate it, he has but a credit in a foreign country.

The original theory of these controls was that they were necessitated by temporary economic conditions; they were a recognition of a lack of foreign exchange to meet all commitments. It was assumed that when relatively small amounts of foreign exchange were available, the national welfare dictated that these should be used solely for the purchase and importation of goods, not readily available within the country, which were essential for the well-being of its citizens and for the maintenance of its industries. Only a government could make these allocations.

Usual priorities granted for the purchase of foreign exchange classify dividends and profits with "luxury items," while capital withdrawals are generally the lowest on the list. This means that capital may not be withdrawn until there is no further need of control.

It would appear the part of reason for a foreign country which is in need of foreign capital to attract it by giving to it some relief from the country's foreign exchange regulations.

"Pegging" of foreign exchange is not strictly a part of foreign exchange control, but it represents a frequent additional detriment. When the currency of one country is depreciated in terms of another, there is the tendency on the part of the government of that country to fix an "official rate of exchange" which overvalues the currency of the country.

Taxation, either by the investing country or by the country where the investment is being made, can be and has been a real obstacle to foreign investment. Naturally a country with lower taxes offers an inducement, where other factors are equal; but the more serious question is raised when foreign capital is subjected to the taxation of both the country of the investor and the country where invested. Generally double taxation is the base of the difficulty. Taxes are generally heavy throughout the world, but this in itself is not necessarily a deterrent; since one would look in vain for more than a few places for investment opportunities where taxes are not heavy. The problem of double taxation has now been recognized, and international efforts are steadily in process to eliminate unfairnesses and discriminations wherein double taxation arises.

INTERNATIONAL AGREEMENTS

It must appear the part of wisdom to create international agreements for the purpose of eliminating these numerous obstacles to foreign investment, which tend to restrict foreign trade and thus retard prosperity throughout the world.

At Bogotá an economic agreement was negotiated and signed on May 2, 1948, which included provisions with respect to private investments. The general statements relating to the rights and duties of government investors seem sound, but it must be noted that they were not passed with any degree of unanimity. Specific statements in most cases proved unacceptable. Although it was stated that "an expropriation shall be accompanied by payment of a fair price in a prompt, adequate and effective manner," the same article provided that no such action shall be "under conditions different from those that the constitution or laws of each country provide for the expropriation of national property." Discussions at the conference made it all too clear that many of the signers carried with them their mental reservations as to the particular meanings to be placed upon this and other passages. It appeared that many of the signers did not feel that their constitution and laws required that payment to foreigners for their expropriated capital should be made in the currency of the investing country or at the current exchange rates at the time of expropriation.

In the absence of multilateral agreement, it appears that the only protection which American investors may have must be under bilateral agreements between the United States government and some country which desires to receive American capital.

CONCLUSION

A basic misconception of industry seems to have arisen throughout the world resulting in an idea that capital can be coerced and that it is necessary for government to pile regulation on regulation to make it perform its function. Historically and logically, this is not true. Capital will always perform its function better by inducement than by coercion. The willingness to take economic risks has always provided, and still provides, the principal argument in favor of the capitalistic system. The imposition of rigid controls or fear of seizure is not part of business and economic risks; and there is no way to insure against resulting losses. When such fear appears, private capital will fail to foster needed economic developments; and this in turn will force the governments to assume these risks.

Foreign countries need and want capital. They can expect it only on terms that give enterprises a reasonable opportunity to make profits and reasonable assurance that next year and for years to come the capital will be theirs to risk and gain therefrom.

DELIBERATE INDUSTRIALIZATION*

HENRY G. AUBREY

THE few existing studies of the course of economic development are restricted by the lack of early statistical material. The very beginnings of industry, the process of transformation to mechanical, power-driven equipment, are shrouded by the tacit assumption that all countries followed the pattern set by England during the industrial revolution: autonomous growth along free enterprise principles. The end of the mercantilist era is presumed to have eliminated the retarding influences of state interference and to have provided free play for the nineteenth-century proc-

* Adapted and reprinted by permission from *Social Research*, Vol. 16, No. 2, June 1949, pp. 158–182.

ess of expansion by rapid capital accumulation.

Close scrutiny of actual events, however, indicates that there was not that complete absence of state intervention, at least in the early transitional stage. It will be shown in this paper that the first steps toward industrialization were assisted and, indeed, often initiated by government at various times between 1775 and 1850 in the industrial countries of western Europe, in the United States, and in Mexico.

Limitation of space precludes a detailed survey of the initial industrial development of all these nations. Only Mexico, therefore, will be presented as a case study, with particular stress on the relative importance of private initiative and government assistance. A cursory comparison with similar phases in other countries will then be made.

I

For a number of reasons the first decades after Mexico's declaration of independence have been selected for presentation as a case in point. The details of Mexico's early industrial development are not widely known and do not seem to have been presented fully in either English or Spanish literature. Official and private opinion holds that Mexico's industrialization dates back not longer than about sixty years. Yet, here is a nation that made a determined effort to match the industrial progress of other countries as soon as it achieved release from its backward colonial status in 1821.

During the colonial regime and the first third of the nineteenth century the textile industry in Mexico consisted of manufacturing workshops (*obraje, trapiche*) and a widely scattered cottage industry. Only hand-spinning and hand-weaving equipment were used. In 1829, three residents of Mexico proposed to the government to set up several thousand hand looms all over the country in return for a seven-year monopoly on the import of equipment and yarn; they offered further to pay a high tax for the privilege. The proposal led to violent discussions in the provincial legislatures, but it was finally decided that the potential detriment to the domestic cotton growing and spinning industry outweighed the fiscal inducements. Also, the legislatures realized that this arrangement would not create a modern integrated industry based on the best spinning and weaving equipment, and feared that the proposed scheme might even delay the eventual establishment of such industry.

Despite the fact that cheap foreign textiles made heavy inroads on native industry, even with the high cost of transportation inland, less than a year after the offer had been made, the embargo on the import of cotton goods was suspended as part of a plan to create a modern industry. One-fifth of the customs revenue from such imports was to be set aside in a fund controlled by a government agency, the Banco de avío, the first Latin-American governmental development agency of a type that was to reappear a hundred years later in various guises. The money was to be used to buy abroad the best machinery available and to pay the transportation charges. The machinery was then to be passed on to prospective manufacturers as a loan, at cost, and additional cash loans were to be granted from the fund to these entrepreneurs for constructing and operating plants. All loans were to be repaid on convenient terms and at an annual interest rate set at only 5 percent.

Ample opportunities for speculation in government loans had driven up the rate of interest to a level at which capital could not be borrowed for productive purposes. The cheap money provided through the Banco de avío was therefore of great importance for the promotion of industry. The capital of the fund was set at one million pesos and it was designed to "revolve" for the benefit of later applicants for loans. When the capital of one million pesos had been accumulated, the embargo of imported textile goods was to be reimposed.

The government offered every encouragement to local private corporations to start new industries. As a result, by 1832 there were nine companies in existence for spinning and weaving cotton, wool, and silk, and one for making paper, though no plants were yet in operation.

A number of other extremely practical measures were taken by the government to stimulate progress in various fields. Wool-bearing animals were brought into the country to improve the native strains.

Silkworm eggs were distributed free of charge, with handbooks on their culture, and the growth of mulberry trees was promoted. Two cotton gins were ordered for the benefit of the industry. Swarms of bees were given away to aid the wax industry, and the latest models of ploughs were acquired for farmers. The mining school was put in charge of exploiting a recently discovered iron mine. Experts were sent to England to study the possibilities of making window glass and hollow glassware, and the problem of making paper from domestic fibers instead of scarce rags was tackled. It was also arranged that European workers would accompany the imported machines in order to train the Mexicans in their use.

Unfortunately these auspicious beginnings of industrial development coincided with one of Mexico's frequent political upheavals. Part of the customs receipts earmarked for the Banco de avío were seized by a revolutionary leader; more were diverted by the government for the civil war. The fund was unable to pay for some of the machines still abroad or for the transportation of others. With the disruption of communications as a result of the Mexican conflict, a number of the machines were left to rust in the port of arrival. Thus the fund never built up to more than two-thirds of the projected million pesos, and much of its investment was eventually wasted on incomplete projects. Finally, the failure was acknowledged officially and the Banco de avío was dissolved in 1842, after a period of several years during which it had been completely inactive.

The undisputed fact of the Banco de avío's bankruptcy led to the conclusion that the experiment as a whole had been a failure and the results negative; it was judged to be just another example of government interference and of a "protectionist policy of isolation." But no attempt has been made to explain the fact that while

no mechanical equipment existed in Mexico before the promotion by the Banco de avío, there were in 1843, less than ten years later, 59 spinning and weaving mills with a total of 125,362 spindles in operation or in process of being installed. Unless this can be accepted as mere coincidence, it is only fair to assume that this industry was built on the very ruins of the Banco de avío and, in fact, partly with its equipment. The first modern cotton mill with mechanical equipment, which started to operate in Puebla in 1835 with a loan of 62,000 pesos, used machines which the Banco de avío had bought in the United States. The equipment for two more small mills was taken over by two individuals in Mexico City, who underwrote all other expenses. The woolen industry was improved by the Merino sheep which the fund had imported, and the first paper factory made use of some of the machines brought into Mexico by the Banco.

Obviously, the government through its agencies had acted as a powerful catalyst, though its limited success in financing the actual operations was achieved only with great waste. Even after the demise of the Banco de avío, the government continued its promotion. In 1842 it established a General Directorate of Industry, and in the following year set up *Juntas de industria* in the provincial capitals. These agencies encouraged and instructed local industry, advised the government on legislative and other action, and collected data which are a rich source of information on this early period of Mexican industrial development.

II

The Mexican *cotton industry*, which had sprung up during the period of direct and indirect government assistance, continued to grow slowly despite the series of wars and periods of civil unrest. A total of 154,-822 spindles was reported by 61 mills in

1866. The number of mechanical looms grew somewhat more slowly, but we have a figure of 4,525 in 1850, a year in which not all the mills reported. In the same year, with only 23 mills reporting on their labor force, the number of cotton mill workers was given as 11,243, but the actual total was probably much higher.

It was fortunate for Mexico's early industrial effort that water power was plentiful, for the steam engine, which had been a major stimulus in promoting the industrialization of Europe, was absent in Mexico. The only available fuel, and that in decreasing quantity, was wood and charcoal; the coal deposits of the north were still mostly unknown at that time and, in any case, were too far removed from the centers of industry to be usable. Thus, if there was no water at hand, it was brought to the factory sites by aqueducts and used to drive a wheel with directly coupled shaft. A few factories continued to use mules or horses for power, but to a decreasing extent. In 1843 two mills reported the use of steam, but in 1850, 32 out of 39 were still operating on water power alone.

One of the retarding elements in the growth of the cotton industry was the periodic shortage of raw cotton. Crop failures occurred frequently and all too often civil unrest hampered the cultivation. The supply of domestic cotton lagged far behind the growth of the industry and the mills were forced either to shorten the working day or remain closed for a part of the year. The embargo on foreign cotton was therefore lifted temporarily in 1843 and again in 1844; in 1838, it was even necessary to permit the import of yarn for a brief period. A battle of words raged almost continuously in local and federal commissions, congress, trade organizations, and newspapers, on the admission or prohibition of foreign raw cotton.

The increases in the price of raw materials, which followed poor crops and the need to import, did not, however, keep the price of cotton piece goods from dropping considerably. Around 1820 the price of manta, the coarse calico which formed the staple clothing of the people, was 3 reales (8 reales = 1 peso) for one vara (a 33-inch length) 22 inches in width. Mechanical looms wove this same material in 34 to 35-inch widths, and the price in 1843, eight years after the first mechanical cotton mill had started operations, was only 2 reales per vara. Taking into account the variation in width, this means a price reduction of nearly 60 percent. An official report of 1851 states that the cost of clothing had been reduced by 70 percent in the past twenty years.

It is important to note that this price drop was not caused by any deflation. Mexico had a silver currency, the value of which did not fluctuate to any appreciable extent between 1820 and 1850. During the last twenty-five years of the colonial regime, payments to Spain had averaged from 9 to 10 million pesos yearly. These, of course, were eliminated with Mexico's independence. An export tax of 2 to 7 percent and a transportation tax of 2 to 4 percent checked the outflow of silver and gold for noncommercial transactions. The influx of foreign loans exceeded the service of existing foreign debt, and the mining and export of silver and gold balanced the import of goods.

Thus, if the price of cotton piece goods dropped so substantially, it is safe to assume that the cause lay in reduced production costs and increased supply. It should be remembered that the pressure of competition from foreign goods was minimized by the government's policy of protection and therefore played no significant role in lowering prices. After 1838, the importation of ordinary cotton goods was again prohibited and every piece of goods sold had to bear the internal revenue stamp. It could be said, of course, that under conditions of free trade prices would have been still lower, but this alternative was never seriously considered at that time, for fear of bringing ruin to native cotton growers and manufacturers. Thus comparison between the prices under preindustrial conditions and those of machine-made goods, at the same level of exclusion of foreign goods, reflects to some degree the technological progress.

Only the most modern equipment had been bought by the Banco de avío. The size of plant considered most suitable at the time the industry started was from 2,000 to 4,000 spindles each. It is interesting to note that mills with fewer than 4,000 spindles were also preferred by private entrepreneurs during the next few decades, as may be seen from the following figures.

perts who accompanied the machinery also taught the flock owners how to improve their breeds of sheep and how to shear and grade according to the best French methods. By 1843, three new mills were under construction or already in operation. Another, added in 1844, was to become the largest woolen mill in the country. At that time, two mills were built to make wool felt rather than the usual woven goods, one of them using a steam engine with peat from a nearby bog as fuel. We have no exact figures on equipment and output, but we do know that the woolen industry grew so much more rapidly than the supply of raw material that the price of wool increased sharply, a phenomenon similar to developments in the early days of the industry in the United States.

The *silk industry* actually dates back to

	1843		1866	
Size of plant	No. of plants	% of total	No. of plants	% of total
Under 1,000 spindles	11	23.4%	12	19.7%
1,000–1,999 "	14	29.8	21	34.4
2,000–3,999 "	14	29.8	20	32.6
4,000–5,999 "	3	6.4	2	3.3
6,000–7,999 "	1	2.1	2	3.3
8,000–9,999 "	3	6.4	3	5.0
10,000–12,000 "	1	2.1	1	1.7

Clearly, the industry did not grow by building larger mills, but by adding more small mills. There is some justification for the conclusion that the smaller mills were best suited to local conditions—that is, the supply of power, labor, raw material, and accessible markets. And this early Mexican experience would seem to confirm recent opinion to the effect that small and decentralized industry may be most suitable for underdeveloped countries.

The *woolen industry* was retarded by the loss of certain machinery en route from France, but in 1840 more machinery and technicians were brought to Mexico with the assistance of the government. The ex-

the early colonial days. In the late Spanish period, however, silk cultivation was prohibited in order to protect the import trade. The republican government took great pains to revive the industry, even after the demise of the Banco de avío, by encouraging the growth of mulberry trees. One of the government-aided special promotion companies owned 3 million trees in 1845. The Jacquard loom and a similar invention by a Spaniard were introduced in 1848 and the industry flourished. About 4,000 workers were employed in throwing, dyeing, and reeling silk, of which about 100,000 pounds could be made annually. The one great threat to the industry was the contraband, which could be easily brought in because of the small volume and which had a high value.

Next to cotton goods manufacture, *paper making* was the oldest industry in Mexico. The first paper mill to be established after the liberation was started in 1822, but took five years to be completed. The Banco de avío ordered two paper mills and became much interested in the feasibility of making paper from wheat straw. This hope did not materialize—the problem has not been solved even today—and the short supply of rags remained a serious obstacle. Most mills added some domestic maguey and istle fibers as stretchers, apparently without harm to the quality, if the good condition of old documents of that day is any indication. Cotton waste was also used to good effect, as were hemp and linen. Actually, paper making was recognized as a good means of using the waste from textile mills, and the owners of some textile plants built paper mills for that purpose.

By 1845, the six factories in existence were producing more than 150,000 reams a year, which was more than the existing print shops could use, even though two years earlier the government had decreed that only Mexican-made paper could be used in public offices. The price of paper dropped substantially and several factories turned to making writing paper and other good grades. During the wars with the United States and France the paper industry seems to have declined again, and in 1866 only four factories reported a total of fifteen machines.

The governments of the new republic realized that a modern *iron industry* was required for the successful development of other industries. For some time, however, the lack or disadvantageous location of proper materials could not be overcome. The right type of refractory clay for lining blast furnaces could not be found at all. Coal was not available; nor could charcoal

be economically transported over long distances. Not until 1846 was the first modern foundry built—a private enterprise with a blast furnace capable of producing 11,000 pounds daily. Equipped with hot air bellows driven by steam, the furnace produced iron described as being of fine grade and similar to steel. The same plant included the first rolling mill in Mexico, completed in 1853 and driven by water power, and also a machine shop in which all foreign machines could be repaired. Two more blast furnaces and another rolling mill and machine shop were ready by 1860. The total estimated pig iron production of all foundries in 1868 was about 10 million pounds, and most of it was locally consumed because of the high cost of transportation.

The absence of an adequate *transportation system* was, without any doubt, a major deterrent to the development of an integrated nationwide economic and industrial system. But in order to understand why large-scale construction of railways was delayed until the last quarter of the nineteenth century, it is necessary to examine the pattern of entrepreneurial initiative over the preceding period.

The Banco de avío was initiated and administered by Lucas Alamán, who later was also Director General of Industries. Politically a conservative, he belonged to the centralist group which stood for strong government, as opposed to the liberals who favored a federalistic system of greater autonomy for the states. The conservatives were the heirs of the Spanish colonial principle of centralized government, initiative by the administration, and paternalism. This tradition was responsible for the public spirit and economic leadership displayed by Alamán and some of his colleagues, as well as for certain negative factors such as self-interest, corruption, and graft. Any overthrow of the conservative regime resulted, quite naturally, in a reversal of policy, as did the many brief interludes of clique rule and the civil and foreign wars which drained the treasury.

Thus the actual period of government promotion and assistance was crowded into the years 1830–35 and 1843–46. Alamán returned to power in 1851 but died shortly thereafter. Following another interval of unrest, Juarez' liberals led the country through a period of political and social reform which culminated in the Constitution of 1857 and the legislation against the power of the church. Direct support of economic development, however, was not a part of the liberal program.

The need for railroads was realized early enough, but the necessary political stability, technical know-how, capital, and fuel were lacking. In 1851 and 1852, the government entered into negotiations with French and Belgian groups, which included vast schemes for railroad building. But little came of these projects. In 1853 one line three miles in length was built from Mexico City to a suburb; in 1854 a line was run from Veracruz to a place twelve miles distant. Between 1853 and 1857, twelve concessions were granted, but most of them lapsed before construction could start. By 1860, only 170 miles of road were in operation. Following the war with France, the government realized that railroad construction had to be subsidized and thus, in 1867, 7 million pesos were earmarked for that purpose. In 1873 the line from Mexico City to Veracruz, 308 miles long, was inaugurated, and that date marked the real beginning of the rapid expansion of the Mexican railway system.

III

The promotion of industrial development by the Mexican government was short-lived and limited, but it stemmed from a philosophy not very far removed from modern economic concepts. Alamán saw clearly the close connection between agriculture and industry in a backward country. His program at all stages included the promotion of agriculture by distribution of seeds and educational pamphlets, importation of improved implements, long-range tax exemptions for new crops, and other such measures. Alamán and his group fully realized the need for stimulating the demand for agricultural products by achieving purchasing power for the population through new industries, even if it meant "forced" [sic] industrialization.

The program was based on the idea of increasing the "wealth" of the country by the "development of its resources." In modern terms this meant industrialization for the purpose of increasing the national income. Unlimited free trade, which had its proponents in Mexico as well as elsewhere, was not seen as a means of achieving this end, nor was the mere exclusion of foreign goods. "Customs protection can remove competition which is harmful to an industry but it cannot start it, provide the capital and the necessary training. It is necessary to create the capital and to guide the industry."

The capital which the government loaned to industry was designed to spread its benefits over the entire economy, a kind of "pump-priming" concept, based on welfare principles. The relatively small total of only 600,000 pesos which was made available to the Banco therefore had beneficial effects beyond its immediate investment value. A great part of it was spent abroad for machinery, but this expenditure brought about a great deal of additional private investment in buildings, aqueducts, installations, and the like—the typical domestic counterparts of equipment imports. While the government provided some of the venture capital, it performed an even more important function: in addition to providing the know-how and the foreign contacts, it freed the entrepreneur of the risk of importing the machines, a lengthy and major undertaking at that time. In this manner, projects quite beyond the scope of the individual industrialist were stripped of their most unmanageable financial risks and placed within his reach.

The Mexican government's initiative also broke through the inertia of the traditional Spanish system of social values, which did not favor industrial investment. Speculation offered better short-range opportunities than production; ostentatious living and the purchase of land brought more social prestige. Industrial venture capital could not be borrowed at reasonable rates. But the Banco's funds, added to the private means of the investment-minded minority, provided the initial stimulus for new enterprises which might otherwise not have been possible, and set an example for others.

This "priming" effect was overlooked by the critics who observed only the Banco's bankruptcy and decided that its funds had been wasted. Nobody will deny that there was waste, but welfare economics would conclude only that the social cost of the experiment was higher than it would have been otherwise. Such failures are quite common wherever the creation of external economies is involved in the early stages of industrialization.

IV

In appraising the extent of state intervention, in general, it will be noted that Mexico lagged several decades behind other nations in applying the innovations of the industrial revolution. The government therefore felt the need of supplementing entrepreneurial initiative in several ways: planning the development, procuring the equipment, encouraging the formation of companies to operate it, and financing a great part of the initial outlay. In other countries it was not, as a rule, necessary to take over all these functions. The amount

of state assistance depended upon the degree of acceleration the government favored for industrial development and on the extent to which private initiative was willing and able to expand unaided.

An extreme example may be found in Japan at the close of the feudal era around 1868. The complete absence of technical knowledge, capital, and modern initiative of the western capitalistic type kept Japan's industrial infancy entirely under state management. From 1870 to 1883 the state owned and operated factories, mines, railroads, shipyards, and textile, paper, and glass plants. Here, even more than in Mexico, the government provided the initiative and the capital; it imported the machines and even operated the plants until private entrepreneurs were in a position to take over the job.

The sudden transition from a feudal economy may explain the high degree of state intervention in both countries. It is surprising to find, however, that the industrial nations of western Europe, which from the outset had easy access to the liberal teachings of the time, also followed a pattern of selective sponsorship by government.

Western European manufacturers were aware of the inventions in the cotton industry that had enabled England to push ahead of her competitors, but did not make use of their knowledge until the pressure of England's low prices compelled them to adopt modern equipment. It is true that an exceptional amount of initiative on their part was required, because England had prohibited, under penalty of confiscation, imprisonment, and even death, the export of machines and emigration of workers. Naturally the outward flow could not be completely checked, but the risk and the required capital outlay involved in getting men and machines out of the country were very great.

Against such great odds private enterprise achieved considerable progress. As was to be expected, however, all innovations were closely guarded by the successful entrepreneurs who wanted to defend their hard-won position. Here government intervened with grants, subsidies, prizes, loans, and other inducements, to spread information and the material means of progress. On occasion, when private development lagged, the government would create a nucleus for new industries by setting up the foreign experts in the business of building machines. Such activities on the part of the state are something more than the ultimate offshoot of mercantilism. Certainly, the tradition of governmental responsibility and protection conditioned the thinking of the crowned heads of the period. But, at the same time, governments eliminated the rigid regulations and controls which had been an essential part of the mercantilistic era.

Governmental intervention in the late eighteenth and early nineteenth centuries should therefore be interpreted in the light of the economic framework existing at the time. The French silk industry, for example, was repeatedly aided by the government during its early history, though only a few instances can be given here. In order to compete with the superior Italian silk industry, Colbert had extended inducements to Italian workers to settle in France. But during the reign of Louis XV the development of a reliable spinning machine became the most pressing problem, and toward its solution many prizes and premiums were offered by the government. The first success, on a large scale, was achieved by the Jubié brothers with the help of a government loan of 100,000 livres and subsidies per pound of cocoons and yarn output. In 1750, within four years after authorization of the subsidies, there were 300 vats in operation, processing 268,000 pounds of cocoons and pro-

ducing 18,600 pounds of *organsin,* a type of yarn which had not previously been made in France with any success. The process was improved by the machinery developed by Vaucanson, who also had a government loan of 100,000 livres. His machine spread, but the weaving of silk remained on a primitive level until Napoleon gave assistance to Jacquard who developed the weaving equipment which bears his name. Jacquard received a yearly pension of 3,000 francs and a subsidy of 50 francs for each loom that was equipped with his device. By 1809, 724 looms were so equipped.

The mechanization of the French cotton industry by installation of spinning frames of the Arkwright type required and received help from the government. Since the machines could not be imported from England, a new industry to build the machines had to be created in France. In 1785, the government made an agreement with the Englishman Jacques Milne according to which he received a building, an initial grant of 60,000 livres, a yearly pension of 6,000 livres, and a subsidy of 1,200 livres for each set of machines he completed. Deliveries started in 1787, and by 1793 sixty-two sets had been sold, each consisting of three machines. A decade later, the introduction of the mule-jenny was effected by the industrialist Bauwens in Gand, Belgium (then under French domination) with a minimum of state assistance, though he subsequently received government loans of 100,000 and 300,000 francs for expansion. These machines were also spread to other sections of France by Richard, the greatest industrialist of his time, who, in 1811, employed as many as 12,000 workers. He too received loans from Napoleon to the amount of 1.5 million francs. By and large, after Milne's day, the French cotton industry required comparatively little aid beyond occasional loans and a large number of small subsidies, prizes, and other such measures of encouragement.

The introduction of machinery into the French woolen industry was delayed by considerable mechanical difficulties. Napoleon's minister, Chaptal, helped the Englishman William Douglas to build and sell wool-carding and spinning machines, giving him a grant of 20,000 francs, a loan of the same amount, free use of a building, and a yearly travel allowance of 5,000 francs to enable him to install the machine throughout the country. Douglas also won two prizes of 60,000 francs each for building the best machines, and 340 of his machines were sold within two years. The French government, however, wanted even speedier distribution. In 1809, it bought Douglas' patent for 100,000 francs so that everyone could build the machine. The government then purchased eight sets of machines for loan to manufacturers, to be paid for in four years; to those who did not want a loan, grants of 4,000 francs per set were offered. In 1810, Douglas listed 949 machines as having been set up in 100 factories within ten years. His machines, however, were soon outclassed by the improved models of the Englishman William Cockerill in Belgium, who prospered without state aid.

Generally speaking, the French government's assistance to the textile industry consisted not only in the great number of small and large direct assistance measures, but in creating conditions under which private initiative could expand. This applies also to the other territories which France then occupied, such as the Rhineland and Belgium, and to which the freedom of industry was automatically extended.

As stated above, the development of the textile industry in Belgium owed much to the initiative of the industrialist Bauwens. He, too, benefited from Napoleon's encouragement by obtaining the greatest part

of a 200,000-franc prize for the first imported cotton spinning machinery. A grant of 60,000 francs was made to the Rousseau family to reopen a damaged factory. A fund of 100,000 francs was also kept available for premiums which were repeatedly granted to Belgian factories.

The Belgian textile industry suffered a severe setback in the loss of the French market after Belgium came under Dutch rule in 1814. A law of 1821 therefore provided that 1.3 million florins from customs receipts be used for the purpose of assisting new and unprosperous industries. The king also granted many subsidies and loans to textile establishments that wanted to expand.

In 1822, the General Society for the Promotion of the National Industry received from the Dutch king real estate worth 20 million florins, for which it planned to sell shares to the public. Although the king guaranteed a yield of 5 percent on the corporate capital, the sale of shares to the public lagged so much that he had to subscribe for 25,800 of the 31,-200 shares. The Society, however, did so well with the real estate that by 1831 it was worth 38 million florins. The Society's investment in mining and metallurgical enterprises rose from 3.7 million florins in 1835 to 38.6 million in 1840, and the capital of companies then under its sponsorship amounted to 65.5 million florins.

The Swiss government stepped into assist the establishment of a domestic cotton spinning industry when it was rumored that England would stop the export of the fine yarn that Switzerland needed. In 1799, the federal government agreed to buy four mules of 204 spindles each and to set them up as models. It also advanced 10,000 livres and granted free space in a former convent for a factory. The canton of St. Gallen promoted the subscription to 26 more mules by commercial houses. When they combined into a joint private company, the government withdrew from the venture but continued for seven years the free use of the factory building and granted a monopoly of manufacture to the company.

The Swiss case is an interesting example of temporary assistance in a country which had a highly developed capitalistic organization. Only during the short period of "gestation" did the government provide a nucleus around which private enterprise could form. Once this was accomplished, the state could step aside.

The United States also has a long history of promotion of and assistance to industry by government at various levels. The concept, which is frequently associated with the names of Hamilton and Gallatin, is really as old as the history of shortages. When the conflict with England took definite shape, the colonies' decision to be self-sustaining and to encourage manufacturing became a matter of national policy. It was laid down at the convention in Virginia in 1774 by Washington, Jefferson, and other speakers, and was reaffirmed by the Continental Congress in Philadelphia. It soon became clear that England's technical supremacy would have to be matched by domestic ingenuity. A vast amount of promotional activity was directed at encouraging the construction of basic machinery, the lack of which retarded the greatly desired rapid evolution. As early as 1775 the Assembly of Connecticut granted a loan for the completion of textile machines, and the first American spinning jenny and stock cards were made there. In 1776, the Pennsylvania Assembly resolved to distribute one spinning machine free to each county. Other state legislation followed. One of the oddest arrangements was the purchase by the Assembly of South Carolina in 1801 of the patent right to the Whitney saw gin for the sum of $50,000, a deal that ended in considerable litigation. (This machine eliminated the bottle-

neck of hand-ginning in the rapidly expanding cotton industry.)

The roster of direct government assistance included not only grants-in-aid to construct certain machinery, to perfect manufacturing processes, or to produce certain goods, but also rewards and other money grants. Many states granted, at one time or another, bounties for increasing the supply of raw materials, such as raw silk, hemp, flax, and Merino sheep for breeding. Premiums were offered by the state legislatures for the first completed plants to make many items ranging from pins to steel and machinery, and including textiles, paper, and even salt. Some assemblies also voted to subscribe to shares in private societies for the encouragement of manufactures. Federal attention to the problem culminated in the famous report which Hamilton made at the request of Congress and in the Gallatin report of 1810. The former also laid the framework for a protectionist tariff policy and tax and duty exemptions for new industries.

The American procedure is an example of a pragmatic and selective policy of state aid to industry. It was not, at any time, designed to supplant the abundant private initiative but to stimulate and supplement it. Numerous small inducements, at strategic points, were sufficient to achieve the accelerated development which the situation so urgently demanded.

Only a detailed monographic study could show the actual effect which each of the minute doses of assistance had in terms of output. We are interested here only in government assistance to the "germination" of infant industries. In each of the examples given, the state withdrew after completion of its "priming" function, irrespective of the extent to which it had intervened.

V

This survey was designed to collect for comparison some widely scattered historical facts. Their evaluation cannot be fully undertaken within the available space. Nor can the thorny problem of free enterprise versus state interference be argued here. It may be sufficient to conclude at this point that some measure of state assistance fostered infant industry in most advanced nations with the exception of England. It is quite true that wars, blocked trade channels, national expansion, personal ambition, pressure of competition, or a combination of any of these motives, were also responsible for a policy of industrialization. It may well be that some industries would have developed sooner or later independently of government intervention. It is not the intention of this paper to decide whether deliberate industrialization is desirable; its aim is only to show that the state did help whenever the forced growth of industry was considered necessary or desirable for any of a number of reasons.

SOME PROBLEMS OF ECONOMIC DEVELOPMENT*

AUGUST MAFFRY

IN THE *International Development Act of 1950* the United States has declared the economic development of underdeveloped areas to be an objective of national policy and has provided both money and men to pursue it. The post-war foreign aid programs of the United States have had important developmental aspects. The Point Four program calls for both technical and capital assistance to underdeveloped countries. Technical assistance is being provided on a small scale under the *International Development Act* and capital assistance through established national and international lending institutions. The Marshall Plan has embraced development projects both in metropolitan areas of European beneficiaries and in their overseas dependencies. Furthermore, the Economic Cooperation Administration, as adminis-

* Adapted and reprinted by permission from *The American Journal of Economics and Sociology*, Vol. XI, No. 3, April, 1952, pp. 327–341.

tering agency for the Marshall Plan, has turned its resources increasingly to development problems in non-European areas, particularly in south and southeast Asia. The *Foreign Aid Act of 1951*, approved by Congress, provides the means for assisting underdeveloped countries throughout the non-Soviet world in developing their resources. The United States Government maintains its own lending institution, the Export-Import Bank, practically the sole purpose of which at present is to assist in financing the economic development of friendly foreign countries.

The United Nations also devotes much attention to the problems of economic development, especially in the forum of the Economic and Social Council. The International Bank for Reconstruction and Development, a specialized agency of the United Nations, has completed the reconstruction phase of its lending operations and now applies itself exclusively to the financing of economic development in member countries. The United Nations has its own program of technical assistance to underdeveloped countries.

The Colombo Plan, named after the capital city of Ceylon in which it was drafted, is an example of a regional development program. It began as a cooperative effort of British Commonwealth countries, with its benefits directed to the underdeveloped areas of south and southeast Asia.

All of these plans, programs, and policies represent a deliberate effort on the part of countries outside the Soviet sphere of influence to systematize and speed up the process of economic development in economically backward areas. It has developed into a broadscale joint effort to bring quickly to underdeveloped areas the material benefits of the industrial revolution which occurred in Western Europe and the United States during the last three centuries.

Now the problems of economic development are legion. They run the whole gamut of national and international economic problems and involve besides the political, social, and religious institutions of underdeveloped countries. It is proposed here to discuss only a few of these problems.

I

THE PROBLEM OF INFLATION

A high rate of investment in an underdeveloped country is almost inevitably attended by currency inflation. The basic reasons for this are the typically low volume of savings, the diversion of savings to purposes other than the creation of new productive facilities, and the consequent inability of private enterprises or governments to sell their securities to the public. Under economic and political pressures to carry out development programs, resort is had to credit creation and the printing press. In other words, since available voluntary savings are inadequate to sustain the desired rate of economic development, involuntary savings must be imposed by means of currency inflation. The alternative may be a lower rate of investment than is politically acceptable or economically desirable.

The monetary authorities of underdeveloped countries must therefore reconcile themselves to some degree of currency inflation if they wish to foster a high rate of investment and corresponding pace of development. Considered realistically, their problem is not to prevent such inflation altogether but to keep it within tolerable bounds—a problem which is complicated by a chronic tendency toward unbalanced budgets characteristic of such countries. They must have a particular care for the damaging effect of inflation on savings and investing habits where, as is usually the case, these are neither well established nor widespread. The problem is rendered more difficult by the sharp effect of a rise in money incomes on imports.

Domestic production in underdeveloped countries is generally inelastic. A rise in incomes therefore has an immediate and strong impact on the demand for imports and causes a drain on foreign exchange resources. Then arises the hard choice between exchange control or depreciation or both, on the one hand, and damping the rate of investment on the other. There is no lack of historic instances of this dilemma.

One solution, or apparent solution, for a country finding itself in this situation is to borrow abroad in order to finance the local-currency expenditures entailed by its development programs. If this can be arranged, the increased import demands generated by currency inflation can be financed without drawing down monetary reserves. There has been much recent controversy over the wisdom and limitations of this expedient, with particular reference to the policies and practices of the Export-Import Bank and the International Bank for Reconstruction and Development.

The Export-Import Bank says in its post-war Policy Statement that "as a general rule, the Bank extends credit only to finance purchases of materials and equipment produced or manufactured in the United States and of technical services of American firms and individuals, as distinguished from outlays for goods, labor, and services in the borrowing country * * *." The situation during the recent war was entirely different. At that time, when the Bank's operations were confined almost entirely to Latin American countries and when these countries needed dollars to finance imports required to stabilize their economies, the Bank permitted the extensive use of its loans to finance local-currency costs of development projects.

The post-war policy against such financing has rarely been breached, even though its observance has made it difficult on occasion for the Bank to facilitate projects involving a very high proportion of local costs. There are several reasons, all cogent from the point of view of the Bank, for maintaining the policy. One is the very desirable objective of putting on the prospective foreign borrower the burden of proof that local-currency expenditures cannot be locally financed. Another is the also desirable objective of conserving the borrowing capacity of a country for loans to finance external expenditures. A third is the statutory purpose of the Bank, which is to finance and facilitate the foreign trade of the United States. (This the Bank wisely prefers to do directly rather than indirectly, although it would be elementary to demonstrate that the financing of local currency expenditures serves to finance U.S. exports at one step removed. However elementary the demonstration, it would not be likely to impress the Congress, to which the Bank must look for the periodic extension and increase of its lending authority.) A fourth reason for the policy is the difficulty in connection with local-currency expenditures of securing satisfactory control and accounting for purposes of the Bank's records.

Local currency loans by the International Bank are governed by the express provisions of its Articles, as follows: "The Bank may, in exceptional circumstances when local currency required for the purpose of the loan cannot be raised by the borrower on reasonable terms, provide the borrower as part of the loan with an appropriate amount of that currency." This provision had its origin in considerations similar to those which have dictated the related policy of the Export-Import Bank. The International Bank has so far not been able to find the exceptional circumstances which would justify loans of local currency to finance economic development.

The monetary authorities of countries undergoing rapid development and, therefore, in all probability currency inflation may find some solace in the chronic inflationary tendencies in industrialized countries. These latter tendencies serve to negate many of the consequences of currency inflation in underdeveloped countries. They tend to keep the terms of trade favorable to raw-material producing countries, of which most underdeveloped countries are examples. They tend to delay or make unnecessary periodic devaluations of the currencies of underdeveloped countries, a circumstance of far-reaching importance. They progressively reduce in real terms the burden of debt incurred by underdeveloped countries towards developed countries. Furthermore, judging by the historical and current record, the authorities of developing countries may determine their monetary policies with fair assurance that inflation in developed countries will continue. As indicated, this is a considerable boon to underdeveloped countries, however deplorable the situation may be for industrially advanced countries.

II

THE PROBLEM OF LOCAL CAPITAL

Where there are great inequalities of incomes, as there are in underdeveloped countries, one would expect a high rate of savings. This is frequently the case, but total savings are nevertheless small because of the low aggregate income of persons in a position to save. Furthermore, the mobilization of savings for investment in productive facilities is attended by very great obstacles. The savings of the high-income classes are typically held in considerable part abroad for reasons of safety and stability of value. Of the part held at home, a large proportion goes typically into real estate for the sake of security or capital gains and into trading and banking enterprises for the sake of a high current return. As to the remainder, investments in manufacturing enterprises in such relatively safe fields as textiles and cement are preferred because of prospective returns ranging from a "normal" 25 per cent to 100 per cent and more per annum. As a consequence, investor interest in low-yielding securities is naturally small or nil. Prospective borrowers must look to foreign sources of long-term capital or, in the case of governments, resort to various devices for forcing the acceptance of their obligations by banks, insurance companies, pension and unemployment funds, and the like.

Under these conditions, the rate of interest plays a somewhat perverse role. The productivity of capital invested in real estate, trade, or manufacturing is often so high, and capital gains equally so, that a little savings will go a long way and provide the means for a good deal of conspicuous consumption by the wealthy classes. On the other hand, high rates of return on invested capital are no inducement to savings by the great majority of populations who live at or near subsistence level. The high level of interest rates also makes it difficult or impossible to attract savings into such generally low-yielding investments as power generation and distribution or into government securities for investment in roads, railroads, drainage and irrigation works, and port improvements. These unattractive fields of investment are also fields in which the capital cost of projects is very great and the proportion of local costs usually very high. These characteristics also constitute enormous obstacles in the way of getting external financing.

Much time and effort has been expended on studies of ways and means of increasing the savings of underdeveloped countries and mobilizing them more effectively for investment in productive facilities. It is clear from these studies, as might have been expected *a priori*, that there is no magic route to these goals. The creation of an appropriate institutional framework for mobilizing voluntary savings is indispensable as are also modern revenue systems to produce involuntary savings for public works. The only fundamental solution is a higher and more evenly distributed level of incomes which will permit the savings habit to become well-established and widespread, lead to a reduction in the rate of interest, and eventually make possible a market for low-yielding securities both government and private.

III

PROBLEM OF GOVERNMENT VERSUS PRIVATE INVESTMENT

In the course of all the planning and implementation of plans for economic development, there has appeared in the United States an heroic contest between the private and government sectors of the country regarding their respective roles in the economic development of foreign countries. This contest has been sharpened by the virtual disappearance of an international capital market in the United States or elsewhere from which long-term funds can be obtained from private lenders by private or public borrowers for purposes of financing economic development.

In objective terms the facts are these:

(1) There is no dependable source of long-term capital for foreign borrowers in New York, in London, or in any present financial market. In countries other than the United States, this is a result largely of enforced official restrictions on the export of capital. In the United States, where the export of capital is free, it is the result partly of the widespread interruption of service on foreign investment during the Nineteen Thirties and particularly the result of the strong attraction of high-yielding domestic investment. American investment banks today show little or no interest in finding capital for placement abroad, and commercial banks avoid long-term foreign financing altogether.

(2) This deficiency in the international capital markets has been made good to some extent by the appearance of national and international lending institutions devoting themselves to the financing of economic development. The United States Government agency for this purpose is, of course, the Export-Import Bank, and the International Bank for Reconstruction and Development is the international institution concerned. The International Bank is restricted by its charter to making loans to its member governments or to others with the guaranty of such governments, while the Export-Import Bank as a matter of policy and practice has also confined its loans largely to governments, to government agencies, and to others under the protection of government guaranties. Both institutions operate therefore essentially on a government-to-government basis, with the qual-ification that the management of the International Bank has achieved a certain autonomy which enables it to escape to some extent from the government-to-government pattern.

(3) The volume of private investment abroad by United States investors, together with the volume of reinvestment of earnings from existing investments, has been relatively high since the end of the recent war. It has considerably exceeded in the aggregate the volume of loans by the Export-Import Bank and the International Bank combined. These private investents have been mainly equity investments and have been heavily concentrated in investments by the major oil companies in Venezuela and the Middle East.

(4) The United States Government has instituted a program of technical assistance to underdeveloped countries and now proposes by the terms of the *Foreign Aid Act of 1951* to provide capital funds on a grant basis and on a government-to-government basis to finance economic development.

(5) In the underdeveloped countries themselves there are strong tendencies for governments to take over larger and larger segments of their economies for development with government capital under government direction. These tendencies are the product in part of the seemingly inherent tendency of bureaucratic operations to spread and in part the result of official and popular impatience with the pace of economic development under private auspices. There is also the fact, mentioned earlier, that it is difficult or impossible to attract private capital, either local or foreign, into low-yielding investments in basic facilities such as transportation, water control, and electric power generation and distribution.

The proponents of private investment and private enterprise contend that the United States Government, by offering technical and capital assistance to the governments of underdeveloped countries, reinforce their tendency to expand the scope of government activity in their economies. They argue, with strong justification, that unless this trend is halted, the underdeveloped countries will be deprived of the dynamic influence of private enterprise, with a consequent retardation of their development, while private enterprise will be deprived of opportunities for profitable operations abroad. The proponents or apologists for government investment and government operations in underdeveloped countries may recognize the advantages of private investment but contend that the economic and political pressures of today leave governments no choice but to take upon themselves many of the pressing tasks of economic development.

There have been a number of ideas put forward for compromising the struggle between the advocates of private initiative, on the one hand, and of government activity, on the other, in carrying out economic development. For example, there have been numerous attempts, to some extent successful, to define and demarcate the respective spheres of government and private operations. There is not much dispute about the field of health and sanitation as a field of activity collateral to economic development. Private concerns have done notable work in the field and will undoubtedly continue to do so. The problem belongs, however, primarily to the sphere of government responsibilities. The same is true, generally speaking, of basic transportation and communications facilities and also of irrigation and drainage schemes. Education in agricultural methods is also usually assigned to the government sphere, as contrasted with agricultural production which properly belongs to private enterprise. The generation and distribution of electric power is a much more controversial item, since there are still a number of privately-owned companies in the field which are struggling to maintain their positions often in the face of prejudicial rate-fixing and competition from government-owned facilities. The ultimate contention of the proponents of private initiative in economic development is that the production of goods and services should be reserved for private enterprise if economic development is to be carried out expeditiously and efficiently. The production of goods and services is considered to include agriculture, mining, fishing, and the forest-products industry as well as manufacturing.

A number of underdeveloped countries have, in fact, officially adopted a demarcation of the fields of development along the lines indicated above and thus, while reserving certain fields for government undertakings, have given assurances that other designated fields are open and will remain open to private enterprise. This device has great merit from the point of view of giving confidence to potential private foreign investors. In essence, it amounts to fixing the rules of the game in advance.

A related device consists of government-sponsored development corporations or financing institutions designed to stimulate, foster, and often to undertake development projects and to obtain the necessary financing from internal or external sources but with a view to selling out their interests to private investors as circumstances permit. There is perhaps nothing inherently wrong in this approach to the government-versus-private issue. It has been used in a number of Latin American countries, in some instances with considerable success and in others with little or no success. The latter cases are generally cases in which political interference or outright venality have made good planning and efficient management impossible.

Another effort to regulate and maximize the role of private initiative in economic development has taken the form of commercial treaties between the United States and foreign countries carrying mutual assurances of fair treatment of private investments and defining the conditions under which outside capital can be invested and earnings and capital withdrawn. These treaties, designed to improve the "climate of investment" in foreign countries generally and in underdeveloped countries particularly, have so far produced small result. Treaties with comprehensive investment provisions have been entered into by the United States with Italy, Ireland, Uruguay, and Colombia. They have in all instances undoubtedly contributed something to improving the attitude of American investors toward investments in these countries. They play a role similar to that of the traditional treaties of friendship, commerce, and navigation in giving formal definition to mutual rights and privileges of the nationals of one country doing business in another country.

As a means of fostering private investment abroad, government guaranties of certain non-business risks of private foreign investment have been urged recently in the United States. A limited experiment has been made in connection with the Marshall Plan in the form of guaranties of the risks of inconvertibility and confiscation in connection with new dollar investments in participating European countries. Partly because of the fact that war risk is not covered and partly for other reasons, the amount of new investment guaranteed under this program has been quite small.

A more ambitious proposal to authorize the Export-Import Bank to issue similar guaranties for productive foreign investment in any area of the world failed of passage in the 81st Congress. The curious feature of the situation was that the business community, in whose interest the measure was ostensibly put forward, not only failed to support it but offered some active opposition to its passage. Many reasons have been advanced for this attitude on the part of business, including the argument that the proposed guaranties would have shifted the burden of giving fair treatment to private investors from foreign countries, where is properly belongs, to the Government of the United States, where it would represent a misuse of government powers and the public credit. The root of the business opposition, however, seems to have been the fear, based on the announced intention of the Export-Import Bank to restrict its guaranties to new investments, that existing investments in foreign countries would suffer from the competition of guaranteed and, in that sense, subsidized new investments. Thus, a proposal which, on the face of it, combined the elements of private initiative and government underwriting of certain non-business risks of private foreign investment fell to the ground and shows little or no present sign of being revived.

Finally, there is the device of preferential tax treatment as a means of stimulating private investment in foreign countries. Again, a limited experiment has been made during the war and post-war years in the United States by giving preferential tax treatment to so-called Western Hemisphere Trade Corporations deriving practically all of their income from operations in the Western Hemisphere. Current proposals for tax incentives to new foreign investment range from those which would extend the Western Hemisphere Trade Corporation concept to other foreign areas to those which would give complete freedom from United States tax to corporate income from investments abroad and preferential treatment to individual investors deriving income from investments abroad. None of these tax proposals has evoked much enthusiasm on the part of the tax authorities, who regard the use of tax preferences for purposes of influencing the direction of economic activity as prejudicial to the basic tax tenets of equal treatment and capacity to pay.

The question of the respective roles of government and private undertakings in economic development is at this date largely unresolved. Yet, by any calculation, all available means, both government and

private, are required to achieve the speedy development of underdeveloped countries which is dictated by the economic and political imperatives of our times. A harmonious combination of government and private effort for economic development would be a major achievement of statesmanship.

Dr. J. Fred Rippy is a Professor of History at the University of Chicago, where he has lectured and directed research for 26 years on the history of Latin America and on the foreign relations of the United States. He has been the author of numerous volumes, among them *Latin America and the Industrial Age,* appearing first in 1944 and in a second edition in 1947.

Mr. William Harvey Reeves is a member of the New York Bar and has been engaged in the private practice of law since 1926 with the exception of the period from 1941 through 1945. He was a special lecturer in the School of Business at Columbia University from 1926 to 1941; during World World II with the U.S. Treasury, 1941 to 1943; and the U.S. Department of State, 1943 to 1945, Washington, D.C. He is the author of various articles in professional journals on foreign trade and finance.

Mr. Paul D. Dickens is Chief of the Far Eastern Division of the Treasury Department. He is the author of several governmental pamphlets on the balance of international payments and foreign investments, and of articles in economic journals.

Dr. August Maffry is a Vice President of the International Banking Division of the Irving Trust Company in New York. Prior to joining the Irving Trust Company, he was Vice President and Economic Advisor of the Export-Import Bank of Washington, was with the U.S. Department of Commerce, and taught at the University of Missouri and Dartmouth College.

IX

TECHNICAL ASSISTANCE TO UNDER-
DEVELOPED AREAS

PRESIDENT HARRY S. TRUMAN's inaugural address in 1949, while a milestone as far as public interest in underdeveloped areas was concerned, was neither a signal putting into motion aid to underdeveloped areas nor a totally new approach to the development of underdeveloped areas. In describing United States government assistance to underdeveloped countries J. Fred Rippy has prepared a painstaking statistical report for the years 1945 through 1953.[1] Unfortunately it is impossible to separate assistance given for economic development from that given for military purposes. It is possible, however, that monies otherwise needed for military programs were made available for economic development due to U.S. military assistance. The total assistance to underdeveloped areas during this period amounted to: Latin America, $1,453,107,000; Africa, $169,249,-000; Near East, $438,987,000; and Asia, $2,027,841,000. Of these sums a considerable amount was spent on economic assistance in each area, much for postwar rehabilitation. However, the postwar rehabilitation programs provided consumers' goods as well as producers' goods and technical assistance. As a matter of fact, the immediate postwar aid consisted in the main of urgently needed consumers' goods, although it can be shown that most everyone with a surplus sought to have their surplus purchased by the U.S. government and sent overseas.

President Truman's Point Four program was distinctive, however, in its emphasis on technical assistance to underdeveloped areas and for that reason emphasis in this chapter shall be placed on that program.

While, at their inception, Point Four and other similar technical assistance programs were defined as being instituted primarily for the benefit of underdeveloped areas, other benefits accruing to developed countries were admitted as well. In a short time the question was raised in some quarters as to whether or not the benefits of such programs to developed countries might not outweigh

[1] "U.S. Government Assistance to the Underdeveloped Countries," J. Fred Rippy, *Inter-American Economic Affairs*, Vol. VIII, No. 4, Spring 1955, pp. 43–57. Rippy compiled his statistics from a variety of publications of the United States Department of Commerce, Office of Business Economics.

benefits to undeveloped countries. As James Baster has pointed out, "Because its aims are diverse and somewhat ill-defined, Point Four is in some danger of coming to mean all things to all men in the underdeveloped areas."[2] Since the dollar gap, that is, the difference between exports of other countries in dollar value to the United States and their imports from the United States, is financed by the United States, any program that would close this gap would be considered highly desirable. Many people seized on Point Four as such a program, for example, without careful consideration of the possibility that it might not have that immediate effect or, for that matter, be able to do it by itself even in the long run. Dr. John H. G. Pierson has summarized the interrelationship of Point Four, dollar gap, and U.S. employment as follows:

Point Four can promote better export-import balance in the world, or it can facilitate our full employment; but it cannot do both simultaneously. The fact that developed countries are better customers than underdeveloped countries shows that Point Four can make world trade expand, but not that it offers a magic formula to banish our "overproduction" worries. Unless the underdeveloped countries' exports increase still faster than their imports, Point Four will not, as we have seen, make any permanent contribution toward closing the gap. If it does make such a contribution, we shall be all the more thrown back on the necessity of perfecting domestic full employment policy. We cannot have it both ways.

In the net investment stage, Point Four can undoubtedly ease our internal problems more or less, depending on the size of the net investment outflow. Private savings going into foreign investment spare the budget the necessity of comparable or greater expenditures or tax reductions that would be required for maintaining the same volume of demand for American products. Heavy-goods industries geared to large export markets need not so suddenly contract. Farm surpluses need not pile up so fast. Readjustment processes are moderated or postponed. Time is gained to work out more lasting solutions. This may well mean that when exports and imports are brought into reasonable balance later on, the balance struck will be at a higher level than could be hoped for, in the face of the natural tendency for our exports to gravitate downward to the level of our imports, if the export surplus had to be squeezed out immediately.[3]

Pierson continues his realistic view of Point Four with,

What needs to be emphasized most is that any claim that Point Four can actually solve our full employment problem is entirely wrong. To think that Point Four is a *sufficient* condition for full employment in the United States is to cherish an illusion. For an American to think that it is a *necessary* condition is to cherish a very dangerous illusion indeed, because such ideas tend to block efforts to find real solutions of our fundamental economic problems.

A vital connection, all too often overlooked, between Point Four and United States full employment runs in the reverse direction. If we can maintain full employment,

      [2] "A Second Look At Point Four," James Baster, *American Economic Review, Papers and Proceedings*, Vol. XLI, No. 2, May 1951, p. 399.
      [3] "Point Four, Dollar Gap and Full Employment," John H. G. Pierson, *Annals of the American Academy of Political and Social Science*, Vol. 290, July 1950, p. 14.

and especially if we can be sure of continuing to maintain it, that will undoubtedly help Point Four. If a business recession develops, or even, it may be, a threat that the level of demand will not keep rising so as to justify the expansion necessary to take care of increased productivity and a growing labor force, wise action will become doubly difficult. In such circumstances the pressure to economize by cutting off assistance to foreign countries, will be second only to the mounting pressure to keep imports out and increasingly subsidize our exports. By contrast, the wealth and the good will flowing from a solidly based full employment will be a major factor in promoting development programs all over the world, because they will allay doubts that we can afford to give generous and continuous aid.[4]

He concludes his analysis of the implications of Point Four by stating that we should support Point Four for its own sake and not for specious or extraneous reasons.

In introducing various articles on the Point Four program, probably none is more fitting than that by Afif I. Tannous, "Positive Role of the Social Scientist in the Point Four Program." This paper was originally delivered before the opening meeting of the American Sociological Society and the Society for Applied Anthropology at Denver in September 1950. In this paper Tannous called for technical assistance based on research and surveys of local culture, appraisals of project progress by social scientists, and proper training of technicians previous to their embarkation on foreign aid missions. Prof. Helmut G. Callis has more recently discussed the role of the social scientists in an even broader context and emphasized the importance of the study of nations in their cultural context as a background for the solution of international problems.[5] In this connection Callis calls for increased emphasis on area research including the possibility of an "Institute of International Study and Teaching." Although not established by the federal government or entirely adequate in their funding by private sources, several institutes for international study have been established in recent years.

An article that serves to sensitize the reader to the problems of Point Four is, "An Anthropologist Views Technical Assistance" by Charles J. Erasmus. This article describes actual attempts to introduce new techniques for solving problems—the successes and failures known to the author are described; hypotheses are set up and suggested as desirable projects for future research.

In summarizing some of the broad problems of technical assistance programs we include "Ten Problems of Point Four," by John M. Hunter and William H. Knowles. This article shows the relationship between the Point Four program for technical assistance and various problem areas in the political, economic, and family institutions. The interrelatedness of social problems is brought out in this article; more questions are asked than answered, testifying to the complexity of the processes of developing underdeveloped areas.

[4] Ibid., pp. 14–15.
[5] "The Sociology of International Relations," Helmut G. Callis, American Sociological Review, Vol. XII, No. 3, June 1947, pp. 323–334.

In "Cultural Barriers to Point Four," Chester L. Hunt suggests that overemphasis of cultural relativity in determining policy may be as harmful to the effectiveness of a development program as the disregard of indigenous cultures which sociologists have traditionally counseled others to avoid. The inhabitants of underdeveloped areas, Hunt contends, often have conflicting values that are to some extent mutually exclusive. If the inhabitants of underdeveloped areas desire the products of industrialization they must forego some of their traditional rewards, attitudes, and values.

Although the United States has maintained a program of technical assistance distinct from that carried on by the United Nations in underdeveloped areas, it has also been a major contributor to the United Nations program. The United Nations program is briefly outlined in "Technical Assistance for Economic Development" by David Owen. The general principles making for the success or failure of such a program have been discussed previously and are also taken up in detail in chapters to follow. This is not the place for a detailed description of the U.N. program for technical assistance which is essentially the same as that carried on by the United States. It has been argued that the U.S. program of technical assistance would be better received and more successful if it were carried out through the United Nations; then recipient countries would be less suspicious of the possibility that political strings were attached to the aid. However, at this point, we are concerned with the general measures suggested for the economic development of underdeveloped areas by the United Nations and specifically by a special committee of United Nations experts.

This committee, consisting of Drs. Alberto B. Cortez, George Hakim, W. Arthur Lewis, Theodore W. Schultz, and D. R. Gadgil, after extensive discussion of the problems of underdeveloped areas in *Measures for the Economic Development of Under-developed Countries,* came fourth with measures for economic development in the form of recommendations to governments. These recommendations were phrased as they were in response to questions implicitly, if not explicitly, put to them by the United Nations representatives of various governments. The general question to be answered was, "What can governments do in order to speed up economic development?" Also, it should be noted, in reference to the earlier discussion of definitions of underdeveloped areas, that this report defines underdeveloped countries as "countries in which per capita income is low when compared with the per capita incomes of the United States of America, Canada, Australia, and Western Europe."

While we may agree with the recommendations of the committee, included as the next article in this chapter, some criticism was almost immediately voiced.[6] Most critical was Professor S. Herbert Frankel. The argument centers, to a con-

[6] "The United Nations Report on the Economic Development of Under-Developed Countries," Peter T. Bauer, *The Economic Journal,* Vol. LXIII, No. 249, March 1953, pp. 210–222; "United Nations Primer for Development," S. Herbert Frankel, *Quarterly Journal of Economics* of the Harvard University Press, Vol. 66, August 1952, pp. 301–326.

siderable extent, upon the feasibility of planning for rapid development of under-developed areas. Frankel, taking what might be termed a conservative economic position, doubts the wisdom, or perhaps wonders if we should pay the price to develop underdeveloped areas through government efforts before they might be placed on the list of profitable places for investment by private developers. His argument is highly critical of the notion that underdeveloped areas may be de-veloped "at will." Prof. Frankel contends that the report reflects

. . . current opinion, and in particular . . . the belief that development is largely a matter of social *will*. The report offers no evidence in support of this belief; nor does it examine its consequences. It seems to me very doubtful whether a history of eco-nomic change, of innovation, or of economic growth in different societies supports this optimistic view of the role and capacities of governments.[7]

At another point Frankel also says,

It is, indeed, precisely because the authors of the report see economic development primarily as an intellectual or artistic exercise by leaders and governments that they fail to do justice to their examination of existing realities in underdeveloped countries.[8]

These brief quotations of course fail to do justice to Frankel's criticisms, but do in-dicate the general trend or flavor of his argument. Frankel's remarks have been answered at some length by W. Arthur Lewis, one of the authors of the United Nations report, and in turn Frankel has replied to Lewis.[9] This exchange, the argument being well presented on both sides, is mentioned because it is repre-sentative of the general debate between those who are inclined to let economic development take its course, with profit or an economic motivation as the deter-minant of the rate and direction of economic growth, and those who believe that economic development has other motivations than profit in dollars, who believe that the profitability of developing an area is not the necessary criterion of whether or not it should be developed. Frankel's position is well summarized when he states,

The mere transfer of capital to underdeveloped regions does not necessarily by it-self insure that the capital will yield *net* income, or even that it will yield a *gross* return sufficient to allow for the replacement of the invested capital. It is essential, if international income disparities (assuming that these can be meaningfully ex-pressed) are to be reduced, that capital should be permitted to fructify wherever it can do so most readily; and this is indeed what has in the past generally occurred when political and social conditions have not erected barriers to the process. To trans-fer capital away from those uses in which it can be most readily multiplied reduces the net *income* from which alone surplus capital can be accumulated for new, more risky, or relatively less or less immediately productive, purposes.

[7] Frankel, *loc. cit.*, p. 303.
[8] Frankel, *loc. cit.*, p. 313.
[9] "United Nations Primer for Development: Comment," W. Arthur Lewis, *The Quarterly Journal of Economics* of the Harvard University Press, Vol. LXVII, May 1953, pp. 267–275 and "Reply," S. Herbert Frankel, pp. 280–285.

Moreover, the only way in which people or communities can be permanently assisted is by supplying them with resources that they will utilize in such directions as will yield *net* income; if they are not so utilized the resources will simply be drained away. This unfortunately is an inconvenient economic dilemma, from which neither economists nor anyone else can escape: be it to please politicians at home or politicians sitting in the United Nations.[10]

In a contrary review of the report, W. Rosenberg writes that the basic reason for the adverse comment of both Frankel and Bauer is the strongly rationalistic flavor of the report. He continues, "In other words, opposition has come from people who do not believe that societies and institutions can be consciously designed. . . ."[11] Rosenberg points out further that

In many instances the experts have been extremely courageous in drawing attention to the interrelation between political and economic institutions and for this alone their report deserves study. Too few people realize that economic development is a sociological matter, not merely an economic one.

On the other hand the report fails to utilize the examples of economic development in the Soviet third of the world. The experts repeatedly stress the importance of a desire for development as a basic pre-requisite. They also make clear that leadership is necessary to carry out a programme which will require the destruction of many established interests, and sacrifices on the part of the whole population, at one time or another. The discussion of the system of party leadership as it has been evolved in the countries adhering to the Soviet social and economic system would have been enlightening in this frame of reference. While it is understandable that in the present world atmosphere such a discussion has not found a place in the experts' report, a document which ignores the most important experiments in economic development cannot be called complete.

Nevertheless, within the socio-economic confines which the authors of the report have set themselves, many useful suggestions have been worked out and an analysis has been offered which cannot be ignored by future students of the problems of underdeveloped countries.[12]

The similarity of Rosenberg's views to those held throughout this volume is readily perceived. In the end, the view that one takes is dependent more or less on one's values, and whether long- or short-run values are determinants in this decision situation.

[10] "Reply," S. Herbert Frankel, *The Quarterly Journal of Economics* of the Harvard University Press, Vol. 67, May 1953, pp. 284–285.
[11] "United Nations Experts on Economic Development," W. Rosenberg, *The Economic Record*, November 1953, p. 264.
[12] *Ibid.*, pp. 264–265.

POSITIVE ROLE OF THE SOCIAL SCIENTIST IN THE POINT FOUR PROGRAM*

AFIF I. TANNOUS

IN HIS inaugural speech, early in 1949, the President of the United States discussed four items of national policy. Under the fourth point (hence, the Point Four Program) he announced to the world the proposal of a "bold new program" of technical assistance, with a view to developing the resources of underdeveloped countries and helping them enjoy higher levels of living.

Finally, after due consideration, Congress, voicing the opinion of the majority of the United States people, passed the bill authorizing the operation of the Point Four Program, on May 25, 1950. On June 5 the President signed the bill into a law entitled *Act for International Development*. Congress appropriated the necessary funds on September 6, 1950, and the implementation of the program in the field is now under way.

Thus the first stage in the fulfillment of the new policy that was proposed about two years ago has been achieved. We are now in a position to see more clearly through the reverberations, critical or favorable, caused by the proposal, and come to some pertinent and pointed observations and conclusions.

1. It is certain, contrary to what a few

still believe, that the technical aid policy was not formulated and proclaimed more or less extemporaneously, in an off-the-cuff fashion. It was the result of serious study and thought on the part of many people sensitive to the real issues at the bottom of world tensions. It was the result of several years of experience in the extension of technical aid in Latin America and in other parts of the world, both by governmental agencies and by private voluntary organizations. It was in reality a direct and simple, yet potent, answer to the challenge posed by the urgent need of the world for the establishment of stability and peace.

2. The global significance and serious implications of this proposal have been amply demonstrated by the keen interest and great hopes it has aroused in the United States, at the United Nations, and among the leaders and peoples of the countries that need the assistance.

3. Thus we can objectively conclude that for about two years the idea has been put to a thorough test of discussion, criticism, and appraisal at the hands of the public and the available national and international leaders, and that it has emerged more seasoned, more clearly defined, with more tangible content, and, above all, overwhelmingly desired by all concerned.

* Adapted and reprinted by permission from *The Scientific Monthly*, Vol. LXXII, No. 1, January 1951, pp. 42–49.

4. As regards the basic objectives of the policy and methods of operation, the law clearly emphasizes the following:

a. That ". . . the United States and other nations have a common interest in the freedom and in the economic and social progress of all peoples."

b. That such progress as achieved in the underdeveloped countries will be mutually beneficial to all concerned.

c. That it is the policy of the United States to aid the efforts of such countries to develop their resources and raise the standards of living among their peoples.

d. That the two major channels for such aid will be the exchange of technical knowledge and skill and the encouragement of the flow of needed capital.

e. That the program will be undertaken cooperatively, with the receiving country contributing a fair share of the required personnel and facilities.

f. That some projects will be undertaken multilaterally through the United Nations, and others bilaterally, through an agreement between the United States and the other country.

g. That the participation of private persons, agencies, and institutions in the program shall be sought and facilitated by such means as grants-in-aid, specific contracts, the creation of an advisory board of representative and professionally qualified citizens, and the appointment of committees in specialized fields.

5. From this brief background statement, we come to the pointed conclusion that the Point Four idea has assumed the form of an extremely significant and challenging reality. It is an avowed policy of the United States government and people, supported by a definite law and by appropriations. Whether it will ultimately attain its major objective of creating prosperity and socioeconomic stability in a large portion of the world, and thus further the cause of democracy and peace, will depend to a large extent upon the backing it will get from the people, institutions, and professional personnel of the United States and of other advanced countries.

In my judgment, there is a real and urgent need for the social scientist to be actively implicated in the program from the beginning. Otherwise, any project of technical aid will run a grave risk of being disrupted, and possibly wrecked, by the ignored forces of local culture, or of creating in the long run more problems than it will have solved.

1. The first basic need that the social scientist is well qualified to meet is the undertaking of related and persistent surveys and research in the local culture. We need to know the organization of its communities, groups, and institutions, its basic values and aspirations, its underlying tensions, its trends of change, before we can safely recommend technical projects for the solution of its problems.

In Saudi Arabia, in Syria, in Iraq, and in Iran, for example, the nomadic and semisettled tribal way of life is either predominant or highly significant in the total economic, social, and political organization of those countries. It is a societal system that is several thousand years old, with deep-rooted traditions and patterns of behavior. At the same time, we find that the knowledge we possess of this type of human organization—i.e., authentic and reliable knowledge—is certainly meager; it is limited to a few classical and temporary studies that are excellent. To be sure, there is a wealth of romantic literature about the nomads of the desert, and there are many superficial observations about their way of life. We cannot depend upon such notions to be our guide in the extension of technical aid to those groups; and any technical aid project will have to be concerned directly or indirectly with the tribal organization in most of the countries of the Middle East.

Stated in more specific terms, the planners, administrators, and technicians of the proposed aid program need to have satisfactory answers to such important questions as the following: Is agricultural settlement (which has become a national slogan in most of these countries) through the development of large-scale irrigation schemes the most effective way of solving the tribal problem? Will the destruction of the grazing economy of the tribe, which makes efficient use of scanty desert growth, result in a net gain or loss to national economy? Are there in the tribal culture certain basic values that should be preserved for the total national culture? How far and how rapidly could the tribal community be transformed into an agricultural community, and by what techniques and methods? What are the chances that such transformation will result in deterioration of health and morale, and in general disorganization? What about the basic land tenure aspect of the matter, which is already the major problem of the Middle East? Will such a program ultimately result in transforming the tribal chief, a democratic leader in the nomadic setting, into a feudal lord, and his tribesmen into landless sharecroppers?

We face the reality that what we know about these village folk and their way of life is fragmentary and inadequate. What are the basic values that are most dearly cherished, and what are the dominant institutions? What are their basic attitudes and prejudices? Is this or that village relatively more ready to absorb technical change, and why? In which one or more of the proposed projects are the people more willing to participate? What are the basic appeals through which the people can be made to go along with the program? By what means could the proposed material aid be translated into higher standards of living? More basically, what standard of living should be defined for

this or that community? What are the chances that this or that technical project might result in destructive disorganization of community life, and by what means could such a development be avoided?

The successful application of the Point Four Program calls urgently for the services of a team of social scientists. They would undertake fundamental research in the local cultures involved, integrate their findings, and present from time to time coordinated and pointed statements for the guidance of the program.

2. The second essential contribution the social scientist can make is to keep in close touch with a certain technical aid project that has been applied, and make periodical appraisals of its development and effects. No matter how carefully a project is selected, and how thoroughly the ground is prepared for it to fit into the local community and into the total culture, unforeseen developments will always arise. This is so because of the dynamic nature of technical change, especially when it is applied to such as the Middle East rural culture, which is highly integrated and stabilized. Reverberations in seemingly remote aspects of the culture will occur, and relatively new situations will develop. A reappraisal of the original project, together with modification of the method of approach, will be necessary. Without the benefit of such appraisal and timely adjustment, the project will run the risk of being wrecked by accumulated tension, or of leading to a point far removed from its original objective.

The grave land tenure problem of the Ottoman Empire is still today the major and basic issue in most of the countries of that region. If it has changed any, it is only in the direction of becoming more acute and explosive. The same factors of tribal and village organization, the same social and economic forces that were operative in those days, are still in full sway there. They are ready to influence and engulf any project of technical aid that is aimed, in accordance with the letter and spirit of the Point Four Program, at the achievement of economic development and higher levels of living for the people of the country concerned.

Again we have to turn to the people best qualified to tell us what these forces and factors are, how to appraise their roles, and how to guide the course of the aid program, with a view to having it achieve its intended objective. Saudi Arabia is moving rather rapidly along the road to modernization. Its way of life is predominantly tribal and nomadic, with minor agricultural activity. Its benevolent government, again basically tribal and Islamic in organization, is all for the introduction of Western technology in agriculture, communications, and other aspects of the country's life. The Arabian-American Oil Company, which holds the huge oil concession in that country, wisely conceives of its mission and responsibility as more inclusive than the mere development of a natural resource, and is actively assisting in the process. An Egyptian mission, three U.S. missions, and more recently an FAO mission have visited the country and rendered assistance in the utilization of water for irrigation and in the expansion of agriculture.

In other words, we witness here a country making a dramatic and drastic departure from a tribal way of life, with a pastoral economy, into a national organization that is based upon agriculture and related industry. The consequences of such a move will certainly be grave; and one with a feel for the historical perspective of the Arab world and for cultural dynamics cannot escape raising such serious and pertinent questions as the following: What effects will these technical projects,

already begun or proposed, probably have upon tribal and national organization? Are those effects really desired by those concerned? If not, what methods and techniques could be utilized to obviate them? As the irrigation projects now under way are realized and expanded, on what socioeconomic basis will they be operated? Private family ownership of the land, collective community cultivation, or large-scale absentee ownership? Which one of these is in the best interests of the country and in keeping with the spirit of the Point Four Program? Are the independent, virile, and essentially democratic tribesmen of Saudi Arabia likely to fall victims to a state of demoralization, loss of cultural values, and economic deprivation, as has happened in the neighboring countries? If this is to be avoided, what techniques, laws, regulations, and policies should be adopted?

Who is going to provide the best possible answers to these and similar questions, now and as the process of development marches on? It would be unrealistic to expect the technician, be he an engineer, an agronomist, a soils man, or a machinist, to do this basic job for us. Nor would it be fair to hold him responsible for the possible ultimate failure of his technical project to attain its original socioeconomic objective, or even to function smoothly in the hands of local cultural groups. This is a task that must be undertaken by additional personnel, especially trained and qualified, who would work hand in hand, step by step, with the technicians and the administrators of the program.

3. The Point Four Program, as clearly stated in the *Act for International Development*, briefly discussed above, rests squarely upon the premise that it consists essentially of a positive and constructive message from Western democracy to the underdeveloped areas of the world. The

need is obvious, therefore, for a clear, unified, and agreed-upon definition of what Western democracy is, what it stands for and what it attempts to do. To be sure, we have many definitions of the democratic idealogy, much literature on its development and principles, many common-sense notions on how it works in various situations of daily life. But this is not sufficient for our purpose; it does not meet squarely, point by point, the challenge of the ideological clash of the present day; it does not satisfy the need of the deprived peoples in most of the world. The usual pedantic and half-hearted way in which we have argued the case for democracy leaves the underdeveloped countries cold.

Hungry, illiterate peoples need to be approached with an unambiguous, positive, simple, yet potent statement of a "Creed of Democracy"—a creed they can understand, and through which they can see hope for the satisfaction of their basic needs and the fulfillment of their aspirations. The proclamation of such a creed will also serve as a dynamic support to the progressive elements who genuinely desire the development of economic resources for the welfare of their peoples.

Furthermore, we need such a clear articulation of the principles, achievements, and aims of the democratic way of life for the benefit of the Point Four Program, and the personnel selected to implement it. Technical projects undertaken within, and as part of, the American or Western culture may not need such a pointed ideological orientation. But an entirely different situation arises when Western technology, part and parcel of Western democracy, is put to function within an Oriental way of life. In order to avoid possible conflict with certain aspects and elements of the cooperating culture— and, more important still, in order to avoid the possibility of compromising the basic principles of the democratic message, and thus defeating its purpose—we need to define our terms of reference and take careful stock of our ideological equipment. It is from this ideological background, clearly and consciously articulated, that every technician will be given the necessary orientation and guidance; and it is against this ideological frame of reference that the selection of every aid project will be made, and its success or failure appraised and measured.

The Technical Aid Program, if broadly conceived, wisely planned, and vigorously and persistently implemented, will make a tremendous contribution to the rejuvenation and growth of Western democracy. It could very well develop into a positive and constructive action program, through which the democratic cultural heritage would reassert itself, strengthen its faith in its basic values, and give them expression on a global scale.

Once more we have to call upon the student of culture and society to assist in this most fundamental task. He will select and give expression to those fundamental values that make up the core of the American culture, and of the democratic way of life as a whole; he will interpret them in terms of the other culture participating in the aid program; he will provide the technical expert with the necessary ideological orientation that will give meaning and direction to his technical achievements; and he will indicate where ideological adjustment and compromise will be desirable and fruitful, and where they will begin to be fatal to the program or to either of the participating cultures.

4. The achievement of economic, social, and political stability, and hence the establishment of peace, often have been declared by responsible people to be the major objective of the Technical Aid Program. This is certainly a fundamental ob-

jective, the attainment of which is urgent. The world is going through a critical stage of rapidly increasing tension, which may explode into a most destructive global conflict. Any action taken with a view to relieving this tension, provided it is genuine, positive, and realistic, will constitute a contribution to the cause of world peace.

In proclaiming the Point Four Program as a major policy, Western democracy has certainly devised a potent tool for the achievement of stability and the establishment of peace. In intent and principle it is positive and constructive, appealing to the basic needs of the underdeveloped countries. Its effectiveness, however, as an instrument of stability and peace, as a contribution to the cause of democracy, will depend entirely upon how straight we keep our ideological aim, and how thoroughly we can grasp the basic issues that really give rise to tension and instability in underdeveloped countries.

Outside ideological forces, from the East and from the West, have been at work in this region for many years. A small but growing middle class of enlightened and progressive elements is increasingly making its weight felt in the national scene. Demands for reform are being made, and the rumblings among the deprived masses are growing in volume and intensity. Maintenance of the *status quo* in the Middle East has become an impossibility. That vacuum in its structure will have to be filled in either by bloody revolutions or by peaceful reform. Western democracy has a grand chance to assist in the latter, through the Point Four Program, provided it keeps its aim straight and acts fast.

More specifically, a major factor that is at the root of this state of affairs is the prevailing system of land ownership. Absentee, large-scale owners hold the major portion of the arable land. In most cases

their hearts are not in the soil, and they make little, if any, contribution to the management and productive development of agriculture. The majority of the cultivators, who constitute the majority of the population, are landless sharecroppers or wage laborers, who produce just enough to keep alive. They are the victims of illiteracy, disease, and general deprivation. Bitterness and resentment have been increasing among them in recent years. They are seeking a way out of their misery. The only hope they see is to own some of the land they cultivate, or to hold decent tenancy contracts that would guarantee their rights.

What services can the social scientist render the program in this respect? He can use the various techniques at his disposal to discover and clearly define those basic problems and those areas of tension that should be given first consideration. He can probe through these problems and point out the responsible factors. He can go directly to the people and find out with a greater degree of reliability how they feel about this or that ideology, about certain policies and about various problems. He is also qualified to suggest measures that would relieve the tension, and to keep a check on the effectiveness of their application.

5. As specified by the *Act*, the program of technical aid will consist largely of the dispatching of qualified personnel to the cooperating countries in order to assist in their fields of specialization. Experts in various branches of agriculture, health, industry, water development, and others, will be assigned as individuals or teams to specific field projects. They will apply their technical skill and scientific knowledge to the job directly, and they will also help in the training of local personnel. In either case, they will be in constant touch with the people of the country, functioning within local governmental systems,

community organizations, and cultural groupings.

In reality the role of these technicians will not be limited narrowly to the imparting of a skill or an item of knowledge. They will be rather the interpreters of Western culture to the peoples of other cultures. They will be the carriers and implementers of a vital message from Western democracy to the underdeveloped countries. Their success or failure in this task will be of grave consequence.

It would be unrealistic, to say the least, to assume that these experts, because they have done a fine job within their culture, would be able to function smoothly and effectively within a foreign culture. They will be faced there with people who think and act differently, who speak a strange language, who eat peculiar things, who have taboos on certain items and acts, and whose religion, family, and other institutions are different from their Western counterparts. Perhaps above all, our technicians will be struck and frustrated by the apparent lack of respect for time, punctuality, and material achievement. They will be irked by a governmental machinery that does not function as effectively as theirs back home.

In other words, we have to expect a major clash in ideas, attitudes, and actions to arise; and the technical expert will have to bear its brunt. He will have to develop a broad, sympathetic understanding of the other culture, and he will have to learn how and when to make effective adjustment. In order to assist him in this difficult endeavor, the Point Four Program must provide him with adequate training and orientation in the culture of the country to which he will be assigned. I see no substitute for this initial period of training of technical personnel. It must be established as an integral part of the total aid program. It would certainly be shortsighted to argue against it on the basis of the time and expense involved or on the basis that the technician must be dispatched quickly to the field. It would be tantamount to saving pennies and wasting dollars in the long run. At the same time it would not be fair to the technical expert to dispatch him to an alien field thus unprepared.

The social scientist, and the available agencies of social science, are very well qualified to shoulder this responsibility. Many of the leading universities in the United States and in Europe, and a few in the receiving countries themselves, can provide facilities for such training, with relatively small financial assistance. A few of them are already providing excellent service in this respect, although on a limited scale. There are also Federal and private agencies, and some organizations of the United Nations, whose services could be enlisted effectively.

The training and orientation program would acquaint the technical personnel with such basic and pertinent matters as the following: Organization and the central values of the American culture, or of another Western culture, and of the democratic way of life; organization and the basic values of the other cooperating culture; the dynamics of technical and social change; essentials of the language used in the country concerned; the outstanding attitudes and behavior patterns of its people; its institutional and community organization; its class structure and means of communication; conditions of daily living; effective techniques through which a technical project, or its products, could be made readily acceptable to the people; and others.

The following are a few illustrations presented in support of our argument for such a training program:

a. The group of technicians who took charge of an irrigation project in one of the Middle East countries, a few years ago, were well selected, highly qualified in their fields, and conscientious workers. One day, in order to speed up work on the project, they issued dog tags to the several hundred laborers involved. An unexpected rebellion ensued, which threatened to wreck the project. Wearing such tags was to the local people a symbol of subservience, and also was against their religious beliefs. They may have had other reasons, too—perhaps a general suspicion of the motives behind the measure.

b. The American or European head of a technical project established in any orthodox Muslim community will have to adjust his budget, output schedule, his sense of achievement, and his temper to what I describe as the "Ramadan Personality." During the Muslim month of Ramadan people go on a complete fast, from sunrise to sunset. It is a holy month, dedicated to prayer and meditation. The local worker or assistant on such a project develops at this time a personality that is irritable and short-tempered. He expects leniency and understanding for his reduced production. To become irked and frustrated in the face of such a situation, as many a Western technician or expert has done, and denounce local labor as lazy, indolent, and hopeless, will get the head of our project nowhere. He will ultimately reap sullenness and rebellion on the part of the local folk, and estrangement between the two supposedly cooperating cultures.

c. In undertaking its vast field operations in Saudi Arabia, the Arabian-American Oil Company has been wisely sensitive to the significance of local conditions, custom, and traditions. It has endeavored by various means to impress this upon its field employees. Its latest development in this respect has been the establishment of a training center for its personnel going abroad. It is a two-way training pro-

gram that is doubly rewarding. It involves the assignment of some of its Arabian employees to the center here in the United States, to teach their American colleagues about Saudi Arabia, and at the same time to learn about American life. The company is now convinced that its training program is paying good dividends in the form of better relationships with the local people and less frequent turnover in its American personnel.

6. The services of social science also will be needed in the training of nationals of the underdeveloped countries, who will come here for specialized studies. This is expected to be a major activity of the Point Four Program. Students, technicians, and scientists of various types will be assigned to Federal agencies, universities, or other private organizations, for periods of study and training.

It is equally imperative that these people be subjected to an adequate program of orientation, similar to the one suggested for American personnel. In the first place, the program will assist them in making the necessary adjustments to the American way of life. The smoother the adjustment, the more effective use of the assignment will be. Second, the program will present them with a concise and sharply outlined picture of the basic values in American culture, and in the democratic way of life in general. We are dealing here with a select group of actual or potential technical and professional leaders of their respective countries. It is essential that they take back with them a true picture of what democracy stands for, and how it functions in the daily life of the citizen. This orientation will provide the necessary frame of reference for their observations and studies. Living with the American people will then become more meaningful.

We know enough now, from years of actual experience, to come to the conclusion that a foreign technician on an assignment in this country tends, in the majority of cases, to see and appreciate the great fruits of American industry and agriculture, but not those cultural roots that made such achievements possible. He tends to conclude erroneously that all his country needs to do to emulate the West is to copy from these achievements. This, of course, is not the message the Point Four Program is intended to convey. The best corrective for this tendency is an orientation and training program.

Third, such a training program will provide the foreign technician with a much-needed orientation in his own cultural background, his own way of life. This is not at all a superfluous proposal,

as it may at first appear. In many cases, the individual concerned, coming from the Middle East, for example, will be a member of a small privileged minority in his country. His knowledge of the tribal way of life, of the rural community, of the conditions of labor, will be extremely limited. Even if he should come from the midst of these groups, it will not be likely that he will possess a thorough grasp of the essentials of his cultural organization, its trends, and the behavior patterns of its people. His consciousness of these matters needs to be heightened, and his knowledge sharpened. It is only then that he will be able to make his technical training fully meaningful, in terms of his culture and the life of his people.

AN ANTHROPOLOGIST VIEWS
TECHNICAL ASSISTANCE*

CHARLES J. ERASMUS

THIS paper is concerned with conscious attempts to direct or to accelerate culture change, and is based largely on personal observations in several Latin American countries. It does not pertain specifically to the work of any one agency or to technical assistance programs directed only by agencies and governments foreign to the countries concerned. Many if not most of the examples used are drawn from cases where local governments have attempted to introduce change within their own countries. The author's purpose is to syn-

* Adapted and reprinted by permission from *The Scientific Monthly*, Vol. LXXVIII, No. 3, March 1954, pp. 147–158.

thesize these observations into a discussion of the patterns of resistance and acceptance demonstrated by the peoples of "underdeveloped" areas in the face of directed attempts to change their ways and to point out the implications of these patterns for the successful and economical operation of technical assistance programs.

EMPIRICISM

Introduced changes that bear clear and immediate proof of their effectiveness and desirability usually achieve a more rapid and widespread acceptance than changes of long-term benefit or changes in which the relationship between the new technic and its purported results is not easily grasped on the basis of casual observation. In agriculture, for example, the introduction of improved plant varieties (higher yielding or more disease-resistant) which result in a greater profit to the farmer has repeatedly resulted in spectacular success stories in many of the Latin American countries, and with a variety of cash crops. A foreign agency in one country developed an improved hybrid corn through local genetic selection. The first year that samples were distributed to farmers, the yield was so much higher than normal that the agency was deluged with requests for seed at the next planting time. In fact, the demand was so great that private enterprise quickly became interested in taking over the job of seed multiplication. In contrast, attempts to introduce soil conservation practices frequently encounter considerable difficulty. Practices that do not bear clear and demonstrable proof of their efficacy in a short period of time usually do not diffuse well on their own, with the result that their diffusion may often be no greater than the range of the agronomist's personal contacts.

The spectacular nature of certain introduced agricultural practices may vary considerably, however, with local environmental conditions. In arid badlands, as those found in some parts of Arizona, for example, where rainfall is confined to one brief season in the form of intense downpours, soil conservation practices may demonstrate remarkable benefits within a very short period. Dobyns shows us how eagerly such practices may be accepted under these conditions, in his case study of a conservation experiment among Papago Indians.

In the tropical lowlands of one Andean country, improved varieties of mosaic-resistant sugar cane have all but replaced the "criollo" varieties since their introduction some ten years ago. The newer varieties demonstrated their usefulness so successfully in the form of higher yields and greater profits that they diffused from one farm to another with a minimum of extension support and promotion. In only two or three small valleys have the older criollo varieties persisted and in these cases because mosaic disease was never a problem, apparently as a result of certain prevailing dry winds. Here the farmers see no advantage to the newer varieties and prefer their criollo in the belief that it is easier to refine.

In public health programs, spectacular curative measures seem to take precedence over preventive ones in the rapidity with which they are accepted. Yaws campaigns carried on by the Institute of Inter-American Affairs, in collaboration with the governments of Colombia and Ecuador, have quickly and successfully overcome the initial resistance of the coastal Negro groups, among which the disease is endemic, and these campaigns are profoundly altering the folk beliefs and the fatalistic attitude formerly surrounding this disease. Even native curers now admit that modern medicine is more effective in the treatment of yaws than their own herbal and magical treatments.[1] In the case of preventive medicine, however, the story in most countries is quite different. For example, the symptoms of intestinal infection in a young child may be diagnosed as "evil eye" by rural populations. In order for these people to be convinced that boiling their polluted drinking water will prevent the symptoms we attribute to intestinal infection, they must be able to observe some measurable decrease in the incidence of the symptoms as a result of the preventive technic. Owing to the conditions under which

[1] Erasmus, C. J., *Southwestern J. Anthropology* 8, No. 4 (1952).

they live and their failure to understand the reasons behind the new device, intestinal infection may take place through other media, and consequently no relationship between the two is empirically established.

In the case of crops, naturalistic explanations are usually and understandably given to insect plagues while ailments due to microorganisms are sometimes attributed to supernatural causes for which magical preventive measures may be employed. However, when a commercial fungicide, which effectively protects one man's crop against the supernatural maladies that afflict his neighbor's, is introduced into a rural farming area, an empirically measurable relationship is established between the preventive device and the malady. Even though the farmers may not fully accept and understand the modern explanation nor completely abandon their former beliefs, they quickly adopt the fungicide (if they can afford it).

From these examples we begin to see that the people of the so-called underdeveloped areas do not reason very differently from those of areas considered more advanced. Unaccustomed or unable to read, they lack the one great avenue by which more sophisticated populations avail themselves of a broader range of experience (including laboratory and statistical analyses) than would be possible if they were limited to the range of their own casual observations. The reasoning processes of both groups, however, are largely empirical and rest primarily on a frequency interpretation of events. Thus, in the case of a preventive measure for plant diseases or a remedial campaign for an easily distinguishable endemic disease such as yaws, the great number of individual cases plus conditions involving fewer variables permits a frequency interpretation in their favor within the lim-

its of casual observation, whereas conditions involving a preventive measure for intestinal infections in a family of two or three children may not. Therefore, where a new practice can demonstrate its relationship to the improvements in such a fashion that a frequency interpretation is possible within the limits of casual observation, it has a much greater chance for rapid acceptance among the populations of underdeveloped areas.

Very often the nature of an innovation will depend upon proper follow-through by the innovator. In most of Latin America, new technics must be adapted to conditions on which few reliable data are available. Under such circumstances, an unknown factor, which would have been known and allowed for in the United States, will upset the results in such a way that the new practice fails to make what might have been a spectacular demonstration. In one country, a U.S. technician who was attempting to introduce the practice of broadbase terracing had no data available regarding maximum rainfall and soil conditions to guide him in calculating slope and channel capacity. By diligently checking his first experimental terraces under rainfall conditions, he corrected all errors before any damages might occur. As a result of this careful follow-through and sense of obligation to the farmers, not a single terrace failed when the area was later subjected to a heavy rain of flood proportions. In fact, the erosive action of the storm on adjoining nonterraced fields was such as to make the terracing demonstrations more valuable.

NEED

The needs felt by the people, as distinguished from those felt by the innovators, constitute one of the most important factors pertaining to the acceptability of an innovation in any particular case. If

298

the people fail to feel or to recognize the need for an innovation, it may prove impossible to introduce it on a voluntary basis.

Several of these examples, pertaining to the introduction of new agricultural practices, involved not only the factor of their empirical verification at the level of casual observation but also appealed to a profit motive. An improved crop variety, which results in a higher yield or a greater margin of profit, appeals to the profit motivation and the desire for greater purchasing power when the improved variety is a cash crop. When it is not a cash crop, the story may be different. From a study by Apodaca of the introduction of hybrid corn into a community of Spanish American farmers in New Mexico, we can see how motives other than those of greater profit may affect the outcome when the crop to be improved is not being grown for market.[2] Within two years after the introduction of the hybrid, three-fourths of the community had adopted it. But after four years, all but three farmers had reverted to planting their original variety. The hybrid had doubled production per acre; the farmers had met with no technical difficulties in planting it, and the seed were readily obtainable. However, the corn was raised by the community only for its own consumption. As these people eat their corn largely in the form of tortillas (unleavened corn cakes), an important mainstay in their diet, and since the new hybrid did not yield tortillas of the same color, texture, and taste as their own corn, they reverted to their older variety. These reasons were more important to them than was the quantity produced. Apodaca notes the fact, however, that the hybrid was dropped with

[2] Apodaca, A., *Human Problems in Technological Change: A Casebook*, p. 35. Edward H. Spicer, Ed. New York, Russell Sage Foundation, 1952.

considerable reluctance by the farmers because of its much greater yield. They had empirically verified the fact that the hybrid was an improvement over the old in one sense, but not in the prime sense which pertained to their particular needs and values. This illustrates what can happen when an improvement that would normally have high appeal under cash-cropping conditions is introduced into a subsistence-oriented cropping pattern.

Let us now turn to examples where subsistence-oriented agricultural improvements are introduced into a money economy. Several years ago the ministry of agriculture in a South American republic sponsored a program to introduce the planting of soybeans in many rural areas. Today, the only place where this crop is planted on any scale is near a city where it is manufactured into vegetable oil. The object of this program was to induce the rural population to improve their diet. Soybeans, considered more nutritious, were to be produced solely for family consumption. The farmers not only found the new food distasteful but discovered that no one cared to buy it, and the movement quickly collapsed. In this case the appeal was made to a better health rather than a greater profit motive, but for the farmers the improvement was not empirically verifiable. Symptoms of malnutrition are often ascribed by the folk to supernatural and other causes which bear little or no resemblance to the medical explanations of the innovators. Therefore, in such cases no feeling of need for a new practice may arise to offset the disagreeableness of changing long-established food habits.

In numerous countries attempts have been made to induce rural populations to cultivate vegetable gardens for home consumption. In all cases observed this, too, usually fails after the program has terminated, if the farmer has found no market for the new product in the meantime. Vegetable crops generally enter an area close to cities and towns, or along reliable communication routes leading to them, where the market is greater. Once farmers grow vegetable crops for profit, they invariably consume some. In one Latin American mestizo community where a health program had enjoyed some degree of success in introducing family vegetable gardens, several farmers said that the best way to pacify government programs was to go along with them and do as one was told; eventually the program would terminate, and then they would abandon the nuisance of vegetable gardens without creating any disturbance.

In another Latin American republic, a government-sponsored agency, designed to look after the welfare of farmers growing a cash export crop of importance to the national economy, instituted a program of aiding farmers to build new homes and improve farm structures that were necessary for properly processing the crop. The agency found that it received many more requests for the processing structures than for the homes, although the cost of both types of units was being borne largely by the agency. The farmers were required to pay a small percentage of the total construction costs, and a majority of them preferred to invest in the labor-saving devices. Frequently the field men of the program scolded the farmers for thinking only of their own convenience and never of the cramped and unsanitary quarters of their families. Again we find an example where the needs felt by the people were not entirely in accord with those felt by the innovators. Farmers accustomed to living under housing conditions which the innovators considered undesirable did not necessarily share this view. The processing structures, however, were already known to the farmers who were aware of their labor-saving advantages. The theory underlying the housing program was that more sanitary living conditions would result in more able-bodied farmers and in higher production. But a majority of the new houses rapidly returned to the same state as those they had replaced, a further indication that the needs felt by the innovators were not generally perceived by the farmers. New houses built on farms located along main highways or near population centers showed better maintenance than those that had to be reached by mule-back. Apparently, greater contact with external influences and the cultural environment of the innovators created a sense of need similar to that felt by the innovators.

Let us turn next to an instance of rapid change independent of any superimposed direction. Near two large cities along a semitropical coast, dairy farming recently has come into greater prominence because of the increasing market for milk. Large and poorly managed haciendas, formerly devoted to the pasturing of beef cattle, are breaking up into smaller and more efficiently operated dairy farms. The dairy farmers on their own initiative have imported improved dairy strains and have adopted improved feeding practices and silage. Some farmers have learned to keep daily records of the milk production of each cow, and on the basis of these records to practice selective breeding of their best producers. These dairymen are sensitive to new technics and knowledge. The local economy already has created an urgent need for new ideas, with the added promise of a high degree of acceptance. Diffusion of ideas from the most advanced to the least advanced farms is proceeding at a rapid rate.

We can see that when the objective of technical assistance is to increase production in an underdeveloped area, it is easier to realize among people who participate in a money economy. Rural people who are cash-cropping for national or international markets frequently tend to specialize. More attention is usually given to a particular crop, such as coffee, sugar cane, wheat, or potatoes. The local group often forfeits a great deal of its self-sufficiency in the process of specialization and consequently grows more accustomed to purchasing specialized products of other areas. An increasing tendency to purchase products external to the area is in turn usually accompanied by an increase in the number of new products and ideas entering the area, and the number of new needs thereby created. This type of situation seems to be more conducive and sensitive to change. Needs created by the process of specialization and the desire for increased production and profit actually seem the easiest for technicians from another culture or subculture to meet. The solution is often largely technical, fewer cultural barriers to a common understanding are presented, and the perception and feeling of needs are more easily shared by the innovators and the people.

However, when change is being attempted in a field not directly related to increased production in a money economy, in other words not directly in terms of profits, the difficulties increase. In the field of public health, for example, the innovator may consider it highly desirable to introduce basic disease prevention measures into an underdeveloped area. But the folk still subscribed to an age-old system of beliefs about the cause, prevention, and treatment of disease, a system so different that the preventive measures of the innovator were meaningless. Lacking an understanding of the modern concepts of the etiology of disease and consequently the reasons for modern methods of prevention, they may feel no need to adopt the prescribed changes. Thus, despite the fact that they feel a general need for assistance in combatting the ailments common among them,

they may fail to perceive the need for the specific measures proposed and may actively resist them.

COOPERATION

Until now this paper has purposely been limited to examples of changes whose acceptance and diffusion are largely an individual matter. As has been seen in the case of spectacular innovations such as improved plant varieties, this type of change frequently spreads with phenomenal rapidity from one individual to another with very little outside stimulus. However, some changes may require group or community adoption, a circumstance that can greatly increase the operational difficulties of introducing them. Not only must the need for the change or changes be perceived by the entire group or a large majority simultaneously, but the members of the group must cooperate for the given end.

Holmberg provides us with an excellent example of an assistance project which depended upon collective acceptance and which failed even though it was concerned with a need already felt by the people.[3] In a community in the Viru Valley of Peru, villagers had petitioned the Peruvian government for aid in obtaining well water to supplement their river supply during periods of shortage in the dry season. A permanent and reliable water supply was important to these people for household and for irrigation and production needs. Although a well was successfully dug, the entire project failed because the technicians did not consult with leaders of local opinion or seek to involve the people. Antagonisms based on local social and political conditions became so great that it was necessay to withdraw the project.

Throughout one Andean country an attempt was made to establish farmer committees, by means of which it was planned

[3] Holmberg, A. R., *Ibid.*, p. 113.

to bring about agricultural improvements. In only one small mountain sector did the movement have success, and here only among farmers who until a few years before had been living in indigenous communities. Accustomed to a measure of independent local government in the past, they were organized with very little effort. Obviously, then, the failure of this program must have been due in part to the organizing technics, for the few successful cases were the result of highly favorable local circumstances.

It would seem that in many parts of Latin America there is a tendency to consider rural populations as more cooperative than they really are, or at least to take their cooperation for granted. However, in Latin America today many of the age-old customs promoting cohesion and cooperation in rural society are being or have been replaced by social relationships of a more impersonal and individualistic nature. Such replaced customs would include the mutual aid and assistance patterns involved, for example, in reciprocal farm labor and the ceremonial kinship obligations of godparenthood. Apparently the economic aspects of such mutual assistance customs were functional in a subsistence-oriented rural economy, where the peasants cropped largely for family and local consumption. As roads increased the possibilities of marketing farm surpluses over larger areas, farmers began to specialize and came to be more dependent on other regions and countries for marketing their products and for the food and goods no longer produced on their own farms. Thus, the interdependencies existing between members of the local group in daily contact were gradually superseded by national and international interdependencies between peoples who never met. When the economic interdependencies between members of the local group were superseded by larger and more impersonal ones, the cooperative

functions of older customs were unnecessary. The rural peasantry became more individualistic and less dependent on their daily contacts.

Actually, it may be fairly argued that the rural populations of Latin America are becoming more competitive than collective. Perhaps one of the clearest illustrations of this may be found in 4-H club work. Results are usually better when the young people work separate plots in competition than when they work the same land together in such a way that they cannot compare their work. Similarly, when earnings of club members are pooled for the purchase of livestock or tools used in common, the results are usually poorer than when each individual has the right to the fruits of his own labor. In such instances we can see how the profit motive coincides with individualistic and competitive tendencies.

When a technical assistance project in a certain country attempted to contour level rice fields across ownership boundaries in order to facilitate irrigation flooding in a pilot area, it was faced with the problem of obtaining the permission and collaboration of all the small landowners within the area. However, the technicians neglected to unite the various landowners concerned, to explain the project to them, and to seek their cooperative support. The project was carried out as if it were a type of change which could be effected on an individual or family basis. One farmer was induced to permit the contouring, then another, and so on. Because of the severe land fragmentation problem, the owners of neighboring plots were not necessarily neighbors in so far as the residence patterns were concerned. Even when a farmer and several of the friends who lived near him were convinced of the benefits of contouring, their plots within the area were found to be widely separated. As planting time approached, the project officials felt obliged

to rush the job through, and so began contouring the individual and widely separated plots as functionally separate units.
As the work progressed, other landowners
began signing up. Eventually, nearly all
gave permission to contour their land and
agreed to pay the costs. But the sequence
of requests was such that practically all
contouring had to be done within, rather
than across, ownership boundaries. Inasmuch as nearly all the farmers eventually
collaborated, there is reason to believe that
with the proper inducement they could
have been encouraged to do so before the
work began. As a result, one of the major
objectives of the project, to contour according to the topography rather than
ownership boundaries, was lost.

INDUCEMENT

The problem of inducement, as we shall
use the word here, refers to the task of overcoming popular resistance to a proposed
change for any of the reasons discussed so
far. Even in the case of new technics or
traits which demonstrate their effectiveness in a spectacular fashion, there is still
the initial problem of bringing them to the
attention of the public. If the problem is
one of introducing an improved plant variety, some farmer or farmers must be persuaded to try it. If these initial experiments
result in a much greater yield, the new variety usually sells itself. Generally, farmers
are suspicious of government authorities
and prefer to let someone else try the new
technic before they adopt it. If a well-
known neighbor obtains satisfactory results, others will often rush to follow his
example. Demonstration farms are not so
readily copied, as the farmers are not sure
what additional advantages beyond their
own means may have biased the results.
When a large brewery in a certain country
found that the home production of barley
was insufficient to supply its needs, it hired
agronomists to stimulate production in

new areas. The agronomists circulated
through the highland regions, promised
farmers a good price for barley, gave instructions for planting, and provided seed.
The first year very few farmers in a given
area tried the new plant on a very modest
scale. However, by the third or fourth year,
after all had been convinced that the
agronomist would keep his word about the
price and that the plant would give profitable yields, barley had become one of the
important crops.

Where the advantages of a new technic
or trait are long term in nature or difficult
to demonstrate empirically, long-term
methods of introduction through formal
education might be considered. Extension work with adolescents frequently
demonstrates that it is easier to instill new
habits among individuals who do not have
to unlearn old habits. Furthermore, young
people usually find it easier to substitute
the prestige of the specialist for the prestige of tradition. Even when introducing
nonspectacular innovations on a long-term
basis through formal educational procedures, it will usually be necessary to take
popular beliefs and practices into account
so that persons may perceive a relationship between the needs they feel and the
remedies proposed. In Quito, Ecuador,
tests were given to school children who had
been receiving formal lectures in health
education, including the use of visual aid
technics for some two years. Results
showed that the period of instruction had
made little or no impression. Whereas
modern explanations of the etiology of disease and its prevention were now familiar
to the children, they were largely related
to modern disease terminologies that had
no meaning to them. The symptoms of
those diseases were still being classified according to a folk system which included
such causes as fright, evil eye, malevolent
air, and witchcraft. According to the school
children, these folk illnesses could not be

caused by modern etiologies, could not be prevented by modern means, and could not be cured by medical doctors. In collaboration with the educators, attempted changes in the methods of instruction were made so as to allow the children to discuss their folk beliefs freely in class. During the discussions the educators attempted to show the children, without deriding their beliefs, that the symptoms they ascribed to fright, evil eye, and the like were the symptoms of the very diseases that the educators had been talking about for the past two years. They also tried to disassociate folk symptoms from folk etiologies and practices and to link them to modern methods of treatment and prevention. Retesting after the lectures gave very different results. Written tests, of course, do not necessarily indicate a change of habits, but these certainly indicated that for the first time the children were cognizant of a relationship between the measures and explanations of the educators and their own maladies. This illustrates the necessity of thoroughly understanding the local culture of a people, in cases where it is difficult for them to perceive the needs felt by the technicians under the ordinary limitations of casual empiricism. Ironically enough, salesmen for patent medicine concerns frequently give very careful consideration to folk beliefs in order to adapt the advertising of their products to the local concepts of disease.

In some cases people can be induced to accept new technics and changes, which they find difficult to accept, by linking them or making them conditional to other changes or services more desirable to them. For example, in anticipation of an irrigation project that they know will materially benefit them, farmers may be more willing to satisfy government wishes concerning secondary improvements which they would ordinarily resist. In the example of the contour leveling of rice fields, it seems very

possible that one of the principal mistakes of the program was in failing to obtain commitments by the farmers for the leveling before the irrigation project was completed. As the farmers had already been provided with irrigation water, the inducement value of the irrigation project had been lost.

Similarly, where public health centers give attention to curative as well as preventive measures, their rapport with the public as well as their influence in implementing changes in disease prevention habits is noticeably greater. At a charity maternity hospital in Quito, it was found that new practices in conflict with popular beliefs—but with which mothers had to conform in order to receive treatment at the hospital—were having an important and permanent influence in altering their beliefs. In agriculture, the distribution of seeds and tools at cost may offer a decisive inducement to adopt recommended new cultivation practices. Where farmers can see no need for a program objective, it may be possible to alter the emphasis of the objective so as to enhance its appeal. In one Haitian valley, agronomists were able to effect measures of soil conservation by appealing to a local interest in coffee planting and by helping the farmers to start seed beds of coffee and shade trees for transplanting to hillside plots.

Where joint and cooperative action on the part of a community is necessary for the success of a project, it would seem that considerable attention should be given to involving the people in the activity at an early stage. Whenever possible, the community should be made to feel that it has participated in the planning of the program. When cooperative programs are simply dropped upon the peoples of underdeveloped areas from some high planning echelon within their government, without any explanation and without any consideration for local opinions, the programs are very likely to fail either partially or totally.

In any technical assistance program one of the most important and most variable aspects of the problem of inducement involves the factor of person to person relationships. Much has been expounded on this subject, but the desideratum usually consists of little more than a consideration for the beliefs and customs of other peoples and a sincere attempt to understand them. Yet understanding can be no greater than allowed by the amount of personal contact and the ability to communicate.

A most effective foreign technician was a U.S. soils scientist attached to an agricultural research station in an Andean country. Good-natured and affable, he set out at once to make a friend of every member of the staff. Within his special field he led the local technicians to adopt several new research procedures, and saw several research projects of considerable importance well under way. Yet he never allowed his name to be attached to any project. He encouraged the local man most interested in the plan to initiate it, carry it through, and take the credit, while he played the part of a counsellor who continued to make suggestions but never gave an order. Three nights a week on his own time he held classes in English because he had discovered that many local technicians wanted to learn the language and that he made friends by helping them.

COMPLEXITY

Frequently a change which seems desirable to the innovator may depend upon so many other secondary accompanying changes that its introduction is difficult. Perishable food products, such as fresh vegetables and fish, are most easily exploited near markets where transportation to markets is reliable, inexpensive, and rapid, or where storage and processing facilities have been developed. Successful adoption of improved livestock may depend upon many correlative changes in husbandry practices. The latter in turn may depend upon the farmer's financial ability to provide better feed and care.

Failure to recognize the factor of complexity is one of the most serious problems in technical assistance work, partly because there are no established principles of diagnosis which can be applied to every case. Oftentimes the standard of living may be so low that the innovator's heart goes out to the evidences of suffering which seems unnecessary to him from his different cultural or subcultural viewpoint. Let us take for example country "X," whose density of population and infant mortality rate are among the highest in the world and whose per capita production is among the lowest. Is the first job of technical assistance to save lives and reduce the immediate evidences of human suffering, or is it to help the country itself to solve its health problems? The answer to this question depends on who provides the funds to build the public health centers, the water purification systems, and the public hospitals, and to educate the doctors and nurses. If the innovators provide these funds, the effort may involve much more than technical assistance; it may involve heavy financial assistance. As a result the population may increase more rapidly than ever, and with it all the existing economic and political stresses may be aggravated. However, if the innovators are concentrating on purely technical assistance, they may endeavor to help country "X" raise per capita production to a point where the country can pay for its own secondary improvements as it feels the need for them. In short, this would mean that technical assistance in country "X" might be aimed first at increasing productivity in agriculture and industry, while assigning the high infant mortality rate to a secondary position on its list of problems.

This extreme case is used simply as an

example and does not mean that technical assistance in public health should be relegated to a secondary position in all countries desiring technical aid. In some countries productivity per capita is much higher than in others and public health services for the population are already well established. In such cases, technical assistance for making these services more efficient is readily grasped and utilized and effects of the technical assistance are far more permanent and far reaching. U.S. public health technicians in one small country have played an important role in a malaria campaign to clean up a wide coastal zone that was formerly poorly exploited. Roads are now being cut through the jungles, exploitation of forest products is intensifying, and new settlers are entering the area to establish banana and other plantations. Thus an entire nation has been benefited by these public health workers.

A price-support program for cotton was adopted in one country in order to induce greater home production for local textile industries. Within a period of three years agricultural changes in some areas have been almost revolutionary. On flat coastal plains to the east, land that was formerly yielding a very low rate of income per acre from an extensive type of beef-cattle ranching is rapidly changing into a zone of mechanized agriculture. Cotton has become white gold. Not only have many farmers rushed to exploit the new opportunities with mechanized farm equipment, but they have adopted new farming technics such as the use of fertilizers, insecticides, and crop dusting. This example is not used to justify price-support programs, but it does show how increased profits facilitate the adoption of new practices. They do not make such change automatic, however, for the same factors of need and empiricism still apply. Many farmers started planting cotton without heeding advice to use insecticides. They suffered serious crop damages the first year and saw the difference between their yields and those where insecticides were used, and then they adopted the practice the second year. Nor did cotton planting itself become generally adopted until a few enterprising farmers had made a handsome profit.

In situations of extreme land fragmentation where farmers must supplement their agricultural earnings by means of other endeavors, it is usually extremely difficult to initiate changes in farming practices. A higher yielding plant variety may be readily adopted, but many other innovations are difficult to introduce on uneconomical farm units. However, a desire to help impoverished farmers may lead administrators and technicians to attempt the introduction of improvements of a subsistence nature which require little or no capital expenditure. Programs may thereby develop with the purpose of introducing the household manufacture of family clothes, home gardening of all food necessities, home food-preservation practices, and inexpensive animal varieties such as rabbits as a source of meat for the family. All such devices are aimed at making farm families more self-sufficient and less specialized, a process contrary to the usual economic trends. Social welfare programs of this type seem to require more extension personnel and promotional activity than those designed to bring production-increasing technics to farmers who have the financial means to exploit them.

In one South American country where soil erosion has become extremely severe, U.S. soil conservation experts found that practically no remedial steps were being taken. In some areas, erosion had reached a point where only such drastic measures as complete reforestation would suffice. In others, the erosion problem was complicated by absentee land-ownership patterns or the exploitation of uneconomical farm units. However, by selecting an area of medium-sized mechanized farms personally administered by resident owners, the technicians were very successful in introducing many new soil conservation practices with a minimum of promotional activity. Farmers responded readily, were quick to recognize the benefits of the new measures, and found them easy to carry out at their level of operations. As a result of the impetus given to soil conservation by the successes in this area, the government created a special soil conservation division, within its ministry of agriculture, to attend to the erosion problems of the country as a whole.

In one sense, the areas of worst erosion in a country might be thought of as presenting the greatest need for correction, or the poorest farmers as the ones most in need of improved agricultural practices. Frequently, however, the persons most in need, in the judgment of the innovator, may be those who feel the need the least. For this reason it may often be more expedient and practical to work where the need, from the innovator's standpoint, is less acute but where there is greater willingness on the part of the people to make the change. The interest shown by the people themselves is more often a better index to their ability to successfully adopt a given change than the judgment of the innovator.

ECONOMIC FEASIBILITY

It would be quite logical to suppose that given unlimited financial and human resources, a technical assistance program could effect any change desired. However, no technical assistance project has such unlimited funds; therefore, in any decision concerning the selection of projects, their feasibility with respect to budgetary limitations must be taken into account.

The kinds of innovations which would seem to be most inexpensive are those which require the least man-hours for strictly promotional purposes. Such innovations include those from which benefits are easily verifiable through casual observation, which are accepted and diffused on an individual basis, which meet a strong need already felt by the people (of particular appeal to a profit motive), and those which are in sequence with local development (not too complex). However, certain circumstances may justify considerable promotional activity. For example, in the case of projects requiring cooperative acceptance and action on the part of the people, the necessary groundwork must be done to involve them in the activities, or the time and money spent in the purely techno'ogical aspects may be lost. In such cases the two deciding factors are the amount of money being invested in the technological aspects, and the need which the people feel. In the case of an expensive irrigation project, about which the people are highly enthusiastic and for which their cooperation is requisite, the extension work necessary to iron out local social and operational problems for the maximum success of the project should be considered a functional requirement. However, where considerable money is to be spent on a project in which the cooperation of the people is essential but for which they do not even feel a need, the project should be reexamined to see if it fits into the local sequence of development. If a project is very inexpensive but would require costly promotional work to secure the necessary cooperation from the people, the project should be reexamined to see if the ends really justify the means. It frequently happens, for example, that innovators like to initiate projects which require cooperative action from the people because they consider the encouraging of cooperation and community spirit as good and worthy projects in themselves.

The principal consideration in questions of economic feasibility is that of the needs felt by the people. When the people do not feel a need for the innovations proposed, promotional activity necessarily must be increased. Fortunately, actual situations are usually neither all negative nor all positive; differences exist in degree, and some persons within the same group or area are more receptive than others. In the case of soil conservation, for example, some farmers with better farm equipment, more capital, and a long-term outlook can be shown the benefits of soil conservation with relatively little difficulty, while neighbors with more modest resources continue to take a skeptical view. However, when a nucleus for change can be permanently established, even though the prospects of diffusing the change outside that nucleus in the immediate future are poor, the long-term gains may justify the modest beginning. Eventually others may come to recognize the benefits of an innovation at a time when conditions make it easier for them to adopt it or to appreciate its advantages. Thus, rather than spend time and money to promote the adoption of an innovation among people who cannot perceive its desirability, it may prove more expedient to establish it among strategically located nuclei or groups who can.

Another long-term alternative to costly promotional activity to establish a sense of need for new measures is that, already mentioned, of appealing to the younger members of the society through existing educational institutions. However, few well trained teachers and extension personnel may be available in some underdeveloped countries. Only highly productive nations can afford to maintain large numbers of competent teachers at salaries sufficiently attractive to make the long years of preparation (five years of university training in some states in the U.S.) worth the effort or the cost. Many persons overestimate the influence of formal education procedures by underestimating the technological and

economic conditions which make them possible. Formal educational procedures become strictly promotional if they require large numbers of foreign personnel on free loan or large numbers of local personnel trained and maintained at the expense of foreign subsidy.

The most unfavorable conditions for introducing innovations are frequently presented by such marginal peoples as Indian groups who more than anything else may simply wish to be left alone. The effort involved in introducing changes among them will be particularly great when their economy is still subsistence-oriented. Their conception of needs may be so different from that of the innovators that the two groups may find it very difficult to establish a common meeting ground for mutual understanding.

In general, the absorption of marginal peoples and cultures into the national sphere seems to follow most rapidly upon their further involvement in the national economy. In many cases it may prove more expedient to develop areas bordering on marginal groups in such a way as to draw them more closely into the national economy than to attempt to superimpose an extraneous need system directly upon them. While living in a Mayo Indian *comunidad* in southern Sonora, Mexico, during 1948, the writer had an opportunity to note the effects produced on an indigenous community by the rapid development of bordering areas. The development of irrigation and a more intensive machine agriculture to the north was creating more job opportunities and prosperity. Not only were members of the *comunidad* going north more frequently to work as seasonal agricultural labor, but they were returning with new ideas and wants. In fact, a growing nucleus was advocating division of the communal land as an incentive for wealthy farmers to extend irrigation into the area. Thus it was hoped that a more intensive and profitable type of agriculture would be possible for all.

A similar situation was encountered at the plantation of an American fruit company in a Latin American republic. The labor turnover the first year or two was extremely high, for individuals worked until pay day or worked only until they had earned enough to buy something they had specifically wanted. However, as new laborers kept replacing the old, some inevitably joined the nucleus of steady workers. These valued the permanent income, the clean and comfortable company housing, the superior company school for their children, and the company medical treatment. Within a few years the plantation had a permanent resident labor force. The company showed an interest in the upkeep and attractiveness of the workers' housing and helped them landscape gardens around their homes; thus a model community had been formed that was influencing the entire area. Workers in neighboring locally managed plantations were beginning to demand the same treatment, as they perceived a need for it themselves.

Not everyone can be induced to share the values and needs of the innovators at once but, by working first with those who already share them, the changes may eventually have far-reaching results without the unnecessary expense of promotional methods. In short, action programs among those who already feel a need for an innovation would seem to be more effective and less expensive in the long run than promotional programs for those who must first be inspired to feel the need.

One of the greatest weaknesses in most technical assistance programs is the failure to recognize the indispensable part played by research in increasing their economic feasibility. In this respect, government might conceivably learn from business. One writer on the subject of business management has said that any company that lacks an organized program of research will eventually find itself out of business. Two major forms of business research,[4] market and engineering studies, might be paralleled by technical assistance agencies to their advantage. Market studies could be designed to get all the pertinent facts about the people to be changed, including their needs and wants, their ability to absorb a given innovation, and their previous reactions to similar programs in the past. Engineering studies might include research in any number of technical fields, as well as comparative research in the methods and results of other agencies in other parts of the world, and the continued self-evaluation by the agency of its own programs to perfect the least expensive and most effective means of realizing its objectives. However, in government assistance programs, research can probably be realized best through an organization pattern that recognizes the difference between staff and line functions. Government reporting is prone to be a line function originating with operations personnel, who execute it with a bias toward justifying the further existence of their programs. By avoiding the disclosure of mistakes in specific operations, short-term benefits may accrue which prevent the self-evaluation and self-correction necessary to avoid those seriously damaging setbacks that result from the accumulation of hidden errors.

[4] Trundle, G. T., Jr., et al., Managerial Control of Business, New York: Wiley, 1948.

TEN PROBLEMS OF POINT FOUR*

JOHN M. HUNTER AND WILLIAM H. KNOWLES

"Economic development" is really "economic history," and when we consider it in this light, the enormity of the task which Point Four undertakes is apparent. It is not surprising that a number of important questions arise from it—some economic, some political; some with answers, some whose answers elude us. We want to suggest here some of the important questions which the Point Four program raises and to suggest the settings in which the problems exist.

(1) *Can sufficient economic progress be achieved in time to serve the political objectives of the program, viz. to prevent the underdeveloped countries from aligning themselves with the Communists?*

Economic development, however technically defined, is not a process which occurs rapidly. It is an evolutionary process; it is the story of economic history. One might well, for example, consider the United States as an underdeveloped area from 1650 or earlier to certainly as late as 1850 and possibly as late as 1914. At least two centuries were required to complete the transition in an environment generally considered favorable to economic development. Today, with the aid of the more advanced countries, the process may be subject to some speed-up; certainly economic development in *one* sense can be obtained under forced-draft circumstances as evidenced by growth in the Russian economy since 1928.

* Adapted and reprinted by permission from *Inter-American Economic affairs*, Vol. VII, No. 1, Summer 1953, pp. 64–81.

Perhaps by examining a couple of the important variables in the process of economic development we can obtain an insight into the interdependencies and complexities which make it such a time-consuming process. One of the reasons why economic development has not occurred more frequently and more rapidly is because purchasing power of the masses is so low.

Some remedies for low purchasing power suggest themselves : (1) better tools (more capital) to work with—but accumulating these requires a higher income so some of it may be saved, (2) a higher level of education—this is a social investment and requires years to accomplish startling results, (3) better transportation—also capital investment and sometimes difficult to get in *advance* of the development of markets, (4) better mass information media—we can hardly expect the very poor to buy newspapers which they can't read or to buy radios when they have never seen an electric light outlet. We do not intend to disparage the Point Four effort, but to point out the complexity and interdependencies of economic development. As we have seen it, it has been a dynamic, sometimes violent process of continued push and pull, and adjustment and readjustment among the many components of one economy. In short, economic development is economic history and is a *time consuming process.*

The real enemy in the underdeveloped countries is not the U.S.S.R. but the tyranny of poverty and the concommitant political and economic feudalism. Desperate measures are necessary to escape this tyranny, and awakening peoples all over the world are ready to take these measures. Essentially two choices confront them: (1) communism, which offers to take over and solve the problems of the masses for them —promises which do not have to be kept once the desired political control is obtained, (2) some form of political and economic democracy which offers to help the masses solve their own problems. Both are revolutionary.

This is one of the major problems of Point Four: can it produce really convincing results before the communists can make their promises convincing?

(2) *Point Four sometimes seems to work at cross purposes with two basic U.S. objectives—economy and building a strong Europe. How can these be reconciled?*

There can be no substantial reduction in the national budget or in taxes so long as the threat of world revolution exists. This does not mean endorsement of wasteful expenditures. The stakes are too high and the costs are too staggering to permit such a luxury. The real issue is whether expenditures for economic development in backward areas represents an extravagance taxpayers can ill afford to bear. Only direct military aid to those with troops ready and willing to fight communism is economical, it is argued. This is penny wise and pound foolish. Such a view looks at our emergency as purely a military problem, one of offsetting the military strength of Russia. When it is understood that world revolution against poverty is the basic emergency, then it becomes apparent that military right is not alone the cure. The ferment of the masses of the world cannot be crushed with military oppression, but it can be channelled into desirable objectives with more productivity, jobs, and dignity. Unless the United States assumes an aggressive role in economic development, the

impoverished and oppressed of the world will turn to the empty promises of communism.

To regain economic strength, England, France, Holland, and Belgium need the raw materials of their colonies at low prices. If the United States competes for the purchase of these raw materials with dollar exchange the "mother country" suffers. If the colonies are assisted in developing their own industries to process their raw materials, the "mother countries" both lose a source of materials and find new competition on world markets. England and France do not welcome our assistance to their colonies unless financial controls remain in Europe. On the other hand, the colonies demand greater independence, more home rule, a broadening of the democratic process, and the end of racial discrimination. In our own revolutionary tradition we sympathize with these aspirations. Positive assistance to turn the world revolution from communism is considered uncalled interference in "internal affairs" by the nations of Western Europe. While in reality the alternatives may not be so extreme nor the promises of success in either course assumed, this is a problem which both the United States and European nations must face. Genuine assistance to economically backward areas may result in the loss of cooperation of the Western European powers. At this point we must decide which policy is most likely to be to our advantage in averting a communist-dominated world revolution.

(3) *How can we reconcile our faith in free, private enterprise with a minimum of governmental interference and the fact that the first step in planning economic development is the establishment of a powerful governmental bureau in each of the underdeveloped countries to do the job?*

There is a difference between government *interference* with and government *service* to private enterprise. The American free enterprise tradition rightly opposes unnecessarily restrictive regulation and governmental favoritism to special interests. In many underdeveloped areas government interference does stifle enterprise and initiative, particularly among those in small businesses who are struggling to expand their operations. Removal of crippling regulation is important in helping underdeveloped areas solve their own problems.

Our free enterprise philosophy, however, has never opposed government assistance in making the free enterprise system function more effectively. Our government has served business by collecting, and distributing vital business statistics, by the services of the Bureau of Standards, Coast Guard, weather bureau, a multitude of research and information services, and providing a monetary system geared to the needs of modern business. Supplying roads, schools, and basic utilities, such as water, sewage, fire protection is a function of government often taken for granted. Regulation of monopoly, misleading advertising, and adulterated products is accepted as necessary to the survival of a free enterprise system. We have not hesitated to subsidize those industries deemed necessary to economic welfare, but which could not survive without assistance. There is no contradiction between free enterprise, capitalism and a government program to create an environment favorable to business.

"Operation boot strap" in many backward areas involves expanded governmental activities to provide conditions which will stimulate private activity. Such a program frequently includes such things as agricultural research, low-cost, long-term loans, market information, an efficient network of roads, good water supply, improved port facilities, and expanded trade school training. The important factor is not the expansion of government bureaus but whether the bureaucracy serves and stimulates private initiative or whether it acts in a condescending and benevolent fashion which creates further dependence upon government action. The blight of many backward areas is that people look to their governments for all assistance and blame their government for all their troubles. Such an attitude is often fostered in colonial areas by a foreign trained civil service which treats the public as wayward little children.

(4) *If we must deal with existing governments, how can we get them to adopt reforms necessary for economic development? Often the existing governments are controlled by the wealthy landowners who strongly resist any land reform, for example, which experts insist is a necessary part of development.*

Many underdeveloped areas are ruled by an aristocracy of landlords and military leaders. Such governments are hardly interested in reforms which would promote democracy and free enterprise capitalism. Here lies a paradox. If we extend aid to such countries with no strings attached, the rich only become richer, basic economic problems remain unsolved, and the United States is regarded as a fool by reactionaries and as an "instrument of fascistic oppression" by radicals. On the other hand, if we demand internal reform, the cry of "capitalistic imperialism" is heard from all sides. Our tendency has been to avoid being branded as imperialists, and to help anyone who is anti-communist. In so doing we fail to solve one of the basic problems of underdeveloped areas, and find ourselves allied with ruling cliques that may prove to be a serious liability to us.

Such a policy is not only self-defeating, but at variance with our revolutionary tradition. The restless masses of the world who clamor for land reform, equality of opportunity, free education, end of dominant military cliques, and greater democracy are fighting for things we have already fought for and won. Unless helped, they will be duped into communism by default. First, we must convince existing governments that reform is necessary for their own survival. We must understand and they must understand that we can not support corrupt and decadent governments simply because they are *currently* against communism. At the risk of being denounced as imperialists, we must insist upon those reforms which experts advise as necessary to development.

A word of caution is needed, however. There are some reforms which the people want, but which their governments oppose for selfish reasons. Other reforms are necessary to development, but are not in harmony with existing values and cultural patterns of the people. Finally, there is danger of imposing the "American way of life" upon foreign cultures whether or not it contains values necessary to economic development. Regarding the first, let us be revolutionaries. In the second case, education to the desirability of change is necessary. In the last instance, let us not be chauvinists.

(5) *Will Malthusian Law of population thwart economic progress in underdeveloped areas?*

Malthus' Law states that population tends to outrun food supply, keeping the standard of living for the mass of people at a subsistence level. Every advance in productivity is cancelled by an increase in population especially through lower infant mortality and infanticide rates and through increase in life span. This grim fact is the number one problem in the development of economically backward areas. Unless this problem is solved there is little point in attempting to solve the other problems. Population pressure has caused many experts to give up in despair, declaring the whole problem of development of backward areas to be doomed from the start.

(6) *How can the dichotomy of interests between the industrial nations and the underdeveloped nations be resolved?*

The underdeveloped countries of the world are primarily producers of certain agricultural products for domestic consumption and one or a few semiprocessed or raw materials for export. Most of their imports have traditionally been manufactured goods from the industrial nations. The fortunes of the raw material producers have been especially poor in the last two decades. Prices received for raw materials, habitually fluctuate more than prices of industrial goods, and consequently during the 'thirties, prices paid for their exports fell a great deal more than prices they paid for imports. Tariffs were raised against their exports as industrial nations sought to provide employment by producing everything possible at home. Events of the 'forties were by no means compensating for the suffering of the 'thirties. Raw material prices went up, and exports increased, but imports were not available; so the underdeveloped countries suffered a continued industrial goods shortage accompanied by severe inflations. Many of them accumulated substantial dollar and sterling balances only to see much of their dollar holdings dissipated in the American inflation after 1946 when exportable goods were just beginning to become available and to have their sterling balances either blocked or at least not convertible into more useful currencies. It is no small wonder that an important motive of the underdeveloped countries is to rid themselves of such a high degree of dependence on the state of foreign markets for the wherewithal to secure industrial goods. In short, they want to diversify their economies or to despecialize.

When one introduces the instability of the real world of international trade where some nations are strong, others weak, some poor, some producers of raw materials and some of industrial and where the pertinent variables behave differently in different countries, one may well reach the conclusion that the benefits of specialization are more than offset by the disadvantages of interdependence. The difficulty here is that neither the gains or disadvantages are measurable; so, as yet at least, it is impossible to compute the costs of a despecialization policy. In short, the underdeveloped countries are buying their pig in a poke.

One of the purposes of Point Four is to increase the raw materials output of the underdeveloped countries while they are explicitly trying to reduce their dependence on the same. There may be no real dichotomy of interest here because it may be possible for them to expand raw material output and at the same time expand output in other sectors of their economies even more so that both their objectives and ours will simultaneously be satisfied. But the problem is an important one and may require considerable astuteness in handling when particular cases arise.

(7) *How can the new American trade philosophy be reconciled with those desired by, and perhaps necessary for, the underdeveloped countries?*

United States commercial policy in the first third of this century was largely the result of unenlightened unilateral interest. It consisted primarily of ever-increasing tariffs on foreign goods with little justifiable logic. Emotionalism and the particular interests of pressure groups were largely responsible. But the beginnings of a lesson were apparent in the decade of the 'twenties. We had at least become a creditor nation and became concerned with how other peoples were going to be able to pay their debts to us and at the same time be able to buy our exports. This lesson was not translated into action due to violent interruption of events in 1929 and 1930. A part of our reaction to this catastrophe was the highest tariff ever—the Tariff Act of 1930 (Smoot-Hawley).

Throughout the world, a wave of trade restrictions were instituted—partly in retaliation and partly just reaction to the tenor of the times. Exchange controls, import quotas, expropriation of foreign investments, administrative impediments to international trade, commodity control schemes, bilateral trade agreements, and other forms of trade restriction and discrimination became the rule rather than the exception to world trade patterns.

By 1934 we were well into the socio-economic experimentation of the New Deal. We were no longer vitally concerned with how foreigners were going to pay their debts—the level of employment and the standard of living became of primary preoccupation. Our experience with the Smoot-Hawley Tariff seemed to indicate that high tariffs might not really do much to improve either. Restricting imports (dollar earnings of foreigners) reduced employment in industries with important export components and at the same time resulted in higher prices for the things we consumed which were either imported or produced behind the iron curtain of tariff protection. In short, we began to realize that our commercial policies had produced painful effects abroad which ultimately rebounded as undesirable effects in the United States economy. As we became more aware of the significance of our export markets, we also became aware of the necessity to buy things abroad in order for foreigners to be able to buy from us.

The Reciprocal Trade Agreements program was passed in 1934 in an effort to undo some of the harm done by the Act of 1930. The Agreements program has been continuously renewed and even liberalized in certain respects since its original adoption. The philosophy responsible for the Trade Agreements Program resulted in a much broader attack on the problems during World War II and in the years thereafter. Not only did we advocate lower tariffs but we advocated freer, multilateral trade throughout the world with such restrictions as exchange controls, quantitative trade controls, etc. being eliminated. Essentially, we were proposing that the world adopt, with us, a system of modified free trade. We had some degree of success in selling this objective as can be seen by examining terms of the Bretton Woods Agreement, the Anglo-American Loan Agreement, the Charter of the International Trade Organization (which was never ratified) and the General Agreement on Tariffs and Trade. That these objectives have not been achieved is well known.

But freer trade, fewer restrictions, lower tariffs are not likely to be useful to small, underdeveloped countries who find their firms small, inefficient, with poorly trained personnel and unpracticed labor having to compete with large, well-established firms of the industrial giants. These infant industries justifiably require protection, and it is almost a certainty that it will be provided by the countries concerned.

Protection has been an important aspect of economic development in the past —examine our own use of it in the nineteenth century—and it will be so in the future.

(8) *Can private investment of sufficient quantity be induced to flow to the underdeveloped countries?*

Foreign investment is generally agreed to be a requisite of rapid economic development for the countries under consideration. It has been estimated that the underdeveloped countries will require $10 billion annually to raise living standards two per cent per year. This very substantial amount cannot likely be made available from public sources; Point Four explicitly places great reliance on the flow of foreign private investment.

The flow of private foreign capital has been small since 1930 because general business conditions were poor and because of fundamental differences in the thinking of investors and recipient nations. We may or may not be able to do something about providing fairly continuous, generally good business conditions, but the schism between the investor and recipient nations is an interesting and perplexing problem.

Essentially, underdeveloped countries have done a good deal to discourage the investment they need so badly. Expropriations, discriminatory wage and labor legislation, refusals of exchange permits (or at penalty rates) for repatriation of earnings or profits, discriminatory taxation, requirements for certain percentages of local capital participation, etc. have all increased risks for the investor and made him unwilling to risk foreign investments. These restrictions have arisen partly for justifiable reasons and partly because foreign investment provides a convenient whipping boy in times of political and economic crisis. Legitimate charges against foreign capital include: improper political meddling, imbalance in the development of economies with overemphasis on the export industries, exploitation of labor and resources without proper benefits accruing to the countries, complete subjection of the interests of the countries to those of the investors.

On the other hand, private investors have reacted to the actions of the underdeveloped countries by abstaining in large numbers. Just recently, for example, a proposal affirming the right of any country to nationalize its resources without obligation to compensate private foreign investors was approved 36–4 in the United Nations General Assembly. Investors are justifiably reluctant to invest in the face of such measures and other threatening legislation.

The problem is simply put: underdeveloped countries need capital; capital will not flow on terms now acceptable to underdeveloped countries; underdeveloped countries will not now accept foreign capital on its own terms. Some compromise is desirable and necessary. But this compromise is one which cannot be made rapidly nor can it rest solely on a legal basis. Essentially, good faith and good will must overcome mutual suspicions, and this is not an easy nor quick process.

(9) *Even if substantial amounts of private foreign investment do become available, it is not likely that it will all be channelled into the proper fields. Particularly, where will the foreign capital necessary for railroads, electric power, highway transportation, and irrigation come from?*

In general, private foreign investment may be expected to shy away from participation in what is loosely called "public utilities" for two reasons. First, these developments usually require a very heavy initial investment which can be recovered only over a very long period of time. The additional risk of foreign investment makes projects of this type fairly unattractive to private firms. Second, because of their nature, these enterprises tend to be monopolistic and are subjected to rather strict governmental controls even in the relatively free enterprise economies. Or they are simply publically owned activities. The almost certain (and likely unfriendly) governmental regulation concomitant with this type of investment is a major deterent factor in this investment area.

It seems likely that most of the foreign exchange necessary for these projects will have to come from intergovernmental loans or grants. Some may object to these interferences with free enterprise and point out that utilities were developed privately (but not without foreign investment) in the United States. This is true enough, but the facts are that we now live in a world

claiming to have a social conscience which will not permit the excesses, gouging, and graft that accompanied our own development.

(10) *Where will the domestic funds come from to finance economic development?*

The process of economic development involves much more than the making available of foreign exchange and "know how" to underdeveloped countries. Most of the expenditures in the process will be in domestic currencies, and most of the resources poured into the effort will be domestic resources. Some means of financing these expenditures and of securing the use of domestic resources must be found.

Essentially there are three possible sources of funds available: savings, taxes, printing press or bank created money. Savings are not apt to contribute substantial amounts to the requisite total because the people are poor and are not able to save much. Those who can save are often reluctant to invest in new and risky ventures. More often they buy land, short term mortgages, or invest in foreign securities. Existing tax structures cannot be expected to contribute great amounts either because, as they are now organized, they extract about all that can be expected. If tax structures could be revised so as to collect taxes from those who control the governments—the aristocracy in these semi-feudal societies—then a great deal more revenue could undoubtedly be attained. This stratum can hardly be expected, however, to submit voluntarily to burdensome taxation. The use of printing presses or the banking system to create money for financing expenditures is most likely to find widespread use. This is an inflationary but rather traditional means.

The use of domestic resources in large scale development projects is also apt to be inflationary. As workers are taken out of the fields and put to work building highways, schools, dams, factories, the production of consumer goods may decline without any decrease in the need for them. In fact, it is even likely that even more money than before will be competing for the reduced number of goods. This, too,

will add to inflationary pressures. Such a situation suggests that a possible solution lies in concentrating first on increasing productivity in existing activities—so that resources can eventually be released without reducing the level of existing output.

CULTURAL BARRIERS TO POINT FOUR*

CHESTER L. HUNT

THIS article is written with all the fear which every heretic must feel when he goes against his ancient vows, for it is an attack on a rather deep-seated tendency of my chosen field, sociology. This field covers so considerable an area that a sociologist has been defined by more restricted academics as "a man who has an alibi for being any place at any time." The apparent difficulty of narrow definition is due to the fact that our interest, together with that of the cultural anthropologist, is in the varied patterns of group organization— a classification which brings all forms of human association within our field of study.

Early in the history of the discipline, we discovered that much of the world's friction was due to a failure to understand that different social institutions may bring people to common human goals. In the course of this discovery, we became advocates of the right of human groups to follow their own patterns, even when these patterns were strikingly different from those of Main Street, U.S.A. The heresy

* Adapted and reprinted by permission from *The Antioch Review*, Yellow Springs, Ohio, Vol. 14, Summer 1954, pp. 159–167.

which prompts this article is a feeling that our emphasis on cultural freedom and the inherent value of the system by which any group organizes its social life has been overdone. To the extent that the charge is justified, it illustrates the danger that the very act of promoting a new concept usually tempts the faithful to push the new insight beyond the limits of its legitimate application.

The basis for this emphasis on social self-determination was a growing appreciation of the value of supposedly "backward" cultures. We learned that the Samoans, at least before the United States Navy came in, did not have adolescent problems and that the Hopi Indians had a social integration superior to that of most modernized social groups. Our message was that every culture must be judged by its own standards and that no bigoted westeners were entitled to offer arbitrary institutional panaceas to the rest of the world. It now seems that sociology has been hoist by its own petard or perhaps I should say, atrophied by its own relativity. Its message has been exaggerated and oversimplified so that it stands in danger of being more of a hindrance to social advance than a tool to attain human understanding. The specific occasion for these laments is the impact of the notion of cultural freedom on the foreign aid program.

Recently, in a cottage on the campus of the University of the Philippines, I read Gardner Murphy's *In the Minds of Men.* His report on the results of the UNESCO Commission which analyzed Indian social tensions ends with a word about the receptivity of India to American help. India, it seems, wants to improve her standard of living and desires technical assistance and foreign capital, but is in no mood to accept uncritically the whole pattern of western culture. Rather than wholesale adaptation of western customs, the Indians desire to pick and choose the cultural elements they will accept. Industrial techniques and public health practices may be valid, but occidental patterns of family life, political institutions, religious movements, and business entrepreneurship may be disregarded as either harmful or irrelevant to the aims of a modern oriental state.

The mixed reactions of the Indians strike a note familiar in many quarters. Even the Philippines, an area more subject to American influence than any other spot in Asia, shows some of the same symptoms. Orators in the Islands mingle quotations from the Gettysburg Address with admonitions against "slavish imitations" of western culture, and politicians speaking in English proclaim the necessity of developing an indigenous national language. The case of language is interesting here, as English has been the language in the schools since the turn of the century and has become the *lingua franca* in a country in which no single local dialect is spoken by a majority of the inhabitants. English became the vehicle through which American culture was spread throughout the educated citizenry, but this does not guarantee its future place in Filipino life. Not only has nationalistic enthusiasm led

to making the Manila language (Tagalog) a required subject in schools throughout the country, but recent legislation also makes mandatory the teaching of Spanish, which, according to the last census, is spoken by less than two per cent of the population. Judging from the treatment of language, one of the first fruits of independence was an effort to minimize American influence in a school system which that influence had brought into being.

India and the Philippines are by no means unique in this respect and the same effort to achieve improved economic standards while rejecting cultural changes associated with industrial development is prevalent throughout the world even including western Europe. Nor is it a case of Americans pushing their institutions against the opposition of a reluctant world, for often Americans abroad are even more solicitous about the local culture than the indigenous population.

All Americans are haunted by the mistakes of those legendary missionaries who are accused of exposing the Polynesians to pneumonia by persuading them to wear Mother Hubbards. Today's missionaries are schooled in anthropology as well as the Scriptures, and other emissaries such as teachers, travelers, businessmen, diplomats and Army officers are all impregnated with the idea that indigenous culture has inherent value which keeps it immune from all criticism. It is a peculiar reversal of values, for Americans have learned to look at their own customs with the coldly analytical eye of the Kinsey report which implies that no traditions are sacred and that every practice must be tested by its current utility.

In looking at America's international efforts, the first thing apparent is the strict demarcation between production techniques and other aspects of the American social pattern. Here, the assumption seems to be that we can export the tools and know-how of mass production, while leaving other aspects of the local culture relatively unchanged. The work of the cultural anthropologists has been so widely disseminated that neither Americans nor others any longer have the notion that the entire universe should be remade in the American pattern. This attitude has prevented the growth of an American imperialism and made visiting experts somewhat more respectful of the strange customs of other countries. Whether it is actually a realistic approach to economic change is another question.

Perhaps we ought to get down to specifics and mention the kind of cultural traits that seem to be involved. One which is often puzzling to Americans is the definition of "materialism." Cultures in which the rich pay few taxes, escape major charitable contributions and live on a sumptuous scale while the bulk of the populace are malnourished, can be classified as "spiritual" in their orientation. Charitable organization, decent wages, public health facilities, businessmen concerned about the living standards of their employees—all this adds up to "materialism." Evidently, the notion that the spiritual has a material aspect is a western heresy.

One part of society which is assumed to be immune from change is the family. In most of the world today, the individual is still submerged in a strong family group which chooses his mate, absorbs his money and makes the major decisions of life on a basis of family rather than individual needs. Such a family usually includes three generations and several households with decisions made on an authoritarian basis by the oldest active family members. It would appear to be more than coincidental that countries with this family system complain of lack of individual initiative and pioneering spirit and of nepotism in both business and government.

While treading on sacred ground, it might be just as well to consider the case of religious institutions. Religion is a touchy subject on which men hold strong feelings and since there is undoubtedly a measure of truth in all religious beliefs, the wise man lets them alone and goes about his business. At any rate, there is no relation between the approach to whatever divine powers there be and the rate of steel production—or is there? The experience of western Europe which saw the Industrial Revolution and modern capitalism develop most rapidly in areas populated by Calvinists might at least raise a question in this regard. Apparently, in this area, religious beliefs which stressed thrift, hard work, simplicity, individual moral responsibility and the achieving of earthly goals walked hand in hand with the accumulation of capital and the development of industry.

Religion in the underdeveloped countries is far removed from any stress on the puritan virtues. The tradition-bound rigidity of Islam, the otherworldly emphasis of Buddhism, the asceticism of Hinduism and the fiesta-laden Catholicism of countries with a Spanish tradition may embody important teachings, but their emphasis is not calculated to produce industrious workers, thrifty capitalists or daring promoters. Since all religious groups claim that religion is the foundation of conduct, one might well raise the question as to how the traits of character essential to a business society may be developed when they are not supported by the dominant religious movements.

Even more exempt from scrutiny than the churches are the institutions of government. In the Wilsonian era, the slogan to make the world safe for democracy seemed both feasible and desirable. Now we have learned the difficulties of exporting our earlier brand of democracy and seem to be concentrating on spreading the concept of the welfare state. The aim is to organize governments which will guarantee the good life and thus offset promises of a communist utopia. The weakness of this procedure is that government cannot distribute the products of industry unless industry has first developed to a point where there are products to distribute. The premature welfare state is driven to inflation by popular pressure for higher living standards and thereby hopelessly retards the essential process of capital formation. A government whose policies favor private enterprise may be difficult to secure, but if industrialization is desired, the choice lies between facilitating the work of private capital or regimenting the country's efforts through a totalitarian regime.

The peoples who wish to avail themselves of the advantages of a higher output of goods while avoiding drastic changes in their life patterns protest that they are trying to avail themselves of the benefits of industrialism while avoiding its evils. Another interpretation is that made by several observers to the effect that underdeveloped countries wish to acquire the end results of economic development while resisting the attitudes which make such development possible.

Cultural relativism has been taken to mean that social traits have to be judged in their total context and that what would be abnormal behavior on Park Avenue might be a perfectly logical type of conduct in Uganda. The difficulty with the application of this concept is the tendency to forget that what makes variation permissible is not the geographical locale or even past cultural history, but the way the specific practice fits into the total system. The fact that the rule of the tribal chief may be hallowed by tradition does not mean that it will be an adequate government mechanism when the way of livelihood changes from hunting to labor in a factory.

While there have been occasional cases in which representatives of western powers ruthlessly ignored the value of local tradition in a blind devotion to their own prejudices, this is not now a major evil. Rather, westerners have encouraged other peoples to minimize the scope of adjustment to a new technological era and to cling to practices which have outlived their usefulness. In the name of cultural freedom, we have ignored the fact that society is a series of interrelated factors, none of which can be changed without alteration in the others.

Most of the maladjustment which has accompanied industrialization has come not from too much tampering with indigenous institutions, but from a reluctance by all concerned to face up to necessary changes. The results are the kind of difficulties that come from trying to teach sanitation to men who do not accept the germ theory of disease, or denouncing dictatorship to those who have never known democratic participation in any area of life.

The consequence is that underdeveloped countries do not seem to generate their own motive power in a way satisfactory either to themselves or the rest of the world. Foreign aid which is supposed to prime the pump of economic development becomes merely a temporary palliative with little permanent effect.

The picture is usually one of a government in which graft is endemic at the bottom and a major malady at the top. In the development of industry, local capitalists decline to take the risks of business enterprise and instead invest their savings in land, or, where possible, in the securities of more fully industrialized countries. Meantime, foreign investors are harried by exchange restrictions, nationalistic requirements on employment of natives and the constant threat of outright confiscation. Labor, at the same time, is irregular and inefficient. Education, all too often, simply drains the best manpower away from agriculture and industry into governmental and professional positions. Finally, the entire populace has been swayed by a Hollywood description of higher living standards and demands to see these standards fulfilled without further waiting.

This failure of business enterprise to become accepted by indigenous groups is reflected in the attitude of foreign capital. The reports of the United States Department of Commerce indicate that petroleum development led the field in foreign investment last year. The petroleum industry is one well adapted to development as a type of cultural island in a country which, as a whole, is not friendly to business enterprise. The industry is developed by foreign engineers who sell most of the product outside the country. Royalties from oil enrich the national coffers, but the industry itself is largely independent of the local economy.

By contrast, heavy industry which requires a long term commitment and an intimate adjustment to the country's economic life, does not attract either local or foreign capital. Most of this type of investment has come from direct governmental action. Since the governments are inexperienced and short of both capital and skilled personnel, the result is likely to be a field day for corruption and inefficiency with limited constructive achievements.

Frequently, education is offered as a cure-all for ills blocking economic progress. Indeed, the formal ideal of education has had considerable acceptance and both by student exchange and local instruction, the percentage of the world's population in school is rapidly growing at all levels of the scholastic ladder. The outcome, however, is not altogether what may be desired. Schooling tends to be formal, verbal and academic with the emphasis unduly on professional training. Its goal is likely to

be considered the acquisition of techniques rather than of the spirit which produced the techniques. Students learn carefully the precepts of their instructors without modifying their knowledge to meet changing local conditions. Verbal instruction is accepted, but libraries and laboratories are regarded as luxuries and research in the physical, biological or social sciences simply fails to develop. The Philippines might be cited as a prime example of this difficulty, with the second highest proportion of college students in the world, the greatest number of lawyers of any country in the Pacific area and the lowest rice production in the Orient. The situation is much the same, however, in other countries in which education has been allowed to reflect cultural stereotypes rather than national needs.

The moral to all this is that the concept of cultural relativism includes the idea that the total culture should be consonant with the type of economic structure the society seeks to develop. This does not mean that American institutions must be exact blueprints for the rest of the world, but it does imply that if an agricultural nation is to be industrialized, the entire culture will be forced to change in a direction in harmony with the new economic ethos. It demands the development of both social and personal attitudes able to cope with the opportunities and problems of mass production. This, in turn, implies that government, education, religion and family structure will encourage a social milieu favorable to industrial development. Such a milieu should promote the accumulation of capital, the development of a labor force able to work with both skill and diligence and the stimulation of a group of entrepreneurs who will become aggressive promoters of business enterprise.

In this setting, the social scientist will have an important place, but his task will shift from the simple effort to understand local institutions to the analysis of ways and means by which they become adapted to the needs of the new industrialism. His job will be to disabuse the naïvete which assumes that one element of society may be subjected to major change while leaving everything else practically static. In brief, he will seek to prepare both countries which give aid and those on the receiving end for the social implications of that new economic order which they seek to attain. The social scientist may be able to indicate methods by which the violence of change can be reduced, but it is too much to expect easy acceptance by all concerned.

This type of cultural analysis is much less pleasant than that which simply describes a society in terms of its own values and is thus able to demonstrate that industrially undeveloped countries have often worked out a beautiful adaptation to the environment of a subsistence-handicraft type of economy. A more critical approach will probably produce irritation, defensiveness and cries of cultural imperialism. It may even reawaken some of the nineteenth-century bigotry associated with the white man's burden complex. Such effects are not pleasant to contemplate, but they are not inevitable and, at their worst, are less painful than the outcome of easy acceptance of all elements of the indigenous society. Intelligent adaptation of the total society to a new economy is a difficult task, but it promises better results than casually attempting to impose modern industrialism on cultures which are basically feudal in character.

One of the early exponents of respect for cultural differences was the late William Graham Sumner who declared that the mores (accepted moral standards) of a society could vary in a fashion that would make any kind of conduct either right or wrong, including murder, slavery and polygamy. This did not mean that he viewed life as a cultural chaos, for he also observed that there was a strain toward consistency within the mores. The good Dr. Sumner was so convinced of this latter idea that he felt that deliberate attempts to modify the patterns of a society would fail because of an inability to incorporate such reforms in the total framework. His complete pessimism was probably overdone, but his analysis of the essential unity of culture might well be kept in mind by our current exporters of industrial technology.

TECHNICAL ASSISTANCE FOR ECONOMIC DEVELOPMENT*

DAVID OWEN

THE United Nations set out to fulfill the mandate in its Charter in a world that was

* Adapted and reprinted by permission from the *Journal of International Affairs*, Vol. IX, No. 2, 1955, pp. 39–49.

wide-awake. The millions of men and women in economically less-developed countries were no longer apathetically resigned to poverty, disease and illiteracy; they were actively seeking a better way of life. Many governments had already made a start on plans for self-development; some had made considerable progress, but nearly all were restricted in their planning by lack of capital. The problem went far beyond that, however, for investment capital, after all, could not work wonders in economic development. It could certainly buy or build factories, manufacture machinery and install it in those factories—but who was to run the factories and tend the machinery? And if capital were used to bring in foreign technicians to do those tasks, what lasting use would it be to the country? The real asset of all these countries was still the potential of their citizens; and the United Nations, which could not dispense large sums of money, was confronted by the vitally important task of realizing this potential.

FOUNDATION FOR A NEW PROGRAM

The method by which the UN undertook this task of mobilizing latent resources was a program of work that has come to be called "Technical Assistance." In simple terms, the United Nations set out to help in transferring skills from people to people and from area to area. It did this in many ways: by sending out missions of experts to give technical advice and services to underdeveloped countries, by awarding fellowships to people from those countries to study abroad, and by organizing training centers and seminars for the exchange of information in vital fields.

The concept of technical assistance did not, of course, originate with the United Nations. It had been practiced on a small scale during much of the twentieth century, both by individual governments and by international agencies. Among the latter was the International Labor Organization. After 1945, other "specialized agencies" were established as part of the system of international organizations working with the newly-created United Nations. Among them, the World Health Organization, the Food and Agriculture Organization, and UNESCO, each gave technical assistance on a limited scale. From 1947 on, the United Nations itself, through its economic and social departments, began to supply technical services that did not fall within the scope of any existing specialized agency. Resolutions passed in 1946 and 1948 by the General Assembly set aside a small portion of the UN's yearly budget so that experts might be sent out and fellowships awarded—first in social welfare, then public administration, and finally in economic development, but the amounts allotted totaled less than $2,000,000 per year.

The decision of the United States in January, 1949 to expand its own technical assistance services into the Point Four Program, and United States action in the UN Economic and Social Council, helped to give positive expression to the belief, previously held by many delegates, that the time had come for the United Nations and its specialized agencies to expand and integrate their technical assistance facilities if they were to carry out fully the mandate of the Charter. By July, 1949 the Economic and Social Council and the General Assembly had worked out and approved the framework of the Expanded Technical Assistance Program, which would make available to underdeveloped countries, at their request, a wide range of technical advice, guidance, and training facilities.

The Expanded Program began in the summer of 1950. It called on the technical resources of seven specialized agencies[1] as well as those of the UN. The International

---

[1] The International Telecommunications Union and the World Meteorological Organization did not begin to operate under the Program until the beginning of 1952.

Labor Organization, the Food and Agriculture Organization, UNESCO, the International Civil Aviation Organization, the World Health Organization, the International Telecommunications Union, and the World Meteorological Organization became participants in the Program, while the United Nations created a Technical Assistance Administration in its Secretariat to coordinate technical assistance services. These eight "participating organizations" covered between them nearly every aspect of economic or social development. Their work was coordinated by a Technical Assistance Board, consisting of the representatives of each of the above-mentioned organizations and an Executive Chairman.

RICE AND STEEL

In practice, the machinery set up was designed to find the best technical skills available and to place them where they were needed. Typically, a project involving the services of an expert or experts would begin with a specific request from a less-developed country, since assistance is given only in answer to requests. Egypt, to take an example, drafted a request two years ago for a rice cultivation expert. The problem was to find a variety of rice that would reach maturity in a short enough time to be adaptable to the climatic and soil conditions in Egypt, and a variety that would thrive without too much water. If this could be done, the country would be able to meet the domestic demand for rice, which had hitherto been largely imported, and might eventually be able to offer rice for export. An important consideration was the fact that Egyptian farmers could earn badly-needed extra income if they could rotate a rapidly-maturing rice crop with their other crops.

Because the request concerned agriculture, it was referred to the participating organization concerned—the Food and Agriculture Organization—which undertook to find a suitably qualified expert in rice-breeding. An expert from Formosa was sent to Egypt, where he began a series of experiments crossing local and imported varieties of rice. When the experiments produced a rice breed which seemed to be suitable, the expert and his Egyptian colleagues in the Plant-Breeding Section of the Ministry of Agriculture started planting the seed in a test area. We have only recently received a report on the success of this test planting, which will now be tried more extensively throughout the country. But the process of sharing skills will not be confined to Egypt. The Government of Iraq has expressed an interest in the results obtained, and the expert has visited that country for consultations on rice-planting problems. Moreover, our tentative plans provide for a number of Iraqi plant specialists to visit Egypt under Expanded Program fellowships; these specialists will then be able to study the progress made at first hand.

The award of fellowships is made, again upon request, to candidates who have some experience in their fields, but who would benefit from further training in up-to-date techniques in more advanced countries. These grants, if wisely applied, can be of great value to the economy of a country, or group of countries, as in the following instance.

Plans were drawn up in 1951 to build a steel mill at Paz del Río, Colombia—the first mill in a country that had hitherto imported all its steel. The plant was to have a potential capacity of 200,000 tons a year, but Colombia was confronted with the problem of training local engineers, foremen and steel workers, since none were available. As a start toward building up the nucleus of such a staff, the Government of Colombia asked for Program aid and the request was passed to the International Labor Organization. Colombia asked the ILO to grant fellowships to her technicians in two stages. In the first stage, fellowships were awarded to ten Colombian trainees to work at the Huachipato steel mill in Chile to learn production techniques. They left for Chile in December, 1953 and returned home six months later. The Paz del Río mill was inaugurated in October, 1954 with these men applying their new skills as foremen and workers in various sections, while at the same time training other men in these techniques. In the second stage, four engineers were chosen by the Government and the ILO early in 1954 to go to France and Luxembourg (the steel production methods used in Paz del Río are modeled on the French system), to learn modern techniques. Having recently returned to Colombia, they are now working with the French engineers who are helping to run Paz del Río. Eventually Colombia will be self-sufficient in steel engineers, as well as in steel foremen and workers.

The implications of this project may not end here, however, as Venezuela in turn starts its first production of steel. The ILO, at the request of Venezuela, is exploring the possibilities of placing Venezuelan trainees in the Paz del Río mills so that they may receive the practical training for operating a newly-established steel mill.

FUNDS FOR HUMAN SKILLS

Since the Expanded Technical Assistance Program was initiated almost five years ago, more than 3,000 such projects have been undertaken, more than 4,000 experts have been recruited, and 4,500 fellowships awarded. In addition, we have organized numerous training centers and seminars to allow specialists of many countries to exchange technical information in vital fields. Some 100 countries

and territories have benefited from United Nations Technical Assistance to date.

To finance this widespread operation, a special conference is called every year, and governments are invited to contribute to the Technical Assistance Account. The funds pledged at this conference are allocated each year among the participating organizations, each receiving a share corresponding to the volume of projects it expects to undertake during the year. Governments invited to the conference may be members of the UN or one of its agencies, and individual annual contributions by governments have ranged from $13,861,000 from the United States (for 1954), to token pledges of $2,000 from the Vatican and the equivalent of $4,000 from Libya. In 1953, we received our first pledge from the Soviet Union, in the equivalent of $1,000,000, followed by pledges from Poland, Czechoslovakia, Byelorussia and the Ukraine. A total of 54 governments, representing developed and underdeveloped nations, pledged $20 million for the first year of operations, and the amount has increased at subsequent conferences until 74 governments pledged a total of over $25 million to carry out the 1954 Program.

The Program's yearly budget is, of course, modest if compared with the resources of other more heavily endowed technical assistance programs. But in spending those funds, we have concentrated on the provision of human skills, allowing only a minimum expenditure for equipment—and then only for demonstration purposes in support of projects. We have, in this way, been able to create an impact far out of proportion to the original investment. The Program has been designed from the beginning to offset the lack of capital in underdeveloped countries by helping governments to use existing resources to greater advantage, conserving capital where its use is not fully justified and making any new capital more effective. A Burmese railway official, for example, who had studied in Britain under a Technical Assistance fellowship, saved his Government a great deal of money by showing that the proposed mechanization of an important freight yard near Rangoon would not be necessary; much simpler and less costly methods which he had learned in Britain could be applied—and capital conserved for use in other fields. In Israel, a soil scientist with the aid of a bulldozer has been able to dam and fill ancient water cisterns originally dug as long ago as 200 B.C. They had been dug to conserve surface water because ground water is either saline or too far down, so that wells are not possible. This project has rediscovered and developed lost ancient technical knowledge uniquely suited to the requirements of the country, and provides "pinch hit" irrigation with minimal capital expenditure.

Examples of how the program is able to help countries make the best use of foreign capital are to be found in both India and Pakistan. Both countries have purchased agricultural machinery with loans from the International Bank for Reconstruction and Development. The machinery, however, is of little use without proper operation, or proper facilities for repair and maintenance. In both these countries, experts assigned under the Expanded Program are advising the Government and helping to train local personnel in the operation, repair and maintenance of its machinery. Ethiopia has obtained a loan from the Bank for the purchase of telecommunications equipment, and UN experts are assisting the Government to establish an institute which will train personnel to operate it. In Indonesia, an expert has advised on the use of equipment for the mechanical extraction of logs, which the Government secured through a loan from the Export-Import Bank.

MANY PROGRAMS— ONE GOAL

Budget limitations have, of course, reduced the possible scope of the program. UN and agency experts can plan and organize hospitals but cannot build them; they can teach people how to run an airport but cannot actually equip and operate it; they can plan roads but cannot build them. Governments are aware that a request for aid does not mean a "handout." On the contrary, they will incur an obligation to provide materials, to make available counterpart personnel so that someone will carry on when the experts leave, and to pay various local costs connected with each project. Indeed, expenditures by governments for projects on which UN personnel have been engaged have far outweighed our own costs. This, then, is a true self-help program, for it can only be applied to supplement the efforts made by underdeveloped countries on their own behalf.

To assure that available resources are used to the fullest, the Program has been directed, with growing success, toward cooperation with other technical assistance programs in the field. A recent report from our representative in Pakistan illustrates what can be done to bring together many different sources of assistance.

In East Pakistan, a vast project to irrigate one-quarter million acres of land is being financed and carried out by the Pakistani Government. Our experts, sent by the Food and Agriculture Organization, are supervising actual field operations. Canada contributed about one million dollars during 1954 to build the necessary power station, and the United

States Point Four Program will ultimately spend some $2,000,000 to supply the large pumps and sluice gates for the irrigation channels.

The impetus for the project was given originally by our agricultural mission, which was asked to go to Pakistan and prepare a detailed irrigation plan for two million acres of the Ganges-Brahmaputra delta. Although the region receives ample rainfall most of the year, a system of controlled irrigation would allow farmers to grow a second and third crop during the heretofore unproductive dry season, and would also prevent erosion of the soil by the sea. When the plan was half completed, the Government asked whether a team of experts could begin to supervise actual field work on one-quarter million acres of the land that had already been plotted out—that is, take the project from paper to the ground and begin cutting canals to get the water flowing. Although our original plans called only for a pilot project, and not an undertaking of this scale, the fact that the scheme would mean another 250,000 acres producing a second crop at a time of great food scarcity was sufficient reason to help Pakistan put it into immediate effect. A considerable number of technical assistance experts are taking part in this important operation—one that is essentially Pakistan's project, but which has drawn thus far on the resources and experience of the Expanded Program, Canadian aid and Point Four assistance.

I have mentioned, as the source of the above project description, the Technical Assistance Board Resident Representative in Pakistan. He is, in fact, one of twenty-four Resident Representatives or Liaison Officers of the Board who are in charge of field offices responsible for the Program in forty-five countries. My appointment of these field officers is made in agreement with the Board. They act as coordi-

nating officials and normally are assigned only to those countries where programs involving several participating organizations are in progress. The Resident Representative provides a point of contact with the government of the country to which he is assigned and with representatives of other technical assistance activities in the same country. The Resident Representative may advise the government on its overall economic development plan, reserving all technical judgments and decisions for the representatives of the individual specialized technical agencies. In particular, he consults with the requesting government to ensure that the program worked out for the country is, as far as possible, an integrated coherent plan rather than a series of individual, unrelated projects, and that it fits into any general economic development scheme which the recipient country may have.

AN INTERNATIONAL EXCHANGE

The United Nations Resolution which created the Expanded Program emphasized that "a sound international program of this character must combine and make use of the experience of many nations, with different social patterns and cultural traditions and at different stages of development, so as to facilitate progress in the less advanced countries . . ." A government can request assistance in any specialized field with the assurance that those experts most suitably qualified for the job will be recruited, be they British, Egyptian, Indian, American, Jamaican, or any other nationality. In practice, this method has led to the establishment of a truly international pool of expert knowledge. To date, some seventy countries and territories have contributed to this pool.

Not only has this interchange of skills

given the Program a richness of resources, but, even more significant, it has given the underdeveloped countries the opportunity of being "givers" as well as recipients—for every country can offer valuable traditional skills to help a neighboring or far-off land. With the help of an Indian textile-printing expert, for instance, Burmese artisans are learning to produce native Burmese fabrics for local use. The bright-colored prints which are traditionally a part of Burmese dress had been an expensive import item for a country which was never a textile-producer. An Indian expert was recruited because India had reached an advanced stage in textile production, but had not advanced so far that it did not remember the problems of starting an infant industry with only the most scanty equipment. The expert has taught silk-screen printing techniques with improvised tools and equipment. He has encouraged the Burmese workers to draw upon their rich folklore and cultural heritage in their choice of designs, and to be critical in their selection of fabrics. To date, the project has trained some fifty people; many of them are already engaged in business or have returned to their villages to teach others. The progress made so far has encouraged the Government to hope that it will eventually be possible to supply the domestic market.

The last time a census was taken in the Kingdom of Libya was in 1936, when the country formed part of the Italian Empire. When Libya became an independent sovereign state in December, 1951 the accurate counting of its inhabitants was one of the many tasks that the new state did not have the "know-how" to handle by itself. Among its manifold requests for UN technical assistance, the Libyan Government included one for a census statistician. In this case it would not have been wise to recruit an expert accustomed to census-taking with elabo-

rate machines and easy access to the population. What was wanted was a man who could deal with the enumeration of a large nomad population, and who could improvise with the staff and equipment available. The UN Technical Assistance Administration therefore recruited an expert from neighboring Egypt. He arrived in Libya in 1952 and worked for two years laying the basis for the census. By July, 1954 the Government was ready to declare a "census day." The counting of the nomadic population, of course, took several months more. With our continued helping the totalling and analysis of the returns will probably take another two years, but when it is done Libya will have vital information on what has been called "its major untapped resource"—the latent skills of its people.

A LONG-TERM PROGRAM SHOWS EARLY RESULTS

I have mentioned above some of our work in the agricultural, labor and industrial fields, but we have done equally important work in the fields of health, education and transport. Teams sent out by the World Health Organization have not only helped to relieve human suffering, but have also helped to restore unproductive labor and lands to a point where they could contribute to the national economy. In Haiti, Indonesia, Thailand and the Philippines, where a crippling tropical disease called yaws has incapacitated large numbers of people, health teams working under the Program have treated some 2,800,000 people with penicillin, generally curing the disease with a single injection. In India's vast Terai region, farms flourished a thousand years ago at the foot of the Himalayas. But malaria made farming impossible. India worked out a large drainage and clearance project to rid the land of mosquitoes. Both WHO and the UN Children's Fund gave a helping hand and the results are now beginning to show. Thousands of people have settled on the fertile soil reclaimed for man.

A number of countries such as Indonesia, Iran, Afghanistan, Ethiopia and Iraq have to overcome their lack of adequate transport by increasing the use of aircraft to cover the great distances involved. The International Civil Aviation Organization has been able to make an important contribution to this work, and what it is doing in Iraq is typical of ICAO missions all over the world. For two years the ICAO staff at Baghdad has helped in the selection and training of air service recruits, who now, after a period of practical training with Iraqi Airlines, have begun actual operational work. The Mission also helped to install a new and more powerful transmitting station.

One of the most challenging tasks undertaken by UNESCO in education was started in the very early days of our existence. On the shores of Lake Patzcuaro in Mexico, a "Fundamental Education Center" was established as a gathering point for education trainees from all over Latin America. Under the guidance of an international staff and experienced Latin American educators, these young people work out the best methods of bringing literacy, hygiene, nutrition and other basic living improvements to rural populations. The students supplement their classroom work by visits to the villages surrounding the Center, where they learn to gain the confidence of members of the community as a first step towards improving their living conditions. The Center has been in operation for five years, and has turned out a large number of graduates fully qualified to return to their countries and play their part in national education campaigns. I have just learned of five Cuban graduates of the Center who have been asked by the Cuban Government to set up a national center to serve as a model for the whole of Cuba. Similar use is being made of the services of Patzcuaro graduates in Brazil, Costa Rica, Honduras, Peru and Guatemala. Indeed, the Patzcuaro Center has been so promising, that a similar center has been initiated for the benefit of Arab-speaking countries at Sirs-el-Layan, Egypt.

EFFECTIVE ADMINISTRATION AND ITS INITIAL PROBLEMS

I have naturally emphasized the good that our work has done, but in its first few years, the Program was naturally attended by the teething troubles that cannot be avoided in the early stages of any complex program. Problems of finance, administration, and staffing, to mention only a few, beset us for most of the five years that the Program has been in operation, and many are still with us. At this point, with a more stabilized and mature Program, we can take stock of what has been done to tighten our administration and programming, and of what still remains very much on our horizon.

The Program started slowly in 1950–51, since many governments were unaware of the services available to them, while others were unwilling to recruit the assistance of an unproved enterprise. But the projects we did undertake in that first eighteen months were doubtless our most effective advertisements, for the volume of projects increased almost four-fold in 1952. Furthermore, we found, upon planning our 1953 Program, that the requests for assistance which we had received represented a potential expenditure of more than $35 million. Since we had only just over $20 million available, we had our first experience with setting up priorities. We were faced with the difficult task of examining requests for assistance from the standpoint of their probable effect on economic development. Would the projects make more food available? Would they make more productive manpower available for agriculture and industry? Would they give the countries added income? Would they improve methods of getting produce to markets?

We emerged from this encounter with priorities with a system of programming which is more realistic, in my opinion, although it could still have been made more flexible. A certain degree of flexibility was imparted by the Economic and Social Council, which translated four years of programming experience into a new procedure, approved at the end of 1954 by the General Assembly. Under this new system, much greater emphasis is placed on the recipient government's own role in determining priorities among projects. Under the old system, the participating organizations and the Board had been responsible for selecting projects from among the many requests received from governments each year. This selection will now be based on detailed preparatory work undertaken, in the first instance, by the requesting government in consultation with the TAB Resident Representative, and with technical advice from the agencies. This new system, which went into effect on a trial basis for 1955 programming, has already resulted in a much greater awareness on the part of recipient governments of the scope and possibilities, as well as the limitations, of technical assistance programs in general.

The recruitment of experts has been, and will remain, a critical matter for us— for the Program will stand or fall on the quality of the experts we send out. Despite an unprecedented area of selection, the task of finding suitably qualified men and women has been a difficult one. They must not only have technical competence but an understanding of the needs of underdeveloped countries and a sympa-thetic attitude towards the varied cultures, hopes and aspirations of other peoples. We have improved our recruitment procedures gradually, enlisting the support of government departments, private organizations, UN associations, and research institutes. But recruitment must be constantly improved if the Program is to remain dynamic.

Finally, we must operate the Program under what has proved to be an uncertain method of finance. The Special Account which I have already described is replenished by voluntary contributions made on an annual basis, with all the uncertainty which that implies. Not only must we plan program ceilings from year to year with little more than a guess as to the amount of funds that we will have at our disposal, but we must also allow during each calendar year for the inevitable delay in collection of pledges. For an operation which is inherently a continuous and long-term one, this year-to-year planning has been most contradictory, but, again, governments have begun to show signs of a willingness to find a solution to this problem. Four governments have already pledged for periods exceeding one year, and we hope to have more such long-term support at subsequent Pledging Conferences.

In spite of these administrative hazards, as the United Nations takes a brief backward glance on its tenth birthday and counts its achievements in the political, social and economic fields, it can afford to feel moderately satisfied with its pioneering work in a unique field of endeavor—technical assistance on a completely international and reciprocal scale. What began as a bold experiment, and was nursed through all the growing pains of a new and complex plan, has now, we believe, been built up into a system which should make a valuable contribution to human progress for many years to come. Governments have given the Expanded Program of Technical Assistance an enthusiastic reception. While it is still too early for a comprehensive appraisal of work that will first begin to show an impact after a long period of years, there are many encouraging signs to indicate that the Program has taken a firm grip on the task that was put before it.

MEASURES FOR THE ECONOMIC DEVELOPMENT OF UNDER-DEVELOPED COUNTRIES: RECOMMENDATIONS*

ALBERTO B. CORTEZ, GEORGE HAKIM, W. ARTHUR LEWIS, THEODORE W. SCHULTZ AND D. R. GADGIL

Throughout our report we have made numerous suggestions of measures for promoting economic development. Not all are equally important. We confine ourselves in this part to selecting those which we wish to put forward in the form of recommendations.

A. NATIONAL ACTION BY UN-DER-DEVELOPED COUN-TRIES

To provide the preconditions and institutional framework of economic development, the government of an under-developed country should:

RECOMMENDATION 1

Make clear to its people its willingness to take vigorous action to remove the obstacles to free and equal opportunity

* From *Measures for the economic development of under-developed countries*. Report by a Group of experts appointed by the Secretary-General of the United Nations, United Nations Department of Economic Affairs, New York, May, 1951.

which blunt the incentives and discourage the efforts of its people. Under this head we include land reform, abolition of privileges based on race, colour, caste or creed, the establishment of taxation upon a progressive basis, and a programme of mass education;

RECOMMENDATION 2

Establish a central economic unit with the functions of surveying the economy, making development programmes, advising on the measures necessary for carrying out such programmes and reporting on them periodically. The development programmes should contain a capital budget showing the requirements of capital and how much of this is expected from domestic and from foreign sources.

In order to promote rapid economic development, an under-developed country should take the following measures:

RECOMMENDATION 3

Survey the ways in which production, distribution and finance are organized in each of the major sectors of the economy and take measures to improve their efficiency;

RECOMMENDATION 4

Survey the prospects of creating new productive employment by industrialization, by bringing more land under cultivation, by developing mineral resources, or by other means; and announce its programmes for expanding employment;

RECOMMENDATION 5

Survey the possibilities of increasing agricultural yields and announce the measures it proposes to adopt in order to effect rapid improvement of yields;

RECOMMENDATION 6

Prepare a programme, covering a period of years, for the improvement of public facilities by capital investment;

RECOMMENDATION 7

Prepare a programme of education and research showing its goals and its proposed expenditures for some such period as five years; and showing separately what is proposed for agricultural extension services, for industrial training, and for the training of scientists and administrators;

RECOMMENDATION 8

Prepare programmes to stimulate domestic savings, including the extension of savings institutions and measures involving taxation; and, in order to ensure that capital moves into the most productive uses, establish a development bank and an agricultural credit system, and if necessary, take other measures for influencing the direction of investment, such as credit controls, foreign exchange controls, or licensing of buildings or capital extensions.

B. NATIONAL ACTION BY DEVELOPED COUNTRIES

RECOMMENDATION 9

The developed countries should desist from commercial policies which hinder the development of the under-developed countries:

(a) They should not fix ceilings for the prices of imports without simultaneously controlling the prices of exports which under-developed countries buy from them so as not to affect adversely the terms of trade of these countries; and

(b) They should not subsidize the production or the export of commodities which are also produced for export by under-developed countries.

RECOMMENDATION 10

Developed countries should consider setting up national institutions similar to the Export-Import Bank of the United States.

RECOMMENDATION 11

Developed countries should facilitate foreign private investment by:

(a) Taking the initiative in making treaties with under-developed countries for the equitable treatment of foreign investments;

(b) Offering to insure foreign investments of their nationals against transfer difficulties; and

(c) Exempting foreign-earned incomes from double taxation.

RECOMMENDATION 12

During periods when there is a general scarcity of supply of goods, the developed countries should establish machinery to ensure that the under-developed countries obtain an equitable share of capital goods and of other materials for maintaining their programmes of development.

C. ACTION BY THE UNITED NATIONS AND OTHER INTERNATIONAL AGENCIES

RECOMMENDATION 13

The International Bank for Reconstruction and Development should set for itself the objective, to be reached within the next five years, of lending $1 billion annually to under-developed countries.

RECOMMENDATION 14

The United Nations should establish an International Development Authority to assist the under-developed countries in preparing, coordinating and implementing their programmes of economic development; to distribute to under-developed countries grants-in-aid for specific purposes; to verify the proper utilization of such grants; and to study and report on the progress of development programmes.

RECOMMENDATION 15

In order to assist the governments and peoples of Africa to analyse and keep under continuous survey the development problems of that continent, the United Nations should establish an Economic Commission for Africa and provide for it an international secretariat.

RECOMMENDATION 16

The United Nations should explore the possibility of establishing an international finance corporation to make equity investments and to lend to private undertakings operating in under-developed countries.

Dr. Afif I. Tannous is Chief of the Africa–Middle East, Foreign Agricultural Service, U.S. Department of Agriculture. He was for many years a regional specialist for the Middle East in the Office of Foreign Agricultural Relations in Washington. Previously he worked and conducted research in Syria, Lebanon, Palestine, and the Sudan. He is the author of numerous articles in professional journals and has written government pamphlets with wide circulation and continuous use.

Dr. Charles J. Erasmus is a Research Associate and Lecturer in the Department of Sociology and Anthropology at the University of Illinois. He was in Colombia as field representative of the Institute of Social Anthropology, Smithsonian Institute, in 1950, and later served as consultant to U.S. technical assistance programs in Haiti, Colombia, Ecuador, and Chile. While in Colombia he taught anthropology at the Instituto Etnologico Nacional. He is the author of a textbook in Spanish on the history of ethnological theory, *Las Dimensiones de la Cultura*, and articles in professional journals.

Dr. John M. Hunter is an Associate Professor of Economics, in the Department of Economics, at Michigan State University. He has just returned from Viet Nam where he was Deputy Adviser (Economics Section) on the Michigan State University, Viet Nam Advisory Team. He is a coauthor of *Principles of Money and Banking* and of *Michigan and Its Foreign Trade*, in addition to articles in professional journals.

Dr. William H. Knowles is an Associate Professor of Economics at the University of California, Berkeley. He has served as a research assistant in Industrial Relations with the Allis Chalmers Mfg. Company and as an Economist with the Chicago Regional War Labor Board. He spent 2 years in the British West Indies studying social economics and political background to labor union development. He is author of *Personnel Management: A Human Relations Approach*, 1955.

Dr. Chester L. Hunt is an Associate Professor of Sociology at Western Michigan College. He engaged in teaching and research in the Philippines and neighboring areas for 2 years under the Fulbright program. He is principal author of *Sociology in the Philippine Setting, Ethnic Tensions in Cotabato*, and of numerous articles on the social problems of underdeveloped areas, race relations, and the sociology of religion.

David Owen is Executive Chairman of the United Nations Technical Assistance Board. Mr. Owens served as a member of the British delegation at the San Francisco Conference and from 1946 to 1952 was United Nations Assistant Secretary-General for Economic Affairs.

Dr. Alberto B. Cortez is a Professor of Economics at the National University of Chile.

Dr. George Hakim is Counselor, Legation of Lebanon, Washington, D. C.

Dr. W. Arthur Lewis is Professor of Political Economy at the University of Manchester in England and author of *The Principles of Economic Planning*, 1949.

Dr. Theodore W. Schultz is Chairman of the Department of Economics at the University of Chicage and author of *Food for the World*, 1945, *Production and Welfare of Agriculture*, 1949 and *The Economic Organization of Agriculture*, 1953.

Dr. D. R. Gadgil is Director of the Gokhale Institute of Politics and Economics, Poona, India, and author of *The Industrial Evolution of India in Modern Times*, 1944.

X

EXPERIENCES WITH MASS MEDIA AND EDUCATION IN UNDERDEVELOPED AREAS

ALTHOUGH numerous experiments in the education of both the young and the old in underdeveloped countries have been conducted in recent years, they have very often been conducted in such a manner that the results were uncertain, or, in cases where a careful experiment has been conducted, the techniques and actual findings have been published in only very general terms.

Helpful, in sensitizing us to the problems of community education, but by no means limited to that use, are articles on extension work in the Middle East by Afif Tannous.[1] The article to which we are presently referring includes a description of the cultural background of the typical community in Egypt, Palestine, Transjordan, Lebanon, Syria, and Iraq. The values of the culture are listed and should be useful as a guide in attempting to motivate change in such an area. Tannous also makes suggestions that should be followed for the success of an extension program in the area. His advice on what kind of project to undertake and how to undertake it appears sociologically sound and is based on his experiences and reasoned judgment. The same may be said for his listing of specific techniques for carrying out projects. Tannous concludes his article with the story of the village pump, a story that is rather typical, and taken from his own field experience. The story goes as follows:

One of our Village Welfare camps was established at the main spring, just outside Jibrail, a foothill village in the extreme north of Lebanon, where most of our work was centered. About two miles away stood Ilat, a small community of a few hundred people. One morning a few of them came to the camp and asked for medical help, saying that many of their children were stricken with "fever," the word they used to cover all sorts of internal diseases. Our doctor and two assistants went to the village to investigate. They came back in the evening and reported several cases of typhoid, malaria and dysentery, and a high incidence of infant mortality. We promised to extend to them medical treatment and to do what we could along preventive lines.

[1] For example, "Extension Work Among the Arab Fellahin," Afif Tannous, *Applied Anthropology*, April–June 1944, pp. 1–12.

Further investigation revealed the probable source of trouble: a tiny spring in the midst of the village, which flowed into a stagnant pool. It was the only source of water supply, and we saw how it was being utilized. One woman after another emerged from the surrounding houses, each carrying an empty jar in her hand. (Hauling water is a woman's job, and a man would be ridiculed if he should be seen doing it.) With bare feet they walked in the dirty street, waded into the pool, drank and gave their trailing children to drink, filled their jars, raised them to their shoulders and walked back home. Animals came to the pool too—cows and oxen, goats and sheep, and donkeys. They waded and they drank. So we thought that our line of action was clear and simple. Dig the pool deeper, cover it with a stone structure and install a hand pump. It was as simple a project as that.

One evening we called the elders to a meeting and informed them of our plan, requesting them to render as much help as they could. There seemed to be general agreement. In our lack of experience, however, we had not yet learned the subtleties by which a "yes" may mean a "no" in certain cases. The following morning, when we came to the village, ready to begin the project, we found the place practically deserted. They had all gone to their fields. The *mukhtar* (headman, a government official) made his appearance to tell us that the people refused flatly to let us install the pump. Let us install the pump! That made us pause and think. So that was how they felt about it; that we were imposing on them something they did not really want. And all the time we took it for granted that we were satisfying their urgent need. Something was certainly wrong.

With much difficulty we were able to bring them to another meeting a few days later. In the course of the discussion we did our best to make them talk freely; and they told us a great deal! The following are more or less direct quotations:

"Our fathers, grandfathers, and great grandfathers drank from this water as it is, and I don't see why we should make a change now."

"You say that you want to install a pump at the spring; but I for one have never seen a pump, nor do I know what might happen if it should be put there."

"I tell you what will happen. The water will flow out so fast that the spring will dry up in no time."

"Not only that, but the iron pipe will spoil the taste of the water for us and for our animals."

"You So and So," put in one of Jibrail's elders, who are much more advanced in their outlook than the people of Ilat, "do you like the taste of dung in your water better?"

"Well, I admit it is bad; but we and our animals are at least used to it."

"You have told us that the water is the cause of our illness and of our children's death. I do not believe that, and I can't see how it could be. To tell you the truth, I believe that the matter of life and death is in Allah's hands, and we cannot do much about it."

"One more thing. We don't understand why you should go to all this trouble. Why are you so concerned about us?"

"You say that the pump will save our women much effort and time. If that happens, what are they going to do with themselves all day long?"

At the close of the meeting we realized that we had blundered. We had to begin from the beginning, taking nothing for granted. An educational campaign was launched, starting with laboratory tests of Ilat's water and samples from neighboring villages. We emphasized to the people that the report on their water was very bad, whereas the other villages received good reports. The way the hand pump worked was demonstrated to them, and they were convinced that it would neither spoil the spring nor dry it up. Quotations from the Koran were cited to the effect that cleanliness was required from every faithful Moslem and that man should do his best to avoid the danger of disease. At the same time, our girl workers visited with the housewives and explained to them how the pump would make their day's work easier and how they could use the time saved in taking better care of their children. They would not get ill so often, and fewer of them would be lost. Finally, we did our best to explain to the villagers that we were doing all this as our patriotic duty, and that it was their duty also to cooperate with us for their own benefit.

It took one whole month before the situation was ripe for action. We advanced the cost of the pump and its accessories, which we ordered from the neighboring town. We insisted, however, according to our working principle, that they should contribute the necessary labor and pay in cash or in kind as much as they could. Two of our volunteers took with them a donkey and went from house to house gathering contributions. Towards the evening they came back with a small sum of money and a heavy load consisting of barley, wheat, eggs, chickens and fruit. The following morning the villagers started working. The pond was cleaned and deepened; a stone structure was built over it, and the village pump was installed at last.[2]

The question remains, will more or less objective, nonquantitative, or at least not rigorously quantified data, give us the information that we need in order to plan large scale extension programs? Could we, on a basis of this kind of information, put into operation a large-scale development program? The answer may be that we cannot wait for all the research and experimentation that we desire but must forge ahead, using the best available data as a guide.

"Professional Problems of Education in Underdeveloped Areas" by Margaret Mead discusses the various alternatives in planning education for underdeveloped areas. Our experience with education in underdeveloped areas has nevertheless not been so extensive that we have definitive answers on either long-run or short-run procedures for increasing literacy or insuring the success of any other kind of educational program. Readers will notice agreement on relevant points between Dr. Mead and Sir Ivor Jennings, whose contribution on education appears in an earlier chapter.

Following Dr. Mead's contribution to the total problem of education is a more specialized and rather long paper, "The Field Program of the Puerto Rican Division of Community Education" by Carmen Isales and Fred G. Wale. This article appeared in a special issue of *The Journal of Social Issues*, one devoted to the program of community change in Puerto Rico. In an introductory statement to this issue, Governor Luis Muñoz Marín points out that the program is guided by two directives contained in the act of the Puerto Rican legislature of May 14, 1949:

[2] *Ibid.*, pp. 11–12.

1) To impart basic teaching on the nature of man, his history, his life, his way of working and of self-governing in the world and in Puerto Rico, thus providing the good hand of our popular culture with the tool of a basic education. 2). To give to the communities the wish, the tendency and the way of making use of their own aptitudes for the solution of many of their own problems . . . to the end that each community can be constantly and usefully employed in its own service, in terms of pride and satisfaction for the members thereof.[3]

In introducing the work of the Division of Community Education, Fred G. Wale calls their program the rural man's "Operation Bootstrap."[4] This program is truly an "Operation Bootstrap" since it offers communities neither consumer's nor producer's goods nor technical assistance as we have described it. The effort is to stimulate the people in a community to organization so that they may solve their problems as a group. The media of mass communication are used in this effort, in fact the Division plans and produces movies, booklets, and posters. It is an extension service but not in the sense that formal classes are offered to the community. Much of the article included here is not scientific in the usual sense of the word; it is loaded with value judgments, statements about how people ought to live— ought to treat other men. But included with these value judgments is the description of an approach to these underdeveloped communities or underdeveloped people as they would prefer it. The reader should accept the exhortations and value judgments as evidence of the seriousness and dedication of the authors. Here we have an intimate glimpse of an attempt by the indigenous inhabitants to raise their level of living. As Fred G. Wale states,

Like all people, the families of these rural neighborhoods are conditioned by the history of their cultural past. Some are indifferent and disillusioned. Some are not sure they have any common problems, and if one does exist, not sure that much can be done about it. Some show little faith in themselves or their neighbors. Some believe that people will act together but only under a leader with authority. But others, with a deep sense of pride in themselves and their neighbors, believe that they can find the solution to some of their own problems. They have found strength in the democratic concept that all members of the community have the right to participate equally in community planning and action. They lack only the ways and means to find the opportunity that will put this faith into a living framework. Our ultimate goal in all of these communities would be to help them develop a maximum of communal self-sufficiency. However, limitations of personnel do not permit us today to reach intensively into more than ten per cent. We try, however, to establish in every community an initial nucleus of democratic action, through showing films and starting groups for the study and distribution of booklets.[5]

[3] "Statement of Motives," Governor Luis Muñoz Marín, *The Journal of Social Issues*, Vol. IX, No. 2, 1953, p. 9.
[4] "Operation Bootstrap" is not treated in this volume because it has received such extensive mention elsewhere.
[5] "The Division of Community Education—An Overview," Fred G. Wale, *The Journal of Social Issues*, Vol. IX, No. 2, 1953, p. 18.

This is a program that may apparently depend for its success upon acquiring personnel with such values that their job becomes a way of life rather than a job.

Within the Division of Community Education an Analysis Unit is studying the effectiveness of procedures and patterns. Among other things they are interested in community self-perception as it relates to behavior as a member of the group when faced with problems. They are interested in the presence of attitudes that may be barriers to participation in community projects. While many people indicated that they liked to be a member of groups, mainly for purposes of recreation, only a few regarded groups as a way of getting things done.[6] The authors continue:

The majority of respondents (69%) had not attended meetings of any kind in the three or four months preceding the survey. Three quarters of those who attended did not, according to their own report, participate in the group's activities and discussion.

From the facts already mentioned it is evident that rural folk have not used in the past, to any appreciable extent, the medium of meetings or group activity as a means for community improvement. They are, however, in general interested in the solution of communal problems, and a considerable sector of the rural population (two thirds) still feel that group activity *may* be effective in obtaining such improvement.

It is surprising that a part of our rural population feels positively towards group participation for community improvement when one views it in the light of past history. Groupings of people were never fostered, always forbidden, during the Spanish domination, because of the fear of the military Governors General of conspiracy and revolt. Only for recreational purposes were gatherings tolerated, because, as one of the Governor Generals put it, 'People who make merry don't conspire.' The lesson of democratic group participation is a very recent development in our history. Even during the first two decades of the American regime little was done in the sense of basic participation by the common man. There was extensive carry-over from the practices of the previous system, especially in the field of politics. It is in connection with this latter activity that the Puerto Ricans, especially the rural, have lately assimilated the concepts and practice of democratic participation and leadership.[7]

In some concluding comments on this program of the Division of Community Education, Charles Cannell and Stephen Withey point out that,

The work of community action necessarily begins on a level quite different from that of most community action programs in the States. For example, the island-wide survey results show the paucity of experience in community participation in anything other than some leisure activities. There are, also, few economic resources available to the Puerto Rican community. Thus the group organizer finds little past experience upon which to base his work and limited economic resources available. Much of his early activity must be spent in bringing the community to the point where it can begin to function as a community. This is one of the main reasons why it is impossible to transfer specialists and accepted methodologies directly from other settings. In general, social scientists have no experience in attempting community action starting from such an elementary basis. Presumably, however, social scientists will be increas-

⁶ "Research and Evaluation in a Program of Community Education," Raúl Muñoz, Belén M. Serra, and Angelina S. de Roca, *The Journal of Social Issues*, Vol. IX, No. 2, 1953, pp. 43–52.
⁷ *Ibid.*, p. 52.

ingly faced with such problems as similar programs gain momentum elsewhere in the world.[8]

From their observation of the Division, Cannell and Withey state that the following principles appear to generally be accepted by the Division's members.[9]

I. The Division's personnel must have a clear, strong and motivating goal. This goal has been described as "community democracy." Although not definable in terms of clear criteria, its acceptance is the basic principle. The following elements, at least, are included:

a. total community involvement
b. unified and cooperative effort
c. satisfaction of community members' individual needs
d. active means for communication and expression
e. inter-individual respect
f. general self-direction
g. positive motivation

Subsidiary principles are, for instance:
1). Progress can only be made at the pace set by the group and cannot be accelerated by an element within or outside the group unless it is accepted and assimilated by the group.
2). The content of action must be the content of community problems: relevance is determined by the community.
3). The stimulus for development must be group stimulus.
4). Progress is impossible without communication and shared perceptions of needs, plans, consequences, goals, means, etc.
5). The process is continuous, requiring continued growth, readjustment, new insights, etc.
II. The clarity and strength of this goal will frequently serve as a sufficiently directive guide to appropriate action. This is the major criterion for the selection of methods. Techniques are consciously evaluated against the above "goal" and against their implications in terms of subsequent developments arising out of their use.
III. The operation of Principles I and II requires certain other characteristics from the group organizer. He should be:

a. identified with the communities
b. accepted by the communities
c. motivated toward community improvement
d. emotionally adjusted
e. adaptive
f. tolerant
g. sensitive and alert to individual and social behavior and its causes

[8] "Concluding Comments," Charles Cannell and Stephen Withey, *The Journal of Social Issues,* Vol. IX, No. 2, 1953, pp. 53.
[9] *Ibid.,* pp. 54–55.

IV. *Experience of "democratic" group functioning is a necessary prerequisite for cognitive clarity and spontaneous emotional involvement in the process.* This is a major factor in group organizer training.

V. *The group organizer needs certain information constantly available as part of his training for him to be an effective agent of growth within the community.*

a. as a necessary element in group functioning
b. to maintain his prestige as a resource person
c. to maintain his motivation
d. to insure the information being available when needed by his community members
e. as the raw material of some aspects of problem solution

VI. *Perceptual growth will be small and, also, the maintenance of goal perceptions can be due to small cues.* This situation will make for slow progress, which should be expected, and will require sensitivity to detail on the part of the group organizer and the mass media producer.

After reading the article by Isales and Wales included in this chapter the reader may check his own analysis of the guiding principles of the program against this list.

The last article in this chapter, "Communications Research on Non-Industrial Countries" by Bruce L. Smith, outlines the kind of research that should be conducted if we are to have a basis for more effective communication with underdeveloped areas. This paper also describes the kinds of social systems that we must expect and the channels of communication that are presented in these areas. The importance of a knowledge of values in planning mass communications is emphasized throughout this article.

PROFESSIONAL PROBLEMS OF EDUCATION IN DEPENDENT COUNTRIES*

MARGARET MEAD

THIS discussion will be confined to the education of those peoples in dependent countries whose tradition is either non-European, because it stemmed instead

* Adapted and reprinted by permission from *The Journal of Negro Education*, Vol. XV, No. 3, Summer, 1946, pp. 346–357.

from one or more of the other great cultural stocks of the world, or because it is primitive, *i.e.*, preliterate, or because the participation of the people in European traditions is of relatively recent date. Thus the people of Indo-China, apart from the French metropolitan residents, would belong to category one, the people of New Guinea to category two, and the inhabitants of the Virgin Islands and of the Seychelles to the last category. Problems of education in all of these areas are furthermore inextricably bound up with the problem of education in the ideas and techniques of Western culture, whatever the goal of the education may be. Among the possible goals we can distinguish several: (1) the education of the peoples of dependent countries so that they become world-mobile in one generation, (2) the education of dependent peoples so that over several generations, and by gradual stages of regional participation and growing political responsibility, they finally become world-mobile and able to participate on a world level and (3) the education of such peoples only to the point where they may be successfully exploited by more advanced economies while they perform relatively simple agricultural or extractive economic functions, subsidiary to the more advanced economy of the countries upon which they are dependent. (4) A fourth possible goal—to leave those groups who have minimal natural resources and which are not of a size or in a position to add to the labor supply of the world, relatively untouched—is so out of the line of the contemporary climate of opinion as not to be worth considering. The third goal defines fairly accurately the past experience and present state of many peoples, the inhabitants of the East Indies, of parts of Africa, of Malaya. It also, however, is incompatible both with world demands and with the demands of the people themselves, enough of whom have been educated in the philosophy of the West so as to be no longer content with such a subsidiary position. The second goal—of gradual change—has much to recommend it to serious students of society who recognize the extreme penalties inherent in too rapid social change, but it recommends itself not at all to the educated leaders of the peoples concerned, and finds little general support in the United States where there is a characteristic desire to hurry the process of maturation— of children, or colonial peoples, or of institutions. In full recognition that the first alternative is the most difficult and poses the most serious problems to the professional educator, it seems nevertheless necessary to consider it as the goal towards which our educational techniques must be aimed, in full recognition of the very poor chance of complete success.

World mobility and world participation in one generation, as an aim for even a section of the peoples whom we are discussing, involves: (1) ability to speak, read and write some "world language," that is a language which will make participation in international conferences and free movement about the world possible; (2) a grasp of the framework of Western economy, use of money and credit, and a recognition of the implications of living in a contract rather than a status society; (3) a modicum of cross cultural sophistication which will enable the individual concerned to work among people with different codes and standards without taking offense or becoming disoriented; (4) a working acceptance of the state of mind roughly summarized in such phrases as "the scientific attitude" with an ability to act within its premises in public interpersonal contexts, political, economic, and technological; (5) some conceptualized view of history which makes it possible to deal with the time perspectives (towards the past and the future) of the great civilizations; (6) a sufficient independence of the living mesh of his own culture to be able to exist outside it without crippling nostalgia. This last requirement is primarily necessary for mobility in space, the others apply to any attempt to deal on a face-to-face basis with members of Western culture, either in the home country or abroad.

In attempting to achieve these objectives, there are two conspicuously divergent methods which have been used. The first and simpler method is to transport individuals from the dependent country to some center where Western world culture is dominant and expose them, as intimately and intensively as possible, to that culture in its formal and informal educational aspects. History is studded with instances in which individuals from exceedingly primitive settings have been reared among people of another and more complex civilization and have successfully mastered its intricacies. The problem of inducting a juvenile member of any people on earth, with the possible but not certain exception of the pygmies, into English or German, or French, or Russian or Chinese culture, is not a serious one. The real problem lies in so selecting the time for temporary expatriation, and the time of repatriation, that the individuals so educated are able to maintain effective contacts with *both* worlds, to speak the new language without forgetting or despising the old, to subdue both of his possible nostalgias in the periods when they are inappropriate, and to become bicultural rather than deculturized —the commoner result. This educational method, in which the technical problems lie not in the country of education, but in the timing and choice of pupils and in the provision which is made for their reintegration into their own societies has, however, serious drawbacks. It is primarily appropriate to an aristocratic people, and has been most successfully applied where both the metropolitan power concerned and the people of the dependent country were aristocratic in practice, or at least in theory. Whether one considers the roster of African and Asiatic students

who have attended Oxford and Cambridge, or the carefully educated sons of the Javanese aristocrats, the importance of the aristocratic element is obvious. If only one party to the educational plan is aristocratic, it is still possible to make an initial success of such an educational plan, as the aristocrats in the dependent country will accept a scheme which takes their nobility away—as a method of selection—or the aristocracy in the metropolitan country will accept a scheme which selects, for special training, the most able and gifted among a casteless and rankless people. Lacking an aristocratic component the system becomes unworkable for the very reason which makes it relatively untenable in the world today, that it is incompatible with the tenets of political democracy. Americans are particularly unqualified to appreciate the high education which a few Javanese have received in Holland, or a few West Africans in England, while the mass of the people remained relatively uneducated and without educational opportunities.[1]

In fact the requirement of preparation for world mobility in one generation is a different one entirely and does not accept the education of a few Burmese gentlemen in the ultimate refinements of English university life as substitute for popular education out of which any individual with ability may receive enough education to make him able to move about and function in the world. We may safely say that the framework within which the article is written, that is an acceptance of the present dominant world opinion with its emphasis upon opportunity for the common people, demands more than the type of selective educational expatriation of the leadership elements in a population, no matter how careful the selection, how

[1] J. F. H. A. de la Court, "Some Proposals for Postwar Education in Indonesia." *Far East Quarterly*, Netherlands Indies Issue, 1946.

adapted the education, and how skillful the reintegration of the privileged individuals so educated. The experience of several centuries in the occidentalization of oriental and primitive peoples is merely valuable data in any controversy which would deny the ability of a people to take on, as individuals, any culture to which they are exposed at a sufficiently impressionable age.

The basic problem of education in dependent countries has become that of devising a system of education which can be applied, on a universal scale, inside the country. While this education may have to rely initially on immigrant teachers, it cannot rely primarily on emigration of students. Within the culture itself—where the very cycle of the seasons and the fluctuations of the weather, the flowers by the wayside and food that is eaten, all reinforce the existing culture—a system of education must be devised which will give the possibility for every child with normal intelligence within it, finally to arrive, within his single educational lifetime, at the six abilities listed above. The idea of pure number will have to be taught, though the language itself may use piecewords, as in Malay, with different numerical particles depending upon the type of object counted. The potentiality for understanding modern credit systems must be developed while the local valuables are bargained for as desirable, individually, in themselves; and a capacity to discount cultural differences in manners must be developed among the exacting nuances of a caste system. Underestimating the extreme difficulty of this task has led to the travesties of education, under Western auspices, which are found in so many parts of the world.

If, however, this exceedingly difficult task is undertaken, what are some of the major factors which must be taken into account? In the first place the educator will need to consider the character structure of the people, those regularities in their behavior, which can be attributed to their having been reared in a common culture. These regularities can be conveniently described under the headings of motivation, incentives and values, on the one hand, and ways of thought on the other. Our educational systems are bound up almost inextricably with our own character structure, so that it seems natural to us to build an educational system on such concepts as competition, reward and punishment, graduated success and failure, etc. But in working within other cultural contexts it is necessary to discard these cultural limitations and study first what are the incentives under which an individual will study and learn, and what are the conditions which may make the use of our methods definitely inappropriate. In Samoa, where precocity is deprecated, parents hung their heads when their children were skipped a grade in the American school, and in the missionary schools it was found impossible to use speed of finishing school as an incentive because custom demanded that the first to enter must also be the first to leave.[2] Dr. Klineberg[3] found that the Dakota Indians considered it bad form to give an answer in the presence of someone who did know the answer. In a Balinese school I once heard a young teacher, discussing the results of an arithmetic test containing twenty examples, say, "One wrong, can be used, two wrong, can be used . . ." up to "*Nineteen* wrong, can be used," but he added in a sad low voice, "Twenty wrong out of twenty, can not be used." In caste societies, the question of who learns a new skill first

[2] Margaret Mead, *Coming of Age in Samoa*, William Morrow & Co., 1928; *Cooperation and Competition Among Primitive Peoples*, Edited by Margaret Mead. New York: McGraw Hill, 1937.

[3] Otto Klineberg, *Race Differences*. New York: Harper & Bros., 1935.

may be crucial, as the high caste may decide that anything a low caste does, he can do better, or conversely, that nothing that a low caste has done is worth doing, and low castes may decide that they cannot do what the high caste does.

In addition to these obvious differences in motivation and conceptions of achievement, there are deeper ones, as between the people whose moral conceptions of right and wrong, for instance, make it also easier for them to handle cause and effect relationships in the material world. Study of the Manus tribe of the Admiralty Islands[4] suggests that a method of upbringing which sternly fixes individual responsibility for wrong doing, also establishes an attitude of mind to which the ways of engines, telephones, and other apparatus of the modern age, are no longer strange. But in other cultures, character structure may be characterized by a capacity to learn by rote methods, but not by analytical ones.[5] The dichotomies which people use, between work and play, between vocation and avocation, between situations requiring effort and those who require no effort,[6] etc., all may have a profound bearing upon the willingness and capacity to learn. After the Japanese have sensitized their children to feel any overt failure as an acute disgrace, it is necessary to give every child a prize,[7] but in certain parts of the orient, a "failed B.A." is said to be as simple a

[4] Margaret Mead, "An Investigation of the Thought of Primitive Children with Special Reference to Animism," *Jour. of the Royal Anthropological Inst.* 62:173–190, Ja. 1932.

[5] G. Bateson and M. Mead, *Balinese Character: A Photographic Analysis.* Special Publication, New York Academy of Sciences, 1942.

[6] G. Bateson, "Social Planning and the Concept of 'Deutero-Learning,'" in *Science Philosophy and Religion,* 2nd Symposium. Conference on Science, Philosophy and Religion, New York, 1942.

[7] Ruth Benedict, *Patterns of Japanese Culture.* New York: Houghton Mifflin & Co. Chapter on Human Feelings.

classificatory statement as the words diploma or some lower degree might be among ourselves. Thus differences in the values given to success and failure, to moral responsibility, to status, etc., form the background, the conditions for learning, and shade imperceptibly into what might be regarded as more strictly intellectual conditions, such as a premium upon the exact use of words, as contrasted with a love of words for their sound and rhythm rather than their precise meaning, the implications of a native language in which direct quotations are used to describe any situation, whether one has been present or not, so that accuracy of narration is virtually impossible, habits of meticulous repetition of verbal materials without any intellectual comment being permitted. Habits such as those common in China of invoking earlier authorities on a subject, may influence and shape any attempt at independent thought. In many cases, when the educator is dealing with previously illiterate people, the problem of attention span is a serious one which has defeated many attempts to measure the intelligence of different races, even when the experimenter rules out the language factor. Only if the experimenter assumes that capacity for an attention span like our own is in itself evidence of intelligence, can tests which involve attention span be regarded as valid. Perhaps one of the most revealing studies of differences in intellectual response to materials, is the recall study done by Nadel[8] among two adjacent African people which shows the contrast in method and style and secondarily in ability to recall a simple story.

It is apparent, therefore, that any system of education should be developed against a very thorough background of a knowledge of the culture of the people to

[8] Nadel, "A Field Experiment in Racial Psychology," *British Jour. of Psychology* 28:195–211, 1937, c.

be educated. This may be attained in two ways, (1) by intensive anthropological study supplemented by the use of social psychological techniques, particularly such projective methods as the Rorshach, Vigotsky, "Draw a Man and Woman," simple recall and completion tests, etc., or when this is impracticable, a great deal could also be learned by a detailed analysis of the methods of education actually being used by native teachers in their attempts to teach alien materials. The gifted native teacher, himself a full representative of his own culture, will both consciously and unconsciously adjust his methods to the emotional and intellectual values and habits which he and his pupils share. Verbatim records of class room situations, using different materials at different age levels, if subjected to intensive analysis, could provide a background for organizing curriculum and program so that it was much more congruent with the local culture. As anthropologists usually lack practical educational experience and educators have not been trained in analyzing educational practices from a cultural point of view, ideally both methods and both types of personnel should be used in combination.

After an initial reckoning with the basic culture in the construction of a school system, which extends, of course, not only to curriculum and incentives but to the whole interpersonal structure of the school, the next most important problem is probably that of literacy. There is now enough evidence in existence on efforts to teach literacy to illiterate and preliterate peoples, to make it possible to say that a basic condition of successful literacy—on any large scale—is that it should be attained in the mother tongue. Literacy achieved in any language other than the mother tongue is likely, except in exceptional cases, to remain superficial and incomparable with the literacy of people who learned to read in the language in which their mothers sang them to sleep. Not only does this fact account for the relatively greater success of the Dutch in bringing native peoples of the East Indies up to college level in one generation, out of village schools, but also for the failure of American efforts to make the American Indian comfortably literate out of the tribal setting. Despite the seeming waste of time involved in teaching children to read and write in languages and dialects in which there is no literature, or at least no contemporary literature, this seems to be the only way in which full literacy can be attained. Once the basic connections are made, the pupils can pass rapidly, as has been repeatedly demonstrated in the East Indies, to literacy in some other language.

Even after this basic requirement of literacy attained in the mother tongue is recognized, serious problems remain in those societies which make special use of other types of script, intermediate forms like Arabic, phonetic syllabic scripts like the Sanscrit scripts, or ideographs like Japanese and Chinese. As each of these types of scripts is the means of perpetuating one or more sacred books, failure to teach the children to read them is exceedingly destructive of continuity in the society, as it breaks the tie between the educated young and their educated elders. Expensive as it may seem to teach young children to use two scripts, it nevertheless would seem worthwhile to proceed by the following steps: a curriculum in which children become literate in mother tongue and local script, even if that script has been restricted in use to scribes and priests, followed by mother tongue in Roman script or whatever more widely used script is to form the basis of their world language skill, then a world language in its appropriate script. In this way the children are never confronted with both strange script and strange language simultaneously, but move by gentle stages from one new skill to another, maintaining their ties with their own culture as they forge ties with other cultures also. Experience has shown that the inferiority which is experienced by westernized young people who can not read and write their ancestral language is too easily translated into defensive contempt and depreciation of their whole cultural background.

A further problem remains when the people for whom a comprehensive literacy program is planned belong to a linguistic group which is too small to warrant the expense of preparing an orthography and text books and training teachers to work in it. Language groups of this sort are found among American Indians, in the South Seas, in Africa and in Asia. Here the principle that true literacy is only achieved through the mother tongue has to be translated into the need for teaching a new alternative mother tongue within which literacy can be established. In fact the literacy of the child must be built upon the ability of the mother to speak a language which is written.

There have been three[9] major methods of solving this problem of the small preliterate language groups and of the dialect speaking non-literate patches among peoples who are literate in some high language. One method is to teach the children to read and write the high language; this has been pursued at different periods in most European countries and has its Chinese analogue. Here—if the dialect is really a dialect and not a separate language—the child learns in terms of a language which is not too unfamiliar and, while probably not making the bridge as perfectly as does the child in whose home the written language is also spoken, nevertheless does become literate. His literacy, however, is

often limited by inability to express emotionally weighted material in the high language. The second solution is through a *lingua franca*. Here also there is usually an already existent bridge as either in grammar or vocabulary the *lingua franca* is likely to resemble the mother tongue of the pupil. There are, however, certain disadvantages[10] inherent in most simplified jargons—the thinness and poverty of the cultural world out of which they spring and the absence of any literature or any tradition to which access may be obtained by learning to read and write the jargon. However, in the case of preliterate areas of great linguistic diversity, such as that of New Guinea, probably the best step is to encourage the women as well as the men to learn the *lingua franca* so that the children will speak it before entering school, and then to take the initial steps towards literacy in the *lingua franca*, followed as rapidly as possible by induction into the appropriate world language. The other method which has been used with indifferent success is that adopted by certain missions, of selecting one small, unwritten language, for a translation of the Bible and other religious books and then teaching literacy to the adjacent peoples in this insignificant and often accidentally chosen language. Such education violates the people's relationship to their own cultural background, gives them no capacity for wider participation in the world, and is generally indefensible. The attempts to go directly from a pre-literate background in some small unwritten language and the level of culture which is associated with pre-literate status, to attempted reading and writing in a world language of totally different structure, seems impossible unless the spoken version of the imported

[9] All such statements are subject to the provision that we have no adequate information about the methods pursued by the Soviet Union in educating their non-Russian speaking peoples.

[10] G. Bateson, "Pidgin English and Cross-Cultural Communication," *Transactions*, New York Academy of Sciences, II, 6, 4:137–141, February 1944.

language has already become current among both sexes and all ages in the population, as in the case with Spanish in some Indian communities in Latin America. Here the imported world language can be regarded as a supplementary mother tongue. It is most important that this preschool experience of the language, in which literacy is later to be attained, should be associated with pleasantly toned experiences for the child. Where the official language of school is neither the language of play nor of family affection, but only the language of an often formidable learning situation, this separation between the emotions associated with the two languages may provide a considerable barrier to effective literacy.[11] Failure to enable a people to become literate in the sense that members of Western countries are literate inevitably handicaps them seriously, and its repercussions can be found all through the individual's life. Many intelligent American Indians, for example, fail to attain the status which they deserve because of the difficulties which they experience in writing reports of any degree of complexity.

The next serious problem which confronts the educator is that presented by the accumulated literary, artistic, philosophic and scientific traditions of the sort which we associate with high civilizations. A certain portion of the population of dependent countries, in fact all of those people whom we describe as primitive or preliterate, have by definition little such tradition. Their view of the past is only as complex as may be transmitted through oral tradition, and while the body of tradition sometimes rises to considerable artistic or philosophical heights, it is not comparable in mass, diversity, complexity or potentiality for new developments, with traditions like the Judeo-Christian, the Graeco-

[11] D. J. Saer, "The Effect of Bilingualism on Intelligence," *British Journal of Psychology* 14:35–38 (1923).

Roman, or the traditions of China, Japan, India, or Islam. When these preliterate peoples come in contact with anyone of these higher cultures, the educational problem arises, how to give them rapidly enough, a familiarity with this rich past which will make them able to use the language and conceptual framework of their new world cultural mentor. This problem has sometimes been seen as merely one of teaching the classics—whichever set of classics is being considered—with the same degree of firmness and repetitiousness with which they are taught in the home schools, with the expectation that such teaching will make such symbols as St. Paul, Charlemagne, Plato, Krisna, Lao Tse, David, etc., available to the local population. The slightest experience with the way in which preliterate peoples handle their contacts with the Bible, the classic to which they are most frequently exposed, proves that this hope is a fallacy. An assimilation of the idea of the Devil to the folklore figure of Coyote does not mean that the American Indian now has access to mediaeval ideas of good and evil, but usually that he is even more effectively cut off from them. It does not increase the sophistication of a Samoan to teach him to recognize the name Egypt, but leaves him believing that Pharaoh still reigns there. What those who expose preliterate peoples to our types of traditional education forget is that our great classics are bedded down in a wealth of common speech and imagery. Shorn of this linguistic and cultural background, their effect on the minds of pupils is often sheerly confusing and disorienting. It is much easier to move from an understanding of the classics of one great culture to an understanding of the classics of another, than to begin to absorb any set of classics into a cultural background from which they have been wholly absent.

It is important to point out that very

serious snobbery often prompts people, recently emerging from a preliterate past, to insist upon having a conventional higher education. If Greek and Roman classics have made the gentleman—who too often is a symbol of a height to which the students have been denied access—then Greek and Roman classics they will have. When a local education department contains individuals smarting under the sting of attributed racial or cultural inferiority, this demand is sometimes impossible to resist, even though in yielding to it whole peoples may be condemned to that very inferiority which they are seeking to avoid.

When, however, fortunate historical accidents make it possible to design an educational curriculum for a pre-literate or recently literate people, without the cooperation of members of their own group whose superior education makes it possible for them to make such complicating demands, the whole question can be usefully side-stepped by planning a curriculum which uses the best of contemporary methods of thought, applied as often as possible to local content. Instead of learning the history of ancient Greece, the student may learn the methods of stratigraphy well enough to make studies in local achaeology which will command the respect of the wider world, and instead of studying Aristotle, he may learn to do studies of local natural history and ecology. For a knowledge of mediaeval dialectics, he may substitute a mastery of contemporary mathematical techniques or a developed photographic skill. If it is recognized that it is easier to teach an untrained mind good modern science than allusion-studded epics, then a careful search can be made for those areas in which local conditions will provide the content on which high level abstractions and highly developed modern techniques can be exercised. In this way the university graduate who belongs to the first class which has ever been graduated from a new

university in a dependent country, stands the chance of facing members of older cultures on a far more equal basis than if he devoted his time to mastering by rote some classic, the basis of which these others learned as children in the casual allusions of mother and schoolmaster.

The problem of education for members of those societies which already possess one high civilization but who now wish to share in another—the well known situation when young people of oriental tradition attempt to become westernized—is a rather different one. Here the demand, both on the part of educators and students may well be for a break with the cumbersome past, but, as in the matter of script, the loss which this will entail in continuity and cultural integrity, is so great that it cannot safely be risked. As the initial hump which any student who is later to be bi- or multi-lingual must get over, is the realization that there are other languages which are as valid as his own, and not merely translations, imitations or approximations of his own, so also it is useful in the case of cultural tradition to introduce fairly early into the education of children who are learning the rudiments of some one high culture, the language and some of the literature of another high culture. This applies today mainly to the introduction of Western languages and cultures in countries where children are being taught within an oriental tradition, but it might equally well be applied in reverse. The children of the occident will never be fully world-mobile until they have an equal experience of some other high non-European culture. With the present world trend, however, towards an approximation to the skills and ideologies of the West, the more recurrent and pressing problem is the education of young people so that they can participate in Western culture without losing touch with their own people.

All of the foregoing discussion makes one assumption which unfortunately is not universally true. It assumes that the peoples to be educated will be members of homogeneous, relatively untouched cultures, with all the internal consistency and harmony which is characteristic of such cultures. In actual practice, more and more of the peoples of the world, in dependent countries and among metropolitan and independent nations, have lost their cultural roots. They exist in a state of deculturation, whether because they have immigrated from one country to another, or from country to city, or from one part of the country to another, or because war, displacement, desolation, and destruction of familiar values and institutions have left them hopelessly disoriented and impoverished even in the land of their childhood. The children of such parents—and one may count them now by the millions, whether one deals with the urban worker in Java or the sugar-cane worker of Puerto Rico, the rural children exploited in the recently-sprung-up factories of the Orient, the wandering Mexican casual laborers in the United States, or the mestizo of so many Latin American cities, the emigrant from the rural Southeastern United States into large and unfamiliar Northern cities, or the mixed African-English groups in Liverpool,—can rely upon no homogeneities of culture, often not even of language. Often the parents have been reared in different cultures and one speaks poorly the language of the other. The words used in the home were formed to deal with a different environment, and often there are no words in the parental language for the material things which surround them. Kin are separated from kin, and the depth of social perception which comes from listening to the tales of grandparents and watching one's own parents' relations to their parents is all lost. The language of the only lullabies a mother knows employs symbols of which she herself has forgotten the meaning, and the children bring in from the streets words and phrases which are equally incomprehensible to her. There are deep gulfs between each individual and his past, between parents and children, and between people and the environment around them which they lack the equipment to interpret and invest with meaning —and these gulfs are so deep that they threaten to become internalized and result in split and disintegrated personalities.

For such children and young people, the educational problem is not to take the coherencies of their cultural heritage and graft onto them whatever new learnings are desired, but rather to devise a curriculum within which they may somehow attain that minimum of personal integration and group belongingness which they must have if they are to learn anything at all. Modern educational trends from Froebel and Madam Montessori through the whole elaboration of the Progressive Education movement may be seen primarily as attempts to recreate in the classroom that closeness to a real world seen through culturally coherent symbols, which members of our deculturated modern society have lost. The Chinese child who comes from a three-generation home, firmly placed in a village where his family have lived for a thousand years, can sit all day and recite the alphabet without damage to his personality, and this is equally true of the French school boy or the Syrian or of the child who comes from a relatively intact primitive community. If what he learns is too alien, he will simply forget it, as do American Indians after returning from boarding school, or adult peasants in whose houses there are no books with which to keep up the little reading learned at school. If what he learns is presented incorrectly, it may disorient him. But in any case, he is a whole personality before he comes to school and only very drastic educational errors can rob him completely of his integration. But the child of rootless parents has no such strengths to fall back upon. Set down in a school room to learn by rote matters which also have no meaning to him, he is likely to be seriously maimed. The schools for these children need to emphasize expression rather than assimilation, for the child is not ready to assimilate anything into the confused, incoherent mental background with which he enters school. A liberal use of the arts, intensive use of the methods by which all skills are integrated about daily life, and the illumination of the processes of food getting, market, exchange, manufacture, etc., are very important here. If such children are given, first, some basis for meeting the world, they may then become more easily world-mobile than those who spring from a more stable cultural background. But there remains a continuous danger that their world mobility will lack depth, that they will move from town to town, or country to country, never making any contact with the people and things they see, because the initial poverty of their childhood robbed them of the means of making a contact with themselves. The lack of introspection, the emphasis on action rather than thought, or facts rather than theory, so characteristic of American culture is itself a product of just such a huge process of deculturation. Without traditional symbols, the individual has no ready means to express himself and so turns away from himself out to the world, which at least in a material form can be dealt with by his five senses if not by his imagination. Modern methods of education do provide ways for repairing this damage, and whereas the introduction to literacy is perhaps the crucial learning situation for children from homogeneous cultures, the introduction to a sense of the self, is equally crucial for rootless deculturized people. Any educator before making a plan should be very sure with which group he is dealing.

THE FIELD PROGRAM OF THE PUERTO RICAN DIVISION OF COMMUNITY EDUCATION*

CARMEN ISALES AND FRED G. WALE

WHAT WE BROUGHT TO THE PROGRAM

THOSE of us who were given the responsibility for planning the field program of the Division of Community Education were

* Adapted and reprinted by permission from *The Journal of Social Issues*, Vol. IX, No. 2, 1953, pp. 23–42.

people who came from three different fields of endeavor: social work, agriculture, and education. However, we shared certain fundamental concepts which helped us achieve a unity of purpose during the initial period of development.

First of all, we were in agreement in what we were doing. We understood its implications. We all believed in the program, in one another, and in the methods we would employ. We were able to communicate our concerns to each other and arrive at common agreements. Having faith in each other, we were able to have faith in the families with whom we were destined to work. Our attitude toward people and problems was a positive one. It began with a deep respect for the individual. We believed that every man had the right as well as the responsibility to share in matters concerning the welfare of the community; that no decision affecting his community should be made for him and brought to him for his endorsement; that regardless of prevailing conditions every community and every member in the community possessed an untapped potential for growth and development providing that the nourishment for this growth came from within the community and not from the outside.

So fundamental is this matter of "respect for people" that we believed any action taken by us could be measured against it as a yardstick. For example, we could not sit in a central office planning the needs of a community, declaring in the same breath that we had unlimited respect for the people living there. We did not believe we could claim to have respect for the judgment of a group of neighbors and at the same time point a finger, no matter how subtly, at the man we wanted them to choose as their leader. We thought it hardly an act of faith to decide for a community that the road they wished to build was too long, or that the store needed for the cooperative had to be rented because the neighbors were too poor to build. We believed that democracy began with the stimulus given each individual to search into his innermost resources, and were it not for the fact that our experience in the field has put this belief repeatedly through a thorough and successful test, we would have been discouraged by those who prefer

to feel that such concerns are idealistic if not imprudent and impractical.

WHAT WE FOUND IN THE RURAL COMMUNITY

We knew that there were many adults in the country who had not had the opportunity to become literate. However, we believed that there were few rural families that did not have one member who could read and write. We saw clear proof of the fact that the countryman had a thirst for knowledge and a natural inquisitiveness with respect to himself and the world around him. We believed that this desire to learn justified our bringing new ideas on broad subjects in booklets and movies as often as the program would permit. Just as we did not go to the country advocating a particular solution to a problem—cooperatives, better nutritional practices, soil conservation—so we did not begin our work by launching a campaign against illiteracy. We do not believe that a man must know how to read and write before he is able to sit with his neighbors on matters of community welfare.

What we actually saw in the rural community was not an indifference to education, but rather a blind faith in it as an insurance for the future. The father with little schooling is ambitious that his children get more formal education than he was able to. He believes that this is the way his child's economic and social standing will be improved. Credits acquired by the son for their monetary worth are too often thought to be of greater value than the natural inquisitiveness and wisdom of the father.

We found in the rural community a freedom of spirit, a generous and open relationship between each man and his neighbor. The stranger is accepted with the dignity he deserves, unless he proves himself to be unworthy. Hot coffee, the leveler of all mankind in the country, is the symbol of friendship and many cupfuls are consumed on one day of visiting from home to home. When a man is in trouble, no matter how great his affliction, he turns to his neighbor to find the comfort and help he needs to solve his problem. We believed that this spirit of individual generosity could grow into one of broad community mindedness.

However, we found that the people had scant experience at working together in groups towards the solution of a community problem; that where such opportunity did exist, too often there was little conscious concern for the democratic process. The all-too-usual attitude was: Look to the government to do the job; the man of influence is the man who can get it done for you; if he cannot help you directly, he will give you a letter to the one who can; every community has its leader to do the planning and to tell the others when to work; the role of the outside professional is to help the leader present arguments to get the people to agree on what is best for them; a good meeting is one in which designated people make stimulating speeches; proof of cohesion in a meeting is the appointment of a board with a president, secretary and treasurer whose function is to act for the community.

WHAT WE FOUND IN THE GROUP ORGANIZER

In establishing criteria for the selection of field personnel we continuously kept in mind the job the group organizer was going to do. Primarily, he was going to build in people a confidence in their worth as members of a community. He was going to help them meet and discuss their problems on an equal basis. What kind of man did we need for this task? The following questions formed the basis upon which we examined the large number of candidates interviewed for the 40 field positions.

Was he a man of the people? A man who wants to build self-confidence in the individual, irrespective of his material value, has first to believe in that individual. We wanted a man of quiet dignity, who spoke of his neighbor as a man like himself. We did not want a man who thought in the "we-they" pattern. We preferred him to live in the country and if he did, to do so by choice rather than by chance. However, where he lived was not as important as how he felt about himself and his fellow man.

Could he work in his own community? Contrary to what some might consider good personnel practice, we believed there were no advantages to be gained by uprooting a man from his environment and sending him to a strange community. If for some reason a worker possesses qualities which make it difficult for him to relate himself to his own neighborhood, they would undoubtedly be the same ones which would make it hard for him to work elsewhere. The man we hoped to find was one who enjoyed working with his own people and would be accepted by them.

What concerns had he shown for the problems of his community? We wanted a man who had seen himself related to the other members of his community and had been active in programs of planning and action. However, we were interested in the way he had been active.

What were his attitudes toward authoritarianism? Toward the "poor man's" right to participate? Toward the concept that more land, more education, and more influence are the accepted criteria for leadership? The candidate who showed disdain or lack of faith in the people's ability and right to think for themselves could hardly be successful at the task of stimulating all people regardless of their station to work together for the common welfare.

Was he a secure person? When challenged, did he rationalize, go on the defensive, or discuss the problem with intelligence and freedom? We needed a man of stability. The depth of our interviews, the walks we took with him, and the observations we made as he entered new situations gave us some evaluation of his security. However, we had to depend upon the three months of training to bring out a greater measure of this concern.

Did he have a set of moral values which he used on all situations and all people indiscriminately? Or was he a person capable of analyzing beyond the single act into the deeper motivations of human behavior? We believed there was no place in our program for the superficial moralist.

What was his attitude toward the opinions of others? Was he a man of intolerant partisan views in such areas as politics, labor, or religion? If so he would not be our man, for we were looking for a man who would permit self-expression in others; a man free to work with all.

Was he a static personality or did he possess the capacity for growth? This was a basic concern. If he had this potential for growth and was not threatened by critical evaluation, he could reach the highest levels of development that the agency could give him.

In the light of these qualifications, such matters as whether the candidate was a man or a woman, the level of his formal education, whether he had a profession or a trade, his age, whether he was married or single, were of secondary importance. All who applied were treated in the same way regardless of how they came to make an application, for it was one of the basic principles of our selection process that anyone who wished to be a candidate had the right to do so and the right to be interviewed.

In part this accounted for the large number who came to the first interview in each town. From this first, large group, a number of more qualified candidates were chosen. These were then visited by a committee of three staff members. The interview was conducted in the candidate's home area, in a place where he was most at ease: on a hillside near his home, under a tree on the grounds of his school, or beside a river in the barrio he had known since childhood. The interview was held without pressure of time. As often as possible he was observed in relationship to his family and his neighbors. In this way the forty group organizers now in the field were interviewed three or more times before coming into training.

The task of selection began December 15, 1949 and ended May 15, 1951. It was accomplished by interviewing successively in the four quarters of the island and selecting four separate groups of 10 to 12 each. During this 17-month period more than 1,200 candidates were interviewed. Of this number more than 400 were interviewed a second time, and more than 100 for a third time before the final selection was made. The candidates chosen were then brought to the Secretary of Education for a final conference and, if accepted, they joined the program for a period of three months of training. At the end of this time they were either employed as group organizers in the field or dropped from the program, depending on the judgment of the committee regarding growth during training.

Thus we finally found the field staff for the program. Of the forty, one was a country peddler, one a fisherman, one the manager of a large cooperative store, one a clerk at the Army Air Base, and one temporarily unemployed though he had recently left the management of an experimental farm. Two had been clergymen and two policemen. Seven were teachers; seven others were small farmers. Seven were former municipal employees in such jobs as auditor, school director-treasurer, hospital administrator. Ten others were employed in the commonwealth government in such agencies as the Department of Public Works, the Land Authority, as a cooperative instructor in the Social Programs Administration, as an inspector for the Department of Health. A small number had ended their formal education at the eighth grade, a larger number below the twelfth grade, and a small group had spent some time at the University. One of the forty had a college degree. The youngest was twenty-eight, the oldest fifty-three. The average age was thirty-eight. All forty were born and brought up in the country and with a few exceptions all lived in the country when selected. All came from the area they now serve with connections since boyhood in most of their barrios. All were men, for the few women who applied soon withdrew when they learned the full demands of the position.

WHAT WE GAVE THE FIELD WORKER DURING TRAINING

During the initial three months of training we followed a very carefully planned outline of study with the following major objectives:

a. To provide the group organizer with an understanding of his historical and cultural past.

b. To give the group organizer a broad view of our present-day social and economic problems.

c. To acquaint the group organizer with the programs of the various agencies working in the rural area.

d. To help the group organizer analyze existing attitudes and practices of community participation.

Two important subjects came under discussion at this time:

Leadership. The group moved gradually from the academic discussion of whether a leader is born or made into a deeper level of concern. If a democracy is to live, why must the leader be selected by the group he represents? In what ways does he serve the best interests of the whole and not a selected few? Why is it his job to help people think and not think for them? The people that the trainee had accepted previously as leaders were seldom ones to be troubled by such questions. If the people were not dissatisfied, why should he be? But for the group organizer it was now a different matter.

As the relationship between leader and group became clear, the organizer's understanding of his role as an educator was sharpened. He saw why he himself had no right to become the leader in any of the communities where he worked, and why it was not his duty, as a "professional" with greater awareness, to choose new leaders for the community or dethrone the ones he did not like. He defined his task as one of providing the people with the opportunities that would lead them to shape their own destiny.

Group Discussion. Of all the subjects brought to training, this was perhaps the only one where all the members of the group became involved in a totally new endeavor. Previous experience in this area had not provided them with a background upon which to make sound conclusions, inasmuch as democratic methods of group discussion were not customary. The analysis of this subject was left purposely for the end of training. By then the group had achieved cohesion, and each man was convinced of the value of good group discussion techniques from the struggle each had experienced rather than from text-book theories.

e. To make a start on the never-ending process of developing methods and techniques for helping communities find democratic means for solving some of their own problems.

f. To help the field worker organize a program of work, keep adequate records, and have a positive attitude toward supervision.

THE GROUP ORGANIZER AT WORK

Visits in the home. Now let us step into the passenger's seat of the jeep and drive with the group organizer to the country. He knows where he is going for he has a planned schedule of his two months of exploration that includes all his 25 to 30 communities. He has a detailed map which shows him every rivulet, mountain, home, schoolhouse and church and he uses it constantly.

He turns off the main highway and follows a barrio road until it ends in a sandbank. Here he leaves the car and continues on foot along a mountain trail. At the first home he comes to, he rests and talks with the family. He hears the answers to such questions as how far the children have to walk to school; whether the barrio has a milk station, medical center or a hot lunch program. He finds out where the churches are located; who the people look to for their leadership; whether the men are fully employed; where they get their water; if the children are sickly, and the many things that people talk about freely. Before he leaves he tells them about himself and his work.

All that day he walks, talks, and listens. He will visit the homes of the men who were named as leaders, but he will not visit them first and he will act no differently than in the home of the man who considered himself the least consequential member of the community. He does this consciously for he has discussed it in detail during training. Had he left his jeep and gone directly to the home of a designated leader, the neighbors might have assumed that he planned to work through the existing patterns. He does not wish to work with the existing leadership nor to work against it; to strengthen it or to weaken it. That right and responsibility belong exclusively to the people themselves. He knows that he must act consciously, for every move he makes and every word he says will be reported throughout the neighborhood. Many discussions will be held in the store, along the roadside, and in the front yard concerning the nature of his visits.

His appearance as well as his approach is another matter he has to keep in mind. He has learned much during training, but he is still the same man. He looks and talks like any other countryman, but he is aware that this manner could be artificially imitated by someone wishing to establish rapport.

During these first visits he wants the people to share with him in deciding the best site for showing the film. He also wants them to join a group to study and distribute the educational booklets he will bring.

The showing of films. Once every ten to twelve weeks the group organizer goes to a community to place posters announcing the coming of a program of movies. The movie showing is an evening of recreation and enjoyment as well as a time for educational growth. The field worker acts as master of ceremonies until a member of the community steps forward to assume this function. His chief concern during the evening is to create the best "ambiente" for all to get the most enjoyment and learning.

The volunteer committee for the study and distribution of books. There were a number of mechanical ways in which the group organizer might have solved this problem. He might have tried to distribute the books himself, going from house to house. He could have asked the teacher to give them to the pupils. He might have left them at a store, one for every customer. Or he could have handed them out at a movie showing. None of these methods, however, would have given the people an opportunity to consider the problem as their own. Instead, during every home visit he showed the neighbors a copy of the book, discussed the subject matter with them, and made clear that the help they could give was for all the people and not just for them.

In general the response from the people is immediate in what is often the first opportunity they have had to render a service to their community. The time and place is decided upon and a group of twenty or thirty neighbors, including the farm owner, the leader and the wage laborer, meet together with a common purpose. The group organizer sees this meeting as the beginning of his work as a discussion leader. He knows that eventually every problem he anticipated during training will show itself in the behavior of the group. But he has the assurance that if he has learned well, the people with his orientation will find a solution. Thus the first seeds of democratic participation are planted. This volunteer committee meets several times throughout the year and between meetings the group organizer continues making home visits. Gradually there is an awakening within the group as it becomes a forum for the discussion of many other problems.

Working toward deeper concerns in the community. Time passes and the group organizer goes more frequently to a community. He finds he is being drawn deeper into the concerns of some of its members. The book committee is now beginning to talk of issues stimulated by the subject matter of the book. The large farm owner is telling him of a dream he has for solving a water problem. A leader tries to persuade him that working together, they can bring a service to the people. A small group of families is eager to "get to work on something." At this point he needs to have clearly in mind some principles fundamental to the objectives of his work and the

methods and techniques based on these principles.

SOME FUNDAMENTAL PRINCIPLES AND METHODS

When the group organizer reaches the point where he is working more intensively with a community, he has already come a long way in understanding people and the problems that surround them. If those of us who helped prepare him for this moment have done our work well and if he has grown into the educator we believed possible, he will have the following beliefs, involving in turn certain methods and techniques.

a. It is the responsibility of the people and not of one person, either from within or outside the community, to decide the problem they wish to solve. Furthermore everyone has the right to be informed and the right to participate if he so wishes.

Generally in each home visit there comes the time when he asks the question, "Well, tell me, how are things with you and your neighbors?" In most cases this is all that is needed for the man to unburden himself. Some talk only of their personal affairs; some talk in generalities. The majority speak of a community problem, though they may not designate it as such. Some clearly state that they alone are concerned about it. Recently, after one group organizer had visited 50 families, an analysis showed that while 13 had talked of personal matters only, 37 had discussed the same thing, the need for a good road. Telling it to the field worker was probably not the first time they had ever voiced this opinion, but it was undoubtedly the first time they had all said it to the same person.

Beginning by such a round of home visits has proved very effective. At the end of this first step the group organizer knows what few of the neighbors know—that many of them have a common concern. Most of the individuals with whom he had talked had mistakenly charged the rest of the neighbors with indifference.

Should the group organizer then become active in calling all of them to a meeting? Or should he follow the same advice he gave to the neighbors—continue talking until the decision to meet comes from the community itself? He decides on the latter, and enters his second round of home visits by going to neighbors he has not yet talked with and by returning to those he has visited previously to inform them of the concerns they shared with others.

Occasionally the group organizer gets the response he is hoping for, "What do you think of all of us getting together to talk about this?" But often it is the group organizer himself who in the end suggests that it might be a good idea if the neighbors were to meet to talk. Usually this suggestion is accepted with enthusiasm, and sometimes with a desire to meet immediately. The group organizer then must help them see that, if the meeting is to be successful, it is important that it be called only when all know the reason for it and after some agreement upon the hour and place most suited to the community. The group organizer and the neighbors who have an interest in meeting accept the task of visiting the families, talking out the problem and letting each person know that he has the opportunity and the right to attend. And even there, as minor as the detail might seem, the group organizer takes care to avoid such impersonal practices as using a loudspeaker to broadcast the news, giving the responsibility to the "leader," or sending a letter home by the school children.

Why does he have so much concern that the people talk together before the first meeting is called? It is because he knows that this will be the testing ground of many democratic principles. The meeting, when it comes, must not be called by him or any other individual, but must be the result of a consensus on the part of the neighbors that they have reached a stage at which they need to meet together.

b. *He believes the neighbors can grow to accept the principle that agreements can be reached through discussion rather than by calling for a vote.* He believes that decisions should be based on common agreement and not the will of a few. He knows that too often in the past the majority have sat back and by default and silence have permitted others to decide for them. He thinks that all decisions of the group should be recorded and respected in subsequent discussions. He is aware of the tendency in some to reach quick decisions by forceful expression or by calling for an immediate vote. He believes that one or two meetings are not time enough to permit a process of growth in which all may share in the final outcome. He is ready to help the community understand that a piece of work that could be completed in a few weeks through the actions of a few may take many months of discussion and planning if there is respect for the rights and wisdom of all.

When a meeting is finally called he is fully aware of the role he must play. He is the discussion leader and as such carries a major responsibility for the development of the meeting. He sees no necessity for a speaker or a movie to get the meeting started. The problem itself is enough.

He has made sure through home visits that those present know well the purpose of the meeting, but at the start either he or a member of the group states this clearly. He also keeps alert to the complexities of the problem-solving process. If the neighbors show that they are looking for immediate action to solve a problem, he will canvass the group to see how representative it is of the whole community. If the problem is a serious one, as is usually the case, he asks questions that bring out related problems few have yet considered. Under his discussion leadership, the people begin to see that a period of study and planning must precede action if they are to succeed. If as often happens certain members at this first meeting urge the election of a board with officers, the group organizer then asks the group to examine the function of a president or treasurer: Why do you wish to appoint a president or a treasurer now; what will that person do; what will the rest of you do; who will be responsible for what happens after this meeting? Such questions help members of the group to realize that they were following the customary procedure which they now see would lead to placing all future decisions in the hands of one or two persons while the rest of the group would return to their homes relieved of all responsibility. They are ready to let the matter of committees and officers rest until there is a clearly understood need for them. However, through this same method of questioning, the group sees the need for a record of each meeting and thus a secretary is usually chosen at the start.

If the community has accepted the purpose of this first meeting, its members will want to continue talking together. The time and place will be decided before adjournment. There now follows a period during which meetings will be held with a frequency depending somewhat upon the urgency of the problem and the eagerness of the members. Experience has shown that this is never less than twice a month and often once a week. The agreed-upon task of the group organizer and all those who were present is to continue talking together between meetings.

*c. He wants to see the neighbors enter into a careful, intelligent study of the prob-*lem. He knows that once the community has agreed on a problem, there will be many different ideas as to its nature and justification. This needs study. At this point technical help may be needed. But here again a learning process is involved, for the people and sometimes for the technician. Undoubtedly the professional could say at a glance the where, what, and how. If the people are helped by him to grow into an understanding of the facts rather than a blind following of a learned voice, he will have strengthened their scientific attitude instead of their superstitious belief of the unfamiliar. It takes patience and understanding for an engineer to have his theories challenged by a layman, but it is worth the trouble if growth comes as a result.

d. When a solution to the problem begins to take shape, he wants the people to plan carefully the steps leading to action. The group organizer believes that action without planning can have no guarantee of success, and that planning which does not include the opinions of the group can become a blueprint reflecting the decisions of a few. This is a phase in the growth and development of the community which tries the soul of the "man of action," for here the temptation to make shortcuts in the democratic process is always present. It may take the community longer to reach down into the depths of its own resources and exhaust these before looking elsewhere, but it is the basis for greater confidence and self-respect.

It is at this time of committee activity that leadership qualities will begin to appear in some of the members. It is part of the group organizer's function to help the people talk out the qualifications for leadership and the best service it can render.

e. He believes action should come only when the community is ready for it. In their eagerness to get started some neighbors may wish to pick up their tools and begin digging as soon as the site of the building has been selected and before the way has been found to obtain the wood and cement. The group organizer helps these neighbors see that action should not begin until the way ahead is clear. Through discussion they understand that democratic procedures for action are as important as for planning and that to guarantee them they must continue to meet. Thus the time of working can become the fulfillment of all the weeks of discussion that lead up to it. In an atmosphere in which man works beside his fellow man, in which women prepare the meals to be carried by the children with each doing his full share, there prevails a spirit of friendship and pride in the task that binds the community even closer in its struggle toward a better world.

HELPING THE GROUP ORGANIZER BECOME A CONSCIOUS TECHNICIAN

After many months of intensive relationship with groups of neighbors, the field worker realizes that there are many questions regarding methods and techniques which he cannot answer alone. He brings his concerns to supervisory conferences and to monthly district meetings, but the time when he has the greatest opportunity to search deeper is during the frequent periods of in-service training.

Following this he examines the question of *how* he works. This is the time when he discusses the details of his methods and techniques. Instead of presenting him with ready-made formulas, we encourage him to draw upon his own capacities for answers to his many problems. This is not to say that we ignore the research that is being done in the field of group dynamics. All such materials as we can adapt from centers like the National Training Laboratory in Group Development, where some of our workers have studied, form the basis

for theoretical discussion, enriched and made more understandable by a wealth of experiencial data.

SOME THOUGHTS CONCERNING EVALUATION

Personnel. Of the 40 originally selected, three did not complete training. Their vacancies were filled by new candidates in subsequent groups. Since these three failures came from the first groups chosen, we were able to examine the process of selection more closely. The reasons for failure differed with the individual, but in general we agreed we were not learning enough of the attitudes and motivations of each candidate. The committee immediately strengthened its techniques of interviewing.

Of the 40 group organizers originally sent to the field, seven have resigned. Analysis of the events which led to these resignations has helped us evaluate our criteria for the selection of field personnel. Although the circumstances differ in each case, there were certain factors common to all. In the first place, the job demanded too much of the man. Sometimes this was due to difficult personal problems and sometimes because of the inner tensions that the job created. In the second place, a deep feeling for rural life was lacking. This was usually due to the fact that although the man had his roots in the country, his interests and values had shifted to the town. And finally, the nature of the assignment created a conflict in the man's personality. His own needs or those of his family diminished the joy with which he went about his work. Sometimes he felt he had to have more money or that he must reach a higher professional level. Sometimes he felt overwhelmed by the creative demands made upon him. A gradual accumulation of these factors finally forced him to the decision that to be at peace with himself he would have to leave.

In our evaluation of these resignations it came clear that in future selections we would have to find a free man, as free as those now working in the field. Free in the sense that he could withstand economic strain and not resent the fact that the quality and amount of work he was asked to perform could not be measured in monetary terms. Free in the sense that if his family complained of neglect, he would know how to draw them into the spirit of his work. And free in the knowledge that the job he was doing was greater than any other and worthy of every sacrifice.

Training. Our training program has been an intensive experience in which growth came from an honest evaluation by the individual of each new awareness. In our analysis of this and of the present level of our field workers, we believe the time has come to challenge their concepts even further. We will do this by bringing to the group a number of people with expert experience in studying such problems as personality development, child growth and care, recreation, and the dynamics of human relations. Lest we become in-grown,

we plan to give our field staff opportunity for fresh insights through the observation of programs similar to our own; through travel; through association with people of vision.

A last look at the field. We are often asked if we believe "we are getting anywhere;" if the communities are responding to the efforts detailed in the preceding pages. It is a fair question. But today it reminds us a little of the maiden aunt who bounces her six-months old nephew in her lap and demands that he tell her what he is going to be when he grows up. We are still in the infant stage; our steps are still halting; our bones not yet formed. There are signs but only signs. A hundred communities under the stimulus of the group organizer have begun the process of working together. Some have failed and stopped. Some have succeeded in completing a piece of work but went no further. Some have finished one project and are moving forward with another. Some see the implications of working together; others see it only as a way to get a job done.

COMMUNICATIONS RESEARCH ON
NON-INDUSTRIAL COUNTRIES*

BRUCE L. SMITH

A PROPAGANDA battle between the Soviet and non-Soviet forces for the allegiance of the peoples of the non-industrial world apparently has been going forward for some

* Adapted and Reprinted by permission from *Public Opinion Quarterly*, Vol. 16, No. 4, Winter 1952–53, pp. 527–538.

years. Intensified efforts have been demanded of the United States Government's International Information Administration in the Middle East and Asia. This brings to the fore the question of just what is known about the processes of communication among the peoples in countries of varying degrees of industrialization. Americans, as relative newcomers in the assumption of heavy international responsibilities, have rather often underestimated the profound differences in socio-political predisposition due to different amounts and sorts of exposure to industrialization. Consequently many of us probably are more baffled than we need to be by the seemingly small effects of our official communications upon Chinese communism, Indian neutralism, Iranian and Egyptian intransigeance, and the enclaves of communism and fascism in Latin America.

This paper is an effort to suggest lines of approach for communication research in this area, across perhaps the next decade. It takes for granted the general validity of the well-known "Who Says What to Whom" approach to communication analysis. For reasons of space, however, it is devoted almost wholly to one of the "To Whom" elements in the formula—namely, the predispositions of non-industrial audiences.

Culturally diverse as the non-industrial areas of the world may be, they appear to possess certain similarities from the standpoint of communication policy. A good case may be made for considering these similarities.

What then, are the main characteristics of the non-industrial audiences of Asia, the Middle East, Africa, and Latin America? How do these characteristics affect the probability that communications by the Great Power nations will get the desired results?

THE THREE-CLASS SOCIAL SYSTEM

The general socio-political characteristics of these countries are well known. Leaving China aside for the moment, there is, in effect, throughout this vast area a three-class socio-political system.

The overwhelming majority of the population, from 80 to 95 per cent, are villagers. Only 5 to 15 per cent belong to the middle class, a class that numbers perhaps 30 per cent of the population of this United States and pretty much sets the tone of the country as a whole. Industrial labor, so prominent and respected in our society, where it numbers about 40 per cent of the population, is of course substantially non-existent in the areas we are discussing now. To mention India as an example, one authority estimates that "the total number of factory workers has never reached 1 per cent of the population."[1] Besides the villagers and the small middle class, there is only one more social stratum in these societies: the tiny group—perhaps 1 to 5 per cent—who belong to the class of landlords and moneylenders and (in a few cases such as Argentina and India) the owners of the very few big industries that exist there. This latter tiny group is, for all practical purposes, the ruling class, by virtue of its highly disproportionate economic power and its near-monopoly on secular and foreign education.

This handful of landowners and moneylenders and their industrialist allies occupies or controls most offices in the legislature, the judiciary, and of course the Foreign Office and the diplomatic service. In coalition with a small and seldom decisive group of urban professionals and businessmen, this group constitutes the National Assembly in almost any Latin American republic, the Majlis in Iran or Egypt, and to a considerable extent the Congress Party in India. They are challenged at times by movements expressing middle-class discontent, but, except in rare cases like the Turkey of Kemal Ataturk, thus far have not been overthrown.

When they are overthrown, it is typically members of the middle class who formu-

[1] W. Norman Brown, ed., India, Pakistan and Ceylon, p. 25.

late the grievances of the masses, carry on propaganda and agitation, and lead the attack—sometimes in the name of vigorous nationalism as in Kemal's Turkey or Gandhi's India, sometimes in the name of socio-economic democracy as in Mao's China or Ho Chih-min's Indochina. Hence the tremendous significance of the middle classes of these areas for communications analysis.

The study of feudalism in the West can easily suggest some possible patterns of social evolution and public opinion in the non-industrial areas of today—provided always that we make allowance for considerable cultural differences, and especially for the fact that in a number of the non-industrial areas there are few of the natural resources that permitted the evolution from feudalism in the West.

THE COMMUNICATION NET-WORK

Communications from the Great Power nations enter this three-class system at all three levels. In the course of dealings with Foreign Offices and other government agencies, and at international conferences such as the United Nations, the diplomats from the industrial nations negotiate day by day with members of landholder and moneylender families.[2]

In the course of efforts to push international trade and economic development, American diplomacy, especially through trade treaties and through the ECA and Mutual Security Administrations, enters

[2] The so-called "extended family" is characteristic of social organization throughout the area we are considering. Family considerations are usually very much more important in the mind of a Latin American, Middle Easterner or Asian than "merely" individual or national considerations. Often, indeed, these people regard *us* as immoral for failing to see the reasonableness of this intense attachment to the family as against a "mere abstraction" like a nation or an international agreement.

into contact not only with the landholder-moneylender class, but also, through them, with elements of the middle class.[3] And as we and the United Nations Organization develop our Point Four programs, our communications come into contact with the villagers—but again, it must be emphasized, through the intermediary of the landholder-moneylender class. For the latter, like Louis XIV, is the State.

Accordingly, an analysis of our communications problems vis-à-vis the non-industrial countries would include discussion of these three chains of communication:

(1) U.S. to Government (to landholder-moneylenders);

(2) U.S. through Government to middle class; and

(3) U.S. through Government to middle class and villagers.

Radio (e.g., the Voice of America, BBC, or Radio Moscow and its satellites) offers a direct channel to all three strata; but access to radio receivers is rather limited in the non-industrial areas.

EXTRA CHANNEL OPEN TO SOVIET UNION

For a full picture of existing communication patterns, it is important to bear in mind the additional communication channel open to those who control the Soviet Union. Being a government, they can of course use the three channels we have just mentioned, in any of the non-industrial countries where they have a diplomatic mission. Since Communists are members of a conspiratorial revolutionary party, they can use an additional channel:

Soviet Union to Communist Party (of the country concerned) to villagers and middle class—and even, in a few cases,

[3] See, e.g., Soedjatmoko, "Point Four and Southeast Asia," *Annals of Amer. Acad. of Polit. and Soc. Sci.*, 270: July 1950, 74–82. Also see Carleton S. Coon, "Point Four and the Middle East." *ibid.*, pp. 83–94.

to selected sympathizers in the landholder-moneylender class.

This extra channel gives the Soviet Union an immense advantage. It enables things to be said that would be extremely *non grata* if expressed through the other channels; and it has the added advantage of being confined primarily to face-to-face propaganda, which probably is far more effective among villager audiences.

CROSS-CULTURAL ANALYSIS OF "VALUE-CONSTELLATIONS"

A very great aid to policymaking in the international communication field would be a tracing-out of what knowledge we have as to the appeals that work or do not work in the channels at present open to the various Great Power nations. To plot the predispositions of the audiences, we could well start with a rigorously comparative catalogue of the value-profiles (or "value-constellations," as I should prefer to call them) most highly prized by representatives of, say, the three strata just named, in the principal non-industrial areas of the world.

These value-constellations could then be laid alongside comparable statements of the value-constellations currently being promoted by the Great Powers. Plotting the areas of congruence and divergence might lead to much better predictions than are now being made.

Particular attention should be paid to the value-constellations preferred by village audiences. We who are products of the industrial cultures are somewhat at home, probably, in fitting our communications to the value-constellations of diplomats, landholders, moneylenders, and middle-classes (who after all have received a large part of their education at Western hands). But in communicating with villagers there are certain things we are likely to underestimate or forget. Yet over the long term, as the case of China shows, both the moneylender-landholder class and the middle-class spokesmen of social reorganization have to work within the limits of the value-constellations of the villagers whom they "govern," or be ousted.

By way of indicating what this research might develop, the rest of this paper will comment on a few of the characteristics of villagers that seem to determine the ways their value-constellations can be affected by political communications from abroad.

THE "VALUE-CONSTELLA-TIONS" OF ILLITERATES

Many items in the value-constellations of the villager are due to the simple fact that he is illiterate. No doubt this is obvious. Everyone knows that from 70 to 95 per cent of the population in these areas are unable to read and write. Yet it may be almost impossible for people like ourselves to grasp the complete meaning of this for our problem of communication. First of all, it obviously means that we cannot use our own habitual media or modes of communication at all. The newspaper, the pamphlet, the book are simply of no avail except through intermediaries (school-teachers, town clerks, tavern keepers, itinerant storytellers . . .) who interpret them orally to the masses. Neither is our usual type of newsreel or radio newscast, for the content of these is based on the unspoken assumption that the audience already has a certain value-pattern derived from elementary reading, at least, in the public schools and the gum-chewers' magazines and the newspapers. Our newsreels and newscasts therefore assume a set of information and values that no villager of the Punjab or Iran or the Gold Coast or Brazil is likely to have.

Our usual media also assume a certain minimum of incentive for paying attention to those aspects of our communication content that *we* consider important.

For example, one of our key values is "political freedom"; another is the military security of the "Free World." Are villagers really interested in what we have to say about the loss of personal freedom under Soviet Communism, or the importance of contributing one's personal iota to the total military defense of the Free World? A good bit of field research indicates that they are not.[4]

Interviews by psychologists may show that there is hardly anyone in a village where the illiteracy rate is 70 per cent or higher who possesses any concepts at all resembling what we mean by freedom, by Stalinism, by total military defense, or by the Free World. Yet it seems almost impossible for *us* to conceive of just what we want to tell these people if we do not want to tell them about these things. And so we have continued to pop in and out of their villages with our movies, jeeps and bookmobiles, extolling the Western way of life, in concepts that illiterate people cannot be expected to understand.[5] In so doing, we seem to have overlooked the apparent fact that the only visual or other sensory image our villager has of the Western way of life is derived from the most violent of Hollywood's motion pictures.

As believers in relatively unrestricted free enterprise, Americans can hardly com-

[4] Much of the best of such research was pioneered by the former Program Evaluation Staff of the Voice of America, under the direction of Dr. Leo Lowenthal. See also the recent international research of Columbia University's Bureau of Applied Social Research, e.g., "Patterns of Communications in a Rural Greek Village," by J. Mayone Stycos, *Public Opinion Quarterly*, Vol. 16, No. 4 (Spring 1952), pp. 59–70. An admirable popular statement of some of the factors involved may be found in Arthur Goodfriend's *The Only War We Seek*, New York: Farrar, Strauss and Young, 1951.

[5] The U.S. International Information Administration has sought in recent months to correct this situation by having documentary motion pictures produced *in the countries concerned* and *about conditions in those countries*.

plain if foreign exhibitors cash in on the discovery that the gangster and cowboy movies are almost the only exhibits of the Western way of life that are very interesting to audiences in the economically less-developed areas. But perhaps it is essential for our Government information programs, if they are to be politically effective, to learn to offset, not reinforce, the existing images of our own values. A great deal of concrete research on a continuous, recurring basis is essential to accomplish this.

SLOW TEMPO AS A CENTRAL VALUE

In part because of illiteracy, in part for other reasons, the non-industrial peoples move through life at a much slower tempo than we, or so it seems to *us*. Recently a member of one of our cultural missions in a Southeast Asian country complained that she found it very boring to go to the native theater or dances or movies. The tempo was too slow. The shows lasted for three or four hours, and they always seemed to deal with the same small set of situations or themes.

If conclusive evidence can be found that this slow tempo is a central value for representative people in these cultures, it might be accounted for in part by their greater dependence on the slow changes of the seasons, and their greater preoccupation with the slowly changing details of plant and animal life and of the family. Their satisfactions in life appear to come to a much greater extent from repetition, meditation, and relatively slow development. If this is true, it is full of implications for our information policy.

For example, it is possible that they experience a frustration-and-rejection reaction when they are exposed to the high and jerky tempo and short attention span of our usual motion pictures and public addresses, and especially to our newsreels and radio programs. The very much slower tempo of the BBC broadcasts as compared with the Voice of America may help to account for the fact that BBC is reported to be more popular with these audiences.

Considering this same factor of tempo, we might also want to ask ourselves about the psychological aspects of our Point Four and "productivity" campaigns among these populations. These are campaigns that demand speedy action on age-old problems. Does our handling of the human relations involved in this tend to reinforce the Russian propaganda which appeals to the predisposition of these people to believe that we are uncultured slave drivers who look down upon the way of life of the Asians, the Middle East and the Latin Americans?

POLITENESS AS A CENTRAL VALUE

A factor associated with the high valuation of slow tempo among these people is their high valuation of politeness. Cora DuBois recently asked some Southeast Asians and Chinese who have studied in the United States just what it is most important for Americans going to their countries to be told. A characteristic answer was:

"Warn them that politeness is very important to us. . . . It is not polite to rush bluntly into a discussion of the purpose of your visit. We like time to make the *sawasti*, to exchange polite remarks while we are getting used to strangers. In the East it is customary and courteous to derogate oneself and one's achievements and possessions. We feel one must be very modest. You must not boast or force yourself on people. If you are very modest and very quiet, then people want to do things for you. That is how to get things done."

Just how these friendly warnings tie in with the tempo, style and substance of our projection of America and American policy through informational and educational media is something that may be brought out by research.

These warnings may also indicate some difficulties that Soviet propaganda may possibly run into in these areas if it insists upon as rapid a rate of technological transformation and as blunt a manner of speaking as it does inside Russia. There is a chance, of course, that the Russian speed-up and bluntness will be softened by the fact that most of their external communication is mediated by Communist Party organizers who are themselves members of the foreign cultures concerned. It is also a fact that the tempo of some of their domestic as well as foreign radio programs has been slowed to what we Americans regard as a snail's pace, apparently to make allowance for illiteracy and for cultural differences in tempo, and also to permit listeners to take notes, or to enable the illiterate to commit a message to memory.

RELIGION AS THE CENTRAL VALUE OF LIFE

Most of these audiences are very much more religious than most of us. To the orthodox Moslem, Hindu or Buddhist in many a village, the only conceivable "way of life" is the Koran, the Vedas or the Eightfold Noble Path.

To say this is to call attention to the obvious. Since Toennies, and especially since Max Weber, it has been a commonplace of social science that the world of the illiterate is of necessity a world peopled by sacred beings and given richness and meaning primarily by sacred values. To him, his government, his social order and his political decisions are likely to appear as religious institutions, while our political efforts appear to be lacking in religious significance, or even to be grossly anti-religious. We often forget this, or we badly underestimate its importance.

In the world of the illiterate, the instrumental and manipulative attitude that we are accustomed to speak of as "scientific rationality," or "business is business," appears not only alien but anathema. Religion is merely an added satisfaction or a consolation to many of us; but its meaning obviously is far deeper to those who are confronted by the horrors of disease, famine, invasion, old age and death, and who have no scientific instruments except their bare hands, and no ways of diagnosis or cure except the lore of an illiterate village.[6]

Some of our Point Four experts are reported to be astounded and infuriated by the grip of ancient religions (or superstitions, as they sometimes call them) on the villagers in Latin America, in the Arab states and in India. Alert and sympathetic information officers have suggested a rewriting of some of the Point Four aims in terms of the Koran and the sacred writings of India. According to reports, a certain degree of success has already been realized in this. Here the relative tolerance of the Western world toward divergences of creed and eccentricities, together with our continually growing understanding of both social and individual psychology, may very well prove to be a great asset.

In regard to the religious question, the

<hr/>

[6] A recent study of villages in Egypt, conducted by the Rockefeller Foundation and reported in *The New York Times*, May 5, 1952, p. 4C, showed that:

"all Egyptian villagers studied had amoebic dysentery; 90 per cent had bilharzia, a parasitic disease that undermines health and energy. Sixty-four per cent had intestinal worms. Five per cent had pellagra. . . . Six per cent had acute infections of the eyes, of the type leading to blindness, and 89 per cent had trachoma, an eye disease that can destroy sight, while 6.4 per cent were blind in one eye. . . . Fifty-six per cent lived on a diet of unleavened bread, skim milk and cheese, plus fresh vegetables approximately once a week. . . . (Another twelve per cent had no vegetables.) . . . Life expectancy at birth is 15 to 20 years of age."

Communist movement has probably had more experience, much better channels of intelligence, and much better channels of communication than the United States. For one thing, it has had a generation of bitter but often successful experience in governing the hundred or more non-industrial culture groups inside the Soviet Union and in Communist China. For another, its main communication channel is the agitator who is himself a member of the non-industrial society.

More than one psychologist has remarked that Soviet Communism can be regarded as a secular religion to a much greater extent than can liberal capitalism. In spite of its emphatic demand for atheism the positive demands and practices of the movement contain many elements that are very close to the more authoritarian religions, such as Islam and Catholicism, and to the religiously sanctioned collectivism and anti-Westernism of the Hindu or Arab villager. Indeed, Communist practice in general contains many more elements of what Toennies called *Gemeinschaft*— the communal psychology of the villager —than does Westernism as practiced in these areas. Therefore, it may perhaps be substituted more rapidly for the traditional practices of the village. These factors may help to account for the relatively rapid spread of Stalinism in the non-industrial areas in the very years when Stalinism has spread very slowly, or even retreated, in the more industrial West.

SOME HYPOTHESES

The foregoing notes have mentioned only a few of the points at which we have some research and need more. We could use much fuller information on the relative intensities and priorities with which the different strata in the various cultures concerned pursue such values as social mobility, physical courage, profit-taking, the sharing of wealth, self-government, the respective roles of the sexes, and the respect due older age-groups. Some research indicates that American behavior and communication in the latter two regards arouse profound antagonism in certain non-industrial cultures. It may be that we already know enough to frame some hypotheses on the relative roles of the United States (or "the West") and the Soviet Union in political communication with these peoples.

We know, for example, that many among the villagers, the middle classes and even the landholders and moneylenders are illiterate, poverty-stricken and ridden with illnesses. But many of them also are sophisticated representatives of ancient, well-rooted cultures whose meditations and accomplishments have enriched philosophy, literature, science and art for centuries. We know that many of their most central values—their races, their cultures, and their dignity as human beings—have for a long time been assaulted and insulted by "the West."[7] We know that a large percentage of the current political leaders of some of these countries have been jailed at one time or another for opposition to such "Western" ways as the wholesale removal of their natural resources. We know that the Communists, who have not yet been in a position to jail them or take away their resources, have a reputation for insisting emphatically upon their "liberation." We can infer that even if Communist propaganda today were highly incompetent—which it is not

[7] See, e.g., F. S. C. Northrop, "Asian Mentality and United States Foreign Policy," *Annals of Amer. Acad. and Soc. Sci.*, 276, July 1951, pp. 118–127 and Vera M. Dean, "How Asians View the United States," *ibid.*, 128–134.

—it would have an easy time among peoples who have been so much offended.

What of America's role in conveying information and education to these people? It may be that whatever information we pass out must, for the time being, be based almost exclusively upon local reporting of concrete actions that we and the United Nations have taken in these areas to help them overcome their haunting tragedies of disease, famine, ignorance, and the loss of human dignity. It might be helpful for the United States and England, and other Powers if possible, to disassociate themselves openly from particular policies and value-symbols hitherto associated by these peoples with "the West," and to speak and act much more in concert with a majority of the United Nations. Gradually a redefinition of the philosophy of political freedom, economic security and human dignity as we *and the non-industrial peoples* understand it might then begin to seem real to them.

Admittedly it is hard to get material or psychological support in America for such a hard-headed communication program. There are many temptations to preach, to accuse, to over-emphasize "the West," and to try to buy friendship. Our country has entered upon its responsibilities in world politics so recently that we are not yet as a nation aware of the scale of the mistakes of this sort that have been made, or how late in the day it is. Yet some elements in the industrialized world are striving vigorously to make up for past mistakes and lost time. We have no choice but to hope that the day can be saved by ingenuity and energy and by a hitherto untapped capacity for investment, mass education, diplomacy—and communication research.

Dr. Margaret Mead is an Associate Curator of Ethnology, American Museum of Natural History, New York, and Adjunct Professor of Anthropology, Columbia University. Dr. Mead is best known for her numerous published works on the

South Seas, for example, *Coming of Age in Samoa*, 1928 and 1949; *Growing Up in New Guinea*, 1935 and 1953; *Sex and Temperament in Three Primitive Societies*, 1935 and 1950; and *From the South Seas*, 1939. More recently among other works, she was the Editor of *Cultural Patterns and Technical Change*, a manual prepared by the World Federation for Mental Health for UNESCO, 1953; and author of *New Lives for Old, Cultural Transformation in the Manus, 1928–1953*. Her articles, expeditions, and professional honors are too numerous to mention.

Carmen Isales is the Chief of the field program of the Division of Community Education of the Department of Education in Puerto Rico. She was formerly with the Division of Public Welfare where she had responsibility for the training of all personnel. She has had several years experience as a social worker both in Puerto Rico and Chicago.

Mr. Fred G. Wale has been Director of the Division of Community Education of the Department of Education in Puerto Rico since its early beginning. He has taught in Greater Boston, served five years in the educational program of the Farm Security Administration, and from 1940 to 1947 was the Director of Education for the Julius Rosenwald Fund.

Dr. Bruce L. Smith is an Associate Professor of Political Science at Michigan State University and a specialist in the study of international and intercultural communication. He has also been on the staff of the Foreign Service Institute in Washington. With Chitra M. Smith he has recently completed a descriptive survey of the entire literature on the above subjects, to be published soon by Princeton University Press.

XI

CHANGING HEALTH PRACTICES AND REPRODUCTIVE PATTERNS IN UNDERDEVELOPED AREAS

ALTHOUGH this subject might well have been included as part of another chapter, interest in public health programs and reproductive control in underdeveloped areas is so intense that an entire chapter is warranted. Since the articles included in this chapter make somewhat similar points, little must be done in order to tie them together. The first article, "Some Social Factors Related to the Success of a Public Health Program" by George M. Foster, offers an explanation for the failure of residents in underdeveloped areas to accept unhesitantly either public health or curative medicine brought to them as a part of various international social welfare or technical assistance programs. Traditional beliefs and, one might say, understanding of folk remedies play important roles in the rejection of what we consider advanced or scientific medicine. The importance of certain common themes in explaining illnesses cannot be underemphasized. If they wish to avoid rejection it seems to be necessary, at least in the beginning, for medical personnel to accept these themes and work within them, or in addition to them rather than against them. Foster also found that mothers stay away from clinics because the importance of preventive medicine, rather than simply curative medicine, has not been dramatized or communicated to them. Other shortcomings of public health programs are presented along with recommendations based on past experience with operating programs in underdeveloped areas.

In recent years people have been willing to accept international social welfare plans because they have been sold on the importance of dealing with problems that they believe threaten group values. All too often, it would seem, interest in solving a problem or dealing with a situation is not followed up with research that even attempts to measure the actual social change taking place. The willingness of residents of an area to patronize a clinic or coöperate with medical personnel attempting to induce changed practices is a beginning and assuredly a step in the right direction if we hope to achieve results. But it should be followed by the precise measurement of change that may be directly or indirectly related to the program in question.

It probably goes without saying that the urgency of aid programs has often precluded careful preparations that would make possible an adequate appraisal of their efficiency. Nevertheless, even when appraisal or objective evaluation of welfare measures is possible, there is often reluctance on the part of participating personnel to have such an operation performed for fear that what to them is most certainly a worth-while program will be damaged by unsympathetic persons who have long opposed welfare programs. Support could probably be enlarged for many welfare programs if it were shown that results are forthcoming for monies and energies expended.

As Sripati Chandrasekhar once pointed out when on a lecture tour in the United States, many people are disturbed about the high birth rate in other countries, many people would like to see other countries reduce their birth rate, but fewer have quite as much concern about their own country's birth rate. Chandrasekhar is concerned about India's birth rate. In his article, "The Prospect for Planned Parenthood in India," Chandrasekhar describes the characteristics of India's population, noted in earlier articles by Kingsley Davis and others. He contends that the motivations for planned parenthood are present in the Indian population, and cites his own research as evidence. He believes that the basic problem is in bringing birth control information to those millions who are now motivated for planned parenthood.

"Studies of Fertility in Underdeveloped Areas" by J. Mayone Stycos reports on the preparations and training techniques that were necessary or at least advisable in setting up a study of birth control practices, a subject matter that, as the author points out, is not approached so easily as buying behavior.

At this time it may be helpful to the reader to refer back to related articles appearing in earlier chapters. These articles, in describing the characteristics of underdeveloped areas, particularly their demographic characteristics, form a background for the articles in this chapter that deal specifically with attempts to change hygienic and medical practices as well as reproductive patterns of behavior.

SOME SOCIAL FACTORS RELATED TO THE
SUCCESS OF A PUBLIC HEALTH PROGRAM*

GEORGE M. FOSTER

I. THE RESEARCH SETTING

THE Health and Sanitation Division of the Institute of Inter-American Affairs[1] operated in 17 Latin American countries as of 1952 through cooperative agreements with one or more ministries. The operational units (except in Brazil) are known as the *Servicio Cooperativo Interamericano de Salud Pública,* usually abbreviated to *Servicio,* a term which has come to be used generically to describe any cooperative program of this type. The original objective of the Division, which began work in 1942, was to provide professional and technical aid and service in the field of public health in Latin America. In line with this policy major programs have been carried out in the fields of preventive medicine, control of specific diseases (malaria, yaws, venereal disease, tuberculosis and others), environmental sanitation and health education. Due to a lack of medical facilities in many places, numerous hospitals and dispensaries have been constructed and maintained, so that an important part of the budget has been devoted to medical care as well as to public health in the more limited sense.

The health center is a focal point of an important part of these services. A typical center, usually a building constructed especially for this purpose, offers pre- and post-natal hygiene, infant hygiene (including inoculations), dental clinic, communicable disease control (including venereal disease and tuberculosis clinics), laboratory analysis, environmental sanitation, home visits by nurses, and vital statistics analysis. Privy construction, milk distribution to the needy, public baths and other additional services are found in some. Maternal and child health services constitute the core of all programs. Families are enrolled, and the appropriate members are expected to come regularly for services according to prearranged schedules. Nurses spend part of their time within the centers, in the several services, and the remainder in home visiting. In theory the work is "preventive," that is, not directly concerned with treatment of illness (except for special diseases). In practice it has been found necessary to offer much clinical care in order to induce patients to avail themselves of the services. Staff members of all health centers are nationals of the countries concerned. They include a head doctor and head nurse whose duties are largely administrative and supervisory, and several full or part time doctors, nurses, nurse's aides, sanitary inspectors, laboratory technicians, and lesser functionaries.

* Adapted from "Relationships Between Theoretical and Applied Anthropology" and reprinted by permission from *Human Organization,* Volume 11, No. 3, 1952, pp. 5–16.
[1] Now the Division of Health, Welfare and Housing of the International Cooperation Administration.

By 1951 it was recognized that, although in general programs had been successful, better understanding of cultural and social factors as related to public health programs might produce a higher level of efficiency. Arrangements were therefore made for the Smithsonian Institution's Institute of Social Anthropology research scientists to analyze selected aspects of *Servicio* programs.[2] Two categories of results were hoped for: (1) practical information and specific recommendations which would be of use to the Institute of Inter-American Affairs in program planning and operations; (2) contributions to basic anthropological theory.

The research setting was almost ideal, and may be summarized as follows: Beginning in 1942, essentially identical cultural stimuli (modern public health programs) were applied to a number of countries which, although of the same super-culture area, show local and national variations in both horizontal and vertical directions. In 1951–52 some of the results of these stimuli were studied simultaneously by cultural anthropologists familiar with the general outlines of each culture, using essentially the same field techniques and methods. Suggestions were made to the administrators of each project as to ways increased efficiency might be injected into programs, and cross-cultural comparison of all results was made. We felt that such a situation, if any, would give us an opportunity to find regularities in cultural processes which, if

[2] The following Institute of Social Anthropology personnel participated in the field work which served as a basis for this report: Charles Erasmus, in Colombia and Ecuador; George M. Foster, in Chile and Salvador; Isabel T. Kelly, in Mexico; Kalergo Oberg, in Brazil; Ozzie Simmons, in Chile and Peru. Dr. Greta Mostny of the National Museum of Natural History in Santiago made important contributions to the Chilean research. Field work was carried out in 1951–1952.

known, would facilitate the development of concepts and operational procedures that might be applied successfully to similar situations in other cultures.

Similar field techniques were used in all countries. Health center personnel, including directors, head nurses, nurses, nurse's aides, doctors, and sanitary inspectors were interviewed. Doctors and nurses were observed in action in the centers, as they received and administered to patients. Home visiting nurses were accompanied on their rounds, they were studied at "BCG" posts where they vaccinated against tuberculosis, at "mothers' clubs" where pregnant women were given instruction in the care of infants, and at volunteer aides' training sessions. Operations of *Servicio* hospitals were analyzed. Random sampling of populations within the area of health centers was done on a door-to-door basis to obtain a cross section of public opinion concerning *Servicio* projects. Health education programs were studied, and limited experimental work in health education was carried out. Tests were given in nursing schools to determine the extent erroneous folk belief was retained by nursing students. Use was made of whatever statistical data were available. Informants were "worked" in typical ethnographical fashion to formulate the basic patterns of folk belief concerning health and disease.

The types of data gathered embrace a rather full description of folk medicine in the seven countries studied, including information on the types of illness for which patients will consult doctors, and those which they prefer to take to the folk curer or treat with home remedies, a good knowledge of health center operations as they impinge upon patients, information on attitudes of patients, potential patients and former patients toward centers and hospitals and the medical profession in general, attitudes of doctors, nurses, sanitarians and other personnel to their jobs, to each other, and to patients, and their ideas of their problems. Statistical data showing the extent to which *Servicio* programs are patronized were analyzed, as were data on community organization and the possibilities of stimulating better organizations as an aid to public health programs.

II. FOLK MEDICINE AND INTERPERSONAL RELATIONSHIPS

Time did not permit the traditional anthropological approach—of many months of study culminating in a well-rounded description of all aspects of life of the peoples concerned. For such aspects as economic organization, income and cost of living, family structure, education and literacy, religion, the prestige complex, and the basic value system, it was necessary to depend largely on the data already on record. Although these fields were by no means neglected, it quickly became apparent that two other categories of data were particularly important for our purposes:

(1). The whole complex of beliefs, attitudes and practices associated with health, prevention of disease, disease, and curing—in the broadest sense, "folk medicine." Though a considerable bibliography on Latin American folk medicine exists, no systematic cross-cultural analyses useful for our purposes existed.

(2). The quality and nature of interpersonal relationships, particularly between patients and public health personnel. These proved to be most effectively studied by analyzing patient reaction to public health services, and by noting characteristic attitudes of all groups of people with the other groups with which they came into contact in the public health situation.

A limited description of data from both categories is essential for an understanding of conclusions reached.

THE NATURE OF FOLK MEDICINE

Almost all groups in Latin America are equipped with a philosophy which explains the cause and cure of disease and the prevention of illness which in many ways is in direct conflict with the teachings of modern medicine. Nevertheless this philosophy forms the basis to explain the action patterns of the peoples in question which must be changed if modern medicine is to prevail. In Latin America there is no single integrated theory of disease, but there is a surprisingly high degree of homogeneity in the sense of common themes and patterns that are so general as to form a framework within which local variations can be studied. These ideas of health and illness are the end result of a long period of fusion of two currents of thought: native American Indian concepts of the universe and man's place in it, and the ancient medical heritage brought to the New World by the Spanish and Portuguese.

Probably the largest single element in the total body of belief is that which has come down through two millenia from the humoral pathology of Hippocrates and Galen. According to that theory each of the four bodily "humors" was characterized by two of the qualities associated with the four elements of fire, earth, water, and vapor. Thus, blood was hot and wet, phlegm cold and wet, yellow bile hot and dry, and black bile cold and dry. The proper balance of these humors resulted in health; imbalance produced illness, which would logically be characterized by abnormal cold or heat and dryness or moistness. This concept, with subsequent modifications and elaborations, reached Spain and Western Europe via the Arab world. It was transmitted to Hispanic America after the Conquest, where it remained the basis of medical classification and teaching until the 18th century. Selected aspects of this theory—particularly the concept of heat and cold as qualities of the body, of types of illness, and of foods and herbs—became part of the folk belief of most peoples. General concepts of humors have also prevailed in some places.

Hence, today, there is a widespread tendency to explain many illnesses in terms of "heat" or "cold," terms which do not necessarily correspond to actual temperatures, but which are innate qualities of substances. Pneumonia, for example, may be classified as a "cold" illness, and typhoid fever as "hot." Frequently, but by no means always, treatment is based on the concept of opposites: "cold" remedies and foods for "hot" illnesses, and vice versa. The "hot" and "cold" distinction provides a general framework of do's and don't's for popular medicine: under what conditions and in what sequence certain foods can be eaten, and what the results will be if the scheme is violated; which remedies can be used for which illnesses, and what the consequences will be if these rules are transgressed.

In each country or area folk medicine has a core of principal illnesses (often with picturesque names) that have no exact equivalent in modern medicine. Each illness has recognized causes, symptoms and cures. Some "folk" causes may be called "rational" in that they are explainable on the basis of the body of empirical knowledge to which the group has access. This knowledge may be erroneous in terms of modern science, but it makes sense in terms of the logical premises of the group. For example, the widespread belief that abnormal cold causes respiratory illness is "rational." Closely related to extreme cold as a causative agent is *aire* or *mal aire* ("air," "bad air"), when this is explained as an actual current of air, a draft, which cools the body, producing various types of illness. Contracting *aire* is almost inevitable if one emerges from a house when warm, or if one breathes air much colder than that breathed a moment before. This in large part explains the belief widespread in Latin America that central heating is unhygienic if not downright dangerous. Violations of "hot" and "cold" food prohibitions which lead to illness may also be classified among the "rational" causes. The role attributed to "microbes," however poorly the term is understood, is another evidence of a rational pattern. For example, the recognizably contagious qualities of such diseases as measles and smallpox put them in this category—as does the belief that gonorrhea comes from intercourse with a menstruating woman, or from sitting on a hot rock, or that malaria comes from eating certain fruits, or not sleeping enough at night. The Colombian belief that "bad odors" cause illness likewise falls in this category, as does the Chilean concept of *empacho*. The latter is one of the most common folk ailments of children and is believed to be caused by green fruit, soft bread, half-cooked food or some similar object lodging in the stomach or intestines.

In general, illness and injury which are explained as due to such "rational" or empirically determined causes are considered by the folk to be "natural." The most common "natural" diseases have names corresponding to those of modern medicine and, in terms of popular syndromes, sometimes etiologies, but only rarely cures, they are essentially the same: whooping cough, colds, grippe, appendicitis, diptheria, measles, chickenpox, smallpox, intestinal worms, diarrhea, venereal disease, typhoid fever, pneumonia, tuberculosis, and so on.

Other causes may be said to be magical

or supernatural in nature, in that they lie outside the body of knowledge empirically verifiable by the group. *Mal de ojo,* or *el ojo* ("evil eye") is the most widespread "illness" in Latin America that is explained in magical terms. Certain individuals have the power, often unintentional and sometimes unknown to themselves, of causing illness in small children by looking at or admiring them. Such a person frequently touches the child at the time of looking, thus preventing the *ojo* from taking effect, or if this is not done recourse may be had to home cures or a *curandero.*

Sometimes *susto* ("fright") is magical in origin in that a malignant spirit or ghost may take possession of an individual, or be the cause of the fright. Bewitchment is not uncommon. For example, rag dolls or images are used to represent the victim, and into them pins are stuck or other injuries inflicted. The belief that a cold essence emanates from a corpse and can cause bystanders to fall ill unless ceremonial bathing or cleansing follow, is another example of a supernaturally-produced condition. In El Salvador this emanation is *hijillo,* and in Colombia *hielo de muerto.*

Folk recognition that strong emotional experiences can cause an individual to fall ill is evidenced by the wide variety of names for sicknesses that are essentially psychosomatic. The emotional experiences which most often produce physiological results include fright, anger, desire, imagined rejection, embarrassment or shame, disillusion, and sadness. *Susto* or *espanto* results from fright, and frequently is explained as a shock which separates the spirit from the body. The cure depends on inducing the spirit to return to its temporal home. *Colerina* is the term often used for disturbances produced by great anger or rage; in Mexico, epilepsy is thought to have this cause. Desires are called *antojos;* unfulfilled food desires of pregnant women

may result in birthmarks, whereas those of small children will give them gastric upsets. (Consequently, in Chile the wise parent never denies a child any food, drink, or sweet it wants, however inappropriate it may be). In most countries sibling rivalry is recognized, often in a form in which a child shows unconscious resentment toward an unborn child of its mother. In Mexico this is known as *sipe,* in Salvador the child *está peche,* in Ecuador *pasión* results and often accompanies weaning, in Peru the term is *caisa,* and in Chile this jealousy is one cause of *pensión.* In Peru embarrassment or shame produce *chucaque,* while in Salvador they cause a bothersome sty known as *pispelo.* The Peruvian *tiricia* is the result of a strong disillusion, and the Ecuadorian *mal de corazón* results from the loss of a loved one, loss of money or property, or some similar saddening experience.

Perhaps the most significant fact with respect to folk illness is that symptoms usually are broad and vague: vomiting, fever, diarrhea, sore throat, aches, and the like. Because of the generality of these symptoms they lend themselves to almost any kind of interpretation, and it would seem that this is precisely what happens in the majority of important folk illnesses. When symptoms appear, the experiences which have preceded them are reviewed and will often reveal the occurrence of an event known to produce a certain illness. Was the patient recently exposed to cold or to a current of air? Did he make an enemy who might bewitch him? Was he frightened? Was he embarrassed or angered? Hence, the symptoms, combined with the supposed causative event, are interpreted as due to such-and-such an illness, and treatment is prescribed accordingly. For example, if a child develops fever and diarrhea the parents may recall that the previous night it had fallen from its bed and cried; since such a fall might frighten a child, it is logical to expect *susto* to follow. Then those symptoms identified with *susto* and characterized by vagueness are seized upon to confirm the diagnosis. Many can be discerned with little imaginative effort: paleness, eyelashes growing long, sadness, and so on. The parents are now sure the child suffers from "fright" and the *curandero* is called in.

In other cases, symptoms which may have been present all the time assume a new significance after an expectancy is created. Once the culturally recognized cause has occurred, occasional crying or vomiting, either one of which is sufficient to diagnose evil eye, are seized upon as proof that the child indeed has been "eyed" by someone. The symptoms of still other illnesses described here appear in considerable part to be manifestations of culturally patterned behavior: for example, the person who experiences great embarrassment may be *expected* to evidence some form of illness. (Of course it is possible that the individual actually develops these or other symptoms as a result of his emotional experience). The functional value of such behavior as being the individual's way of escape from an unpleasant situation is apparent. In Peru he takes refuge in *colerina* from the embarrassing or unpleasant aftermath of a fit of anger, and thus renders himself immune from possible retribution.

Folk medical practitioners most commonly are called *curanderos* (feminine *curandera*) in Latin America, though other terms are encountered: in Salvador, *parchero* is also used, and in Chile, *meico* and *meica* (from *médico*, "doctor"). Midwives are called variously *parteras, comadronas,* or *curiosas.* Usually these men and women have come to occupy their positions after long periods of formal or informal training, not infrequently as apprentices or assistants to older practitioners. Only rarely do they claim divine or supernatural powers to aid in their cures, or combine their work with black magic. Their clinical perspicacity is often astonishing—beyond doubt they frequently cure sickness and alleviate suffering—and they have considerable knowledge of herbs, as well as of psychology. In general they are honest, sincere practitioners, and respected members of the community. In most cases they cannot be looked upon as witch doctors, frauds, or shams.

Folk cures make use of a variety of techniques the most common of which are herb teas. Massage is often resorted to, and usually is explained as an action that removes the illness or poison from the body, in a mechanistic sense. The famous egg-rubbing of the body of a child believed to suffer from evil eye falls into this category. A warm, freshly-laid egg is passed over the body of the little patient, broken open and examined, and if a spot appears on the yoke it is assumed that *el ojo* has struck the child. This diagnostic practice also has therapeutic value and frequently is believed to cure the child. Poultices often are used, sometimes for mechanical effects, but more commonly for magical reasons: in Peru and Colombia a live pigeon is split open and applied to the body for certain illnesses. Diet is important in all areas, with special attention to the "hot-cold" qualities of the foods. Often, certain days are used for curing (Tuesday and Friday, especially in Peru) and certain hours of the day. Religious orations and creeds frequently are recited.

Most of these techniques and cures are worthless in a clinical sense; at best their therapeutic value is psychological. Nevertheless, a good deal of significant knowledge has been contributed to medicine through primitive or folk pharmacopoeias, and a number of general symptomatic curing practices appear to be of sufficient value for the entire complex of folk medicine of a people to be critically examined by competent judges before it is decried as worthless.

The pervasiveness of folk medicine, its vitality, and its self-sufficiency are noteworthy. It is not just a question of a random collection of old beliefs and superstitions. Folk medicine flourishes today because it is a functional part of the people's way of life. It is believed in, it is practiced, it is given credit for its own cures—as well as many for which it cannot claim credit —and is recognized, consciously or unconsciously, by its practitioners as a legitimate expression of popular culture. Almost every informant was able to describe with little effort a large number of household remedies and their uses, and had well defined ideas about the causes, symptoms and cures of a wide variety of illnesses. Informants frequently spoke of their children as having been recently *ojeado* or *asustado* (attacked by the evil eye, or "frightened"), and cited cases of friends or relatives who had suffered from one or another of the folk illnesses here described and who had been cured by folk remedies. *Curanderos* do a brisk business in all places studied.

INTERPERSONAL RELATIONSHIPS

A majority of *Servicio* programs work well, some outstandingly so. Many doctors and nurses manifest a high degree of sense of duty. Pride in the physical equipment of plants and genuine sympathy for patients are felt by many of the personnel. Nevertheless, in many cases there are serious problems of personal relations to be overcome: some centers do not operate to full capacity, in others there is an unnecessarily high turnover of patients, and patient criticism of health services frequently is sharp. Three general criticisms are leveled at health centers, varying in intensity from country to country and center to center, but present in some degree in all places studied: frequent lack of tact and diplomacy on the part of doctors, nurses,

and other personnel toward patients; time lost in going to and from centers; failure of many centers to treat sick children who were not previously enrolled, or who had not kept routine appointments.

(1). Lack of tact and diplomacy. In many cases doctors and nurses are impersonal to the point of frightening patients, and in some cases they are consciously or unconsciously rude. Part of this stems from ideas of class and status found in Latin America, with rigidly preconceived ideas of the manners and intelligence of people in all other classes, particularly those one considers below one. In other cases, apparent rudeness is completely unconscious and results from the desire of a nurse or nurse's aide to do a thorough job: she rushes through a long questionnaire, which bears little relationship to the family situation, meticulously fills it out, scolds the mother for her failure to do the impossible, reiterates ad nauseum the importance of keeping center appointments. In some cases mothers have come to centers begging to have their names stricken from the roles to avoid being annoyed by overly conscientious nurses.

(2). Loss of time. This is the most frequent single complaint about center services. Most appointments are by the day, and the patient must wait until he or she is called. For a busy housewife with many small children, a hungry husband coming home at noon, and morning marketing to be done, the loss of up to half a day is a well-nigh insurmountable difficulty, frequently resolved by not going to the center at all.

(3). Failure to treat sick children. This is the most bitter of all criticisms of center services. It illustrates the failure of the people served to understand the fundamental distinction between preventive medicine —the basic goal of health centers—and clinical treatment of the sick and ailing. In most centers doctors will examine and prescribe for sick children if they are already enrolled. But in many, a mother may not enroll a sick child, so that in her hour of need she is turned away, to become a bitter critic of health centers. Unquestionably, whatever the philosophy and logic behind health center programs, parental anger at being refused treatment for sick children has resulted in active antagonism to center activities on the part of many people.

III. PROGRAM RECOMMEN-
DATIONS

The success of public health programs depends to a very great extent on persuading a majority of people in a given area to cooperate with health authorities, to change certain habits, to give up old practices, and to adopt new ones. All cultures are resistant to change, including those of Latin America. As has been pointed out, most of the people toward whom public health programs are directed are equipped with a strong philosophy about the nature of health and illness, and have essential faith in their own system of folk medicine. They believe, as does the public health specialist, that health is a desirable state, but they often differ with him as to how it can be preserved or, if lost, regained. A basic problem, then, is re-education rather than education. Ways must be found to drive out those characteristics of folk medical practice and belief which are in fundamental conflict with the teachings of modern medicine, and to utilize those which are or can be made consonant with the goals of the medical doctor. This means imbuing the recipient peoples with the realization that hygienic living and modern medicine, particularly preventive medicine, are forms of personal health insurance which will help keep them in better health, help to lengthen their lives, to work more efficiently, and to enjoy life more fully than will adherence to traditional health practices. It means educating peo-

ple who consider illness to be due primarily to magical causes or to divine will to believe in scientific concepts of cause and effect, of microbes and their power, and to act accordingly.

There is no easy way to achieve this goal. It seems quite obvious, however, that one important approach lies in recognizing the importance of folk medicine to the peoples concerned, and understanding its nature and function. If public health personnel are acquainted with prevailing concepts of folk medicine, in many cases these beliefs can aid rather than hinder the doctor—the good or the useful can be separated from the bad and the useless, and programs planned with this in mind. There are at least two ways such knowledge may be utilized:

(1). The ability of trained personnel to utilize folk concepts in interpreting and making intelligible modern medical treatments and preventive measures, and in persuading patients to adopt and follow through with recommended practices. This suggestion is based on the premise that people accept new ideas or techniques more readily if something exists in their culture which is or appears to be similar to the foreign element.

(2). The confidence which will be instilled in patients if it is apparent to them that the trained personnel understand folk concepts, even though they believe scientific ways are superior.

Occasional examples illustrating the validity of the first manner were found already to be in use. In Chile, as in the other countries, herbal teas form an important part of the *curandero's* pharmacopoeia, and popular confidence in them is great. For infant diarrhea some *Servicio* doctors prescribe, in addition to other remedies, the herbal teas in which they know the people have confidence. Drinking quantities of liquid is part of the treatment for diarrhea, and by the device of teas it is possible to ensure that the water is boiled and therefore safe. Were the doctors to say "Give the child lots of boiled water," mothers would be much less likely to follow instructions; but because the treatment is interpreted in terms of local belief they are convinced that the doctors know what they are talking about, and the child is therefore well taken care of.

Other examples in which a similar psychology might be employed were suggested by the anthropologists to Institute of Inter-American Affairs personnel:

(1). Ritual numbers, particularly "3," are frequently interwoven into folk curing. It was suggested that treatment might be prescribed in terms of injections or internal medicines on three successive days, or three times a day, or for three weeks. Thus, deeply ingrained folk ideas of therapeutic measures might be utilized to ensure that the doctors' instructions are followed.

(2). In many parts of Latin America the placenta must be disposed of in ritual fashion. In some places the impersonal hospital disposition appeared to be keeping women from utilizing available maternity services. It was suggested that arrangements might be made to deliver the placenta to the family so that disposition could be made in the traditional fashion.

(3). In some places it is believed that a postparturient woman should eat only those foods she ate during her first confinement. Some women expressed hesitancy about going to hospitals for delivery for fear they would be forced to eat other foods which they felt would harm them. It was suggested that as far as possible mothers be promised the diet they felt they could eat, and that meantime primiparas be sought who had no such restrictions and could eat normal hospital fare.

(4). In Peru the concept of the "dirty stomach" is widespread. It was suggested that doctors' prescriptions might be more faithfully followed if, in the case of illness defined by the people as due to "dirty stomach" is widespread. It was suggested that doctors' prescriptions might be more faithfully followed if, in the case of illness defined by the people as due to "dirty stomach," the doctor were to remark that the medicine would clean out the stomach. Or, if the problem were to convince someone of the need for a changed diet, it might be efficacious if he remarked that the prescribed diet was a preventive against "dirty stomach."

These suggestions aroused in *Servicio* personnel both interest and opposition. The principal question was, how far can or must one go in compromising the standard medical approach? We were much impressed with the pragmatic nature of the peoples toward whom these health programs are directed. If a practice is observed to work well, regardless of how much it may conflict with folk belief, people tend to accept it. An illustration comes from the new maternity hospital in Quito. About one-third of all births in the city occurred in the old hospital. The new one has sufficient capacity for about two-thirds. A survey revealed that many complaints against the new hospital were based on folk belief: fresh air, considered dangerous, is admitted to the hospital; patients are bathed; they are sent home in five days, whereas the culture pattern calls for a stay in bed of up to two weeks. Nevertheless, in less than a year the new hospital was operating at capacity, and comments of the following nature were volunteered by townspeople: "Fresh air is dangerous, but there is plenty of it at the *Maternidad* and it seems to harm no one, so maybe after all it isn't dangerous." Bathing of patients, and their short hospitalization period were also criticized, but it was remarked that neither mothers nor children seemed to suffer as a result. Apparently in many cases if a good service is offered, not only will it be accepted, but the very act of acceptance does more to destroy erroneous folk belief than any conscious educational campaign. There seems to be no single rule to indicate the extent to which medical services should cater to or be recast in terms of folk belief, but the limit is considerably lower than we were inclined to believe at first glance.

In other ways the failure of public health personnel to understand folk medicine appeared to seriously jeopardize health programs. Although there were noteworthy exceptions, a majority of the doctors interviewed had only the slightest grasp of the importance of folk belief to their patients, and little concrete knowledge of customs and practices. Moreover, they possessed an almost universal tendency to deprecate such beliefs and to ridicule the people who hold them. Not infrequently in the presence of patients doctors remarked on their lack of culture, their ignorance, and their brutishness in failing to cooperate with him. In general, the doctors operated as if folk medicine did not exist, that as far as their goals were concerned it could be ignored. Though they generally felt that patients distrusted them, they did not realize that their attitude actually reinforced rather than broke down folk belief. By ridiculing their patients' ideas they contribute to a more or less pronounced dichotomy that already exists in the minds of many Latin Americans between "folk" illnesses and those recognized by medical science.

Because they have seen conclusive demonstrations the "folk" know that certain types of disease can be cured or prevented by the doctor, and so in spite of their natural distrust of him they seek his services when they feel he can help. At the same time they feel that there are other illnesses that are best treated by home remedies or *curanderos*, illnesses which are not understood by the doctor and whose existence he

denies. These illnesses are generally those here described as having magical or psychological etiologies. If a child's illness is diagnosed as evil eye, obviously it is poor judgment to take the child for treatment to an individual who denies that there is such a thing. For example, in Valparaiso a public health nurse visited a home and found a child suffering from bronchial pneumonia. She asked why the child had not been brought to the health center for treatment and was told "the child is suffering from evil eye, and you know as well as I that the doctor does not know anything about the evil eye."

This dichotomy in the minds of the people is not hard and fast. Yet the common tendency of the doctor (or nurse) to ignore or ridicule folk concepts of illness undoubtedly reduces his effectiveness, for patients become more firmly convinced than ever that he has blind spots and, as a result, many genuinely sick persons do not receive proper medical treatment. There is a growing awareness of microbes in Latin America, but there is a marked tendency to understand by "microbes" those things that cause the illnesses the doctor can cure. Microbes have nothing to do with the evil eye, *susto*, and the like.

If patients could come to believe that doctors and nurses are familiar with folk ideas of health and sickness, and approve of some of its treatments (such as isolation, bathing, specialized diet, herbal teas), but feel that for many things they have better methods, it is very likely that the folk would have greater tolerance for modern medicine. There must be great numbers of people who would like to follow a doctor's recommendations but who fear to do so because of the accumulated repressive weight of folk tradition and the doubts which arise from feeling that the doctors are not familiar with the type of sickness with which they are afflicted. If an obviously sick child suffering from fever, headache, and vomiting were brought to the doctor, and the mother did not hesitate to say "I suspect it is the evil eye," the doctor should lose none of his professional integrity by replying, "Well, let's see. There are many illnesses with similar symptoms, and my examination convinces me that in this case it is such and such, and I recommend the following treatment." The doctor is neither ridiculing nor sanctioning the mother's belief—he is diplomatically bypassing it. As a specialist he points out why it is more likely to be something else, and as a sympathetic specialist his advice may very well be followed.

Other cultural factors of a more general nature also affect *Servicio* programs. A striking example comes from Mexico. In one large urban health center 43 percent of registered women desert prenatal treatment before delivery, the majority dropping out after the first gynecological examination. In a nearby semi-rural health center the loss is only 21 percent. Even if allowance is made for some variation because an urban population is more mobile and less stable than a rural one, there is a significant difference between the two centers. The explanation seems based on Mexican (and Latin American) ideas of decorum and modesty. The first prenatal examination comes as a great shock to most women. The intimate examination itself is embarrassing, and is doubly so because it is made by a man. In the small center the woman is carefully prepared for the experience: the nurse explains just what will be done, why it must be done, that it probably will happen only once during the course of treatment, and that she (the nurse) will be present all the time. In the large center the patients have little idea of what to expect. "It's best just to take them by surprise," was the joking attitude expressed by one doctor. In one Colombian center there is, practically speaking, no gynecological examination. The women refuse to submit to it partly because of their own feelings, and partly because their husbands are outraged at the idea of any other man having such intimate contact with their wives. Even in Chile, where health services generally are well advanced, it was noted in one large center that the gynecological examination, such as it was, was made by a midwife; the doctor barely looked at the patient beyond taking her pulse and listening to her chest. On the other hand, in a small center in El Salvador where, as in the case of the small Mexican center, women were well prepared by the nurse, little embarrassment was shown during examinations, and relatively few women abandoned treatment.

The impersonality of modern medicine here runs into a cultural barrier of considerable importance; prevailing concepts of modesty are incompatible with the requirements of medical treatment. It was suggested to The Institute of Inter-American Affairs that, at the very least, in all prenatal cases a thorough and sympathetic explanation be made to each woman. Ideally, women doctors should make gynecological examinations whenever possible.

In all countries communication between doctors and patients is a problem of greater or lesser magnitude. For a variety of reasons a significant number of patients after seeing the doctor do not understand what they have been told to do. In many cases the patient is nervous and uneasy in the presence of a man, particularly since she usually is of humble origin, and he of a much higher social status; she is unable to concentrate or to grasp what is being said. Development of greater rapport between doctors and patients will partially solve this problem. But it must be realized that the *manner* in which instructions are phrased is highly important. What appears simple and logical to an educated person may not be at all simple to a less well educated, often illiterate, individual. In the United States it is taken for granted that patients will understand what is meant by doing something "every three hours." Yet in much of Latin America such instructions are meaningless. For example, in a Mexican center the doctor told a mother to nurse her infant "every three hours." The anthropologist asked the mother at what hours she would feed the child. "At six, seven, eight, and so on," replied the mother. The startled doctor repeated his instructions, but upon being requestioned the mother still gave the same answer. Instructions in terms of time as defined by hours were meaningless to this woman. She had no clock, she was unable to tell time, and in her life experience it had never been necessary to grasp the import of time as understood in hours. In many other cases time was found to be meaningless, as far as instructions were concerned.

When significant numbers of a center's patients come from illiterate and low income groups unused to clocks, it would seem wise to work out local adaptations of the time concept in terms of things that have meaning to the people. In most cities there are factory whistles, municipal sirens, church bells, and so on, that sound at regular hours. Time points could be established with meaning for each area and instructions might be phrased in such terms.

A similar case was noted in Temuco, Chile, where pregnant women are told by the doctor to walk three kilometers a day if they feel well. This phrase appears to be taken directly from medical text books designed to be read by students and doctors. At a meeting at which volunteer nurse's aides were being trained, the nurse asked "How much exercise should a pregnant woman take every day?" All trainees promptly replied, "Walk three kilometers daily if you feel well." The anthropologist

asked, "How far *is* three kilometers?" This precipitated a lively discussion. The women remembered that they had heard both the numbers nine and 27, and multiplying each by three decided that a pregnant woman should walk nine, 27 or 81 blocks. But they were unable to agree on which distance. (Apparently they had been told that a kilometer is equal to nine city blocks). As in the case of time instructions, what appeared to the doctor and nurse to be simple, clear expressions were of no use whatsoever because the people were not trained to think in the same terms as the doctors.

Bureaucratic hours and practices were found to constitute a considerable cultural barrier to full acceptance of some *Servicio* projects. In many parts of Latin America, government hours are from 8 A.M. to 2 P.M., or a similar time period. Allowing for the time it takes to "open" shop, as well as to close it, the effective hours are considerably reduced. Moreover, since full time doctors are the exception rather than the rule, many doctors put in only an hour or two a day at health centers, with considerable latitude with respect to arrival time. To be reasonably sure of attention, a patient must come early and await her turn. If some services could be re-scheduled for the afternoon (and this is done in a few centers), when mothers are less occupied, it is very likely that they would attract more patients, with a resulting increase in goodwill.

The humble pit privy may also be used to illustrate the importance of understanding the general cultural configurations of a country in which one proposes to work in public health. Privy campaigns of one sort or another probably have been carried out in all Latin American countries. Public acceptance in some cases has been good, but all too often they end up as chicken coops or grain silos. Customary posture in defecating is perhaps the single most important fact bearing on the acceptance or rejection of privies. A coffee planter in El Salvador, in the interests of his employees, built a series of privies, one for each house, according to the standard American "riser" model. He was upset when his employees refused to use them. Finally an old man offered the suggestion, "Patrón, don't you realize that here we are squatters?" The planter ripped out the seats, replaced them with a perforated slab floor, and was gratified to find that public acceptance was general. Riser privies, for psychological or physiological reasons, seem to cause constipation among squatters. Similar cases could be cited from most other Latin American countries.

As a general rule in Latin America the perforated slab privy should be the basic working premise on which a campaign is planned, but other factors may override the traditional posture factor. Attempts to popularize this type in Xochimilco have met with little success. The village is sufficiently close to Mexico City for the inhabitants to realize that the bowl-seat toilet is used by cultivated people, and that the use of the slab marks one as a country yokel. Hence, in this village success of a privy campaign probably will depend on the development of cheap bowl-type equipment. Prestige here is more important than posture.

But other attitudes may also enter the picture. After an earthquake in El Salvador in 1950 the government built temporary camps for the homeless, including fine, modern privies. Their acceptance was limited. Finally it was realized that the people were accustomed to satisfying their bodily needs in the bushes, under the shade of trees. They liked the outdoor atmosphere. When the privies were moved from open fields and placed under trees, with roofs left off, the psychological requirements for defecation were met and everybody was happy. Twenty years earlier Rockefeller Foundation doctors in Java had discovered precisely the same thing!

In La Dorado, Colombia, *Servicio*-built privies appear to meet all cultural specifications, but they are not well accepted. The anthropologist found an important factor was the belief that bad odors in themselves are carriers of infection and causes of illness. Many people avoid privies because they usually smell badly; they feel they are observing good hygiene in not using privies, because they are avoiding contact with sources of illness.

In many respects the most interesting conclusions derive from the comparative analyses of results from all countries. The question of preventive medicine versus curative was particularly revealing. Following standard North American practice, in health centers the emphasis has been on preventing rather than curing illness. As previously pointed out, this has given rise to the bitterest of all criticisms leveled at health centers. We felt that improved health and better living conditions may very well come more rapidly through a process of education and persuasion which frankly recognizes the sick individual as an initial target. Fundamentally the preventive medicine specialist must gain the sympathetic ear of the people. Movies, lectures, and demonstrations will be treated with suspicion, and attendance at them will be small among people who are inherently skeptical of the apparent good intentions of government programs. But the mother who has seen a dangerously ill child restored to health will probably have more faith in the doctor's advice to boil milk than the mother who has been turned away because the center does not treat the sick.

Whatever the merits of a public health program based on preventive medicine, the fact remains that the average Latin American is interested in doctors and nurses because they can cure his ills. In most cases he avails himself of *Servicio* services, not primarily to remain healthy, but to get well. A survey of 100 families was taken in the area of the Beatríz Velasco Alemán Center in Mexico City to find out who patronized the center, and why. Half of the people interviewed had never been to the center. Of the approximately 50 families that had gone, 25 went because they had a sick child that needed attention. An additional one-fourth went because they could get free milk. A number of others went because they needed chest X-rays or other clinical services. Only three or four gave as their main reason for going their desire for a routine examination of an infant. Conversely, one of the principal reasons why mothers had not taken their children was the fact that they were well, and why should one take healthy children to see a doctor?

This reluctance to avail one's self of medical advice when one obviously is healthy is deep-rooted in Latin American concepts of well-being. Health, it is thought, consists in feeling well; it is not possible to be ill if one feels well and has no evident symptoms of disease. Since sickness is due in large measure to fate or luck, or carelessness in personal habits, there is very little a healthy person can or ought to do to keep himself in this condition, at least as far as a doctor's attentions are concerned. Treatment is sought when a person becomes unmistakably ill. This feeling about health is akin to the Latin American concept of machinery maintenance: if a machine runs well obviously it is in good condition and needs no attention; it is clearly logical to repair it only when and if it breaks down and ceases to function properly. With such a point of view, periodic check-ups simply have no logical explanation in the minds of the people; they feel they are doing the center a great favor in keeping appointments, rather than that they are being helped. At present, there seems to be no stimulus sufficiently strong to keep healthy people coming to health centers, unless certain concessions are made toward what the people believe they need.

Moreover, in much of Latin America there is a deep-seated distrust of the motives and knowledge of doctors. Many people feel that the native *curandero* knows more than a medic, that doctors are conceited and actually know very little. Everyone can and loves to tell examples of how the doctor failed and the *curandero* effected a cure. At the same time, the average Latin American is pragmatic by nature. One of the reasons why *Servicio* programs should also stress curative medicine is that it is about the only way the doctor can show the patient that he knows what he is doing. To illustrate, in Temuco, Chile, a bad whooping cough epidemic started in 1951. Fortunately, health authorities were in a position to vaccinate a large number of children and arrest the spread of the epidemic in a graphic fashion. There is no doubt in the minds of most mothers in that town that the doctor is a good man to know when whooping cough threatens. And this faith spreads to other inoculations as well; BCG vaccinations are being carried out with a high degree of co-operation from all.

The satisfaction of the patient in receiving a public health service which he or she wants, and the satisfaction of the doctor and nurse in offering a service the public desires, seem to promote an atmosphere in which suspicion and tension are reduced to a minimum, and in which, as a consequence, really good preventive measures can be effected. In the Cerro Barón Center, Valparaiso, Chile, where there is frank recognition that curative is just as important as preventive medicine, and where no sick child is ever turned away, more than half of the visits are "well baby" visits where the mother has brought the child for a routine check up.

If the premise is accepted that in the long run better world health will come from preventive medicine, the fact must also be recognized that in Latin America, at least, a sizeable amount of curative services must be available to develop the conditions essential for a preventive program.[3]

The problem of good interpersonal relationships between *Servicio* staff members and patients turned out also to be linked with the question of relative emphasis placed on curative versus preventive medicine. When the initial studies were made in Mexico, Colombia, Peru, and Brazil, significant differences in the quality of these relationships were noted. To illustrate, in Brazil there seemed to be a closer understanding between staff members and patients than in Peru. The first hypothesis

[3] The importance of understanding the basic cultural premises of a people in planning health programs is emphasized by comparing the Latin American picture with that of India. In the latter country the Hindus are said to be "more concerned with health than with illness, and prevention of disease is thought to be of greater importance than the treatment of disease." In the prevailing *Ayurveda* system of medicine "there has always been a strong emphasis on the prevention of disease." (Carl E. Taylor, "Hindu Medicine and India's Health," *The Atlantic*, Vol. 190, No. 1, July, 1952, pp. 38–42. Quotations from pp. 39 and 42 respectively.) A public health program based largely on preventive medicine presumably would stand a greater chance for success in this cultural milieu than in Latin America.

advanced to explain this situation was rooted in the question of class structure. In Latin American countries with considerable Indian populations one finds that educated city people tend to look upon the lower classes, and particularly Indian groups, as beings from another world, condemned by nature to an inferior existence, and incapable of being assimilated as useful members of national life. At first glance it seemed as if in countries where these conditions prevailed the quality of interpersonal relationships was generally poor.

Following subsequent work in El Salvador, Ecuador, and Chile it became apparent that this tentative formula did not hold. In Ecuador the social gulfs are about as marked as in any American country, and yet doctors and nurses on one hand, and patients on the other, appeared generally to get along well. Tensions and frictions seemed much less marked than in Colombia, where the socio-economic level is much higher, and where class differences are less marked. Our present tentative hypothesis—and it should be further tested —is that in those countries where there is frank recognition that for a long time to come curative medicine must be an integral part of any public health program, relations between staff members and the public tend to be good. Conversely, in those situations where curative functions are grudgingly accepted, or avoided entirely, interpersonal relations are poor, and public health programs are much less successful.

THE PROSPECT FOR PLANNED
PARENTHOOD IN INDIA*

S. CHANDRASEKHAR

OF THE many major socio-economic issues facing present-day India, none is more grave or more urgent than her population problem. Although a country's demographic situation may have many aspects, India's over-population—taking the form of tremendous pressure on her limited land and other resources—is the basic issue, since all programs for improvement are either deferred or frustrated as population overstrains the capacity of education, public health, sanitation and rural recovery. While the general economic context of the problem in terms of the ratios between the number of people and the available resources or between man and land has remained basically the same, the new data provided by the 1951 Census has modified the factual framework somewhat. India's area and frontiers, as well as the political divisions of the states and their populations, have changed in the wake of independence.

Since 1881, when the first regular census was taken in India, there have been decennial censuses without a break. The 1951 Census was the eighth regular census and the first in free India. With the exception of a certain amount of heat and emotion displayed in connection with recording the language spoken by the citizen interviewed, the 1951 Census operations were as efficient, smooth and peaceful as

could have been expected in a heterogeneous country marked by irrepressible cultural pluralism.

The total population of India on March 1, 1951, was 361.8 million, on a total land area of 1.27 million square miles. This figure includes the estimated populations of Jammu and Kashmir (4.41 million) and of the Part-B Tribal areas of Assam (0.56 million), where the administration rests lightly and where the 1951 Census was not taken. The 1951 population represented an increase of about 42 million, or 13.5 per cent, over the 1941 Census figure.[1]

The factors responsible for the growth of India's population are too well known to permit detailed discussion here, but some knowledge of these factors and of how they operate is necessary for an appreciation of the difficulties certain to confront any scheme for controlling the birth rate. They include: political stability and peace, even if these terms are defined as merely the equivalent of averted wars; control of famines, largely through the introduction of a modern railway system; a measure of public health services; and the cumulative effect of certain sociological institutions, such as the universality of the married state, early marriages and the Hindu Joint

---

* Adapted and reprinted by permission from *Pacific Affairs*, Vol. XXVI, No. 4, December 1953, pp. 318–328.

[1] In 1901 the population of India, excluding the area of Pakistan and Jammu and Kashmir, was 235.5 million; in 1951 it was 356.83 million. Thus in half a century the population had increased by 121.3 million or by about fifty-one per cent.

Family system. While the available public health services and the machinery for fighting famines are inadequate and unsatisfactory, they have been sufficiently effective to reduce the toll of epidemics and the rigours of famines. In fact, the population growth has been due more to a fall in the death rate than to a rise in the birth rate. For, although these rates are still very high, in the last twenty years the birth rate has registered a perceptible, if very gradual, fall—according to official figures. Available data regarding reproduction rates indicating fertility and net reproduction rates reflecting the replacement trend show that, while the net reproduction rate is high (1.30 for 1941), the gross reproduction rate is even higher (2.76 for 1941), and thus reveal a considerable and unnecessary wastage of life.

For whatever reason, the population has been growing during the last half-century at an average annual rate of 1.25 per cent. At this rate, the total may reach 500 million in another twenty-five years. Such a projection must of course be based on certain assumptions regarding fertility, mortality and migration. It is possible that in the future, as in the past, the rate of growth may not be abnormal in comparison with certain countries both in the East and the West during periods of comparable socio-economic development; but the net addition, in view of the existing massive population, has been abnormal and will continue to be so for some decades.

Examination of vital and other statistical data, such as they are, reveals an unhealthy state of affairs in the country as a whole. In 1950 India's estimated crude birth rate per 1,000 was around 40, although the reported rate was only 26; while for the United States and the United Kingdom the figures were respectively 12 and 10.6. The Indian death rate per 1,000 in 1950 was 16.5—definitely a matter of under-registration—compared with 9.6 in the United States and 11.6 for England and Wales. The infant mortality rate per 1,000 live births—a sensitive index of the state of public health and services and of over-all socio-economic conditions—was 127 in 1950 in India as against 29 in the United States and 30 in England and Wales.

The expectation of life at birth in India is among the lowest in the world. In the United States in 1950 the expectation of life at birth for white males and females was 65.27 and 70, respectively; in England and Wales the figures were 66.39 and 71.15, respectively. In India, where the calculations are based on certain approximations, the 1951 figures were 32.45 for males and 31.66 for females. While these figures represent some improvement over those of 1901, when they were 22.59 and 23.31, respectively, the great disparity between Indian experience on the one hand and American and British on the other is obvious.

Death rates among the particularly vulnerable groups in the population—children and women—are high. About forty per cent of total deaths are of children below ten years of age, and what is more disconcerting is the fact that nearly half of the deaths in this age group occur during the first year of life. In 1949, of the total deaths of all ages, 20.5 per cent occurred under one year, 15.8 per cent between one and five years, and 5.6 per cent between five and ten years.

The total number of maternal deaths per year, again a matter of under-registration, is about 200,000. That is, maternal mortality is estimated at about twenty per 1,000 live births. The total morbidity resulting from what should be the normal physiological function of childbearing in women is more than twenty times greater than the number of maternal deaths, or about four million.

The reasons for this distressing picture

of public health are well known. For instance, there is only one doctor for every 6,500 of population, and one nurse for every 43,000. While eighty-two per cent of the population is rural, seventy-five per cent of all doctors and ancillary medical personnel work in urban areas. Other disadvantages include the unsatisfactory hygienic environment; low resistance due to poor nutrition; sub-standard housing; want of an adequate and potable water supply, especially in the hot summer months; lack of medical care—preventive, diagnostic and curative; and, above all, poverty, in the shape of incredibly low incomes, which starts the whole vicious circle.

In spite of this depressing state of public health and allied factors, the population has been consistently growing. The population problem of India therefore boils down to this: How can the country raise the standard of living and reduce its death rate when it is unable to support the existing population even at a miserable level of living, if at the same time the population continues to increase by four or five millions every year? Some effort must be made to reduce the growth of population, and among the practical means of achieving this end planned parenthood is the most important.

A decade ago, controversies raged over the question: was India overpopulated or not? Some years later the controversy shifted to the question whether birth control was good or bad. Today the issue is not whether India wants birth control, but how best to disseminate knowledge of it among the people. This welcome change became apparent in 1951, when the first All-India Conference on Family Planning was convened under the presidentship of the present writer. The nation-wide response and support from the public and the press were so spontaneous and abundant as to surpass the fondest hopes of the organizers. The conference offered conclusive proof that the country was disposed to endorse planned parenthood.

Despite the persistent misgivings of Rajkumari Amrit Kaur, the Central Health Minister, the government was not slow to appreciate the changed atmosphere. It requested the World Health Organization to provide a planned parenthood specialist for the purpose of organising a "pilot study of the rhythm method of birth control on the assumption that if this method were to prove successful on a large population basis it would represent a simple method for dealing with family planning in India." The Ministry of Health informed the World Health Organization that it was "definitely for the moment unwilling to consider any other type of family planning." Dr. Abraham Stone, of the Planned Parenthood Federation of America, came to India as a World Health Organization consultant, and helped the government to establish five centres in which the rhythm method is taught to selected couples. When the follow-up histories of these couples have been completed, they may provide some evidence for judging whether this method of birth control is suitable and effective for India. In any case, it is of interest that India was the first country to give official sponsorship to a policy of population control.

The government's Planning Commission, which issued its final Report on the First Five Year Plan in 1952, went a step beyond the Ministry of Health and recommended planned parenthood, involving the use of scientific contraceptive methods. The Planning Commission asserted that "a rapidly growing population is apt to become more a source of embarrassment than of help to a programme for raising standards of living. In other words, the higher the rate of increase of population, the larger are likely to be the efforts to raise per capita living standards."

On the assumption that the population

is likely to grow in the next ten years at the rate of about 1¼ per cent per annum —the rate registered in the last decade— the Commission estimates that at the end of the Five Year Plan (1956) the population will total 378 million. If this rate continues for a longer period, India's population in 1971 is likely to be 450 million. In other words, twenty-five years hence the population may reach 500 million. This rate of growth is viewed with disapproval, if not with alarm, by the Planning Commission, for "the reduction in the rate of growth of the population must be regarded as a major desideratum." Therefore, the Five Year Plan recommends certain measures for inculcating the need for, and the techniques of, family planning. The Commission believes that progress in the field of family planning will depend, first, on the creation of a sufficiently strong motivation in favour of birth control and, second, on the provision of acceptable, harmless, cheap and efficient methods.

According to the Commission, two requisites for the implementation of such a policy are (1) intensive studies both of attitudes and motivations affecting family size and also of techniques and procedures for public education in family planning, and (2) field experiments in different methods of family planning, as well as medical and technical research. A programme of family limitation and population control should "obtain an accurate picture of the factors contributing to the rapid population increase in India; discover suitable techniques of family planning and devise methods by which knowledge of these can be widely disseminated; and make advice on family planning an integral part of the services offered by Government hospitals and public health agencies."[2]

[2] Planning Commission, *The First Five Year Plan*, Government of India, New Delhi, 1952.

The programme envisaged by the Planning Commission includes:

(1) the provision in Government hospitals and health centres of advice on methods of family planning for married persons who require such advice. Medical officers working at hospitals and health centres such as maternity and child welfare clinics should give advice to women regarding family planning when such advice is necessary for health reasons. If a doctor feels that a woman patient cannot undergo again the strain of pregnancy, it is obviously the duty of the doctor to give such advice as is necessary to enable the person to prevent conception. . . .

(2) Collection from representative sections of the population of information on reproductive patterns and on the attitudes and motivations affecting the size of the family. . . .

(3) Collecting and studying information about different methods of family planning (based on scientifically tested experience in India and abroad) and making such information available to professional workers.

(4) Research into the physiological and medical aspects of human fertility and its control.[3]

To execute this programme, the government has allocated Rs.6,500,000 for expenditure by the Ministry of Health during the period of the Five Year Plan. On its part, the Planning Commission has appointed two committees, one to deal with problems of policy and approach, and the other with research and programme requirements; these committees, having only recently begun to function, have not as yet produced anything concrete. It is proposed to appoint in due course a Population Commission, which will "assess the population problems, consider different views held on the subject of population control, appraise the results of experimen-

[3] *Ibid.*

tal studies and recommend measures in the field of family planning to be adopted by the Government and the people."

A careful perusal of these recommendations of the Planning Commission will demonstrate that they are reasonable, realistic and unhampered by preconceptions or prejudices. With regard to the rhythm method as an effective means of achieving planned parenthood in India (and the only means advocated by the Ministry of Health), the Commission has maintained an open mind in the sense of wishing to explore its scientific possibilities. Here is an area of possible disagreement between the Planning Commission and the Ministry of Health.

Because the entire field of family planning in a broad (and particularly in a clinical) sense is new in India, many of the foregoing recommendations are of a pioneer nature. The only legitimate complaint concerning them has to do with the meagreness of funds allotted for this great task. But then, this appropriation must be viewed in the larger context of the Five Year Plan, and one must not forget that, since India is a poor country, execution of part of the Plan is necessarily dependent on deficit financing.

Now that the Planning Commission has declared itself in favour of planned parenthood, the next most important single factor will be the attitudes of Indian mothers (of all religious beliefs and denominations), since after all they are the persons most intimately involved.

In Baroda City, a provincial city in Bombay State, with a 1951 population of 211,-416, the present writer conducted an attitude survey in 1952 based on a five per cent random stratified sample. The schedule was addressed to Gujarati and Marathi mothers between the ages of fifteen and forty-five. Sixty-three per cent of the Gujarati and seventy-seven per cent of the Marathi respondents favoured birth con-

trol; eighteen per cent of the Gujarati and five per cent of the Marathi mothers preferred "moral restraint"; nineteen per cent of the Gujarati and eighteen per cent of the Marathi mothers opposed "any kind of control of family size."

Similarly, a joint study conducted in Ramanagaran village in Mysore State by the Indian government and the United Nations showed that "in 78 per cent of the couples interviewed one or both partners expressed a desire to avoid or postpone pregnancy and to learn a method for doing so."[4] Again, in Lodi Colony (in New Delhi), which houses junior civil servants, seventy-two per cent of the wives interviewed expressed a desire to learn a method for postponing or avoiding pregnancy. The Family Planning Pilot Research Project conducted in the villages of Lucknow, Meerut, Etawah and Almora districts in Uttar Pradesh revealed that sixty-two per cent of the mothers and fifty-seven per cent of the fathers in these rural areas approved of birth control and were eager to learn methods of family planning. Thus, generalizing from the findings of these random sample surveys, it would appear that the majority of Indian mothers favour planned parenthood.

Any plan for a national network of birth-control clinics must take into consideration the aids and obstacles peculiar to the Indian scene. The mere mention of birth control for India conjures up notions of all kinds of difficulties—religious, cultural and social. The truth is, however, that India is more advanced than many countries in the West as far as the public reception of this idea is concerned.

The foremost aid is the fact that the government has never objected to the dissemination of information about birth control or to the establishment of clinics. This

[4] Report submitted to the Third International Conference on Planned Parenthood, Bombay, November 1952.

was true under the British Raj and it is true today. Indeed, the Indian government is more progressive in outlook than the government of any other country confronted with a comparable socio-economic situation. In most countries there have been severe battles—legal, social and moral—before birth-control practices became acceptable and were made available to those who needed it. India is fortunate in being able to enjoy the benefits of battles fought elsewhere years ago.

In the second place, the religious attitude on this question has been relatively unimportant, for the Hindu position in general is one of tolerance. Careful examination has convinced the present writer that the Hindu scriptural texts, properly interpreted and understood, do not oppose but in fact favour control of the size of families. Since the Catholic community in India constitutes a very small minority, organized and vocal opposition to birth control has been practically nonexistent.

Finally, the periodic famines and the semi-chronic food shortages existing in the country have dramatized the population situation, and have aided greatly in giving a fillip to the educational effort launched by the present writer some seven years ago.

If these aids are impressive, the obstacles confronting a birth-control programme are no less so. First, the low level of living is both an asset and a liability—an asset because it underscores so vividly the need for birth control, and a liability because it makes the practice of such measures difficult. Birth control is usually associated with a high level of living. But since India cannot wait to introduce it until the level of living has been raised, birth control must form a part of an over-all programme for economic development. Secondly, this movement should start in the villages—the base of India's socio-economic structure; in reality, however, it has begun at the apex—in the cities. The fact that birth-control facilities exist in most large cities, where they cater to the needs of the middle and upper classes, represents more of a problem than a solution, for it only aggravates the implications of the rural-urban and inter-class fertility differential. This situation is bound to affect the quality of the population. The families that are now most severely handicapped in terms of economic resources, health and education, are precisely those that are most poorly equipped to rear the nation's future citizenry. Yet, it is these families that at present have the major burden of nurturing more than their proportion of the next generation.

Taking birth control to the villages is, unfortunately, more easily said than done. Not only are the villages deficient in basic health and medical facilities, but they are plagued by unhygienic conditions, insufficient running water (and often any readily available water), lack of privacy, illiteracy, ignorance, and above all poverty so extreme as to make the price of a contraceptive prohibitive. Some knowledge of these and other difficulties is necessary to appreciate the efforts needed to make planned parenthood workable in India.

Without losing sight of these aids and difficulties, there may be some point in examining the progress made in planned-parenthood work in certain areas since 1950. As has been pointed out, real clinical work is of recent origin, and acceptable statistical data are as yet insufficient to permit a serious evaluation of the programme. It will be of interest, however, to note briefly the experience gained thus far in one or two projects.

In Bombay, in addition to the seventeen birth-control clinics operated by the Bombay Municipal Corporation in Greater Bombay since 1947 in conjunction with municipal maternity homes and hospitals, the Family Planning Association of India in 1952 inaugurated a Family Welfare

Centre, operating on modern, scientific lines. The Centre provides services in connection with advice on contraception and infertility, marriage counselling and sex education. It has gathered revealing information concerning Hindus, Muslims, Protestants, Catholics, Jews and Parsees—all Indians of course. Of a total of some 3,000 individuals who sought contraceptive advice, one-third visited the clinic more than once. A majority of the callers were of middle-class economic status. About sixteen per cent of the fathers and mothers applied not for contraceptives but specifically for sterilisation. Some six per cent of the women who requested contraceptive advice were found on examination to be pregnant; though they did not ask for abortions, they were under the erroneous impression that the Centre's activities included this service.

It is too early to evaluate the effectiveness of these services, but follow-up records of the individual cases are being maintained, so that two or three years hence information should be available on the degree of success achieved by these mothers in preventing or postponing pregnancy. The percentage of failures recorded will then afford an idea of how effective contraceptives are proving when utilised by Indian mothers.

Some evidence is available also for the State of Hyderabad, where a family-planning association and three birth-control clinics have been operating since the end of 1950. During the first sixteen months the attendance at these clinics was 2,035. Diaphragms and jelly were supplied to 1,324, and 711 received pads and oil (the indigenous and cheaper contraceptive method). Of these, 760 revisited the clinics after a few months to report that they had conceived.

Since 1950, birth-control clinics of one kind or another, under either official or private auspices, have been functioning in Madras, Bangalore, Mysore, Lucknow, Allahabad, Delhi, Calcutta and in the Punjab, but unfortunately these pioneer projects maintain no accurate data concerning the fertility history of the mothers, the acceptability of the method employed, the difficulties encountered in its use, and, most important, its effectiveness or the reason for its abandonment. Because the case sheets used in these different clinics are rather haphazard and lack uniformity, they are gravely defective from the statistical standpoint. For want of reliable, comparable statistics, it is difficult to assess the over-all value of the work done in the years since 1950. From both the clinical and the statistical standpoints, the major weakness lies in the lack of trained personnel. An attempt is now being made to remedy this defect.

Wherever a scientific contraceptive method has failed, the distressed expectant mothers have advanced such reasons as: "I forgot to use it once or twice"; "It was inconvenient"; "I used it carefully as taught, but the diaphragm was probably in an incorrect position"; "I didn't use the jelly"; or sometimes, though rarely, "My husband objected to it" or "My mother-in-law objected to it." These reasons for failure are not all peculiarly Indian; birth-control workers in other countries encounter similar explanations.

As for certain other material difficulties in semi-rural and smaller places, the following may be regarded as representative comments: "The jelly was used up, and no local shop carries it"; "There was no light, and I couldn't find the diaphragm." One mother complained that she had forgotten to wash the diaphragm after use, and that in consequence a band of black ants had eaten it! In almost all of the centres the mothers who seek contraceptive advice are not very happy with diaphragms or other mechanical and chemical contraceptives; they invariably ask for a "mixture" or "a pill" that will induce temporary sterility. And, to be sure, the real need is for just such a contraceptive—an oral and a biological one that will be simple, cheap, harmless and effective. When such a contraceptive is discovered, the Indian population problem will be much more easily solved.

Two obvious conclusions emerge from this brief and necessarily incomplete survey. India has become aware that her population growth constitutes a problem and jeopardizes the realization of her desire for a better level of living. Moreover, this awareness has induced a perceptible change in individual and group attitudes and motivations in favour of planned parenthood.

STUDIES OF FERTILITY IN UNDERDEVELOPED AREAS*

J. MAYONE STYCOS

SAMPLING AND CASE-FINDING

SAMPLING for fertility surveys in an underdeveloped area involves at least two problems: (1) The problem of *locating* cases in a probability sample; and (2) the problem of locating cases when sampling by special fertility categories. We were fortunate in being able to procure listings of some type for sampling purposes, both in Puerto Rico and Jamaica. However, in these underdeveloped areas, case-finding from such records is difficult, costly, and hard on interviewer morale. In trying to locate cases, interviewers have temporarily been lost in fields of sugar cane, swept downstream while fording rivers, and drenched in tropical downpours. In one case where I accompanied an interviewer, we climbed rugged, muddy hills for three hours, only to find the respondent not at home. Moreover, addresses from these listings are usually highly inadequate, often

*Adapted and reprinted by permission from *Human Organization*, Volume 13, No. 1, Spring 1954, pp. 9–12.

giving only the parish or general neighborhood. One system devised in Puerto Rico was to go to the nearest school, moving from class to class until we found a child who knew the respondent. Then the teacher would talk the child into being a guide. My feeling is that more unorthodox sampling methods are greatly needed in such areas. Let me describe one sampling procedure worked out in Puerto Rico, which tried to simplify case-finding while insuring representativeness from different categories of birth control use.

Our problem was to do about 1,300 one- and one-half-hour interviews, but we wanted equal numbers of users, non-users and past users of birth control. Not only could we not finance the necessary pre-listing; but we felt we could not finance 1,000 final interviews if they had to be conducted in the home. Moreover, a pre-list screening on birth control is not the same as a pre-list on education or buying behavior. One could not very well knock on a door and ask what types of contraceptives were being used. Finally, we required a system which would guarantee a maximum of privacy for the interview, no simple matter where the advent of an interviewer often creates great excitement and curiosity on the part of neighbors and relatives. Consequently, we devised a system whereby the respondent would come to *us* both for his pre-list and final interview, and one in which he would be willing to answer the intimate questions of a five-minute screening questionnaire.

The population chosen for pre-listing consisted of patients attending general clinics of seven public health centers and two hospitals. The centers, located in different parts of the island, reasonably close to rural areas, give free medical care of practically all types to all who desire it. Patients waiting to see the doctors were shuttled to the interviewer's desk, where, with little or no introduction, the pre-list questionnaire was administered as if it were part of the normal health center routine. In this way, intimate questions could be asked without lengthy preliminaries, patients were pleased at a diversion from waiting, and we secured 3,000 cases at very little cost. Moreover, comparison of the characteristics of the sample with census figures showed no serious biases.

From this sample we drew the sub-sample of different birth control types. Letters were then sent out on Department of Health stationery, signed by the physician in charge, requesting the patient to come into the clinic at a particular day and hour. If the patient did not show up, a second letter was sent with a reappointment. If this failed, an interviewer was detailed to conduct a home visit. In general, the system can be considered a success.

However, two assumptions caused difficulties. The first was that mail would reach rural respondents within 10 days. Actually, some did not come to the nearest general store or post office for two or three weeks,

and it never occurred to others to look for mail. A cheap messenger system and the entrusting of delivery to neighbors or respondents was finally employed. A second assumption was that the hour and day of appointments would be taken seriously. In practice, interested individuals often came hours or days early, and less interested individuals came hours or days late. Fortunately, these tended to balance each other, and interviewers were not too frequently left without work.

RAPPORT AND INITIAL CONTACT

Interviewing in the health centers eased the problem of securing the confidence and cooperation of respondents. In other surveys, however, home visits were the rule. In terms of approach, one factor which may have been in our favor was the higher class level of the interviewers. For many poor families, it was flattering to have an educated middle class person show an interest in them, and even more flattering to be visited in their homes; some considered it to be an educational experience. In Jamaica, interviewers were occasionally badgered by people in the community who wanted to know why they were not being interviewed; one Puerto Rican woman, after being interviewed in the clinics, brought in a whole group of female relatives the next day with the request that they be asked "all those interesting questions."

In Jamaica, where class and color are of great importance, we were advised by some informants to use white interviewers because they would presumably get more respect and cooperation from respondents. It was felt, however, that the combination of higher class and color might be too much, so no white interviewers were used.

In both Puerto Rico and Jamaica, since groups of cases were often clustered within relatively small areas, the fear of gossip preceding the interviewers prompted the adoption of a "hit and run" method. Enough interviewers were sent to each area to enable its completion in a few days. Moreover, every effort was made to conduct interviews in private, and both at the beginning and end of the interview, respondents were assured of the confidential nature of the project. The confidentiality approach seemed to work well enough in Puerto Rico, but boomeranged in a few instances in Jamaica. In one case a reluctant and rather sullen respondent finally asked the interviewer if she were a nun. "All this sounds too much like confession and the Catholic Church," she explained.

A more serious boomerang occurred in a sugar cane area, where interviewers made the mistake of setting up their appointments the night before. On the following morning they were greeted by an angry crowd brandishing machetes. Many of the inhabitants of the area had been up all night discussing the matter and had decided to kill the group or run them out of the area. "All that talk about how secret and private it's going to be—that sounds like Black Art." Unused to privacy, their only interpretation of it was witchcraft.

What other content was conveyed in the initial approach? Interviewers were instructed to introduce themselves, to strike up conversation about the respondent's children, crops, and so forth. Most important was to give the impression of being comfortable in the lower class home. The content of questions themselves was only given in general terms—they concerned "family matters, bringing up your children, and things like that."

The explanation for wanting to talk with the respondent combined truth and flattery:

"The doctors have studied the rich people too long. Now they want to know more about the troubles of ordinary people like yourself—good, typical (Jamaicans or Puerto Ricans). We pulled your name out of a hat, just like in the lottery, and that is how you got picked."

In Puerto Rico, where most of the population is aware of the University and respects it highly, the mention of its sponsorship was an open sesame. In Jamaica, the concept of the University often had to be put in simpler terms.

"You know down in Kingston we're proud to have a new college—a school that trains our own people to be teachers and doctors. They want to find out more about the *real* Jamaican, so they can train our doctors and teachers better."

In Puerto Rico, it was felt that to associate the study with "Americans" might do more harm than good. In Jamaica, the interviewers unanimously opposed the exclusion of American sponsorship holding that many look to America for aid and employment. Consequently the following approach was frequently used:

"You know the Americans want to help us. They employ our boys on the farms up there and they are very interested in us. They gave money to our doctors to do this study."

Something also had to be said about what was to be gained by the respondent in answering the questions. In Jamaica, where the lower class population is even more impoverished than in Puerto Rico, respondents often asked bluntly, "What do I get out of it? Other people have been around here asking questions and nothing ever happens." Because of the unusual length of the interviews (about six hours), the Jamaicans were given 75 cents each in cash or food, but were also told:

"All these questions probably won't help *you* any right now, but they're going to help your children to have better families. Don't you think that's good?"

Of 100 female and 50 male Jamaicans, we encountered only a half-dozen refusals. In the qualitative study of 72 Puerto Rican families there were no refusals, and only a dozen from the 1,300 clinic-based interviews.

In general, the approach, which put the sponsorship, purpose and value of the project in simple and somewhat flattering terms, appeared to be successful in both areas.

QUESTIONNAIRE CONSTRUCTION

There are just two points I would like to make about questionnaire construction: (1) The necessity of employing unstructured interviews prior to construction of a poll-type questionnaire, and (2) the need for more careful pre-testing than in studies in the States.

The first point needs little comment. In another culture, the unanticipated response is almost the rule, and the armchair questionnaire can be disastrous. The reasons people do not use birth control in Puerto Rico, for example, appear to have relatively little to do with such expected factors as ignorance, availability of materials, and religion, but have much to do with such complexes as modesty, superstition, lack of communication between spouses, and suspicions of infidelity. Let me give one quotation from a Puerto Rican interview to show how inadequate the poll-type questionnaire would be if not preceded by some exploratory work.

I brought condoms home from the Health Center and he used them for about two years. After I had my last child I got some more but haven't used them yet, becaue I haven't menstruated again, my husband might think I had contact with another man. So I cannot use them until I know whether I am pregnant or not.

Closely allied to the above points is the importance of careful pre-testing. This is particularly important because of the translation problem. Ordinarily, even the trans-

lations of natives to the culture cannot be fully trusted. Such individuals tend to have as little or even less understanding of their lower class than we do of ours. Moreover, they have as often as not been trained in Britain or the United States, further removing them from an understanding of their cultures. As just one instance of terminological difficulties, I might cite the case of a Jamaican woman who was asked when she first slept with her present mate. "After we had our second child," she replied.

Fortunately, after questionnaires have been worked out with local assistance, I have been able in both areas to try out problem parts myself, a revealingly different experience from reading pre-test returns. Even where the study director is not familiar with the language, I would recommend that pre-test interviews be observed to catch respondent confusion, embarrassment and hostility to items. These points are seldom picked up by pre-test interviewers.

Where the level of education is especially low, even the relatively unstructured interview may break down. In Puerto Rico, where the average education of our respondents was four years, difficulties were considerably less than in Jamaica, where the respondents were both less educated and less cosmopolitan. I recall one respondent, very eager to cooperate and described by his wife as very intelligent, who, after giving his own age as 35, gave his son's age as 40 and could not understand the contradiction. When asked for his idea of a good son, he replied, "You mean the one that shine in the sky?" For such types, more anthropological techniques may be desirable, or at least, very unstructured interviews.

INTERVIEWER-TRAINING

The usual problems of whom to hire and how to train them are even greater in another culture, particularly where the survey deals with fertility patterns. In neither place was it possible to recruit individuals with interviewing experience. While it was relatively easy to find college graduates in Puerto Rico, this was not possible in Jamaica. In Puerto Rico, where women tend to be guarded carefully by husbands or fathers, it was very difficult, and in some cases impossible, to get women to stay overnight on a field trip. In Jamaica, where women wield more power in the family, this was not a problem.

In screening applicants in both areas, a good deal was learned by having them demonstrate briefly for me their approach to an interview. I played the role of a lower class respondent, and they had the task of explaining the project to me, getting my cooperation and asking a few questions from the questionnaire. While the method has obvious limitations, it did give a fairly good indication of how the applicant would handle a lower class person, how he reacted to the more intimate questions, and how he handled himself when certain interviewing difficulties arose.

The training program itself had three major objectives: (1) Convincing the group that the study was important for their island, and was not just an academic investigation conducted by outsiders. Consequently, the problem of over-population was discussed for them by various officials of the local Departments of Health and Statistics. In class meetings the practical implications of the study were discussed. (2) Weakening their inhibitions about discussing sexual matters. This was a greater problem in Puerto Rico than in Jamaica. One Puerto Rican male confessed that he had never discussed such things even in the presence of men. This problem was met first by readings, introduced early in the course, where the interviewer could see that such studies in Puerto Rico and on the continent had been conducted success-

fully. Then little by little the group was encouraged to discuss intimate points in class. (3) The major objective of training was, of course, to teach interviewing skills. In the light of the difficult content and form of the questionnaires, and in consideration of the special problems involved in dealing with personnel of other cultures, two weeks were devoted to training in Puerto Rico and in Jamaica. In addition to the usual lectures, readings, discussions and field practice, several other techniques were used:

A. Practice interviews in front of the group, with discussion and criticism by the group. The interviewer-trainer occasionally acted as interviewer or respondent.

B. Small group sessions where one person acted as interviewer, another as respondent and a third or fourth as critics. This presumably took away the stage fright of performing in front of the group and "the Boss."

C. Audio-Visual aids of various sorts served to dramatize interviewing errors and make them more accessible for discussion.

1. Recordings of staged interviews containing most of the usual interviewing errors were played and the group asked to pick out the errors.

2. Recordings of practice sessions were played back and discussed by the group. In addition to hearing the interview, an opaque projector enabled the group to see what the interviewer actually wrote.

3. A recording of an interview not previously heard was played back to the group, which filled in a questionnaire. Their errors were subsequently discussed privately.

Subsequent to the training, a training evaluation questionnaire was filled out by members of the group: in Puerto Rico, a test measuring extent of learning was also

398 UNDERDEVELOPED AREAS

given. These were compared with subsequent field performance.

That an investment in careful training pays off is indicated by the differential results achieved by our own personnel and by public health nurses whom we occasionally used to conduct screening interviews. In the 500 questionnaires administered by the nurses, close to one-fourth of the cases had never heard of a birth control method. Questionnaires done by our own personnel in the same clinics showed that less than half of one percent knew no methods.

Whether or not such extensive training is necessary is a matter yet to be tested, but it is our impression that it is, although its major impact may be on motivation and morale rather than on any specific skills.

Dr. George M. Foster is a Professor of Anthropology and Lecturer in Public Health at the University of California, Berkeley. From 1946 to 1952 he was Director of the Institute of Social Anthropology, Smithsonian Institute, and in 1952 served as an adviser to the American delegation to the fifth World Health Organization in Geneva. He has observed community development programs in India, Pakistan, and the Philippines for the International Cooperation Administration and is currently a member of their Health Committee. His principal publications are A *Primitive Mexican Economy*, 1942; *Sierra Popoluca Folklore and Beliefs*, 1945; and *Empire's Children: the People of Tzintzuntzan*, 1948; and various articles on ethnography, folklore and culture change on Mexico, California, Latin America, Spain, and India.

Dr. Sripati Chandrasekhar is a former president of the All-India Conference on Family Planning and a Professor of Sociology at Baroda University. He has been educated in India, England, and the United States and is internationally known as a lecturer on the subject of India's population problems. He is the author of *Hungry People and Empty Lands*, 1954 and *Les problèms démographiques dans l'Inde et dans le Pakistan*, 1950, and editor of *Population Review*, a journal of Asian demography.

Dr. J. Mayone Stycos is an Associate Professor of Sociology at St. Lawrence University. He has worked with the Bureau of Applied Social Research at Columbia University, at the Social Science Research Center at the University of North Carolina, and at the University of Puerto Rico. He is the author of *Family and Fertility in Puerto Rico*, 1955, and of numerous articles of both a substantive and methodological nature on population in various professional journals.

XII

EXPERIENCES ATTEMPTING TO IN-
TRODUCE SOCIAL CHANGE IN UNDER-
DEVELOPED AREAS

THIS chapter is concerned with the general subject of planned social change. In his article, "Problems of Adapting and Communicating Modern
Techniques to Less Developed Areas," Bert F. Hoselitz has extracted, from a
variety of contemporary researches, those principles that seem crucial to the success
of a technical assistance program; he has attempted to formulate some principles
for effectively planning social change. His article also serves as an introduction to
those following it. It should be noted that we have devoted at least one chapter
to each of the fields of social action mentioned by Hoselitz, i.e., economic, political,
and social innovations.

Although Ernest Beaglehole, in his article "Cultural Factors in Economic and
Social Change," makes the problem of developing underdeveloped areas an interdisciplinary problem, he emphasizes the basic role of the anthropologist in interpreting a culture so that action may follow cultural themes rather than run
counter to them. He sees the anthropologist in the role of an adviser, one to
whom the technician may turn for suggestions on how the values of another culture may be used as vehicles for innovation rather than as obstacles to social
change.

Although its title might seem to belie the contents, McKim Marriott's "Technical Change in Overdeveloped Rural Areas" describes some villagers' reactions to
an outsider entering a village in India and behaving in such a way that his
motives are ambiguously perceived. The villagers had been tuned to development
schemes and had expected some grandiose plan, from Marriott or the government that they believed him to represent, that would lead them out of the wilder-
ness of poverty. Although their village is in an area usually thought of as underdeveloped, overdevelopment of scarce resources seems to be the case. Marriott is
showing variation within the larger underdeveloped area, the existence of an area
that has few resources to be developed, intensive development of these resources
agriculturally, but continued poverty due to the relative absence of resources.

On the other hand, Henry F. Dobyns, in "Blunders with Bolsas," describes an underdeveloped area in the southwestern United States, an area within a country that would probably be considered one of the most developed in the world. This article is included because it not only deals with some of the more general difficulties that have been experienced in attempting to introduce technological change but, in addition, is an example of some specific troubles encountered by a large government bureaucracy in its own back yard. The generalizations made by Dobyns may be placed along with those by others who have conducted their field work in the larger underdeveloped areas. But more important, this paper suggests that experience in underdeveloped areas in the United States may well be instructive to those going abroad. We cannot go so far as the well-known sociologist who said that he could find out anything that he wanted to know about human behavior by observing half a dozen people interacting in Gravelswitch, but we can say that the principles of effective communication in underdeveloped areas may be learned at home. Experience in an underdeveloped area in the United States might well be a testing ground for those who are interested in service abroad. Success in introducing changes in a test area here may be predictive of ability to operate successfully elsewhere. No attempt is made to summarize the findings of the various pieces of research contained in this chapter. Each study complements the other and numerous cross-references show the interrelations of the articles as well as a considerable consensus among their authors.

PROBLEMS OF ADAPTING AND COMMUNICATING MODERN TECHNIQUES TO LESS DEVELOPED AREAS*

BERT HOSELITZ

I. INTRODUCTION

THIS paper presents an outline of some basic considerations which may be helpful to technical experts and technical assistance workers in their endeavour to adapt and communicate modern techniques to the peoples of less developed areas. In

* Adapted and reprinted by permission from *Economic Development and Cultural Change*, Vol. 2, No. 4, Jan. 1954, pp. 249–269.

order to discuss our problem more meaningfully, I shall present first a somewhat restrictive classification which may enable us to describe the various innovations in the culture, economy, society and political structure of the less advanced countries in more general terms.

The criteria by which innovations, with which we will be concerned in this paper, may be classified, are (1) the field of social action in which the innovation is predominantly located, (2) the degree of change called forth by the innovation, that is, the difference between ways of acting if it is adopted and traditional modes of behaviour, and (3) the group of "primary participants" in the innovation, that is, the class of persons whose social behaviour is directly and immediately affected by its introduction.

In the fields of social action into which an innovation may be placed we distinguish again three classes. Innovations may be (1) in the area of productive activity, (2) in the field of government, i.e., public administration, or (3) in the field of social welfare, notably health and education. Many innovations cannot be placed sharply and exclusively into any one of these classes, but require for their introduction alterations of social behaviour in more than one field. This classification is nevertheless useful, because it permits us to distinguish at least between innovations which are *primarily* economic, political, or social. It also draws attention to the fact that an innovation which may be thought of as being purely economic has political or social welfare dimensions, and vice versa.

The second criterion of our classification needs little explanation. As a rule, one would expect that the introduction of tools made of better materials than those customarily used in a less advanced society would be an easy matter and would be quite generally accepted, especially if these tools can be used in the same way and for the production of the same things as the qualitatively poorer ones. At the other extreme are institutions which represent total innovations in a culture and for which there exist no even approximate equivalents. The introduction of machines, in the operation of which skills are required which are not present in the adopting country, will understandably be a job of quite different proportions than the re-

placement of one type of tool by an externally identical but qualitatively improved one.

The third criterion of classification presents probably the greatest difficulties. Whatever secondary and tertiary ramifications a particular innovation may produce, the crucial stage of its acceptance or rejection is the transmittance to the group whose social behaviour is directly and immediately affected by it. Unless this group, which becomes the carrier of the innovation, actively engages in behaviour supporting its introduction, it may never be adapted to the conditions of the less advanced country. Although, as will be shown, some innovations may not take root or may require for their successful adoption continuing technical assistance, the first and original impact and the response of the group upon which this impact is exercised occupy a strategic position in the eventual success of technical assistance work.

II. INNOVATIONS IN THE FIELD OF PRODUCTIVE ACTIVITY

In considering the group of primary participants to which a new technique is addressed we may distinguish three types of innovations. In the first group are those which call for cooperation on a mass basis; in the second group are those which require the action of several individuals, among whom some selection is possible, so that only specially qualified persons are chosen as carriers of the innovation. In the third group are innovations addressed to a very limited number of individuals usually in central administrative or governmental positions. An example of the first type of innovation is the introduction of a new seed or a new fertilizer in the agriculture of a less advanced country. Another example is the introduction of new tools, for example, the replacement of wooden or stone implements by metallic ones, or the replacement of soft and easily blunted iron tools by others made of steel. In all these instances no demand is made upon the population of the under-developed country to alter significantly its traditional working habits, nor does the innovation lead to a replacement of traditionally consumed objects by others. On the surface, interference with traditional forms of work and social action appear minimal, and yet net productivity increases may be considerable. It is clear that the new technique must be one which can meaningfully be communicated even to illiterate persons, that it must be designed to meet a strongly felt need, and that its successful introduction may often require the participation of large numbers of technical assistance workers, agricultural extension agents, or other welfare workers, that is, an administrative service which may as yet be unavailable and would also have to be created.

The effective communication of the kind of innovations we are discussing here thus requires often efforts of considerable magnitude. It is not sufficient for a particular new technique to be "made available" to the people concerned, in the sense that information about it can be easily had or that the objects needed to apply it can be obtained locally. It may be necessary to carry the new technique literally into the houses and onto the farms of the people who are to use it. Mr. Rudra Datt Singh reports the very instructive, and ultimately very successful, experiment of introducing fertilization by means of green manure in the Etawah district of Uttar Pradesh, India.[1] Here the farmers were reluctant to buy *sanai* seed (which was to provide the green manure) in government stores, al-

[1] See Rudra Datt Singh, "The Village Level," in Edward H. Spicer, *Human Problems in Technological Change*, New York, 1952, pp. 55–67.

though they knew about its availability and the price at which it could be bought. Only after the seed was carried to their homes and farms by the workers on the project did they use it. Instances like this give a serious shock to the traditional convictions of some western trained social scientists, who assume, almost unquestioningly, that people will choose the better production function if they know about it, and if they can calculate that by using it they can increase the net results of their operations. Although the farmers knew that in spite of the expense for *sanai* seed their output of grain would increase sufficiently to leave them a larger net income, they refused to adopt the new method because of distrust, fear, and, perhaps, disbelief in the unselfish motives of the government and the members of the project.

This example raises a problem in the communication of modern techniques to less advanced countries which has wide applicability. Behaviour such as that described which from the standpoint of productive efficiency may appear irrational is found in many under-developed countries, and not infrequently even in advanced countries. Usually, if all the underlying resistances to the introduction of a new technique are fully explored, clear reasons for this seeming irrationality appear. The successful introduction of the new technique then depends upon whether or not the underlying resistances can be successfully removed. This means that the mere demonstration of a better way of doing things is often an inefficient means of introducing a new technique, because it depends upon the passage of a long time period in which values or social behaviour patterns are changed. It is possible, and perhaps even probable, that eventually the farmers of the Etawah district would have adopted the method of using green manure after some of the more venturesome among them had accumulated favorable experience with this method. The new technique might have spread slowly, and after several years or perhaps decades this method would have been generally adopted. But Indian agriculture must be made to improve its output rapidly. By bringing the *sanai* seed to the farmers years of experimenting were saved and output was increased within a short time. But the very success of the Etawah experiment in turn serves as an instance of demonstration of new techniques for other parts of India. It might be argued that since this method was successful in one district, people in other districts will hear about it and wish to adopt it also. This effect may by no means take place and it may be necessary to engage in extensive agricultural field work also in other parts of India in order to improve their method of fertilizing the fields.

An example of the second type of innovation in the field of productive activity is the introduction of tools and other productive equipment for which there do not exist equivalents in the less developed country. Such equipment may be designed to be employed in the manufacture of traditionally used products in an entirely new way, or even in the production of new products hitherto not produced in the less advanced country. These new productive techniques usually require the development of new skills—and hence the provision of training facilities where the skills can be acquired—and may lead also to the creation of new forms of social division of labor. Concrete cases in point are the introduction of power-driven machinery in place of hand tools, or the introduction of new transportation facilities.

The third type of innovation in the realm of productive activity is exemplified by the setting up of medium or large scale productive installations which involve not only an alteration of the kinds of products traditionally turned out, but which also require a fundamental restructuring of social relations. The most characteristic instance of this kind of innovation is the creation of a modern factory in a region inhabited by peasants or primitives. This third type of innovation is distinguished from that discussed in the previous paragraph in that here capital resources of such magnitude are required as normally are in the command of only very few persons in a less advanced country. These persons already form a special, quite limited, social class, because of their wealth. To the extent to which industrialization is envisaged on the basis of private enterprise, we must take account of the expectations and interests of this class as a significant factor in determining whether the innovation will be adopted or not. In the absence of private initiative, the carrier of the innovation is the government or some agency partially sponsored by the government (e.g., a development corporation), and here again the primary participating group differs significantly from that discussed before. We need not enter in this place into a detailed discussion of the complexities arising in the course of industrialization on a sizeable scale of a less advanced society. This problem has received much attention and the many ramifications of it have been excellently summarized in a recent book by Professor Wilbert Moore.[2]

III. INNOVATIONS IN THE FIELDS OF SOCIAL WELFARE AND PUBLIC ADMINISTRATION

So far we have been concerned with innovations in the field of productive methods, that is, economic activity. Economic problems are acknowledged to be among the most crucial for less advanced areas, whose lack of development is precisely in the field of production and economic or-

[2] Wilbert E. Moore, *Industrialization and Labor*, New York, 1951.

ganization. But the economy is only part of the general social relations of a country and the development of economic relations of a country must be supplemented by changes in other factors closely associated with the economy. The introduction of new productive techniques without the simultaneous improvement of education, health, and general governmental services would lead to completely barren results. Hence, just as we have classified techniques in the field of productive activity in terms of the primary participating groups, we will do the same for new methods of procedure in the fields of social welfare and public administration.

Examples of the first type of innovation, those requiring for their successful adaptation the cooperation of large masses of the population, are certain new methods of curing or treating diseases endemic in many parts of the tropics. The use of injections of anti-biotics against certain communicable diseases (e.g., treatment of yaws with penicillin, or vaccination against smallpox), and treatment of malaria by means of quinine are instances in point. Similarly the use of X-ray equipment in the diagnosis of tuberculosis and the active participation of a population in such diagnostic health programmes require that the meaning and importance of these new techniques be communicated meaningfully and effectively to large masses of often illiterate persons.

Innovations of the second type are exemplified by more elaborate methods or installations requiring longer range care and control. A swamp drainage programme to control malaria requires an installation which must be supervised by some local governmental authority. Moreover an agency must be created for its continued upkeep whose members appreciate the significance of long-range maintenance of the new installation. In its report the United Nations Technical Assistance Mission to Haiti states, for example, that in the Petit Goave district a successful drainage project for the control of malaria had been set up in 1942–44 under the auspices of the Rockefeller Foundation. The report continues:

On a visit to the spot by the Mission's expert on public health it was found that some of the main drainage channels were filled with sand, a dike was broken, and in consequence the once perfectly drained area had been inundated and become marshy. If necessary measures are not taken in due time, the purpose of this malaria control drainage project will be frustrated. The sanitary inspector in charge of the maintenance of the project has but four day-laborers at his disposal, a number just sufficient for the regular digging out of the obstructed outlets of the drains, but absolutely inadequate for emergency repairs.

"Needless to say, this neglect of maintenance of expensive malaria drainage projects seriously affecting the malaria control in the area concerned, must be considered a grave shortcoming of the administration responsible. If the upkeep of existing public health installations is not effectively attended to, the undertaking of further projects of this nature would be of doubtful value.[3]

An instance like this demonstrates that the problem of adapting a new technique of public health control requires a receptive audience on the level of local administrative agencies. The transmission of the new technique is incomplete unless persons can be found who clearly understand the long-range implications of the innovation. Such people need not be members of the central government, but, on the other hand, not just anyone in a less developed country would be a suitable person to be entrusted with the supervision of such a programme. Some of the more intelligent,

[3] United Nations, Mission to Haiti, New York, 1949, pp. 68–69.

and perhaps more literate, members of a local community form the primary manpower pool among whom local leaders of this type must be recruited. Similar observations could be made about the administration of educational services, irrigation installations, and the supervision of public health measures, such as sewage disposal systems, local hospital facilities, and first aid stations.

The third type of innovation in the welfare of public administration field centres around techniques requiring innovations of considerable size and complexity and having often far-reaching secondary consequences in administrative procedures or institutions. The agency which becomes the carrier of this type of innovation is usually the central government. The development of new administrative or welfare services, the remodeling of the tax system of an underdeveloped country, the establishment of a development corporation or other institution charged with the financing of developmental projects, are all innovations which require government sponsorship and responsibility. Although in their immediate impact these projects require action only by members on the upper levels of the administrative apparatus of a less advanced country, they have wide ramifications and may affect profoundly the daily lives of the masses of the people. Though their implementation is often a matter of internal policy, it is part of a foreign expert's task to draw attention to such possible ramifications and to suggest ways of dealing with them.

It is not suggested, of course, that this classification of innovations in terms of groups of persons in the less advanced country, whose response is a primary factor in making their adoption effective, provides us with tight and mutually fully exclusive classes. But I believe that it has the merit of pointing to three fairly distinctive groups in the population of less ad-

vanced countries whose active cooperation and interest is necessary for the effective introduction of various innovations. At the one end are innovations which require some positive action on the part of all, or at least large portions, of the population of less developed countries. At the other end are new techniques or institutions of such magnitude or basic importance that only governments can assure their introduction. Between these two extremes is a class of innovations which requires the action of local leaders or individuals endowed with special vision, education, intelligence, or venturesomeness. Here the availability of persons who present characteristics somewhat deviant from the prevailing norms in under-developed countries may be desirable. Small-scale industry and many public welfare programmes of local dimensions fall into this group. In these areas the successful communication and adaptation of new techniques is dependent upon the discovery and strengthening of a new "elite," and sometimes on alterations of social values in order to provide adequate rewards for the performance of these innovators.

It should also be clear that many programmes of technical assistance contain portions which are addressed to different groups of primary participants.

IV. RESISTANCES TO THE ADOPTION OF INNOVATIONS DUE TO ECONOMIC AND CULTURAL FACTORS

The preceding analysis suggests that the transfer of modern techniques in the productive, administrative, or welfare fields is not a simple, strictly isolable, process, but a many-sided complex affair. This is true not merely of technical assistance programmes which, like the rural rehabilitation project in the Valle de Cuzcatlán, or a sizeable industrialization project, are many-pronged programmes, but even in cases where much more narrowly limited objectives are sought. Any transfer of modern technology is a form of acculturation. It occurs, in general, at several points of contact simultaneously. A clear example of how far-reaching, in a special situation, may be the introduction of a relatively simple new technique is provided by Professor Lauriston Sharp's account of the introduction of steel axes, in place of the traditional stone axes, among the Yir Yoront of the Cape York peninsula in Queensland, Australia.[4] Although the economic role which the newly introduced steel axes performed was identical with that previously played by native stone axes, the social and magical relations surrounding stone axes did not attach to steel axes. The consequence of the introduction of the new technique led, therefore, to serious social stresses and strains and severe cases of anxiety, bordering on *anomie*, especially among the older Yir Yoront males. This clearly required the provision of additional "processes of acculturation"—in the form of social services of various kinds— in order to protect the tribe against full social disintegration. Although the consequences of a simple technological innovation are so far-reaching among the Yir Yoront precisely because of the "primitiveness" of these people, the case analyzed by Professor Sharp is merely an extreme example of a process which is present, to a more limited extent, in many instances of actual or attempted modernization of parts of the culture of less primitive groups than the Yir Yoront.

This interdependence of various strands in any culture explains also why often an innovation which appears to fill an obvious need of the population in a less advanced country is not adopted, or, if adopted, meets with serious resistances. The best

[4] See Lauriston Sharp, "Steel Axes for Stone Age Australians," in Edward H. Spicer, *op. cit.*, pp. 69–90.

way of making clear this problem may be to describe a few characteristic cases, especially those in which innovations leading to increases in output of badly needed and much desired objects have not been adopted. We may group these cases into several classes.

(1) In the first group fall instances in which innovations leading to increased output were not adopted because, in the view of the members of the adopting culture, the innovation entails losses outweighing, or at least counterbalancing, its advantages, although from the viewpoint of the person or group recommending the innovation these disadvantages are non-existent. It is, of course, not surprising that a technical assistance worker who recommends the adoption of a new technique in a country with whose culture he is only imperfectly familiar may value things differently from the valuations put on them by the natives. It is by now a commonplace to cite the many past "sins" committed by European colonizing powers, in parts of Asia and Africa, which resulted from their attempt to impose a European system of values on populations to whom this system had no meaning. As is well known this often led to serious trouble. To some extent the misunderstanding of different valuations in different cultures is due to semantic difficulties, but it is due primarily to cultural bias. The members of the more advanced (European) culture tend to interpret social roles and social relations in terms familiar to them and thus increase the strains already imposed on the native society by the introduction of the new technique. I shall return to this problem later.

Misunderstandings of this sort are, however, not confined to persons belonging to different cultures. Sometimes the promoters of new techniques in the government of a less advanced country adopt a "modern" outlook which is not shared by their countrymen who cling to more traditional values and beliefs. An excellent case in point is an incident reported by Mr. Mc-Kim Marriott from a village in the Ganges plain in India.[5] The region about which Mr. Marriott writes is located some 100 miles from Delhi and is devoid of industry. It is so heavily populated that people may be said to live under conditions in which further population growth would call forth the positive checks envisaged by Malthus. An increase in the production of food, possibly by means of higher yielding seed, is, therefore, a prime necessity, profoundly felt by all villagers. Here is what Mr. Marriott says:

The native wheat seed, used universally in my village, produces only half the yield that the available improved seed will produce, given good conditions. The improved varieties are hardy ones, carefully selected and tested over many years. They are "available" in the sense of being present in nearby government seed stores. Peasants know about the stores and know about the seed. Why then do they not rush to get and use the improved varieties?

In part the fault may be with the operator of the seed store, a harsh and unkindly man. In part it may be due to the fact that loans made from a government store must be repaid punctually, whereas those owed to a private money-lender may be renegotiated with greater informality. But the crucial reason for the refusal of the introduction of the new higher-yielding seed seems to be an economic reason:

The grains are indeed big—so big and tough that the women cannot grind them well in the old stone flour mills. Dough made from the new flour is difficult to knead and hard to bake into good bread.

The new bread, which is all a poor farmer has to eat, does not taste like the good old bread . . . Next look at the cows and bullocks! They do not like to eat the straw of the new wheat; they will die of hunger if we grow it. The straw is worthless, too, for thatching roofs. It does not even make a good fire.[6]

This is a clear case in which the valuations of the Indian government and those of the Indian farmers in Mr. Marriott's village clash squarely. An innovation may not be worth while, because in spite of its meeting an acknowledged need, its cost in detracting complementary satisfactions is too high. Mr. Marriott cites still another case of the same region in which the use of animal manure as fertilizer, although known to have beneficial effects on crop yields, is foregone because of alternative, apparently more important uses of the manure as fuel, as an ingredient in plaster for houses, and as part of the "tobacco" used in the villager's water-pipe.

Cases like these occur more frequently than is generally assumed. They occur even on levels where supposedly more accurate economic calculations have been, or can be, made. For example, Mr. Peter G. Franck reports that in Afghanistan the conflicting valuation of American contractors of public work projects, used to relatively high labor costs, and the native government which prices native labor very cheaply, led to a situation in which the contractor was accused of waste, and in which, partly for this reason, serious difficulties arose.[7]

(2) The second group comprises instances in which output-increasing innovations are not adopted, or meet with resistances, because their introduction would

[5] See McKim Marriott, "Technological Change in Over-developed Rural Areas," *Economic Development and Cultural Change*, Vol. I, No. 4 (December 1952), pp. 261–272.

[6] *Ibid.*, pp. 265–266.
[7] See Peter G. Franck, "Economic Planners in Afghanistan," *Economic Development and Cultural Change*, Vol. I, No. 5 (February 1953), p. 338.

require the relinquishment of certain traditional customs, habits, or behaviour forms. This is especially pronounced if an innovation centers around the introduction of new foods or altered forms of traditionally consumed foods. One of the reasons for the rejection of improved seed in Mr. Marriott's Indian village was, as we have seen, the fact that the new bread tasted flat and uninteresting. Another quite similar case, in which the difference in taste and consistency of the flour was apparently the decisive factor is reported from New Mexico by Mr. Apodaca.[8] Here also a higher yielding hybrid of maize was rejected, because even those farmers who planted the hybrid corn repeatedly found that "after three years they had not become accustomed to the flavor or texture, and their wives were up in arms."

In all these instances, as well as in the case of the refusal to use animal dung for fertilizer in Mr. Marriott's village, the problem lies partly in the nature of finding technological solutions which will fit better the needs of the people. If the two main competing uses for animal dung are as fertilizer and as fuel, especially for the manufacture of clarified butter, the problem might perhaps be met (as Mr. Marriott suggests) by introducing an apparatus by means of which clarified butter can be produced with less fuel. Similarly, if higher-yielding varieties of maize are rejected because of the taste or texture of the tortillas made from it, it would be important to apply research in the innovation of strands which are both higher-yielding and, at the same time, allow the production of dough or *nixtamal* of the same or very similar consistency and taste as those customarily used.

All these examples are only special instances of a more general problem: The

role of the technical expert does not consist invariably in trying to introduce the seemingly most suitable technology available in more advanced countries. This is the difference between communication and adaptation of modern techniques. The former looks merely to finding ways and means of introducing already available processes and objects into a less developed country. The latter requires often a greater inventive effort. It calls for the development of new strains of plants and animals, of new tools and implements, of new productive and administrative methods which may have no exact counterparts in advanced countries. It is readily granted that such alternatives may often be unavailable. But this means that the task of communicating and adapting modern techniques to the less advanced areas is not fully accomplished by field work of technical experts and other technical assistance workers, but that it has its ramifications in the agricultural and industrial laboratories of the advanced countries and in the wisdom of its social scientists and administrators to devise new methods and procedures which may as yet be untried anywhere, but which may be the very things needed in a particular spot in the less developed portions of the world.[9]

In even more profound terms this problem may be regarded as one in which the optimum result of adapting modern techniques to the less advanced countries consists not merely in the transfer of the techniques developed in the west to the underdeveloped areas of the world, but in the transfer of the technique of developing improved methods of production and administration. A higher-yielding seed developed locally, under local climatic and soil

[8] See Anacleto Apodaca, "Corn and Custom," in Edward H. Spicer, ed., *op. cit.*, pp. 35–39.

[9] See on this problem the very pertinent remarks by Harvey S. Perloff, "The Requirements for an Effective Point Four Program," *Economic Development and Cultural Change*, Vol. I, No. 3 (October 1952), pp. 212–213.

conditions, starting with locally available varieties of grain, may be more easily adapted to the needs of the people in a less advanced country than an imported type. The ultimate aim of communicating technical procedures in these cases might thus be regarded as being the transfer of techniques of seed improvement or techniques of tool development. Western scientific and technological methods then become guides for analogous procedures engaged in locally in the less advanced countries by personnel recruited from the less advanced countries.[10]

It is evident that the failure to accept output-increasing innovations because customs or behaviour patterns stand in the way is not confined to cases in which dietary changes occur. It seems that food habits are particularly difficult to change, but there are many other culture traits which resist the introduction of innovations. A wide variety of cases has been presented by Professor Walter R. Goldschmidt, and it would be useless to repeat his account in this place.[11] Some Indian tribes in the southwestern United States or the Central American highlands, have proved to be especially impervious to innovation from the outside. Others, residing in the same general locality and belonging to similar ethnic and linguistic stocks have readily adopted innovations. On the basis of our present theoretical knowledge of processes of acculturation it is impossible to indicate clear reasons for this difference in behaviour.[12] What is of importance for tech-

nical assistance work is not so much the full clarification of the social variables involved in acculturation, but the awareness that certain cultures have shown themselves more resistant against outside influences than others, and that these differences are of crucial significance in the approach to problems of introducing new techniques to less advanced populations.

V. RESISTANCES TO THE ADOPTION OF INNOVATIONS DUE TO SOCIAL-STRUCTURAL FACTORS

(3) The third group of resistances against output-increasing innovations is composed of instances in which a new technique is rejected because of the fear that it would interfere with traditional social or kinship relations. In a certain sense all innovations produce alterations in social structure. This proposition is almost tautological. But the strain to which existing social relations are subjected differ with the kind of innovation. In most cases societies achieve a creative adjustment to the introduction of new culture traits. The literature on diffusion of culture traits is full of examples of the processes involved. But in some instances the expected strains to which social relations will be subjected by an innovation are so great that it will be rejected. In other cases the society is not capable of fending off the innovation and its introduction results in serious social disorganization. These instances are different outcomes of a single social situation, the balancing of the force of cohesiveness of a social structure against that of innovations which tend to destroy this cohesiveness. In the case of the Yir Yoront, referred to earlier, the attractiveness of the innovations tended to outbalance cultural

[10] I gratefully acknowledge my indebtedness to the valuable suggestions made by Dr. Mosher in a private communication on the matters discussed in this paragraph.

[11] See Walter R. Goldschmidt, "The Interrelations between Cultural Factors and the Acquisition of New Technical Skills," in Bert F. Hoselitz, ed., The Progress of Underdeveloped Areas, Chicago, 1952, pp. 135–151.

[12] On the relative newness of the study of acculturation in general and the absence of a

generally accepted theoretical framework in this field, see Ralph R. Beals, "Acculturation," in A. L. Kroeber, Anthropology Today, Chicago, 1953, pp. 621–641, esp. 621–625.

cohesiveness and here acculturation led to disruption. In other cases the malleability of social relations is strong enough to accommodate an innovation without leading to a major disruption of social relations, and in some limiting cases, social structure is so rigid and hard as to lead to the rejection of the innovation.

The most famous example of a social arrangement which has stood in the way of innovations is the caste system of India. Although in many instances the rigidities of the caste system have been overcome, and although noble leaders like Gandhi and others have contributed to mitigating its effectiveness, it still is operative as a deterrent to innovations in many areas. These are so well known that they need not be discussed here extensively.

A number of other, similar instances could be cited, most striking among them one which has been described by Professor Allan R. Holmberg.[13] The locale is Viru, a village in Peru some 300 miles north of Lima. In 1947 the Peruvian government decided to drill several wells in order to supply the farmers of the Viru valley with water for household use and irrigation as well as for use in a sewage system. Although there was considerable need for water, especially in the dry season, and although many inhabitants of the valley had complained vociferously about the scanty water supply, the project had to be abandoned after only one technically successful well had been drilled, primarily because of lack of favorable response from the very people whom it was intended to benefit. As in many such instances several factors were responsible for the failure of the project. But the overriding reasons seem to have been the opposition of many persons in the valley whose informally held prestige

was violated by the procedures used and the fact that the first well had actually been drilled on the land of a large landowner against whom there was considerable hostility on the part of several other large and many small landowners.

Although the failure of the water-supply project at Viru exhibits certain ecomplexities, we may say that the chief obstacle to the successful completion of the project was the disregard of social-structural relations in the area. From the report of Mr. Marriott on the Indian village in which he resided we can gather a similar impression. Here also the introduction of tube wells and irrigation canals was resisted because of the increased stresses on social relations that were released by their use.[14] These stresses often result in mutual recriminations, and tensions may become so great as to cause the complete failure of an innovation.

The path to industrialization in many less advanced countries is strewn with obstacles of this kind. Wherever new factories are built alterations in social structure are obvious. The gradual proletarianization of an agricultural population is a process which has imposed everywhere great sacrifices on large numbers of persons. Often outright compulsion was used, frequently threats, supported sometimes by a strong ideology coupled with promises of special rewards for those who conform. Industrial entrepreneurs, as well as capitalist planters in underdeveloped countries were almost uniformly facing an unstable, uncertain, and often unwilling labor force. The motivations impelling European workers are lacking and the commitment to the life of an industrial worker is acquired only gradually. This problem appears to present the greatest obstacles to the introduction of new tech-

[13] See Allan R. Holmberg, "The Wells that Failed," in Edward H. Spicer, ed., op. cit., pp. 113–124.

[14] See McKim Marriott, op. cit., esp. pp. 270–271.

niques. Large masses of people are involved who not only must be induced to acquire new skills, but also to move often from their homes to other places, thus destroying or weakening existing kinship relations. They must learn the discipline and punctuality without which work in a factory is almost impossible, and, ultimately, they must become committed to the life of an industrial worker in a city. In other words, they must be induced to embrace an existence which is fundamentally different from their traditional mode of life.

(4) Closely related to the impact exerted by social-structural relations on the adoption of new techniques is the refusal to adopt output-increasing innovations because their introduction threatens the power or prestige of certain privileged groups. In the preceding paragraphs I mentioned difficulties in the path of industrialization because of the reluctance of peasants and primitives to commit themselves to a life as industrial workers. But there exist strong resistances against industrialization also on the entrepreneurial side. My own observations in Latin America have led me to conclude that among the wealthy classes land-ownership has apparently such high status-conferring attributes that persons who have acquired wealth in trade or finance will attempt to acquire land rather than investing their funds in industry. The strength of this behaviour pattern varies, of course, from country to country. There is no doubt that it is still very strong in the less advanced portions of Latin America, notably the countries in the Andean chain and Central America. Even in Cuba, which is geographically and economically closely tied to the United States, this lack of dynamism and the reliance on the alleged security provided by the status-quo has been commented upon by a Mission of the International Bank for Reconstruction and Development.[15]

The observation of this phenomenon in several countries, not merely in Latin America (where it appears to be most conclusively verified), has led me to state in another context, that the manpower pool for a rising class of industrial entrepreneurs in under-developed countries is not likely to be made up of the presently wealthy merchants, bankers, or landowners, but rather of persons whose social origin and present economic role is more marginal.[16]

Another phenomenon, particularly prevalent in some Middle Eastern countries, is the refusal by wealthy owners of investment funds to apply them in the modernization of their own (agricultural) enterprises, because they fear that modernization and the consequent increases in output will expose them to a series of uncertainties which they wish to avoid. These uncertainties are based on the fear that modernization may be accompanied by restructuring of social relations which will impair the power positions now held by large landowners or regional sheiks. They fear also that markets for increased output may not be easy to find and that a tightly controlled monopoly position provides greater safety, even though perhaps somewhat smaller profits, than could be reaped by expansion. Finally they are afraid that modernization, by requiring the simultaneous installation of educational and other social services, will lead to a greater secularization of the popular masses, and hence make them less submissive and more susceptible to political

[15] See International Bank for Reconstruction and Development, *Report on Cuba*, Washington, 1951, pp. 779 ff.

[16] See Bert F. Hoselitz, "Entrepreneurship and Economic Growth," *American Journal of Economics and Sociology*, Vol. XII, No. 1 (October 1952), pp. 105–108.

propaganda threatening the privileges of the upper classes.[17]

All these instances, as well as the resistances opposed to industrialization by peasant peoples, exhibit the depth to which some cultural restraints against innovation go. This does not mean that the introduction of new techniques is impossible, but that certain forms of it are of such magnitude and complexity as to provoke secondary and tertiary adjustments in spheres of social behaviour often far removed from the initial impact of the innovation. Neglect of these secondary and tertiary effects may sometimes lead to dire consequences.

VI. GENERALLY APPLICABLE PROPOSITIONS WITH REGARD TO THE COMMUNICATION AND ADAPTATION OF MODERN TECHNIQUES

In the instances of colonial administration or the introduction of an overall industrialization programme we deal, admittedly, with processes of all-embracing magnitude. But from what has been said in this paper it is clear that even if certain limited items of a culture are transferred, secondary and often tertiary effects will ensue, some of which may be and some of which may not be anticipated. Let us again emphasize the statement, made earlier in this paper, that culture contact occurs at several points simultaneously and that even the apparently isolated transfer of a culture trait is a complex process because of the functional relationships existing between different traits in any culture. Thus, although in practice the tasks of a technical expert or a technical assist-

[17] These factors are suggested for some Moslem countries of the Middle East by Peter G. Franck, *op. cit.*, p. 336; and by Hedley V. Cooke, *Challenge and Response in the Middle East*, New York, 1952, pp. 40–41 and 176.

ance worker will vary greatly with the type of modernization project with which he is associated, some generally applicable propositions may be made which are relevant to all cases of communicating and adapting modern techniques to less advanced areas.

Above all, it should be remembered that usually modern techniques are not transferred piecemeal, but that every transfer of a new technique implies changes in several dimensions. The primary change may be technological, but it is accompanied by associated changes in the fields of social relations, customs, and habits, and often values and beliefs. No matter how strictly circumscribed is the culture item which is transferred, the adopting culture must make adjustments to integrate it into the cultural whole. This adjustment may take place sometimes in areas of social behaviour far removed from that of the innovation. The introduction of steel axes among the Yir Yoront is a particularly striking example of this point. Another example is the introduction of immunization of cattle against diseases carried by the tsetse fly in East Africa. Here was a people which maintained lifelong relations with cattle, living in a region which abounds in suitable pastures. If cattle strains could be improved and the health of cattle made more secure, if, in other words, longer-lived and better cattle and, as an end result, more cattle could be produced, the region, it was thought, could become another Argentina, and supply the meat-hungry parts of the world with beef.

There was no resistance on the part of the people of East Africa against the vaccination of cattle. Cattle was wealth and they understood that vaccination of cattle would improve their chances of becoming and remaining wealthy. But with one or two exceptions the improvement of the health and strains of cattle did not lead to a marketable surplus of beef, but rather to the economically undesirable effects of partial overgrazing. For the value system of the East Africans places emphasis on the number of heads owned by a person rather than on the returns he can gain by marketing them.

The discussion so far suggest a series of practical considerations which should be borne in mind by technical experts and technical assistance workers participating in programmes of communicating and adapting modern techniques to economically less advanced peoples. There is, of course, no assurance that even if all these points are observed a new technique can be introduced in all cases. Indeed, I fear that I have stressed obstacles to, and difficulties in the way of, innovations more than factors favoring their adoption. I do not wish to give the impression that I believe the transfer of modern techniques is impossible or even excessively difficult. In all of the less advanced countries there is a very genuine and widespread desire to learn new and better techniques, to improve production, and to raise standards of health, education, and general welfare. This desire assures that native populations will give full cooperation, within the limits of their understanding, to technical assistance workers, especially those representing the United Nations or one of its specialized agencies. The chief purpose of my insistence on difficulties is to show that in spite of mutual willingness to arrive at favorable solutions, in spite of goodwill exhibited on the part of those who come to help and those who need help, there arise often rigidities, misunderstandings, and gaps in communication, which prevent the successful accomplishment of technical assistance. A clear recognition of these hurdles is necessary in order to overcome them.

VII. PRINCIPLES FOR THE INTRODUCTION OF NEW TECHNIQUES

Professor Walter R. Goldschmidt has listed a series of "principles," chiefly of a theoretical nature, which may "guide us to success in bringing our technology to peoples" still lacking many of the modern techniques.[18] The principles listed by him are restated in a form to make them more applicable to the practical needs of the technical assistance worker.

(1) New techniques should be fitted, wherever possible, into the organizational principles of the native society. The case of the wells in the Viru valley exemplifies that failure ensued because, among other things, this fact was disregarded. On the other hand, Professor Morris E. Opler has reported that in Uttar Pradesh the ancient village assemblies or *panchayats*, which for a long time had been virtually in disuse, have been revived after independence, and have been selected as the chief vehicles for the introduction of new techniques in Indian villages.[19] Here an institution with which the villagers are familiar and in which they have confidence, a part of their own customary organizational structure, has been selected as an instrument in the process of innovation.

(2) Optimum use should be made of local values. Their rightout destruction is likely to lead to severe strains and, in extreme cases, to *anomie* and social disorganization. This was the case in Burma during the first part of this century. Many innovations are supported by local values, or these are at least neutral. Better health, more food, better education,

[18] See Walter R. Goldschmidt, *op. cit.*, pp. 149–151.
[19] See Morris E. Opler, "The Problem of Selective Culture Change" in Bert F. Hoselitz, ed., *op. cit.*, p. 134.

greater welfare, are greatly desired by populations living in poverty and distress. Technical assistance programmes which meet these objectives will normally not encounter resistances, if properly explained.

At the same time, it should be recognized that innovations which are contrary to existing values will prove almost impossible to introduce, except perhaps by harsh dictatorial measures. But social values are not permanent and unchanging. The very fact that innovations do get accepted brings about a gradual alteration in social values. As the physical and technological environment changes, values will change and this process must be exploited judiciously. Hence too great timidity in interfering in the cultural arrangements of a population is as much a vice as too much interference. For example, although there are still many areas in India in which the caste system holds sway, Gandhi's teachings and example, and perhaps, equally importantly, the needs of industrial organization have mitigated or removed its effect in other spots. An entering wedge has thus been created which should be enlarged, so that ultimately caste will not stand in the way of material or social progress of India.

Similarly, as industrialization proceeds it is accompanied by growing urbanization. The migration of rural people to the cities, even if only temporary, has the effect of dissolving, at least in part, traditional kinship ties and breaking up the joint family where it exists. This again provides an opening wedge. In areas in which individual, rather than tribal or kinship responsibility are important, the gradual breakup of the joint family has the effect of fostering individual responsibility. One of my colleagues, who held a United Nations Technical Assistance post in Burma, relates that in some government offices duplications in staff occur, because many positions are held by relatives of a section chief; since their only qualification for the job is their kinship relation to the section chief, they must be given assistants who have the technical qualifications to perform the necessary administrative functions.

(3) An effort must be made to single out the person or persons who are most appropriate as carriers of the innovation. Again the failure to introduce successfully an improved water supply in the Viru valley is a case in point. Here persons with local prestige as experts in the location of wells were not consulted, with the result that they worked against rather than for the project.

In Viru there were persons who already had positions of prestige and who would have been suitable primary participants in the innovation programme. Sometimes a slight change in the conception of their social role by persons who occupy elite positions may be necessary to make them accept the role of carriers of an innovation. For example, the introduction of iron plows in a district of Northern India met, for some time, with serious opposition of the blacksmith caste. Normally blacksmiths fitted steel tips to the traditional wooden plows. They saw the introduction of a different implement, which they did not know how to service, as a threat to their economic position. The technical assistance workers decided to engage the blacksmiths to become agents for improved implements and to train them in servicing the new tools with the result that the opposition against the introduction of iron plows was converted into active cooperation.[20]

This point touches closely upon another topic of this conference, the problem of eliciting local participation in development programmes. As I have

[20] This experience was kindly communicated to me by Dr. A. T. Mosher in a private letter.

shown earlier, in some situations the new techniques must be brought into the homes of the people who are to adopt them. Fortunately, this is not always necessary. But in all cases the selection of local leaders whose cooperation is necessary for the introduction of an innovation becomes crucial. Thus the introduction of many innovations will have the tendency of creating new élites. This, in turn, may imply the creation of a greater degree of social fluidity so as to permit persons to gain rewards for behaviour which, on the basis of traditional valuations, are regarded as deviant or at least marginal. An excellent example of this process is provided by the social and economic history of England. Owing to the increasing weakness of the guilds, and their absence in certain parts of the country and certain industries, the rapid development of some branches of production, e.g., cotton manufactures, was made possible. The entrepreneurs in the new industries operated in a social environment sufficiently fluid, and the gradual permeation of British society with some aspects of what has been called the protestant ethic, permitted them to reap rewards, which made the extension of this form of activity attractive, and hence contributed to economic advancement of astounding proportions.

(4) A technical assistance worker should look at the problems of introducing a new technique not from the purely specialized view point of the science or art in which the technique is located, but he should be aware of the totality of the adopting culture and the interdependence of its parts. In particular, he should try to become aware of the function which the new technique will play in the cultural whole and what other parts of social behaviour will be affected by it. Mr. Marriott's examples from India suggest that the introduction of improved seed

necessitated consideration of the supply of fuel and cattle feed in the locality. His report on the problem of using dung for the fertilization of the soil shows that due consideration must be given to such apparently remote problems as the supply of ingredients for plaster of houses and pipe mixtures for the villager's hubble-bubble.

Closely associated is a semantic problem. To people with specific tastes, such as the Spanish-American farmers in New Mexico, about whom Mr. Apodaca writes, traditional Indian corn is not the same thing as the improved hybrid variety. To the agricultural extension agent, who sponsored the introduction of the hybrid seed, this distinction did not exist. This suggests, however, that the language used by a technical assistance worker, and his understanding of the meanings given to different objects by the population with whom he is in contact, may sometimes be of great importance. Probably every technical expert and technical assistance worker is familiar with the fact that it makes considerable difference what words he chooses to recommend a specific innovation. Sometimes a slight change in wording may make an innovation acceptable which, if stated in different language, may be rejected.

It is of crucial importance, therefore, to avoid rigorous dogmatism, to look for those aspects of a culture which seem to offer the best "peg" on which to hang an innovation.

(5) The overriding requirement for the technical assistance worker is that he gain the trust of the people with whom he works. Familiarity with their culture and habits, non-ostentatious behaviour, humility, consideration, and kindness, are only some of the external traits necessary to achieve this result. Fundamentally, technical assistance, although designed to improve ultimately the welfare position

of the people to whom it is extended, unavoidably leads to social disorganization of varying intensity. The more narrowly a particular technical assistance project is designed, the more likely it is that its secondary effects will be neglected. Hence technical assistance work may produce frustration and irritation, and blame for the failure may often be sought in the recalcitrance of certain individuals. These conditions are not designed to increase a feeling of mutual trust and to extend the desire to cooperate.

These difficulties on the personal level can only be overcome if two important factors are constantly kept in mind. One relates to the selection of personnel for technical assistance work, and the other to the unit in terms of which a technical assistance project is to be defined. Although these factors may be analyzed separately, they are closely related.

In this paper repeated emphasis was placed on the proposition that technical assistance programmes provoke secondary and tertiary effects. Higher-yielding seed can be introduced, if milling practices are improved. New fertilizer will be accepted if the problem of alternative uses for manure can be solved by appropriate additional technical changes. Irrigation projects, and land reclamation projects will be successful if the resulting water and land claims can be satisfactorily adjusted. A technical assistance project in agriculture, confined purely to the introduction of a new seed, or fertilizer, or water supply, usually centers on too small a unit to be really effective. At the same time, a technical assistance project which contemplates a remodeling of the entire national economy of a less advanced country may not be workable either, because of its overwhelming magnitude. Hence a solution for the appropriate size of field projects somewhere between these two extremes must be found. No general

statement can be made of what is the "right" unit for technical assistance projects. They will vary from country to country, and will depend on the kind of innovation that is introduced. The agricultural development program in the Valle de Cuzcatlan in El Salvador is an example of an integrated, many-pronged project in which sub-projects in most, if not all the relevant aspects of social life are consciously planned. Gradually the American Point Four Administration has come to the viewpoint that special projects, at least in agriculture and health, are not as effective as integrated community projects, and these, in turn, are not as effective as regional projects.

As the magnitude of a project increases, the personnel engaged in technical assistance work increases, and the need to recruit extension workers from among the local population becomes strongly felt. In this manner technical assistance projects are, at the same time, means for the training of local individuals in all or some of the techniques which are to be communicated to the population at large. It should not be surprising that this development leads to readier acceptance of many projects by the mass of the population, because the field workers who contact them come from the same culture, speak the same language, and have the same skin color.

One might say, therefore, that the determination of the appropriate size of assistance projects, which in turn influences the culture traits interfered with, and specifies the personnel needs, forms a crucial factor in the problem of communicating and adapting modern techniques to less advanced countries. If the practice of undertaking integrated projects of industrial or agricultural development, on a regional basis, becomes more widespread, a means may be found of achieving that result which alone insures the ultimate and long-range success of technical assistance work: the accommodation of the societies of less advanced countries to the use of procedures by means of which they themselves can develop, with personnel drawn from their own ranks, technical and scientific improvements which will provide a better and richer life for their own populations.

CULTURAL FACTORS
IN ECONOMIC AND SOCIAL CHANGE*

ERNEST BEAGLEHOLE

THERE is no contradiction between the work of the anthropologist and that of the economist. The practical problem is always a field problem: how shall we go about interesting an indigenous people in doing new things, practising new habits, using new pieces of machinery, planting a new type of seed? In attempting to solve this kind of problem, the skills of many experts are required. The skill of the anthropologist is basic for the solution simply because he can bring to a team of experts a knowledge of the existing indigenous social and economic life. This pattern of life is one factor in the social change equation. Without an understanding of the factor one may never learn to solve the equation. But without other kinds of knowledge also the equation will never be solved. Cultural integration without economic integration can never be successful; conversely economic integration may fail because of the blockages and resistances human beings place in the way of an economic integration that may do violence to their cherished values. Economic integration and the fullest possible knowledge of indigenous cultural life are complementary factors that must be kept to the fore at every stage in the development of an indigenous group.

This principle becomes more obvious when one recalls that man is the only culture-using animal species in the world. His culture is a design for living. In Tylor's now classic definition, culture "is that complex whole which includes knowledge, belief, art, morals, law, custom and any other capabilities and habits acquired by man as a member of society."[1] This complex whole is the social heritage of a group. It is a reasonably efficient instrument for solving the problems of survival that face any human society. But the design is really a design, the whole a complex whole. This means that various parts of the pattern mesh with each other so that a balanced equilibrium is maintained between the various parts of the whole. Studying one aspect of a culture—say, the economics of getting a living in an African tribe—inevitably and

* Adapted and reprinted by permission from the *International Labour Review*, Vol. LXIX, No. 5, May 1954, pp. 416–430.

[1] E. B. Tylor: *Primitive Cultures* (London, Murray, 1891), Vol. 1, p. 1.

very soon forces the investigator to study the ramifications of economic life as the trail leads him through marriage to kinship and from gardening to religion. Similarly in a more complex society, such as our own, the impact of total war does not begin or end with a military machine but is to be traced in morals and religion, social life and changed ways of earning a living. It is just because culture is a complex whole that attempts to change one aspect of a culture, say the economic, introduce a whole series of interacting changes in other interrelated aspects of the culture. The final result will be a new social equilibrium that supports and makes possible the desired change in economic life. Without this new equilibrium economic change would hang in a sort of social vacuum, and its effects would be superficial rather than profound.

The fact that one is always dealing with a "complex whole" in initiating economic change leads to the further observation that changes in culture can best proceed through the consent and participation of those whose life one wishes to alter. Change can be brought about by force, but such change produces resistances and blockages which often nullify the result that one seeks to achieve. Securing the consent of indigenous peoples before embarking on action projects may often appear time-consuming; none the less such consent, freely given, will secure more lasting effects than coercion.

Very often the problems involved in developing public health programmes can be met by adding new therapeutic practices to the already existing, customary, semi-magical indigenous procedures or by widening the functions and increasing the skills of indigenous persons already specialised as traditional curers. New therapeutic practices may be rather readily accepted provided that they can be integrated into customary ways of think-

ing about disease. The principle involved seems to be that new practices are more easily introduced to an indigenous people than new ideas underlying the causes of disease. Instead, therefore, of waiting for a long process of re-education to take place, the practical task of the expert is to try to graft European therapeutical techniques on to the body of religico-magical practices and beliefs already existing in an indigenous group. Re-education should not be neglected, but in this field of public health it should not receive priority. Folk concepts of illness, including even folk attitudes to hospitalisation, must be understood and not ridiculed if popular confidence is to be gained and public health work succeed. This general principle seems universally valid. It does not, of course, preclude efforts to improve the health of an indigenous people by large-scale projects aimed, for instance, at nullifying the effects of disease by treating pathological symptoms.

THE ROLE OF ANTHRO-
POLOGY

Just as anthropology can throw new light on public health problems, so it helps to elucidate the adjustments necessary in developing new forms of economic organisation.

One aspect of indigenous life that must always receive attention because of its profound effects on the possibilities of social and economic change is the close relation that exists, according to indigenous thought, between magic and economics. In a chance-ridden world, subject to all sorts of natural disasters, where a man may sometimes, but not always, expect to reap what he sows, it is natural that indigenous peoples should look for some form of insurance against the blows of ill-fortune, the disfavour of malignant spirits or even the hostility of fellow men. This insurance is most often found in a well-developed indigenous system of magic and sorcery. In times of social change, however, such magical practices may hinder the introduction of new and better agricultural techniques or even operate to prevent economic initiative.

The customs of the Pondo of South Africa may be taken as an illustration of the effects of magic on animal husbandry. In the life crises of birth, initiation, marriage and death, as well as on occasions of sickness, or of thanksgiving for having escaped danger, or again to make rain in times of drought, an ox or a cow is killed ritually. In sickness it is believed that an essential part of the cure is the violent bellowing of the beast as it is stabbed in the stomach over the aorta. Such bellowing summons the ancestral spirits to a ritual feast. After being well fed the spirits are apparently agreeable to releasing the patient from his illness. Since scrub cattle can bellow as loudly as good dairy cows or a pedigree bull and since more scrub cattle can survive on impoverished and overgrazed land than quality animals, improvement in stock is hindered, and over-grazing continues to menace the pasture lands of the Pondo.[2] Again, the Nyakyusa of South Tanganyika believe in a magical association between rams and thunderstorms. Since rams fight when they meet, a herdsman always hurries home with the rest of his sheep when a thunderstorm approaches, leaving the ram of his flock in the pasture to fight the thunderstorm. Sometimes the ram prevails, the storm passes. Sometimes the storm wins and the ram is destroyed.[3] But it is never worth taking the animal home, nor would it be worth investing, presum-

ably, in well-bred sires if a poor quality ram can fight the thunderstorm with a reasonable chance of success. Thus the magical association of rams and thunderstorms or the similar magical association elsewhere between agriculture and the violation of Mother Earth must be taken into account before improved techniques of agriculture or animal husbandry are likely to be effective.

In the field of incentives, magic may have the effect of dampening economic initiative while at the same time guarding the individual against the risks of failure. Magical security may be of more importance than a competitive striving to get a better position than the next man. Thus for those Bantu natives settled in a town like East London, the need for money earnings to pay taxes, augment food supplies, or satisfy the new wants which contact with the European has created is a very strong incentive to effort. But the magical part of the old Bantu economic organisation is fitted into the new economic system. When the scientific control over the process of earning wages ends, there magic begins. Magical medicines are bought which are believed to ensure that the worker will find a job or will not be dismissed from his position; or witchcraft is used against rivals for employment—witchcraft which is thought to cause blindness or a septic finger, even death—so that persons will not accept positions of high responsibility or well-paid jobs if they think that their action would cause jealous rivals to have recourse to sorcery. Sorcery is believed to account for unlet rooms in a boardinghouse; sorcery is used to obviate the necessity of paying bills or by the storekeeper to attract custom to his shop.[4] Everywhere the Bantu's association with modern economic life is hedged and supported by magical practices. Hence technological change cannot

[2] Monica Hunter: *Reaction to Conquest* (Oxford University Press and International Institute of African Languages and Cultures, 1936), pp. 79–84, 240–253. See also G. and M. Wilson: *The Analysis of Social Change* (Cambridge University Press, 1945), p. 94.

[3] G. and M. Wilson, *op. cit.*, p. 94.

[4] Monica Hunter, *op. cit.*, pp. 455–458.

"sell" itself by its utility alone. Such change has almost literally to become incorporated into an already pre-existing body of economic values and practices. This process of incorporation may well take time if, as with another Bantu people, the Lovedu of the Transvaal, business enterprise is associated with subterfuge and deceit because the people have been conditioned to, and value highly, mutual helpfulness and non-competitive bartering as the only respectable means of obtaining consumer goods.[5]

PITFALLS FOR THE EDUCATOR

Just as public health, new forms of economic organisation and training for leadership will depend for their ultimate success upon the capacity of a people to absorb new ideas and learn new habits, so in the field of education a successful attempt to introduce fundamental education will depend upon prior understanding of folk practices. The experience of U.N.E.S.C.O. in its Marbial Valley (Haiti) pilot project suggests most strongly that in many ways, some obvious and some more subtle, a clear knowledge of social conditions not only shows the educator where he should step lightly but also how fundamental attitudes of the peasants may be used to support a programme of education and social change. Thus, intense religious rivalries superimposed upon intense interest in magic and voodoo indicate that the educator must be careful neither to alienate the deeply religious nor ride roughshod over the folk beliefs of the peasant. Again, a knowledge of the customary relations between parents and children gives the educator insight into attitudes that will inevitably determine relations between teacher and

[5] E. J. and J. D. Krige: *The Realm of the Rain Queen: A Study of Lovedu Society* (Oxford University Press, 1943), pp. 67–68.

pupil. Similarly the interest with which Haitian parents follow the progress of their children in school can be used to secure the support of adults for new programmes.

The very open-mindedness of Haitian peasants, however, to new explanations and ideas in itself poses dangers. The peasant may find no incongruity between new ideas and old folk beliefs, particularly when new ideas come with all the power and prestige of the international expert behind them. Yet the peasant may soon over-exaggerate the new and become completely dependent on the outsider, with the risk that, when the educator leaves, his ideas are in turn abandoned in favour of other innovations.

Finally experience in Haiti suggests that it may be unwise for the educator to foster progress by emphasising competition and rivalry. Just as the Pondo Bantu uses sorcery to humble a competitor, so competition appears to arouse deep anxiety feelings in Haiti and competitive success leads to envy, malevolence and a desire to pull down a possible rival by fair means or foul before he succeeds. Incentives based on competition therefore have no place in plans for social improvement. Rather must the educator in Haiti strive to stimulate native forces in the local culture so that non-competitive cooperation becomes the lever whereby the peasant is not only helped to develop self-respect but also to evolve a new way of life that combines the advantages of a simple technology with the rich values of a traditional peasant social organisation.[6]

[6] *Unesco, The Haiti Pilot Project, Phase One*, Monographs on Fundamental Education, No. 4 (Paris, Unesco, 1951). The organisation and functioning of the typically Haitian co-operative working association are described in A. Metraux: *Making a Living in the Marbial Valley (Haiti)*, Unesco Occasional Papers in Education, document ED/OCC/10 (Paris, 1951), pp. 68–86.

Experience from other parts of the world reinforces the conclusion that education must be an integral aspect of social and economic development if the village teacher is not to find that his education produces more frustrations than satisfactions.[7]

PRINCIPLES TO BE OBSERVED

There is one very significant set of signs that it is important to recognise in indigenous groups as giving clues to the relative success with which social and economic changes are being accepted and absorbed by these groups. These signs are part of a social complex of action that recurs from time to time in various parts of the world and constitutes to the anthropologist evidence for the existence of revivalistic, messianic or nativistic movements. In general it may be said of such movements, whether they take the form of the Ghost Dance of the Plains Indians, the Ringatu and Ratana revivalisms of the Maori, the Vailala madness or the more recent cargo cults and "Masinga Rule" movements of New Guinea and the Solomons, that they all represent the response of an indigenous people to the threats, frustrations and disorganisation produced by exposure to social and technological change. With the loss of their hunting territories as the white settler pressed westward over the great plains of the United States, the Plains Indians, for instance, found their customary economy no longer possible. The Ghost Dance represented a revival

[7] See, for instance, J. van Baal: "Educating the Netherlands New Guinea Village," in *South Pacific Commission Quarterly Bulletin*, Vol. III, No. 3, July 1953, pp. 18–22; and for the Middle East, A. S. Eban: "Some Social and Cultural Problems of the Middle East," in *International Affairs*, Vol. XXIII, No. 3, July 1947, pp. 367–375.

and adaptation of aboriginal ceremonies and ritual in order to strengthen and support the Indians in their disorganised social and economic life. Again the Vailala madness, so-called because of the automatisms, spirit-possession and dancing that characterised the movement, was the reaction of a socially disorganised Papuan people whose economic life had been undermined and its social life broken by the loss of traditional religious rituals. Thus the development of new religious movements, the rise to power of religio-political prophets and the swift dissemination of irrational cults all need careful analysis and appropriate social action if the energies of an indigenous people are not to be frittered away in useless protest against changes they can neither understand nor cope with, and constructive social development is not to be blocked by rebellion instead of being furthered by co-operation.

The outlook for planned social change might in fact be pessimistic were there not in fact sufficient examples of the adjustment of indigenous groups by their own endeavours to prove that such adjustment is possible and to suggest the probability that adjustment can be helped through the use of anthropological knowledge and techniques. The widespread development of co-operatives in New Guinea seems to be pointing the way to an economic change that will provide the necessary incentives for the indigenous people of this part of the Western Pacific to adjust themselves to the demands of a new economic system; the people of Nayón, a Quechua Indian village on the outskirts of Quito, Ecuador, are by-passing mestizo culture and working out a reasonable economic adaptation to Ecuadorean urban life; finally Indians from Tepotzlan have shown evidence that they can without social or personal disorganisation adjust themselves to the complex demands of living in Mexico City.[8] In all these instances of reasonably successful adaptation careful analysis reveals at least one probable cause: there has existed a latent congruence between the values, attitude-systems and forms of socio-economic organisation characteristic of the indigenous people and those of the culture bringing the new ways of social and economic life. Thus a graft has been possible and a new growth has taken place that represents a sturdy integration of the traditional with the new.

One of the most important problems of contemporary social science is simply the problem of ensuring that, as far as knowledge and goodwill can take us, the process of adapting the customary social and economic patterns of indigenous people to the demands of technological change shall proceed with the minimum stress, frustration and blockage, with the least possible violence to the traditional values and the greatest possible consideration for the human beings whose ways of life are being changed. It is not without significance that realisation of this problem has led U.N.E.S.C.O. to establish a committee of experts to study the principles that should be taken into account in

[8] A brief summary of the situation in Palau is given by O. Lewis: "The Effects of Technical Progress on Mental Health in Rural Populations," *América Indígena*, Vol. XII, No. 4, Oct. 1952, pp. 299–307. For Yucatan see Robert Redfield: *A Village That Chose Progress: Chan Kom Revisited* (University of Chicago Press, 1950), pp. 46–66 and 113–138. Quecha experience is noted in R. L. Beals: "Acculturation, Economics and Social Change in an Ecuadorean Village," in Sol Tax, (ed.): *Acculturation in the Americas: Proceedings and Selected Papers of the XXIXth International Congress of Americanists* (University of Chicago Press, 1952) pp. 67–73. An analysis of the case of the Tepotzlan Indians is provided by O. Lewis: "Urbanization without Breakdown: A Case Study," in *Scientific Monthly*, Vol. LXXV, No. 1, July 1952, pp. 31–41.

furthering economic change.[9] In a very summary form these principles are: every culture is a living unity, and a change in any one aspect will have repercussions on other aspects of the culture; changes within a culture will produce changes in the personality of individuals living within the changing culture; purposive technological change involves responsibility for the effects of such change upon the lives of the people concerned; each change is unique, and therefore it is impossible to lay down general prescriptions but, through an identification of the process as it occurs, experts will be able to act in terms of the fullest knowledge; changes should be introduced with the fullest possible consent and participation of the people and in ways that are familiar and acceptable.

Once these principles are accepted then the role of the social scientist in technological change becomes clear. In co-operation with a team of experts and administrators the anthropologist, for instance, has the task of ensuring that the experts are fully aware of the cultural values of the people whose culture it is sought to change. It is of equal importance that the experts should become aware of their own cultural values and prejudices so that, for instance, tensions and discriminations between racial and minority groups, closely connected in the West with industrialism and technology, are not diffused to an indigenous people as unsuspected appendages to desired innovations.[10] The anthropologist, through

[9] The main conclusions of the committee, under the chairmanship of Dr. Margaret Mead, are to be found in the report "Unesco and the Social Consequences of Technological Change," in *International Social Science Bulletin* (Paris, Unesco), Vol. IV, No. 2, Summer 1952, pp. 370–380.

[10] Brazilian and foreign observers have the impression that unless the dangers and pitfalls are known and steps taken to avoid them,

his detailed knowledge of indigenous life, can note the areas of resistance, blockage and susceptibility to change, so that local patterns will be circumvented or utilised in order to reduce friction and resistance. Thus the evaluation of an on-going process becomes an important contribution of the anthropologist to a team approach. Finally in bridging a possible gap between administrators and the indigenous people the anthropologist can make sure that planning and action both proceed with the fullest possible consent of the people and on the basis of a complete communication between all those concerned with projects of social and economic change.

TECHNOLOGICAL CHANGE IN OVERDEVELOPED RURAL AREAS*

McKIM MARRIOTT

WHEN in America, we think of "rural areas" in remote parts of the world we are inclined to imagine rugged, crude, partly developed spaces—in the official phrase, "underdeveloped areas." It is usual, too, to think of technology as something that can be added to a rural area to develop it. I want to suggest that we will come closer to understanding the real problems of technological change in most of the world if we reverse the emphasis. From the point of view of the people in them, many rural areas are not so much underdeveloped as they are overdeveloped.

The problems of technological change in an overdeveloped area are not the same as our familiar additive problems. Rarely does technological change merely add new things; more often, it alters the pattern and the structure of people's lives. It does not just add, but creates a new structure or pattern, and often destroys an old structure or pattern. In this fact lie some of the most serious practical problems of technical change. Some problems of technical change are involved in finding the appropriate new technique, others may be involved in teaching and explaining the technique once it has been found, but major problems always await us in the overdeveloped context into which the new technique is introduced.

What I mean by technological "overdevelopment" is the pressing of techniques up to and beyond the point of an optimum relation between man and environment. In an overdeveloped area, too many techniques are too exhaustively applied by too many people to too little land.

Western attitudes and concepts of "racism" may be unsuspectingly smuggled into Brazil along with Western industrial organisation and improved technological processes. See C. Wagley (ed.): Race and Class in Rural Brazil (Paris, Unesco, 1952), pp. 154-155.

* Revised and reprinted by permission from Economic Development and Cultural Change, Vol. I, December, 1952, pp. 261-272.

This phenomenon of overdevelopment affects the spread of new techniques in several ways:

(1) Development in an overdeveloped area is an old story. Much development has occurred in the past, often too much development. Techniques have reached what seems to be a static equilibrium. A new technique has little room in which to spread.

(2) Overdevelopment leads generally to tight interconnections among techniques. Thus the introduction of an additional new technique may disrupt or require readjustments in many old techniques.

(3) Technology in an old, overdeveloped area is likely to have become interconnected with many patterns of personal and social behavior—groupings, ideas, beliefs. Introduction of a new technique may be followed by acceptance or rejection according to criteria which are not directly technical at all but social, cultural, and political.

(4) Finally, overdeveloped areas have technological problems and their people know that they have them. Technological change itself is likely to have become an institution with a regular social organization, national or even international. The spread of new techniques will therefore be affected not only by the local situation, but also by the culture, society, and politics of the people who introduce the new techniques. Those who introduce changes may have to deal personally with all of these four effects of technological overdevelopment.

I will discuss these four problems of technological change as they appear in one overdeveloped rural area of India. Problems in other places will not be identical, but Indian overdevelopment demonstrates, in extreme form, the kinds of problems which are likely to attend the introduction of technical changes anywhere.

The observations which follow were made in remote villages of the Ganges plain about one hundred miles from the capital at New Delhi. The immediate area had undergone no industrial development and there were no obvious signs of any program for technological change. Rural population numbered six hundred per square mile, the people being jammed into tight little villages. Wheat, barley, and peas supplied most of subsistence by means of what appeared to be very primitive techniques. The area was so conservative, and my presence so frightening, that I was politely thrown out of three villages before I was finally allowed to settle in a fourth.

A LONG HISTORY OF TECH-NOLOGICAL DEVELOPMENT

Although this area had seemed at first to be very backward and unchanging, I was struck soon afterwards by evidence of a great amount of recent development. Indeed, the very existence of a population problem implied that there had been extensive technological expansion and change.

I was impressed very early by evidence of American influences—influences much older than those of Point IV. Farmers were cultivating potatoes, maize, tomatoes, and a strain of improved cotton, all of them imported from America. I was surprised, too, to find many other crops in the village which I knew were not native to the Ganges valley. Carrots, originally from Central Asia, were being eaten in huge quantities by men and beasts instead of the native turnip. Mustard oilseed plants were crowding wheat and barley in the grain fields; villagers told me that there had been none two generations ago. Sugar cane of an improved variety was being cultivated in my village as a valuable small cash crop, while it had become the only crop in other villages beside the canal a few miles away.

I noted also that certain mechanical innovations were being used in this seemingly static agricultural village. A homemade seed drill was being used for sowing wheat in place of the broadcasting by hand which had once been traditional. Big hand-cranked, rotary iron chaff-cutters were cutting half the fodder fed to the village animals. A gasoline-powered flour mill was grinding one-third of the village grain and was beginning to replace the hand-operated stone querns formerly used in every house. There were also a few modern jim-cracks: flashlights, kerosene lanterns, a phonograph, a Japanese banjo, a harmonium, European-style shoes and shirt-tails.

There was all this evidence of technological change both in crops and in machines, but it stood out against a background of poverty, malnutrition, poor health, and extreme inefficiency in most of the essential agricultural activities. Plowing, for example, was done with great labor using a three-inch iron point set in a wooden share. Irrigation required drawing up one bucket at a time: a week's labor by three men and two oxen was needed to irrigate a single acre of wheat. Sickles the size of a man's hand were used for harvesting all the grain, and the grain was threshed under the slow treading of the hooves of oxen.

The change which had occurred has not penetrated very deeply, but had gone far enough to permit a slow growth of population in the village during the past century. There is now scarcely a spare square foot of land to be found. In the present generation, pastures and forest plots have all been cleared and sown with grain. While I was in the village, the last bits of interstitial land—roadways, cremation grounds, shade trees, gravel pits, and the like—were leased out for cultivation. This was clearly desperation. Agricultural development had now gone so far that every new organic element is completely extracted from the soil once, twice, or many times each year. Almost every plant is fully used. Grass and weeds are carefully dug up, roots and all, to be used as animal fodder. All useable leaves are stripped off the trees systematically. The entire land lies absolutely bare and brown for three months of each year; the air, too, is brown, for it is full of the precious soil, dried and blown about as dust. I learned that one family of every ten had been compelled to leave the village in this generation in search of food. Yet many economists have represented this generation in northern India as one of relative "agricultural prosperity."

Despite obvious crisis, there is great hope to be derived from knowledge of the history of technological development. Without anyone growing crops recommended by government, without anyone having seen movies or slides or listened to radio propaganda for higher food production, many changes and much expansion of food supply have actually come about. Through the centuries, quietly and without urging, the peasant has made many changes on his own. And the changes have stuck. Sticking is surely one criterion of effective technological change.

INTERCONNECTIONS OF TECHNIQUES

There is hope in this picture of past development, and yet there is also great difficulty in adding anything more to the total complex of technological equipment used by such a people. To make room for anything new, one would first have to uproot something old. To improve on something old, one would have at least to modify its older form. Every improvement requires a minimum of experimentation, but the technology of an overdeveloped area allows very little free room for experimentation. An overdeveloped village has room only to subsist. It has no room to try, and certainly none in which to err; the margin is too small.

What is more, each part of an overdeveloped technology is likely to have come to have positive connections with many other vital parts of the total technology. If one incautiously adds some new element, not just one old part, but many connected parts of the old technology will be affected, sometimes for the worse as much as for the better.

New items and new techniques may succeed if they prove viable in the total context of interconnections. I have already noted several instances of successful additions to the village's repertory of crops. Potatoes and carrots, for example, replaced cotton and turnips. As human food, both potatoes and carrots proved to be popular substitutes for turnips, and were in time favored far beyond them. Carrots found favor among the livestock and have become an important fodder crop. Potatoes can be preserved and sold for cash, making it possible for the peasant to buy much of the cotton which formerly occupied his potato fields. What had seemed to be mere additions to the technology were thus in fact replacements. Most additions of new crops must become replacements, for resources of land, labor, and water in an overdeveloped area are strictly limited.

Another more complex instance of successful replacement, this in the recent past, is the replacement of an old native variety of sugar cane by an improved new variety. The new variety, which yields much more sugar to the acre, is thin-stalked and very tough. It is so tough, in fact, that it cannot be properly crushed by the old wooden presses which were formerly used. Its successful replacement of the old cane depended upon the introduction of a new heavy iron cane crusher. Fortunately, iron crushers were introduced at the same time as the improved cane. The improved cane brought part of its context along with itself. Sugar yields were increased materially, enough to pay the increased cost of

renting the iron crushers, and enough to provide slightly higher profits than before.

Carrots, potatoes, and improved sugar cane were successful because they fitted into the old contexts of the items which they replaced, or where they did not fit, they provided good, realizable, economical alternatives. Because they successfully met the criterion of total adaptation to the context of an overdeveloped technology, these successes were achieved without the intervention of any government officials, without consulting high-priced experts, without the necessity of anyone's travelling half way around the world.

These successes point the way to further successful change, but in themselves they do not begin to touch some of the most desperate technological needs of the village. Despite the ready presence of what seem to be obviously better techniques, despite explicit study, despite energetic government propaganda, the desperate problem of making further increases in food production remains unsolved. To get more food, three necessary technical changes have been stressed above all others: more manure, better seed, and more water for irrigation. Technicians hold that food production in India could be increased as much as 100 per cent if all three of these technical changes were made. But the peasants of my overdeveloped village, like the people of most Hindu villages, have not seen the light. Let us see why they must look upon the proposed improvements so darkly.

Manure, for instance. Farmers are urged to put more of it on their fields. The peasant farmer in my village knows the value of manure very well, all popular writing to the contrary notwithstanding. And here let me incidentally indicate the problem of obtaining reliable information about peasant life. There is a common belief among foreigners that the Chinese, like the Europeans, appreciate the value of manure and particularly of human night soil, while the Hindus, for some religious reasons, do not. Nothing could be further from the truth. Most of my farmers took special pains to defecate in their own fields, walking as far as a mile to do so. I was many times cordially requested by one or another Hindu farmer to please perform my natural functions in his field, so as to enrich it. The manure of the bovine is also treasured and is actually worshipped. Twice a year each farmer pays to have his household trash and his surplus animal dung carried to his distant fields. Knowledge of and belief in the value of manure are clearly present; no educational campaign is needed.

But remember that the elements of an overdeveloped technology are likely to be interconnected. Manure in this village is connected as one of a set of alternatives with many other possible uses of animal dung. Manure competes therefore with cooking, especially with the cooking of clarified butter (ghee), which requires slow-burning dung as fuel; it also competes with plastering a house, which requires a plaster made of dung, and even with smoking the hubble-bubble, which requires a sweet dung fire in the bowl of the pipe. The supply of manure has a direct connection with population and with the pressure of population on land. Because of pressure on the land for food, forest land and scrub jungle were cleared and turned into cultivated fields. Thirty years ago, those same lands had furnished free and ample fuel wood for cooking many families meals on the village hearths. Now that the wood supply has been cut away other sources of fuel must be found. Only dried leaves and the stalks of certain crops are left. And dung. More and more dung has had to be expended to fill the gap in cooking needs left by the loss of wood as fuel. Less than half the dung remains to be used as manure for

the fields which need it more desperately with each passing year.

One reformer about a generation ago discovered that the manure problem was connected with cooking needs. He tried to solve the problem by inventing a kind of insulated box that would keep milk almost at the simmering point for an hour or two after it had been brought to a boil on a quick fire of crop refuse. That device should have permitted housewives to manufacture clarified butter without burning precious dung cakes. The reformer worked hard to get some boxes made in a city and then showed many village housewives how to use the box. But village carpenters did not know how to make the box, and so the idea did not spread. When the first boxes broke they were not repaired, and housewives went back to burning dung cakes. The change failed because the technological problem was not solved in its full context.

Better seed is a second main road to greater food production. Why have so few hungry villagers travelled that road? The native wheat seed, used universally in my village, produces only half the yield that the available improved seed will produce, given good conditions. The improved varieties are hardy ones, carefully selected and tested over many years. They are "available" in the sense of being present in nearby government seed stores. Peasants know about the stores and know about the seed. Why then do they not rush to get and use the improved varieties? The replacement of an old, inefficient seed by an improved seed of the same plant would seem to be the simplest kind of technological change, a change so simple that one might easily ignore the complexities of the total context. How could there be elaborate technical repercussions from so simple a change? But we are discussing an intensely overdeveloped technology in which there is no waste, in which most organic elements are exploited to the last calorie. In such a tightly-knit technology there can be no change, not even the smallest, which does not have repercussions.

Let me list some of the objections which farmers in my village, and in other nearby villages, have raised against the improved wheat seed. It is true, they said, that if the Lord pleases, one will get a better weight of fat wheat from the field sown with Government's improved seed: the yield in weight is really very good. One or two farmers had tried it. However, they had no intention of doing so again. The operator of the seed store was an impossible man. He gave the seed at a low enough rate of interest, but he demanded that it be paid back on a certain date, which might not be at all convenient if one had other debts to pay after the harvest. What was most unreasonable, the seed store operator demanded that the seed should be grown and returned pure, not mixed with the barley, peas, gram, and oil seeds that guaranteed against complete crop failure in a bad wheat season. Aside from these impossible conditions governing the loan and use of the seed, look at the resulting crop? The grain is indeed big—so big and tough that the women cannot grind it well in the old stone flour mills. Dough made from the new flour is difficult to knead and hard to bake into good bread. The new bread, which is all a poor farmer would have to eat, does not taste like the good old bread: it is flat and uninteresting (the explanation being in part, of course, that it does not contain that potpourri of barley, peas, gram and mustard seeds that "wheat" contained in the old days). Next, look at the cows and bullocks! They do not like to eat the straw of the new wheat; they will die of hunger if we grow it. The straw is worthless, too, for thatching roofs. It does not even make a good fire to warm our hands in winter.

An improved wheat seed thus does not appear to the Hindu farmer as a simple addition, or a simple replacement or improvement on one item of his technology. The new seed brings along with it a whole new plant; the many parts of the plant and their many uses lead to an unknown series of threatening consequences. When techniques are so tightly interconnected we must admit the wisdom of the Hindu farmer's conservatism. He rightly feels that even small alterations in his precarious, overdeveloped technology may lead to catastrophe. Somehow, the peasant's legitimate technical fears must be answered by the innovator. Only by taking the larger technological context into account can the introducer of new techniques claim that he is acting responsibly. Only when he does so is he likely to be operating effectively—introducing changes that will not raise more problems than they solve, changes that will stick.

SOCIAL AND CULTURAL CONNECTIONS OF TECHNIQUES

Considering how to get more water to irrigate the crops—the third main road to greater food production—brings us to another kind of observation about overdeveloped technologies: that the elements of technology tend to be tightly connected not only with one another, but also with other aspects of rural life which are not technological at all. Thus the sacred cow cannot be manipulated without regard for her position in Hindu belief and social custom. Thus, too, techniques of agriculture, since they occupy so much time in the total lives of Hindu peasants, often have a direct and important effect on social groupings. People's developed attitudes towards each other and people's developed beliefs may be so deeply involved in technological matters that possible advantages of a new technique may be outweighed by the threat of personal and social disruption.

I shall cite only one example of this principle from the field of irrigation. Reformers of Indian agriculture, both private and governmental, have long attempted to stimulate wider use of a mechanical irrigation device known as the Persian Wheel. The PW is a device for raising water from a dug well by means of an endless belt of pots on a rope, or more recently, steel buckets on a chain. Its gears are operated by a camel or an ox. It can raise about five times as much water in twenty-four hours as can an ordinary well which is operated by drawing up one leather bucketful of water at a time. The PW is common through most of Punjab, but its distribution stops rather suddenly about forty miles north of my village. A large number of PWs which had been installed a few miles to the west twenty years ago by an agricultural reformer now lie unused and broken. Why does use of the PW stop where it does? Why is it not used in every place where the water level in the wells is sufficiently close to the surface of the ground? There are, of course, real technical problems of construction, finance, and provision of facilities for repair of the PWs. More than that, there are serious problems of social organization, law, and supernatural belief. The PW is such a valuable and expensive investment, and has such power to affect a large plot of land that it requires cooperation among several peasant families to make its use profitable. The cooperating families who have adjacent fields must agree on terms of investment, and later on terms for the use of the water, for sharing the costs of repairs etc. In those western parts of Punjab where the PW is most at home, the system of land tenure has had to be reshaped, making the block of fields around each well rather than the lands surrounding a central residential site the unit of tax assessment. A new type of ownership of fractional shares in water rights along with rules for buying and selling, borrowing and renting water have had to be worked out so that all the scattered fields of a waterowner will be irrigated. Over and beyond these legal problems of controlling the well that has a PW, there arise special social problems within the working group of people who will operate it. To bring real profit on the investment, PWs in many places have to be worked twenty-four hours a day. Someone has to sit up all night prodding the ox or camel around the towpath. And many Hindu villagers believe that the dark fields are populated by thieves, ancestral ghosts, and dangerous animals. To offset such fears, to provide for taking turns on the PW, and to organize some control over use of the precious water, it has been necessary for farmers in West Punjab to split up their houses and build them right beside their wells. This splitting-up of houses conflicts sharply with the scheme of village organization which is usual near my village in the upper Ganges plain. There all houses are crowded into the smallest possible space at one point in the centre of the village's fields. My villagers looked to their old, fortress-like plan as offering them maximum security in a threatening world. The old laws of house-building, too, have until recently discouraged the drastic rearrangement of dwellings that the PW would demand. If the PW were to be introduced effectively, provision would have to be made for solving the problems of law, social structure, and belief that are directly involved.

Such involvement of non-technical elements in the technology of an overdeveloped area may be stated as a general truth. Sometimes problems of social organization may retard the adoption of technical change, sometimes they may speed it, and occasionally they may be approximately neutral. But they are always likely to be involved. They demand to be considered before a large effort at introducing any specific technical change is launched.

Thus far I have suggested that (1) much technological change can occur and has occurred in the overdeveloped areas of the world that now appear to be static; (2) any one technical item tends to be connected with many other parts of the total technology; and (3) technical matters may have very important connections with wholly non-technical matters of social organization and the like.

TECHNOLOGICAL CHANGE AS A POLITICAL INSTITUTION

We move now to the fourth point, that in overdeveloped areas technological development itself has often already become something of an institution. Villagers and government people both have rather definite ideas about technological change in general and about specific new items of technology in particular. Development in such a nation as India has become a very well-developed institution: definite people are concerned with the business of development, and villagers are coming to have definite expectations about such developers. The question of development has come to be much mixed with questions of power and status.

When I sought out my remote village in 1951 and casually settled there, I had not heard anything of the American technical assistance program later called "Point IV." I was astonished at what my villagers told me. I simply said I was a student from America who had come to learn how they lived. They were not only convinced that something like Point IV was sure to happen, but seeing me in a Jeep were further convinced that I was, personally, the first wave of the American Empire. Just as the British had begun their conquest of India by seizing the island of Bombay two hundred years ago, so I had begun my conquest with their village, some told me in

all seriousness. The Government of India had called me to solve the problems of change that the Government could not solve by itself; or, conversely, Pandit Nehru had taken a big loan of grain from America, and I was here, in the conventional manner of village grain-lenders, to make a credit-rating of the debtor, perhaps to seize all grain from the coming harvest as repayment. Many villagers predicted what would happen next. Two hundred—three hundred—five hundred Americans were already on the way or were in Delhi even now. I would take over the village houses, buy or seize (by virtue of my secret weapons) the best, or all of the village lands. I would then carry on all agricultural work of the village by machines, harvesting the crops and disposing of the grain. Families would cease to exist: everyone would now have to eat at a great cafeteria and sleep only in hotels, as they do in America. Many villagers thought that they might have more food to eat, but just what would the food be? Would it be those strange loaves of English bread? Would they be forced to eat the forbidden beef? All the children would, of course, be taken from their parents and raised apart in schools as in America—this they knew. Would I pay their wages, and how much? Incidentally, I would handle all law suits, dispense criminal justice, abolish all the old Hindu rites and ceremonies, and deliver moral lectures from time to time, for I was—and this phrase summed up matters pretty well for many villagers—I was their Mother and Father.

Most persistently through the following months, villagers whispered among themselves that I was about to introduce a revolution in agriculture by means of machines. For instance, they hoped to have the secret device which had made American farmers so wealthy—four times the amount of surface land, to be achieved by digging a basement under the fields and by erecting two or three stories of artificial fields, supported on poles above the present ones. That is how Americans get such remarkable yields per acre! On a more credible and practical level, villagers often begged me for seeds of strange American plants and for the most minute descriptions of how the technology of agriculture, and all the other necessary works of life, were carried on in America. For them, these were tales of wonder and delight that had to be repeated hundreds of times. Such a response to the mere presence of one official-looking person might be understood in part as an expression of courtesy and respect. From their reactions, one might also easily conclude that villagers in the old, overdeveloped village of India are psychologically prepared for technological change on a grand scale, that they are ready for an accelerated program of technical assistance.

Some are prepared for change in the sense that they have fantastic hopes and wild expectations. Others are prepared in the sense that they are afraid and hostile, in the sense that they feel they are being attacked. Many are prepared in the sense that they know enough of the outside world to realize that their own technology might be changed for the better. But most see change as something that is to be handed down to them from above, as indeed, has been often attempted in the past. Villagers in this overdeveloped area know that their technology is precarious and are therefore conservative; confronted with the enormous consequences of technological change, they can only throw themselves upon the paternalistic mercy of the innovator, making him totally responsible for the possible effects of his great power on them. These are the kinds of attitudes that may shape the innovator's role in villagers' eyes. For the introducer of change who is hoping that there will be some modest efforts on the part of the peasants themselves, such attitudes and such a role present both difficult obstacles and interesting opportunities.

Without discussing some of the possible ways of handling such attitudes towards change, I do want to point out that these are attitudes of dependency—attitudes which are justly famous in India as *ma-bap*-ism, the "mother and father" attitude. This *ma-bap* dependency is a source of continual distress to Indian workers on projects of technological change. Gandhi's philosophy of technological change by pure self-help is a direct challenge to the passive fantasies of *ma-bap* attitudes. Gandhi knew and his followers today know that motherandfatherism not only reduces people to a rather undignified condition of apathy, but prevents effective mobilization of energies to put new techniques across, in a practical sense. Gandhi's program of change through self-help is one on which tens of thousands of social workers are operating in India today. Their aim is to develop agriculture not on a great industrialized scale, but rather on a scale that will be within the technological competence, knowledge, and control of ordinary, poor, illiterate farmers. Since the country is poor in industrial resources, really effective changes in techniques must be those which are desired, understood, and willingly carried out by the masses of peasants without elaborate superior direction. In this connection, they have talked a good deal about "cottage industries," and worked to get them started.

Now whether or not one believes that the Gandhian program can solve all the technological problems of raising production in overdeveloped areas, it is important to realize that peasant feelings may be strongly in sympathy with certain parts of Gandhian doctrine. Peasants want to be in control of their technology, old or new.

They react with passive motherandfatherism when they are threatened with the power of a new technology, which is completely out of their control.

Let me illustrate this by describing villagers' attitudes towards certain technological changes which have been markedly outside their spheres of knowledge and control. Great mechanical changes have passed over their society, bringing ruin to many old ways and slight or no profit to the peasant. Irrigation is one of the most striking instances: canals and tube wells are capable of bringing vast supplies of water to the thirsty crops, yet villagers of the upper Ganges plain often look on canals and tube wells with deep distrust. In many places a sizeable proportion of villagers are not willing to use water from canals and tube wells that stand at their very doors, or will use it only when their land taxes are increased to the point that they must grow a crop of sugar cane, which requires more irrigation than an old-fashioned well can produce. The canal, then, seems to them to be a coercive device by which government can extract more work and more money from the peasants. The canal is bad, many villagers say, because all must pay higher taxes to support the canal which distributes its water very inequitably. There is usually fighting among the farmers who have to use water from the same canal distributary channel, the ones at the far end complaining that most water is taken by those at the near end. What is more, the canal agents are said universally to demand small bribes from the farmers, who are helpless to resist them. The farmers cannot send up complaints against the petty officials who are exploiting them without incurring great cost, and without perhaps suffering ultimate reprisals which may be far worse than the day-to-day costs and troubles suffered in the past. Tube wells are even worse, since entire control of the tube well's water lies

in the hands of one outsider who operates the electric pump machinery. He normally takes large personal fees for giving the water on time and in full quantity, which raises the cost of tube-well water to an amount more than double the government's rate. Operators of tube wells are generally suspected of being criminals or of being in league with criminals, since they not only have power and take bribes, but move about the rural areas in trucks, sometimes at night, and associate with literate urban people of the landlord class.

What villagers often say about the new technology then is that it is operated by corrupt people who have come to prey upon them, the ignorant and helpless ones who are forbidden to open a canal lock and do not know how to run an electric pump. Villagers feel much the same way about tractors, gasoline-powered flour mills, and hospitals. All of these complicated devices are beyond the range of their social control. The mechanic, the canal agent, the clerk, and the doctor are able to exploit the peasant without check or redress and are therefore immoral. The range of activities within which the villager can exercise some moral control is, to be sure, a very narrow one; this range may not even be as large as the village itself. It is more likely to be the range of the family, or the clan, or the ward of the village. This, then, is one reason why in India Gandhi's program of small-scale industry—industry on the scale of the family or small group of families—makes sense to villagers. If enthusiasm and self-acting energy are to be mobilized from villagers in programs of technological change, then this problem must be considered: that large-scale centralized programs are doomed to a minimal or negative response so long as they leave the villager dependent upon persons who are utterly beyond his familial type of group controls. Public health, medicine, improved seeds, more water, and fertilizers must somehow be worked into the area of social control within the village where they will be handled morally and for the maximal good of all. Or, conversely, village organization must be trained upward to handle such new jobs; it is not now competent. What is clear is that the villager's dependency cannot be realized in fact. The outsider can never really bring prosperity to the village in the simple, one-directional way in which a mother and father feed and clothe a child.

Technological change in overdeveloped areas has stimulated not only latent dependent attitudes and several competing philosophies, but also regular social institutions with their own structures of rank and power. Such institutions have made deep inroads into the structure of government. Government is, of course, the biggest motherandfather of them all, one principal source, in fact, of motherandfatherism—although my villagers were more apt to refer to government agencies obscenely as their "step-mothers" or their "mothers-in-law." Indian government officials especially deputed to create development and change are legion. Their agency is being extended downward so that many a village now falls within the sphere of a whole hierarchy of development officers, development inspectors, development leaders, development trainees, etc. Many of these developers were selected for their political work during the independence struggle. Few have yet been able to do much beyond the writing of programs and slogans. Most lack any technical knowledge, and few are competent in the social and administrative techniques which would be essential to transcend the inherent handicaps of a government department in the rural countryside. Most serious of all, these developers have until recently lacked material resources. National planning and foreign aid will bring some of the material resources with which to carry out the programs that the regular officialdom has been dreaming of for years. But new development projects in many lands such as India cannot and will not be operated entirely by the local persons who had formerly functioned as regular administrative officials. To the extent that development projects import outside experts and hire technicians who are not regular officials, they will be setting up a development bureaucracy which rivals the regular bureaucracy. Cutting around the regular officials does not, however, abolish them; the regular administration will be there carrying on its work long after any temporary, special staff has gone. Diplomacy in this difficult competitive situation may have a large influence on the ultimate success and spread of the new techniques which are introduced. Potentially the situation is fraught with jealousy; either side may try to discredit the other's claim to be the real leader of successful change. I know of one great development project in India where rivalry between the temporary but effective development workers inside the project and the ineffective regular officials outside it has led to discontent and wrangling on a scale which has threatened to cripple the technical work. Solution of such intergroup problems of power is not just a matter to be settled by directives of higher policy, but one requiring administrative adjustment and day-to-day good politics on all levels.

Technological change in overdeveloped rural areas implies a redevelopment, a restructuring of patterns. The course of that redevelopment may be determined by the pre-existing technology of the rural people, by the way in which redevelopment is connected with the rest of rural social life and culture, and by the way in which those who introduce new techniques manage the problems of their own peculiar structure of power.

BLUNDERS WITH BOLSAS*

HENRY F. DOBYNS

PHIL HEAD was a guy with character, sure. But you wouldn't expect him to be at the bottom of all this fuss. After all, he was just a well-driller working for the CCC out on the Papago Indian Reservation back in the thirties. To understand how this all started, you've got to understand how things were on the Reservation then.

The Superintendent, T. B. Hall, was full of enthusiasm. He was a man with a mission—putting the Papago Indians on their feet. The men around him had caught fire, too. The work relief programs of the thirties "afforded the first real opportunity for improvements and rehabilitation of the reservation range lands."[1] Hall and the rest of the staff were on the lookout for ideas to help the Indians.

Head talked to Hall about those strange Mexican farms, and Hall was interested. In fact, he was so interested that he and Head and three other Agency officials drove across the border one day. They rattled along the wagon-track Sonoran roads to Guaymas on the Gulf of California, then south to Huatabampo. They looked over Head's exotic farms, called bolsas, and talked to their operators. Entranced with the idea that this commercial farming technique would enable the Papagos to raise bigger crops, they went back to work on the reservation.

"So thoroughly convinced are we of the

practicability of the Bolsa and of its adaptability to Papaguería that we plan an experimental Bolsa as a project of our three-month E. C. W. program in order to have it ready to catch next summer's rains."[2]

In 1939, another group of U.S. employees from the Papago Indian Agency and CCC personnel dropped below the border for a look at the Sonoran bolsas.

THE MEXICAN "SECRET"

The Indian Bureau agents found that the Sonorans had a way of making floodwaters from a single storm raise a crop on a commercial basis. The bolsa system of agriculture is essentially one of impounding floodwaters in basins made with earthen walls, and then growing a crop in the basin.

The crux of the bolsa technique is catching the water, and dust-mulching the soil after the water sinks in to conserve it:

The Mexican 'Bolsa' system of utilization of flood waters for crop raising is a very ingenious way to make the most of a meagre rainfall. . . . The Bolsa impounds water in a lake or pond and is designed to supply moisture sufficient to grow a crop without further irrigation. From 12 to 36 inches of water is run into the Bolsa and allowed to remain until it has soaked into the ground, producing deep moisture penetration. In years of subnormal rainfall, frequently water from a single shower can be collected into a Bolsa and enough moisture secured to make a subsistence

---

* Adapted and reprinted by permission from *Human Organization*, Vol. X, No. 3, Fall 1951, pp. 25–32.

[1] Papago Indian Agency, 1950, p. 1.

[2] Head & Holloway, 1937, p. 15.

crop of corn, beans, chiles and melons, where the conditions are right and the owner is willing to work.

The Spanish term 'Bolsa' means 'pocket.' The water is literally run into a pocket and left there to soak into the ground, after which the ground is plowed and harrowed and well-pulverized, and the seed planted. Fine corn, beans, and cotton are raised without any more water being used. If the crop is cultivated and the soil kept loose, the moisture does not evaporate.[3]

At Guaymas, Sonora, the Robinson family raised crops with the bolsa technique for four generations. In 1937, they showed the curious U.S. Indian Agents flourishing garbanzos, wheat, barley, and watermelons growing in dark, heavy alluvial soil which is ready for plowing about two months after receiving three or four feet of late summer floodwater. The surface is plowed, harrowed and dragged with brush to form a dust mulch. Seeds are drilled in, and a brush drag used again after seeding. Cultivation must follow any winter rains to prevent surface cracking and loss of moisture. A ditch brings water from a diversion dam on the Matape River, with a main gate, and ditch gates control the flow to each individual bolsa.

The Matape River floods heavily during August and September rains, backing up into tributary arroyos. Then it is dry until light winter rains in January or February cause local flooding. Then it is dry again until July.

Ten miles south of Huatabampo, Sonora, a 60,000 acre project was irrigated by floodwaters when the Americans saw it in 1937. The Valderrain hacienda included 1,000 acres in bolsas of about 15 acres each. When the Americans were there, English peas had been picked twice for marketing, and were expected to yield two more pickings before the vines were fed

[3] Head & Holloway, 1937, p. 10.

to cattle. A bolsa planted to English peas on August 25 had produced a crop and had been planted to a local type of bean on February 1. Excellent corn and pumpkins were grown on this fine sandy loam, watered from the Mayo River, which rises in the foothills of the Western Sierras and empties into the Gulf of California. As soon as the water soaked in and before the soil cracked, a dust mulch was established by discing and dragging. This eliminated further weed seed germination.[4] The Mayo River flows the year round, falling to a trickle in May and June just before summer rains begin.

BUILDING BOLSAS

The bolsa technique is so unusual it has tremendous appeal. It is strange to the U.S., and Indian Bureau administrators discovered it during a period of Good Neighborliness and appreciation of things Latin American. The special qualities of bolsas were not overlooked by a Congress-conscious Bureau.

Fundamentally, the Bureau employees were convinced of the value of bolsas to the Papagos. The environment of the Papaguería—the desert home of the Papago Indians—was much like that of Sonora. There was a wet and dry season, and the vegetation of Sonora continued north into the Papaguería. Both regions were extremely arid, although southern Sonora did have a few streams coming down from the Sierras, while the Papaguería had no surface water.

The bolsas utilized flood waters, and the administrators knew there were troublesome flash floods in the Papaguería. The earthen-diked basins made more efficient use of such floods than the Indian method of farming. For centuries the Tohono Au'autam—Desert People—as the Papagos call themselves, have been irrigating their farms with flood waters. More accurately,

[4] Head & Holloway, 1937, pp. 11–13.

they farm where the floods spread out, letting the waters irrigate their crops automatically.

With the rainfall available, the Desert People couldn't raise a good sweat. But they know that little of the summer rain stays where it falls. It drives down hard and fast, and runs off before the dry-packed soil can absorb it. Each mountain received higher rainfall than the valleys around it, since precipitation increases with altitude in the Papaguería. The summer rains course down the slopes into stream channels that are dry, except for a few hours after a storm. These arroyos carry the floods to level valleys where the water spreads out and slows down, dropping most of its silt load.

The Desert People centuries ago learned to plant their crops where the *arroyos* spread out. They clear the thorn-studded brush off a small plot, plow it, and plant corn, or tepari beans, or squash or melons and, in winter, wheat. The first summer rains may come in late June or not until early August. The Papagos plow and plant after the first flood softens the ground so it can be worked. If they are lucky, rain falls often enough to irrigate the field sufficiently to mature a crop before first frost, usually before mid-November.

The Desert People build low earthen dikes to spread the flood waters evenly over their fields, or to divert water from a small gully into the field. Crops require no further attention except the hard work of weeding. If rain comes, the field is irrigated automatically.

The administrators thought the *bolsa* technique surer and more efficient than Papago flood-farming, since water from only one flood was needed to mature a crop, because it was retained on the field and absorbed.

While the Indians made no attempt to retain water on their fields beyond the amount naturally flooded over them, it

looked like a short step from their spreader-dikes to water-retaining dikes. The Papagos were famed for their adaptability to American ways.

"It was not until 1938 that a work classification was established under the CCC program of authorized work for the development and improvement of small subsistence farm tracts."[5] In the four years after 1938, until the end of the CCC program, improvements were carried out on 921 acres of flood farms. Of this area, 222 acres went into *bolsas*.[6]

At the Agency headquarters town of Sells, a 14-acre *bolsa* was built. A few miles south, at Choulic, another 14-acre *bolsa* with two fields was put in. At Rusty Shovel, a tiny two-acre project was built, and a modified form was made at Sikulhimatk. A structure for Pipyak was washed out by a flood before completion.

The main *bolsa* project was on the Valshni Wash at San Miguel, south of Choulic, near the Mexican border. This covered 193 acres, divided into several interior basins. Construction began on the west bank of Valshni Wash across from San Miguel in 1938.

Crawler tractors with blades scraped dirt on the site up into dikes some eight feet high for exterior walls, and half as high for interior dikes separating the 15- to 20-acre basins. Lined up one behind another, the basins were connected by culvert pipes through the dikes to allow water to flow through.

An intake gate at the south end of the series threw water into the first basin, which emptied into the second, and so on to the last basin, which was equipped with another gate to drain excess water back into the wash. On the wash, which flows northward from its origin in Mexico, a concrete diversion structure with a 20-inch radial gate and supplementary spillway

[5] Papago Indian Agency, 1950, p. 1.
[6] *Ibid.*, p. 2.

turned water into a canal with lateral turn-outs into the *bolsa*.

CCC officials made a conscious effort to familiarize San Miguel men with the principles of operation of their *bolsa*. San Miguel residents were employed in its construction, although leaders, machine operators and tradesmen on the project were Papagos from other parts of the reservation. San Miguel workers included men who were to receive assignments in the *bolsa*. Land assignments were made by the District Council, composed of representatives of the villages in Chukut Kuk District where San Miguel is located.

The CCC worked on the San Miguel *bolsa* three years.

SHOWING THEM HOW

The Papago Agency has an Extension Division carrying on adult education activities in farming and stock raising. Extension agents operated the Choulic 14-acre *bolsa* as a demonstration project in 1939. It was planted to beans and wheat during the summer. Pink beans yielded at the rate of 1,100 pounds per acre.[7] The Indian Bureau day school at Agency headquarters planted half the Sells *bolsa* that year as a demonstration. An Indian farmer planting the other half had an excellent stand of winter wheat.[8]

LUCKY BOLSEROS[9]

The Papago Agency staked quite a bit of its local reputation on its big *bolsa* at San Miguel. The administrators figured they'd done San Miguel farmers a big favor. In their enthusiasm they neglected to experiment with the smaller *bolsas* before plunging into the San Miguel venture.

San Miguel people were part of a large movement to seek employment away from

[7] Papago Indian Agency, 1950, p. 2.
[8] *Ibid.*, p. 2.
[9] Bolseros: *bolsa* farmers. A term coined for ease of expression not actually used.

ancestral lands. With greater experience with Europeans and earlier education, they could compete for better jobs than most Desert People. They were able to pay cash for their staples instead of swapping a meagre and fluctuating flood-farm surplus. They could afford luxuries such as canned fruit.

Outside their reservation the nadir of employment of Papagos seems to have been reached during the depression years of the thirties, when most of them were forced back on reservation resources. Then large numbers worked for the Indian Division of the CCC.

War reversed the employment situation, and off-reservation jobs reached a peak. Young English-speakers found high-paying defense industry jobs in Arizona and California. Older men who spoke a little English took their families into the southern Arizona cotton fields to replace migrant pickers from the Oklahoma-Texas region who no longer made their annual harvest treks. Papago women can always find domestic work in Anglo cities, and Indian yardmen are considered desirable. With many young men in the armed forces, more cash flowed through Papago hands during the war than ever before or since.

HOMES AND HORSEMEN

When the CCC decided to build the San Miguel *bolsa*, the administrators went to the Chukut Kuk District Council to obtain permission to use necessary land. The Council gave its blessing.

The area west of Valshni Wash, where the *bolsa* began to take shape, had been grazing lands of three politically powerful cattle-rich San Miguel families. While these families couldn't own the land—all lands of the Papago reservation are in tribal ownership status—their use-rights to it were fully recognized.

Later on, as the operation of the *bolsa* became clearer, the Indians realized someone had to be there all the time to operate the gates if it rained. Men assigned lands in the project began looking for homesites there. The CCC administrators looked at their cost-sheets and refused to allow house construction in the *bolsas*. They felt investment cost was too high to waste *bolsa* land in homesites.

San Miguel really became a permanent settlement in 1915 when the Indian Bureau drilled a deep well there. The San Miguel Spokesman, then a comparatively young man, went around to talk to the people, and found they wanted the well on the east bank of the wash where they would build homes. A few people suggested different spots, but they were talked around, and the Spokesman told the Americans where to sink the well. Today, that well is still the only source of water in San Miguel (except for the artificial basin used to store flood water before the well was drilled). Everyone must haul his water from the hydrant at the well to his house in barrels on a truck or wagon.

Then the administrators went to the District Council seeking additional acreage for homesites on the west bank of the wash near the *bolsa*. At this point some of the cattle families with grazing rights on the west bank called a halt. Having given up lands for the *bolsa* itself, they did not wish to yield more pasture land for assignees of rival families to build on. Under their pressure, the District Council declined the CCC request for re-assignment of the pastures.

THE BOLSEROS WEREN'T GRATEFUL

When it became clear that no homesites were to be had west of Valshni Wash, some men who had been assigned land in the *bolsa* were discouraged and wanted to give up their assignments. CCC officials persuaded them to hang on in hopes the political balance would shift.

Farming began in the *bolsa* in 1939, although construction work continued. Despite the problem of crossing Valshni Wash after a flood, men tried to raise crops in the new structure. Valshni is formidable in flood, as the villagers have learned from experience. The Spokesman once attempted to cross the flooding stream to shut off the *bolsa* gate. He had a big, strong riding horse, but it went down in mid-channel and the Spokesman was left to swim out of the raging flood in midnight darkness. After that, he stayed home when the wash ran.

Yet, someone had to be at the *bolsa* to operate the gates when the floods came. The intake had to be opened to let water in. Or if it were left open, someone had to come shut it before the *bolsa* washed out from over-filling. Of course, the drain gate could be left open as a safety valve, but then someone had to close it in time to keep the *bolsa* full when the flood began to subside. Regardless of family, fiesta, or other work, someone had to turn the gates when the wash ran full.

This constant attention to the *bolsa* was very different from the traditional Papago technique of flood irrigation that let the flood do all the work. No one had to be within 100 miles of his field when the flood came. San Miguel men didn't like being tied down so, but they were game.

The alternative to crossing the flooding wash was to camp at the *bolsa* until a flood came down the wash. A Papago Tribal Council member from San Miguel tried that. He stayed for weeks waiting for rain. Finally, he ran out of supplies and made a quick dash to a trading post for supplies. While he was on his 50-mile trip, rain hit the watershed in Mexico. When he reached San Miguel the flooding wash had cut him off from the *bolsa*.

The San Miguel farmers began complaining about the construction of their *bolsa*:

Another thing I don't think is right is that ditch, that big canal. Where it starts, it goes up, and then drops, so the water almost goes over the top before it runs through. If it were made right, we could open the gates and let the water in to run evenly, and everyone would have enough water, instead of one *bolsa* getting all the water that does come in. If it were made right you could let all the water in you want. As it is, everyone goes to irrigate, and has to watch his own water and the main ditch, without being able to be both places at the same time.[10]

This gripe shows that the *bolseros* were using their project not as a *bolsa* but as an irrigation project!

Another *bolsa* farmer explained his technique in cropping:

You see, the idea in these *bolsas* is to fill up your *bolsas*, and then either drain the water out or let it soak in. Then you are supposed to plow the moisture in as soon as you can get on the land. I don't do that, because the *bolsa* is slanted. I got them to make me a ditch so I could irrigate that upper part. I soak the lower part but irrigate the upper part.[11]

In using the *Bolsa* for irrigation, the San Miguel farmers found new problems. In 1939, the people of the village requested the CCC "to clear and level the flood control subsistence farm." (The *bolsa*.)[12] Yet the CCC did not capitalize on this opportunity to draw the people into planning. The leveling wasn't done. While it wouldn't make much difference in a *bolsa*, it was very important in an irrigation operation.

The *bolsas* are awfully uneven. When you irrigate the first time it is all right. But then, after you've planted, it is hard to irrigate because of the unevenness. The plants on the low spots are flooded out

trying to force the water up to the plants on the high spots.

The government should have leveled the *bolsas*, or put in small dikes in each *bolsa* field, like white farmers do in planting alfalfa.[13]

The Indians found that their *bolsa* fields were not very productive: "I plant five to eight acres at the most in beans. I got 15 sacks off eight acres once—the most."[14]

And the farmers were not slow to realize why their yields were low in the *bolsas*:

When they made those *bolsas* they took the fertilizer—all the rich soil, top soil, off to make the dikes. They left hard soil with little fertilizer.

Since then we haven't been doing good. You'll see people with *bolsa* assignments not using them—they farm their fields somewhere else. I farmed in the *bolsa* in 1941, 1942, and 1943. I did pretty well. Mostly I raised barley in the fall. I planted corn, watermelons, pinto beans, and a very little squash. When I couldn't do good in the *bolsa*, I cleared this small field and planted corn.[15]

The *bolsa* farmers gave up in this way until at the end of the war no one at all was farming in it.

BOLSTERING A BOLSA

In 1946, the Papago Indian Agency had a new Extension Agent on its staff. He was in charge of teaching the Desert People modern methods of farming and stock raising. He felt the *bolsa* project was worthwhile and could be salvaged. So he encouraged the Tribal Councilman from San Miguel who had always been interested in the project. The Councilman had "outing" experience on New Jersey farms during his Carlyle school days. (Indian students at the time he went to school were farmed

---

[10] Bolsero No. 1.
[11] Bolsero No. 2.
[12] District Program, 1939–40.

[13] Bolsero No. 1.
[14] Bolsero No. 2.
[15] Bolsero No. 1.

out with a farmer or tradesman for the summer to learn through experience). Over 70, he was a staunch Presbyterian and a political power.

On the advice of the Extension Agent, the Councilman purchased a tractor and embarked on an ambitious program to put his *bolsa* assignment into full production.

When the Councilman's corn was at its best, the grasshoppers descended on it. "He had green corn and everything and I did too, before. But the grasshoppers ate it all up. They're new too, a new pest. So this year I'm not planting. I'm not sure I want to plant to feed the grasshoppers."[16] The Extension Agent obtained two tons of grasshopper poison bait from the Pima County Extension Agent. Some of this the Councilman used on his *bolsa* field in September, but the results were only fair.[17] The Councilman didn't get a crop. In 1947, his crops failed again. The Extension Agent had given up by 1948, and the Councilman didn't plant at all. In 1949, he planted beans, watermelons, a little corn and a few pumpkins. During these years he was the only man trying to farm in the *bolsa*.

In planting season at San Miguel, the head of one of the powerful families said:

If those people would come out here and tell us how to farm the *bolsas*, I'd be interested in farming. They should be out here at this time of the year, knowing that the water may come at any time, but we don't see them.[18]

EXIT THE BOLSA

The Councilman's 1949 crop failed when the *bolsa* itself failed. The final chapter in the history of the San Miguel *bolsa* was written in September by an unusually large flood which swept down Val-

[16] Bolsero No. 1.
[17] Papago Indian Agency, 1946, p. 25.
[18] Bolsero No. 1.

shni Wash and washed out the *bolsa* completely.

No one will ever again farm in the San Miguel *bolsa*. It no longer exists.

ANALYSIS OR: HINDSIGHT IS CLEARER THAN FORESIGHT

Leaving aside the human relations involved for the moment, the project failed for technical reasons. It didn't work in its new environment.

This points up an administrative principle that would seem too obvious to need statement. Since in this case it was ignored, let it be stated:

To be accepted by a group of people, any technological change offered them must be workable and practical in their environment.

It follows that an administrator who wants to introduce a questionable technique should test it before introducing it full-scale. While the Papago administrators, at the beginning, realized the need for experimentation, their enthusiasm apparently ran away with them. The San Miguel project was a large-scale introduction, committing Indian Bureau prestige. The attitude of the San Miguel people toward the Bureau was determined, to a very great degree, by the success or failure of the *bolsa*. The Bureau risked its prestige with the San Miguel people, and also with Congress. As the *bolsa* failed, people in San Miguel have come to feel the Bureau is fallible, making administration there much tougher.

Technological failures—Aside from its final destruction, the San Miguel *bolsa* exhibited a number of technical failings which contributed to the sparing use made of it by the Desert People.

Climatic capers—When the government officials borrowed the *bolsa* idea from Sonora, they seem to have underestimated the difference in climate between the Papaguería and southern Sonora.

Sonoran *bolsas* are several hundred miles south and several hundred feet lower in altitude than San Miguel, which means their climate is considerably warmer. In fact, they are almost frost-free. Papago farmers must reckon with mid-November to mid-February frosts.

The streams filling Mexican *bolsas* have a much larger flow than any ephemeral Papago *arroyo*. The Mayo River is permanent, though quite small at times. The Matape is much larger than any stream in the Papaguería, flooding regularly every August and September, with smaller peaks in January or February. In contrast, smaller local drainages in the Papaguería may be skipped entirely by rainstroms in any particular year. Some years the San Miguel *bolsa* was dry. Valshni Wash has high flood crests occasionally, as the destruction of the *bolsa* shows, but often it doesn't rise enough to irrigate the *bolsa*. Villagers say only the basin nearest the intake has been adequately watered any time since the war. This indicates that either the project was over-built for the normal flow (and certainly under-built for flood peaks) or the Papago estimate of the intake mechanism quoted above is correct.

The frost season created problems for *bolsa*-type operations in the Papaguería. The growing season, from the first summer rains in July or August to frost in November, is short enough to catch the flood farmer who plants as soon as he can plow after the first rain. For the *bolsa* farmer, who must wait for a couple of feet of water to soak into his impervious soil, growing summer crops becomes almost impossible. At best, he can succeed only in years of early summer rain.

The difficulty of filling a *bolsa* with enough water from one flood to raise a crop, further mitigated against a *bolsa* technique. Probably these two factors, plus the great amount of extra work involved in maintaining the dust mulch required in *bolsa* farming, explain the irrigation operations of the San Miguel farmers.

A change in crops might have overcome these difficulties, but no one ever suggested changing. The *bolsas*, although copied from large commercial operations, were never envisioned as anything more than subsistence farms raising traditional Papago foods.

Leveling—Since the *bolsa* was actually operated as an irrigation project, it was important for fields to be level. The experience of the San Miguel farmers with high and low spots leaves no doubt that the construction crews left the fields very uneven, and the condition was not remedied.

Fertility—When the *bolsa* was constructed, the scrapers simply scooped the fertile, loose topsoil off the site and piled it up in dikes, covering it with tight subsoil. This left hard subsoil for the Papagos to farm, illustrating the lack of technological mastery of the CCC crews and engineers. Every farm boy of 15 knows the value of topsoil. An administrator who intends to change farming habits needs to be better informed than the farmers he wants to change.

Summary—These technical failings of the San Miguel *bolsa* all added up to low production. Inadequately and unevenly watered fields of low fertility could hardly produce more than undisturbed flood fields. Yet *bolsas* meant much more work.

The Papagos are, after all, intelligent human beings. It is not to be wondered that they returned to flood farming techniques, producing more with less work.

LANGUAGE, THE VEHICLE THAT BREAKS DOWN

The manner in which the *bolsa* concept arrived at San Miguel furnishes an intriguing study in the process of diffusion— the movement of ideas from one people to another. Originally *bolsas* formed part of the economic system of the Spanish-speaking social system in Sonora. They were seen by Phil Head, a member of the U.S. social system. But Head did not become an innovator by introducing *bolsas* to his own Anglo-group. It was not until he became part of the sort of twilight social system existing where Papagos meet Anglos that he became an innovator. In the Indian Division of the CCC he introduced the *bolsa* idea to the English-speaking side of the cross-cultural social system on the reservation. Then other Anglos in this contact social system went to Mexico for first-hand examination of the *bolsas*.

Finally, *bolsas* were constructed as part of the physical equipment of the Anglo part of the reservation social system. They failed to become part of the Papago social system because the Desert People were never made to feel the *bolsas* were their own. *Bolsas* remained in the twilight zone between Anglos and Papagos, defined by the Indians as one of the things Anglos could do.

In the diffusion of the *bolsa* concept from Sonoran Spanish society to the English-speaking Papago contact society, communication was faulty. The English-speakers in Papago administration failed to grasp from their Spanish-speaking guides the entire complex of knowledge, practices and attitudes associated with the physical structure of the *bolsa*. When, in turn, they attempted to communicate their partial knowledge of the complex to Papago-speaking Desert People who were to operate the *bolsas*, another partial failure of communication occurred. The Papagos knew less than the administrators of the total necessary for successful *bolsa* operation. At the same time, the administrators knew less than the Papagos of local circumstances affecting the success of the project.

Human Failures—Administrators didn't bring San Miguel people into the preliminary planning of their *bolsa*. As one result, the project failed to fit into the current socio-cultural situation of the village in many respects. Since they did not participate in the planning enough to modify the project to fit their needs, San Miguel farmers have never felt it to be their own. No Papagos were taken to Sonora to see *bolsas*, so their knowledge had to be derived at second hand from administrators. Lacking first-hand knowledge of *bolsa* techniques, the Indians were unprepared for complications of operation, and couldn't foresee some problems which arose. To them, the *bolsa* remained government property—it put it there, it should make the *bolsa* work.

Had Papagos been brought into the planning, they would probably have foreseen problems involved in constant residence at their *bolsa*. The *bolsa* probably wouldn't have been built on the west bank, across the wash from the village. The administrators didn't foresee this problem, and went to the District Council for homesites across the wash only after the project was underway. The villagers could have told them early in the planning, before construction began, that the land control pattern would prevent settlement across the wash by *bolsa* assignees. The villagers would also have pointed out that even if assignees could move across the wash, they would need a new well, since they would be cut off from the old one, and the *charco*, during every flood.

Another principle of administration may be stated:

An induced technological change will succeed to a degree proportionate to the extent to which the administered people feel a need for it, are brought into its planning and execution, and feel it to be their own.

The problem of yield in the *bolsa* has already been touched upon, but needs another look from the point of view of incentives.

Although Mexican *bolsas* were large-scale commercial enterprises raising crops for sale, the administrators viewed the projected Papago *bolsas* as subsistence farms. The San Miguel project was large enough to be operated commercially, but was split up with one or even two farmers to each 20-acre or less basin. As subsistence farms, they had to show increased yield to compete with flood farms, since they required more work. This they didn't do, so farmers went back to flood farms.

A subsistence-farm concept led to neglect of the *bolsas* in another way. During the war years, work at high wages off their reservation attracted many Papagos, especially those speaking English and with some knowledge of a trade. Many young men were in the armed services. Not only were *bolsas* neglected, but flood farming decreased sharply. Wages offered a high living standard, far above a subsistence level. So a man who could find work was foolish to gamble on farming at the subsistence level. This sudden change in economic situation on the Papago reservation was totally beyond the control of the Indian Bureau.

However, a different approach to *bolsa* operation might have kept the project in use. If it had been operated commercially, as a unit, it might have offered sufficient incentive to one or two men to keep them in San Miguel. Subsistence assignments were not large enough to accomplish this end.

The readiness with which Desert People abandoned subsistence farming when wage labor became readily available to them points out another guiding thought for administrators:

In any cross-cultural administration, unless the agency directing cultural change is the only institution of the dominant culture in contact with the subordinate culture, it will never be able to control the changes in the subordinate culture.

The contacts the administered people have with other institutions of an impingent culture produce reactions far beyond the control of an agency attempting to direct cultural changes.

In this case, administrators paved the way for the ultimate failure of one of their directed changes, the *bolsa*. In hiring San Miguel men to work on their project with the intention of teaching them its operations, administrators hastened the transformation of Papago economy from a gift-exchange and barter basis to a cash surplus basis. Working for the CCC accustomed San Miguel men, on a large scale, to a regular pay check, and to the luxuries those checks represented at the trading posts or nearby Anglo cities. To some extent the administrators foresaw the change in economic pattern, and favored it. But they didn't foresee its direct effect on the change they sought to make in farming patterns.

This illustrates the view that *since each social system is in equilibrium, any change in it will produce other changes until a new balance is reached.* These resultant changes cannot always be predicted.

Despite the power of wages in drawing *Tohono Au'autam* men away from subsistence farming, and despite the number of young men in armed service, the *bolsa* basically didn't fail to attract farmers because all the farmers were working for wages. Even at the peak of manpower loss, there were still older men in San Miguel growing crops on flood farms. They could have farmed in the *bolsa*, except for the errors in human relations committed by the administration in planning the project, which led to errors in the technology of the *bolsa*.

Ultimately, failure to fully grasp the principles of the *bolsa* technique, and failure to bring San Miguel people into project planning in a way that would have enabled adaptation of the technique to the peculiar circumstances of San Miguel, caused the failure of the *bolsa* as a cultural change.

However, there is one more piece of this puzzle to be put in place. This is the experience of the Extension Agent in persuading the Councilman to farm the *bolsa* in 1946 and 1947. In spite of all the technological shortcomings of the *bolsa*, in spite of all the previous shortcomings in bringing farmers into project planning, and in spite of his past experiences in the *bolsa*, the Councilman was persuaded to try once more. The Agent's effort even had some carry-over effect, for the Councilman actually tried to farm the *bolsa* in three of the next four years. He bought a tractor, a huge investment for a Papago. He would have leveled his own field had he known how or had the Agent shown him how.

The willingness of the *bolsero* quoted previously to try *bolsa* farming, if instructed by the farm agent, helps place this bit of the puzzle: *In cross-cultural administration the amount of change produced by any program of directed change will be proportionate to the amount of* *face-to-face contact between administrators and administered people.*

As a principle of administration, this is advanced as more tentative than the preceding ones—as a hypothesis. (If the people are resistant, the effect might well be the opposite, for example.) But in this case, face-to-face contact between the Extension Agent and Councilman produced change in the Councilman's actions proportionate to the amount of time and effort the Agent spent with him. As the Agent, disheartened, let up, the speed with which the Councilman changed his attack on the *bolsa* problems slacked off.

The success of the Agent again emphasizes the necessity for an administrator *knowing* that a change will work in its new environment before attempting it. The tractor for use in the *bolsa* purchased by the Councilman with the Agent's encouragement, has been a total loss as far as *bolsa* operations go. Fortunately, the Councilman is also a cattleman, and has been able to use the machine for hauling fence posts on his range.

Dr. Ernest Beaglehole is a Professor in the Department of Psychology, Victoria University College, Wellington, New Zealand. He was Chairman at the Second Session of the I.L.O. Committee of Experts on Indigenous Labour in 1954 and the leader of the joint field mission on indigenous populations of the United Nations and the specialized agencies that visited the Andes in 1952.

Dr. McKim Marriott, a Social Anthropologist, has devoted 3 years to field studies of town and village life in rural India. Trained at the University of Chicago, he has lectured and conducted further research at the Institute of East Asiatic Studies at the University of California. His publications include *Village India*, dealing with traditional patterns of peasant culture, and *Pilot Project, India*, of which he is coauthor, on India's pioneer effort in rural community development at Etawah.

Mr. Henry F. Dobyns is an independent research anthropologist whose main interests have been in programs of directed cultural change, particularly in bisocietal situations. He has conducted ethnohistorical studies of southwestern Indians and published widely in scholarly and professional journals in his field. He has an M.A. degree in anthropology and is now engaged in further work at Cornell University.

XIII

MEASURING THE DEVELOPMENT OF
UNDERDEVELOPED AREAS

FROM time to time we have raised the question of measuring development and have without going very deeply into the subject postponed it for more comprehensive treatment in the present chapter. Several measuring instruments, their rationale and suggestions as to how they might profitably be used are presented in this chapter. These measuring instruments or scales are general in nature, in that they include in their measure of development a variety of different indices, but in a sense not quite so broad as some might think since they are indices that appear important relative to our own culture. Although we have admitted that these scales are culture bound just as are intelligence tests, that in itself does not mean that they are useless. Each of the scales mentioned in this chapter measures a particular kind of development, i.e., the kind of development represented by the indices included in the scale.

As an introduction to the papers included in this chapter we shall first have a look at the scale that we employed in measuring the development of political entities in order to classify geographical regions as generally developed or underdeveloped. The scale was first mentioned in the introduction to Chapter I. In constructing a scale of this nature one realizes that an almost infinite number of items might be suggested for inclusion, as indicative of development. It will be recalled that we have discussed the present stage of international social bookkeeping and that, for many of the items that might be considered pertinent, comparable economic or other data are unavailable for a large proportion of the 195 political entities of the world. However, we shall assume the available data to be acceptable rather than no data at all. In constructing this simple scale of development we have used 17 items for which adequate data could be obtained on a fairly large proportion of our 195 political entities.[1] Each of the 17 items has been treated previously on an individual basis in earlier chapters and their relationship to our classification of political entities as developed or underdeveloped has been shown.

[1] We now speak of 195 political entities although in 1949 previous to some consolidation there were 198 political entities, i.e., at the time that the earlier studies commenced.

In some cases they have correlated very highly with the classification of entities as developed or underdeveloped, and in other cases they have not.

The items included in this scale and their individual correlation with the developed or underdeveloped dichotomy is repeated in Table 35.[2]

While any single variable or combination of several variables might be used as an index of development in this fashion, as is frequently done, we have chosen

TABLE 35.   Phi Coefficient of Correlation of Individual Variables with
Developed or Underdeveloped Dichotomy

Variable	Phi Coefficient of Correlation
Tons of railway freight per 1000 population	1.228
Pieces of railway rolling stock per 1000 population	1.202
Grain and food production *per capita*	1.144
Number of inhabitants per physician	1.128
Commercial energy consumption *per capita*	1.122
Number of radios per 1000 inhabitants	1.022
Crude birth rate	.964
Production of commercial and noncommercial energy *per capita*	.925
Steel production	.888
Number of telephones per 100 inhabitants	.856
Commercial energy production *per capita*	.848
Motor vehicles in use per 1000 population	.791
Percent of population in urban areas	.787
Iron ore production	.731
Percent of population enrolled as students	.678
Infant mortality rate	.478
Number of inhabitants per hospital bed	.436

to combine a variety of indices in order to obtain an overall score of development, a score that is likely to be more representative. The rationale for combination of items into a scale may be found in articles appearing in this chapter or in greater detail in any modern textbook on methods of social research. The scoring technique is simple in the example to follow in that each political entity received 2 points for each item on which it fell in the "most favorable subcategory" and 1 point for each item on which it fell in the "least favorable subcategory" from a standpoint of development. The score on items for which no information was available was determined for each political entity on a pro rata basis, i.e., each political entity received 2 points or 1 point for each "no information available" item in proportion to the number of 2's and 1's that they already had received. A developed political entity such as the United States fell in the most favorable subcategory each time, receiving a score of 34. On the other hand, Angola fell in either the least favorable category or in the no information category, so that

[2] As previously stated, the phi coefficient of correlation is used as an index of relationships for comparative purposes; the fact that its upper limit may be greater than 1.000 is neither here nor there.

only the minimum score of 17 was obtained. This simple scale, simple in the sense of the scoring technique, is presented as an example of the general relationship between overall development and our dichotomy as developed or underdeveloped rather than as an example of sophisticated scaling technique.

The rationale for setting up cutting points dividing the continuum of scores on each item has been presented in Chapter III and is the same in this case. Each item has the same weight. A considerable body of research data has shown that a score derived from a number of equally weighted items has about the same predictive value as a score derived from a number of items with different weights. An example of each is presented in one of the articles reprinted in this chapter.

TABLE 36.   Development Scores by Geographical Areas

Area	(1) Unweighted Mean Scores	(2) Mean Scores Weighted by Population of Each Political Entity	(3) Number of Political Entities in Area	(4) Percent of World's Population in Area	(5) Percent of World's Land in Area
North America	28.75	33.99	5	6.89	16.02
Europe	28.23	31.62	34	16.31	3.67
Oceania	23.54	30.06	24	.55	6.39
South America	23.60	24.28	14	4.58	13.28
Central America and Caribbean	22.25	23.65	24	2.12	2.06
Central, East and South Asia	19.47	20.85	15	51.07	28.90
Africa	18.44	19.03	50	8.20	23.56
Middle East	20.37	18.36	19	3.18	3.52
Southeastern Asia	19.40	18.11	10	7.10	2.59
			195	100.00	100.00

While no single item had greater weight than others, certain areas of interest were represented to a greater extent than others. For example, production of energy appeared in 2 different series, one including noncommercial energy and the other only commercial energy. Both series were included because, although one was partially included in the other, one seemed to reflect a different type of productive effort than the other. There were also 2 series on railway transportation and 2 on the media of mass communication. It might also be said that the items for which information was available were weighted more heavily than others because they determined the score for areas without available information on other items. That is, inferences were made about some kinds of development in a country in proportion to its development in other respects.

The score of each of the 195 political entities may be found by turning to Appendix II where they are presented by geographical regions.

In order to summarize and parsimoniously represent the findings, these scores are presented by geographical region in Table 36.

Column (1) of Table 36 contains the mean weight of all political entities in that geographical area, without regard to the size of the political entity in population. In other words, Canada, St. Pierre and Miquelon, Alaska, and the United States were of the same importance or weight in determining the average score of North America. In Column (2) the average or mean score is weighted by the size of the population of each area. Thus, the score of North America is determined to a very great extent by the United States. This generally permits a more realistic view of the development to be found in a region. Columns (3), (4), and (5) are presented as a matter of convenience for comparative purposes. Remembering the classification of regions as developed or underdeveloped in Chapter I, the regional development scores are in almost complete agreement with what we would expect. Some of the difference can be attributed to the heterogeneity of regions and the fact that political entities with large populations were weighted out of proportion to the weight that they would have had if the number of political entities alone had been used in working out the regional score. North America and Europe, for example, score as expected but Oceania's score is greatly influenced by Australia and New Zealand, giving Oceania a higher score than might have been expected.

The development scale shown here could well serve as a basis for construction of additional scales, scales which when applied would give us a bench mark from which to measure the development of a political entity. And as attempts were made to develop political entities we could measure their progress with various scales and subscales.

The first article in this chapter is by Stuart C. Dodd, "The Scientific Measurement of Fitness for Self-government." This article is reprinted not so much for the substantive area in which it provided a rationale for measurement, but for the excellent presentation of a rationale and methodology that may be applied to the problem of measuring general development.

Additional research on the same problem is presented as a follow-up in "A Quantitative Approach to Political Decision." It should be read not for its substantive content alone but likewise for its application of the general approach suggested by Dodd. The efficiency of weighted and unweighted scoring systems are also shown in this paper.

The original research on non-self-governing political entities was continued with manipulation of more recent data in much the same manner as in the earlier study but with some modification of orientation and differences in variables for which data were available. The third paper in this chapter consists of excerpts from a restudy of non-self-governing political entities, "A Re-examination of the Concept, 'Capacity for Self-Government.'" Its treatment of United Nations data using the self-governing or non-self-governing dichotomy sheds some light on the question of self-determination for nations.

Although the focus of attention in this chapter is on economic and political development an examination of the broad areas considered for measurement shows that there is room for a variety of subscales permitting closer measurement of various areas of development.

THE SCIENTIFIC MEASUREMENT OF FITNESS FOR SELF-GOVERNMENT*

STUART C. DODD

WHEN is a dependent people fit for self-government or independence? The mandate system and now the trusteeship system are intended to give a dependency either self-government or independence in the course of time, increasingly because of the fitness of the dependency and decreasingly because of international power politics or imperial interests of the controlling power. To carry out this policy of democratic concern for the welfare of the inhabitants requires that fitness be so specified that the inhabitants know what efforts or achievements by them will result in specified advances toward full self-government. There is need for a procedure to make this transition from dependence to independence a pacific and constructive one and to provide an alternative to the appeal to force that was the sole resource of the dependency in the past. If fitness can be defined and measured and degrees of it set as goals, the trusteeship system is likely to work with less friction and probability of bloodshed in the future.

THE FACTS TO DATE

The officially declared purpose in the United Nations Charter and Trusteeship Agreements that the dependency shall be developed toward eventual self-government or independence has taken cognizance of this problem and suggested its solution. The outlook for its solution is made more hopeful by the increased willingness, occasionally evident in the modern world, of some nations under certain circumstances to give up their dependencies and sincerely work toward developing them, not for exploitation, but for the welfare of the inhabitants.

The first step toward the achievement of self-government for dependencies is to set up criteria for measuring their fitness. We analyzed[1] this question to find the criteria that had been agreed upon by both the dependency and the controlling power in the cases of the Philippines, India, and Iraq. There resulted agreement on some eleven criteria, five dealing with internal affairs and six with international obligations of the dependency. These criteria included such requirements as the ability of the dependency to maintain (a) its civil government, (b) its territorial integrity, (c) its financial solvency, (d) a competent judiciary, and (e) a public opinion wanting self-government; and to guarantee

* Adapted and reprinted by permission from *The Scientific Monthly*, Vol. LXXVIII, No. 2, February 1954, pp. 94–99.

[1] Ritsher, W. H., "Criteria of Capacity for Independence," *Social Science Series*, p. 152. Lebanon: American University of Beirut, 1934.

the rights of foreigners and minorities and other international obligations of debts, treaties, and so forth, legally contracted. These criteria thus analyzed were the identical set that were later adopted by the Mandates Commission of the League of Nations. This official declaration of the criteria of fitness for independence is the first step in working toward a solution of the problem of peaceful transition from dependency to self-government.

The analysis was materially aided by technics developed by the social sciences in the last decade or two for measuring such complex and qualitative phenomena.

A PROPOSED MEASURING INSTRUMENT FOR SELF-GOVERNMENT

(a) How to measure the criteria for self-government. The instrument here described for measuring fitness for self-government is based on several assumptions which it is well to state clearly at the start. It assumes that: (1) self-government is often a desired goal; (2) measuring fitness can be a useful step toward self-government; (3) this step can reduce conflicts; and (4) fitness can be measured by suitable statistical indices. This paper is mostly concerned with giving evidence in support of the last assumption—that fitness can be measured.

Before describing the indices for measuring fitness a review of the theory of measurement on which they are based may be useful for political scientists.

Our theory of measurement, which is applicable to any social phenomena and is not limited to dependencies nor even to governmental phenomena, may be described in three cycles: the qualitative, the quantitative, and the correlative.

For the qualitative cycle, one begins by naming classes of phenomena and their subclasses in a classification scheme. A sub-classification may be carried to as many

levels or degrees of fineness as may be needed.

For the quantitative cycle one begins by observing whether a given qualitative class is present or absent in a particular situation. This makes it an all-or-none variable which may be assigned the numerical values of one or zero and then may be weighted later as desired in combining with the other variables. Wherever possible such all-or-none variables should be observed more exactly in an ordinal series, or ranks, such as in stating whether there is none, some, more, or most of that variable in a given situation. This ordinal variable in turn should be still more exactly observed wherever possible by converting it to a cardinal variable which is a multiple of equal and standardized units. Ordinal variables are designated "first, second, third . . . ," while cardinal variables are designated "one, two, three. . . ." When the cardinal variable has been calibrated, that is, when its limits, reliability, validity, and so on, have themselves been measured, it becomes the most exact type of variable and is the ideal in the quantitative cycle.

For the correlative cycle the indices of the quantitative cycle, whether all-or-none, ordinal or cardinal, have all their intercorrelations calculated by appropriate technics. This determines the structure or pattern of the indices or classes of phenomena that are involved in the total situation under study. In proportion as the determinant of the table of intercorrelations vanishes, the system of observed variables can be considered a closed system, since any one variable within it can be completely predicted from the other variables, that is, its multiple correlation with the others is unity. This serves to measure how completely or adequately, for the predictive function of science, the variables in the situation have been observed.

Now apply this theory of measurement

which, in its broad outlines, can be shown to subsume all measurement that exists in any science, to the problem of measuring fitness for self-government. The eleven criteria adopted by the Mandates Commission were subclassified through seven levels into a resulting 350 subclasses, or items, of objectively observable phenomena. These 350 items were then converted into quantitative indices by observing them either as present or absent or present in ordinal degrees or present in cardinal amounts. Consider, for example, three sample indices at these stages of precision. These three indices measure, for instance, the three major internal criteria of a competent judiciary, a favorable public opinion, and financial solvency.

For a qualitative index converted into an all-or-none quantitative index, consider the criterion that the dependency must possess a judiciary commanding the confidence of the people. Alongside the courts of the controlling power, let parallel native courts be set up with alternative jurisdiction as formerly was the case in various Near Eastern states. Let the native courts try those cases where both litigants agreed to take their case there. At the end of each year, the percentage of all the cases in the court that went to their own native courts could be calculated and judges appointed for the next period, such that the native judges would be that percentage of all the judges. Thus, as people gained or lost confidence in their native courts, the percentage of native judges in the country would increase or decrease. When they attained full confidence in their own judiciary, all judges would automatically become nationals; and the dependency would have achieved complete control of its judiciary by demonstrated confidence in it. The action of taking the case to the native court is a qualitative item of behavior. Coupled with its absence, the not-taking-the-case-to-a-native-court becomes an all-or-none item of behavior. The arithmetic mean of such items is the percentage of cases taken to the national court. (Every percentage is the arithmetic mean of an all-or-none frequency variable.)

For an illustration of an ordinal variable, consider a public opinion poll determining the criterion that there shall be a predominant public opinion in favor of self-government or independence. Here, instead of asking the question, "Do you approve or disapprove?" the question could be asked more exactly in ordinal degrees specifying the degree of self-government that is favored or as the degree of intensity of approval or disapproval of self-government. Of course, such a question should be carefully phrased in alternative forms, penetratingly analyzed by supplementary questioning to make sure that the opinion expressed on the question at issue is adequately reflected in all its complications and is independent of the particular phrasing of the question. The questions should elicit the "give/get" ratios or price of independence which the citizens are willing to pay. This cost of what they want can be measured in eight types of indices that we have developed.[2] Thus indices of willingness to pay higher taxes, have military service, and put up with possible specified degrees of lowered efficiency in government services, can gage the strength of the public opinion in terms of what the people will give for what they want to get.

For a third illustration, this time a cardinal variable, the financial solvency of the budget can be determined in cardinal units of money.

For the correlative cycle, the 350 indices need to be combined in successive stages until eventually they yield a single index or scale of total fitness. This combination is usually made additively with some kind of weights. Ideally, the weights should be

[2] Dodd, S. C., *American Sociological Review* 16, No. 5, (1951).

regression weights determined by multiple correlation, which is calculated by correlating the indices against some accepted measure of dependence-independence such as the difference between a set of dependent areas and another comparable set of independent areas. As a first approximation, these weights may be secured as ratings by a panel of competent specialists.

For this weighting, a decimal system has been developed that distributes 100 points among the subclasses of each class wherever it may fall in the hierarchy of classification which breaks "fitness" down into subclasses and sub-subclasses in successive levels. The number of percentage points given to each subclass is according to the judge's estimate of its relative importance among the other subclasses of its class in contributing toward fitness for self-government. In this way the weights of all the subclasses of any one class add up to 100. Provision may be made for an extra unidentified subclass in the event the judges feel that the given specified subclasses are an inadequate analysis of their class. The weight assigned by the judges to the unidentified class measures the degrees of inadequacy of the other subclasses. With this decimal weighting system, the net weight of any class, anywhere in the hierarchy on any of the seven levels, toward total fitness is simply the product of its percentage and the percentage of all classes above it in the hierarchy. This yields indices for every item or combination of items up to the total fitness so that the whole, as well as any of its parts, is measurable. This decimal weighting system is flexible in permitting the insertion or removal of any items above or below it, with consequent shift of weighting only in the subclasses.

It remains to be seen whether the ratings would transcend the raters, that is, to what extent the ratings assigned by different panels of judges with different ideologies would differ from each other or give a constant result. Thus, in constructing attitude tests it has been found by Thurstone that panels of judges with very different attitudes themselves will yet agree on rating the meanings or scale positions of statements of attitude so that the attitude scales they construct transcend or are independent of the attitudes of the judges who constructed them. If it should be found that the ratings do not transcend the ideologies of the raters and that they yield significant differences, then the scale could still be applied but with specified weighting systems, for example, Communist weightings, Republican weightings, or a UN Trusteeship Council weightings system.

The reliability of this weighting system has been experimentally measured. Shannon[3] secured weightings from social science faculty and student groups. He found no significant differences in mean weights when he subclassified his data into expert raters and inexpert raters. They correlated 0.9 together (± 0.008). The ratings differed significantly from chance, which would assign equal weights in every subclass in a class. On repeating the ratings, correlations of ratings of individuals between first and second ratings ran as low as 0.41, but correlations of the mean first ratings and the mean second ratings ran up to 0.997 (± 0.002). The split-half correlation of odd versus even items was 0.93 (± 0.006). These studies proved that the weights could be highly reliable if they are the mean weights of a panel of judges.

(b) *Reliability, validity, and norms.* The next steps still to be taken in constructing the scale of fitness are to determine its reliability, validity, and norms.

Reliability can be determined for one index of it as the correlation coefficient be-

[3] Shannon, L., "Measuring Capacity for Self-government," Unpublished M.A. thesis, University of Washington, 1947.

tween one determination of the scale and a second determination of it on presumably the same phenomena, as when one set of a person's determination of the indices is correlated against another set's determination of the same indices.[4] To the extent that this correlation is high, say above 0.9, the scale is judged reliable; that is, it is free of errors of observation due to the observer. Many of the indices are fixed by censuses, school, tax, budget, and other statistics that would not vary much if reobserved. But other indices which are mean ratings by experts or polls of samples of the population might vary more on reobserving them. Hence their degree of reliability must be experimentally isolated and measured.

Validity is definable as the correlation coefficient between the scale and an accepted index of dependence-independence. How high does the scale, when applied to a group of independent and a group of comparable dependent areas, correlate with the all-or-none variable of independence or lack of it? The higher this correlation, the more valid the scale, that is, the more closely it is proved to measure what it claims to measure in society. At present the validity of only a few indices has been explored. Shannon[5] has found correlation scattergrams with correlations in the 0.2 to 0.5 range between dependent or independent states as the one criterion variable to be predicted and illiteracy, gold reserves, and other factors as independent or predictor variables. These preliminary findings suggest that by multiple correlation technics a scale can be built and

[4] The more the two sets of observers represent different viewpoints or cultures, the more their degree of agreement will establish the objectivity or rerating reliability of the scale, of course.

[5] Shannon, L., "The Non-self-governing Political Entity," Unpublished Ph.D. thesis, University of Washington, 1951.

proven to measure more accurately the degree of independence.

For this purpose of determining the norms, a "para-nation technic" is proposed. It may be sketched here in oversimplified summary; eventually the Trusteeship Council might work out details. Let the degree of fitness demanded of a candidate dependency, in order for it to qualify for full self-government or independence, be some preassigned amount

TABLE 1.   A Schematic Distribution of Nations by Their Fitness Scores
(x = 1 para-nation)

↑		x		
Number of		x		
nations		x		
↓	x	x	x	
	x	x	x	x	x

| 0 | 50 | 100 | 150 | 200 | 250 | 300 |

Fitness score, a weighted average of 350 indices of fitness
↑
mean
score
Range taken as standard
←――――――――――→
and divided into percents

0%   100%
↑   ↑
totally   ←―%―→   fully
unfit   of   fit
point   fitness   point

such as the average degree of fitness of ten para-nations, which are nations comparable in as many respects as possible to the candidate area. Let these nations be measured by the scale, and their arithmetic mean determined. Call this point "100 percent fitness" for the candidate nation (Table 1). This means that the dependencies must be more fit than the less competent independent nations of its class, yet need not measure up to the most competent, but only attain the average.

With this 100 percent point on the scale of fitness determined for a given nation, subdivisions of it, when reached, could determine when that candidate would reach specified increments of autonomy. Thus, it could progress gradually toward self-government by peaceful, rational, and predetermined steps.

APPLICATION OF THE MEASURING INSTRUMENT

(a) *Possible administration of testing.* In order to try out the extent to which a measuring instrument can contribute to the peaceful evolution of a dependency toward self-government, the instrument must be applied and developed further under field conditions. Administrators of dependent areas must become more interested in applying social science technics to their practical problems. It is to be expected that such interest will grow sporadically but may be encouraged by clear statement of the goal and available means. The goal here would be a controlled experiment for testing the hypothesis implied in the second and third assumption above.[6] This fitness scale hypothesis might be stated as: It is expected that in proportion (1) as a people's fitness for self-government is well measured; (2) increments in fitness are preannounced as the precondition for increments in self-government; and (3) increments in fitness are at least partly attainable by the people's own efforts then, self-government is likely to be achieved sooner, with less conflict, and with more satisfaction to most people,

[6] The proposals here may seem a little naive to some political realists. The author recalls, however, proposing in Geneva in 1927 that criteria for terminating a mandate should be specified. Sir Austen Chamberlain replied that that was a job for the academic people before political administrators could move. The fact that when criteria were then worked out with a fellow academician (Professor Ritsher) these were the ones adopted by the Mandates Commission, gives hope that now in measuring these criteria the statesmen may again find the social scientists' technics useful.

than without this measurement and motivation plan.

In order to test this hypothesis scientifically, controlled experiments would be designed, ideally, but in practice only crude approximations may be possible. These may be less crude, however, if the administrators have the plan of a controlled experiment in mind, even though they may lack the power to execute it cleanly. A controlled testing of the hypothesis implies finding two similar or matched dependencies. One of them would then have the aforementioned measurement and motivation plan applied to it while the other would not (or at least would get much less of it.) In a few decades the satisfactory and peaceful progress of the former toward self-government should be visibly greater than in the latter, if the hypothesis holds.

(b) *Possible administrators of testing.* There are four types of authorities, each of whom could contribute a part to the full testing of the hypothesis. These authorities are the United Nations Trustees, national colonial offices, bureaus for research on government, and political scientists with statistical training.

(1) Trustees of United Nations trusteeships should be the first to apply the hypothesis and its implementing scale to their trusteed lands. Thus a technic is offered that can help fulfill the official purpose of trusteeships—to prepare the trusteed lands for self-government or independence. It offers a substitute for agitation, rebellion, and the appeal to force which have all too often in the past been the only course open to a dependent people wanting their freedom. It offers an evolutionary method of gradual growth toward self-government in place of revolution. It provides a definite constructive procedure which can motivate the inhabitants to those efforts and achievements that fit them best for taking over the man-

agement of their own affairs. In short, it offers a way to make the trustee's task easier. Of course, this fitness is not the only consideration in granting self-government or independence. Considerations of strategic defense and other self-interests of the trustee may still play a part, but the measuring and isolating of fitness removes the question of fitness from the realm of controversy and makes it less possible for any trustee to rationalize imperialistic policy by the claim that the trusteed land is not yet fit for autonomy. Above all, the scheme would stimulate the development of fitness as a conscious, implemented goal.

This is a bit of the scientific method applied to administration, namely, the isolating of factors so that, with the causes and effects of each factor separately known, any one factor can be controlled even when other factors are still uncontrolled.

Trusteeships should begin this process of planned, peaceful transition to self-government by writing an article to this effect into the charters that set them up. The principle of measured and motivated fitting of oneself for self-government could be established by some such article as the following:

In order that the inhabitants may be constructively guided in their efforts to fit themselves for self-government by peaceful steps and without recourse to force, the Trusteeship Council shall advise and recommend to the Administrative Authorities as to the procedure for determining: the inhabitants' current degree of fitness for self-government, and what efforts or achievements by them, and what other conditions, are considered prerequisite to specified increments in self-government.

(2) Farsighted colonial administrators can use the fitness yardstick to simplify their problems. Nationalistic agitation tending toward demonstrations involving bloodshed can be headed off by agreement, at an early stage, upon fitness goals with the representatives of the inhabitants when such agreement is more possible than later when nationalist emotions and demands go to the extreme. With political, economic, educational, and social development mapped out in definite detail and the energies of the nationalists harnessed to cooperate in achieving them, the colonial administrator will have intelligently solved his future problems in large part by preventive action.

Considerable progress in this direction has been made. The Trusteeship Council has prepared elaborate and searching questionnaires for securing detailed information from the trustees. But the motivating of effort by the nationals is little developed, since what they must achieve to earn specified increments in autonomy is not stated definitely and in advance.

(3) Bureaus for research on government and governing could test the hypothesis and also expand it. They should research to refine the scale of fitness toward making it a more realistic and exact instrument for prediction and control—the functions of science, whether political science or any other. Further, they could expand the scale from government of dependencies to any governmental unit as many of the indices would be equally pertinent in a self-governing or a non-self-governing area. By appropriate choice of indices, variant versions of the scale could measure the excellence of functioning of any governmental unit.

Indices of municipal political functioning could be developed and synthesized into a scale for the efficiency of municipal government. Indices of county or provincial or state governing could be collected more systematically than hitherto by the technics developed here to form scales for county or state government. Appropriate indices of national or international government could eventually yield scales for measuring the excellence of national and world governing. The method of scale construction, based in part on our theory of measurement, is applicable to any size of governmental unit. It may well be that self-government is best developed on a local scale first and later extended to larger units.

This method of scaling is also applicable to any department or function of government for which separate diagnosis and treatment may be wanted. Subscales for administrative, legislative, judicial, or party functioning, or any of their subfunctions, can be progressively developed by research. Bureaus for research on the government process itself can greatly improve that process in the long run by systematic research to measure it, so that its degree of excellence can be factually determined

with less controversy and less frustrating of the voters' wishes.

(4) Political scientists, authorities on government more than in government, also should help in testing this hypothesis. They should get beyond mere description of government and achieve more of that prediction and control that science gives to man. Toward this, more exact generalizations or laws of political behavior are required, and such exact observing involves a precision instrument such as our scales of government. To the extent that political scientists expand the indices of fitness for self-government to measure the excellence of any government, the resulting governance scales can help to make political science an exact science.

A QUANTITATIVE APPROACH TO A POLITICAL DECISION*

LYLE W. SHANNON

IN DISCUSSING the possibility of political independence or self-government for colonial or other non-self-governing areas it is frequently contended that non-self-governing entities lack the capacity for self-government. It is argued that colonies and trust areas differ in many fundamental and important respects from self-governing political entities. Oftentimes, because these differences are only alleged and have not been demonstrated to be crucial factors differentiating self-governing from

* Adapted and reprinted by permission from the *Journal of Human Relations*, Fall 1954, pp. 44–55.

non-self-governing political entities, the arguments of self-governing powers may only be considered rationalizations for a previously determined course of conduct. On the other hand, when differences exist and have been acknowledged by both self-governing and non-self-governing entities it remains difficult to determine the progress of a non-self-governing entity in the direction of capacity for self-government.

The approach described in this study substitutes an objective, quantitative and rational technique for determining the factors that differentiate self-governing from non-self-governing entities and also suggests a method for measuring development and determining when the appropriate level of development has been reached.

However, while the study is concerned with quantitative techniques of handling political data no attempt is made to discount numerous meritorious historical studies of the problem, detailed anthropological descriptions of tribal life in non-self-governing areas, or the many volumes that deal with political aspects of the problem of non-self-governing entities.

DEFINITION OF THE POPULATION

If the 196 major political entities of the world were placed on a continuum according to the degree of self-government which they possess, they would range from self-governing, fully sovereign states such as the United States to the opposite extreme of little or no self-government as typified by many African or Asiatic possessions of the colonial powers. The population may be dichotomized into self-governing and non-self-governing entities in order to simplify statistical treatment. Closely following *Nomenclature of Geographical Areas for Statistical Purposes*,[1] we have 85 self-governing and 111 non-self-governing political entities. These exact definitions and our dichotomous division of political entities need not be accepted, but some definition of the population and some division according to the criterion self-governing or non-self-governing, must be made if the problem is to be approached on an objective level. Persons engaged in the decision-making process must therefore come to agreement among themselves or must be willing to accept the definitions and classification of an independent group of

researchers charged with technical details of the problem.

SELECTING THE CRUCIAL VARIABLES

All interested parties must agree upon the set of variables that are to be considered crucial in determining whether a non-self-governing entity is capable of self-government. This set of variables may be determined in several ways. By consultation between interested persons the variables may be selected and agreed upon in a more or less arbitrary manner. This has been the case on several occasions in the past when self-governing powers were able to come to some agreement with their colonies or territories in discussing conditions that must be present in an area in order for it to gain political independence. On the other hand, the self-governing power may lay aside its preconceived notions, as may the non-self-governing entity, and request that a study be made of factors differentiating self-governing from non-self-governing entities. This latter approach selects items from a universe of attributes that characterize political entities and seeks those factors that are differentiating, hypothesizing that a non-self-governing political entity is ready for self-government only when it has the characteristics of a self-governing entity. Studies based on the first approach have attempted to establish "criteria of capacity for self-government,"[2] have broken these criteria into observable and measurable indices,[3] and have established the relative importance of various criteria

[1] The definitions used in this article were previously presented in Chapter II.

[2] Walter Holmes Ritsher, *Criteria of Capacity for Independence* (Jerusalem: Syrian Orphanage Press, 1934).
[3] Felicia Fedorovicz, *Measurement of Fitness for Independence* (M.A. Thesis), (Beirut: Library of the American University of Beirut, and Washington: American Documentation Institute, Document 2425, 1946).

by using a panel of competent judges.[4] Closely related to this approach is the Provisional Questionnaire of the Trusteeship Council.[5]

The second approach has been used and tentative findings indicate that there is a wide variation in the degree to which other quantitative variables or qualitative attributes differentiate self-governing from non-self-governing entities.[6] In this preliminary study some fifty items were selected from the available sources of information; the criterion for acceptance of the specific items used was simply that a more complete enumeration of the population was possible on these items than on others in which we were likewise interested. It would be difficult to attribute any randomness to the sample and a complete enumeration was not possible for all of the variables selected. Nevertheless the study may be used as a model of the objective, quantitative approach to our problem. If we are concerned with the relationship of certain attributes to the criterion self-governing or non-self-governing and desire something more than intuitive feelings, hunches, theories, or an occasional case study, these are the available data.

A combination of the first and second approach might be to take variables that the controlling self-governing powers believe to be crucial in determining capacity for self-government and see to what extent they actually are found in self-governing entities and not in non-self-governing entities. Factors that were found only remotely related to political status, it would be previously agreed, would no longer be considered useful factors in determining whether or not an entity was capable of self-government.

STATISTICAL TECHNIQUES AND EXAMPLES

The most important point is to secure agreement by all concerned that a specific procedure will be acceptable in determining the importance of various items or attributes. There are numerous statistical measures that may be used in comparing the relationship of various attributes to the criterion self-governing or non-self-governing. We are, of course, not only interested in the relationship of single attributes to the criterion but also in the relationship of various attributes in combination to political status. It is here that more complex methods must be used.

As an example of the manner in which the data may be treated we shall now present a discussion of the relationship of size of the population of political entities to the criterion self-governing or non-self-governing. The world's population and political entities have been dichotomized in Table 1.

TABLE 1. Distribution of Persons According to Political Status of Entity in Which They Reside

Political Status	Population	Per cent	Number of Political Entities	Per cent
Self-governing	2,059,407,000	88.6	85	43.4
Non-self-governing	265,570,000	11.4	111	56.6
Total	2,324,977,000	100.0	196	100.0

After arranging the 196 political entities on a continuum according to the size

---

[4] Lyle W. Shannon, *Measuring Capacity for Self-government* (M.A. Thesis), (Seattle: University of Washington Library and Washington Public Opinion Laboratory Library, 1947).

[5] *Provisional Questionnaire*, Approved by the Trusteeship Council of the United Nations at the twenty-fifth meeting of its first session on 25 April 1947 (Lake Success: United Nations Publications, 1947).

[6] Lyle W. Shannon. *The Non-self-governing Political Entity* (Ph.D. Thesis), (Seattle: University of Washington Library, 1951).

of the population, a cutting point was established by careful inspection of the continuum in such a manner as to reduce the amount of overlapping of the distribution of self-governing and non-self-governing entities to a minimum.[7] The data may then be presented in a 2 x 2 association table as seen in Table 2.[8]

TABLE 2. Distribution of Political Entities According to Size of Population and Political Status

Population	Self-governing	Non-self-governing	Total
−1,130,000	15	84	99
1,130,000 or +	70	27	97
Total	85	111	196

The mean of the self-governing distribution is 24,228,317 and the mean of the non-self-governing distribution is 2,392,522. The mean or average population of self-governing political entities is thus about 10 times as large as the mean of non-self-governing entities. The phi coefficient of correlation is .895, indicating that population size is closely related to political status. Were this a prediction problem, using the modal category of the marginal totals or category of the greatest frequency in order to predict the political status of an entity would give us 85 errors for we would predict that every entity is non-self-governing. By introducing the *predictor*, population size, we may increase the efficiency of our predictions by decreasing the 85 errors that we would make without it. If a political entity has less than 1,130,000 persons we would predict that it is non-self-governing and be incorrect 15 times. If a political entity has

[7] For details see Paul Horst, Louis Guttman, *et al.*, *The Prediction of Personal Adjustment* (New York: Social Science Research Council, 1941), pp. 271–272.

[8] Data from *Demographic Yearbook—1948*, Table 1 (Lake Success: Statistical Office of the United Nations, 1949), pp. 75–85.

1,130,000 or more persons we would predict that it is self-governing and be correct 70 times and incorrect 27 times. Thus we would have a total error of 42 rather than 85 or a reduction of errors by slightly more than 50 percent. Our predictions would be correct 78.5 percent of the time, using the predictor. Measures such as the two that we have just mentioned are useful in treating single variables.

We shall now turn to techniques of combining variables in order to more accurately describe the characteristics of self-governing and non-self-governing entities. The Guttman type of scale, also known as the Cornell Technique of Scale Analysis, is a useful method of bringing out meaningful relationships (although our data do not fulfill the necessary assumptions). By giving each item the weight of 1 and ranking our political entities from high to low we are able to determine if the general response pattern of self-governing entities differentiates them from non-self-governing entities. The score that each member of the population receives in a scalable area has a definite meaning with respect to the actual items on the scale. If an area of content is scalable in the Guttman manner it is meaningful to say that a political entity with a higher score than another has a more favorable response pattern than another political entity. A higher scale score means that an entity has an equivalent or higher response to each item than other entities with lower scores, within certain limits of error. A single index could not represent the characteristics of a political entity on other types of scales. Two political entities could have the same score on the scale and have quite different characteristics.

In order to facilitate arrangement of the data according to the scalogram technique all items were first reduced to a di-

chotomy. If an entity fell in the most favorable subcategory it received one point
and if it fell in the least favorable category or no information was available, it
did not receive a point. This more or less
ethnocentric technique defined "most favorable" as the category into which the
largest number of self-governing political
entities fell; it may be justified on a common-sense basis by the fact that entities
not having data available were usually
those same entities which fell in the least
favorable subcategory on those items for
which data were available. No data was
an indication that the entity would probably be in the least favorable response
category even if the data were available.
The coefficient of reproducibility when
calculated in the Guttman manner was
82.5 percent and therefore remained below the acceptable level. Although our
data do not meet the assumptions necessary for scale analysis as defined by Gutt-

TABLE 3. Distribution of Political Entities According to Scale Scores

Scores	Self-governing	Non-self-governing	Total
−22	28	108	136
22 or +	57	3	60
Total	85	111	196

man and do not come up to his standards
of reproducibility, the scalogram technique suggests the existence of a systematic pattern of attributes that is related to
the criterion self-governing or non-self-governing.

Approaching the problem according to
more conventional methods and with an
interest only in the extent to which scale
scores discriminated between self-governing and non-self-governing entities, the
distribution of scores was dichotomized as
in Table 3. The score in this case does not
tell us anything about the characteristics

of an entity except that it fell in the most
favorable category a certain number of
times. This type of scale does, however,
enable us to measure development in a
particular direction, i.e., the direction defined by the items included in the scale.
The mean score for self-governing political entities is 26.2 and the mean for non-
self-governing entities is 8.9. Using the
scale score of a political entity we can predict its political status correctly 84.2 percent of the time.

Assuming that we wish to increase the
efficiency of a political entity's score in
predicting its political status, certain
techniques are available that enable us to
give unequal weights to items depending
on their relationship to the criterion self-
governing or non-self-governing. Multiple
correlation techniques should be used
when the criterion to be predicted is
quantitative. If the criterion to be predicted is qualitative it is generally agreed
that the discriminant function provides a
relatively easy manner of selecting weights
that will most efficiently predict the criterion.

TABLE 4. Distribution of Political Entities According to Abbreviated Scale Scores

Scores	Self-governing	Non-self-governing	Total
−6	21	102	123
6 or +	64	9	72
Total	85	111	196

In order to illustrate this approach, 15
items were selected for an abbreviated
scale. The efficiency of scale scores in predicting the criterion with each item given
a weight of 1 was compared with the efficiency of scale scores using a system of
weights derived from the relationship of
the various items to the criterion. The
scores of the abbreviated scale with a
weight of 1 for each item are presented
in Table 4. Political status may be pre-

dicted from scale scores 84.7 percent of the time without error. The item analysis technique has been suggested as a first approximation to the discriminant function where an assumption of independence of the predicting variables seems reasonable.[9] The computations are simple and result in weights that enhance the power of discrimination of a group of items over their predictive efficiency with equal weights.[10]

The sum of the item analysis weights for each subcategory in which a political entity falls becomes the score of each entity. These scores are dichotomized as were other scale scores and their efficiency in discriminating between self-governing and non-self-governing entities is revealed by Table 5. The mean score for self-gov-

TABLE 5. Distribution of Political Entities According to Total Scores Using Item Analysis Weights

Scores	Self-governing	Non-self-governing	Total
−2.824	18	104	122
2.824 or +	67	7	74
Total	85	111	196

erning entities is 4.517 and for non-self-governing entities it is 1.217. The item analysis weights enable us to correctly predict political status from scale scores 87.3 percent of the time.

Indonesia scored highest among the

non-self-governing entities on our final scale using item analysis weights. Algeria was second, followed by Hawaii, Hong Kong, Alaska, Southern Rhodesia, and the Bermudas. Other non-self-governing entities with comparatively high scores were those entities in which considerable agitation for self-government had already existed. Some of them follow in order of decreasing scores: Nigeria, French Morocco, Malta, Malayan Union, Puerto Rico, Jamaica, and the Gold Coast. Libya, a non-self-governing entity that received self-government from the United Nations had a score of 1.006, less than either the mean or median of non-self-governing entities and much lower than many other non-self-governing entities in Africa.

The lowest scoring self-governing political entities are for the most part limited to small Middle Eastern kingdoms and European principalities that in the past were more or less dominated by larger powers but in recent years have evidenced a greater degree of self-government and have been classified as self-governing. Those scoring lowest are: Bhutan, Bahrein, Kuwait, Trucial Oman, Muscat and Oman, Qatar, San Marino, Nepal, Yemen, Ethiopia, Andorra, Trans-Jordan, and Saudi-Arabia. Had we used a criterion with more than 2 subcategories, i.e, self-governing and non-self-governing, we probably would have had even greater predictive efficiency.

DETERMINING LEVELS OF ACHIEVEMENT

Up to this point we have been concerned with methods of selecting criteria of capacity for self-government or political independence. Let us assume that some acceptable technique has been used and that a scale has been constructed that purports to measure capacity for self-government. What level of achievement

[9] Louis Guttman, "Supplementary Study B," in Paul Horst, et al., The Prediction of Personal Adjustment, pp. 282–285.

[10] The theory of scales and weighting systems with methods of computing weights, the discriminant function in particular, is discussed in some detail by Horace W. Mooney, The Quantification of Social Attributes by the Use of the Discriminant Function and an Application for Predicting Response to Treatment in a Mental Hygiene Clinic (M.A. Thesis) (Seattle: University of Washington, 1949).

should be reached by a non-self-governing entity before it can be given self-government? Considering the great diversity in development of both self-governing and non-self-governing areas from region to region it is doubtful if we should have a universal standard of development. It is doubtful if non-self-governing entities should be required to attain the same level of development as the most advanced self-governing entities in an area. Before the criteria have been decided upon, the scale completed, and the scores of various political entities known, agreement must be reached on the relative level of development that will be required if an entity is to be given self-government.

One more or less objective approach might be to divide the world into areas and arbitrarily decide that a non-self-governing political entity having a score equal to or above that of the average of self-governing entities within an area, is capable of self-government, in so far as any discussion of its development is concerned.

TABLE 6. Scale Scores of Self-Governing Political Entities in Southeast Asia with Item Analysis Weights

Australia	7.038
New Zealand	6.723
India	5.470
Philippine Republic	4.979
Ceylon	4.406
Thailand	4.338
Burma	3.566
China	2.871
Pakistan	2.690
Nepal	1.577
Bhutan	.475

As an example, we can select the scores of self-governing and non-self-governing entities in Southeast Asia. The scores in Table 6 were used in establishing a mean of self-governing political entities in Southeast Asia.

The mean or average score of these self-governing entities is 4.120. Using the general approach that we have described in this paper, only one non-self-governing entity in the area has a score surpassing the mean and that is Indonesia with a score of 4.217. It should be remembered that most of the data used in this study are from the 1947 period and that the dichotomy of political entities was established as of January, 1949. Since that time Indonesia has obtained self-government.

Taking Africa as another example we find four self-governing entities with the scores shown in Table 7.

TABLE 7. Scale Score of African Self-Governing Political Entities with Item Analysis Weights

Union of South Africa	5.385
Egypt	4.750
Liberia	2.950
Ethiopia	1.577

The mean or average score of these self-governing entities is 3.666. Algeria, a non-self-governing entity, has a score of 3.921 and would be granted self-government according to the procedure that we have described. It is already a Department of France, a political status that places it close to being a self-governing entity. Other non-self-governing areas with comparatively high scores are Southern Rhodesia 3.216, Nigeria 2.782, French Morocco 2.723, Gold Coast 2.564, Tunisia 2.500, and Madagascar 2.392. It is interesting to note that these entities have been gaining increasing increments of self-government in recent years or have been the scene of violent struggles for increasing self-government. Only Libya has received self-government and it has a score of 1.006. The political nature of the decision to give Libya self-government contrasts with the more objective procedure that has been outlined in this study.

Obviously any decision of self-governing and non-self-governing entities to use a procedure similar to that described here would require a completely new study. The various political entities would be classified as self-governing and non-self-governing according to their present political status. New data would replace the 1947 data. It is possible that a more complete enumeration of the various political entities could be made and that a larger sample from the universe of attributes of political entities could be selected. The study that we have described is merely used as an example of the general procedures to follow although some of its findings appear to be validated by subsequent happenings.

CONCLUSION

The various steps that must be taken to put such a scheme as we have described into effect may be summarized.

1. The administering powers or self-governing political entities must be agreed that increasing increments of self-government or complete self-government is the goal toward which tutelage of the non-self-governing entity is intended to lead and that these goals may be reached in the foreseeable future.

2. The administering powers must indicate whether the decision to grant self-government is to be made independently by consultation with the non-self-governing entity or with one or more disinterested parties. If the decision is to be an independent political decision, then there is no need for the procedure that we have suggested.

3. If the decision is to be made with the aid of other parties the administering power must indicate its willingness to establish criteria in some way that will be acceptable to all persons taking part in the decision. If the criteria are to be acceptable to all parties taking part in the decision, assuming that non-self-governing entities are represented, the method of establishing criteria must not be entirely arbitrary on the part of either self-governing or non-self-governing entities.

4. The administering power and others must be willing to accept certain more or less established procedures of a technical nature for setting up norms and determining when a non-self-governing entity has reached the norm or appropriate level of development. It must be agreed that fulfillment of these criteria will mean that an entity is capable of self-government. It must be willing to accept the decision of scientific observers as to whether a political entity has reached the level of development entitling it to self-government.

If the administering authority is unwilling to make these or similar commitments before knowing the comparative score of self-governing and non-self-governing entities and before the determination of norms, we may only assume that the administering authority is interested in questionnaires and scales in order to provide a pseudoscientific rationalization for the decision to maintain control of certain non-self-governing entities.

A REËXAMINATION OF THE CONCEPT, "CAPACITY FOR SELF-GOVERNMENT"*

LYLE W. SHANNON

I. INTRODUCTION

WHEN the term "capacity for self-government" is used, or as is more frequently the case, when references are made to lack of capacity for self-government, the concept usually remains undefined. An appraisal of current and past behavior of administering powers might result in operationally defining lack of capacity for self-government as that state of affairs, whatever it may be from time to time and place to place, which appears to make the granting of self-government inadvisable, according to the views of the controlling powers. Since such an operational definition may well be sufficient for self-governing powers in practice, it may behoove non-self-governing areas to direct their energies along the lines suggested by the administering authorities or other controlling powers. Thus it can scarcely be said that they are working toward capacity for self-government in any other way than in reference to the peculiar or particular operational definition just mentioned.

A reëxamination of the concept may be made from several approaches. An historian, militarist, or logistics expert might be concerned with the relative strength of a controlling power in terms of dis-

tance from a non-self-governing area, the help that the latter might be able to secure from other powers in sympathy with the desire for self-government, the morale and general attitude of the controlling power's troops which might be sent to quell a revolt, and the various military commitments that a power has previously made on the continent and in foreign areas. Using this approach, capacity for self-government would consist of the ability to throw off the control of another power and not whether the conditions thought necessary for self-government by a controlling power were present. Ability to revolt successfully would be the crucial content of capacity for self-government, the necessary and sufficient condition for attaining self-government.

Another approach has arbitrarily attempted to set up criteria of capacity for self-government based on a consensus of opinion, criteria that are relative to the culture of the persons establishing them. While such an approach avoids the capriciousness inherent in the traditional attitude of controlling powers, the non-self-governing area must either conform to certain culturally defined criteria or remain dependent. One advantage is that definite standards are set up with some universality in goals toward which dependent people should work. In order to make the criteria more relevant to regional standards, it has been proposed that the determination of cutting points

* A portion of this article has previously been published under the same title in the *Journal of Negro Education*, Vol. 25, Spring 1957. It has been adapted and expanded from the original by permission.

be based on the relative development of self-governing entities in each cultural or geographical area. However, if differences between self-governing and non-self-governing areas, assumed to be present on a basis of what has been said by statesmen and experts, are not present, then it would be capricious and illogical to say that non-self-governing areas must have certain conditions or characteristics in order to be "capable" of self-government. It could only be said that capacity for self-government of a particular type was facilitated, in the opinion of self-governing powers, by the presence of certain attributes.

Assuming, on the other hand, that certain factors differentiate self-governing from non-self-governing areas, one still cannot say that these factors are necessary for self-government. It may be possible that the differentiating factors are a product of varying political status and that only the self-governing area is capable of developing these specific conditions. Perhaps the policy of controlling powers is such that development follows the acquisition of self-government. It might be shown that differences disappear when one controlling power is replaced by another. We must conclude that much interpretation is necessary even if marked differences are found between self-governing and non-self-governing areas.

This introduction should not be taken as an attempt to cut the ground from under other studies but to place previous research in its proper perspective. Two things may be accomplished by the research already conducted and by that now to be described. Some myths about what is necessary for self-government may be rejected. Statesmen may have perpetuated them in an effort to rationalize their continued control over non-self-governing areas. Secondly, the research has descriptive value; the characteristics of non-self-governing areas are contrasted with those of self-governing areas.

While the term "prediction" has been used in earlier writings on this problem, a true prediction problem does not exist; rather it should be referred to as a taxonomical problem. It is possible to classify areas very accurately as self-governing or non-self-governing, if their characteristics are known. It is also possible to make statements about an area, knowing its political status. But the data cannot be said to predict capacity for self-government; the data presented do not allow us to say that those non-self-governing areas with characteristics similar to self-governing areas are most capable of self-government. We may be able to say that non-self-governing areas with characteristics similar to those that are self-governing will have the least difficulty in convincing controlling powers that they are capable of self-government. But, in actual experience, even this has not always been the case. We may also find that non-self-governing areas with characteristics similar to those of self-governing areas have been and are at present more troublesome to administering authorities than less developed areas. This phenomenon is related to the second general definition of self-government presented in the paper, i.e., capacity for self-government is capacity to successfully revolt. The most developed non-self-governing areas are more likely to have this capacity. If we desire to measure the development of non-self-governing areas in the direction of the characteristics of self-governing areas, the data presented here make possible the construction of such a measuring instrument.

II. THE DATA, PROCEDURES, AND TYPE OF SINGLE-FACTOR ANALYSIS INVOLVED

Eighty-eight political areas are classified as self-governing and 110 are classified as non-self-governing. Most of the data on each of these political entities have been obtained from various United Nations publications such as the *Statistical Yearbook* and *Demographic Yearbook* of the United Nations. One difficulty has been the lack of data on small, isolated self-governing and non-self-governing areas, the non-self-governing in particular.

Tests of statistical significance are difficult to apply to the findings. It might be possible to reason that our data are a sample in time of a universe of data on the 198 areas, but this puts us on treacherous ground because the years represented were not selected in a random fashion, simply being the latest data available and as close as possible to the year 1950. About all that we can do is to set up some expected distributions based on statements or inferences from statements by those who believe that development in a certain direction is essential to self-government. Using chi-square, for example, we might then say that the observed characteristics of self-governing and non-self-governing areas are significantly or not significantly different than expected. This is done with hesitation and it would be better to think of chi-square only as an index. Any test of this type will be a "conservative" test and will be all in favor of those who say that differences exist, because the political entities have been dichotomized on the principle of selecting the point on a continuum that most efficiently discriminates between self-governing and non-self-governing areas.

Population size has been held to be crucial in determining capacity for self-government. We would thus expect self-governing areas to be larger than non-self-governing areas. If we dichotomize the 198 areas according to population size, the self-governing areas should fall above some point established as the crucial minimum size. No one has ever suggested a crucial minimum size that an area must have in

order to be self-governing, but size has always been referred to in general terms. If size is crucial, then there should be a break or at least a definite tendency to break at some point, the self-governing areas falling above and the non-self-governing below. The theoretical distribution of political entities should be as follows.

TABLE 1. Theoretical Distribution of Areas According to Political Status and Population Size: Perfect Correlation

Population Size	Political Status Self-governing	Non-self-governing	Total
Falls below cutting point	0	110	110
Falls above cutting point	88	0	88
Total	88	110	198

Selecting as a cutting point that place which most sharply differentiates self-governing and non-self-governing areas on a basis of size, we find that 1,200,000 persons minimizes the number of areas that are incorrectly classified, according to this theoretical scheme. With this as a cutting point, which differs only slightly from that in the earlier paper, we have a minimum amount of overlap of self-governing and non-self-governing areas according to their population size. The question then arises, how much deviation from the model shown in Table 1 may be tolerated before we must say that the observed or actual distribution of political entities is significantly different than that hypothesized, assuming that "capacity for self-government" is based upon the existence of certain attributes in an area, absence of which precludes the possibility of self-government? Observation of the values in Table 2 enables one to readily see that it is appreciably different than Table 1. With a total number of 198 political entities or less, any combination of 5 in the 2 cells that should have zero value will result in a significant chi-square so that inspection alone enables us to determine if the observed distributions are significantly different from the theoretical at the 1 percent level.[1]

TABLE 2. Observed Distribution of Areas According to Political Status and Population Size

Population Size	Political Status Self-governing	Non-self-governing	Total
Less than 1,200,000	17	83	100
1,200,000 or more	71	27	98
Total	88	110	198

While this approach enables us to reject the hypothesis that there is a crucial population size separating self-governing from non-self-governing areas, it is also apparent that population size is correlated to some extent with political status.[2]

Using chi-square in a different way, we might say that there is a significant relationship between population size and political status. If population size was unrelated to political status, the distribution found in Table 3 would be expected. Testing for the significance of the difference between Tables 2 and 3 we find that the chi-square value is 61.65 and therefore significant at the 1 percent level. The phi coefficient of correlation for Table 2 is .867.

The median size of self-governing areas was 6,500,000, while the median size of

[1] For example, if one of the hypothetically zero cells contains 2 political entities and another contains 3 political entities, then the chi-square value would be 14.26 and of course significant at the 1% level.

[2] Data from *Demographic Yearbook—1951 and 1952*, New York, United Nations, 1952 and 1953, Table 1.

non-self-governing areas was only 289,000. Self-governing areas ranged in size from 5000 to 300 million population, while non-self-governing areas ranged from 100 or more persons to 30 million persons. A comparison of size with other variables reveals that it is one of the most closely related to political status.

The entire list of 56 variables was manipulated in the manner that we have de-

TABLE 3. Theoretical Distribution of Areas According to Political Status and Population Size: No Correlation

Population Size	Political Status Self-governing	Non-self-governing	Total
Falls below cutting point	44	55	99
Falls above cutting point	44	55	99
Total	88	110	198

scribed.[3] It should be emphasized at this point that not a single variable failed to have a distribution significantly different than the theoretical distribution presented in Table 1. This means that none of our variables has a one-to-one relationship to political status. Chi-square values and phi coefficients of correlation were computed using only those areas for which data were obtained. They were also computed with the areas for which there was no information available placed in the least

[3] The 56 variables were measures of the following general factors: size of population, land area, crude birth rate, crude death rate, crude rate of natural increase, infant mortality rate, urbanism, iron ore resources, iron ore production, steel production, fuel production, fuel consumption, food production, livestock production, arable land, railway development, motor vehicles, hospital beds, doctors, proportion of students in population, telephones, literacy, radios, movies, daily newspapers, and foreign trade.

desirable category of the dichotomy if there appeared to be a rationale for so doing.

III. FINDINGS

Before engaging in any discussion of specific factors or groups of factors and their relation to the criterion, several general findings should be mentioned. Variables that were significantly related to the criterion either declined in their significance or were not significant when placed on a *per capita* basis. This emphasizes further the importance of size in its relationship to being self-governing. In about 50 percent of the cases, the inclusion in the least desirable category of areas for which no information was available, increased the significance of the relation of that variable to the criterion. And as previously mentioned, although none of the variables had a one-to-one relationship to the criterion, self-governing or non-self-governing, most of them were significantly related to the criterion on a basis of the tests applied to the data.

In order to facilitate a discussion of the variables observed, certain percentage and *per capita* data have been selected and ranked in Table 4 on a basis of their correlation with the criterion. Each of the variables in Table 4 is relatively independent of population size, or at least not directly dependent upon it.

It immediately becomes apparent that non-self-governing areas are relatively small and underdeveloped in comparison with self-governing areas. Although many factors were directly related to the size of the population of an area and thus not included in Table 4 as independent variables, other factors could be shown to have an indirect but yet considerable dependence upon population size. Steel production would be such an example. The development of railroad transportation systems is related to both population size, area of the country in square miles, and

the development of production facilities. Studies have shown that the size of the population is related to the percent of the population that is urban; even more closely associated with size would be the existence of cities of 50,000 population.

Various demographic and economic factors have been found to be related to each other. This relationship appears in the data at hand. The crude rate of natural increase is dependent upon both birth and death rates. The death rate is greatly influenced by the infant mortality rate. The percentage of illiteracy is related to the proportion of the total population in school, and the circulation of newspapers is related to both of the former. Imports and exports are related not only to each other but to other factors in Table 4.

It should be noted that many of the coefficients of correlation in Table 4 are very low. Some of these correlations are increased by placing areas with no information available in the least desirable category of the 2 by 2 tables. Some of these are factors that in the past have been hypothesized to be very highly correlated with political status.

IV. SUMMARY

The findings of the study thus far may be briefly summarized before proceeding to a more complex analysis using multivariate techniques applicable to dichotomized quantitative variables.

1. Each of the 56 variables observed had a significantly different distribution from that which would be expected if we assume that each self-governing area must have a higher score than that obtained by non-self-governing areas.

2. Forty-three of the variables were significantly related to political status as self-governing or non-self-governing at the 1 percent level, if only those areas for which data were available were used in the computations.

TABLE 4. Representative Factors and Their Correlation with the Criterion Political Status

Variable	Only Areas with Data Available	Areas Without Data Included in Correlation
Per capita production of sources of commercial energy	.882	.833
Population size	.876	
Percent of population urban	.785	
Percent of population in cities of 50,000 or more	.870	
Area in square kilometers	.745	
Production of grain and food in tons *per capita*	.772	.909
Livestock in tons *per capita*	.345	.435
Steel production in kilograms *per capita*	.699	.697
Pieces of rolling stock per 1000 population	.560	.725
Crude birth rate	.592	
Crude death rate	.355	
Crude rate of natural increase	.542	
Radios per 1000 population	.565	.712
Percent of population literate	.392	.606
Daily newspaper circulation per 1000 population	.290	.634
Cinema seats per 1000 population	.300	.499
Telephones per 100 population	.216	.342
Percent of students in total population	.209	.152
Population per physician	.567	.265
Population per hospital bed	.140	.056
Imports in dollars *per capita*	.369	
Exports in dollars *per capita*	.304	
Percent of total area arable land including fallow, orchards, permanent meadows, and pastures	.211	.250
Motor vehicles per 1000 population	.128	.289

3. Forty-eight of the variables were significantly related to political status as self-governing or non-self-governing at the 1 percent level of significance when areas for which no information was available were placed in the least desirable category, if there appeared to be a rationale for so doing.

4. Variables that were significantly related to political status either declined in significance or lost their significance when placed on a *per capita* basis, leading us to conclude that size is an underlying vari-able running through many of the differences found in self-governing as contrasted to non-self-governing political entities. Not only is population size of great importance, but area is likewise crucial and seems to underly other variables.

5. Many factors held to be of importance from time to time in determining capacity for self-government had very low correlations with political status.

6. Non-self-governing areas are relatively underdeveloped in comparison with self-governing areas, but lack of development

does not seem to preclude self-governing status.

V. A NEW APPROACH

It is doubtful if any one should have expected to find a single factor explanation of the differential status of political entities, considering all that we have learned from various disciplines about the complexity of human behavior. The possibility of various combinations of factors differentiating self-governing from non-self-governing areas must also be considered. How is it possible to accept or reject the hypothesis that hidden in the vast amount of data collected by the United Nations is some complex configuration of traits differentiating the self-governing from the non-self-governing areas? And if it is possible to reject the hypothesis by analysis of the United Nations data, can we assume that uncollected data on a multitude of other characteristics would give us the same results, were they available?

One approach that might be useful is scale analysis. Although, as indicated elsewhere, it will not be possible to apply scale analysis in the usual fashion or meet the assumptions, it may still be a useful tool.

This approach assumes not only that the response pattern of self-governing political entities is different than that of non-self-governing entities but also hypothesizes that a single dimension, capacity for self-government, is present in degrees and underlies the varying response pattern. This is usually known as the hypothesis of unidimensionality. Since our dichotomy, self-governing or non-self-governing, is probably a dichotomized continuum, ranging from the most completely self-governing entities like the United States and the U.S.S.R. to those with little self-government at any level such as some African colonies, capacity for self-government will be present in varying amounts. In place of

2 distinctive patterns or configurations, the pattern would gradually change as we proceed from those political entities with the greatest capacity for self-government to those with the least capacity for self-government. One characteristic of scale analysis is its ability to rank each member of the population in a meaningful fashion, i.e., each political entity will have at least as favorable or a more favorable response on each item than all political entities below it. This means that political entities with the maximum capacity for self-government, assuming that the area is scalable, will have a more favorable response pattern on each item than those with a minimum capacity for self-government. If the data that we have are scalable, the set of scores that we have will represent varying degrees of a single dimension composed of the items on the scale. This is in contrast to score differences on the additive type scale where differences may be due to the presence of several dimensions or to differences in kind rather than degree.

The possibility of self-governing areas scoring higher than non-self-governing areas in every case will be reduced by errors in classification according to political status. In perhaps 5 percent of the cases one could argue the classification of a political entity as self-governing or non-self-governing. Some have changed their political status through revolution or negotiation since the United Nations' classification was published.

Deviations from unidimensionality will be measured in a manner to be described later in the paper. Should the data that we have meet the requirements of scalability and, in addition, more or less separate the self-governing entities from the non-self-governing entities, we will accept the data as indicating the presence of a dimension, "capacity for self-government." If the area is not scalable, following the rules to be described, we can turn to other techniques that may reveal the existence of an under-lying factor or factors. Its limited ability to reject hypotheses is, of course, one of the criticisms that may be made of scale analysis.

Using this approach, one assumes that any randomly selected sample of items or characteristics of political entities will ob-tain the same results as any other sample from a universe of their characteristics. Out of the multitude of major and minor characteristics of political entities, it is dif-ficult to randomly select a sample of items and then proceed to determine the char-acteristics of each particular political en-tity for the items selected. The difficulty in obtaining the necessary data preclude such an approach. On the other hand, it is pos-sible to take a sample of items from vari-ous United Nations sources such as the *Statistical Yearbook* or the *Demographic Yearbook of the United Nations*, assuming that the data collected are fairly reliable and representative of the important char-acteristics of political entities. Rather than sample the various data at random it is also desirable to select those items for which the data are available for the largest percentage of the population of self-gov-erning and non-self-governing political en-tities. We have moved quite far from hav-ing a random sample of the universe of characteristics of political entities, but these are the data with which we must work. Neither are we working with a sam-ple of the population of political entities. Our goal in each case is a complete enu-meration of the political entities for each item, but we must be content with less than that. If there is any bias in the selec-tion of items according to the method de-scribed it is in the direction of selecting those items which are considered most pertinent by international social bookkeep-ers. If there is any bias in the population of political entities on which data are avail-able it is a bias due to another characteris-tic of political entities, i.e., their relative development of social bookkeeping. Since these variables are quantitative in most cases but qualitative in some, each was re-duced to a dichotomy, with "no informa-tion" provided as a third possible response in the same fashion as in earlier studies.

In each case we assigned 2 points to the subclass of the item or characteristic in which self-governing entities fell. For ex-ample, each political entity received 2 points on the item, inhabitants per physi-cian, if it had less than 5,500 inhabitants per physician. If a political entity had more than 5,500 inhabitants per physician it re-ceived 1 point, and if no information was available it received 0 points. Each po-litical entity could be scored on each item and the scores totaled, providing a basis for ranking them from highest to lowest. If the data constituted a perfect scale the response pattern should have appeared similar to Table 5. This diagram employs only 5 items for simplicity.

It is readily seen that the example pre-sented does not sharply differentiate be-tween self-governing and non-self-govern-ing areas although it illustrates the hypoth-esis of unidimensionality. Each score is a scale type and, knowing the score of a po-litical entity, it would be possible to de-scribe its response pattern without error. Had we expected distinctly different scalo-gram patterns for self-governing and non-self-governing entities the result should have appeared as in Table 6. We have re-tained a perfect scale but it is sharply di-vided into 2 halves on a basis of political status. Self-governing political entities have distinctly different response patterns than do non-self-governing entities. The ranking of political entities is meaningful and, in addition, the response pattern of any entity may be described by knowing its scale score alone.

What do we find upon examination of the actual data? The 56 variables from the

TABLE 5.   A Perfect Scale

Political Entities	Items Making up the Scale			Scale Scores	Scale Types
	2 Most Favorable Subcategories 1, 2, 3, . . . n	1 Least Favorable Subcategories 1, 2, 3, . . . n	0 No Information 1, 2, 3, . . . n		
Self-gov. a	X X X X X			10	I
Self-gov. b	X X X X	X		9	II
Self-gov. c	X X X	X X		8	III
Self-gov. d	X X	X X X		7	IV
Self-gov. e	X	X X X X		6	V
Non-self-g. f		X X X X X		5	VI
Non-self-g. g		X X X X	X	4	VII
Non-self-g. h		X X X	X X	3	VIII
Non-self-g. i		X X	X X X	2	IX
Non-self-g. j		X	X X X X	1	X
Non-self-g. k			X X X X X	0	XI

TABLE 6.   A Perfect Scale

Political Entities	Items Making up the Scale			Scale Scores	Scale Types
	2 Most Favorable Subcategories 1, 2, 3, . . . n	1 Least Favorable Subcategories 1, 2, 3, . . . n	0 No Information 1, 2, 3, . . . n		
Self-gov. a	X X X X X			10	I
Self-gov. b	X X X X X			10	I
Self-gov. c	X X X X X			10	I
Self-gov. d	X X X X X			10	I
Self-gov. e	X X X X X			10	I
Non-self-g. f		X X X X X		5	II
Non-self-g. g		X X X X X		5	II
Non-self-g. h		X X X X X		5	II
Non-self-g. i		X X X X X		5	II
Non-self-g. j			X X X X X	0	III
Non-self-g. k			X X X X X	0	III

earlier study had been dichotomized in the manner described and manipulated following the procedures suggested for this type of scale analysis.

If the coefficient of reproducibility is computed as originally suggested by Guttman, the large amount of reproducibility guaranteed by the distribution of the marginal totals is not taken into consideration so that both the marginals for political entities and the marginals for items create an additional reproducibility above what we might call "inherent" unidimensionality.[4] The coefficient of reproducibility was 74.8, but when the coefficient of scalability suggested by Menzel was computed it dropped to 33.1. This coefficient tells us the relative improvement in reproducibility that re-

[4] This problem is discussed in Herbert Menzel, "A New Coefficient for Scalogram Analysis," *Public Opinion Quarterly*, Vol. 17, Summer 1953, pp. 268 ff.

sults from the ordering of categories and individuals in a scalogram. The data have such a large amount of error that scale scores do not permit accurate reproduction of response patterns.

If the continuum of scores is divided into a dichotomy at that point which most efficiently separates the self-governing from the non-self-governing, the result in Table 7 is obtained. If some measure of the relationship of these scale scores to the variable, self-governing or non-self-governing is desired, the phi coefficient of correlation is .970. If we combine categories so as to reduce their numbers, it is usually possible to increase the coefficient of reproducibility. There is a rationale for rescaling the data by combining the category "no information" with the least desirable half of the dichotomy or "least favorable subclass"

TABLE 7. Scale Scores on Fifty-Six Items

	Self-governing	Non-self-governing	Total
−70	27	99	129
70+	61	11	69
Total	88	110	198

for each variable; this is also the subclass in which non-self-governing entities tended to be found. In this case each political entity received 2 points if it fell in the "most favorable subcategory" of the variable, as in the scoring system previously offered, but received 1 point if it fell in either the "least favorable subcategory" or the "no information" subcategory. In this fashion a political entity was not so heavily penalized on the scale for its lack of social and economic bookkeeping. The relation of these scores to the variable, self-governing or non-self-governing is presented in Table 8. The lower limit of the scores was raised by this change in the scoring system but at the same time the relationship between scale scores and the variable

self-governing or non-self-governing was increased; the phi coefficient of correlation became 1.000. In the example at hand the coefficient of reproducibility was 83.8 when computed as originally suggested by Guttman but the modal categories were so large that computation as suggested by Menzel dropped the coefficient of scalability to 24.4. Ordering individuals and items in a scalogram resulted in relatively little improvement in reproducibility over that obtainable from the modal categories of either the items or the individuals.

TABLE 8. Scale Scores on Fifty-Six Items

	Self-governing	Non-self-governing	Total
−78	24	99	123
78+	64	11	75
Total	88	110	198

While neither the correlation obtained from Table 7 nor 8 is greater than that of many of the single factors, it cannot be said that an additive scale is entirely without use since such a scale may correlate more highly with the general social and economic development of an area than any single index, i.e., the sum of the scores may be more representative of that which we are trying to measure than any single item correlating highly with the variable self-governing or non-self-governing.

At this point the hypothesis of scalability has been rejected for the 56 items selected from the various United Nations publications. This does not mean that we have exhausted all possibilities with the data at hand.

It is possible that some of the variables aside from those representing "capacity for self-government," variables representing quite a different dimension, have reduced the scalability of the data. What would happen if we eliminated them? This procedure would be criticized by those who would follow the steps originally detailed by Guttman and others. There is some merit, however, in removing certain items which it is hypothesized are responsible for the lack of unidimensionality in the original 56 items. If we remove all items except those expressed in *per capita* terms and all items except those expressed in per square kilometer, wherever relevant, 29 items will be left, including land area as a single item and population as another single item. In this fashion the score obtainable by a political entity is largely based on stages of development or conditions of living. Instead of hypothesizing that any available set of data on the population will have unidimensionality on one hand and on the other the characteristic of discriminating between political entities according to their status, we hypothesize that *per capita* and per square kilometer data will have unidimensionality and discriminatory ability. If we score each political entity 2, 1, 0, as in the first example of scoring, we find that the 29 items have a coefficient of reproducibility of 71.6 but a coefficient of scalability of only 29.5 If the continuum of scores is dichotomized so as to yield the maximum prediction of political status we have the distribution found in Table 9 with a phi coefficient of correlation of .906.

TABLE 9. Scale Scores on Twenty-Nine Items

	Self-governing	Non-self-governing	Total
−37	34	102	136
37+	54	8	62
Total	88	110	198

It is apparent that population size and area were not separate elements impairing the unidimensionality of the items in the first scale.

If we combine categories as we did with the 56 item scale it is possible to increase the coefficient of correlation between scale scores and political status as shown in Table 10. The phi coefficient of correlation is .930 and the coefficient of reproducibility is 82.3. The coefficient of scalability is 23.4. Combining categories so that we have the dichotomy of "most favorable subcategory" and "least favorable subcategory or no information," decreases error but does so by increasing the size of the modal categories. This takes us nowhere that we desire to go.

TABLE 10. Scale Scores on Twenty-Nine Items

	Self-governing	Non-self-governing	Total
−42	38	106	144
42+	50	4	54
Total	88	110	198

It is not the purpose of this paper to go into what might be called substantive matters but it should not go unmentioned that high scale scores among non-self-governing political entities are related to our conceptions of which political entities are capable of self-government or political independence. In fact, high-scoring non-self-governing areas are usually those making an effort in some manner or another to obtain political independence.

Unfortunately, or perhaps fortunately, depending on our inclinations, numerous other alternative hypotheses remain to be considered, each of them being reasonable hypotheses about the relation of our data to the criterion, self-governing or non-self-governing. We might hypothesize that a set of economic variables, or a set of demographic variables or any other set of variables would present a unidimensional scale differentiating self-governing from non-self-governing political entities. This involves, theoretically, the selection of a new set of variables on economic characteristics or any other area that we hypothesize to be related to political status.

On the other hand, it is very possible that application of latent structure analysis might show that there are different kinds of political entities and that some types are invariably, within certain limits of error, self-governing, while other types are non-self-governing.[5] Such an arrangement need not be scalable in the Guttman sense, since the Guttman model is only a special case of latent structure. It is very possible, as we have previously suggested, that some complex ordering of political entities may underlie what appears to be an unordered or random distribution of characteristics of political entities. What may be the apparent lack of order turns out to be a complex arrangement that does not fit

ble 11. While the different patterns of self-governing and non-self-governing areas are readily seen in the diagram, one must realize that 200 political entities and 56 or 29 variables, whichever we might choose to use, would present a far more complex pattern, one impossible to discern by visual inspection, a pattern which could only be brought out by the use of latent structure analysis or some equally sophisticated technique.

We must conclude that more complex models should be tested as possibly being representative of the hypothesized relationship between certain variables and the self-governing or non-self-governing dichotomy. We have rejected the hypothesis of unidi-

TABLE 11. A Complex Model

Political Entities	Items Making up the Scale							Scale Scores	Scale Types
	2 Most Favorable Subcategories 1, 2, 3, . . . n		1 Least Favorable Subcategories 1, 2, 3, . . . n		0 No Information 1, 2, 3, . . . n				
Self-gov. a	X X		X X			X		6	I
Self-gov. b		X X	X X	X				6	II
Self-gov. c	X X		X	X		X		6	III
Self-gov. d		X X	X X		X			6	IV
Non-self-g. e	X	X	X X		X			6	V
Non-self-g. f	X	X	X X			X		6	VI
Non-self-g. g	X			X X	X		X	4	VII
Non-self-g. h	X		X	X	X			4	VIII
Non-self-g. i	X		X X		X	X		4	IX

such a simple model as that which we have first tried to relate to the data. It may well be that a variety of combinations of factors differentiate self-governing entities from non-self-governing entities. If this is the case, then certain combinations of factors are related to "capacity for self-government" and other combinations of factors are related to absence of self-government. An example of such an arrangement as we have been hypothesizing is shown in Table-

[5] See Stouffer *et al.*, *op. cit.*, Chapters 10 and 11.

mensionality of a sample of characteristics of political entities. Differences are present, however, as evidenced by the correlation between simple additive scale scores and political status. A systematic description of these differences must now be made. One further note of caution should be added. To what extent any differences found are "causes" of lack of self-government and to what extent they are "results" of self-government has not been answered even when systematic patterns of differences are found. We are left with the choice of accepting observed differences as the factors making up "capacity for self-government," or as consequences of differential opportunity arising from political status, or more likely, as the result of an interplay of both "causes" and "consequences."

Dr. Stuart C. Dodd is Director of the Washington Public Opinion Laboratory and Professor of Sociology in the Department of Sociology at the University of Washington. Professor Dodd is the author of numerous books and monographs, among them A *Controlled Experiment on Rural Hygiene in Syria,* 1934, and *Dimensions of Sociology,* 1942. He has been particularly active in recent years in the World Association of Public Opinion Research and has also supervised extensive contract research for the U.S. Air Force. He was Chairman of the Department of Sociology and Professor of Sociology at the American University of Beirut for many years before coming to the University of Washington.

APPENDIXES

APPENDIX I

Proportion of World Population in Various Regions According to Population Type, Development, and Political Status
Population Type* and Political Status‡

		I SG	I NSG	II SG	II NSG	III SG	III NSG	V SG	V NSG	VII SG	VII NSG	VIII SG	VIII NSG	TOTAL SG	TOTAL NSG
North America	Developed	U.S. 11.77	.00	Canada 1.06	Alaska St. Pierre & Miquelon .01						Greenland −.01			12.83	.01
	Underdeveloped	.00	.00	.00	.00					.00	.00			.00	−.01
Central America	Developed	.00	.00	.00	.00									.00	.00
	Underdeveloped	.00	Barbados .01	Cuba .41	.00			Panama Costa Rica Dom.Rep. Honduras Nicaragua .47	Trinidad & Tobago Puerto Rico Neth. W.I. Bermuda Br. Hond. Jamaica Canal Zone .36	.00	Virgin Is. Bahamas −.01	El Salvador Mexico Guatemala 2.34	Leeward Is. Windward Is. Br. Guiana .07	3.22	.44
South America	Developed	.00	.00	Paraguay .10	Falkland Is. .00			.00	.00	Chile .45	.00	.00	.00	1.49	.00
	Underdeveloped	.10	−.01	Peru .66	.00			Venezuela .38	Surinam .01	.00	.00	Bolivia .23	.00	.33	.01
Europe	Developed	Austria Belgium Bulgaria Czechoslovakia Finland Denmark France Germany Greece Hungary Luxemburg Ireland Italy Liechtenstein Norway Monaco Netherlands Portugal Spain Sweden Switzerland U.K. 25.86	Channel Is. Gibraltar −.01	Poland Yugoslavia Iceland 3.20	.00	Romania 1.24	.00	Malta & Goza .00	.02					29.69	.00
	Underdeveloped	.00													

Table (rotated 90° on the page). The row stub shows region (Africa, Middle East, Southeast Asia, Central and South Asia, Oceania), each split into Developed / Underdeveloped. The column heads are Types I–VIII, each divided into SG (Self-governing) and NSG (Non-self-governing), with a final Total (SG / NSG). Values are proportions; named political entities are entered in their cells.

Region	Status	I SG	I NSG	II SG	II NSG	III SG	III NSG	IV SG	IV NSG	V SG	V NSG	VI SG	VI NSG	VII SG	VII NSG	VIII SG	VIII NSG	Total SG	Total NSG
Africa	Developed	.00	.00	.00	.00	.00	.00	.00	.00					.00	.00	.00	.00	.00	.00
Africa	Underdeveloped	.00	Spanish Poss. in N. Africa .01	.00	Seychelles, St. Helena −.01	.00	.00	.00	.00					Egypt, Algeria 2.25	Sierre-Leone, Madagascar .48	.00	Mauritius .03	2.25	.49
Middle East	Developed	.00	.00	.00	.00	.00	.00	Israel .09	.00					.00	.00			.09	.00
Middle East	Underdeveloped	Syria .24	.00			.00	Aden Colony −.01	.00	Cyprus .03									.24	.03
Southeast Asia	Developed	.00	.00	.00	.00	.00	.00	.00	.00					.00	.00			.00	.00
Southeast Asia	Underdeveloped	Philippine Republic 1.42	.00	Thailand 1.54	Hong Kong .17									.00	Malaya, Singapore .47			2.96	.64
Central and South Asia	Developed	.00	.00	Japan 6.43	.00	.00	.00	.00	.00									6.43	.00
Central and South Asia	Underdeveloped	Pakistan 5.82	.00	.00	.00	India 27.78	.00	Formosa, Ceylon 1.16	.00			Korea 2.29	French India .02					37.05	.02
Oceania	Developed	Australia, N. Zealand .78	.00	.00	.00			.00	Hawaii .03					.00	.00			.78	.03
Oceania	Underdeveloped	.00	Norfolk Is. −.01					.00	Fiji, Tonga, A. Samoa, Guam, Pac. Is. (U.S), Western Samoa .10					.00	Cook, Niue, Gilbert & Ellice Is. −.01			.00	.07
Total	Developed	37.80	.00	11.35	.01	1.24	.00	.47	.06			.45	.00	.00	.00	.00		51.31	.07
Total	Underdeveloped	8.14	.02	1.95	.17	27.78	.34	1.63	.49			2.29	.16	4.82	.54			46.66	1.72

* = most favorable subcategory on item, i.e., + = low birth rate, + = low natural increase, + = low death rate

(Data presented here for 100 of 195 political entities; data unavailable for others.
SOURCE: *United Nations Demographic Yearbook—1952* and *United Nations Statistical Yearbook—1952*.)

* Type I	= + + +	35
Type II	= − + +	13
Type III	= + + −	3
Type IV	= + − +	27
Type V	= − − +	0
Type VI	= + − −	8
Type VII	= − + −	8
Type VIII	= − − −	14

‡ SG = Self-governing; NSG = Non-self-governing

APPENDIX II

DEVELOPMENT SCORES OF POLITICAL ENTITIES BY GEOGRAPHICAL REGIONS:
Based on Seventeen Items Listed in Chapter XV

AFRICA

32   Union of South Africa

26   St. Helena

25   Southern Rhodesia

23   Tangier

22   Seychelles

21   Reunion, Mauritius, Spanish Possessions in North Africa

20   Algeria, French Somaliland

19   Basutoland, Ruandi Urundi, Tunisia

18   Morocco, Belgian Congo, Moroccan Protectorate, French Cameroons, Sierra Leone

17   British Cameroons, British Togoland, Swaziland, Bechuanaland, South West Africa, Spanish West Africa, Spanish Guinea, Libya, Northern Rhodesia, Liberia, Zanzibar and Pemba, Cape Verde Is., Italian Somaliland, British Somaliland, Portuguese Guinea, Sao Tome and Principe, Ethiopia, French Equatorial Africa, Tanganyika, Angola, Mozambique, Gold Coast, French Togoland, French West Africa, Madagascar, Nigeria, Anglo-Egyptian Sudan, Uganda, Nyasaland, Kenya, Gambia, Egypt

NORTH AMERICA

34   United States, Canada

30   Alaska

28   St. Pierre and Miquelon

23   Greenland

EUROPE

34   Austria, Germany, United Kingdom, Norway, Sweden, Luxembourg, Belgium

33   Italy, Czechoslovakia, France, Netherlands

32   Finland, Iceland, Switzerland, Ireland

31   Poland, Spain

30   Denmark, Hungary

29   Monaco

26   Malta and Gozo, Gibraltar, Romania

24   Yugoslavia, Portugal, Channel Is., Lichtenstein

23   Bulgaria, San Marino

20 Greece, Albania
17 Isle of Man, Andorra, Svalbard and Jan Mayan Land

SOUTH AMERICA

33 Argentina
32 Chile
27 Uruguay, Falkland Is.
26 Venezuela
25 Peru
23 French Guiana
22 Brazil
21 Surinam
20 Paraguay, Colombia
19 British Guiana
18 Ecuador, Bolivia

CENTRAL AMERICA

29 Netherlands West Indies, Canal Zone
27 Cuba
26 Mexico, Trinidad and Tobago, Bermuda, Barbados
25 Puerto Rico, Virgin Is.
24 Panama
23 Bahama Is.
21 British Honduras, Martinique, Guadeloupe
20 Leeward Is., Jamaica, Honduras, Costa Rica
19 Dominican Republic
18 Nicaragua
17 Haiti, Guatemala, Windward Is., Salvador

SOUTHEAST ASIA

25 Singapore
22 Thailand
20 British Borneo, Philippine Republic, New Guinea
18 Federation of Malaya, Burma
17 French Indochina, Indonesia, Portuguese Timor

OCEANIA

34 Australia
31 New Zealand
29 Guam
28 Hawaii, New Caledonia
27 Nauru, United States Trust Territory of the Pacific
26 Norfolk Is., Tonga, American Samoa
24 Cook Is.
23 Tokelau
22 Papua, Niue, French Oceania

21 Gilbert and Ellice Is., Fiji
20 Western Samoa, Ryukyu Is.
19 British Solomon Is.
18 New Hebrides
17 Pitcairn, Bonin Is., New Guinea

SOUTH AND CENTRAL ASIA

31 Japan
30 USSR
22 Formosa
19 Ceylon, India
18 Hong Kong
17 Nepal, French India, Mongolian People's Republic, Bhutan, China, Korea,
    Macau, Portuguese India, Maldive Is.

MIDDLE EAST

28 Israel
25 Bahrein
24 Kuwait, Cyprus
22 Lebanon, Saudi Arabia, Iraq, Qatar
20 Turkey, Iran, Aden Colony
19 Syria
17 Trucial Oman, Muscat and Oman, Yemen, Aden Protectorate, Jordan, Afghan-
    istan, Pakistan

INDEXES

INDEX OF NAMES

486

Hunter, John M., 283, 309, 332
Hunter, Monica, 79, 419

Isales, Carmen, 336, 340, 350, 368

Jennings, W. Ivor, 100, 114, 119, 336

Kaur, Rajkumari, 388
Kellogg, Charles E., 66
Kelly, Isabel T., 372
Keukjian, E. A., 46
Kimball, Solon T., 91
Klineberg, Otto, 343
Knowles, William H., 283, 309, 333
Krige, E. J. and J. D., 420
Kroeber, A. L., 409

Laubach, Frank C., 112
Leonard, Olen E., 174, 175
Levy, Marion J., Jr., 186
Lewis, Oscar, 422
Lewis, W. Arthur, 284, 285, 330, 333
Linton, Ralph, 38
Longmore, T. Wilson, 158, 174, 178, 195
Loomis, Charles P., 158, 174, 195
Lowenthal, Leo, 364
Lugard, F. D., 40

Maffry, August, 246, 273, 280
Mair, Geo. F., 90
Mandelbaum, K., 227
Manners, Robert A., 158, 166, 167, 195
Marbach, Fritz, 182
Marin, Governor Luis Muñoz, 336, 337
Marriott, McKim, 399, 407, 410, 415, 423, 444
Marshall, Alfred, 151, 156
Mayo, Selz C., 180
Mead, Margaret, 35, 336, 340, 343, 344, 367, 422
Meier, Richard L., 200, 232, 240
Menzel, Herbert, 472, 473
Metraux, A., 420
Mintz, Sidney, 166
Mooney, Horace W., 461
Moore, Wilbert E., 60, 71, 79, 95, 181, 403
Mosher, A. T., 409, 414
Mostny, Greta, 372
Mukerjee, Radhakamal, 70
Muñoz, Raúl, 338
Murdock, Geo. P., 89
Murphy, Gardner, 317
Murray, R. L., 235

Nadel, Siegfried, 344
Northrop, F. S. C., 367
Notestein, Frank W., 63

Oberg, Kalergo, 372
Oliver, Vere Langford, 153
Opler, Morris E., 413
Owen, David, 284, 321, 333

Padilla, Elena, 166
Patel, I. G., 199, 208, 240
Patnaik, Nityananda, 99, 100, 119
Perloff, Harvey S., 73, 408
Pierson, John H. G., 282, 283
Piquet, Howard S., 69

Redfield, Robert, 422
Reeves, William Harvey, 244, 253, 280
Riesman, David, 193
Rippy, J. Fred, 241, 242, 243, 244, 247, 280, 281
Ritsher, Walter H., 449, 454, 457
Roca, de, Angelina S., 338
Rodriguez, Justo Diaz, 174
Rosenberg, William, 286
Rottenberg, Simon, 128, 149, 154, 156
Russell, Josiah C., 90
Russell, William F., 112

Saer, D. J., 347
Salter, Robert M., 65, 66
Scheele, Raymond, 166
Schuler, Edgar A., 174
Schultz, Theodore W., 284, 330, 333
Semmons, Robert L., 256
Serra, Belén M., 338
Sharp, Lauriston, 406
Shannon, Lyle W., 448, 452, 453, 456, 458, 464
Simey, T. S., 152
Simmons, Ozzie, 372
Singh, Rudra Datt, 402
Smith, Adam, 150
Smith, Bruce L., 340, 361, 368
Smith, T. Lynn, 174, 175
Soedjatmoko, 362
Solomon, Morton R., 128, 131, 156
Spengler, Joseph, 129
Spicer, Edward H., 402, 406, 408, 410
Staley, Eugene, 3, 4
Steward, Julian H., 158, 166, 167, 195
Stone, Abraham, 388
Stouffer, Samuel, 58, 475
Stycos, J. Mayone, 93, 364, 370, 393, 398
Sumner, William Graham, 321

Taeuber, Irene B., 63
Tannenbaum, Frank, 158, 160, 194
Tannous, Afif, 283, 287, 332, 334
Tax, Sol, 422
Taylor, Carl E., 385

INDEX OF SUBJECTS